S0-FSO-372

Ethnoperspectives in Bilingual Education Research, Volume I:

Bilingual Education and Public Policy in the United States

Edited by Raymond V. Padilla

Ethnoperspectives in Bilingual Education Research:

BILINGUAL EDUCATION AND PUBLIC POLICY IN THE UNITED STATES

Edited by Raymond V. Padilla

Bilingual Bicultural Education Programs
Eastern Michigan University

Ethnoperspectives in Bilingual Education
Research Series Volume I

Cover design by Martín Moreno. The design reflects various cultural symbols, including the pyramid of the sun, the yin and yang principles, and the African symbol for life.

The activity which is the subject of this report was supported in whole or in part by the National Institute of Education, Department of Health, Education and Welfare. However, the opinions expressed herein do not necessarily reflect the position or policy of the National Institute of Education and no official endorsement by the National Institute of Education is inferred.

Library of Congress Catalog Card
ISBN Number: 79-9265

Published and Disseminated in the United States of America by:
Department of Foreign Languages and Bilingual Studies
Bilingual Programs
106 Ford Hall
Eastern Michigan University
Ypsilanti, Michigan 48197

First Printing December 1979

ACKNOWLEDGMENTS

This publication would not have been possible without the interest and efforts of all those persons who responded to the call for papers. The authors whose works are included here deserve special mention not only for the papers which they contributed but also for their excellent participation in the two national forums on "Bilingual Education and Public Policy in the U.S." Valuable support was provided by Dr. Gwen Baker, head of the Experimental Program for Opportunities in Advanced Study and Research in Education, National Institute of Education. The members of the advisory committee were very helpful in selecting presenters for the forums.

Staff from many offices at Eastern Michigan University provided welcomed support. Dr. Anthony Evans and Dr. Jean Bidwell were especially helpful and supportive. Margo MacInnes and Martín Moreno contributed technical services as consultants. Staff from the Bilingual Programs performed with their customary efficiency and cheerfulness.

CONTENTS

INTRODUCTION

This book is a collection of papers that were presented during April and June of 1979 at two national forums on *Bilingual Education and Public Policy in the U.S.* The forums were part of an on-going multi-year project called *Ethnoperspectives in Bilingual Education Research.* The project is sponsored by the Department of Foreign Languages and Bilingual Studies at Eastern Michigan University with support from the National Institute of Education through its Experimental Program for Opportunities in Advanced Study and Research in Education.

The *Ethnoperspectives in Bilingual Education Research* project serves two main purposes. First, the project is intended to materially encourage and promote research related to bilingual education. Secondly, minority viewpoints, or perspectives, in bilingual education research are fostered and supported. These purposes in turn are aimed at increasing the involvement of minorities and women in educational research.

In recent years, there has been strong advocacy from diverse groups for increased research in bilingual education. This advocacy is largely the result of a perceived need to strengthen the pedagogical basis for bilingual education. At the same time, bilingual advocates want to develop informed arguments for use against the onslaught of politically and ideologically motivated criticisms that have been leveled against the bilingual education movement over the past decade. As a result of this advocacy effort, the 1978 amendments to the federal Bilingual Education Act place a greater emphasis on research than ever before.

Since research in bilingual education is clearly in its formative stages, it is necessary to develop a broad conceptual framework for encouraging and conducting such research. Obviously, any given conceptual framework will be colored by the preferences and needs of those doing the initial conceptualizing. For example, one can perceive a strong emphasis on evaluation in the research mandated by the 1978 amendments to Title VII of the Elementary and Secondary Education Act. On the other hand, research conducted by doctoral students often reflects narrow disciplinary concerns or is limited by the scarcity of resources which usually afflicts such research. This is not to say, of course, that either the Title VII mandated research or doctoral research is unimportant. The point is that any research approach or strategy reflects certain preferences, limitations, and biases, and that there is a need to understand these factors so that eventually one or more optimal research strategies may be devised.

The conceptual approach encompassed by the Ethnoperspectives Project is premised on a broad view of the research needs in bilingual education. Basically, successful research must result in the significant advancement of knowledge and understanding in three distinct but interrelated global areas in bilingual education. These are (1) theory, (2) technology, and (3) public policy.

Few informed persons today would deny the need to develop a sound theoretical framework within which to develop the field of bilingual education. Such persons recognize that theory is especially important because it provides a conceptual and analytic framework within which to interpret and understand the underlying principles and elements of bilingual education. Theory in bilingual education also is fundamentally important because it may well set intrinsic limits for further development and growth in the field. In its practical applications, theory is used to analyze, explain, support, and change bilingual learning activities in the classroom and in natural settings outside of the classroom. Hence, the advancement of theory in bilingual education is a basic necessity for the field as a whole. One of several key problems currently facing bilingual education is the egregious lack of attention to the construction of theories applicable to the numerous phenomena and events which occur in bilingual education.

Bilingual technology implies procedures, techniques, materials, and instrumentation. In short, bilingual technology includes all of the skills and paraphernalia which are utilized in the teaching enterprise. Much that is important to teaching has to do with technique because technique is a key element in the formation of skills and patterned behavior. To the extent that teachers control skills, techniques, and technical products, they are technicians. As technicians they must be able to understand, utilize, and evaluate the growing technology that applies to bilingual learning and the management of a bilingual classroom. In this context, the proper role of research is to contribute to a greater understanding of the technological basis for bilingual education, and certainly to promote the refinement and expansion of that technology. Today, bilingual education is supported by a broad technological base, but the usefulness and applicability of much of that technology remains unknown. There is a critical need to establish specifications and standards for most of the existent bilingual education technology. Perhaps it is not too farfetched to suggest that today there is also a need to place warning labels on certain untested materials in order to inform people about possible dangers in the use or misuse of those materials.

By definition, public education occurs in a public setting and is a public activity. As such, public education, including bilingual education, is subject to prevailing public attitudes and values. In a formal sense, bilingual education is derived from, and continuously affected by, public policy. The most significant aspect of public policy is its impact on resources and their allocation. Resource allocation in turn greatly influences the nature of opportunities and limitations imposed on any activity.

Yet public policy is not often formulated through purely rational processes. It is quite clear that public policy sometimes depends as much on prevailing social attitudes and values—not to say bias and prejudice—as it does on theory, sound reasoning, or empirical findings. From a research perspective, then, it is essential to generate a refined body of knowledge that illuminates the basic contours of the policy-making processes that have an impact on bilingual education. It is necessary to find out how effective bilingual education practices can be incorporated into public policy. It is equally necessary to find out how to eliminate ineffective bilingual education practices that have been sanctioned by existing but outdated public policy.

These three areas—theory, technology, and public policy—outline, if only briefly, the project on *Ethnoperspectives in Bilingual Education Research.* Activities in the area of theory are currently being implemented while activities in the technology area are planned for the future. Public policy was the focal theme of two national forums held during 1979. This volume contains the papers that were presented at those forums.

In reading this volume, the reader should keep in mind not only the conceptual framework outlined above but also the current objective conditions of research in bilingual education public policy. In spite of the fact that the contemporary phase of bilingual education was initiated almost two decades ago, an astonishingly small amount of research has been done which specifically investigates the many dimensions of the policy-making process in bilingual education. The limited research that has been carried out is largely confined to doctoral dissertations and a few federally funded studies. Journalistic exposés and congressionally inspired committee reports on bilingual education are also a source of accumulated data. But these products are more properly classified as quasi research in part because of the former's staccato performance and the latter's peripatetic features.

In view of these objective limitations, it may well be useful to identify—if only in a preliminary way—the elements that may contribute to the public policy-making process for bilingual education in the U.S. As identified for the two national forums supported by the Ethnoperspectives Projects, the following elements are considered important:

1. federal legislation
2. state legislation
3. the federal courts
4. the mass media
5. bilingual communities

These elements all seem to have an impact on the policy-making process, but most have scarcely received any attention from researchers. Some, such as the mass media, have been almost totally ignored. To begin to remedy this situation, and to gain more accurate knowledge about what is actually "out there," a call for papers was made for theoretical, conceptual, analytical, or empirical studies that relate to the five areas identified. Not surprisingly, the response to the call demonstrated clearly that current research efforts relating to bilingual education public policy are very uneven with respect to the areas of research interest identified for the forums. Most notable was the extremely low response for papers relating to the mass media. This is especially significant in view of the intense debate on bilingual education which the media have provoked, encouraged, and sustained.

The response to the call for papers also demonstrated that, with notable exceptions, the present research efforts tend to be in areas that are *related* to bilingual education policy, but they seldom clearly focus on policy as the primary issue. Thus, it can be concluded that while there exists some research that can support the bilingual education policy-making process, much of the research is focused on other concerns of the bilingual education field. The contents of this volume reflect this state of the research art. As a result, the reader may encounter material in some of the articles presented in this book that appears tangential to the focal concerns of policy making. For the same reason, this volume may appear to some to lack the conceptual and analytic elegance expected in a more narrowly focused and well-developed field. Nevertheless, the papers presented here are an important beginning for the advancement of serious research on the public policy aspects of bilingual education.

The reader also will note that this volume does not contain a statement or position which details a recommended national policy on bilingual education. Such a statement would be difficult, if not impossible, to formulate through the activities which constituted the forums. Moreover, it is evident that, from a research perspective, we are a long way from even articulating clearly the policy questions that need to be answered and identifying the elements of the policy-making process itself.

An important concern of the Ethnoperspectives Project is not only to promote more and better research in bilingual education, but also to raise questions about *who* performs or should perform the needed research, and the *context* in which such research is to be implemented. Here we are focusing attention on the idea that research is an activity which is profoundly affected by the social and cultural patterns in which the research act takes place. Thus, issues and questions of policy in bilingual education can have very different meanings and answers depending upon the individual researcher and the context in which those questions or issues are raised.

Questions are never absolutely objective, and those who ask a question may assume very different premises from those who ultimately answer the question. It is said that the famous Spanish writer Francisco Quevedo once bet a friend that Quevedo would tell the queen of Spain to her face that she was a gimp. Naturally, such an audacious and irreverent act seemed impossible, so Quevedo's friend accepted the bet. Quevedo, famous for his boundless wit and resourcefulness, was quick to find a solution. It is said that he took two flowers—one in each hand—and presented them to the queen. In his left hand Quevedo held a *clavel* (carnation) while in his right hand he held a *rosa* (rose). He then asked the queen to choose between the two flowers by saying, "Entre el clavel y la rosa, Vuestra Merced escoga." (Of course, *escoga* means "choose" but is homophonous with the Spanish expression for female gimp—*es coja*.). Quevedo eventually languished in prison for his insolent behavior, but the lesson to be learned here is that the very act of asking a question, especially a research question, already has potential policy implications. The decision maker may be led down a rosy path by a clever researcher who has a hidden agenda. So it is quite legitimate to question the motives and perspectives of researchers, because these elements ultimately are conditioning factors in the research act.

The two national forums on bilingual education and public policy were definitely concerned with raising issues and questions which could form the basis for a legitimate national agenda and public policy on bilingual education. Already there is evidence to show that some modern-day writers, such as the Epsteins and the Quiggs, who have access to powerful means of communication, are only too willing to pose loaded questions about bilingual education public policy. Although this volume represents a preliminary attempt to begin to raise proper questions about bilingual education policy, it is far too early to present an exact formulation of those questions. And clearly it is premature to attempt to speak for the numerous bilingual communities in this country who ultimately must not only raise the proper questions but formulate some practical answers and solutions. Perhaps the most appropriate question that can be expressed today harks back to the wily Quevedo. As Don Francisco might say before *la corte del pueblo:* "Entre español e inglés el pueblo es el juez." Researchers can only hope to enlighten that decision and help to develop effective educational practices consistent with the verdict.

Part I

LA LEY/THE LAW

THE LEGAL DIALECT OF BILINGUAL EDUCATION

Steven R. Applewhite, Ph.D.

> Laws not enforced cease to be laws, and rights not defended may wither away.
>
> —Thomas Moriarity

The Supreme Court of the United States in 1954, *Brown* v. *Board of Education,* declared that compulsory racial school segregation and its principle of "separate but equal" was unconstitutional.[1] Any policy that encouraged a dual educational system could no longer be tolerated nor be sanctioned in public education. Nearly a generation later, the nation's highest court is now wrestling with the issue of equality of educational opportunity and the right of all individuals to a "meaningful education" vis-à-vis bilingual education.

Despite the foot-dragging, state and federal legislation, litigation, and administrative mandates continue to pave the way in determining the legal status of bilingual education. It is evident from a judicial standpoint that denial of educational opportunity to non-English-speaking students is discriminatory when it bars students from effectively participating in educational programs offered by a local education agency. Further, the provision of equal treatment of students with different needs, based upon an analysis of equal access, will no longer satisfy statutory, or arguably constitutional mandates when the results are unequal distribution of education benefits. Educational policy must focus its concern not on the goal of providing an education for *all* students, but rather on providing an education for *each* child.

With the knowledge that not all students come to the starting line with equal preparation, the uniform delivery of services alone cannot be used as the sole basis for the distribution of educational benefits unless each individual has been provided an equal opportunity to develop his abilities and skills. Accordingly, meritocratic principles must be re-examined carefully in order to incorporate an egalitarian perspective that emphasizes "alternative means of learning" that are "adaptive to and . . . in some ways matched to, the knowledge about each individual . . . his background, talents, skills, interests and the nature of his past performance."[2] To this end, the Supreme Court has affirmed that educational parity can no longer prevail since "there is no greater inequality than the equal treatment of unequals."[3]

In recent years, a number of cases have demonstrated the impact of litigation in identifying the intent of bilingual education in the context of equal educational opportunity. The judicial pronouncements in five landmark cases have provided a precedent for interpreting the legal dialect of bilingual education. Among the major court decisions that address the civil-political perspective in this area are: *Keyes* v. *School District No. 1, Denver, Colorado*;[4] *Lau* v. *Nichols, San Francisco Unified School District*;[5] *Serna* v. *Portales Municipal Schools, New Mexico*;[6] *Aspira of New York, Inc.* v. *Board of Education of the City of New York*;[7] and *Rios* v. *Reed, New York.*[8]

This paper focuses primarily on providing a summary of the legal findings related directly to bilingual education. In addition, this paper will provide a synthesis of observations and recommendations, based on a cursory review of the literature, relating to the legal issues surrounding bilingual education and public policy in the United States and its prospect for the future.

THE LEGAL DIALECT

Keyes v. School District No. 1, Denver, Colorado

The issue of desegregation and bilingual education is often difficult to interpret according to the principles set forth in judicial rulings. The *Keyes* decision has done much to clarify the legal dialect and the position of the courts on this matter.

In the *Keyes* ruling, plaintiffs contended that the racial imbalance that existed in the Denver schools resulted from purposeful segregatory actions rather than normal shifts of residential patterns and "racially neutral" assignment criteria. Therefore, the segregative conduct in Denver resulted in a "dual system" and subsequently barred identifiable minority groups in Denver from meaningful participation and benefits of educational opportunities.

The opinion expressed by the trial court stated that segregation, as it existed in the district, was not a unique and isolated case, but represented the practices of an entire educational system in Denver. To this end, desegregation was required "root and branch" in order to dismantle the dual school system existing in Denver.

The district court decision of Judge Doyle focused its attention on mandating an equitable and feasible plan of desegregation.

Of significance in the *Keyes* decision was the reaffirmation that Hispanics in this country represent an "identifiable ethnic minority group," an opinion that was advanced in 1970 in *Cisneros* v. *Corpus Christi*[9] and *United States* v. *Texas*.[10] The court added that ". . . though of different origins, Negroes and Hispanics in Denver suffer[ed] identical discrimination in treatment when compared with the treatment afforded Anglo students."[11] Accordingly, the segregation of Hispanics, or any identifiable minority group or class, is prohibited according to *Brown*, and thus Hispanics must be afforded protection under the Equal Protection Clause of the Fourteenth Amendment. As in *U.S.* v. *Texas*, the District Court in Denver clearly ordered that bilingual programs be included in the desegregation plan in order to address the specific educational needs of Hispanics.

The trial court, in considering part of the remedy in the desegregation plan, included the Cardenas Plan—based on Dr. Jose Cardenas' Theory of Incompatability—as a model for addressing the educational needs of Hispanics in Denver.

Briefly, the Cardenas Theory of Incompatability states:

> [T]he educational failure of minority children is attributable to a lack of compatability between their characteristics pre-supposed by typical instructional programs tailored for a white, Anglo-Saxon, English-speaking, middle-class school population. Rather than changing the child to fit the instructional program, the theory proposes changing the instructional program to fit the child.[12]

The Cardenas Plan proposed the elimination of incompatability factors by "requir[ing] an overhaul of the system's entire approach to education of minorities and touch[ing] virtually every aspect of curriculum planning, methodology and philosophy."[13] It was anticipated that the ultimate goal of this plan would be to enable a child to accept his own cultural and linguistic characteristics in lieu of adapting negatively to an educational system imposed upon him.

A major issue surrounding the *Keyes* case involved the interpretation of a district's "equitable powers to intervene" in establishing a suitable remedy. In *Keyes*, the district court contended that intervention and reparation of past wrongs was necessary since the plans proposed by the school district failed to address the entire issue of desegregation and equal education, though it was given every opportunity to discharge its duty. The trial court ordered the school district to develop a bilingual-bicultural program consistent with the model proposed by the Congress of Hispanic Educators.[14] Further, the court, acting in the interest, and upon the request of the Mexican-American community not to be desegregated, declined to include five schools (seventy-seven to eighty-eight percent minority) in the Denver desegregation plan if it meant the elimination of existing bilingual education programs.

However, the controversy surrounding the court's intervention was not settled in the lower court, but was resolved in the United States Court of Appeals for the Tenth Circuit. The circuit court found that the lower court failed to establish sufficient evidence that the existing academic curricula or its methods of educating minority students discriminated and effectively barred Hispanics from equal education.[15] The appellate court added that the refusal of the school district to establish bilingual education programs tailored to meet specific cultural and developmental needs of minority students *could not* be considered a constitutional violation of the Equal Protection Clause of the Fourteenth Amendment. The appeals court did, however, address the issue of "identifiability" in considering the rights of Hispanics, adding that a "meaningful desegregation plan" must help "Hispano school children to reach the proficiency in English necessary to learn other basic subjects."[16] In addition, the appeals court concluded that a system-wide remedy is appropriate when a dual system is identified, and the use of "broad percentage guidelines" is an appropriate measure for determining a solution.[17]

However, the continued segregation of bilingual programs in the five pilot schools was viewed as illegal segregative conduct and as such was to be reevaluated to determine whether these programs could be "justified on grounds other than the institution and development of bilingual-bicultural programs at the school."[18]

Of equal significance, the court noted that the adoption of the Cardenas

Plan was not "removing obstacles to effective desegregation . . . [but rather] would impose upon school authorities a pervasive and detailed system for the education of minority children."[19] Thus, the Cardenas Plan could not be justified as a remedy for a violation of Section 601 of the Civil Rights Act of 1964 since the court's mediation "overstep[ped] the scope of remedy properly directed to the violation."[20]

Indeed, the legal dialect between desegregation, bilingual education and courts of law was established. The message in *Keyes* was clear:

> *Bilingual education . . . is not a substitute for desegregation.* Although bilingual instruction may be required to prevent the isolation of minority students in a predominantly Anglo school system . . . such instruction must be subordinate to a plan of school desegregation.[21] (Emphasis added.)

Therefore, the *Keyes* ruling struck down bilingual programs in segregated settings but made clear the role of bilingual education in the United States and can best be summarized in the following statements:

1. Hispanics, like black Americans, represent an *identifiable ethnic minority group* subject to the same rights afforded all citizens of the United States.
2. The maintenance of segregated schools in the name of bilingual education is not justified since bilingual education is not a substitute for desegregation.
3. The concentration of bilingual students in a school district that is otherwise integrated, does not represent a segregated dual system.[22]
4. Faculty desegregation; standards for reduction, demotions and dismissal of staff; and recruitment of minority teachers, staff and administrators, constitute an appropriate remedy in order that the ratio of minority personnel in each school is substantially closer to the ratio of teachers in the entire system and more truly reflects minority student ratios.[23]
5. Although the right of national-origin minority children to a bilingual education was not established, the basis for determining identifiability provided a firm basis for identifying further the educational needs and rights of Hispanics in future litigation.

Lau v. *Nichols*

The District Court for the Northern District of San Francisco found in 1971 that 2,856 students of Chinese ancestry in the San Francisco Unified School District spoke little or no English, and could not, therefore, comprehend the language of instruction. Of this total, approximately 1,790 received no instruction or special help in English and the remaining 1,066 students were provided supplemental courses in the English language on a part-time basis.

The non-English-speaking students filed a class action suit against the school district, seeking relief against the unequal educational opportunities which allegedly violated their legal rights guaranteed under the Fourteenth Amendment of the United States Constitution and the State of California. The plaintiffs (Chinese students) requested that the school district provide special English classes for all non-English-speaking children, utilizing bilingual teachers. The defendants (school district) admitted that the failure to teach the English-deficient children bilingually meant poor performance in schools and that the placement of students in special English classes was an arbitrary decision in the absence of reliable testing procedures to ascertain language proficiency. In addition, special classes for non-English-speaking children was not a matter of "right and duty" but a gratuitous effort by the school district contingent upon availability of money and personnel.[24]

In rebuttal, the plaintiffs contended that equality of education goes beyond equal access to educational facilities and resources since access alone cannot be the sole determinant of a child's educational rights. In support of the *Lau* petitioners, the federal government was granted permission to endorse the plaintiffs as *amicus curiae,* contending that statutory mandates provide for educational opportunities designed to meet the specific needs of non-English-speaking children. The plaintiffs attempted to establish a fundamental argument of discrimination based upon their guaranteed rights under the Constitution of the United States, the State of California and federal and state legislation promulgated under Title VI, Sections 601 and 602 of the Civil Rights Act of 1964. However, Edward Steinman, counsel for the plaintiffs, added that the Circuit Court of Appeals silenced all arguments, maintaining that the alleged discrimination programs experienced by the Chinese students were "not the result of laws enacted by the State . . . but the result of deficiencies created by the plaintiffs (children) themselves in failing to learn the English language."[25]

The District Court and the United States Court of Appeals for the Ninth Circuit agreed with the defendants and denied relief to the plaintiffs stating that there was no evidence to substantiate a violation of the Equal Protection Clause of the Fourteenth Amendment, nor Title VI, Section 601 of the Civil Rights Act of 1964. The court sympathized with the plaintiffs, but added that equal educational opportunities were provided each student since "they (appellants) received the same education made available on the same terms and conditions to the other tens of thousands of students in the San Francisco Unified School District."[26] Steinman added that the court callously concluded:

> Every student brings to the starting line of his educational career different advantages and disadvantages caused in part by social, economic and cultural background, created and contributed completely apart from any contribution by the school system. That some of these may be impediments which can be overcome does not amount to a 'denial' [by the school authorities] of educational opportunities within the meaning of the Fourteenth Amendment should they [school authorities] fail to give them special attention.[27]

In December, 1973, the plaintiffs requested and were granted consent to present oral arguments to the Supreme Court. In corroboration with the Chinese students, *amicus curiae* briefs were filed by the United States government, the Lawyers Committee for Civil Rights Under the Law, the National Education Association, the Puerto Rican Legal Defense and Education Fund and the Harvard University Center for Law and Education.

The Supreme Court heard arguments and in January, 1974, ruled in favor of the *Lau* plaintiffs and unanimously reversed the lower court ruling. Relying solely on Title VI of the federal Civil Rights Act of 1964, the

Supreme Court *first* noted that according to Section 601, "No person in the United States shall, on the ground of race, color, or national origin, be excluded from participation in, be denied benefits of, or be subjected to discrimination under, any program receiving Federal financial assistance."[28] The court added that since the San Francisco School District had received federal funds for education, it must comply with the contractual regulations of Section 601, and enforced in Section 602 of HEW regulations, which insure that recipients of federal funds comply with Section 601. The HEW regulation 45 CFR Section 80.3 (b)(1) further specifies that recipients may not:

> iv) Restrict an individual in any way in the enjoyment of any advantage or privilege enjoyed by others receiving any service, financial aid, or other benefit under the program.

Since Chinese students were receiving fewer benefits than English speaking students, the school system effectively denied Chinese students the opportunities to participate in educational programs, "earmarks of discrimination banned by the regulations."[29] The Supreme Court, in its analysis of the case, rejected the notion that the equal provision of, or access to, educational services is synonymous with equal education stipulated under Title VI. The Court observed that offering the same services to *all* children cannot be construed to mean that *each* child was receiving educational benefits equitably. In dismissing the equal access argument advanced by the lower courts, the Supreme Court found a denial of a meaningful opportunity to participate through the utilization of the same texts, classrooms and teachers without considering a language barrier. The Supreme Court opined:

> . . . [T]here is no equality of treatment merely by providing students with the same facilities, text books, teachers and curriculum; for students who do not understand English are effectively foreclosed from any meaningful education.[30]

The Supreme Court, in a clear display of irritation with the school district, denounced the classroom experiences of non-English-speaking children as "wholly incomprehensible and in no way meaningful," and added that ". . . [the] imposition of [a] requirement that before a child can effectively participate in the educational program he must have already acquired those basic [English] skills is to make a *mockery* of public education."[31] (Emphasis added.)

It is important to note that the Supreme Court in reversing the appellate court decision *did not* require bilingual education nor did it specify the course of action to remedy the problem. Rather, the Supreme Court remanded the problem to the District Court to decide upon the appropriate relief, asserting that school boards and not courts of law should be involved in educational planning, since no specific remedy was urged upon the Court.[32]

A second major point in *Lau* is that by relying on a statutory rather than a constitutional violation, the Court surreptitiously limited its scope of involvement. The Court deferred its enforcement to the Department of Health, Education and Welfare, Office of Civil Rights, which relied heavily on a memorandum issued on May 25, 1970, which states in part:

> Where inability to speak and understand the English language excluded national-origin minority group children from effective participation in the educational program offered by a school district, the district must take *affirmative steps* to rectify the language deficiency in order to open its instructional program to these students.[33] (Emphasis added.)

In retrospect, it can be surmissed that most school districts did not actively take affirmative steps to remedy the language deficiencies of their constituents due to the Court's apparent reluctance to define what constitutes an appropriate plan of affirmative action and the punitive action that would be assessed in cases of noncompliance.

Lastly, the Court touched on the issue of numerical guidelines in educational planning and development. The legal controversy was reduced to one of numbers—when does the number of affected students become so significant as to warrant special programs?

Expressing a minority view, Justice Blackmun concluded that numbers were "at the heart of this case . . . [adding that] . . . when, in another case, we are concerned with a very few youngsters . . . who speak . . . any language other than English, I would not regard today's decision . . . as conclusive."[34] The opinion of Justice Blackmun was not to be taken lightly in the battle to dismiss bilingual programs, as was apparent in *Otero* v. *Mesa County Valley School District No. 51*.[35] In this case, the Court noted that few students in the district experienced any "real language difficulty." Therefore, the lack of evidence to substantiate a violation of Title VI or the Fourteenth Amendment, and the lack of numbers, resulted in the dismissal of the claimed right to bilingual education.[36]

Regardless of the dissenting opinion, the Supreme Court mandated the San Francisco Unified School District to present an equitable plan to meet the special needs of the plaintiffs.

In October, 1977, a consent decree was entered in the District Court of Northern California providing for bilingual-bicultural programs for 10,903 students in San Francisco—including Chinese, Filipino, and Spanish groups—who spoke little or no English.

Serna v. *Portales Municipal Schools*

In the wake of the *Lau* decision, the *Serna* case in Portales, New Mexico, was the first test of bilingual education where segregation was not an issue. In *Serna*, the District Court of New Mexico found a violation of the Equal Protection Clause of the Fourteenth Amendment of the United States Constitution. The District Court observed that although an equal type of education (same teachers, classrooms, texts) was provided the Spanish-speaking students, the Portales school district failed to reassess and enlarge its educational program for students deficient in the English language.

Using test results administered to first and fifth grade students, which reflected language expression and intelligence quotient scores, the court concluded that the school district failed to establish a meaningful bilingual education program. In effect, this action denied Spanish-speaking students an equal education and thus constituted a violation of the Equal Protection Clause. As with *Lau*, equal education was given to unequal students. As a result, students of limited-English-speaking ability were unable to reach levels of academic performance equal to Anglo students since language barriers severely restricted those students and accounted for eighty percent of the achievement difference between Anglo and Chicano children.[37]

The school district responded to the plaintiffs' plea with a plan to remedy the educational program. The court rejected the district plan and mandated the adoption of a new bilingual education program.

On appeal to the Tenth Circuit Court of Appeals, the appellants (school district) contested the trial court's decision to specify the type of educational relief for the school district. The Circuit Court did not concur with appellants and observed that the *Serna* and *Lau* cases were nearly identical in that a totally English language curriculum had the effect of discriminating against students of limited English language ability. The Court of Appeals, therefore, upheld the trial court in a landmark ruling that established bilingual education programs as viable solutions in language related cases. The court clearly recognized the appropriateness and rights of Chicano school children to receive bilingual instruction under Title VI of the Civil Rights Act of 1964.

Predictably, however, the appeals court did not reach the constitutional Equal Protection Clause argument, but relied totally on the statutory violations of Title VI that were advanced in the *Lau* decision.

Of major significance in *Serna* was the fact that the court also denounced the appellants' proposed program as a "token" plan that would not really benefit students. In addition, the court recognized that since the Portales School District had not applied for federal educational funds under the Bilingual Education Act, nor accepted similar funds offered by the State of New Mexico, the court's duty to fashion a bilingual program for Spanish-surnamed children was necessary in order to assure that Spanish-surnamed children received a meaningful education.[38] As a result, the educational remedy developed by the court was properly directed to the violation, since the school district defaulted in its responsibility to provide bilingual education programs.

Aspira of New York, Inc. v. *Board of Education of the City of New York*

The effects of *Lau* and *Serna* were evident in the *Aspira* case filed in 1972. *Aspira* plaintiffs argued that the linguistic and cultural needs of Puerto Ricans and other Hispanics were not being fully addressed. The Board of Education relied upon the equal benefits analysis to deny the alleged district violations of the Equal Protection Clause and/or Title VI. The District Court rejected the defendant arguments and ruled in favor of the plaintiffs and mandated the Board of Education to conduct a survey of needs and resources to meet the linguistic and cultural needs of the plaintiffs.

In the aftermath of *Lau* and in consideration of the legal mandates imposed upon the Board of Education, a consent decree was reached between the plaintiffs and the defendants without appeal to a higher court. The decree acknowledged the rights of bilingual students and provided for the development of a bilingual program "for all New York City public school children whose English language deficiency prevents them from effectively participating in the learning process and who can effectively participate in Spanish."[39] The program was designed to provide emphasis upon curriculum development and reinforcement of Spanish language skills.

In order to measure language proficiency, students whose dominant language was other than English were administered an English standardized test. Those who fell below the twentieth percentile of all students tested and who, when tested in Spanish, scored higher in Spanish than English, were placed in bilingual programs. Students who scored above the twentieth percentile and who were no more proficient in Spanish than they were in English would not be placed in bilingual programs.[40]

It is evident that the problem of identifying and placing students with English language deficiencies was a major weakness of the decree, but was admissable in the absence of a better criteria for determining language proficiency. The court commented on the limitations of the decree:

> As has been noted, the assertedly "ideal" view of plaintiffs—to test all Hispanic students in Spanish and give the bilingual program to all who do better in Spanish than in English—is not accepted. The setting and the goal remain *a course of English language instruction* so those who can now participate *effectively* in English are outside the plaintiffs' case, whatever their relative fluency may be.[41] (Emphasis added.)

The *Aspira* plaintiffs regarded the consent decree as a poorly devised process to determine eligibility for the bilingual programs since many Hispanics who should receive instruction would be excluded. In dismay, the plaintiffs strongly voiced their opinion regarding the identification, classification, and evaluation of students when the results were illicit tracking, grouping, or placement of students in compensatory classes.

The weaknesses, however present, were recognized and included in the decree under the watchful eyes of educators and Hispanics, and implemented in the New York public school system.

Rios v. *Reed*

The impact of the previous court decisions related to affirmative action were most visible in the *Rios* decision. Spurred by the *Lau* and *Serna* rulings, plaintiffs in the school district of Patchogue-Medford, Long Island, questioned the "effectiveness" of the school district's bilingual programs. The plaintiffs requested information from the students' records to determine whether the program "effectively promoted academic progress and second language fluency."[42] The argument, identical to *Serna,* was that a program is "meaningless without a concommitant emphasis on the quality of instruction."[43]

Responding to the plaintiffs' request, school authorities noted that *Lau* stipulates that districts must take affirmative steps to rectify language deficiencies. The decision did not, however, describe the steps to be followed in order to rectify the problem. Hence, the obligation to disclose students' records by school authorities was not considered within the purview of the *Lau* decision. School authorities further maintained that the establishment of a bilingual program in itself satisfied the requirements under *Lau.*

The District Court noted the efforts of the school district to address the problem confronting non-English-speaking students. However, the trial court reminded the defendants of the *Serna* decision and its implications. The court added that the establishment of token programs that do not have the effect of benefiting students cannot be considered an act of compliance. The court stated:

It is not enough simply to provide a program for disadvantaged children or even to staff the program with bilingual teachers; rather, the critical question is whether the program is designed to assure as much as is reasonably possible the language deficient child's growth in the English language. *An inadequate program is as harmful to a child who does not speak English as no program at all.*[44] (Emphasis added.)

In the aforementioned opinion, the court clearly established criteria for defining, explicitly and implicitly, the meaning of "affirmative step." In addition, the court acknowledged the importance of bilingual education and the Bilingual Education Act of 1974.

Following the *Rios* decision, a definite pattern of judicial intervention was established: *Keyes* stipulated ethnic identifiability; *Lau* determined the need for affirmative steps; *Serna* identified the remedy—bilingual programs; *Aspira* established the usage of proficiency tests to identify students in need of bilingual education; and *Rios* affirmed the rights of bilingual students through school accountability.

OBSERVATIONS AND RECOMMENDATIONS

The enactment of the Bilingual Education Act in 1968, the subsequent Bilingual Education Act of 1974, and the anti-discrimination provision of Title VI of the Civil Rights Act of 1964 have strongly determined the means and method for implementing bilingual education. In addition, other federal and state legislative sources have provided funds for bilingual-bicultural education, including such programs as the Vocational Education Act of 1963 (Bilingual Vocational Training); Emergency School Aid Act, Title VII (Desegregation Assistance, Bilingual Programs); Elementary and Secondary Education Act, Titles I, III, and VII (Bilingual Education Basic Programs, and technical assistance in coordination); Higher Education Act, Title V (Teacher Training); and the Equal Educational Opportunity Act of 1974.

The surge of programs that have developed, directly or indirectly, from the legislation is not, however, indicative of the continuing resistance by school districts to these programs. Legal battles are still waged against further implementation and new arguments have resulted.

Despite the unanimous decision of the Burger court in the *Lau* case, many school districts do not yet consider deprivation so severe and educational neglect so defined to merit bilingual programs. Obviously, the issue is not an educational concern but a political problem.

Budgetary Argument

The question of economics and the *lack of funds* to implement bilingual programs (whether mandated or voluntary) is continuously raised by school districts. If one identifies the cost factor as a measure of defense, the overriding concern is the determination of statutory or constitutional violation. If a district receives federal funds for educational services, that district must comply with the federal legislation and guidelines promulgated under Title VI. Districts failing to comply with civil rights mandates, or suspected of noncompliance, will run a risk of immediate termination of federal funds, deferral of future federal funding or refusal by federal funding agencies to support future grant proposals submitted by those districts.[45]

At the state level, the argument of insufficient funds is equally dismissed. State education agencies must also comply with the federal statutes imposed upon them if they are recipients of federal educational funds. Since the state serves as a major contractor of federal funds and channels monies to subcontractor agencies (districts), it must recognize an affirmative obligation or suffer the consequences of noncompliance.

A second argument regarding finance involves the cost per pupil expenditure determined by the state's system of financing education. A district that fails to provide a meaningful education to students of limited English language abilities is in effect spending state educational funds unjustly and ineffectively. For example, the San Francisco Unified School District was spending $1,900 for educational services for each non-English-speaking child in the school system. As a result, approximately $9.5 million was spent on 5,000 non-English-speaking children (including the Chinese students) who were effectively excluded and denied an education.[46]

It should be noted that the question of added costs in implementing bilingual programs is readily apparent and costly to districts. However, the Supreme Court stood moot on this issue and its silence may therefore be interpreted as an implicit rejection of the districts' defense regarding budgetary constraints.

The case of the *United States* v. *Texas Education Agency,* which concerned a desegregation issue in the Austin public schools and the need to fund bilingual programs, also addresses this funding issue.[47] In Austin, the Court of Appeals noted that "cost is not relevant at the liability state and . . . although cost is a factor . . . a constitutional violation must be rectified."[48] To this end, the ultimate responsibility of the school district, not the state, is the equitable (re)distribution of funds to implement bilingual programs. Similarly, a court in the District of Columbia, concluded that "[i]f sufficient funds are not available to finance all of the services and programs that are needed and desirable in the system then the available funds must be expended equitably in such a manner that no child is excluded from a publicly supported education consistent with his needs and ability to benefit therefrom."[49]

Teacher Integration

The need for bilingual programs has become a highly contested issue among teachers in most school systems. Reassignment criteria have become a major concern among school teachers who often feel the pressure of being placed in totally bilingual settings with minimal interaction with monolingual English students and faculty. Conversely, a major concern among minority teachers involves the dispersal of faculty to schools in ratios that do not reflect the percentage of minority children in the school district. Without careful teacher placement, the dispersal of teachers and students as a plan of desegregation, can have the effect of matching bilingual teachers with students experiencing no language difficulties while other children experiencing linguistic and cultural interferences receive no special instruction. Further, the prospect of bilingual education programs is often minimized under the argument that integrated schools should not have segregated programs (bilingual or otherwise) nor segregated faculty. The separation of minority and non-minority students through bilingual programs often threatens to become a divisive issue in schools, as in communities. The issue that must be considered is whether the bilingual programs are within themselves integrated with minority and non-minority students. Since it is unlawful to have segregated programs, there should be bona fide ability grouping, heterogeneous grouping in the daily scheduling, staff/faculty integration and other integrative measures. Efforts should be made to insure that bilingual programs address the language deficiencies of children rather than separate and ultimately exclude children from participation in school activities, since regulations, such as the Emergency School Aid Act (ESAA), clearly forbid the separation of minority group from non-minority group children for a "substantial portion of the school day." Secondly, according to the *Lau* remedies, racially/ethnically isolated or unidentifiable classes per se are also not permissible when the result is "segregation and separate treatment."[50]

Finally, it should be noted that according to federal regulations, it is not educationally necessary or legally acceptable to *establish separate schools* of racial and ethnic composition in order to respond to the educational needs of Hispanic students. Therefore, the only viable solution is to establish bilingual programs within an integrative system in order to have an equitable remedy for children experiencing English language difficulties.

Numerosity Issue

Perhaps the most difficult issue to deal with is the question of establishing programs for a "substantial" number of students. Since *Lau* did not stipulate what constitutes a sizeable number, the only Supreme Court opinion on this matter was voiced by Justice Blackmun and supported by Chief Justice Burger, stating that, "numbers are at the heart of the case." The contention is that the *Lau* decision is applicable *only* when there are *many* children who do not comprehend English. It is important to note that regardless of their definite views, that opinion represents a minority view since the majority concurring opinion rejected the numerosity issue.

In *Otero* v. *Mesa County Valley School District No. 51*, the plaintiffs argued for bilingual education on similar arguments as those advanced in *Keyes* and relied on the Cardenas Theory of Incompatability to advance their position. The results were unfavorable to the plaintiffs and the court rejected the claims advanced by Chicano students. The court added the dimension of numbers, concluding that only a small number of students actually experienced language deficiency. Hence, the *Otero* decision affirmed that the Fourteenth Amendment does not mandate bilingual programs regardless of numbers.

In spite of the arguments against numbers, Hiller and Teitelbaum note that a legal basis exists for determining the individual rights of all students.[51] In the language of the Constitution, the Fourteenth Amendment states:

> [N]or [shall any state] *deny* to *any person* within its jurisdiction the equal protection of the laws.[52] (Emphasis added.)

The wording from Title VI of the federal Civil Rights Act of 1964 adds that:

> *No person* in the United States shall . . . be excluded . . . denied the benefits of . . . or be subjected to discrimination . . . under any program . . . receiving Federal assistance.[53] (Emphasis added.)

Lastly, the Equal Educational Opportunity Act of 1974 specifies that:

> No state shall deny equal educational opportunity to an *individual* on account of his or her . . . national origin . . . by . . . the failure . . . to take appropriate action to overcome language barriers . . .[54] (Emphasis added.)

Clearly, it should be evident that educational opportunities must be made available to any student. State and local education agencies should assume a major responsibility in determining the educational needs, the demand and feasibility of implementing bilingual programs in order to initiate equitable programming for their constituents.

To conclude, in viewing bilingual education and its prospect for the future, it is necessary to separate the legal issues from the philosophical principles of egalitarianism. The latter substantiates the rights of individuals to equal educational opportunity while the former determines the conduct of the courts in interpreting this issue. It is also essential to interpret the legal obligations of educational institutions in concert with the identifiable resources that will facilitate program development and management.

The overriding concern in bilingual education must continue to be the educational needs of all students. Language cannot be a barrier to participation or a tool of discrimination. Bilingual programs must be integrative in design in order to encourage children to participate and compete equitably in the public schools.

Beyond these major considerations, four patterns must be established in order to facilitate the adoption and implementation of language-related programs.

First, the advocacy position of the federal government must be emphasized and the power of enforcement made apparent. Investigative reviews of districts not complying with the federal and state mandates must be increased in order to justly interpret the spirit and the letter of the law.

Second, accurate assessments of the language proficiency and needs of students must be made. The performance levels of students must be evaluated and a determination must be made regarding the most suitable educational program to meet the needs of each child. Above all, programs should be designed with the students and parents in mind, since bilingual education may not be the solution for every child experiencing language difficulty.

Third, the curriculum and instruction within a school should be examined carefully to insure that courses and scheduling are not racially or ethnically identifiable. In-service training should be instituted to prepare all teachers, administrators, parents, aides, and other ancillary personnel to understand the concept and methodology of bilingual programs in order to improve their knowledge in this area.

Finally, school districts should avoid any tracking and misclassification of linguistically different children. Hispano children should not necessarily be placed in special programs on the assumption that language is a barrier, or that all parents desire bilingual education for their children. Hispano children and other minority children should share with their Anglo counterparts as much as possible the educational activities provided by that school. Regardless of the type of program (Transitional, Bilingual-

Bicultural, English as a Second Language or Multilingual-Multicultural), students must participate in the common curriculum to the greatest extent and in a most harmonious fashion.

It is unquestionable that countless other considerations must be addressed in bilingual education. Consonant with their commitments, school districts, state and federal education agencies, and judicial bodies must exemplify a concern for identifying the needs and rights of all citizens. Finally, we must take a pragmatic view toward law, education, and society in the context of justice according to the principles of democracy in order to serve the constituency of this nation. In the words of Justice William J. Brennan: "The law is not an end in itself, nor does it provide ends. It is preeminently a means to serve what we think is right."

NOTES

1. Brown v. Board of Education, 347 U. S. 483 (1954).
2. Glaser, Robert. "Individuals and Learning: The New Aptitude," *Educational Research*, Vol. 1 (June, 1972).
3. Steinman, Edward. "Lau v. Nichols: Implications for Bilingual Education," *Bilingual Bicultural Education: Conference Papers,* Ann Arbor: Program for Educational Opportunity, The University of Michigan, (1977):27.
4. Keyes v. School District No. 1, Denver, Colorado, 480 F. Supp. 673 (D. Colo. 1974) Rev'd; 521 F. 2d 465 (10th Cir. 1975), cert. denied; 423 U.S. 1066 (1976).
5. Lau v. Nichols, 414 U. S. 563; 39 L. Ed2d 1, 94 S. Ct. 786 (1974).
6. Serna v. Portales Municipal Schools, 351 F. Supp. 1279 (D. N. M. 1972), aff'd; 499 F. 2d 1147 (10th Cir. 1974).
7. Aspira of New York, Inc. v. Board of Education of New York, 58 F. R. D. 62 (1973).
8. Rios v. Reed, 75 C. 296 (E. D. N. Y., Jan. 14, 1977).
9. Cisneros v. Corpus Christi Independent School District, 324 F. Supp. 599 (S. D. Tex. 1970); 457 F. 2d 142 (5th Cir. 1972) (en banc) cert. denied; 413 U. S. 920 (1973).
10. United States v. State of Texas, 342 F. Supp. 24 (E. D. Texas 1971), aff'd per curiam; 446 F. 2d 518 (5th Cir. 1972).
11. 413 U. S. 189, 198 (1973).
12. Teitelbaum, Herbert and Hiller, Richard J. "Bilingual Education: The Legal Mandate," *Harvard Educational Review,* Vol. 47, No. 2, May, 1977:151.
13. Pressman, Robert. "Annotation of Northern and Western Desegregation Decision," *Overcoming Segregation and Discrimination,* Ann Arbor: Program for Educational Opportunity, The University of Michigan, (1977):123.
14. 380 F. Supp. 692
15. 521 F. 2d 482
16. Id., p. 465.
17. Pressman, "Desegregation Decision," p. 123.
18. Ibid.

19. 521 F. 2d 482
20. Pressman, "Desegregation Decision," p. 123.
21. 521 F. 2d 465 (1975).
22. Roos, Peter. In *Desegregation and Education Concerns of the Hispanic Community* (Conference Report), Washington, D.C.: The National Institute of Education, Department of Health, Education and Welfare, (1977):31.
23. Pressman, "Desegregation Decision," p. 123.
24. Steinman, "Bilingual Education," p. 24.
25. Ibid.
26. Id., p. 25.
27. 483 F. 2d 797
28. 42 U. S. C. 2000d (1970)
29. 414 U.S. 568, In Teitelbaum, Herbert and Hiller, Richard J. "Bilingual Education: The Legal Mandate," *Harvard Educational Review,* Vol. 47, No. 2, May, 1977:143.
30. 414 U.S. 566
31. Steinman, "Bilingual Education," p. 27.
32. 414 U. S. 564
33. 35 Federal Register 11595 (1970).
34. 414 U. S. 572
35. Otero v. Mesa County Valley School District No. 51, 408 F. Supp. 162 (D. Colo. 1975).
36. Teitelbaum and Hiller, "Legal Mandate," p. 151.
37. Levin, Betsy, *et al.* "Legal Issues Related to School Desegregation and the Educational Concerns of the Hispanic Community," In *Desegregation and Education Concerns of the Hispanic Community* (Conference Report), Washington, D.C.: The National Institute of Education, Department of Health, Education and Welfare, (1977):87.
38. 499 F. 2d 1154.
39. Aspira of New York v. Board of Education, Consent Decree, August 29, 1974 at 4.
40. 394 F. Supp. 1161 (1975).
41. Grant, Joseph. "Bilingual Education and the Law: An Overview," paper submitted to The Dissemination and Assessment Center for Bilingual Education, Austin, Texas.
42. Teitelbaum and Hiller, "Legal Mandate," p. 149.
43. 75 C. 296 at 16
44. Id., p. 15.
45. Teitelbaum and Hiller, "Legal Mandate," p. 153.
46. Steinman, "Bilingual Education," p. 32.
47. 467 F. 2d 848 (5th Cir. 1972).
48. 532 F. 2d 398 (5th Cir. 1976).
49. 348 F. Supp. 866 (D. C. C. 1972).
50. Teitelbaum and Hiller, "Legal Mandate," pp. 159-160.
51. Teitelbaum and Hiller, "Legal Mandate," pp. 158-159.
52. U. S. *Constitution,* amend. XIV.
53. 42 U. S. C. 2000d (1970).
54. 20 U. S. C. 1703 (f)(Supp. IV, 1974).

THE FEDERAL MANDATE FOR BILINGUAL EDUCATION

María Eugenia Matute-Bianchi

Achieving equality of educational opportunity continues to be a battle in this country. Bilingual education is only one of many efforts waged to establish public responsibility for achieving equal educational opportunity. While earlier efforts to equalize educational chances were aimed at equalizing resources and facilities, bilingual education joined the national scene at a time when compensatory efforts were considered to be the key to providing equality of educational opportunity.

Support for bilingual education as a process through which to achieve equality of educational opportunity springs from a variety of complex sources:

1. pressure from Hispanic communities for educational change and cultural recognition
2. this nation's ideological commitment to equality of educational opportunity
3. Supreme Court decisions, especially *Brown* v. *Board of Education* (1954), *Swann* v. *Board of Education* (1971), and, perhaps most importantly, *Lau* v. *Nichols* (1974)
4. official recognition of the problems facing Mexican-American children in schools which were documented and thoroughly researched, and hence, legitimated by the Office of Civil Rights
5. pressure from various sources to establish the principle of federal responsibility for non-English-speaking children in public schools
6. advocacy on the part of many large school districts needing increased fiscal support as a result of pressures mounted by declining tax bases and enrollment changes

These factors have not only legitimized federal intervention in public schools—an intervention that was unknown prior to the passage of the Elementary and Secondary Education Act of 1965 (ESEA)—but have committed the federal government to assume a responsibility for the education of linguistically different children. That all these factors contributed to the passage of the 1968 Bilingual Education Act and the 1974 Bilingual Education Amendments underscores the fact that the resulting Title VII programs have not been oriented to a single, homogeneous purpose. The legislation, the controversies, debates, and congressional hearings that have gone on behind the initial entitlement and subsequent amendments reflect these various interests and the competitive social and political priorities.

The record is clear. Despite numerous philosophical, fiscal and administrative controversies, the federal mandate in support of bilingual education has been established and expanded. The 1968 Bilingual Education Act initiated the federal responsibility for assuring equal educational opportunity for linguistically different children and defending the legitimacy of their native language and culture in the school. The 1974 Bilingual Education Amendments not only affirmed but expanded this responsibility. Title VII programs continue to manifest this established federal responsibility.

Let us now turn to a more focused discussion of the 1968 Bilingual Education Act. It is often hailed as a masterpiece of ambiguity, raising more conflicts than solutions to the problems of linguistically and culturally different children in the schools. It was instituted as a demonstration program with funds allocated on the basis of potential for development of pilot projects designed to test the effectiveness of new and imaginative curricular plans, and the development and dissemination of special instructional materials for use in bilingual education programs. The intent of Congress in promoting this demonstration concept was the development of model programs which could be replicated once their effectiveness had been established. The assumption was that, before committing large amounts of money and before attempting to serve all limited-English-speaking students, the federal government should sponsor experimental pilot projects. Indeed, in 1969, the first year of Title VII funding, there were seventy-nine projects funded for a total of $7,500,000 serving some 26,500 students.[1] This funding level and scope of offered services were merely a token effort in light of the fact that estimates place the number of school-age (preschool to age eighteen) limited-English-speaking pupils in the U.S. at about six percent of the total school-age population in the United States.[2]

The 1968 legislation is unclear and imprecise from a variety of standpoints. Not only does it fail to define bilingual education and the type of bilingual programs the federal government was interested in sponsoring, it is decidedly ambiguous with respect to the goals of federally sponsored bilingual education. There is no doubt that the ambiguity of this landmark piece of legislation is a reflection of the legislative process whereby the language of intent contained within the legislation is deliberately unclear in the sense that no one wants it deliberately clearer. For example, in the original legislation there was no definition of bilingual education. Nor was it clear whether the goal of the legislation was transition into English or native language maintenance or both. The ambiguity of the language allows more legislators and advocacy groups to buy into the action without having to compromise needed political alliances tied to other pieces of legislative and political activity. This is the nature of the legislative process but it does complicate the implementation of legislation when there is no single, clearly stated congressional intent. Moreover, since there is confusion over congressional intent, there is confusion and controversy over the goals of bilingual education, the eligible recipients of program support, and the level of fiscal support.

According to Bruce Gaarder, three major goals have emerged out of the 1968 Bilingual Education Act, and each one is in basic opposition to the others:

1. the development of a more effective, more just one-way bridge to English by building upon content instruction first in the mother tongue (transitional bilingual instruction)
2. the development of more effective education for limited-English-speaking children, in addition to the long-term development and maintenance of both English and the mother tongue (maintenance bilingual education)
3. the provision of a source of jobs in education and of preferential treatment for members of the ethnic groups involved[3]

The original 1968 legislation was unclear as to the purpose of this new funding. Was it to speed up the assimilation of linguistic and cultural minorities by means of a humane transition into English? Or was it to support the development and maintenance of the minority language in addition to the English language? Advocates for both types of programs base their advocacy on their own interpretations of the legislation, as well as succeeding legislative amendments and judicial decisions. The differences between the two competing approaches (transition versus maintenance) are open to bitter debate, unevenly divided along ethnic lines, and fueled by the changing economic and political realities of the day. The "can do" philosophy and optimism which sparked the War on Poverty efforts in compensatory education, has now changed to a "can't do" orientation, largely as a result of the more constraining political and techno-economic realities facing the nation. The recently completed U.S. Office of Education Impact Study on Spanish-English Title VII Programs (known as the A.I.R. report), and Noel Epstein's attack on the inappropriateness of federally sponsored programs of 'affirmative ethnicity' (bilingual maintenance) have raised the ante of the transition versus maintenance debate.[4] But back in 1968 the differences between the two approaches and their controversial implications were either unknown or unvoiced.

In 1968 the debate centered over whether bilingual education represented an appropriate, innovative response to the educational needs of limited-English-speaking children of poverty or whether it represented an un-American, counterproductive intrusion on the "English only" instructional policies in schools and institutions all across the land. Up until the passage of the National Defense Education Act of 1958, the federal government had little interest in reversing its traditional "English only" national language policy, reflecting the discriminatory legislative history, as well as nationalistic and isolationist foreign policies affecting linguistic and cultural minorities residing within U.S. boundaries.

The 1960s ushered in the civil rights movement with its accompanying ideology of ethnicity, and the political context in which domestic Third World groups operated, changed dramatically. The rise of Chicano consciousness followed on the heels of the black civil rights movement, and coincided with the worldwide processes of decolonization and Third World consciousness movements, the flowering of an aggressive U.S. imperialist involvement in Southeast Asia, and deteriorating economic conditions. The ideology of ethnicity, a ritualization oriented to reaffirming and perpetuating a new sense of history and a new interpretation of reality, sparked an interest in bilingual education as a quest for identity, cultural status and political power.

Chicanos focused upon bilingual education as part of a process of defining interests as they related to issues of power in this society. It was a way of creating an awareness of a shared fate, a comprehensive "place" from which to search out a niche in space, time and relation. By focusing on the urgent need for bilingual education, many Chicanos were able to make use of the ideology of ethnicity as a political resource, one of the few resources available to the politically powerless in this society. The politics of ethnicity, however, obscured the need to examine carefully the various philosophical approaches, the competing goals, or the programmatic issues involved. Rather, the politics of ethnicity tended to romanticize and reify a single, homogeneous Chicano culture which ignored differences between groups and classes of Chicanos and recent Mexican immigrants. As Gerald Rosen points out:

> Creating an awareness of a shared fate in spite of many potentially divisive group characteristics is essential to successful unified action. This is most particularly the case when unity is the one political resource that must be available in the de-colonization struggle.[5]

One consequence, then, of this situation was the assumption that what must be good for the goose must be good for the gander, i.e., that Chicanos and recent Mexican immigrants could all profit and succeed educationally with the implementation of bilingual education. Such an assumption ignored the fact that many urban Chicanos—and the Chicano population is decidedly urban—are monolingual English-speakers with few perceived economic, political, or social reasons for learning Spanish. Moreover, the assumption ignored the class and racial basis of relations between Chicanos, Mexicans and whites which influence the form and process of schooling. Bilingual education has been based on the assumption that the problems facing Chicanos and Mexicans in schools are primarily those of language differences. This is made quite clear in the introductory paragraph of the 1968 Bilingual Education Act:

> The Congress hereby finds that one of the most acute educational problems in the United States is that which involves millions of children of limited English-speaking ability because they come from environments where the dominant language is other than English . . .[6]

While the analysis of the educational problems facing Chicanos and Mexicanos in the schools was incomplete and rooted in superficial assessments of language differences and cultural conflict, bilingual education was very much a product of the War on Poverty optimism and heightened concern for the Spanish-surnamed population. The 1960 census documented the dramatic increase of Spanish-speaking constituents. By 1967 the federal government had established the Interagency Committee on Mexican American Affairs and the Mexican Affairs Unit within the Office of Education in response to the growing recognition of the problems facing Spanish-speaking people. The hearings before the U.S. Civil Rights Commission on Mexican-Americans and the publication by the Equal Employment Opportunity Commission of a study entitled *Spanish-Surnamed American Employment in the Southwest,* documented that Spanish-speaking persons faced enormous educational, economic and political problems. It was clear that something had to be done.[7]

The passage of the 1968 Bilingual Education Act was a reflection of all these forces. The emerging voices of ethnic lobbyists and strong civil rights advocacy found in the Johnson administration and in the Congress paved the way for its passage. The political and social implications of the legislation, while never clearly or precisely articulated, accompanied the purely educational issues and have been an intimate part of the history of bilingual education since 1968. For this reason alone it is improper as well as impossible to attempt an understanding of federally supported bilingual education without a thorough exploration of the social-action features accompanying the passage of the 1968 Title VII program.

There was, of course, some resistance to the legislation. For example, the Office of Education was initially reluctant to support Title VII legislation on the basis that the need of non-English-speaking children could be met through existing provisions in Title I and Title II of ESEA.[8] This reluctance in part reflected the apprehension felt in other quarters over the federal government assuming responsibility for non-English-speaking children as a protected class. In other words, there was a fear that once the federal government had assumed even this limited responsibility for supporting demonstration programs in bilingual education for a limited period of time, the door would then remain open for continued, perpetual federal subsidy of what should be a state-supported endeavor. And of course there was some resistance to the legislation based on racist fears over the presumed anti-American or un-American approach of bilingual education. "If they want to speak Spanish, let them go back to where they came from," was a commonly voiced refrain, which conveniently ignored the fact that many Spanish speakers came from El Paso, Corpus Christi, Calexico and other Spanish-speaking bastions in the United States.

The 1968 Bilingual Education Act, then, was a major victory for those who felt the federal government should assume an important responsibility for the educational problems of linguistically and culturally different children of poverty. One assumption of the legislation was that poor children could be helped out of poverty if they could overcome the language barrier. Hence, the monies authorized by the bill were earmarked specifically for low-income students. As Bruce Gaarder noted, the act provided for financial assistance for children of limited-English-speaking ability and defined the eligible population in such an ambiguous way as to attract the support of ideologically diverse camps.[9]

In addition to the political and social climate which supported bilingual education, court decisions have also played a prominent role in expanding the federal role—especially in the years after 1967. The *Lau* v. *Nichols* decision in 1974 did not advocate bilingual education, but did establish the notion that equality of educational opportunity does not mean equality of treatment and that students who do not understand English are effectively foreclosed from meaningful education if they are instructed in a language they do not understand. In the aftermath of *Lau*, *Serna* v. *Portales Municipal School District* (1974) the court ruled in favor of the Spanish-speaking plaintiffs who charged that the English-only instructional program denied them equal educational opportunity and was a violation of their constitutional right to equal protection under Amendment Fourteen.

In *Aspira of New York, Inc.* v. *Board of Education of the City of New York* (1974), a consent decree which is probably the most far-reaching court-ordered bilingual program since the *Lau* decision, forced the school board to set up a bilingual program for all children whose English-language deficiencies prevent them from effectively participating in the learning process. According to a report by the U. S. Commissioner of Education, judicial decisions such as these three reflect a general trend in favor of plaintiffs who charge that school districts do not adequately address the special needs of limited-English-speaking children:

> Although the courts do not always require bilingual education as a remedy, their actions are in accord with the more general trend for support of bilingual education in the United States.

The judicial climate in support of bilingual education is based in no small measure on the May 25, 1970 memorandum issued by the Office of Civil Rights. This memorandum has played a crucial role in the development of federally supported bilingual education in that it clarified OCR's responsibility in enforcing the provision of the 1964 Civil Rights Act (Title VII) which requires that there be no discrimination in any federally supported program. The decisive element of this memorandum is as follows:

> Where inability to speak and understand the English language excludes national origin-minority group children from effective participation in the educational program offered by a school district, the district must take affirmative steps to rectify the language deficiency in order to open its instructional program to these students.[11]

The significance of the memorandum was primarily affirmed in the *Lau* decision and has been a cornerstone for subsequent court decisions. The document assumed an even greater significance with respect to the federal role in light of the language survey conducted by the Commissioner of Education, which found that of the more than 15 million persons from non-English-speaking households, more than 5 million (or forty percent of the group four years of age or older) were from Spanish-speaking homes, and made up sixty-nine percent of the school-age population among the 15 million non-English-speaking homes.[12] As the federal government began to document the extent of educational problems confronting the Spanish-speaking population, through various Office of Education reports, studies by the Office of Civil Rights, and the report by the Comptroller General's Office, it became clear to those in the federal bureaucracy that the government could not ignore the problems.

With varying degrees of interest and advocacy, various groups and agencies within the bureaucracy—specifically within the Office of Education and the Office of the Secretary of HEW, and the legislative branches—began to assess the growing federal involvement in support of bilingual education. The immediate aftermath of the passage of the 1968 Bilingual Education Act, the May 25 Memorandum of the Office of Civil Rights, and the *Lau* v. *Nichols* decision introduced a number of controversial issues which framed the debate over the 1974 Bilingual Education Amendments.

In 1968 the passage of the Bilingual Education Act suggested the permissibility, even the desirability, of instruction in the native language, but by 1974 the controversies and implications generated by the ambiguity of the original legislation began to emerge. This was the setting which ushered in the 1974 Bilingual Education Amendments.

The 1974 Bilingual Education Amendments

The first major revision of the Title VII program occurred with the passage of the 1974 Bilingual Education Amendments. Although the original bilingual legislation was amended twice before 1974, the changes were relatively minor. However, by 1974 the conflict emerging out of the 1968 legislation, the diversity of approaches, definitions and competing philosophies forced the debate in Congress and in the administration into a major revision of the statute.

By 1974 the issue of transition versus maintenance was clearly out in the open, with debate growing increasingly more intense. Supporters of transitional programs argued that the proper goal of a bilingual program should be to promote the fastest possible assimilation of the limited- and non-English-speaking children into the English-speaking mainstream. Supporters of the maintenance concept argued that bilingual programs must be designed to maintain the linguistic and cultural resources of this culturally pluralistic society by maintaining the linguistic and cultural identity of the limited- and non-English-speaking. The federal regulations governing the application procedures for Title VII proposals reflected this controversy. The official Project Manual, issued by the Office of Education as an interpretation of the legislation, implied two opposing positions. On the one hand, the manual affirms the primacy of the English language in the bilingual program, and on the other hand recognizes that the use of the child's mother tongue might prevent academic retardation.[13]

The implications of transition versus maintenance brought to the fore other unresolved issues surrounding federally sponsored bilingual programs:

1. How much instructional time should be accorded each language?
2. What role did ESL (English as a Second Language) play in a bilingual program?
3. Since Title VII guidelines established a poverty criterion, how could a bilingual program be designed which did not segregate children according to language, origin or race?
4. What was bicultural education and what role did it play in a bilingual program?
5. Was the federal government to continue to sponsor Title VII as a demonstration program (limited funds allocated on a competitive basis for the development of dissemination models) or as a full-service program based on the formula grant nature of Title I (non-competitive funds allocated on an established formula basis)?
6. In light of the May 25, 1970 memorandum and the 1974 *Lau* decision, just what should be the appropriate goal of federally sponsored bilingual education?

The significance of these questions is compelling; their answers have yet to be resolved and continue to predominate the national debate over federally supported bilingual education. However, by 1974 the federal government was committed—if only nominally—to require that the needs of limited-English-speaking students be met on penalty of loss of federal assistance.

The process of amending the Elementary and Secondary Education Act (ESEA 1964) began with the introduction of four distinct pieces of legislation in both houses of Congress (H.R. 69, S. 1539, S. 2552 and S. 2553), and was ultimately resolved by a conference committee of both Houses. Throughout the 1974 reauthorization process, both bodies engaged in an intensive overall review of elementary and secondary education legislation. Title VII was but one of several federally sponsored education programs subjected to intensive scrutiny.

There were eleven major areas of difference which had to be resolved in the Conference Committee (policy; definition of bilingual education programs; expiration and authorization of funding; distribution of funds; local educational agency grants; training grants; state educational agency grants; research and demonstration grants; participation of Indian reservation school children; national advisory committee on bilingual education; administration[14]). The following results were accomplished by the new legislation:

1. an increase in appropriations and in the number of local education programs funded
2. an increase in funding awarded for fellowships, teacher in-service training and paraprofessional training
3. an increase in funding for classroom materials development, with awards going to two national dissemination assessment centers, nine materials development centers and seven resource centers
4. the upgrading and reorganization of the Division of Bilingual Education to an Office of Bilingual Education, with the director of the Office reporting directly to the Commissioner of Education
5. the formation of the fifteen-member National Advisory Council on Bilingual Education, composed of professionals and practitioners in the field (but no parents)

Moreover, the passage of the 1974 bilingual education revisions resolved certain simmering philosophical issues dealing with bilingual-bicultural education and the federal responsibility. The issue over the appropriateness of the federal role was resolved in favor of retention of the role established in 1968, i.e., that of sponsoring demonstration programs. In addition, the federal role was expanded to include sponsorship of capacity-building projects, especially in the areas of teacher training, curricula, and research which would stimulate local community capacity to eventually take over the programs.

The issue of transition versus maintenance was "resolved" but with little clarity. The new legislation affirmed a transitional goal of bilingual programs but did not specifically exclude maintenance programs. Consequently, both types of programs could be promoted. However, within the framework of both transition and maintenance programs, the issue of whether bilingual education and cultural enrichment must be required was clearly resolved: Federally supported bilingual programs specifically *could not* be E.S.L. efforts alone, and had to include both native language instruction and cultural enrichment.

The process of resolving all these issues, culminating in the passage of the 1974 amendments, was an arduous one, complicated even further by a variety of political, personal and partisan considerations.[15] New issues and problems surfaced, specifically in the areas of research, administration and civil rights compliance. In the years immediately following the passage of the amendments, the national debate over bilingual education has taken up a number of the issues surfacing out of the 1973-74 reauthorization process, and has been reflected in the current 1977-78 reauthorization process, revolving around four emerging basic problems:

1. the well-established controversy of transition versus maintenance goals
2. demonstration versus full-service project
3. effectiveness of the administration of the program by the Office of Education and the Office of Bilingual Education
4. effectiveness—as demonstrated by conclusive research findings—of bilingual-bicultural education as a curricular and pedagogical innovation

In sum, then, the 1974 Bilingual Education Amendments represented the first major revision of the original 1968 legislation and an attempt to resolve the major conflicts and problems in federally supported bilingual education. According to Schneider in her thorough account of the 1974 reauthorization process:

> . . . the 1974 Bilingual Education Act represented a reform of existing law and existing Federal practice in the field of bilingual-bicultural education. It would be difficult to make a quantitative measurement of that reform. The proponents of such reform in the Congress and Administration were enthusiastic. The opponents were somewhat dissatisfied but not, other than the Office of Management and Budget, outraged. The lobbyists viewed the final compromise as having achieved some desirable goals, but not all. However, all shared the sense that the law presented a continuing and expanding Federal role in bilingual-bicultural education.[16]

The passage of the act was, in the final analysis, a temporary truce between various constituencies within the federal bureaucracy. The mediating influence of the truce was the *Lau* v. *Nichols* decision handed down in January, 1974. This decision had a profound effect on the bilingual education debate, emphasizing the federal role in ensuring compliance with the 1964 Civil Rights Act. The *Lau* decision reaffirmed the federal commitment to providing equal educational opportunity. The Bilingual Education Act, which was signed into law in August 1974, affirmed the federal commitment to providing equal educational opportunity for limited- and non-English-speaking children.

The Legislative Process, the Federal Bureaucracy and Bilingual Education

The federal bilingual education effort is in no small measure affected by the interplay between personalities, political interests, institutional constraints and outside lobbying groups. It is an intensely political process but no more so than the legislative and bureaucratic maneuvers that affect other governmental activities. The intensity of the process and the sophistication of the strategies employed reflect the high stakes for which the game is played. The game is one for power between the various legislative, bureaucratic and administrative factions—a game of win or lose with the outcome determining the relative status of one group vis-à-vis the other groups.

The game is, in essence, a four-way ping pong game between members of Congress, the incumbent administration, the professional bureaucrats and the special interest groups, with alliances and hostilities within and between the various factions coloring both process and outcome. Each faction advances or undermines a particular program, expands it or reduces it as much as possible, and attacks it or defends it against all challenges. The dynamics of the interplay assume a life independent of the world outside Washington, insulating the players of the game from sustained contact with life outside. It is within this climate that the business of government is transacted. It is from within this environment that federally supported bilingual education must be understood.

As soon as huge sums of money have been made available, there are swarms of supporters and lobbyists descending on Washington. Inevitably a bureaucracy of advocates springs up to carve out and institutionalize a section of "turf" as a toehold within the system. In the case of bilingual education, a Hispanic bureaucracy has grown up which is battling its way up the ladder of prestige and status. Bilingual education has been the rallying cry. Within the complex system of patronage and status within the federal system, the Hispanic bureaucracy and specifically the Office of Bilingual Education, ranks relatively low within the system. This low status and prestige of the OBE has a profound effect on the interplay between this office and the Office of Education, the various offices directly under the Secretary of HEW, and the several legislative committees on Capitol Hill. The OBE is not highly regarded by the more powerful factions higher up in the HEW bureaucracy. It is not highly regarded by legislative factions on Capitol Hill. Moreover, it is not highly regarded by other Hispanics (primarily Chicanos) in Washington who consider the OBE as a source of embarrassment.

I spent several weeks in Washington collecting data for this study. While there I interviewed various individuals, many of them Chicanos who have been involved in policy-making aspects of the federal bilingual education effort. Some have worked as lobbyists, others as Congressional liaisons, others with the Department of Health, Education and Welfare, and still others as White House liaison with Hispanic constituencies. When the Office of Bilingual Education was brought up for discussion, most of the people I talked to were critical of this office for not having exerted more leadership, for not having developed a more effective political constituency, and for not having broadened the level of discussion surrounding the federal role in bilingual education. In the words of one Congressional liaison I spoke with:

> . . . the Office of Bilingual Education has not taken care of business. How can you have a program if you have no sense for policy?

A lobbyist I spoke with said:

> If there is no policy there really can be no program. Those people over there in the Office of Bilingual Education have no training, no understanding and hence, can provide no leadership.

There was the sense among many persons I spoke with that the Office of Bilingual Education was staffed by career bureaucrats who have been a source of embarrassment to a "collective Hispanic effort." Consequently, the activities of the OBE and groups supporting its activities (such as the National Advisory Council on Bilingual Education) are seriously circumscribed and are the object of constant derision. For example, the NACBE is closely affiliated with the personnel in the OBE, and has publicly applauded OBE's efforts in its annual reports on bilingual education. The recommendations issued in these annual reports have been ignored by the HEW bureaucracy. Also, the A.I.R. interim results were released at a time when they could be most damaging to the bilingual reauthorization, in the spring of 1977 when the process was just beginning. The study, which was commissioned by the Office of Planning, Budgeting and Evaluation within the Office of Education, is critical of Spanish-English bilingual education. It is widely believed that the preliminary findings of this study were released in early 1977 precisely as a strategy to weaken the support for bilingual education in the reauthorization process.

Be this as it may, it does not necessarily mean the demise of the Hispanic bureaucracy. As with other bureaucracies, once established they are difficult, if not impossible, to dismantle completely. The institutionalization of the bilingual education bureaucracy in Washington has to do with the idiosyncracies of the demonstration project - full service project continuum. Although demonstration projects are funded on the basis of competition for limited duration, they have a way of developing into entrenched full-service programs, funded on a noncompetitive basis for an unlimited period of time. Meredith Larson, professional staff member on the House Committee on Education and Labor, explained the continuum this way:

> The law is clear that Title VII was established as a demonstration program. But equally clear is that demonstration programs lead to service programs. You go through demonstration because you know that once a program gets installed it never goes away. A bureaucracy grows up and it will never go away. Look at the example of Follow Through. Each year it goes through the death throes, but we will never get rid of that program.[17]

The advancement along the demonstration-service continuum was mentioned in the May, 1976 Comptroller General's report on bilingual education, commenting on a 1971 Office of Education task force report which indicated that Title VII had become more and more an educational service program than a demonstration one.[18] As the report states:

> Bilingual education was relatively new in the U.S. when the program was established in 1968, and accordingly the Congress intended that it be a demonstration program. The goals of the program were sound in that, before committing large amounts of money and attempting to serve all children needing these services, effective bilingual education approaches should first be developed. However, the program has evolved into a small service program and little progress has been made in achieving original program goals.[19]

Despite the fact that the bilingual education bureaucracy is advancing along the continuum from demonstration to full service, it does not mean that Title VII has been firmly institutionalized within the federal bureaucracy. As noted by Leticia Chambers, legislative aide to Senator Pete Domenici:

> Title VII money is funny money. It is not stable money. It is hard to institutionalize a demonstration program.[20]

Regardless of the tenuousness of the bilingual education bureaucracy within the federal system, it has achieved a toehold and will probably continue to inch its way up the ranks. In many respects, the demonstration-service continuum is analagous to the transition-maintenance split, and it is likely that as the program inches toward the service end of the continuum, it will at the same time be inching toward federal support of bilingual maintenance programs. The final outcome of this process is still in doubt, but clearly the seeds for full-service maintenance have been planted and will continue to be nurtured to the extent possible by the bilingual education bureaucracy.

The intricacies of the legislative process within the federal bureaucracy profoundly effect bilingual education in a number of other ways. The partisan politics between a Republican administration and a Democratic Congress has influenced not only the scope of the funding but the level of actual expenditures in Title VII, although it doesn't necessarily follow that a Democratic President with a Democratic Congress will produce significantly different funding levels or expansion activities. Bilingual education is also influenced by the interplay between various personalities within the various offices of the Secretary and the Under Secretary of HEW, alliances and hostilities between bureaucrats in the aforementioned offices and the Office of Education, legislative committees, the Office of Bilingual Education, and certain officials in the White House. Additionally, all of these relationships and official involvements are shaped and influenced by the lobbying efforts of such groups as Mexican American Legal Defense Education Fund (MALDEF), El Congreso Nacional de Asuntos Colegiales (CONAC), the Chicano Education Project of Colorado, National Council of La Raza, the Hispanic Affairs Unit of the Democratic National Committee, the American Federation of Labor, the National Education Association, and the American Federation of Teachers.

How successful any one lobbyist group is in advancing its particular position with respect to bilingual education depends on a variety of factors, but either its success or failure will have an impact on the development of the administration's position, the outcome of both House and Senate committee deliberations, the passage of subsequent legislation and the development of ensuing rules and regulations guiding the implementation of the legislation. For example, during the 1977-78 reauthorization, the Chicano Education Project of Colorado was very successful in lobbying a reluctant Carter administration with respect to certain issues in bilingual education, particularly as they related to community participation in bilingual education. So successful were they in their efforts that a special White House meeting was convened in early October of 1977, attended by various Hispanic groups, HEW Secretary Joseph Califano and Vice President Mondale. The meeting represented the significance of the effort made by the Chicano Education Project—a significance which subsequently paled when the action shifted over to the Congress. While there are at least a half dozen or more Hispanic groups in Washington that have had an impact on the course of federally sponsored bilingual education, the practitioners of bilingual education in the field, particularly the National Association for Bilingual Education (NABE) and the California Association for Bilingual Education (CABE), and the National Advisory Council on Bilingual Education (NACBE) which was established in the 1974 Bilingual Education Act, have had little impact on either the course of legislative activity or on the implementation and articulation of federal policies within the bureaucracy. *Presumably,* the practitioners are the ones who are most closely affiliated with the rank-and-file recipients of Title VII monies and who could, *presumably,* articulate some of the issues and concerns of this voiceless group into the federal decision-making arena. But to date, these groups have demonstrated a profound naivete and unsophistication about the political processes of legislative activity and bureaucratic maneuverings.

This naivete and unsophistication has been all the more dramatically underscored during the last two reauthorization processes (1973-74 and 1977-78) when bilingual education was subjected to ever-growing attacks and challenges. The 1977-78 reauthorization has been particularly controversial given the impact of the A.I.R. study, the backlash of both *Lau* and *Bakke,* the criticism of Noel Epstein, and the apparent resistance of both Jimmy Carter and Joseph Califano to support an expansion of federal activity in bilingual-bicultural maintenance programs. According to several informed Spanish-speaking lobbyists and bureaucrats in Washington, NABE and CABE have been remarkable in their political ineptitude, having no sense of the current political scene. As one of them noted:

> Down at NABE's conference in Puerto Rico in April, they were talking about the future of bilingual education as if in a fantasy world. How can they talk about bilingual education without taking care of business here in Washington! And these are all we have in terms of organized advocates for bilingual education. The other Spanish-speaking lobbies have many other agenda items to watchdog.

Whether or not NABE, CABE and the NACBE seek to act in this capacity is unclear. But they do represent the only organized potential to link the Spanish-speaking barrios to Washington, which could have enormous political impact on many issues, not just bilingual education. However, the development of this potential does not look especially promising given the fact that both CABE and NABE are victims of the same professionalization and insulation which plagues the schools.

It should be clear by now that the legislative process, together with the machinations of the federal bureaucracy and the incumbent administration generate consequences for bilingual education at an exponential rate. What happens to bilingual education in the next several years will ultimately depend on a variety of interlocking factors, including the following:

1. court decisions which favor bilingual education as an appropriate remedy in cases of violations of the 1964 Civil Rights Act, Title VI
2. the federal role in enforcing desegregation and the impact this will have on both federally and state-supported bilingual education
3. conclusive research evidence which supports bilingual-bicultural education as a pedagogical innovation

4. the development of more sophisticated political strategies on the part of organized and emerging bilingual lobbyist groups to influence legislative activities and subsequent reauthorizations
5. the politics of ethnicity as they interact with the ever-changing dynamics of power within the halls of Congress, in the White House, and among the ranks of the professional bureaucrats. This factor is especially critical with respect to the relatively low prestige of the Hispanic bilingual education bureaucracy (specifically in the Office of Bilingual Education) among other influential Hispanic groups and among higher-ranking officials in HEW and on Capitol Hill.

The discussion up to now has been concerned with the major themes and issues which have developed in federally sponsored bilingual education since 1968. The discussion has also explored the manner in which these themes and issues have made their way through the legislative process and the federal bureaucracy. Throughout the discussion, a good deal of attention has been focused on the nature of the political issues attending to the focal issues of transition-maintenance and demonstration-service. Thus, a framework has now been established which allows us the opportunity to explore in detail the federal mandate for parent-community involvement in bilingual education.

The Federal Mandate for Parent-Community Involvement in Bilingual Education

At best the federal mandate for parent and community involvement in bilingual education is a weak one. It has never been a priority in Title VII, although it received more attention during the last reauthorization (1977-78) than at any other time in the history of Title VII. Several facts emerge upon reviewing not only the literature on parent-community involvement in bilingual education, but the machinations of the legislative and bureaucratic labyrinth as well:

1. There is no consensus on the purpose, function or goals of the parent and community advisory councils.
2. There is no policy, either in HEW, the Office of Education or in the Office of Bilingual Education, on citizen or parent participation in educational decision making.
3. There is no theory of involvement upon which to generate policies or develop models which can then be evaluated.
4. There is no reliable body of data of research findings which could help clarify and reformulate policy issues.

The federal mandate for parent-community involvement in bilingual education, then, reflects a lack of commitment, a lack of policy, a lack of purpose:

> There is, in fact, no mandate for parent or community involvement in educational decision making.

Despite the rhetoric as to its importance, the absence of policy, the absence of data, the absence of theory, the absence of specifically worded governing rules and regulations, the absence of established models of involvement, the absence of training programs or technical assistance to parent-community councils, all point to one undeniable conclusion: There is no federal interest in promoting meaningful, substantive parent-community involvement in bilingual education. In the words of one Hispanic official in the Office of Bilingual Education:

> . . . as long as it threatens the bureaucrats, you'll never have community involvement. If it threatens the bureaucrats, forget it . . . By bureaucrats, I mean us. We keep them out.

Evidence in support of this statement is overwhelming.

The history of parent and community involvement in federally sponsored bilingual education parallels that of other Department of Health, Education and Welfare sponsored social action programs—a history of no policy, lack of commitment and disinterest. The review of the literature on citizen participation indicates that many social action programs with mandated community and parent involvement have experienced problems, conflicts and inadequacies generated, for the most part, by the ambiguity, the tokenism, and the condescension surrounding these efforts.

What has occurred in bilingual education has followed a by now well-established pattern in the Department of Health, Education and Welfare: interpretation of the galaxy of Congressional intentions which are then reformulated or ignored by disinterested policy makers within the various offices in HEW, particularly the Office of Education and Office of Bilingual Education, who have very little stake in the actual outcome of citizen participation on local communities. The nature of the federal bureaucracy, a leviathan of enormous proportions, offers no practical incentive for an agency's investment in participatory structures at the local site level.

Once in a while there appears on the scene in Washington a person or group of people who are thoroughly committed to the concept of sustained, substantive involvement of the community at the local level. This appears to have been the situation with the recently completed Urban/Rural Project administered through the Office of Education under the Education Professions Act of 1968. No such committed group has advanced the cause of parent-community involvement in bilingual education.

Since there is no federal policy or interest in parent-community involvement in bilingual education, it comes as no surprise that there is apathy and confusion, as well as frustration and controversy at the local site level. The San Jose Bilingual Consortium-C.O.M.E. controversy has been the most polarized of the struggles, but there is growing indication that the issues raised in the San Jose struggle are felt in other communities. The strength of the Colorado Chicano Education Project's lobbying efforts during the 1977-78 bilingual education reauthorization was based in part on parent-community involvement issues.

Despite the fact that there is no direction, leadership or interest in parent-community issues at the federal level, there is some evidence to support the claim that in the early 1970s the Department of Health, Education and Welfare was interested in at least looking at the problems of citizen participation in all of its programs. Elliot Richardson, then Secretary of HEW, requested a study that would review HEW goals, review prior experiences and research relevant to various forms of citizen participation. The purpose of the study was the development of information that would assist HEW in drafting regulations and models for citizen participation in specific HEW programs. In making his request, Richardson proposed three goals for the department in the area of citizen participation:

1. to devolve power to clients
2. to reduce alienation of clients to the service agency
3. to improve program effectiveness

It is difficult at this point to ascertain how far down the bureaucratic maze this request filtered, or the impact it had on the thinking of the various constituent agencies within the department. There is little evidence of any impact on the Office of Education or on personnel within the office charged with administering bilingual education. Presumably there was no interest at this level in responding affirmatively to Richardson's call. Any other departmental interest in Richardson's study apparently vanished when he left HEW during the brewing Watergate crisis.

Let us look once again at the three goals of citizen participation promulgated by the Richardson study: to devolve power; to reduce alienation of clients; to improve program effectiveness. While there is no evidence to support the endorsement of these goals within the organizational hierarchy administering bilingual education, there is some evidence that it affected the rhetoric attending to the issue of citizen participation. To have taken these goals seriously would have meant, at the very least, the development of tentative strategies and policy statements, or the sponsorship of pilot programs to test the efficacy of implementing such goals. But the fact remains that the Office of Bilingual Education has not been addressing itself to strategies. It has been relatively passive on the issue of parent-community involvement in bilingual education. This passivity continues to exist.

The original bilingual legislation in 1968 made no provision for parent or community involvement. This omission parallels the history of parent-community involvement in ESEA Title I, passed in 1965. In the late 1960s all that was suggested in the ESEA guidelines was that parents and other groups be *consulted* about the program, but it was not clear how this consultation was to be accomplished. There were no formal requirements for parent involvement. In 1968 the ESEA amendments required the local school agencies to establish an "appropriate organizational arrangement" to involve parents and community members, with the suggestion that an advisory council was an appropriate way to comply with this requirement. In November the regulations were again changed, this time requiring "maximum practical involvement" but there was no clear statement as to what this meant or how to implement it. Since the early 1970s, the ESEA amendments dealing with Title I have been the revisions of Title VII, which reflects in part the strong advocacy for parent-community participation in the National Council on the Education of Disadvantaged Children.

In bilingual education, the 1973 governing federal rules and regulations required only that a community advisory committee be established, that it be afforded an opportunity to review and comment upon proposed programs prior to submission of the proposal, and that at least fifty percent of the advisory committee be made up of parents of children served by project funds.[21] The only evidence required by the guidelines as evidence of compliance with this component of the regulations was the following:

1. a membership list of advisory council members which had been published in a newspaper of general circulation or otherwise made public
2. a statement of the date the application was submitted to the advisory group for review and comment

3. the written comments or recommendations, if any, made by such a group with respect to the application

Although the regulations call for the local educational agency to consult periodically with the advisory group, there is no indication as to what this consultation should mean or how it could be implemented. The school could call for a public meeting, hand out a proposal (written in English), verify that some parents did, in fact, attend the meeting and submit comments—and thereby comply with the federal requirements for parent-community involvement.

In 1974 there were no major changes in these federal regulations, although there was a change in the requirement of group membership. Prior to 1974 the membership requirement stipulated that fifty percent of the group had to be made up of parents of children served by the project. In recognition of the fact that many limited-English-speaking parents were thereby being excluded from participation on the council, the 1974 revisions mandate that the ratio of English-dominant parents to limited-English-speaking parents on the council had to approximate the ratio of such persons in the program.[22]

In the 1976 revisions of the governing regulations there are a few changes in the parent-community participation component. In addition to asking for assurances that the LEA would provide the advisory council periodic opportunities to observe and comment upon the bilingual program's activities, the LEAs were also asked to make provisions to involve the committee in the evaluation of the program.[23] There is no statement or suggestion as to how this might be accomplished. The one other major change in the 1976 regulations dealt with the membership requirements. This time the regulations clearly state that only parents of limited-English-speaking children served by the project could serve on the council. This change was prompted by the widespread trend for English-dominant parents to dominate the council's limited-English parents.

We can see from this brief examination of the federal regulations governing parent-community participation in bilingual education that the requirements are nothing more than vaguely worded requests for compliance. Furthermore, at the federal level, there has been no assessment as to what constitutes consultation between the parents and the school or how to implement the consultation. There is no requirement that the school incorporate the recommendations of the council in the submission of the Title VII proposal. And, most importantly, there is no requirement that parents and community members be trained to promote their active participation. At best, the regulations reflect some vague notions that parents and community should somehow be consulted in the program's activities and in the development of the funding proposal. But at worst, the regulations provide for the abuse, manipulation and exploitation of the parent-community councils because they fail to provide specificity, support, or policies to protect the rights of parents. And while there is provision within the statute to allow for the training of parent-community advisory members, there is no leadership or interest in the Office of Bilingual Education to promote training of any kind for parents.

Programmatic considerations aside, the lack of interest in promoting parent-community training represents a strategic political mistake, a political unsophistication and naivete on the part of the Hispanic bureaucracy in bilingual education. Whatever their political persuasion within the federal bureaucracy, the Hispanics in bilingual education might have promoted the training of parent-community councils which in turn might have generated a sizeable lobbying effort for bilingual education.

Perhaps one reason why the Office of Bilingual Education has never really promoted the idea of training is that there is some reluctance, even fear, in the higher echelons of HEW to promote any activities which might activate the political consciousness of council members. There is a tendency within the department to make a distinction between parents and community, with the distinction based on a level of political activism. There is real feeling among various high-ranking HEW officials that community groups—a euphemism for political activists—will use the Title VII advisory council as political vehicles for ethnic power. In a memo to Secretary Joseph Califano, dated October 1, 1977, Michael O'Keefe (Assistant Secretary for Policy and Evaluation) wrote:

> While parent involvement is certainly desirable, it should probably not be a principal focus of the statute. . . . The degree of emphasis [on strengthening parent-community advisory councils in Title VII] promoted by the Colorado legislators [of the Chicano Education Project] might politicize projects to the detriment of educational objectives.[24]

Another HEW staff person, in an off-the-record interview, revealed similar sentiments:

> We have gone as far as we can go at the federal level. We can require parent-community involvement and then just hope it is meaningful. Parents should be involved, and so should the community—but within certain limits. They shouldn't be involved in issues over control, like hiring and firing. Only on issues that pertain to education.

Still another HEW staff person in an off-the-record interview underscored the above statement:

> The major problems in implementing parent-community participation revolve around the politics of it. They [the community activists] want to use it as a political vehicle for other things. I don't see any way to get the community involved at the local level. It really is a local issue. The community should not be involved . . . only the parents. They're the only ones with a vested interest in the outcome of the program.

The comments of these individuals, which are representative of other staff persons within the department, indicate how far we have come since the initial exuberance and optimism of the 1960s War on Poverty. When ESEA was initially promulgated, it was seen as a social reform using educational intervention strategies as an aid to eliminating poverty. Moreover, the legislation also provided for political changes by creating a *promise* of increased public access to institutional decision making. In the decade since the passage of ESEA Title VII, the exuberance and optimism have turned to suspicion, mistrust, and wariness. Within the agency itself there is the semblance of a half-hearted interest in parent (but not community) participation in bilingual education, as if to say, "We want parents to be informed, but not too informed. We want them to be involved, but not too involved. We want them to be organized, but not too organized." The implicit assumption here is that parents are to be involved as long as they are acquiescent and non-threatening—the making-tamales-for Cinco de Mayo syndrome. Once the participation begins to make strides in parent education and training, interest in supporting, maintaining and institutionalizing the participation wanes.

One effective mechanism which militates against the institutionalization of substantive parent participation is the absence of any formal grievance procedure or hearing procedure to resolve disputes at the local level. If parents raise substantive issues over questions of program finances, expenditures, personnel actions and the like, there is no procedure for a formal hearing or review. According to Steve Winnick, an attorney in the Education Division of the Office of the General Counsel in the Office of the Commissioner of Education:

> If there are questions like an audit dispute, misspending of money, there is a formal appeal process. But the Office of Education determines this and decides whether a formal review is necessary. A parent group does not have a right to bring a formal suit against the LEA. Only OE can.[25]

If the Office of Education determines that a formal appeal is unwarranted, the only recourse the disaffected parent-community groups have is to write letters to the Commissioner of Education or to the Secretary of HEW. Some groups have given up in frustration and disgust. Other groups, notably C.O.M.E. in San Jose and the Chicano Education Project in Colorado, have used more sophisticated extra-legal lobbying strategies outside HEW. However, the success of these efforts remains to be seen. Only with the final outcome of the 1977-78 bilingual education reauthorization and subsequent revisions in the governing regulations will we learn of the impact these and other community groups have had in changing the administration, implementation and monitoring of parent-community participation in bilingual education.

In this section the federal mandate—*the lack of a federal mandate*—for parent-community participation has been presented in great detail. The background for understanding the federal position was developed in an overview of the original federal Bilingual Education Act of 1968, dealing specifically with the ambiguity of the legislation, the influences of the War on Poverty and Civil Rights Movement on the concept of equal educational opportunity and bilingual education, the implications of the transition versus maintenance controversy, and the effect of the key court decisions favoring bilingual education as an effective remedy for limited-English-speaking children.

The framework for understanding the federal position was then explored with respect to the major revisions in the federal legislation contained within the 1974 Bilingual Education Act. The issues of transition versus maintenance were again considered as they influenced the demonstration versus service project continuum in bilingual education. Attention was also given to a consideration of the major areas of difference which had to be resolved in favor of passing the 1974 bilingual education revisions. While these issues are not central to an understanding of the federal position on parent-community participation in bilingual education, they are important insofar as they illuminate the intricacies of the legislative process and bureaucratic operations.

The next major section dealt specifically with the intricacies of the legislative and bureaucratic processes effecting bilingual education, informing the reader as to the complexities of the interplay. In the final analysis, it is this complexity which shapes and directs the federal role in parent-community participation in bilingual education.

The concluding section was an analysis of the federal position in directing and implementing parent-community participation in bilingual education. Specific consideration was given to the absence of policy, data, theory, established models, training programs, and legal recourse in the federal role. The conclusion to the analysis is that there is no federal mandate, that there is no federal position favoring sustained, substantive parent-community participation in bilingual education.

NOTES

1. *Bilingual Education: An Unmet Need,* Report to the Congress by the Comptroller General of the United States, p. 3. Washington, D.C.: May 19, 1976.
2. *The Condition of Bilingual Education in the Nation,* First Report by the U. S. Commissioner of Education to the President and the Congress, p. 21. Washington, D. C.: 1976.
3. Bruce Gaarder. "Bilingual Education: Central Questions and Concerns," in *Bilingual Education,* eds. LaFontaine, Persky, Golubchick, p. 36. Wayne, New Jersey: Avery Press, 1978.
4. Noel Epstein. *Language, Ethnicity, and the Schools: Policy Alternatives for Bilingual-Bicultural Education*. Washington, D. C.: Institute for Educational Leadership, The George Washington University, 1977; American Institutes for Research, *Interim Report, Evaluation of the Impact of ESEA Title VII Spanish/English Bilingual Education Programs*. Palo Alto, California: February, 1977.
5. Gerald Rosen. "The Chicano Movement and the Politicization of Culture," *Ethnicity*. 1 (July 1974):292.
6. *Elementary and Secondary Education Amendments of 1967, Statutes at Large 81,* secs. 701-706.
7. Arnold H. Leibowitz. "Language Policy in the United States," in *Bilingual Education,* eds. LaFontaine, Persky, Golubchick, p. 8. Wayne, New Jersey: Avery Press, 1978.
8. Ibid., p. 9.
9. Bruce A. Gaarder. *Bilingual Schooling and the Survival of Spanish in the United States,* p. 105. Rowley, Massachusetts: Newbury House Publishers, Inc., 1977.
10. *The Condition of Bilingual Education in the Nation,* p. 12.
11. May 25, 1970, Memorandum of the Department of Health, Education, and Welfare, *Federal Register* 35, 11595 (July 18, 1970).
12. *The Condition of Bilingual Education in the Nation,* p. 23.
13. *Manual for Project Applicants and Grantees,* U. S. Department of Health, Education, and Welfare, Office of Education, Washington, D. C., p. 7.
14. Susan Schneider. *Revolution, Reaction or Reform: The 1974 Bilingual Education Act,* pp. 127-137. New York: Las Americas Publishing Co., 1977.

15. Ibid., p. 147.
16. Ibid., p. 163.
17. Personal interview with Meredith Larson, Professional Staff, Minority Side, House Committee on Education and Labor, Wednesday, May 31, 1978, Washington, D. C.
18. *Bilingual Education: An Unmet Need,* p. 9.
19. Ibid., p. 29.
20. Personal interview with Leticia Chambers, Legislative Assistant to Senator Pete Domenici (R. New Mexico), June 6, 1978, Washington, D. C.
21. *Federal Register,* Vol. 38, No. 189, Monday, October 1, 1973.
22. *Federal Register,* Vol. 39, No. 100, Wednesday, May 22, 1974.
23. *Federal Register,* Vol. 41, No. 141, Friday, June 11, 1976.
24. Memorandum from Michael O'Keefe, Assistant Secretary of Health, Education, and Welfare, Policy and Evaluation, to Secretary Joseph Califano, October 1, 1977.
25. Personal interview with Steve Winnick, Attorney, Educational Division of the Office of the General Counsel, Office of the Commissioner of Education, Department of Health, Education, and Welfare, June 1, 1978, Washington, D. C.

CHOICE OF LANGUAGE AS A HUMAN RIGHT— PUBLIC POLICY IMPLICATIONS IN THE UNITED STATES

Reynaldo Flores Macías

This essay is a *tactical* exploration of the legal bases for bilingual schooling and bilingual public services in the United States. I am not advocating, at this point in time, a national language policy, but that this tactical exploration may contribute to the debate about whether to have one, and if so, what it might consist of. I am indicating, as well, that the debate over the language choice of schooling and other social services, has been dominated by bilingual schooling and has been a narrow debate. It has excluded the issues of language choice as a daily reality—both positive and negative—that non-English-speaking persons enjoy throughout the country.

Any discussion of language policies, whether at the local or national level must include the effects of that policy on all areas of a person's life: employment, contact with social services, the law, and health institutions, to mention a few. The debate must be broader. The notion of human rights is one way to broaden the debate, even though it has been primarily tied to discussions of international affairs and foreign policy.[1]

In the last few years, as attention has increased on human rights in the international community, the language situation of non-English speakers in the United States—particularly in schooling—has also drawn attention. Few have brought the two themes together. Heinz Kloss (1971, 1977), A. Bruce Gaarder (1977), and Shirley Brice Heath (1977) have drawn our attention to this nexus between human rights and language choice, but little else has been done.

This essay covers the nature of the human rights debate in the international arena, its implications for the domestic situation of non-English speakers, and the elements of a United States human-rights language-choice policy, with a focus on Spanish-speaking people in the United States.

International Review of Human Rights Concerns

Prior to the establishment of international organizations in this century, the international legal protection of linguistic minorities was slight, though language as a basis and mechanism of social control and exploitation has a much, much longer history.

The first significant legal/constitutional protection of language groups came with the organization of the League of Nations. The nations

> undertook to "assure full and complete protection of life and liberty" to all their inhabitants "without distinction" of "language," and to assure all their nationals equality before the law and enjoyment of "the same civil and political rights" without distinction as to "language" (McDougal, Laswell, and Chen 1976: 161, citations omitted).

These countries assured each other that no discrimination based on language would be sanctioned, by also providing protection for the freedom of "access," or use of the language in particular domains—in any private intercourse, commerce, religion, press, publications of any kind, and public meetings. Non-discrimination in the courts was provided by allowing speakers of the non-official language recourse to their own language verbally or in writing, in court proceedings (McDougal, Laswell, and Chen 1976: 162). The international agreements of the time also provided linguistic minorities the right to establish, manage and control, at their own expense, organizations and schools in which they could use their languages. Member nations were also obliged to provide adequate mother-tongue primary school facilities, where there were significant concentrations of non-official language speakers.

Present day protection of linguistic groups comes primarily from the United Nations Charter and related documents. "The Charter consistently enumerates 'language' along with 'race, sex, religion' as an impermissible ground of differentiation" (McDougal, Laswell, and Chen 1976: 163).

Another document is the Universal Declaration of Human Rights, adopted by the U.N. General Assembly in 1948, which also makes language an impermissible ground of distinction. The declaration "makes no explicit reference to freedom of access to languages," but "such freedom would appear inherent in the policy of fundamental freedom of choice, which pervades the entire declaration" (McDougal, Laswell, and Chen 1976: 164). Singled out for particular reference to language would be the following rights enumerated in the Declaration.

1. the right to effective remedy (Art. 8)
2. the right to due process of law (Art. 10)
3. the right to privacy, family, home or correspondence (Art. 12)
4. the right to freedom of religion (Art. 18)
5. the right to freedom of opinion and expression (Art. 19)
6. the right to education
7. the right to participate in the cultural life of the community

Other international instruments involving human rights which afford protection to language minorities include

1. The Convention Against Discrimination in Education (1960)
2. The International Covenant on Economic, Social, and Cultural Rights (agreed to 1966, in force 1976)
3. The International Covenant on Civil and Political Rights (agreed to 1966, in force 1976)

In addition to these agreements, which expressly mention language, some noted jurists of international law feel that

> since language is often a prime indicator of a "national, ethnical, or racial" group, that the various prescriptions designated for the protection of ethnic or racial groups, such as the Genocide Convention

> (1948) and the Convention for the Elimination of Racial Discrimination (1969), might on occasion be invoked to protect groups in the enjoyment of their home language (McDougal, Laswell, and Chen 1976: 167).

There are also the regional conventions which include language groups, as a class, among those groups to be protected—The European Convention on Human Rights and the American Convention on Human Rights.

McDougal, Laswell, and Chen (1976: 152-153), indicate the various ways of language discrimination.

> Deprivations imposed in relation to language may be manifested in a variety of modes, notably—denial of opportunity to acquire and employ the mother tongue, the language of the elite, or world languages; deprivations imposed upon individuals through group identifications and differentiations effected by language; deprivations resulting from arbitrary requirements of specified languages for access to different value processes (as, for example, employment); the conduct of community processes and enterprises, especially of enlightenment and power, in languages alien to members of the community; and, finally, the coerced learning of specified languages other than the home language.

Before proceeding to discuss the status of international human rights agreements in the United States, the following brief points should be kept in mind. There is much vagueness on the interpretations of these documents and how they should be applied, even though there is general agreement that they reflect an emerging international norm of minimal human rights in relation to government conduct.

These rights are also reflective of the changing nature of international law as well. International jurisprudence is moving away from only mediating relationships between governments and their citizenry—from an *international* law to a *world* law, where the impact of governmental action on the quality of individual and human life is on review.

In reflecting these changes, these international agreements begin to include a greater concern for implementation (and enforcement) and so governments raise greater cautions about participation in these multilateral agreements, and raise fears of meddling in the domestic affairs of member nations. Human rights agreements have been variously viewed as *desirable goals* for the world community and as *legally binding norms* on the parties to the agreements. Selectively, countries have been spotlighted for their violations of human rights. At the same time, individuals are beginning to make inroads in being given legal standing before international bodies, thus bypassing their governments. This international legal concern for human rights is relatively new, is developmental, and bears watching and shaping.

A second point one should keep in mind is that the notions of "language rights" must be clarified. There are here two kinds of rights: (1) the right to freedom from discrimination on the basis of language; and (2) the right to use one's language(s) in the activities of communal life. There is no *right* to *choice* of language, of governmental service for example, except as it flows from these two rights above in combination with other rights, such as due process, equal enforcement of the laws, and so on. But, the identifiability and, if you will, legal standing, of a class based on *language* is recognized throughout the international community.

A third point is the ranking of human rights. While all can be viewed as formally or conceptually "equal," there are more immediate ones which have, for political and other reasons, been focused on, such as freedom from racial discrimination (Veenhoven 1975: xvi). Others are ranked according to the resources needed to meet them, such as the right to schooling and to an adequate standard of living. Still other reasons for ranking involve the compatibility of various rights with the legal/political system of a country, or with cultural/social traditions of a society. For example,

> while the Western tradition of human rights centered on the individual, it was sometimes forgotten that the vast majority of the world's peoples had not been raised in this tradition . . . , and that they therefore viewed human rights issues from a different perspective. . . . Marxism, almost by definition adopted a collective view of human rights. Many Third World leaders felt the extension of civil liberties had to take second place to economic development (Veenhoven 1975: xix).

The United States, International Treaties, and Human Rights

The United States government through the current administration, has recently made much of the human rights situation in the world and has, thus, focused greater attention on the issue, internationally and domestically. As part of its *foreign* policy, the United States government recognizes three categories in human rights.

First, the right to be free from governmental violation of the integrity of the person. Such violations include torture, cruel, inhuman or degrading treatment or punishment, arbitrary arrest or imprisonment, denial of a fair public trial, and invasion of the home.

Second, the right to the fulfillment of such vital human needs as food and shelter, health care and schooling, while recognizing that these depend on a nation's economic development.

The third category of human rights recognized by the United States government, is the right to enjoy civil and political liberties including freedom of thought, religion, assembly, expression and movement (Derian 1978: 244; and Schachter 1978: 75-76).

The status of international human rights *within* the United States, however, bears upon those international agreements to which the United States is a party. The United States has signed the United Nations Charter, and voted for the Universal Declaration of Human Rights, but only in the Fall of 1977, did President Carter sign the International Covenant on Civil and Political Rights, the International Covenant on Economic, Social and Cultural Rights, and later the American Convention on Human Rights, and the International Convention on the Elimination of All Forms of Racial Discrimination (1969) (Weissbrodt 1978: 35-36). These treaties all await ratification by the Senate along with the Genocide Convention (1948), which had been submitted to Congress earlier (Commerce Clearinghouse, *Congressional Index,* "Treaties," July 12, 1979).

These treaties were not ratified earlier, in part due to an administrative policy based on early congressional opposition to the treaties in the 1950s. Some members of Congress feared the treaties might (1) encourage international scrutiny of the racial discrimination in the United States, and (2) infringe on prerogatives of the states in the United States federal system (Weissbrodt 1978: 38-39, footnote 45).

> The enactment of domestic civil rights legislation, the announcement of court decisions to eradicate some of the worst injustices of racial discrimination, the related decrease in concern for state's rights, and the increasing interest in international human rights, have considerably improved the climate for ratification of these multilateral treaties (Weissbrodt 1978: 41).

On February 23, 1978, President Carter also submitted a letter, with memoranda on the Covenants, that recommended a series of reservations and understandings, which, among other things, would take away from these multilateral agreements any legal force they might gain in United States domestic courts (cf. Weissbrodt 1978; and Lillich 1978).

Without entering the complicated vagaries of international and national politics and strategies, the question of human rights—as it stands now—is legally bifurcated between a developing international standard and a national standard. This is still an open question, however, since the Senate has not yet ratified the treaties, and it warrants the informed concern, if not the involvement, of this country's citizenry, including its non-English-speaking citizenry.

It is important because treaties and federal law possess "equal dignity" under the Constitution. If they conflict, the most recently adopted, controls. Further, federal law, including treaties, controls state law if the two conflict (Weissbrodt 1978: 54-55). But this holds only if the treaties are considered "self-executing," that is, binding on domestic courts without the aid of implementing legislation. President Carter has recommended an understanding they be *not* self-executing.

Federal courts, in facing other treaty and United Nations issues, have lately been very reluctant to declare international agreements self-executing, citing the judicial lack of jurisdiction due to the separation of powers, which makes the treaties part of the executive branch's responsibility in foreign affairs (cf. Lillich 1978; and Weissbrodt 1978).

One can argue that there are sufficient domestic sources to protect human rights in the United States so that Carter's reservation that the covenants are not laws applicable to United States courts without implementing legislation, is not so severe. There is a great overlap between those rights derived from the constitution and the civil rights legislation, and those human rights listed in the international agreements. However, there are significant differences in the recognition of a right to education, and identification of language issues, if not the legal standing of a class based on language.

The Constitution guarantees many things, but does not give language rights nor a right to an education (Foster 1976: 158). For example, the right to equal protection of the laws has been the basis for much of the legal pursuit for bilingual schooling. Language issues have been heard when related to discrimination of *fundamental* rights, such as voting and due process.

> The relative success of litigation seeking bilingual services is determined by the nature of the rights involved. Voting, for example, has

> been traditionally viewed as a fundamental right, and any infringement on its exercise is subjected to exacting judicial scrutiny. Inequality in the criminal justice area is also scrupulously probed. Cases involving the unequal delivery of social services, such as welfare, have received less favorable treatment by the courts (*Bilingual Education—Current Perspectives*, Vol. 3—Law, 1977: 35, footnotes omitted).

One court has summed up the equal protection doctrine as follows—"... government action which without justification imposes unequal burdens or awards unequal benefits is unconstitutional" (*Hobson* v. *Hansen*, 269 F. Supp. 401 (D.D.C. 1967) as quoted in Foster 1976: 164). There is and there will be, differences as to "what government action is, and on what makes an unequal burden. And the application of this rule depends also on the prior identification of a class upon which the inequality falls" (Foster 1976: 164). One observer noted a couple of years ago, that "a class based on language distinctions, such as 'non-English speakers,' may be too broad to warrant special attention from the courts; however, a class based on 'national origin' would be distinctively considered" (Foster 1976; and *Bilingual Education* 1977: 38-39).

Consequently, not only must language rights issues be related to "fundamental rights," but a language group must be consonant with a national origin or racial group in order to pursue language equality through the courts. We will further address the problem of classification of language groups below.

The courts have generally rejected the Constitutional arguments in bilingual schooling cases (except for the District Court in *Serna* v. *Portales School District*, 351 F. Supp. 1279 (D.N.M. 1972), *aff'd* 499 F. 2d 1147 (10th Cir. 1974), which was upheld by the Circuit Court but *not* on constitutional grounds). They have also rejected them in lawsuits seeking bilingual government services and equal employment opportunity. Some federal courts have found the due process clause of the Fourteenth Amendment to the Constitution to apply in criminal trials where the defendant speaks no English and there is no interpreter. "This Constitutional approach, however, has not prevailed" (Bergenfield 1978: 550). State courts have not done any better in applying constitutional doctrine, particularly where the class was defined by the court based on language only and not in terms of national origin (*Bilingual Education* 1977: 37-39).

There has been greater success in language litigation based on legislative grounds, especially the 1964 Civil Rights Act and administrative interpretive memoranda, and the 1965 Voting Rights Act. The key cases in this area are highlighted by the U.S. Supreme Court decision in *Lau* v. *Nichols*, 414 U.S. 563 (1974), where the Court did not reach the Constitutional arguments, but held that the San Francisco Unified School District, which received federal financial assistance, violated section 601 of the 1964 Civil Rights Act, which bans discrimination based on race, color, or national origin in any federally funded program, and U.S. Department of Health, Education and Welfare (HEW) regulations outlining that non-attention to the language situation of non-English-speaking students constituted national origin discrimination. The class suit had been brought by "non-English-speaking students of Chinese ancestry." Three of the concurring justices, however, indicated that the Civil Rights Act alone may not have sustained the decision, but when regulations are "reasonably related to the purposes of the enabling legislation," and they require (as in this case) affirmative or special attention to a situation or problem, they will be upheld.

It is tempting to say that somehow the *Lau* decision created some language rights for the plaintiffs, but it did not. The plaintiffs sought no specific remedy by the school district and the Court demanded none. Although federal funds are flung wide among most school districts, the 1964 Civil Rights Act is limited to those districts where federal funds are in use. At least for two of the justices, the magnitude of the numbers of the affected non-English class "was at the heart of this case." It is heartening, however, that the interpretation of the HEW regulations (that non-attention to the language needs of students constitutes national origin discrimination) has been codified in the United States Education Code (20 U.S.C.A. sec. 1703(f)). Whether the concern for "substantial numbers" would be an issue under the statute is an open question. It is binding, however, as federal law and not dependent on a district receiving federal funds.[2]

The *Lau* holding has been extended to apply in cases involving welfare rights and governmental services as well (*Bilingual Education* 1977: 36-37). But, here again, a language group must coincide with a national origin group for the court to consider the case and the language argument must be tied to discrimination based on national origin to win.

The 1965 Voting Rights Act and its 1975 Amendments, now provide for determining if an election is in violation of the Act and thus discriminatory, if it is exclusively in English.

> Five percent of the voting age population within any state or political subdivision are members of a single language minority, and the rate of illiteracy of the particular language minority exceeds the national average of voting age citizens (*Bilingual Education* 1977: 36, citations omitted).

The Voting Rights Act, however, applies only in certain parts of the United States. Also, the implementation of the "remedy," bilingual elections, may be less than satisfactory.

> Unfortunately, the Voting Rights Act and the guidelines interpreting the Voting Rights Act's bilingual provisions do not assure a completely bilingual process. The guidelines may encourage election officials to translate selected passages in an election document, which could result in translations being incomplete or misleading. Even if there is a complete bilingual translation, election officials may decide not to translate all election documents and notices.
>
> Also, there is the concept of "targetting" which involves the extent of bilingual distribution. Although there may be complete bilingual translation, election officials may decide to target or distribute the bilingual materials only in certain areas. Instead of blanketing an entire area, only certain parts of the political subdivision may receive bilingual election materials and oral assistance (MALDEF 1977: 48-49).

There is another language-related law that does not address language rights, but has singularly drawn most of the attention on the language situation in the United States—the Bilingual Education Act of 1968. This law, recognizing a social need, authorizes the expenditure of public funds for the development of model school programs for limited and non-English-proficient students. The Act does not create any language rights nor bilingual schooling rights, but has had the effect of (1) encouraging many states to repeal and remove school laws which prohibited the use of non-English languages, or which mandated the exclusive use of English; and (2) focusing national and international attention on the situation of language groups in the United States, especially the Spanish-speaking and the Amerindians. This was not an easy achievement, but went hand in hand with increases in federal bilingual schooling funds, as well as the passage of similar state bilingual schooling legislation.

A possibly related activity is the increase, since 1970, of language-related state legislation. California, for example, considered ninety bills between 1971 and 1974, which in some way affected linguistic minorities (Blaine 1974: 659). Few of the bills passed, but the concern for language groups has been spreading, although the extent is not known, as the political power of certain language groups increases.

This growth in legislative consideration of language issues is important, even if not always beneficial to language groups, for it pursues the situation on the basis of *social policy*. The courts are hesitant to form new social policy to meet social needs outside the frameworks of the Constitution, case, legislative, and administrative law (even though many times their decisions have wide-ranging social policy implications). Legislation, however, can generally be drawn up once enough politicians have been convinced of the social need.

The overlap, then, between international human rights and domestic sources of similar rights is great in general, but very limited when it comes explicitly to language. The legislative guarantees of language "rights" follows that of the Constitution in that (1) language per se is not a sole basis for the identification of a group as an affected class in discrimination, but most often has been included as part of a national origin classification; (2) the language discrimination claimed must be made explicit and must also be causally tied to the deprivation of a "fundamental freedom" as defined in domestic law. The Constitution and federal law do not provide for, nor guarantee, language choice or language rights directly or explicitly.

Approaching a Human Rights Language Choice Policy for the United States

In the above brief review we noted the lack of standing a language group has as a class before United States courts, as well as the court's requisite of an association with "national origin" as a category before granting standing. It seems very little legal or other attention has gone into the differentiation of language groups in the United States. What are some of these differences and how do they relate to language rights?

Heinz Kloss (1971, 1977), has brought this problem the most light. He provides us with a summary of language rights as derived from the status of the groups themselves.

Kloss (1977: 22-25) first makes a distinction between tolerance-oriented language rights and promotive language rights. The tolerance-oriented language rights are based on the formal equality of language groups. They ensure the right to preservation of one's language in the private, non-governmental sphere of national life. The tolerance-oriented rights are applied either widely or narrowly. The widest in scope is that based on pursuit of life, liberty, and the "fundamental rights" of which we spoke earlier, such as voting. Next is the right to use one's mother tongue at home or in public; then freedom of assembly, organization, and the right to establish private cultural, economic, and social institutions and to use one's mother tongue in these. Most narrowly, there is the right to cultivate one's own language in private schools.

The widest of these rights assumes all citizens have the same needs and treats all the same. In the narrowest sphere of tolerance-oriented rights, the state accommodates itself "to the continued existence of the particular language among future generations," by allowing private mother tongue schools (Kloss 1977: 23).

Promotion-oriented language rights are based on the material equality of the groups and "regulate how public institutions may use and cultivate the languages and cultures of the minorities" (Kloss 1977: 22). There are simple promotive rights in which the government makes limited use of the mother tongue for the dissemination of public or specific information to the language minority. These documents have no legal authority, nor are they distributed to other groups.

Expediency-based promotive rights are a low-level promotional form designed to serve state ends rather than those of the linguistic minority (e.g., translation of tax notices; bilingual schooling designed to lure students away from private schools; time limitations on minority language promotion). The state otherwise ignores the minority language.

Expanded promotive rights may be granted by the state when it (1) allows for a language minority group "to care for its internal affairs through its own public organs, which amounts to the state allowing self-government for the minority group" (Kloss 1977: 24); or (2) uses the minority language in governmental relations with the majority group, thus putting them on equal legal footing.

The major difference Kloss makes among groups is between indigenous, old settler language groups, and immigrant language groups. These groups correspond to a scale of language claims, pretensions, or demands (Kloss 1977: 18-19).

Kloss indicates that, historically, the United States old settler groups who singly occupied an area, claimed and enjoyed promotive rights. All the language groups enjoyed tolerance-oriented rights. Kloss argues that,

> Such tolerance-oriented nationality rights have to be granted whenever an ethnic group is ready to make sacrifices for the necessary private institutions (Kloss 1977: 289).
>
> Only when the immigrant generation has succeeded in giving its native languages firm roots among the grandchildren, only when the immigrant generation has made the sacrifices for a private cultivation of the language, only when they have taken root in the new country while retaining their native language, can they demand that the state come to their aid and promote their language. Such claim to promotion can be considered a natural right only beginning with about the third generation (Kloss 1977: 289-290).

Such is the distinction of language groups made by Kloss. If a group first settled an area by itself, at the same time as the Anglo immigrants, or if they are at least third generation with a proven language maintenance track record, then they are entitled to promotive language rights.[3] Otherwise, tolerance-oriented rights should be respected for all groups. Citing a similar conclusion reached by a United Nations-sponsored seminar on the Multinational Society in 1956, Kloss (1977: 300) states that "it would seem that a worldwide consensus regarding this principle is not entirely beyond reach. . . ."

If this is the case, then we have additional criteria at hand to apply in the formulation of a human-rights language-choice policy. If we compare the distinction of tolerance-oriented and promotive-oriented rights with some of the international human rights documents discussed above, we see that (1) the right to freedom from discrimination on the basis of language can variously be interpreted, and when it is related to a denial of a fundamental right, it can be viewed as tolerance-oriented. Thus, the right is only explicitly pointed to when it has been violated, and (2) the right to use one's language in communal life can also be viewed as tolerance-oriented. But, tied to this second right is the right of *access* to the mother tongue, the elite tongue, and world tongues. Without access, the heart of the right to use one's own language is offered as sacrifice at the legal altar of *formal* equality. It is the denial of language access in all spheres that is lifted in promotive-oriented language rights. The minimum criteria for entitlement to these promotive rights, however, according to Kloss (1971, 1977) and others, is the three-generational commitment to the maintenance of the language made by immigrant groups themselves. But what about non-immigrant groups? What about Chicanos (and Puerto Ricans and Native Americans)?

This question leads us into an area of problems and biases I will only briefly explore here, and strictly within the context of the United States situation. This country is basically an immigrant country and its view of language and cultural minorities has been affected by this as well as its experiences in racial oppression, which have been dominated in the national consciousness by black-white relations.

As an immigrant country, the notions of language and cultural change lead one to assume non-English language loss over time. To speak another language is only a temporary phenomenon. The prototypical example and justification given for this assumption—when it is dealt with explicitly—is the European immigrant experience of the turn of the century. As it turns out, the statistics and the major study on language loyalty (Fishman et al. 1966) bears this out on a broad scale. To consider a "maintenance" language policy, then, is often viewed as only temporarily delaying the inevitable loss of the non-English language and is unfairly juxtaposed to not learning English. Tolerance-oriented laws are then viewed as appropriate, while expediency-based promotive rights may be called upon occasionally to soften the harshness of the changeover, hence we have transitional language policies, especially at the federal level.

When contemporary language groups have sought more beneficial language policies, especially through the courts, they have met the obstacle of *formal equality* as well. The notion of formal or legal equality has been biased and buttressed by major racial and social events—the Civil War, the 1954 *Brown* decision by the U.S. Supreme Court, the 1964 Civil Rights Act, and related or similar legislation. Formal equality has been equated with *sameness* and has been generalized to national-origin discrimination as well, and, thus, to language issues. With the introduction of the national origin classification, we view a further reinforcement of the assumption of non-English language loss by immigrants—and occasionally there is stated the explicit assumption by a judge or policy maker handling national-origin discrimination, that the persons involved are not citizens; often an erroneous assumption.

This situation, not of policy but of the social context for policy making, has important implications for Mexicans, Puerto Ricans, and Amerindians, the latter two being groups that are occasionally, if not often, excluded from the "immigrant" category. These groups, along with Asians, are often the ones involved in the current litigation of language issues or for whom social policy in the form of language legislation, is considered.

Two important sociolinguistic studies should be mentioned here. Fishman et al. (1966) is a study on language loyalty in the United States. It often excluded the Spanish-speakers from its conclusions. Whereas, there has been a general decline in the number of non-English speakers over time, and a fragmentation of the supportive cultural/social matrix or "ethnic community" for the non-English languages, Spanish speakers have increased over time and still maintain a cohesive cultural/social framework for the language.

The monograph by Kloss (1977) on language policy and traditions in the United States makes a distinction between nationality law (language/cultural law), racial law, and immigration law, the latter dealing with the regulation of immigration, aliens, and naturalization/citizenship. Indians are not treated in this study and blacks are excluded as well. For Kloss "immigrants constitute a national minority only after having become American citizens" (Kloss 1977: 21). Up front, Kloss also indicates that

> a tense and double polarity exists where separate ethnic groups differ from Anglo Americans by both language and race, as is the case for Hawaiians among the original settlers and the Mexicans among the late settlers (Kloss 1977: 20).

Kloss makes a further distinction among Mexicans—those whom he calls late settlers (the "Spaniards," especially in New Mexico), who settled an area prior to Anglo colonization, and those he calls immigrants, who settled in an area after it had become the United States. This affects the status of the group and thus its "language rights." It is a convenient distinction but a specious one.

Neither Fishman et al. (1966), nor Kloss (1977) explore systematically the reasons for making Mexicans an exception to their conclusions or their evaluations. Nor do these studies explore systematically the differences between Mexicans and the basically European immigrant data base or focus they are dealing with. As social science and sociolinguistic sources for legal and legislative proceedings, they thus reinforce the two assumptions of social context mentioned above (non-English language loss over time and formal equality). This general state of affairs is further complicated by the general lack of information on Mexicans (and Puerto Ricans), the social stereotypes engendered over the years of group contact with "Anglos," and the oppressed economic and political status of the Spanish-speaking.

There are significant differences between Spanish-speaking peoples and the turn of the century European immigrants. Here, let it suffice to mention a few.

1. Both the Mexican and the Puerto Rican, along with the Amerindian were integrated into the political jurisdiction of the United States by military conquest.
2. There is a Spanish-speaking historical continuity of 350 years, across political sovereignties, within the primary contemporary areas of these populations. (What is now the U.S. Southwest and Puerto Rico.)
3. Among Latinos there is a confluence of racial, cultural and linguistic, and immigrant/citizenship status.
4. Unlike the period between 1880-1920, when the linguistic diversity of the United States immigrant and non-immigrant populations was high, the recent influx of Central and South Americans, and the greater rate of increase among the Latino population in the United States, produces a lower linguistic diversity among the non-English and immigrant population.
5. There is an inter-generational co-mingling, partly as a result of the continuing in-migration and partly as a result of internal migration.
6. The development, rather than retardation, of an institutional language infrastructure (as opposed to the fragmentation of ethnic community [Fishman et al. 1966] or solely the appearance of a community-based organizational infrastructure) has continued. For example:
   a) Schools:
      (1) bilingual schooling
      (2) Spanish as the most popular "foreign language"
   b) language issues have forced the liberalization of voting and due process (court interpreters for limited- and non-English speakers)
   c) the Spanish language mass media—particularly broadcast media—continue to grow, being characterized as the "5th Network"
   d) Chicano literature, and the arts, in Spanish and bilingually, are experiencing a resurgence.
7. Increasing importance of Latino América in the world; the parallel loss of prestige of the United States; the increasing focus on human (including cultural/linguistic) rights in the international community.
8. Spanish speakers in the United States are the northern-most segment of over 200 million Spanish speakers in Latino América. This is an additional factor in the historical contiguity between the domestic Spanish speakers and their "country of origin."

There are other differences, the presentation of which will have to wait for another time. These differences between racial/linguistic groups and previous European immigrant groups, however, are indicative of a need to more closely and clearly explore the basis of language rights and policy in the United States.

In conclusion, the review of international activity and thinking on human rights and language, the sources for similar rights in the United States, and an appeal for a broader based language policy, constitute this discussion of language choice and human rights in the United States. These are, in effect, policy matters, and they are distant oftentimes from the human *needs* of the populations we have just discussed. It is not a question of legality or of rights solely, but of justice and quality of life—in the areas of political institutions (governmental services), public service institutions, the schools, mass media, and the economy.[4]

There is a need to reconceptualize the *nature* of language and human rights within the United States. Sociolinguists, bilingual educators as professionals and as part of a committed citizenry, and others, can and must contribute to that work. As policy matters, these concerns are not entirely separated from the work in language census/demography, sociolinguistic interactional analysis, functions of language, pragmatics, ethnography, the structure of the languages, bilingual schooling, political economy, and other areas as well.

There is also a need to expand the domestic discussion of language issues by looking at the developing norm of international conduct as a *source* for human rights. Language issues must be viewed as legitimate concerns in their own right. Language-based groups should enjoy greater legal standing domestically as well. With these steps we can contribute to a greater social justice for language groups within the United States.

NOTES

1. An earlier, slightly different version of this paper was read at the 1979 Georgetown University Round Table on Languages and Linguistics—"Language and Public Life," under the title of "Language Choice and Human Rights in the U.S." This essay came, in part, from conversations I had with Eduardo Hernández-Chávez, and I would like to thank him.

   I am aware that the use of the term "rights" is in danger of being so overused as to become meaningless. In this essay, the notion of "right" is part of the topic. It includes the idea that, if one has it, one can demand accountability and enforcement, such that the "legal" institutions must recognize it as such. There are other bases for "rights," philosophical, moral, etc. I do not deal with these areas here.
2. There have only been a few cases litigated under this statute—*Deerfield* v. *Ipswich, Guadalupe* v. *Tempe,* and *Martin Luther King, Jr. Elem.* v. *Michigan,* (see bibliography for the full citation). The first two cases were found wanting in arguing the violation of 20 USCA sec. 1703(f). *Deerfield* involved German-speaking Hutterites in South Dakota, while *Guadalupe* involved Mexicans and Yaquis in Arizona. *Martin Luther King, Jr. Elementary School* involved black youngsters arguing under "race" and "Black English" language barriers. The court in the case held that the section of the law required a showing of (1) the denial of an educational opportunity on account of race, color, sex, or national origin; and (2) the educational agency's failure to take action to overcome language barriers that are sufficiently severe so as to impede a student's equal participation in instructional programs. *Deerfield* also adopted this requirement.
3. One can ask the question, if the group has maintained its language without government support, why should promotive language rights be necessary? Official recognition of a language should not be taken lightly. It is, in part, a shift of resources directed to the maintenance effort. It is also a "matching" of government with its constituencies. What may be more important to ask here, is whether there will be a loss of "control" by the language group of some language resources, once the government officially recognizes its duty and intervenes.

4. Each of these institutional areas is the focus of other research I am doing in institutional language policy and language as a mechanism of social control. Preliminary profiles have been completed for political institutions, public service institutions and schooling. An additional area of future research is domestic treaties with racial linguistic indigenous groups, Native Americans and Mexicans in particular—The Treaty of Guadalupe-Hidalgo (1848) as an example of "rights" and privileges assigned and agreed to for Mexicans in the conquered Mexican territory after the U.S. invasion.

SELECTED BIBLIOGRAPHY

TABLE OF CASES.

Schnell v. *Davis,* 336 U.S. 933, aff'g, 81 F. Supp. 892 (S.D. Ala. 1949).

Hobson v. *Hansen,* 269 F. Supp. 401 (D.D.C. 1967).

Lopez Tijerina v. *Henry,* 48 F.R.D. 274 (D. New Mexico 1969) *appeal dismissed* 398 U.S. 922 (Douglas dissenting).

Castro v. *State of California,* 2 Cal. 3d 223 (1970).

United States v. *Texas,* 342 F. Supp. 24 (E.D. Texas 1971).

Carmona v. *Sheffield,* 475 F. 2d 738 (9th Cir. 1973).

Lau v. *Nichols,* 483 F. 2d 791 (9th Cir. 1973) *rev'd and remanded* 414 U.S. 563 (1974).

Serna v. *Portales Municipal Schools,* 499 F. 2d 1147 (10th Cir. 1974).

Morales v. *Shannon,* 516 F. 2d 411 (5th Cir. 1975).

Keyes v. *School District No. 1, Denver, Colorado,* 521 F. 2d 465 (10th Cir. 1975).

Parents' Committee of Public School 19 v. *Community School Board of Community School District No. 14 of the City of New York,* 524 F. 2d 1138 (2d Cir. 1975).

Frontera v. *Sindell,* 522 F. 2d 1215 (6th Cir. 1975).

Otero v. *Mesa County Valley School District No. 51,* 408 F. Supp. 162 (D. Colo. 1975) *rev'd in part* 568 F. 2d 1312 (10th Cir. 1977).

Pabon v. *Levine,* 70 F.R.D. 674 (S.D. N.Y. 1976).

Evans v. *Buchanan,* 416 F. Supp. 328 (D. Delaware 1976).

Rios v. *Read,* 73 F.R.D. 589 (E.D. N.Y. 1977).

Armstrong v. *O'Connell,* 74 F.R.D. 429 (E.D. Wisconsin 1977).

Deerfield Hutterian Association v. *Ipswich Board of Education,* 444 F. Supp. 159 (D. South Dakota 1978), 468 F. Supp. 1219 (D. South Dakota 1979).

Martin Luther King Jr. Elementary School Children v. *Michigan Board of Education,* 451 F. Supp. 1324 (E.D. Michigan 1978), 263 F. Supp. 1027 (E.D. Michigan 1978), ____ F. Supp. ____ (July 12, 1979).

Guadalupe Organization, Inc. v. *Tempe Elementary School District No. 3,* 587 F. 2d 1022 (9th Cir. 1978).

STATUES/CODE

Voting Rights Act of 1965—Extension, Pub. L. No. 94-73, 89 Stat. 400 (Aug. 6, 1975), codified at 42 U.S.C. sec. 1973 b, 1973aa-la to 1973aa-4.

Court Interpreters Act, Pub. L. No. 95-539, 92 Stat. 2040 (Oct. 28, 1978), codified at 28 U.S.C. sec. 1827, 1828, and sec. 602.

Bilingual Education Act, Pub. L. No. 90-247, 81 Stat. 783, 816 (Jan. 2, 1968), as amended by the Education Amendments of 1974, Pub. L. No. 93-380, 88 Stat. 484, 503 (Aug. 21, 1974), and as amended by the Elementary and Secondary Education Amendments of 1978, Pub. L. No. 95-561, 92 Stat. 2268 (Nov. 1, 1978).

Equal Educational Opportunities Act of 1974, 20 U.S.C.A. sec. 1703(f).

Bibliography

Acuña, Rodolfo. *Occupied America: The Chicano Struggle Toward Liberation.* San Francisco: Canfield Press, 1972.

Bergenfield, Glenn. "Comment—Trying Non-English Conversant Defendants—The Use of an Interpreter." *Oregon Law Review* 57 (1978): 549-565.

Bilingual Education—Current Perspectives. 5 vols. Rosslyn, Va.: Center for Applied Linguistics, 1977.

Blaine, Carl. "Comment—Breaking the Language Barrier—New Rights for California's Linguistic Minorities." *Pacific Law Journal* 5 (1974): 648-674.

Bloomfield, Morton, and Haugen, Einar. *Language as a Human Problem.* New York: W. W. Norton and Co., 1973.

Brière, Eugène. "Limited English Speakers and the Miranda Rights." *TESOL Quarterly* 12 (September 1978): 235-245.

Castro, Raymond. "The Bilingual Education Act—A Historical Analysis of Title VII." In *Perspectivas en Chicano Studies I,* pp. 81-122. Edited by Reynaldo Macías. Los Angeles: National Association of Chicano Social Science and the UCLA Chicano Studies Center, 1977.

Claydon, John. "Internationally Uprooted People and the Transnational Protection of Minority Culture." *New York Law School Law Review* 24 (1978): 125-151.

Cohen, Andrew. "Assessing Language Maintenance in Spanish Speaking Communities in the Southwest." In *El Lenguaje de los Chicanos,* pp. 202-219. Edited by Hernández-Chávez et al. Rosslyn, Va.: Center for Applied Linguistics, 1975.

Commerce Clearinghouse, Inc., *Congressional Index, 96th Congress, 1979-1980,* Vol. 1, No. 26 (July 12, 1979), Chicago, Ill., p. 1007.

Derian, Patricia. "Human Rights and United States Foreign Relations—An Overview." *Case Western Reserve Journal on International Law* 10 (1978): 243-249.

Downes, Richard. "The Future Consequences of Illegal Immigration." *The Futurist* (April 1977): 125-127.

Estrada, Leobardo F. "A Demographic Comparison of the Mexican Origin Population in the Midwest and Southwest." *Aztlán—International Journal of Chicano Studies Research* (Special issue on the Chicano in the Midwest) 7 (Summer 1976): 203-234.

__________. "The Extent of Spanish/English Bilingualism and Language Loyalty in the United States." Unpublished ms, 1977.

Fedynskyj, Jurij. "State Session Laws in Non-English Languages—A Chapter of American Legal History." *Indiana Law Journal* 46 (1971): 463-478.

Fishman, Joshua, et al. *Language Loyalty in the United States—The Maintenance and Perpetuation of Non-English Mother Tongues by American Ethnic and Religious Groups.* The Hague: Mouton Publishers, 1966.

Fong, Kevin. "Comment—Cultural Pluralism." *Harvard Civil Rights-Civil Liberties Law Review* 13 (1978): 133-173.

Foster, William. "Bilingual Education—An Educational and Legal Survey." *Journal of Law—Education* 5 (1976): 149-171.

Gaarder, A. Bruce. *Bilingual Schooling and the Survival of Spanish in the United States*. Rowley, Mass.: Newbury House Publishers, 1977.

García, F. "Language Barriers to Voting—Literacy Tests and the Bilingual Ballot." *Columbia Human Rights Law Review* 6 (1974): 86-106.

Grubb, Erica Black. "Breaking the Language Barrier, The Right to Bilingual Education." *Harvard Civil Rights-Civil Liberties Law Review* 9 (1974): 52-94.

Gutiérrez, G. "The 1975 Voting Rights Act—Lessons Learned and Tomorrow's Imperatives." *Agenda* 8 (January/February 1978): 18-21.

Haugen, Einar. *Bilingualism in the Americas—A Bibliography and Research Guide*. American Dialect Society, Publication No. 26. University of Alabama Press, 1956.

———. "Bilingualism, Language Contact, and Immigrant Languages in the United States—A Research Report, 1956-1979." In *Current Trends in Linguistics*, pp. 505-591. Edited by Seboek. The Hague: Mouton Publishers, 1973.

Heath, Shirley. "Language and Politics in the United States." In *GURT 1977 Anthropology and Linguistics*, pp. 267-296. Edited by Saville-Troike. Washington, D.C.: Georgetown University Press, 1977.

Hernández, Antonia. "Chicanas and the Issue of Involuntary Sterilization—Reform Needed to Protect Informed Consent." *Chicano Law Review* 3 (1976): 3-37.

Hernández-Chávez, E.; Cohen, A.; and Beltramo, A., eds. *El Lenguaje de los Chicanos—Regional and Social Characteristics of Language Used by Mexican Americans*. Rosslyn, Va.: Center for Applied Linguistics, 1975.

Hippchen, L. "Note—Development of a Plan for Bilingual Interpreters in the Criminal Courts of New Jersey." *Justice System Journal* 2 (Spring 1977): 258-269.

Hymes, Dell. "Models of the Interaction of Language and Social Life." In *Directions in Sociolinguistics—The Ethnography of Communication*, pp. 35-71. Edited by Gumperz and Hymes. New York: Holt, Rinehart, and Winston, 1972.

Irizarry, Ruddie. *Bilingual Education—State and Federal Legislative Mandates—Implications for Program Design and Evaluation*. Los Angeles: National Dissemination and Assessment Center, SCULA, 1978.

Jewell, Malcolm. "Formal Institutional Studies and Language." In *Language and Politics*, pp. 421-429. Edited by O'Barr and O'Barr. The Hague: Mouton Publishers, 1976.

Johnson, Jacquelyne. "Illegal Aliens—Big Threat to Black Workers." *Ebony Magazine*, April 1979, pp. 33-40.

Johnson, William. "The Constitutional Right of Bilingual Children to an Equal Educational Opportunity." *Southern California Law Review* (1974): 943-997.

Kloss, Heinz. "German American Language Maintenance Efforts." In *Language Loyalty*, pp. 206-252. Edited by Fishman et al. The Hague: Mouton Publishers, 1966.

__________. "Language Rights of Immigrant Groups." *International Migration Review* 5 (1971): 250-268.

__________. *The American Bilingual Tradition.* Rowley, Mass.: Newbury House Publishers, 1977.

Language Policy Task Force. *Language Policy and the Puerto Rican Community.* New York: Centro de Estudios Puertorriqueños, 1977.

Leibowitz, Arnold. "English Literacy—Legal Sanction for Discrimination." *Notre Dame Lawyer* 45 (Fall 1969): 7-67.

__________. *Educational Policy and Political Acceptance—The Imposition of English as the Language of Instruction in American Schools.* Washington, D.C.: ERIC Clearinghouse for Languages and Linguistics, ED 047321, unpublished MS, 1971.

__________. "Language as a Means of Social Control." Paper presented at the Research Committee on Sociolinguistics, VIII World Congress of Sociology, University of Toronto, Canada, August 1974.

__________. "Language and the Law—The Exercise of Political Power through Official Designation of Language." In *Language and Politics,* pp. 449-466. Edited by O'Barr and O'Barr. The Hague: Mouton Publishers, 1976.

Lieberson, Stanley, and Curry, Timothy. "Language Shift in the United States—Some Demographic Clues." *International Migration Review* 5 (1971): 125-137.

Lillich, Richard. "The Role of Domestic Courts in Promoting International Human Rights Norms." *New York Law School Review* 24 (1978): 153-177.

Macías, Reynaldo. "Opinions of Chicano Community Parents on Bilingual Preschool Education." In *Language in Sociology,* pp. 135-166. Louvain: Institut de Linguistique, 1976.

__________. "Public Schooling and Language Policy in the U.S.—A Brief History and Its Contemporary Configurations." Paper presented to course on sociolinguistics and education, Georgetown University, Spring 1977.

__________. "Language Policy and Social Control in the United States from Colonial Times to 1900." Long term paper, Dept. of Linguistics, Georgetown University.

__________. "U.S. Hispanics in 2000 A.D.—Projecting the Number." *Agenda* (National Council of La Raza) 7 (May/June 1977): 16-19.

MALDEF (Mexican American Legal Defense and Education Fund). *A Voting Rights Act Handbook for Chicanos* (English and Spanish). San Francisco: MALDEF, 1977.

McDougal, M.; Laswell, H.; and Chen, L. "Freedom from Discrimination in Choice of Language and International Human Rights." *Southern Illinois University Law Journal* 1 (1976): 151-174.

McWilliams, Carey. *North From Mexico.* New York: Greenwood Press, 1968.

Montoya, Joseph. "Bilingual-Bicultural Education—Making Equal Educational Opportunity Available to National Origin Minority Children." *Georgetown University Law Journal* 61 (1973): 991-1007.

National Center for Education Statistics. *Bulletin.* "The Educational Disadvantage of Language Minority Persons in the U.S., Spring 1976." HEW, July 26, 1978.

———. *Bulletin.* "Geographic Distribution, Nativity, and Age Distribution of Language Minorities in the United States, Spring 1976." HEW, August 22, 1978.

———. *Bulletin.* "Place of Birth and Language Characteristics of Persons of Hispanic Origin in the United States, Spring 1976." HEW, October 20, 1978.

O'Barr, William. "Boundaries, Strategies, and Power Relations—Political Anthropology and Language." In *Language and Politics,* pp. 405-420. Edited by O'Barr and O'Barr. The Hague: Mouton Publishers, 1976.

Pousada, Alicia. "Interpreting for Language Minorities in the Courts." Paper presented at the 1979 Georgetown University Round Table on Languages and Linguistics—"Language in Public Life," Washington, D.C., March 22-24, 1979.

Reeber, Christopher. "Linguistic Minorities and the Right to an Effective Education." *California Western International Law Journal* 3 (1972): 112-132.

Rios, Antonio, ed. *Immigration and Public Policy—Human Rights for Undocumented Workers and Their Families.* Los Angeles: UCLA Chicano Studies Center, 1977.

Ritvo, R.; McKinney, E.; and Chatterjee, P. "Health Care as a Human Right." *Case Western Reserve Journal of International Law* 10 (1978): 323-357.

Rubin, Joan, and Shuy, Roger. *Language Planning—Current Issues and Research.* Washington, D.C.: Georgetown University Press, 1973.

Schachter, Oscar. "International Law Implications of U.S. Human Rights Policies." *New York Law School Law Review* 24 (1978): 63-87.

Shuy, Roger. "Language Policy in Medicine—Some Emerging Issues." Paper presented at the GURT 1979, Georgetown University, Washington, D.C., March 22-24, 1979.

Silko, John. "Beyond the Law—To Equal Educational Opportunities for Chicanos and Indians." *New Mexico Law Review* 1 (1971): 335-351.

Sugarman, Stephen, and Widdess, Ellen. "Case Commentary—Equal Protection for Non-English Speaking School Children—*Lau* v. *Nichols.*" *California Law Review* 62 (1974): 157-182.

Teschner, R.; Bills, G.; and Craddock, J., eds. *Spanish and English of U.S. Hispanos—A Critical, Annotated, Linguistic Bibliography.* Rosslyn, Va.: Center for Applied Linguistics, 1975.

Thompson, Roger. "Mexican American Language Loyalty and the Validity of the 1970 Census." *International Journal of the Sociology of Language,* "The American Southwest" 2 (1974): 7-18.

U.S. Commission on Civil Rights. *Counting the Forgotten—The 1970 Census Count of Persons of Spanish Speaking Background in the U.S.* Washington, D.C.: USGPO, 1974.

———. *Puerto Ricans in the Continental United States—An Uncertain Future.* Washington, D.C.: USGPO, 1976.

U.S. Commissioner of Education. *The Condition of Bilingual Education in the Nation.* Washington, D.C.: HEW, 1976.

Van Dyke, Vernon. "Human Rights Without Distinction as to Language." *International Studies Quarterly* 20 (1975): 3-38.

———. "Human Rights and the Rights of Groups." *American Journal of Political Science* 18 (1974): 725-741.

Veenhoven, Willem. "Introduction." In *Case Studies on Human Rights and Fundamental Freedoms—A World Survey*, pp. xii-xxi. Vol. 1. The Hague: Martinus Nijhoff Publishers, 1975.

Waggoner, Dorothy. "Non-English Language Background Persons, Three U.S. Surveys." *TESOL Quarterly* 12 (September 1978): 247-262.

__________. "Resources to Meet the Educational Needs of Language Minorities—Teachers in Public Schools." Paper presented at the NABE Conference, Seattle, Washington, May 4, 1979.

__________. "Resources to Meet the Educational Needs of Language Minorities—Teachers in Public Schools." Paper presented at the TESOL Conference, Boston, Massachusetts, February 28, 1979.

Wald, Benji. "Bilingualism." *Annual Review of Anthropology* 3 (1974): 301-321.

Weinberg, Meyer. *A Chance to Learn—The History of Race and Education in the United States.* Cambridge: Cambridge University Press, 1977.

Weissbrodt, David. "United States Ratification of the Human Rights Covenants." *Minnesota Law Review* 63 (1978): 35-78.

LAW AND BILINGUAL EDUCATION: AN EXAMINATION OF THE LITIGATION STRATEGY

Manuel del Valle
Ruben Franco
Camille Rodriguez Garcia

INTRODUCTION

This article was written by members of the National Puerto Rican Task Force on Educational Policy in order to highlight some aspects of the litigation process and problems involved in obtaining bilingual-bicultural education relief. Presented for the consideration of the actors in the litigation process, the educator, parent, community worker, community organization and civil rights attorney, it is a brief exposition of the roles of these actors, that portion of the process denominated as *el vacío* (the void), aspects of relief that should be scrutinized, and considerations in desegregation and bilingual-bicultural education that should be examined. Appended to this article is a list of questions that should be examined by each of the major actors in the litigation process which we believe will stimulate further discussion regarding the respective roles of each actor and the efficacy of the litigation strategy itself.

THE ACTORS IN THE LITIGATION PROCESS

In all civil rights litigation, including bilingual-bicultural lawsuits, there are several actors or participants, each playing a very definable role. Depending on the role which the actors play in the lawsuit or the benefits which they derive, they can be categorized as class members, clients, attorneys or educators.

The Class and Clients

Generally, class members* in a bilingual education lawsuit are those ultimately affected by the outcome of the lawsuit. All Puerto Rican and other Hispanic children who attend schools in the school district where litigation is contemplated and who cannot learn or communicate effectively in the English language, and who are not enrolled in bilingual programs, or who are enrolled in inadequate programs, are members of the class. Likewise, the parents of such children are members of the class since they are directly concerned with the quality of education which their

*The term "class" used herein does not refer to a socioeconomic grouping. It is a legal term used to refer to a very large category of persons who have a similar problem, or, as the legal writers say, "are similarly situated."

children receive and are aggrieved by the failure of the school district to provide their children with adequate educational programs. In any event, they are the legal representatives of their minor children. Because the size of the class is usually too large to make it practical for all of them to join in the lawsuit, their interests are represented by the named plaintiffs. A plaintiff is a person who sues another. The person who is sued is the defendant.

Clients are those persons in the class who have signed a retainer authorizing a lawyer or group of lawyers to represent them in a lawsuit. The retainer is a contract signed by the prospective client(s) as well as the attorney. It states that the attorneys have agreed to be "retained" to handle the case. It also states the conditions, if any, under which he is taking the case, and the fee, if any. This contract allows the lawyers to use the names of the persons in the lawsuit as named plaintiffs. However, not all those who sign retainers will become clients. For one reason or another the lawyers may decide that an individual or organization that signed a retainer will not be used as a plaintiff. It may be that there are already too many plaintiffs; or a particular individual or organization, in the lawyer's view, does not fit into the category of plaintiffs that the lawyers feel will best exemplify to the court the problems in the particular school district.

When we refer to "the community organization," we mean those groups which exist in many of our communities and are usually formed to fight against social injustices and to seek reform.

Civil Rights Attorneys

One of the prime actors in any legal action is the lawyer. Ultimately the community worker, the parent and the educator must deal with the civil rights attorney.

The civil rights attorney has probably gained expertise in the area during his first year or two out of law school while working for a legal services office, or for one of the six major civil rights defense organizations.[1] Very few civil rights attorneys are from minority groups. One reason for this is that the field is not financially rewarding for the few minority graduates of law schools who are usually deeply burdened by debts incurred in financing their education.

Most of the civil rights attorneys that the Puerto Rican and other Hispanic client will come in contact with will be non-Puerto Ricans and non-Hispanics. They will normally have little or no knowledge of Spanish and must depend on interpreters for their communication with non-English-speaking clients. Moreover, their law school training has not prepared them to deal with clients who are unable to articulate precisely the nature of their grievances and desires.

Client/Attorney Relationship

The traditional relationship of client and attorney is that the client hires an attorney to solve a particular problem or to provide a specific type of advice. If the client is not satisfied with the lawyer's work or advice, he/she can dismiss the lawyer at will. In the civil rights field this relationship becomes distorted. Rather than hire and pay for the services of a lawyer, a community or group of parents ordinarily attempts to interest a civil rights organization or a legal services group in the merits of their case.

The agencies usually do not commit themselves to taking the case until they investigate and determine that filing the suit will be profitable,[2] or that the case can be won.[3] Moreover, these agencies do not charge clients. They rely on foundation, corporate or government contributions to conduct litigation. Consequently, these agencies do not take on all cases brought to them. Indeed, many meritorious cases are turned away.

Once the agency decides to take the case, the lawyers may disqualify potential plaintiffs for various reasons.

When a community organization or a group of parents is attempting to interest a law agency in a particular lawsuit, in the initial contact, or shortly after the retainer is signed, ground rules for the working relationship should be discussed. It should be clear that the attorneys are conduits for the community's legal desires, and that they are not independent policy planners for the community. The community group should demand that its members be present and active at all news conferences, and that they be consulted before all major legal and non-legal decisions are made. If the community does not take charge from the beginning, or establish itself as the guiding force that moves the lawsuit ahead, the lawyers will make all the important decisions and will be free from any type of accountability. It is important that the basis of the future relationship be set out at the very beginning, in order to avoid any misunderstandings that might arise later. It is also important to realize that the lawyers do not have all the answers and that they must and should depend on their clients for guidance.

The legal profession, for all the training that its members get, is the last bastion of the generalist. It is a profession whose members are confronted with new topics or concepts each time they take a case. Experts are continually used to instruct attorneys. Whether these be experts on vinyl chloride, noise, homicide, medicine or bilingual education, their role is to educate the lawyers as to the particulars, so that they can successfully prepare for trial. Despite the fact that lawyers may become extremely knowledgeable in any one of these areas, they should not be considered experts in the area. They lack the years of training, research, keeping up with the new literature in the field, and the particular sensitivity in the topic that the trained expert has. Accordingly, it is best for any community to identify experts for the lawyers, to review experts proposed by lawyers, and to be wary of lawyers claiming expertise in any area other than law. What must be maintained in the civil rights area, as in any traditional area of law, is a healthy client-attorney relationship, with the client exercising the same role and authority as in any private litigation.

Active and Inactive Clients

Once litigation has commenced with the filing of the Complaint in court, the clients who have been named in the Complaint usually assume either an active or inactive role. After the suit is filed, there may pass a long period of time during which the maneuvers and strategy being pursued by the attorneys of both sides are almost exclusively legal and technical in nature. During this period, which we call "el vacío" (the void), much interest is lost in the lawsuit because the attorneys usually may not inform the clients of the developments in the suit nor seek their help and participation. The active clients and active non-clients, however, come forward to fill the void.

Active clients play a very important role in bilingual-bicultural education litigation. They maintain constant communication with the attorneys and serve as the attorneys' contact in the community; they obtain information for the attorneys relative to other clients or to the school system; they organize meetings between the attorneys and the clients and inform the other clients, the community and the press about developments in the lawsuit. When the attorneys feel comfortable working with the active clients, they will rely upon them heavily and the active clients will have great influence in determining the type of educational program implemented as a result of the lawsuit.

The inactive clients are those who, once the lawsuit is commenced, may never be heard from again. Nor are they usually sought out by the attorney, except when absolutely necessary, such as when the defendants request additional information regarding all the named plaintiffs. Inactive clients fulfill their function by being representative of the problem that affects Hispanic children in the school district and merely lend their names and characteristics to the lawsuit. They may have little influence in determining or selecting the type of bilingual program which will result from the suit. The inactive client category comprises by far the largest group of persons named in the lawsuit.[4]

Sometimes the inactive clients become "active" to the extent that they are gathered for a meeting by the active clients to be informed of any important developments; or for a meeting with the lawyers; or for the client-children to be tested for English or Spanish proficiency. It should be noted that without the inactive clients the lawsuit could not be won. The children of inactive parent-clients generally have the most difficulties in functioning in the English-only school curriculum, and would benefit the most from bilingual education programs. The lawyers use the educational plight of the inactive clients' children to dramatize to the court that the right of Hispanic children to equal educational opportunity has been violated and that the implementation of bilingual education will help to rectify the problem.

Another category of actors involved in the bilingual-bicultural education lawsuit is what we call the "active non-client." The active non-client is a person who is not a named plaintiff and who has not signed a retainer authorizing the attorneys to represent him/her in the suit. The active non-client may not even be a member of the class, that is, a person ultimately affected by the outcome of the lawsuit. Active non-clients are, usually, sophisticated, articulate individuals who are often involved in almost all community issues. They are sometimes teachers, sometimes members of the organizational plaintiff or some other community group.[5] They may or may not be Puerto Rican. Active non-clients play a very important role in the litigation—identical to the role played by active clients. Attorneys usually feel most accountable to active clients and active non-clients.

In some cases, the active non-client, such as a particular group of teachers, may have greater influence in determining the type of bilingual program which results from the lawsuit than the inactive clients. This is generally due to their particular expertise, interests or the rapport they may establish with the attorneys. The active non-clients oftentimes are most compatible with the attorney since they can bring to the lawsuit their own experiences with the community and can articulate comprehensive answers to the questions of the attorney. It is important that all clients be active clients. It is the active client who is most informed about the complexities of the lawsuit and its progress. In addition, the client who is informed and active is more likely to influence the progress and outcome of the lawsuit.

Teachers and Administrators

The educator plays a very important role in bilingual education lawsuits. The lawyers and clients call upon educators to articulate the educational problems of the school district and to help formulate pedagogical and legal arguments in support of bilingual education. Educators also help to equip the attorneys with the educational jargon and some of the expertise needed to initiate a bilingual lawsuit. Since educators can explain the community's position in both professional and layman's terms, the lawyers use educators to reinforce their arguments, and clients utilize them to interpret their situation and the possible solution.

In a bilingual education lawsuit, teachers can assume an interpretive or intermediary role. They may be required to:

1. interpret the problem to the lawyers;
2. interpret what the lawyer says about the problem to the client;
3. interpret the problem to other educators and professionals;
4. interpret the problem to the courts as professional educators or as expert witnesses;
5. interpret to the courts possible solutions as expert witnesses and as participants in the formulation of educational plans submitted to the courts;
6. interpret the solution to the named plaintiffs and to the community;
7. interpret to other educators the final educational plan ordered by the court; and
8. assist in implementing and monitoring the final educational plan ordered by the court and to interpret this plan to parents and students on an ongoing basis.

Civil rights attorneys usually assign these teachers and administrators to expert and interpretive roles, which places upon them the burden to produce evidence of the harm suffered by Puerto Rican and other Hispanic children in the local schools. This may require that the teachers and administrators testify in court to show, for example, that non-English-speaking Puerto Rican children in the school system score several grades lower on reading tests than English-speaking children of equal intelligence, or that the former are several grades behind their age group.

The teachers or administrators who are the best witnesses in court for the plaintiffs are those who favor the implementation of bilingual education and who can document and articulate the problems that non-English-speaking Puerto Rican children have in the school system. The teacher or administrator should be very familiar with the bilingual education concept and should be prepared to state why it is preferable to English as a Second Language (ESL) or traditional methods.

One major problem which often faces teachers and administrators who get involved in bilingual education litigation is their inability to ascertain whether or not a viable and comprehensive education plan which they favor may be legally acceptable by the courts. To the extent that teachers and administrators do not understand what types of relief are legally acceptable, they may compromise a sound educational plan in the name of legal expediency. In this regard, it is the responsibility of teachers to give to the community a full explanation of the concept of bilingual education as well as of the different permissible options, so that they can be in a position to support or reject the proposed educational plan with complete knowledge. It is important that teachers, administrators and community members explore the various alternatives available before deciding what plan they feel is acceptable from an educational viewpoint, which at the same time is acceptable to the court. They should determine whether the constraints articulated by the lawyers are limitations imposed by the law or by the attorney's educational philosophy or view of the case. It is the teachers and administrators with the community members who are the experts in the formulation of the educational plan and not the lawyers. Where these roles are reversed, and the lawyers are permitted to formulate an educational plan or are given a veto power on the plan to be submitted to the court, then the community, teachers and administrators have abdicated their role as primary movers of the lawsuit and the affected school children may ultimately be recipients of an education which is no better than the one under attack.

THE LITIGATION PROCESS

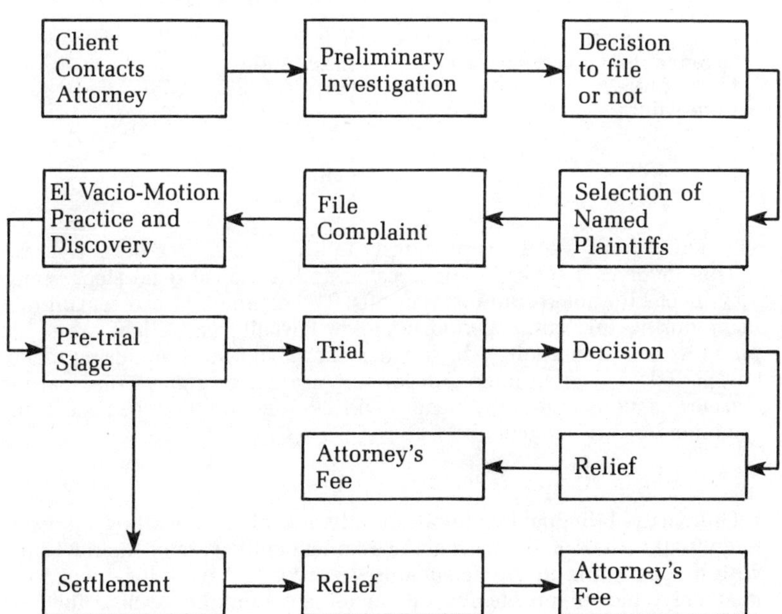

Finally, teachers and administrators must be sure to maintain constant communication with students and members of the community to receive input and feedback on their proposed educational plan. It is members of the community, the teachers and administrators who will have to apply and implement whatever educational plan is ordered by the court, and, while the lawyers may walk away from the community and school district at the end of the lawsuit, the community members, the teachers and administrators cannot.

THE PROCESS: *El Vacío (The Void)*

In bilingual-bicultural education litigation there is a long period which lasts anywhere from one to three years, which is filled with legal and technical maneuvers by the attorneys of both sides and during which the majority of the members of the class and clients lose interest in the lawsuit. We call this lull *el vacío* (the void). *El vacío* begins almost immediately after the Complaint is filed and ends several years later when the court decides the case or when the lawyers from both sides announce that they are going to enter into a consent decree or settlement.

The following is an attempt to describe superfically the legal events which occur during *el vacío*. More importantly, some suggestions are offered to potential clients and community people for utilizing their time and efforts in order to maximize their participation in the lawsuit and thus increase the likelihood of getting a favorable judgment from the court or a viable settlement agreement from the opposition.

In graphic form, *el vacío* includes the following stages:

A	*B*
Defendants' answer to plaintiffs' Complaint	Class Action Certification
C	*D*
Discovery	Other Motions

The period from A to D, as previously indicated, can drag out for years.

This involves a series of complicated and technical legal steps which may be of little interest to the plaintiffs. The community can remain dormant during this entire period, and the lawsuit can still be won. But plaintiffs or a community which choose to remain inactive during this or any period of such an important lawsuit, are taking a grave risk that the attorney or non-community people will assume complete control of the litigation and its outcome.

A. Defendants' Answer to Plaintiffs' Complaint

Ordinarily, bilingual-bicultural lawsuits are filed by mailing the Complaint to the Clerk of the Court of the pertinent United States District Court, with a copy going to the defendants. In order to have a big impact immediately, and to educate and organize the community around the suit, it is suggested that the Complaint be taken personally to the Clerk of the

Court, and that just prior to filing, a news conference be held by the lawyer and community leaders at the courthouse steps. Within thirty days from the filing of the Complaint, the defendants will file their answer. The defendants may deny each and every allegation in the plaintiffs' Complaint: denying that plaintiffs cannot function effectively in an English-only curriculum; denying that certain plaintiffs read below grade level; denying that they have violated plaintiffs' rights, etc. Or, defendants may contend that they offer bilingual education. Upon close scrutiny and with the help of plaintiffs and their allies in the school system, the attorneys may determine that in fact what defendants offer is ESL. If this is the case, then defendants may be in violation of federal law, since the Department of Health, Education and Welfare (HEW) has dictated and, for the most part the courts have agreed, that ESL is inadequate at least for the elementary school level.

Instead of answering the Complaint, defendants may admit all of plaintiffs' allegations and move to dismiss the lawsuit on the grounds that the Complaint does not state a cause of action upon which the court can fashion an appropriate remedy. In other words, in every lawsuit, the plaintiff must set forth an injury, or claim (in legal terms, cause of action) which is recognizable by the courts and upon which an appropriate and proper remedy can be granted. For example, if one is injured by a speeding automobile, one can bring a negligence suit (which is a cause of action recognizable by the courts) and ask for compensatory damages (money damages to compensate him/her for injuries). In the bilingual suit, defendants would be claiming that the cause of action which plaintiffs are attempting to make out in their Complaint is not one recognizable by the courts and therefore not one in which relief can be granted. Of course, given the precedents which have been established in this area of law, defendants' claim would be frivolous and would be denied by the court.

B. Class Action Certification

After the defendants have answered plaintiffs' Complaint or have moved to dismiss, plaintiffs will file a motion with the court to have the lawsuit certified as a class action. When plaintiffs ask the court to permit them to grant class action status to the lawsuit, they are requesting to be permitted to represent all other individuals who are similarly situated. In other words, plaintiffs want to represent all parents and their school children who attend schools in the district, who cannot function effectively in the English-only curriculum; and who are provided either no programs or inadequate programs to help rectify their situation. The defendants will try to persuade the court that the problems which plaintiffs raise are different from the problems of the rest of the class, and thus, that plaintiffs are not representative of the rest of the class. At this point, defendants may also attempt to have the court dismiss the organizational plaintiff from the lawsuit for lack of standing.[6]

Plaintiffs and other community people can be very helpful during the class action certification stage. There should be an attempt to test all plaintiff school children to determine the extent of their English-language proficiency. The attorney should be invited to the community for a meeting with the plaintiffs, and he should become familiar with every parent and child who is a named plaintiff, as well as with all courses which the school district offers that are supposedly designed to meet the needs of plaintiff school children. The attorney should also be introduced to all members of the organizational plaintiff and should be briefed on the structure, as well as on activities and functions of the organization. The Certificate of Incorporation of the organization or other pertinent documents should be given to the attorney. If the court certifies the lawsuit as a class action, a press conference should be held in the offices of the organizational plaintiff or in some other convenient and accessible location in the community. The purpose of the press conference would be to announce the favorable decision, to inform the community of the development and to further solidify the community behind the lawsuit. The attorneys should be present at such a news conference.

C. *Discovery*

After the class certification motion, the lawsuit enters the stage in the process known as discovery. This stage exists in every lawsuit. Its purpose is to permit each side to discover as much as it possibly can about the opponent's case and position, so that neither side will be surprised at trial, if there is a trial. During the discovery stage, each side will send written questions (interrogatories) to the other side, requesting the submission of documents and the answering of specific questions. Discovery also entails the taking of oral questions and answers under oath (depositions) of the opposing parties. If plaintiffs wish to take the deposition of the superintendent of the school district, plaintiffs' attorneys will issue formal papers to the court and to defendants' attorneys requesting that the superintendent appear on a certain date and time, and usually in the offices of the defendants' attorneys. On that date and time, in the presence of a court reporter, the superintendent will be sworn in by the reporter and he will be asked questions by plaintiffs' attorneys. All questions and answers are recorded by the reporter. It is like court testimony, but it is not in court and the judge is not present. The defendants' attorneys will be present and can object to any questions asked by plaintiffs' attorneys and can direct the superintendent not to answer objectionable questions. If a party does not answer specific interrogatories, or does not submit a particular document which was requested, or does not answer certain questions during deposition, the attorneys for the opposing side can file a motion in court requesting the judge to compel the party to comply. Defendants' attorneys can submit written interrogatories to plaintiffs' attorneys and can also take the deposition of any or all plaintiffs.

The plaintiffs' role during the discovery process can be critical. Plaintiffs and members of the organizational plaintiff should help their attorneys frame the interrogatories and the questions asked at depositions. Of prime importance is the aid that they can render in determining the accuracy and truth of defendants' responses to plaintiffs' interrogatories and depositions. Defendants may submit old or inaccurate documents or may give responses to interrogatories or depositions which are not truthful. Since plaintiffs probably deal on a day-to-day basis with the school system, they probably know the proper answers. Plaintiffs should inform their attorneys that they wish to see defendants' answers to interrogatories and depositions as soon as they are available. It is the plaintiffs' obligation to inform their attorneys of any inaccuracies or untruths.

Plaintiffs and/or members of the organizational plaintiff should also be present when their attorney takes the depositions of defendants. The defendants are more than likely to tell the truth when they are sitting in front of people from the community, who probably know the answers to the questions, and, if not, can certainly find out.

D. Other Motions

After the discovery stage is closed, there may be a series of motions filed and argued in court. Plaintiffs should make it a point to be informed of the topic of these motions and the dates during which they will be argued. They should inform the community of such motions and try to be in court when they are heard, offer the attorney help that he may need, and after each such event have a press conference.

The following are some suggestions for plaintiffs, organizational plaintiff members and community people for keeping active during *el vacío;* for maintaining community interest in the lawsuit; and for increasing the likelihood of a favorable disposition:

1. Keep in close contact with the attorneys. Insist on being apprised of all developments in the lawsuit.
2. Insist that the attorneys go to the community occasionally to inform the other plaintiffs as well as the community of progress and developments in the case.
3. Publicize all developments in the news media.
4. Help the attorneys to:
   a) prepare interrogatories,
   b) answer defendants' interrogatories,
   c) prepare depositions.
5. If a plaintiff is to take a deposition from the other side, be sure that he or she is well-informed on all aspects of the case and is well-prepared to answer questions.
6. Help the attorneys to determine the accuracy and truth of defendants' answers to plaintiffs' interrogatories.
7. Be present when the attorneys take the depositions of school officials and other defendants.
8. Encourage as many people as possible to be present in court each time there is a court hearing.
9. Give the attorneys guidance and direction.
10. Help the attorneys make the decisions.
11. Conduct massive publicity campaigns in the community to inform people of the existence of the lawsuit and of any progress or developments.

THE PROCESS: *Relief*

Relief is the stage of the lawsuit at which plaintiffs will seek to obtain a remedy for past wrongs committed by the defendants. At this stage the plaintiffs have already shown that they are entitled to a court-ordered remedy since the court has found that the defendants' practices and policies discriminate against them. Before the court adopts a final bilingual education plan, both the plaintiffs and defendants are usually asked to submit proposed plans. In some instances, the defendants may choose not to submit a plan. In other instances, the defendants may submit a plan

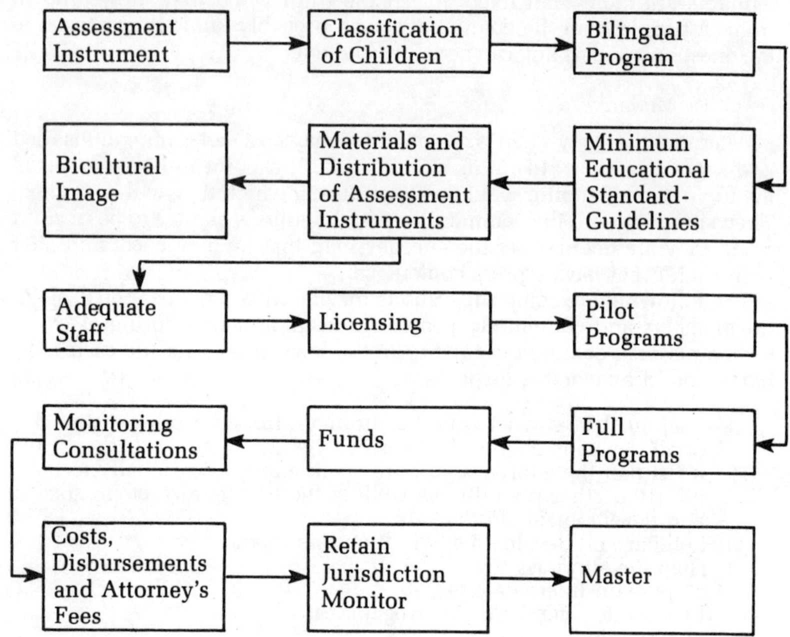

seeking to minimize the plaintiffs' victory, while the plaintiffs will tend to submit a proposed plan that will maximize their victory.

The parameters of the proposed relief have already been determined by the way the Complaint was framed, the manner in which the case was tried, and the evidence which was introduced at trial, especially the evidence upon which the court based its decision. Of major importance is the definition of the class adopted by the court, since those included in the class will now constitute the group eligible for any program ordered by the court. Also critical is evidence presented at trial as to the number of Hispanic teachers in the public school system and the number necessary for a viable bilingual education program.

Before members of the Puerto Rican community even approach lawyers, they may have a good idea of the type of program they are seeking to preserve, enhance or initiate. Many Puerto Rican parents may feel that the program should admit as many students as possible; that the teachers must be bilingual and have a deep understanding of the students' culture; that teachers and administrators be responsive to parents, children and community; and, that there be parent participation in the administration of the program. Some of these elements are in place to one degree or another where a bilingual-bicultural program is already in existence. What may be missing is a permanent funding source for the program, a network for recruitment and hiring of personnel, a procedure for expansion of the program to include a larger number of students, strengthening of the curriculum with the aim of making the bilingual-bicultural program a more effective means of bilinguality, or a proper testing (assessment) procedure to insure that all students who need bilingual education are included in the program.

In those school districts where no program exists, community members should look at model programs in other districts and the best features of each should be adopted. Experts should also be consulted so that the latest developments and worthwhile innovations can be incorporated into the program.

The definition of the class presented to the court in the Complaint will become critical in the relief stage. Where the class has been too narrowly defined, as has been the case in several lawsuits where language, such as "those Puerto Rican children with English language deficiencies who can more effectively learn in Spanish," has been used, then the relief may be limited to only those children who can: (1) speak and write Spanish at a certain level of competence; and (2) who have English language deficiencies. Under this definition, a child who may benefit from the program would not be eligible unless he meets the two requirements. The definition also creates a need to measure Spanish competence and English-language deficiency, thus in effect, setting a double barrier (filter).

Words such as "deficiencies," "difficulties," and "educationally deprived" should be avoided in the Complaint. They cause people to view bilingual education as compensatory in nature and tend to stigmatize those students who participate in the program. A more appropriate way of defining the class would be: "Puerto Rican children who attend the public schools who, by reason of their national origin or their inability to effectively function in the English-only curriculum, are prevented from equally participating in the learning process." In this case, the argument will be that the child's language is an integral part of his national origin and that he should be entitled to a program of bilingual-bicultural education in order to receive from the public school the full education to which he is entitled. This definition also expands the class to include any Puerto Rican child who could benefit from the program without requiring proof of "proficiency" in Spanish. The HEW guidelines promulgated pursuant to the Civil Rights Act of 1964, and which have been the basis upon which the courts have ordered the implementation of bilingual education, speak to the needs of national-origin minority group children.

Identification and Eligibility for the Program

The assessment of a child's eligibility for the bilingual program must seek to examine the child's abilities, skills, mode of behavior, language usage and not merely how well a child does on a pre-determined standardized test. The testing process should include aural examinations, participant observations and linguistic analysis of the child's use of language. Individual teachers as well as outside experts may be used to supplement information on the child. Instead of locking themselves into a particular test or method of assessment, the community should insist that any consent decree or court-ordered program be flexible enough to allow for review of a testing or assessment method chosen so that these may be replaced as they are improved and made more comprehensive. Where the public school seeks to make use of a test, the community should be aware that HEW's Office of Civil Rights has developed criteria to ascertain the validity and reliability of these tests, and proof should be sought from public school officials that they have conformed to these criteria.

The fundamental requirement then, in selecting a method of identification and eligibility, is flexibility in the use of criteria in order to allow for the creation of a reliable data base which contains accurate background information on each child.

Hiring and Recruiting Bilingual Teachers

A bilingual-bicultural program to be effective must be able to attract and retain a teaching staff sufficient in numbers and quality to meet the needs of the children enrolled in the program. It is always difficult for any school system to attract teachers who have mastered a subject and possess the skills to teach the subject well. Teachers in bilingual-bicultural programs must meet these two requirements, and must also have mastered two languages as well as be familiar with the child's culture.

These teachers should be required to meet five criteria, all of which are equally important: (1) fluency in English; (2) fluency in Spanish; (3) mastery of the content area to be taught, e.g., science, history, etc.; (4) mastery of the teaching skills necessary to teach a content area; and (5) an informed and complete understanding of the child's culture, customs and the Island's history. These stringent requirements will reduce the pool of teachers from which a local school system can draw. The school system may have to expand its recruiting activities to other parts of the country, to Puerto Rico and possibly even to Latin American countries. The logical starting point for such recruitment is the local community itself, and no simple assumptions should be made about the ability of bilinguals from other Hispanic cultures to understand the cultural forms that heritage may take in United States urban settings.

Many colleges that train teachers are increasingly varying their curricula to provide for the skills required by bilingual programs. Public school officials and the community can recruit from these institutions as well. The basic aim is to have an applicant pool of sufficient size so that the best possible candidates for the program are chosen. It is clear that simply because a teacher is Hispanic does not mean that he or she possesses the skills necessary to teach in a bilingual-bicultural program. Only those candidates who most closely approximate the requirements of the program should be hired. There should be no compromise on this point.

An effective program requires that the public school system have full input from community organizations and that the efforts and resources of local colleges be used. Community organizations should be cognizant of the need the schools have for particular types of bilingual personnel and should gear their efforts toward obtaining such persons from as large a recruitment area as is necessary. Community people must be prepared to balance immediate needs in the program with future needs in recruiting a well-trained and adequate staff. In this sense their concern and concerted action must reach beyond local schools to the training institutes preparing professionals for such programs.

The relief ordered by the court should require the public school system to undertake affirmative recruitment efforts for teachers and administrators and insure that a sufficient number of bilingual-bicultural teachers will be hired to meet the needs of the children enrolled in the program.

Bilingual-Bicultural Curriculum

The prime feature of a bilingual-bicultural program is its curriculum design and course content. A bilingual-bicultural program must be able to offer instruction in substantive courses in Spanish. Such subjects as mathematics, science and social studies must be taught in Spanish. The aim is to have the child receive instruction in a language which facilitates his/her effective participation in learning. A child who already has skills in Spanish should be allowed to develop his/her knowledge of substantive courses in Spanish. In some bilingual-bicultural programs, music, art and physical education are taught in English exclusively. This is done, not so much so that the children learn English—which is actually accomplished in other courses—but so that Hispanic children can mix in a classroom setting with other school children who are not in the bilingual program.

However, some feel that in these cultural courses the child should be taught in Spanish so that the socialization process will be accelerated. There is much in the Hispanic child's culture that can be emphasized and studied in art and music and the child should have an opportunity to obtain mastery of these. These courses can be used to further implement the bicultural aspect of the bilingual program.

In designing a bilingual-bicultural curriculum that meets the needs of a specific school system, community representatives should examine what has been done elsewhere. As has been mentioned, the best features of these models should be adopted. The court should receive a proposal which details the curriculum design for the elementary school, the junior high school and the high school. This proposal may also outline the subjects to be taught exclusively in English. It may include the proportions of time in a given course that will be bilingual, e.g., a mathematics course at the first grade level may be 100% in Spanish; at the second grade level may be 75% in Spanish and 25% in English; at the third grade level may be 50% in Spanish and English, and continue at this level until the sixth grade.

Whichever particular design is proposed, the aim is to seek to foster the child's equal development in both English and Spanish. This may mean a course such as music or art will be fifty percent in Spanish and fifty percent in English, or some other ratio, but which in either case will allow for the use of the child's abilities in Spanish for acquisition of English. It is understandable that a variety of curriculum designs abound throughout the country and that a school system may begin with one design and grow into another. The relief ordered by the court should set forth the guidelines for these programs, but should allow for flexible growth in design and curriculum.

Evaluation and Monitoring of the Program

It is very important for the success of the program to incorporate a mechanism in the remedy ordered by the court for evaluating the bilingual-bicultural program. Such evaluation should occur on a periodic basis, possibly annually, in order to determine what changes, if any, are necessary. The evaluation should take into consideration the flexibility which a bilingual-bicultural program requires as it develops and becomes responsive to the particular characteristics of the school system and the children enrolled in it.

Such an evaluation will also provide documentation of the progress which has been made with respect to the implementation of the program and its effectiveness. Yet, it is no substitute for the monitoring which must be done by the community to insure the proper implementation of the program. The court-ordered plan will set forth certain dates by which students are to be identified for the program, by which teachers are to be hired, by which the curriculum is to be in full operation. Whether these goals are actually met may be a direct result of the community's ability to monitor the progress taken with each one.

In one case, for example, the community monitored the implementation of a bilingual program and found (1) that thousands of entitled students were not provided the program; (2) that the school system had failed to hire the necessary available personnel; (3) that the school system was using unqualified personnel in the program; (4) that the school system had failed to complete testing of the eligible student population; and, (5) that school officials had failed to submit information to the plaintiffs which had been required by the court. This effort required the community representatives to review and analyze hundreds of pages of reports supplied by the school board with respect to its implementation of the bilingual-bicultural program. Hundreds of hours went into the analysis of these reports. Many hours were also spent interviewing teachers in the program and parents in different schools to find out how the program was being implemented. Many of the curriculum designs for the programs were no more than replicas of what had actually been in place before the lawsuit was filed. As a result of this work, the defendant school system was held by the court to be in contempt of its order to implement the plan; was ordered to take immediate steps to implement the plan; and was liable to plaintiffs' lawyers for attorneys' fees.

Thus, there will be a need for the community representatives to assess the progress of the school system in obtaining funding, hiring personnel, identifying students, providing the appropriate curriculum, and insuring that all eligible students are given an opportunity to participate in the program. In addition, community representatives should be available to receive complaints from parents, teachers and others regarding the program and its implementation. All of this work involves the ascertainment of facts to determine whether a contempt action or other legal move is warranted to obtain full compliance.

The community's work then, begins in earnest once the lawsuit has been won and the program has been developed on paper. The community must receive periodic information from the public schools, while having accessibility to parents, students, teachers, administrators and others who can identify what the problems are with respect to the program. The task is time-consuming but it must be assumed by members of the community, because no one else will be willing to do it.

Allocation of Funds for the Program

The fundamental basis of any bilingual-bicultural program is sufficient funds to carry out the objectives of the program. To the extent possible, funds used should be tax levy funds (tax monies derived from income taxes) since these are not apt to be cut off as are federal monies for temporary programs. The school system must be placed under a duty to obtain and expend the funds required to implement the program, and to safeguard the positions of existing bilingual-bicultural personnel, as well as to hire new personnel when the need arises. In case tax levy funds cannot be obtained, the school system should be required in the relief ordered by the court to seek alternative sources. The school system's obligation should be specifically outlined in the court's order. Ambiguous wording, such as "defendants shall use their maximum efforts," should be avoided since such wording is open to various interpretations.

It is of major importance that the community be informed of any and all obstacles relating to the securing of adequate funds for the program. As funds are needed, failure on the part of the school system to provide them should be immediately brought to the court's attention.

Without adequate funding there may be no program and all that is contained in the court's order will be no more than a list of unfulfilled promises. If a program is created with inadequate funds, it is surely doomed to failure.

DESEGREGATION AND BILINGUAL-BICULTURAL EDUCATION

Most Puerto Rican and other Hispanic parents would agree with the Supreme Court's interpretation of the significance of equal educational opportunity which was set out in the landmark *Brown* v. *Board of Education* case of 1954:

> Today, education is perhaps the most important function of state and local governments. Compulsory school attendance laws and the great expenditures for education both demonstrate our recognition of the importance of education to our democratic society. It is required in the performance of our most basic public responsibilities, even service in the armed forces. It is the very foundation of good citizenship. Today it is a principal instrument in awakening the child to cultural values, in preparing him for later professional training, and in helping him to adjust normally to his environment. In these days, it is doubtless that any child may reasonably be expected to succeed in life if he is denied the opportunity of an education. Such an opportunity, where the state has undertaken to provide it, is a right which must be made available to all on equal terms.

In this decision, the Supreme Court announced the fundamental principle that segregation in public schools is a denial of the equal protection of the laws and declared that racial discrimination in public education is unconstitutional.

Since 1954 there have been many lawsuits brought by children and parents with the intent of stopping local school boards from forcing their children to attend segregated public schools. The courts maintain that school boards have an affirmative duty to desegregate schools. This includes "whatever steps might be necessary to convert to a unitary (non-segregated) system in which racial discrimination would be eliminated root and branch."[7]

Hispanics also brought lawsuits to terminate the segregation which they too had suffered. In *U.S.* v. *Texas*,[8] the courts declared that the principles of *Brown* v. *Board of Education* applied to the practice of segregation of Mexican-Americans. The District Court also found that "Mexican-American students are an identifiable, ethnic-minority class. . . ."

In *Keyes* v. *School District #1*,[9] as a result of efforts by Hispanic intervenors, the Supreme Court held that Hispanic students should be grouped with blacks under a "minority" category for the purposes of school desegregation, thus preventing a school which was predominantly comprised of students from the two groups from being considered desegregated. The practice of school districts had been to classify Hispanics as whites, thus, predominantly black schools were "desegregated" by assigning Hispanic students to these schools. In the case of Puerto Ricans, the use of the standard racial classifications of black and white makes no sense. Using these classifications, a Puerto Rican family with dark-skinned and light-skinned children may find one child classified as white and one as black for desegregation purposes. Such a classification would have a traumatic effect on an otherwise unified family.

It is thus evident that Hispanics have either actively pushed for desegregation remedies of their own, while at the same time seeking some form of bilingual education as a remedy for past discrimination, or have found it necessary to actively collaborate with blacks in desegregation lawsuits initiated by the latter when it is obvious that such suits can affect existing or contemplated bilingual programs. A community that seeks to preserve or expand its bilingual programs must often decide in a relatively short period of time whether to intervene in the desegregation lawsuit. This must be done to insure that student assignment procedures will give special consideration and priority to the distinct educational needs of Hispanic children, especially those in need of bilingual instruction.

Intervention

If an Hispanic community or its representatives decide that it is best to intervene in a desegregation lawsuit already in progress, it must secure attorneys for representation in the legal process. In such cases, the community organization(s), parents on behalf of their children, and the children themselves will be known to the court as "plaintiffs," "plaintiff-intervenors," or simply "intervenors." The attorney for Hispanics must make a motion to the court seeking permission to allow them to intervene, that is, to join the lawsuit. This motion must be accompanied by a Complaint similar to the one previously discussed. The proposed intervenors must show the court, among other things, that they have an interest in the outcome of the existing litigation; that the attempt to intervene is timely; that the existing parties do not represent their interests; and that the existing parties will not be prejudiced if the intervention is permitted.

To be permitted to intervene, the Hispanic parents and community organization must show that their children who attend public schools have a clear interest in the outcome of the lawsuit. This can be done by showing that whatever decision the court makes on a proposed educational plan will have an impact upon them, especially if bilingual programs may be dismantled or adversely affected by the assignment of Hispanic students to schools without such programs. If intervention is sought before a final remedy has been ordered by the court, the motion should be considered timely by the court, that is, not too late in the proceedings to adversely affect the original parties. It will also have to be demonstrated that the interests of the original parties are not impaired by having the court consider the interests of Hispanic children. Finally, it is usually the case that the parties who brought the original lawsuit are not expert in and have not addressed the issue of bilingual educational programs in the school district. Thus, it can be pointed out that original parties in the lawsuit have failed to represent the interests of Hispanic students.

In certain instances, the court must allow intervention because the intervenors have a right to become part of the suit. In other instances, intervention is allowed at the discretion of the court. If intervention is permitted, it may be for all purposes or for only a limited purpose. In other words, the judge may permit the plaintiff-intervenors to participate in all aspects of the litigation, or he may restrict the participation of the plaintiff-intervenors to only one stage of the court proceedings.

The danger with intervening in a desegregation suit or of bringing a bilingual education lawsuit in a school district where a desegregation suit is pending, is that there is a long line of well-established court precedents in the desegregation area which plainly state that maintaining segregated schools is a violation of the Fourteenth Amendment to the United States Constitution. A finding of segregated schools in a particular community is thus a finding of a constitutional violation. On the other hand, bilingual education litigation is a new field and while courts have held that failure to provide bilingual education to school children of limited-English-speaking ability is a violation of federal law, the courts, including the United States Supreme Court, have not held it to be a constitutional violation. This means that when a judge is presented with a segregation case and at the same time a bilingual education case, the court will place more importance on the segregation case because it has its basis in the Constitution and bilingual education may be subordinated. Its basis is in federal law, but not in the Constitution.

In sum, Hispanic communities considering litigation to achieve bilingual education and/or desegregation are faced with several alternatives. They can intervene in an existing desegregation lawsuit as has been discussed. Or, they can initiate a separate bilingual education lawsuit without intervening in the desegregation case. However, the court may consolidate these two lawsuits and treat them as one. In addition, the Hispanic community may bring a desegregation lawsuit of its own and request bilingual education as part of the remedy. In fact, in the Southwest, in a number of desegregation suits, courts have ordered the implementation of bilingual education programs as affirmative relief for past discrimination. However, bilingual education cases have, to date, not been decided on the original constitutional grounds argued, but rather as a violation of federal law.

There is a need for those seeking desegregation and those desiring bilingual education to work together and reconcile any differences. The two concepts are not incompatible, for both seek the same end: an equal opportunity for quality education. Effective bilingual education programs can be implemented in a desegregated school system; desegregation is not adversely affected by the presence of bilingual education programs. Advocates of desegregation and bilingual education live in the same community, and they must take the lead to avoid conflicts and confrontations.

The area we have sought to describe is a very sensitive one which must be given much thought and planning by the Hispanic community. The most important task of providing form and direction to the goal of obtaining effective school desegregation and bilingual education is one which ultimately rests on the Hispanic community.[10]

EPILOGUE

The strategy discussed in this paper—litigation in behalf of bilingual-bicultural education premised on the right to equal educational opportunity—is only one avenue in the quest to insure quality education for Puerto Rican children. But this strategy has limitations. As has been repeatedly noted, the courts and school personnel tend to view bilingual education as compensatory. They see its goal as merely to remedy the child's lack of English-language skills. For this reason, and because of other misconceptions about the maintenance model, the transitional model is the basic program that has been achieved through litigation. The mere mention of implementing bilingual education makes many English monolingual teachers and their unions uneasy and insecure because of fear that they may be displaced by bilingual teachers, or, because of ethnic prejudices, ignorance and other attitudes. Court intervention in educational matters may serve to further alienate many teachers and their unions to the extent that the merits of court-ordered programs become muddled.

In addition, since bilingual education lawsuits are many times filed while desegregation suits are pending, the bilingual education claims may be subordinated or even rejected by the courts. While the courts have ruled on the unconstitutionality of segregation, the right to bilingual education rests on federal laws and HEW guidelines that interpret those laws, and not on the United States Constitution.

Furthermore, attaining bilingual education through litigation in one school district does not effect children who may direly need it in other districts in the same state, indeed, in a neighboring school district. And, of course, litigation takes a long time. Advocates of bilingual education, if they pursue the legal route, must wait years from the time the decision is made to seek redress until final disposition. During this time, Puerto Rican children continue to languish in the schools without any programs that will insure their effective participation in the educational process.

As this paper attests, of course, we do not reject the litigation strategy. Bilingual education, although not yet a constitutional right, is well-embedded in the law by virtue of the favorable court decisions that have been gained. Lawsuits can be a tool for powerless communities to organize against school officials who fear the negative publicity and who are concerned with the costs of defending a lawsuit. They may also provide the stimulus for the passage of state legislation for bilingual education. However, it is our position that, although use of the legal process should be maximized, its limitations should be kept clearly in view and other alternatives, especially continuous pressure for administrative and legislative actions, should be simultaneously explored in all cases.

APPENDIX

Questions the Actors Must Address

To ensure optimum involvement in the lawsuit (that is, to participate comfortably and effectively), those intending engagement in the lawsuit should seek answers to the questions which we pose here. Some of the questions can be answered for the client(s) or the community person(s) by the educator(s) or the lawyer(s). Others, they will have to answer for themselves.

Some of the questions should be directed to the attorneys. This can be done by members of the community organization, those who are initially seeking lawyers who are willing to file the suit, or the clients. The answers to many of the questions intended for the attorneys will help to determine the type of relationship that will be had with the attorneys and the input and influence that the community will have in directing the lawsuit.

We also suggest questions that the educators can ask themselves. These will hopefully aid them in planning the extent of their involvement, as well as in preparing for what may be stormy confrontation with school board members and school administrators.

There may come a time during the course of the lawsuit, or during the implementation of the resulting program, when those who had a hand in the lawsuit will have to answer these questions for someone.

Questions to be posed by prospective clients:

A. To what extent should I become involved in this lawsuit?
   1. Should I become a named plaintiff?
   2. Should I allow the lawyers and other community persons to meet with and test my children to see if they would benefit from a bilingual-bicultural program, but not become a named plaintiff?
   3. Should I actively participate but not lend my name or that of my children to the lawsuit?

B. What does my role as a named plaintiff entail?
   1. Will I attend court proceedings?
   2. Will I have to give an affidavit (sworn statement)?
   3. Will I have to give a deposition (answers to oral questions outside of the court under oath) to the attorneys of the school district?
   4. Will I be consulted on any final settlement?
   5. Will I be called to testify as a witness in any trial or hearing?
   6. Will meetings be held in the community, and will I attend?
   7. Will I be consulted by the lawyers? the teachers? the community organization?
   8. Will I be involved in demonstrations?

9. Will there be a newsletter to inform us of the progress of the lawsuit?
10. Will there be one person I can call for information on the lawsuit?

C. How shall I monitor compliance with the terms of the lawsuit or any order of the court?
    1. Will I help make reports to the community organization on compliance or violation of a court-ordered program?
    2. Will I help gather information on the programs established by the school district?
    3. Will I report the results of the program on my children to the parents' organization?
    4. Will I assist the community organization in preparing reports on the state of compliance?
    5. Will I testify as a witness in any proceedings to enforce the court-ordered program?
    6. Will I help raise funds to pay for the costs of monitoring?
    7. How will I work with the teachers in the program and the administrator of the program to insure that the terms of any court order are in fact met?

D. What does my role as a member of the community organization involved in the lawsuit entail?
    1. Will I help to find parents whose children cannot function effectively in the English-only schools so that these can become involved in the lawsuit?
    2. Will I interview children to identify those with the kinds of needs to be addressed by the lawsuit?
    3. Will I participate in demonstrations?
    4. Will I be involved in any negotiations with the school authorities?
    5. Will I give depositions to the attorneys of the school district?
    6. Will I be called to testify as a witness in any trial or hearing?
    7. Will I be called upon to provide an affidavit or to assist the lawyer in obtaining the affidavit of others who have the information sought?

E. What should I be thinking about during the implementation of the bilingual program?
    1. What is the extent of parental involvement that any program should have?
    2. What are the purposes to be served in any educational program?
    3. What do I want my child to learn from an educational program?
    4. What types of educational personnel should be recruited for the program?
    5. What level of funding should be provided to meet the needs of this program?
    6. Do I favor maintenance bilingual education or transitional bilingual education?
    7. How should my child be tested for progress in the program?
    8. Who should appoint the administrators of the program?
    9. Who shall the administrators of the program remain accountable to: parents? teachers? school authorities?

Questions to ask the lawyers:

1. Under what conditions will they take the case?
2. What role, if any, will the community play in shaping the Complaint?
3. Will the legal organization allow the community to select which attorney(s) will be assigned to conduct the lawsuit?
4. Will the community help to develop the plan for relief which will outline the type of program the school children may receive?
5. Can the community share in any attorneys' fees that the legal services or defense fund will receive?
6. Will the community be permitted to oversee and/or monitor the implementation of any program secured by litigation?
7. Will resources be made available to the community to monitor the implementation of any program, including but not limited to sharing in any attorneys' fees?
8. Will the attorneys consult with the community on any and every motion brought by or defended by the attorney?
9. Will the attorneys invite the participation or the attendance of the community at each court proceeding in the litigation of the lawsuit?
10. Will the attorneys meet with members of the community and keep them informed of each step taken in litigating the lawsuit, including discovery and the shaping of a final program for relief?
11. Will the community be able to veto a particular litigation strategy and/or types of programs or final plans proposed by the attorneys and their experts?
12. Will the attorneys allow the community to meet with experts engaged in their behalf, in order to discuss the nature of the suit as well as the experts' contribution?
13. What will be the extent of the involvement of the organizational plaintiff in the lawsuit?
14. Will the community be permitted to issue press releases and public notices regarding the litigation?
15. Will community members receive copies of all legal papers filed in the lawsuit as well as explanations prepared in language understandable to laypersons?
16. What will be the role of any local counsel? Will the out-of-state defense organization attorneys be accountable to the community and to the local counsel; and, if so, in what form?

Questions to be posed by educators:

What will be the extent of my involvement in the lawsuit?

1. Will I help organize parents for the lawsuit?
2. Will I assist the lawyers to organize meetings with parents and children?
3. Will I identify children who are Hispanic?
4. Will I identify Hispanic children who cannot function effectively in the English-only curriculum?
5. Will I become a member of the community organization?

6. Will I attempt to obtain and evaluate for the lawyers statistics and facts which may be available from the school system which tend to portray the educational plight of Hispanic children in the school system?
7. Will I identify what programs are in need of improvement?
8. Will I work with the Parent-Teacher Associations on behalf of the lawsuit?
9. Will I encourage parents to attend meetings of the community organization?
10. Will I participate in demonstrations?
11. Will I attend court proceedings?
12. Will I be called upon to give an affidavit regarding information I may have about the school system?
13. Will I be called as a witness in any trial or hearing?
14. Will my activity on behalf of the lawsuit be protected by the First Amendment of the Constitution of the United States and by other laws and cases?
15. Will the attorneys involved in the lawsuit represent me or bring a suit on my behalf if the school board fires me or disciplines me because of my activities in connection with bilingual education?

Some general questions that the educator should consider for implementing the program:

1. What should constitute a model bilingual-bicultural program?
2. Which bilingual program model best meets the educational needs of children and the aspirations of the community?
3. How should students who need the program be identified?
4. How will the progress of students in the program be measured?
5. What should be the student/teacher ratio in the bilingual program?
6. What courses should be taught in Spanish? in English? in different combinations of English and Spanish?
7. What activities should the children in the program share with other students who are not in the program?
8. How should the bilingual school curriculum change from year to year?
9. What kind of materials will be necessary in order to support the needs and aims of the curriculum?
10. How will teachers be recruited for the program? Will they have to meet any licensing requirements? Will current licensing requirements have to be changed in order to obtain the necessary number of teachers?
11. Will community and senior colleges be encouraged to train prospective personnel for the program?
12. How will teachers keep up with new developments in bilingual education in the rest of the country?
13. What methods should be employed in teaching students in bilingual programs?
14. When should a student enter a bilingual program? When is the best time for him/her to leave?
15. How do you measure a teacher's competence in Spanish and English? A student's competence?

16. What kind of measure will be developed to assess the effectiveness of the program?
17. What level of funding will be necessary to support this program?
18. What should be the source of such funding (city tax levy, state or federal)?
19. What will be my role in monitoring compliance with the court-ordered program?
20. How will my involvement in the lawsuit affect my independence as a teacher and educator?

NOTES

1. The Puerto Rican Legal Defense & Education Fund, Inc.; the Mexican American Legal Defense & Educational Fund, Inc.; the Center for Constitutional Rights; the NAACP Legal Defense & Education Fund, Inc.; the American Civil Liberties Union; and the National Association for the Advancement of Colored People.
2. There is a possibility that if the case is won, the court may allow such agencies to gain attorney's fees from the defendants.
3. Since these agencies generally employ small legal staffs and since their funds are not unlimited and since, generally, it is their policy to attempt to persuade the courts to make new and/or good law, whether or not a case can be won and whether it has potential for establishing good law are important considerations.
4. In one lawsuit in Connecticut there were approximately twenty named individual plaintiffs, all of whom were inactive. There was also an organizational plaintiff, three of whose members were active. The latter three were all Puerto Rican. One was a female in her sixties with a daughter who attended college. The other two were males. One of these males did not live in the Puerto Rican community and had two young children, neither of whom would be eligible for bilingual education under most present state or federal standards. The other male had high school- and college-age children, none of whom would be eligible for bilingual education. In a lawsuit filed in New York State, there were approximately twenty named plaintiffs and one organizational plaintiff. Members of the community organization were active while named plaintiffs were not.
5. Members of the organizational plaintiff may be active non-clients. The organizational plaintiff which is also active is, of course, properly characterized as an active client since it has retained the lawyer and is a bonafide client. On the other hand, most of its members are non-individual clients of the lawyer. However, some of its members may also be clients—active or inactive.
6. All parties who bring a lawsuit must have "standing" to sue. This means that they must be sufficiently injured or aggrieved. Here, defendants would allege that the organization has not been harmed or injured by the alleged conduct of defendants; or, that it does not have authority from its membership to bring the lawsuit.
7. *Green* v. *County School Board,* 391 U.S. 430, 437-438 (1968).

8. 342 F. Supp. 24 (E.D. Tex., 1971). *aff'd* 446 F 2d 518 (1972).
9. 413 U.S. 189, 197 & N.6 (1973).
10. For further discussion on the bilingual education/desegregation issue, see *Bilingual Education and Desegregation: A New Dimension in Legal and Educational Decision-Making,* Ricardo R. Fernandez and Judith T. Guskin, pp. 1-10; 16-21 and footnotes. In *Bilingual Education,* LaFontaine and Golubchick, editors.

NEW JERSEY REQUIREMENTS FOR BILINGUAL EDUCATION CERTIFICATION AS THEY RELATE TO FEDERAL AND STATE LEGISLATION

Ana María Schuhmann

On January 8, 1975 the New Jersey Bilingual Education Act (Senate Bill No. 811) was signed into law by Governor Brendan Byrne. The N.J. Bilingual Act, modeled after the Massachusetts bilingual law, is transitional in nature and mandates the establishment of a bilingual education program in any school district having more than twenty pupils of limited-English-speaking ability in any one language classification. Before the Bilingual Education Act was enacted, work had proceeded toward establishing certification requirements for bilingual education teachers. After more than a year of planning and deliberation, a statewide subcommittee on Bilingual Education and English as a Second Language Certification[1] submitted two separate proposals to the State Board of Education. These regulations were approved on October 1, 1975.

According to bilingual-bicultural certification regulations (Authority NJSA 18A:6-34 et.seq.-NJSA 18:35-15-26), to receive an endorsement in bilingual education in New Jersey, a teacher must hold both a bachelor's degree based upon a four-year program in an accredited college and a regular teaching certificate in another field. In addition, a teacher must complete twenty-four semester-hour credits in bilingual-bicultural education and demonstrate verbal and written proficiency in both English and the other language used as a medium of instruction. The State Department of Education Bureau of Teacher Education and Academic Credentials maintains responsibility for monitoring the implementation of these regulations (Brown, 1978-A).

In March 1979, more than three years after the enactment of certification regulations, almost one-third of New Jersey's bilingual education teachers were in danger of losing their jobs. These teachers could not be certified under these regulations because they had not achieved the minimal levels of language proficiency set by the N.J. Department of Education. The situation was complicated further because a great many of these 307 teachers were tenured and, because of seniority and other certification, have "bumping rights" over other personnel who were in regular classrooms (Brown, 1978-B). Language proficiency is *not* a requirement for regular elementary or secondary certification in New Jersey. It is a requirement only for bilingual education and for English as a Second Language (ESL).

Why does this situation, which the New Jersey Education Association has classified as an "emergency," exist in New Jersey?

This paper will examine the development of federal and state bilingual education legislation in an attempt to determine its effect on language policy, on the regulations and implementation of programs, and on certification requirements for teachers in New Jersey. Special emphasis will be given to the controversial language proficiency requirements, an issue that has polarized the advocates of bilingual education in the state. The 1968 Bilingual Education Act will be discussed first, followed by the amendments of 1974, the Massachusetts Transitional Law, the New Jersey Bilingual Law and, finally, the Bilingual Act of 1978.

Federal Legislation

The 1968 Bilingual Education Act (Title VII Amendment to the Elementary and Secondary Act of 1965) provided funds to local education agencies to "develop and carry out new and imaginative" programs to meet the special needs of children of limited-English-speaking ability (U.S.C. 880B., 1968). However, the implementation of bilingual programs under the 1968 Bilingual Education Act has revealed that one of its weaknesses is the lack of explicit language (Molina, 1978). Gaarder (1977) stresses the ambiguity with which the Bilingual Act was worded, noting that "Congress couched its extraordinarily generous and innovative legislation in support of dual-language public schooling in terms that permit both the ethnocentrists and the cultural pluralists to see what they want to see in the Act." Gaarder (1978) adds that, under the stress of creating proposals for the Act by 1969, differing patterns of federal and local administration of the program were quickly developed.

New Jersey chose to see cultural pluralism in the Act. Federally funded bilingual education pilot projects were started in 1969 and 1970 in Union City, Newark, Jersey City, Perth Amboy and Vineland (a four-district consortium); and Paterson, Elizabeth and Lakewood (another consortium) to serve large populations of Spanish-speaking children (*N.Y. Times,* 1972). In their haste to develop bilingual education programs funded under Title VII, local school districts "minimized the importance of employing in bilingual education programs only well-prepared teachers and administrators, strongly literate in the non-English tongue and highly knowledgeable of the other culture" (Gaarder, 1978).

Gaarder cites as the first explanation for this phenomenon the fact that "most Spanish speakers were victims of an educational policy that had previously denigrated their mother tongue, discouraged them from using it and virtually assured their illiteracy in it." This was not the case in New Jersey. By the time the first Title VII projects were implemented, some 100,000 Cuban refugees had settled in the state, more than half of them in the twin cities of Union City and West New York, where they became a majority of the local population (Mackey and Beebe, 1977). Many of these Cuban refugees were professionals and many had long teaching careers behind them. When bilingual education programs started in New Jersey in 1969 and 1970, these professionals were tapped.

Many native Spanish teachers, who had degrees from their native countries, revalidated their credentials by going back to college. Because there were no bilingual education teacher training programs at the time, many enrolled in Spanish as a Second Language programs and received certification and master's degrees in Spanish. A suit has recently been instituted by the participants in one such program implemented by a state college. In a class action suit, the graduates of that program claim to have received a "monolingual" (Spanish) rather than bilingual education, an education that did not prepare them to pass the proficiency exams later required for certification (Hidalgo, 1978).

The model for bilingual schooling adopted by most programs in New Jersey in the beginning years under Title VII was the team-teaching approach where (a) in a partially integrated full-day program, two teachers were used per classroom, one a native speaker of Spanish, the other a native speaker of English, or (b) in a team-teaching half-day program, two teachers, one Spanish-dominant and one English-dominant, exchanged class groups at a certain time of the day. (These two approaches have been discussed by Reyes, 1975.) In either case, the English-dominant teacher was responsible for instruction in English and ESL, while the Spanish-dominant teacher conducted the curriculum content in Spanish, and taught Spanish as both first and second languages. Newark's Bilingual-Bicultural Program Description (1970) states: "Based on the principle that a child will learn better and faster in the language in which he is dominant, children have been grouped according to language dominance and receive instruction in the subject area by a teacher who masters that language. The native English-speaking teacher teaches ESL and English as a first language and the Spanish-speaking teacher teaches Spanish as a second language and Spanish as a first language. They also teach basic content areas in the language of the students' dominance."

In the early 1970s, proficiency in two languages was not a criterion for the hiring of teachers for the bilingual education programs in New Jersey. Instruction in two languages was achieved by employing two teachers, each proficient in one of the languages of instruction.

In 1971, the U.S. Division of Bilingual Education attempted to assist school districts more extensively by issuing guildelines describing the purpose of bilingual education and the use of two languages of instruction (Molina, 1978). These guidelines and the philosophical position of Title VII suggested a language-maintenance approach to bilingual education, seeking fluency and literacy in both languages. This early maintenance philosophy was reflected in the bilingual programs in New Jersey at the time. Teachers who worked in the federally funded projects and who were interviewed for this paper recall no pressure from the administration to develop the English skills of the children so that they might be integrated into the "regular" program as quickly as possible. As a matter of fact, teachers interviewed recall being "forbidden to teach in their second language."

The federal Education Amendments of 1974, which expanded the original Bilingual Education Act of 1968, were clearly transitional in nature. In a transitional program, the language of the children is used in the early grades to the extent necessary to allow pupils to adjust to school and/or to master subject matter until their skill in English is developed to the point where it alone can be used as the medium of instruction (Fishman, 1976).

The 1974 Act encouraged and provided financial assistance for the establishment and operation of educational programs using bilingual educational practices, techniques and methods designed to enable children of limited-English-speaking ability to achieve competence in the English language. Furthermore, the act specified that in a program of bilingual education "there is instruction given in, and study of, English and, to the extent necessary to allow a child to progress effectively through the educational system, the native language of the children of limited-English-speaking ability" (P.L. 93-380). The Bilingual Act of 1974 thus established the learning of English and effective progress in school as goals for bilingual education (Molina, 1978).

State Legislation

The first mandatory bilingual education legislation passed by a state, the 1971 Massachusetts Bilingual Act, "contributed much to institutionalize the concept of transitional bilingual education" (Gonzalez, 1978). This law provides that a child of limited-English-speaking ability shall remain in the program for a period of three years or until such time as he or she achieves a level of English language skills that enable him or her to perform successfully in classes where instruction is given only in English, whichever shall occur first (Irizarry, 1978).

In 1975, New Jersey enacted its Bilingual Education Law, following the transitional model set by Massachusetts and by the federal Bilingual Act of 1974. The New Jersey law establishes bilingual programs to meet the needs of children of limited-English-speaking ability (LESA) and to "facilitate their integration into the regular public school curriculum" (Senate Bill No. 811). This law, like its Massachusetts predecessor, states that every pupil participating in a bilingual program shall be entitled to continue such participation for a period of three years.

With the enactment of the mandatory transitional New Jersey Bilingual Law, the adoption of certification guidelines and the development of rules for bilingual education (Administrative Code), many changes occurred in the implementation of programs in the state:

1. The number of bilingual education programs expanded greatly. From demonstration projects serving only Spanish-speaking children in nine districts, there are now bilingual education programs in twenty counties, serving over 23,000 students and employing approximately 1,000 teachers (Palsha, 1978). Even though the majority of the programs are Spanish/English, languages of instruction now include Portuguese, French, Italian, Japanese, Korean, Greek and Arabic.
2. The early team-teaching approach with two teachers per classroom was abandoned. Despite the educational benefits of the model, e.g., keeping the two languages separate, it is immediately obvious that the cost of providing two teachers for the same classroom discourages administrators from adopting it (Blanco, 1977). The model currently used by most bilingual programs in New Jersey utilizes a bilingual education classroom teacher with an ESL specialist who comes into the classroom daily for thirty-five to forty-five minutes[2].
3. The bilingual education classroom teacher became responsible for teaching the native language of the children and for instruction in the content areas in that language and also, for the first time, in English (though not necessarily for ESL).
4. Furthermore, because of the transitional nature of the law, teachers were encouraged to increase the amount of English spoken in the classroom. Even though not specified in the Administrative Code,

the percentages generally recommended to bilingual education teachers are eighty percent of instruction in the dominant language and twenty percent in English in the first year of the bilingual program, a fifty-fifty split in the second year, and twenty-eighty in the third year. For those teachers who taught in the federally funded projects, this policy is quite a change from giving instruction in only their dominant language. Today, bilingual personnel are subject to increasing pressure to develop the English language skills of the children, a job for which many of the pioneer teachers interviewed do not feel adequately prepared.

5. In the early federally funded projects, there was utilized a two-way approach to bilingual education, where both dominant and minority language group children learned curricula through their own languages and through a second language. That approach changed to a one-way bilingual schooling (Cohen, 1975), where only the minority group learns bilingually. Even though the New Jersey law states that bilingual education programs "may include children of English-speaking ability," the majority of the programs now in existence in the state have few, if any, children whose native language is English.
6. Teachers, even those who had been teaching since 1969, had to be additionally certified. The Commissioner of Education decided in 1975 against a "grandfather clause" under which teachers already in bilingual programs could be certified automatically. However, in July of 1976, the N.J. Board of Education revised its certification requirements "in response to complaints that the requirements were discriminatory" (*New York Times,* 1976). The revisions allowed for work experience to be substituted for some (but not all) of the twenty-four semester credit-hours required for an endorsement in bilingual education.
7. The language proficiency requirement became a serious issue in the state.

New Jersey Certification Requirements

In October 1975, certification regulations for bilingual education, including oral and written language proficiency requirements, had been approved. However, it was not until a year later that oral language proficiency examinations began, after the State Department of Education had contracted with Educational Testing Service (ETS) to develop a method of determining language proficiency and after language proficiency centers had been established at six colleges and at the state university (memo from Dr. Richard Brown, 1976).

The system developed for the New Jersey Department of Education by ETS to measure oral language proficiency is known as the Language Proficiency Program. The program utilizes the Language Proficiency Interview (LPI) developed by linguists at the Foreign Service Institute (Brown, 1978-B). Current users of this face-to-face interviewing procedure and associated rating scale include the Peace Corps, CIA, Chula Vista (California) School District, and Cornell University, (Clark, 1978).

The intent of the Language Proficiency Program is to provide scores (on a scale of zero to five) descriptive of various levels of language performance (ETS, 1976). The score levels required for certification in New Jersey, as set by the Department of Education, are the following: three (minimal professional competence) in English and four in the native language of the children (i.e., the other language used as a medium of instruction) for those engaged in bilingual education; and four in English for ESL instructors.

The procedure followed for the LPI is as follows: a candidate for certification is interviewed for about twenty minutes in each language by a trained interviewer at one of the language proficiency centers (bilingual education teachers are interviewed in the two languages of instruction, ESL teachers in English only). The interview generally begins at a relatively simple level and becomes progressively more complex. The vocabulary, structure and comprehension required to continue the conversation become increasingly difficult (Brown, 1978). The interview is recorded and the resulting tape is mailed to ETS, where trained raters score it.

The State Board of Education set August 31, 1977 as the date by which all bilingual education and ESL teachers had to take the language proficiency examination and August 31, 1978 as the date by which teachers had to attain minimal levels of oral proficiency. The written proficiency requirement was never implemented, although it is still part of the Administrative Code (Brown, 1978).

Even though bilingual education programs in New Jersey involve languages other than Spanish (e.g., Portuguese, French, Italian, Korean, Greek, Japanese), the State Department of Education, as of this writing, has made provisions for development of language proficiency examinations in Spanish and English only. This situation has caused many problems and ill feelings among bilingual personnel. On the one hand, Spanish/English bilingual teachers feel discriminated against because they are the only ones for whom an examination is required. On the other hand, bilingual education teachers for the other language groups also feel discriminated against because, even though they have completed the twenty-four credit-hours in bilingual education needed for an endorsement, they cannot be certified because they cannot fulfill the language proficiency requirement.

Spanish/English bilingual education teachers, then, had a year in which to take the oral proficiency test in two languages and two years in which to pass it. They were urged to complete their interviews as quickly as possible to give themselves sufficient time to upgrade their language skills if they were unable to attain minimal proficiency (Brown, 1976). In the first year of language proficiency exams (end of 1976 through November 1977), 688 candidates completed an interview in both English and Spanish for bilingual education certification. Of those 688 interviewees, 353 reached the minimal levels in both languages, 164 reached the minimal level (three) in English but not in Spanish, and 171 reached the minimal level (four) in Spanish but not in English (figures released by ETS, 1977).

It is the contention of this writer that the teachers who failed were primarily those who worked in the early bilingual projects in the state, where, because of the team-teaching approach of the programs and the language maintenance philosophy, proficiency in both languages of instruction was not expected.

In April of 1978, because so many bilingual education teachers had been unable to reach the oral proficiency levels required for certification, the

State Board of Education adopted a resolution extending the deadline for passing the language proficiency examination from August 1978 to April 1979. For the year 1978-79, teachers employed in bilingual education classrooms could be issued substandard certificates if they had achieved a two plus in English and a three in Spanish (rather than three and four, respectively), and provided they enrolled in a language training program established by the Bureau of Bilingual Education (Brown, 1978-C). This language training program, offered in the summer of 1978, was the first attempt by the state to improve the language skills of the bilingual teachers.

Bilingual education teachers who have not passed the language proficiency requirement for certification are now teaching (in the 1978-79 school year) with substandard certification. However, they have been told that contracts for the 1979-80 school year will not be offered if the minimum proficiency levels have not been reached by April 1, 1979. Deputy Commissioner of Education Ralph Lataille requested county superintendents in New Jersey to contact all public school districts that offer bilingual and ESL programs to determine the number of teachers who had not met the proficiency levels. On March 2, 1979, the results of that survey showed that 307 presently-employed teachers had not yet reached the minimal levels required for certification (Burke, 1979). The Commissioner of Education recommended to the N.J. Board of Education in March of 1979 that the April 1 deadline be maintained.

The New Jersey Education Association, an early advocate of bilingual education[3], has filed a suit against the State Board of Education in an effort to exempt from the bilingual education certification requirements (including that of language proficiency) those teachers who were working in bilingual programs prior to the approval of certification regulations.

The Federal Bilingual Act of 1978

The issue of dual-language proficiency as a requirement for bilingual education teachers will be given great attention at the national level as a result of the 1978 federal Title VII Amendment to the Elementary and Secondary Education Act. This newly-enacted legislation states that "the program will use the most qualified available personnel, including only those personnel who are proficient in the language of instruction and in English." This is the first instance where federal legislation promotes the hiring of teachers who are bilingual for bilingual programs (Gonzalez, 1979). The regulations developed for the Bilingual Act will have to specify a workable definition of language proficiency.

Language proficiency in both languages of instruction as an area of competency for bilingual education teachers is prominent in all guidelines for teacher-training programs (CAL *Guidelines for the Preparation and Certification of Teachers of Bilingual/Bicultural Education,* 1974; *Competencies for University Programs in Bilingual Education,* U.S. Department of Health, Education and Welfare, 1978; Sutman, et al., *Educating Personnel for Bilingual Settings: Present and Future,* 1979.). Dual-language proficiency is also one of the personnel requirements identified in state bilingual education legislation.

Thirteen states have adopted certification requirements for teachers of bilingual education programs: Arizona, California, Delaware, Illinois, Indiana, Louisiana, Massachusetts, Michigan, Minnesota, New Jersey, New

Mexico, Rhode Island and Texas. Most of these states specifically require teachers to have competence in both English and the language of the LESA children served by the program (Irizarry, 1978). Most of these states specify that personnel must have communicative skills in both English and the other language. Some say teachers must have communicative skills in English and the ability to speak and read in the language other than English. Rhode Island requires the ability to speak or read the other language (Irizarry, 1978). The means by which proficiency in the two languages is determined varies from state to state. Some states use standardized tests designed for "foreign language" teachers, other states use the face-to-face interview procedure such as the one utilized by New Jersey (Woodford, 1977).

In writing regulations for the Bilingual Act of 1978, the Federal Office of Education could play an important leadership role by setting standards and establishing criteria for measuring a teacher's competence in two languages.

Recommendations

From this brief look at the development and implementation of certification requirements, particularly those for language proficiency in New Jersey, this writer now lists the following recommendations:

1. The language-skill levels of personnel already in bilingual programs must be determined.
2. Funds must be provided for advanced language training in both English and the non-English language for existing bilingual teachers who might not be able to meet language proficiency levels.
3. There must be an allowed period of time during which bilingual teachers already in the classroom can improve their language skills.
4. Representatives of all statewide interest groups, including public school teachers and administrators, must be involved in the development of regulations. (This was the procedure in New Jersey. Brown, 1978.)
5. An instrument must be developed to assess language proficiency in all language groups represented in the bilingual programs.
6. The chosen language proficiency instrument must be pretested prior to the implementation of such a program. (Brown says this should include conducting validity and reliability studies.) Also, the minimal levels of proficiency must be established carefully.
7. If a face-to-face interview is chosen as a measuring instrument, training of interviewers and particularly of raters assumes paramount importance. Woodford (1977) states that rigorous training and regular inter-rater reliability studies must be carried out when this procedure is used.
8. If an interview procedure, such as the one in New Jersey, is used, tapes should be listened to, or judgements should be made, by more than one rater.

In conclusion, federal and state legislation now advocates transitional bilingual education. In New Jersey, bilingual education has moved from a policy of language maintenance to a policy of language shift; from a model teaming two teachers, of whom bilingualism was not required, to a model utilizing one bilingual classroom teacher who must give emphasis to developing English skills. These changes in policy are reflected in teacher certification regulations and in the numbers of teachers who are unable to meet the new language proficiency requirements in the state.

Proficiency in both languages of instruction is demanded by both state and federal legislation. Bilingual educators must establish what a "bilingual" teacher is, must develop criteria for assessing communicative skills in both languages, and, finally, must insure that the instruments used to measure the language proficiency of teachers are reliable and valid.

REFERENCES

Acosta, R. and Blanco, G. *Competencies for University Programs in Bilingual Education.* Washington, D.C.: U.S. Department of Health, Education and Welfare, 1978.

Bilingual Education Act, 1968 (20 U.S.C. 880b.), January 1968, Public Law 90-247.

Bilingual Education Act, 1974, August 1974, Public Law 93-380.

Bilingual Education Act, 1978, Amendment to Title VII of the Elementary and Secondary Education Act of 1965, November 1978.

Blanco, G. "The Education Perspective," *Bilingual Education: Current Perspectives - Education.* Rosslyn, Va.: Center for Applied Linguistics, 1977.

Brown, R. W. Memorandum to Deans and Chairpersons of N.J. College and University Teacher-Education Programs. July 1, 1976.

Brown, R. W. "Oral Proficiency Testing in New Jersey Bilingual and English As A Second Language Teacher Certification," *Direct Testing of Speaking Proficiency.* Clark, J. L. D., Ed., Princeton, N.J.: Educational Testing Services, 1978.

Brown, R. W. "New Jersey Bilingual and ESL Certifications." Paper presented at William Paterson College, November 1978.

Brown, R. W. Memorandum to County Superintendents. April 21, 1978.

Burke, F. Report to the New Jersey Board of Education. March 7, 1979.

CAL *Guidelines for the Preparation and Certification of Teachers of Bilingual/Bicultural Education.* Arlington, Va.: Center for Applied Linguistics, 1974.

CAL ERIC/CLL Series on Language and Linguistics, Number 23. *The Current Status of U.S. Bilingual Education Legislation.* Arlington, Va.: Center for Applied Linguistics, 1975.

Clark, J. L. D. *Direct Testing of Speaking Proficiency: Theory and Application.* Princeton, N.J.: Educational Testing Services, 1978.

Cohen, A. *A Sociolinguistic Approach to Bilingual Education.* Rowley, Mass.: Newbury House, 1975.

Fishman, J. A. *Bilingual Education - An International Sociological Perspective.* Rowley, Mass.: Newbury House, 1976.

Freda, R. A. *The Role of the New Jersey Coalition for Bilingual Education in the Enactment of the 1974 New Jersey Bilingual Education Law.* Doctoral Dissertation, Rutgers University, 1976.

Gaarder, B. A. *Bilingual Schooling and the Survival of Spanish in the United States.* Rowley, Mass.: Newbury House, 1977.

Gaarder, B. A. "Bilingual Education: Central Questions and Concerns," *Bilingual Education.* LaFontaine, et al. eds., Wayne, N.J.: Avery Publishing Group, 1978.

Gonzalez, J. M. "Bilingual Education: Ideologies of the Past Decade," *Bilingual Education.* LaFontaine et al. eds., Wayne, N.J.: Avery Publishing Group, 1978.

Gonzalez, J. M. "The New Title VII: Implications for ESL in Bilingual Education." Talk presented at the Thirteenth Annual TESOL Convention, Boston, Mass., March 1979.

Hidalgo, H. Address to the New Jersey Statewide Conference of Hispanics in Higher Education. Princeton, 1978.

Language Proficiency Program. Bulletin of Information. Princeton, N.J.: Educational Testing Service, 1976.

Lipshires, J. B. Letter to the Editor - *NJTESOL/NJBE Newsletter.* December 1978.

Mackey, W. T. & Beebe, V. N. *Bilingual Schools for a Bicultural Community.* Rowley, Mass.: Newbury House, 1977.

Molina, J. C. "National Policy on Bilingual Education: An Historical View of the Federal Role," *Bilingual Education.* LaFontaine et al. eds., Wayne, N.J.: Avery Publishing Group, 1978.

Narvaez, A. A. "Certification Rule Revised for Bilingual Teachers," *New York Times.* July 15, 1976.

Newark, N.J. *Bilingual Bicultural Program Description.* Newark, N.J.: 1970.

NJEA *Bilingual Education.* Policy Statement by NJEA Delegate Assembly, Trenton, N.J.: 1974.

New Jersey State Department of Education, Bureau of Bilingual Education. *New Jersey Bilingual Law.* Trenton, January 8, 1975.

New Jersey State Department of Education, Bureau of Bilingual Education. *Regulations for Use in Administering Programs in Bilingual Education as Provided for in Chapter 197 of the New Jersey Laws of 1974.* Trenton, 1975.

New Jersey State Department of Education, Bureau of Teacher Education and Academic Credentials. *New Jersey Bilingual/Bicultural Teacher Certification Regulations.* Trenton, October 1975.

New York Times. "Bilingual School Lowers Language Hurdles." March 19, 1972.

Palsha, A. D. Letter to Kean College of New Jersey. October 18, 1978.

Reyes, V. H. *Bilingual-Bicultural Education: The Chicago Experience.* Chicago: Bicultural-Bilingual Studies, 1975.

Sutman, F. X., Sandstrom, E. & Shoemaker, F. *Educating Personnel for Bilingual Settings: Present and Future.* The American Association of Colleges for Teacher Education, 1979.

Woodford, P. "The Importance of Testing," *Bilingual Education: Current Perspectives - Education.* Arlington, Va.: Center for Applied Linguistics, 1977.

NOTES

1. The subcommittee consisted of public school teachers, college and university staff, Department of Education staff, Educational Testing

Service staff, NJEA representatives, and members of state-wide bilingual interest groups (Brown, 1978).

2. The New Jersey Administrative Code states that the bilingual education program required by statute shall be provided by one or more of the following:
   i. A bilingual class, defined as a class for LESA children, where students are initially taught in their dominant language. The second language is gradually introduced and included as one of the languages of instruction.
   ii. A pure bilingual class, with equal numbers of students from two different language groups.
   iii. A team-teaching approach, where a class is taught by two teachers, one a certified ESL teacher and one a certified bilingual-bicultural teacher.
   iv. Learning centers, located within a classroom and designed to serve LESA students. Instruction for LESA students would be provided in their dominant language and ESL, instruction for English-speaking students would be in English and in the language of the LESA children.
   v. Partner classrooms, two classes at the same grade level, one of LESA students and the other of English-dominant students, who will merge for instruction in areas that do not need a high level of verbalization.
   vi. An ungraded bilingual class, a group of LESA pupils with the same dominant language but of different age groups or educational levels.
3. The NJEA was part of the New Jersey Coalition for Bilingual Education, an organization instrumental in the enactment of the N.J. Bilingual Law (Freda, 1976). The NJEA also was part of the subcommittee that worked on certification requirements, including those for language proficiency. It is interesting to note that, in its 1974 Policy Statement on Bilingual Education, the NJEA included the following requirement for basic teacher preparation in bilingual education: "Language Preparation - native or near-native proficiency in the language or languages to be taught (English and/or the other language) in all four skills (listening, speaking, reading and writing)."

Part II

LA POLITICA/POLITICS

A CHRONICLE OF THE POLITICAL, LEGISLATIVE AND JUDICIAL ADVANCES FOR BILINGUAL EDUCATION IN CALIFORNIA AND THE AMERICAN SOUTHWEST

Lawrence J. Estrada

Historically, bilingualism in the United States has been perceived as either a recent phenomenon, or as a result of immigrants from Europe, (i.e., Germans, Italian, French, Dutch, Greek), arriving in the Northeastern part of the United States, and consequently developing into enclaves of "white ethnic" communities. The focus was primarily given to the European without regard for the linguistically and culturally diverse Spanish and Indian groups that already had settled Mexico, the Southwestern United States, and as far north as Kansas.

Although many American school children of diverse ethnic background now attend schools which offer bilingual classroom instruction, bilingual-bicultural education has historically been associated with the educational and developmental needs of Chicano school children in the Southwest. Unlike other regions of the nation, bilingual education in the Southwest is part of a long political and historical process whose roots precede the first Spaniards who arrived on the North American continent.

The foundation of bilingualism and bilingual education in the Americas has its roots in the period known as "Pre-Cortesian." It is interesting to note that Pre-Cortesian educational policy encouraged language and cultural diversity throughout the Aztec Empire. Emphasis was placed on "respect and obedience" for authority. Language played a significant role in the socialization process of the child and became an important part of his or her education. An example of this educational system was Doña Marina, Cortez's translator, who spoke several of the Indian languages in addition to Nahuatl, the official language of the Aztec rulers. Although bilingualism flourished in the fluid empire of Mexico-Tenochtitlan, the government maintained a monolingual language policy. The position of the Aztec empire at that time was a clear tolerance for language and cultural diversity as long as it did not interfere with official governmental business.

When the first Spaniards arrived in the New World they found neither a wilderness nor a cultural vacuum. There were already millions of people representing many different cultures, languages, and civilizations. Conservative estimates place their numbers from 10 to 15 million, although many estimates go far beyond this number. The early Meso-American civilizations—the Toltecs, Olmecs, Mayans, and Aztecs—built splendid cities and developed literature, philosophy, mathematics, and fine arts to a high degree. When Cortez first discovered the valley of Mexico, one member of his group exclaimed, "To many of us, it seemed doubtful whether we were asleep or awake. Never did man see, hear, or dream of anything equal to the spectacle which appeared to our eyes this day" (Bernal, 1975: 1-2). In time, the heterogeneous invader and conqueror of Mexico would mix with the heterogeneous Indian. The mixture was to become the present-day Mexican and Chicano (Lozano, 1970).

By the time the Mayflower and its religious dissenters reached Plymouth Rock, the Spaniards had already founded a university in Mexico City, built a series of missions along the California coast, and settled as far north as the American Midwest. As early as 1538 there was a printing press in Mexico City. St. Augustine, Florida, settled in 1565, is the oldest settlement of Europeans on the mainland of the United States. The history of the United States was to be enriched by the names of Cabeza de Vaca, Coronado, Cabrillo, Piñeda, De Soto, Father Serra, and many others.

Language as a Function of Colonialism

During the settlement of "Nueva España" which included the Southwest, several significant laws were enacted by the Spanish monarchy to address the issue of colonizing an indigenous population. "The Castilian Crown's official language policy for Nueva España derived not from any rational assessment of the prevailing dominant language (Nahuatl) as a '*lingua franca*,' but rather from politics and philosophy of the Spanish Crown," (Heath,1972: 5). The use of Nahuatl by the Indio could be compared to the use of Latin throughout Europe. "This Mexican language (Nahuatl) is the common tongue which runs through all the provinces of New Spain, inasmuch as there are innumerable languages within each province, and even within sections of each village. Moreover, throughout all parts of New Spain there are interpreters who understand and speak Nahuatl, since this language is spread here just as Latin is through all the realms of Europe," (De Mendieta, 1870: 552).

Although the communiques sent by the royal messengers clearly indicated the existence of diverse linguistic groups in Nueva España, the policies prevailing under Ferdinand and Isabella in Castile in the late fifteenth and early sixteenth centuries were continued and expanded in the newly conquered territory. The final attack (1482-1492) on the Moorish state of Granada signified the end of the 700-year Spanish *reconquista*. The next step in solidifying Isabella's kingdom was to develop a national identity, and to this end Isabella and Ferdinand were determined to "Castilianize" their nation and those territories acquired through conquest. This forceful position projected by the Spanish government was to have profound influence on the language planning and policy directions followed by royal magistrates and religious leaders in Nueva España.

Due in large part to the influence of Elio Antonio de Nebrija, Isabella's royal historiographer, the dominance and propagation of the Spanish language was to become a paramount objective for future colonial magistrates (De Nebrija, 1492). Nebrija's development of a Latin-Spanish dictionary and the first modern primer for Spanish grammar established the foundation for linguistic purity in the minds of Spanish policy makers, educators, and colonizers. He "nationalized" Castilian in his *Gramatica Sobre la Lengua Castellana* in which he advocated teaching the "things of the nation, in the language of the nation" (Heath, 1972). Nebrija's linguistic contribution to the policies of Isabella set a principle which succeeding

Spanish monarchs would adopt in their official language policies at home and in Nueva España (Hanke, 1959). The impact of language emphasis in fifteenth and sixteenth century Spain was both to increase and reinforce cultural chauvinism by redefining and reasserting Castilian as the official tongue for *el indio* and later the *mestizo* in Nueva España.

The Castilianization program in Spain rested on very idealistic reasoning which prevailed in the Spanish post-*reconquista*. This mood quickly disappeared as conquistadores and the variety of persons and classes who came in the aftermath of the conquest met the realities of Nueva España and found it impossible to carry policy into practice. The development of the Spanish government's exoglossic language policy toward *los indios* of Nueva España reflected a determination to incorporate all Indians into the Spanish system under one language. Colonial planners disregarded the advanced state of the Indians in Nueva España and the fact that there were probably several hundred linguistically different Indian groups during this period of Spanish imperialism.

The formulation of a national language by Isabella and Ferdinand and the resultant language planning in Spain would eventually continue into the seventeenth and eighteenth centuries in the islands of the Caribbean, South America, and into the American Southwest.

The Mission System: The Origins of Bilingualism In The American Southwest

With the establishment of the mission system in Baja and Alta California in the late seventeenth and early eighteenth centuries, the importance of bilingualism would become pronounced. The history of occupied California dates back to 1769, but the history of the missions can be traced to 1493, just after the landing of Columbus. "Between these two dates there is an interval of almost 300 years during which the mission system grew to be a philosophy of human rights, put forward and defended by the religious orders and bitterly opposed by the secular elements among the colonists" (Wright, 1950). The primary goal of the mission system was military, and the main function of each of the missions was to maintain political stability (Guest, 1961).

As an integral part of the mission system it was the policy of the Spanish government and the church to keep the *indios* in *pueblos*, or at the mission in separate *rancherias*. The Indian women lived in *monjerias* and were trained in domestic services (cooking, sewing, etc.), while the young children received training in reading, writing, and technical trades. Generally, life for the *indios* was difficult since their traditions, customs, and beliefs differed from the Spaniards considerably. The issue of assimilation among the Indians proved to be an imposition placed upon them by the Spanish priests (Wright, 1950).

Each of the missions developed polytechnic schools which concentrated on trade skills. The learning of a trade (carpenter, blacksmith, tailor, stone mason, etc.) was emphasized in order to maintain the mission facilities and to engender "citizenship" and community life. Actual bilingual instruction at the missions was primarily restricted to religious and work-related activities (Bolton, 1917).

Although bilingualism was officially banned by royal edict, most of the missionaries did not strictly adhere to government policy because they realized that many of the older Indians could never hope to learn Castilian and that many of the young were simply not interested. It became standard policy within each of the missions to teach the young Indian boys Spanish so that they could become proficient interpreters for the padres. At most missions, mass and daily affairs were conducted in two languages. At Mission Santa Barbara, for example, "the missionaries taught religion daily at the mission in Chumash and Spanish" (Geiger, 1960: 24). Because of the diversity of languages in the surrounding missions, most priests and Indians were bilingual or in some cases trilingual (Kroeber, 1953).

In contrast to the mission schools and the teachings of the Franciscans, secular training in the Southwest and in California was primarily monolingual. As the furthest outpost of Nueva España, the Southwest territory received very little in the way of funds for educational training. Except for a limited number of fundamentalist schools in San Jose, Monterey, Santa Barbara, and San Gabriel, most education was informal and passed on from generation to generation on the ranchos or by military personnel in the presidios (Bolton, 1964). One of the early fundamentalist schools was vividly described by General Mariano Guadalupe Vallejo:

> The teacher was almost invariably an old soldier, brutal, drunken, bigoted, and except that he could read and write, ignorant. The schoolroom was dark and dirty, and the pupils all studied aloud. The master's ferule (rod) was in constant use, even for blots on the writing paper or for mistakes in the reading. Serious offenses such as laughing aloud, or playing truant, or failure to learn the Doctrina were punished by use of the scourge, a bundle of hempen cords, sometimes having iron points fastened to the end of the lashes. It was a horrible instrument that drew blood, and if used with severity, left a scar for life. The only volumes used for reading were the books of religious formulae, which the pupils used cordially to hate all through their later life, for the torments of scourging were recalled.
>
> The Escuela Antigua was a heaping up of horrors, a torture for childhood, a punishment for innocence. In it the souls of the whole generation were inoculated with the virus of a deadly disease . . ." (Ewing, 1918: 59).

For a few of the more prominent families in the Southwest formal instruction was given in the home with the aid of textbooks and novels sent from Mexico City. These texts, which sometimes took from six months to a year to arrive, were regarded as family treasures (Bolton, 1964).

With the outbreak of the Napoleonic Wars in Europe in the early 1800s and later Mexico's struggle for independence beginning in 1810, the lack of a consistent educational policy was a reflection of the overall political instability of the Spanish regime in Nueva España and its inability to efficiently govern its imperial domain. Later, under Mexican rule, the status of formal education would not change appreciably. For more than twenty years Mexico and its outlying territories would be torn by internal dissent and warfare with Texas and the United States which would virtually drain the nation of its financial resources. Further, the strong anticlerical posture of the Mexican government proved ruinous to secular education and heralded the demise of vocational training within the mission system.

In fairness to the Spanish and Mexican governors, some of whom had encouraged and even imposed education, they faced unyielding problems, not the least of which was lack of money. Not until 1838, for example, was a system of rate bills established in Los Angeles that produced sufficient funds to support a school (Guinn, 1909: 195-196). Nor was money forthcoming from the national government. The last Mexican governor, Pio Pico, was one of many who had sought educational funds from Mexico City. Pico's request was denied because Mexico already was preparing for its disastrous war with the United States (Geltner, 1972: 52-53).

Post-Annexation—The Struggle for Bilingualism and the Preservation of Cultural Integrity

Under the Mexican regime, education in the American Southwest suffered from an absence of competent teachers; supplies and paper were difficult to obtain; and the people showed little interest in what education was available (Guinn, 1896). Disinterest in education, regardless of the reason, would afflict California's Spanish-speaking citizenry for decades.

The Treaty of Guadalupe Hidalgo, which ended the Mexican-American War on February 2, 1848, granted U.S. citizenship to all Mexicans remaining in the American Southwest if they chose to accept it. In California, at the beginning of the war, the Anglo population had been barely 1,500 compared to 6,000 *Gente de Razon* (those considered fully part of the Hispanic community and subject to its laws) and another 4,500 primarily comprised of Spanish-speaking persons of European, Mexican, Indian, and African backgrounds. In addition, there were perhaps 200,000 Indians, most of whom lived in the interior (Borah, 1970). At the war's end, except for the U.S. soldiers who had taken their discharges in California, the population distribution was roughly what it had been two years earlier. Had it not been for the discovery of gold at Coloma on January 28, 1848, the Spanish-speaking Californians would likely have retained their eight-to-one ratio over the Anglos for a considerable time. Instead, the gold rush swelled the Anglo population to approximately 80,000 on the eve of the constitutional convention in September 1849. The Mexican population, although boosted by a migration of Sonorans to the gold fields, was only about 13,000 (McWilliams, 1968). Within a period of about three years the Spanish-speaking population had fallen from a role of dominance to that of a defeated and conquered people.

The Hispanic population of Southern California and the Southwest had been warned early in the American period that its influence would diminish with the influx of large numbers of Anglos. The rush to the gold fields had temporarily delayed the Anglo immigration, and it also had reduced the population of Los Angeles from about 5,000 to 1,610 in 1850 (Newmark, 1929). Many of those who had gone to the northern part of the state were Americans who would return when the placers ran out and would be joined by other Anglos. It was clear to the more perceptive "Californios," that education would be essential if the Spanish-speaking were to hold their own with the ambitious and aggressive Anglos.

The Spanish-speaking people of Los Angeles, who would remain in the majority until the late 1870s, noted with tentative pleasure, then, that the first school established (in June, 1850) by the Common Council after the American occupation was a *Spanish* school. Unhappily for them its teacher, Francisco Bustamente, who was paid but sixty dollars per month to instruct "twenty poor children," stayed only until the end of the year. Bustamente's school was followed by an equally short-lived bilingual school, and in November, 1850, the council—demonstrating a shift in ethnic composition—contracted with a Rev. Henry Weeks to conduct a school *in English* at $150 per month. Weeks remained at the post until 1853 (Splitter, 1951: 101).

Henry Splitter reports that as many as a half-dozen "little educational groups" were maintained privately by the Spanish-speaking "natives" in 1851, but that attendance was lax (Splitter, 1951: 102).

In 1849, and again in 1851, the Common Council had granted the Catholic church a two-square-block site (near the present-day Dodger baseball stadium) for the construction of a *colegio*. The church evidently gave serious consideration to the opportunity, for in the summer of 1851 a priest fluent in Spanish, English, French, Hebrew, and several other languages arrived in the city to inspect the area. When nothing came of the plan, the bilingual *Los Angeles Star*, the city's leading newspaper from 1851 to 1879, deplored the failure and added in warning:

> What will the Spanish-speaking population do, as more and more Americans arrive, and ranches are cut up into farms, and merchants put out their wares? Unless educated, they will inevitably sink to the status of house servants and *vaqueros*, which would be a pity, since there are many bright though undeveloped talents among them (*Los Angeles Star*, July 12, 1851).

In May, 1851, after the council had agreed to a partial subsidy of three Spanish-language parochial and private schools until the city could erect its own schoolhouse, the *Star* issued an "invitation of learning" to the Spanish-speaking citizens, reminding them of the advantages of education (Splitter, 1951: 104).

But by March, 1855, when the schoolhouse was opened (at the corner of Second and Spring Streets, on the site of the present Times Mirror Building), the legislature had enacted a law specifying that instruction in California public schools was to be conducted *only in English* (Pitt, 1966: 226). This action, intended apparently to guarantee "Americanization" of all children, instead excluded most Spanish-speaking children from public education and had the unintended result of spurring creation of parochial schools in the state (Pitt, 1966: 226-227).

In Los Angeles, for example, the church moved almost immediately to develop its own schools. By December, 1855, Bishop Thaddeus Amat had organized a committee to create a home for six Daughters of Charity of St. Vincent de Paul, who had arrived in October from Emmitsburg, Maryland. The pueblo's leading citizens, Yankees and Californios alike, paid $8,000 for a house with a vineyard and orchard, and in January the sisters—three Americans and three Spaniards fluent in French—opened a girls' orphanage and school they called *Institucion Caritativa de Los Angeles*. It stood at the corner of Macy and Alameda Streets (today part of the site of the Union Passenger Terminal). The pupils were taught both in English and Spanish. Although *El Clamor Publico* failed in an attempt to obtain a subsidy for the orphanage from the Common Council, the newspaper was successful in raising $6,000 for an additional house for the sisters. So vigorous was *El Clamor's* campaign that even Protestants and Jews contributed to the fund (Pitt, 1966: 224-225).

The creation of a permanent parochial school in Los Angeles was not without its setbacks. The first attempt was made in 1855 by Antonio Jimeno del Recio who, with a small subsidy from the council, taught Spanish-speaking children in the parish priest's home. Del Recio's plan was to hold out until Jesuits could be summoned by the church to assume control. The Jesuits, who had been expelled from New Spain in 1768, were not forthcoming, however, and the school was terminated when the limited appropriation was exhausted (Pitt, 1966: 225).

Although the initial efforts to form bilingual schools for the Californios were resisted by the dominant Anglo population, a number of California educators would hold strong to their beliefs that bilingual and predominantly Spanish-speaking schools would ultimately benefit the entire community. Early in 1855 J. R. de Neilson started a Catholic bilingual school for boys in a print shop. Although he charged as little as one dollar per month tuition, he was not able to attract more than thirty-five students, and some of these attended free. When the school began to fail because of lack of resources, the leading Hispanic citizens petitioned the Common Council for a small salary for de Neilson. They were refused, however, and the school closed after less than one year (Pitt, 1966).

In January of 1859 Father Bernardo Raho, at the request of Bishop Amat, bishop for the city of Los Agneles, opened the *Escuela Parroquial de Nuestra Senora de Los Angeles,* a bilingual grammar school charging two dollars per month for instruction. It was so successful that many Americans, including Protestants and Jews, enrolled their children, although with the understanding that non-Catholic students would be excused from religious instruction. In spite of the fact that public education in California officially banned instruction in the Spanish language, Los Angeles and other major cities in the Southwest would form permanent parochial school systems which would offer instruction in both languages (Pitt. 1966).

California never officially excluded Chicanos from public schools, nor were they ever required by law to attend the separate schools established for blacks and Indians. Nevertheless, as W. Henry Cooke pointed out, the law excluding Indians from the schools between 1860 and 1880 was sometimes applied to Mexican-Americans. "To many an administrator this (law) included 'Mexicans,' " wrote Cooke. "This pattern was followed principally because majority groups in the local communities wanted it done that way" (Cooke, 1948: 417). Of greater importance, of course, was the fact that the Spanish-speaking in California, as well as in Texas, Colorado, New Mexico, and Arizona, in effect would be *excluded* from public education because of the unwillingness of the Anglo majority to maintain a bilingual public school system (The Official Associated Press Almanac, 1975). Coupled with a traditional absence of formalized education among Mexican families in the Southwest, the eventual result, wrote Carey McWilliams, was that Mexican-Americans "lacked the education and training, the institutions, the organizations, and the leadership which might have made it possible for them to compete on more equal terms" (McWilliams, 1968: 5).

In spite of the official edict denying the use of the Spanish language in the public school system in California, the Spanish-speaking peoples of California wished to preserve their culture and to promote their language. While *El Eco de la Raza Latina,* published in San Francisco, urged Latins to learn English, it was an exception to the majority of Spanish-language newspapers which supported bilingualism. In 1872, *La Crónica* published all Los Angeles ordinances in Spanish and asked that the provisions of the 1849 California Constitution be honored so that all laws would be published in both English and Spanish (Neri, 1973). A few years earlier the Los Angeles Superintendent, Dr. T. H. Rose, had proposed that Anglo teachers working in southern California learn *Spanish.* In an 1868 letter to State Superintendent O. P. Fitzgerald, he wrote, "Many, indeed, most of the children are Spanish, and a teacher, to succeed, should know something of that language. A large number of very good teachers have been here lately and left in disgust. Some have been assisted by me to get away" (Splitter, 1951: 101). A century would pass and the cry for bilingual teachers would still be heard in California.

In other parts of the Southwest, bilingualism and language diversity was to gain partial acceptance as a medium for communication and instruction during the late nineteenth and early twentieth centuries. In 1884 New Mexico passed a school law which recognized the viability of public Spanish-language elementary schools. In addition, the U.S. Congress authorized funds for the translation into Spanish of bills, laws and journals of the New Mexico state legislature, on condition that legislative proceedings and laws be printed in English. In 1911, the newly ratified constitution of the state of New Mexico specified that all laws passed by the legislature had to be printed both in Spanish and English and that public school teachers were required to be trained in Spanish to teach Spanish-speaking students. This was to be the first legislative act in the Southwest which set forth mandatory language training for public school teachers who taught Chicano school children.

The Amalgamation Period—Monolingual Education and the Shaping of the "American Identity," World War I to 1960

This period was characterized by the almost complete abandonment of bilingual education in the United States and by a declining interest in the study of foreign languages. The reasons for this were several: (1) the advent of mandatory attendance laws for public schools, (2) the elimination of public funding for church-affiliated schools, and, most importantly, (3) the isolationism and nationalism which pervaded American society after World War I. These factors led to the implementation of English-only instructional policies in many states. In 1903 only fourteen states had regulations requiring that English be the sole language of instruction; by 1923 thirty-four states had such provisions. In some states the laws that were passed forbade the use of other languages for instruction in all subject areas except foreign language classes. The state of Nebraska attempted, unsuccessfully, to go even further by passing a law severely restricting the teaching of foreign languages. The new regulations imposing English as the only language of instruction affected not only the Southwest and Chicanos residing there but German-Americans and Japanese-Americans as well, two groups which had practiced bilingual education extensively prior to World War I.

During this period educational practices reflecting the philosophy of the "melting pot"—the "school of 400" (Nava, 1975) and ESL (English as a Second Language)—were created. Acceptance of segregation and the fears generated in the McCarthy era added to the ignorance and influenced the refusal by government and educational systems to accept language and cultural diversity. For example, the "school of 400" was based on the false premise that a person can only learn a language by learning words or a specified vocabulary. The schools of 400 were set up in various Southwestern states, especially along the Mexican American border towns. A crash course would be given in English to Spanish-speaking students in an effort to familiarize them with at least 400 English words. Once this was accomplished they would be able, supposedly, to compete and achieve just as well as their Anglo counterpart.

Contemporary Milestones and Landmark Decisions in the Implementation of a Dual-Language System

In 1964, following the example of the bilingual education effort made in Dade County, Florida to assimilate Cuban refugees after the political takeover of Cuba by Fidel Castro, two bilingual programs were launched to serve the Chicano population in the state of Texas; one in the Nye school of the United Consolidated Independent School District in Webb County (outside Laredo), and the others in the San Antonio Independent School District. By 1965 bilingual education programs were begun in Pecos, New Mexico and in Edinburg, Texas. During this same year the Elementary and Secondary Education Act (ESEA) was passed. Title I of this act, which deals with the education "of the disadvantaged," eventually provided funding for bilingual programs of the type stressing ESL and the rapid transition to English.

The first nationwide victory for bilingual education and dual-language competence came in 1967 with Senator Ralph W. Yarborough's (D-Tex) Bilingual Education Act, which was authorized under the Title VII Amendment to the Elementary and Secondary Education Act and represents a milestone in the progress toward bilingual education programs in the United States. Through the funding of exemplary projects, the act is expected to help all children in the United States who come to public school speaking a language other than English. Other programs which support the bilingual education effort are:

1. The Emergency School Aid Act (1972) which provided funds for bilingual education as a means of securing equal educational opportunity for non-English-speaking children.
2. The Commission for Teacher Preparation and Licensing, (October, 1973) which, under the authority of California Assembly Bill No. 122 (Ryan Act, 1970), established guidelines for issuing a bilingual/cross-cultural specialist credential to enable credentialed teachers to obtain specialist skills for working with culturally and linguistically different children.
3. California Senate Bill No. 1335 (1973) which provides for the implementation of programs for training bilingual/cross-cultural teacher aides and specialists and provides funds for programs and professional development purposes.
4. California Education Code, Article 3.3, Section 13344, which requires schools with substantial proportions (twenty-five percent) of minority students to provide inservice training for teachers in the history, culture, and current problems of students with diverse ethnic backgrounds.

5. California Assembly Bill 2817 enacting the state bilingual Teacher Corps Program, which seeks to provide teachers and school administrators who are qualified to meet the needs of the limited-English-speaking and non-English-speaking children in the state. The program furnishes stipends and tuition to teaching aides who are providing public school classroom instruction and who are pursuing approved teaching credential programs.

6. California Assembly Bill No. 1329 (1976) would require each school district, other than community college districts, to undertake a census of the number of pupils of limited-English-speaking ability in the district and report its finding to the department of education. The bill would also require each limited-English-speaking pupil, as defined, enrolled in the California public school system in kindergarten through grade twelve to receive instruction in a language understandable to the pupil, which recognizes the pupil's primary language in addition to teaching the pupil English.

Since the 1954 *Brown* v. *Board of Education* decision that segregation according to race is unconstitutional, the courts have continually refined the concept of equal educational opportunity. A listing of judicial decisions clearly points to the recognition by the courts that equal education opportunity for the culturally and linguistically different requires multicultural education:

1. In *United States* v. *Texas* (1972) it was decided that the failure of school districts in Texas to provide bilingual-bicultural education to Chicano students violated the constitutional rights of these students.
2. The *Serna* v. *Portales Municipal Schools* Case (1974) revealed discrimination against Chicano students in the schools and led the Portales Public Schools to implement bilingual education programs.
3. In *Lau* v. *Nichols* (1974) the U.S. Supreme Court ruled unanimously that the San Francisco Independent School District was in violation of the Civil Rights of 1,800 non-English-speaking Chinese children since it failed to provide instruction in their native language. The *Lau* decision has national ramifications and affects every federally supported school with non- and limited-English-speaking children.

The issue of dual-language instruction is an intrinsic feature of the history of the United States. From the arrival of Cortez in Nueva España, to current issues concerning non- and limited-English-speaking students in American public schools, various commitments and approaches have attempted to meet the needs of minority language students. However, the recent language policies adopted by both state and federal officials in support of bilingualism do not recognize the need to support judicial mandates with careful planning and coordination. History shows that language diversity can be used effectively in educating non- and limited-English-speaking students; since it appears that the struggle for bilingualism and biculturalism will increase rather than diminish, we should pay heed to the lessons of history.

The issues in Mexican-American or Chicano education must be viewed in the framework of psychosocial and cultural-linguistic phenomena. No *one* approach to the educational problems of Chicanos can achieve significant results. Even the linguistic "disadvantages" of Chicano children are basically the product of a thoroughly lexocentric society; they are in large part caused by the ignorance about language and its social function that has arisen from the distortion of Chicano culture and history.

When one examines typical educational instruction designed for the Chicano, one finds that it is frequently premised on the "cultural differences" or on the "cultural substitution" models and is justified by the philosophical corollary of the American "melting pot." Such instructional emphases suggest that Chicano culture interferes with the intellectual and emotional development of the child in the school system, and has led to the belief that the central mission of education is to mold those "damaged" and "disadvantaged" children into the image of the Anglo middle class. Even in schools which propose having bilingual and bicultural programs, the emphasis of the instruction is many times placed upon the transition from the parent culture to that of the school and the prevailing society. Success is then measured in terms of how well the individual student has transcended to and mastered the concepts, value structures, and mores of the dominant group. In such instances bilingual-bicultural education becomes merely a device for further socialization rather than a vital tool for learning and instruction. Opposing this view is the Chicano-proposed alternative that the total educational *system* must become sensitive and supportive to the culturally unique personality dynamics of Chicano children by developing a culturally diverse learning environment consistent with those dynamics.

The great bulk of enlightened current research in the field of bilingual-bicultural education validates the demand that school systems respond to the distinctive Chicano learning modes in three domains: (1) incentive-motivational, (2) human relational, and (3) cognitive style. The end goal is to foster a creative bicultural self-image to displace the negative images which continue to haunt the Chicano.

Essential to this argument is the notion that language is an inextricable element of culture. If we accept cultural differences, then we must consequently be prepared to accept language differences. The personal, familial, and cultural ramifications of a sound learning theory tell us that the child must be secure and that the value orientations the school imparts should fulfill the expectations he has already learned in the three domains mentioned above. To the Chicano this means his cultural heritage and linguistic background must be understood by the school and academically reinforced by the school.

REFERENCES

Bernal, I. *Mexico Before Cortez,* Doubleday, 1975.

Bolton, H. E. *H. E. Bolton and the Spanish Borderlands.* University of Oklahoma Press, 1964.

Bolton, H. E. "The Mission as a Frontier Institution in Spanish American Colonies." *American Historical Review,* October, 1917.

Borah, W. W. "The California Mission." In C. Wollenberg (ed.) *Ethnic Conflict in California History,* Los Angeles: Tinnon-Brown, 1970.

California Archives, P.R., 520-521, VI. Letter of Appointment: Bancroft Library, Berkeley, California.

California Archives, P.R., VI, 25-252.
California Archives, S.P., VII, 462-463.
California Archives, P.R., VII, 441-443, Bancroft Library, Berkeley, California.
Cooke, H. W. "The Segregation of Mexican-American School Children in Southern California." *School and Society*, (June 5, 1948) 67.
Emanuel, Sister Rose, I. H. M. "The Parish Schools of Our Lady Queen of the Angels." *Historical Society of Southern California Quarterly*, (December, 1961) 42.
Ewing, A. K. "Education in California During the Pre-Statehood Period," *Annual Publications, Historical Society of Southern California*, (1918) 11.
Geiger, M. *The Indians of Mission Santa Barbara*. Santa Barbara, California, 1960.
Geltner, Sharon O. The Common Schools of Los Angeles, 1850-1900: Variations on a National Pattern. (Unpub-Ed.D. Dissertation, University of California, Los Angeles) 1972.
Guest, F. F. *Municipal Institutions in Spanish California: 1769-1821*, University of Southern California Press, 1961.
Guinn, J. M. "The Beginnings of the School System of Los Angeles." *Publications, Historical Society of Southern California*, VIII, (1909) 195.
Guinn, J. M. "The Old Time Schools and Schoolmasters of Los Angeles." *Annual Publication, Historical Society of Southern California*, (1918) 11.
Hanke, L. *All Mankind Is One*. Northern Illinois University Press, 1974.
Heath, S. B. *Telling Tongues*. Teachers College Press: Columbia University, 1972.
Kroeber, A. L. *Handbook of the Indians of California*, California Book Co., Ltd., Berkeley, California, 1953.
Los Angeles Star, July 12, 1851.
Lozano, D. Office of the Secretary, U.S. Department of Health, Education and Welfare, Washington, D.C., 1970.
McWilliams, C. *The Mexicans in America: A Student's Guide to Localized History*, Teachers College Press; Columbia University, 1968.
Nava, A. & Sancho, A. Bilingual Education: Una Hierba Buena. *The Claremont Reading Conference Yearbook*, 1975.
Neri, M. C. "A Journalistic Portrait of the Spanish-Speaking People of California, 1868-1925." *Southern California Quarterly, Summer*, (1973) 55.
Newmark, M. H., & Marco, R. *Census of the City and County of Los Angeles, California: For the Year 1850*. The Times-Mirror Press, Los Angeles, 1929.
Pitt, Leonard, *The Decline of the Californios: A Social History of the Spanish-Speaking Californians*. University of California Press, 1966.
Splitter, H. W. "Education in Los Angeles: 1850-1900." *Historical Society of Southern California Quarterly*, (1951) 33.
Wright, R. B. *California Missions*. Hubert A. Lowman: Record Printing, Covina, California, 1950.

THE ENACTMENT OF BILINGUAL EDUCATION LEGISLATION IN TEXAS: 1969-73

José E. Vega

Federal support for general and specific educational reforms, such as bilingual, does not seem likely to decrease in the 1980s. Moreover, states are increasingly assuming a greater role in educational leadership, support and control of such programs (Mosher and Wagoner, 1978: 145-170). Since the enactment of the Bilingual Education Act of 1968, twenty-six states have passed similar education laws which either permit or mandate the use of bilingual education instruction for public school children with limited-English-speaking competence (*A Study of State Programs in Bilingual Education*, 1977). In spite of this continued interest on behalf of linguistically and culturally different children in many states, little research has linked the process of ethnic group political behavior to educational legislative policy outcomes in the states which have enacted such laws.

Why was the first mandatory bilingual education law enacted in Massachusetts and not in Texas? Were the tactics and aims of the various groups who supported this kind of legislation the same or different? How did such things as government structure, attitudes or the political environment in each state influence the organization and strategy of these pressure groups? What was the nature and extent of the federal influence on those states which enacted language education laws? These and other questions dealing with bilingual education interests and state curriculum policy-making outcomes have not been examined. The literature of politics and education has given this phenomenon scant attention.

On the other hand, ethnic related politics has been a major theme in political science. In the eastern and northern sections of the United States the persistence of cultural, religious or linguistic similarities has often been the basis for political organization (Handlin, 1944). The character and persistence of ethnicity in American society has most often been measured in terms of election voter turn out rates and the tangible benefits of support (Bailey and Katz, 1969: 86-94). Since the early 1920s social scientists were convinced that it was only a matter of time before cultural distinctions based on language, religion or some other ethnic associated belief system would disappear (Wirth, 1928). Efforts to explain the causes of black activism and its impact on other minorities during the 1960s, however, challenged the commonly accepted notions of assimilation and political pluralism in American life (Litt, 1970).

Ethnic group politics has been a distinctive feature of Texas political history since the earliest days of the Republic. It has been noted that although Texans have had "little cause to be obsessed about the Negro," as has been the case in Mississippi, they have been concerned about "Mexicans" (V.O. Key, 1949: 254). Social and political voluntary associations such as the League of United Latin-American Citizens and the American G.I. Forum have often played a major role in articulating the concerns and demands of Mexican-Americans in Texas since the mid 1920s (Garcia, 1973). Among the many social concerns, education has always been a high priority. The need to improve the educational status of the Mexican-American has never been a disputed issue. The differing views regarding the role of language and culture in the public school curriculum, however, have often been the basis for contention among Chicanos and Anglos.

The use of another language other than English as a medium of instruction in the elementary public schools of Texas was a common practice dating back to 1926, yet it was not until 1969, with the support and persistence of two Mexican-American legislators, that the legislature authorized the use of another language for instructional purposes. Texas had the greatest number of bilingual education programs in the United States prior to 1968, and also a considerably long history of bilingual schooling. However, it was not until 1973 that the legislature enacted a mandatory bilingual education law (Zamora, 1977).

The great bulk of the literature on state educational policy making has dealt with the influence of professional groups and elites on the legislative process and its effects on the level of state funding. Research on the federal influence on state educational innovation has judged the success or failure of federal programs according to preconceived federal criteria. Most studies have ignored the phenomenon of ethnic political participation and its effect on state legislative policy outcomes in the field of bilingual education.

Fishman has suggested that there is a need to know how the various parties interested in bilingual education legislation "went about trying to get their way: proposing, compromising, bargaining, threatening, influencing, rationalizing, withdrawing or advancing; and their reasons, public and private, for so doing." The need is all the more pressing because "most of the recent policy decisions concerning U.S. bilingual education have remained largely undocumented in terms of the *processes* and *pressures* that transpired in connection with them . . ." (Fishman, 1977: 1-2).

Lacking in the research literature is documentation of the factors which led various state legislatures to redefine the government's role in education, and most particularly in terms of the language of instruction. What prompted state legislatures to revise old statutes which prohibited the use of any language other than English as a medium of instruction in public schools? What factors account for the acceptance of demands by ethnic group leaders that their language be used as a legitimate medium of instruction? How were these groups able to obtain funds from the legislature for such bilingual programs?

An historical case study approach was utilized in order to gain an understanding of how the Texas legislature responded to the demands of Mexican-Americans for bilingual education in 1969, and then again in 1973. The collection, organization, and analysis of the data in this study was guided by Easton's general systems model. More specifically, Philip Meranto's conceptual framework for describing and analyzing the factors which contributed to the enactment of the Elementary and Secondary Education Act of 1965 is used in this study (Easton, 1965; Meranto, 1967).

Meranto's model for explaining legislative actions included two categories of environmental changes: circumstantial conditions, and demand articulators. Circumstantial conditions referred to those unexpected changes in the political system which impinged on the policy making. Demand articulators identified those actors which directly affected the policy-making process through direct lobbying, letter writing and formal legislative recommendations. The model also called for an examination of those changes which occurred within the legislature itself. The following diagram illustrates how some of the data collected in the study were organized.

MODEL OF STATE CURRICULUM POLICY MAKING

ENVIRONMENTAL CHANGES

A. *CIRCUMSTANTIAL CONDITIONS* 1. Bilingual Education Act of 1968 2. Office for Civil Rights May 25th Memorandum 3. Sharpstown Scandal 4. 1972 Elections	*NEW INPUTS*→	*LEGISLATIVE CHANGES* 1. Election of Reform minded Legislature in 1972 77 House Members 15 Senators 2. New Legislative Leadership a) Speaker of the House Price Daniel, Jr. b) President of Senate William P. Hobby c) Governor Dolph Briscoe 3. Collaboration of House and Senate Human Resources Committee Chairmen: Carlos F. Truan: House Chet Brooks: Senate	*NEW OUTPUT*→ TEXAS BILINGUAL EDUCATION AND TRAINING ACT OF 1973
B. *MAJOR DEMAND ARTICULATORS* 1. League of United Latin American Citizens 2. American G.I. Forum 3. Texas Association for Continuing Adult Education 4. Texas Education Agency 5. Governor's Office	*NEW INPUTS*→		

Source: Meranto: page 11

This study sought to demonstrate how at least four environmental events which took place between 1968 and 1972 helped to alter the highly cautious attitudes of Anglo Texas legislators toward Mexican-American demands for educational change. The four unexpected conditions included the enactment of the federal bilingual education law in 1968, the Office for Civil Rights May 25th Memorandum on the civil rights of national origin minorities in the United States, the Sharpstown Scandal, and the election results in 1972.

The second category used by Meranto under environmental changes was the demand articulators. Although circumstantial changes may have a direct impact on the way legislators' perceive the various demands and the need for change, the need for change is often more effectively channeled through known and newly formed interest groups. Under this category, attention was focused on the political activities of two well-established Mexican-American voluntary associations: The League of United Latin-American Citizens (LULAC), and the American G.I. Forum. A third factor was the impact which the lobbying efforts of the Texas Association for Continuing Adult Education had on the enactment of the bilingual education bill during the Sixty-Third Legislative Session. The last two factors considered were the activities and influence of the Texas Education Agency and the governor's office. Each of the factors under this category played an important role in bringing about significant educational change in the state of Texas.

It should be noted that not all of the possible factors which may help to account for the enactment of bilingual education legislation in 1969 and 1973 were included in the model. Their omission, however, in no way minimizes their importance. It did suggest the necessity for narrowing the scope of the study to a discrete and more manageable number of variables. Thus, the model focuses on the legislative changes which occurred in 1973 rather than on the events which transpired in 1969 during the Sixty-First Legislative Session. Both events are clearly important. However, the enactment of permissive bilingual legislation in 1969 represented but a first step in legitimizing the demands of Mexican-Americans for educational reform. The passage of the mandatory provisions of the bilingual education bill in 1973 represented both the cumulative effects of the various factors mentioned as well as the distinctive events which occurred during the Sixty-Third Legislative Session in 1973.

Three major changes occurred during the Sixty-Third Texas Legislative Session. They were: (1) the election of seventy-seven new, reform minded House members and fifteen new, reform minded Senators, (2) the election of a new and supportive legislative leadership (governor, lieutenant governor and speaker), and (3) the collaboration of Senate and House Human Resources Committee chairmen, Chet Brooks and Carlos F. Truan.

Meranto's model of legislative innovation was used in this study as a framework in which to analyze educational curriculum policy making in the state of Texas in 1973. The investigation sought to examine environmental factors and changes which occurred during the Sixty-Third Legislative Session which decided the destiny of the bilingual bill. Thus, the related factors of environment and legislative change were joined to account for the enactment of the Texas Bilingual Education and Training Act of 1973.

Circumstantial Conditions

The enactment of the mandatory bilingual education act by the Texas Legislature in 1973 was as much a product of the legislative process as it was an indication of the political, social and economic changes which had occurred in Texas over a period of twenty years. The political and social changes which considerably altered the Texas political environment during the period 1966 to 1972 account in part for the enactment of what can be considered landmark legislation in the area of state educational curriculum policy making.

In a 1953 study of the political and social status of the Mexican-American in Texas, Clinchy noted that there seemed to be little evidence of interest by Texas legislators in the educational problems of this group. Most of the work which had been done on behalf of Mexican-Americans had been shouldered by state educational agencies, but on a piecemeal basis. With the sole exception of one bill, which established the Good Neighbor Commission in 1945, actual legislation which addressed itself solely to the needs of Mexican-American citizens did not exist. Texas legislators, it was noted, were cautious when it came to enacting legislation which would directly benefit minority students. The sentiment of the legislature at the time seemed to be marked by "a resistance to direct governmental action . . . , but (with) a willingness to experiment with gradual change. . . ." (Clinchy, 1974: 124; 180; 202).

One such experiment came in the form of two bills which were introduced in the legislature in 1943 and 1945. The first bill, House Concurrent Resolution 105, was introduced in the form of a resolution. The first part of the bill stated that "All persons of the Caucasian Race" within the state of Texas were entitled to equal access and use of all accommodations in public places. The second part of the resolution admonished its readers that those persons who failed to abide by this principle would be "violating the good neighbor policy" of the state. The bill was a harmless concurrent resolution with no law enforcement provision. It omitted the blacks and safely avoided mentioning the other victims of discrimination in Texas, Mexican-Americans.

In 1945, Senator J. Franklin Spears of San Antonio introduced Senate Bill Number 1. The bill differed from the previous resolution in two respects. It specifically mentioned Mexican-Americans, commonly referred to as Latin-Americans, as being the victims of discrimination in Texas. The bill's prohibition of discriminatory practices applied to all public accommodations and imposed a penalty of imprisonment, a $500 fine, or both for persons who violated its provisions (Clinchy, 1974: 180-181). The bill never left committee.

With the exception of the 1959 pre-school bill, known as the Little School of the 400, Mexican-American educational problems were not addressed or seriously considered by the Texas legislature until the convening of the Sixty-First and Sixty-Third Legislative Sessions in 1969 and 1973. Much of this interest in the educational condition of the Mexican-American in Texas can in part be attributed to the influence of the federal government.

The Federal Bilingual Education Act of 1968

The Bilingual Education Act (Title VII of ESEA) was enacted into law by the ninetieth Congress on December 15, 1967. It was the first federal categorical grant ever legislated that addressed the unique educational needs of the Spanish-speaking minority in the United States. The law's enactment came as a direct result of Mexican-American lobbying, the support of the National Education Association, and the expert and energetic leadership of Texas Senator Ralph Yarborough (Sánchez, 1973; Schneider, 1976).

The Bilingual Education Act was signed into law by President Johnson on January 2, 1968. The act provided for the financial assistance of those public schools engaged in the development of "imaginative elementary and secondary programs" that would meet the "special educational needs" of children of "limited-English-speaking ability." The law specifically provided that such programs would be available to those children who came from families whose annual income did not exceed $3000. The kinds of activities suggested under this program included instruction which imparted to students a knowledge of the history and culture associated with their language, closer ties between parents and school authorities and the establishment of early childhood education programs. In addition, the law provided for the creation of programs that would help reduce the high dropout rate of Mexican-American students. Adult education programs for the parents of children participating in bilingual programs were also encouraged.

Another important aspect of the federal law was financial commitment. The Congress appropriated a total of $85 million for implementation of the law for a three year period beginning in 1967 and ending in 1970. For the fiscal year ending in June 30, 1971, the Congress appropriated $80 million (*A Better Chance to Learn*, 1975: 180-181).

Texan legislators have traditionally opposed increased federal interference in local government, but they seldom have displayed similar opposition to receiving federal funds (Kirst, 1972: 249). The availability of federal funds was one of the strongest arguments which House member Carlos F. Truan, Corpus Christi, and Senator Joe J. Bernal, San Antonio, used to encourage Texan legislators in 1969 to vote in favor of a state permissive bilingual education law. They repeatedly emphasized that the law's enactment would allow Texas to receive up to $3 million in new Title VII federal funds. They also stressed that participation in such federally funded programs would be optional.

Serious demands for educational reform and interest in the educational problems of Mexican-American students in Texas public schools probably would not have readily been accepted or adopted by state legislative and education officials had it not been for federal initiatives and financial assistance. This was the case with the enactment of the first Texas bilingual education law in 1969 (Interview, Truan, 2/20/79).

The enactment of the Bilingual Education Act in 1967 was seen as a major achievement by many Mexican-American educators. The federal law not only approved the use of native home languages as legitimate vehicles of instruction in public schools, but also encouraged changes in the curriculum which reflected the historical and cultural contributions of Mexican-Americans in the southwest. The adoption of these innovative changes, however, made little impact on the problem of Mexican-American school segregation in the southwest. The persistence of segregated educational facilities in Texas at that time was acute.

Since the 1930s and earlier, Mexican-Americans had consistently opposed and resisted segregationist practices in and out of court. In 1970, when the education division of the Office for Civil Rights issued its national origins memorandum, the segregation of Mexican-American students in public schools was still a very serious problem (Rangel and Alcala, 1972: 111-311).

Office for Civil Rights and Bilingual Education

Prior to 1970, the Office for Civil Rights had been primarily concerned with attacking black-white school segregation. Neither the federal courts nor the President had seriously considered the widespread practices of segregation affecting Mexican-Americans and other non-black minority students. In 1968 HEW only required racial statistics on blacks and whites. The following year OCR began to require statistics on Mexican-Americans and other national origin minorities (Gerry, 1974: 228-230). Much of the evidence documenting the continued segregation of Mexican-Americans in public schools came from testimony which was offered at the civil rights hearings in San Antonio, Texas at the end of the year (U.S. Commission on Civil Rights, San Antonio, December 9-14, 1968).

In 1969 HEW law enforcement efforts against districts found to be in violation of the 1964 Civil Rights Act were slow and ineffective. It was not until the following year that HEW administrative officials began to pay attention to the complaints of Mexican-Americans. One reason for the change in attitude was the rising militancy of Chicanos seeking relief from local restrictive practices. Another rationale offered for this switch was the continued success which HEW had experienced in the South, thus enabling the agency to release staff to work on the problems which were still plaguing Mexican-Americans in Texas. A third reason for the change in policy is attributed to the incessant number of complaints by Mexican-American leaders that OCR had failed to identify and investigate serious charges of discrimination and segregation in its communities (Rangel and Alcala, 1972: 365-369; Gambone, 1973: 13-25).

On May 25, 1970 the Office for Civil Rights issued a memorandum to school districts with more than five percent national origin minority children who were found to be deficient in the English language. The memorandum outlined four basic areas by which future Title VI compliance reviews would be judged. The first criteria stipulated that school districts had to take affirmative steps to rectify the language deficiency of those children who could not understand or speak English. Second, school districts could not assign students to classes for the mentally retarded or exclude them from taking college preparatory courses on the basis of tests measuring only English language skills. Third, ability grouping for the purpose of dealing with special language needs were permissable as long as they were temporary arrangements. Fourth, school districts were responsible for adequately informing the parents of national origin minority children of school activities in a language other than English if it were necessary (*A Better Chance to Learn:*, 1975: 204-205).

The new guidelines influenced both the Texas Education Agency and the proponents of bilingual education in the legislature. When TEA submitted its recommendations to the legislature in the fall of 1970, it adopted some of the language of the Memorandum. It urged the adoption of a bilingual program for those students whose inability to speak and understand English excluded them from full participation in the school's program of instruction (*Recommendations for Legislative Consideration on Public Education in Texas,* November, 1970).

During the Sixty-Second (1971) and the Sixty-Third (1973) Legislatures, Representative Truan introduced House Bill 495 and 146 respectively.

Both bills were almost verbatim copies of the May 25th Memorandum. On both occasions the bills were referred to the House Committee on Public Education, but were never reported out. However, not all of the memorandum criteria were discarded. The provision which called for informing parents of linguistically different children, of school activities in their own language was kept and incorporated into the body of Senate Bill 121 in 1973. This bill became the mandatory bilingual law which was enacted by the historic Reform Session of the Texas Legislature. Much of the interest in governmental reform which occurred during this session was directly attributable to the stock fraud disclosures which were made during the previous legislative session.

The Sharpstown Scandal

On January 18, 1971, the day before the inauguration of the Texas State leadership, the Securities and Exchange Commission filed a law suit which implicated high Texas political officials in a stock fraud scheme. The case affected the proceedings of the Sixty-Second Legislature, and influenced the enactment of progressive social and political legislation during the Sixty-Third Legislature. One of the more liberal educational measures passed during this session would be the Bilingual Education and Training Act.

What became known as the infamous Sharpstown Scandal grew out of a scheme by Houston financier and real estate developer, Frank W. Sharp, to artificially increase his bank's deposits through a series of illegal stock manipulations through interconnected insurance and bank companies. The suit would not have surprised nor angered most Texas citizens had it not been for the disclosure that elected officials had contributed to the success of the scheme and had benefited from the fraudalent business transactions devised by Frank W. Sharp (Kinch and Proctor, 1972: 1-36).

Preliminary results of the investigation revealed that the Governor, Preston Smith; the Lieutenant Governor, Ben Barnes; the Speaker, Gus F. Mutscher, along with two of Mutscher's aides were all directly or indirectly implicated. Bill Heatly, the powerful chairman of the House Appropriations Committee was also linked to the scheme. With the exception of Ben Barnes, all of these individuals had benefited handsomely as a result of the investments which they all had made during the summer of 1969.

The political phase of the scandal took place during the Second Called Session of the Sixty-First Legislature, which met between August 27 and September 9, to consider the matter of passing a tax increase (Kinch and Proctor, 1972: 45).

When Governor Smith called the Second Session of the Sixty-First Legislature, he, along with six other politicians, had purchased stock in the National Bankers Life Insurance Company with loans obtained from the Sharpstown State Bank in Houston. Both companies were owned by Sharp. Sharp was interested in getting the legislature to pass the state's own bank deposit insurance during this session of the legislature. The passage of such a law would have permitted him to evade the scrutiny of Federal Deposit Insurance Corporation officials who were at the time investigating his bank's questionable loan practices (Kinch and Proctor, 1972: 41).

On September 5th, Representative Shannon, Mutscher's right hand man, introduced House Bills 72 and 73, the bank deposit insurance bills. Three days later Governor Smith submitted the subject of additional bank insurance to the legislature for its consideration. The matter would not have been considered by the legislature at this time if the governor had not explicitly mention it in his purpose for convening the legislature. On the same day, House Bills 72 and 73 were passed by the House. The next day they were quickly passed by the Senate. On September 29 Governor Smith vetoed both bills, but not before he and the others who had bought large amounts of stock in the National Bankers Life Insurance Company had sold their stock for substantial gains (Kinch and Procter, 1972: 41-51).

The scandal which shook the foundations of Texas government in 1971 resulted in two very significant outcomes. First, it contributed to the formation of a mixed coalition of thirty House members who viewed the Speaker's leadership as tyrannical and sought to bring about "procedural reforms and ethical standards that would weaken the Mutscher team's, or any team's, control over the legislative process" (Kinch and Proctor, 1972: 87). Their opposition throughout the session kept the issue of political corruption in government and the need for reform very much alive in the minds of the voting public. Second, the revelations also dramatically shaped the outcome of the 1972 elections. In turn, the elections contributed to the rearrangement of the internal power structure of the House. These events inadvertently aided the proponents of bilingual education legislation during the Sixty-Third Legislature.

The 1972 Election Year

The Sharpstown incident, the activities of the Dirty Thirty throughout the entire sixty-second legislative session and judicial intervention, contributed to the election of a reform minded legislative body in 1972. When the Sixty-Third Legislature convened on January 9, 1973 the top leadership of Texas government had totally been changed. Conservative Dolph Briscoe, a millionaire rancher and banker from Uvalde, won the race for governor. William P. Hobby, president and executive editor of the *Houston Post,* and a moderate conservative, was elected lieutenant governor. The Speaker's position went to Price Daniel, Jr., a liberal, member of the Dirty Thirty, and son of a former Texas governor.

The elections in the fall of 1972 also affected the composition of both Houses of the legislature. Seventy-seven new House members were elected. In the Senate fifteen new senators had been elected. The new and different Sixty-Third Legislature would respond to the demands of Mexican-Americans for educational reform more than any other in Texas legislative history (Clinchy, 1974: 124).

The elections of 1972 resulted in one of the largest turnovers in Texas legislative history. The Sharpstown Scandal created an atmosphere that damaged the hopes of many of the incumbents who ran for re-election. Although no perfect cause and effect relation can be drawn between election results and the Sharpstown incident, the role of the Dirty Thirty and the connection of defeated incumbents with the Speaker cannot be underplayed. Of the fifty-six members of the Sixty-Third Legislature who had been elected, fifty-one had had the endorsement of the Dirty Thirty (Deaton, 1973: 139-150).

Another major change affecting the outcome of the 1972 elections in Texas was a federal court ruling which prohibited the use of multimember districts in Dallas and Bexar counties. Multimember districts restricted the choice of candidates to conservative, business backed members of the Democratic party. Chicanos, blacks, and Anglo liberals challenged the legality of this system and won their case. The court ruling would have resulted in a legislative challenge, but Governor Preston Smith decided not to defy the decision, sensing that the legislature would be unable to draw up a plan that would be acceptable to the court in time for the February 6th deadline and the upcoming primary elections in May ("U.S. Court Revises Texas Districts," *New York Times,* 23 January 1972: 30). The results of the court ruling became evident in the fall.

Out of the 150 member House, 53 representatives were from the three most heavily populated counties in Texas: Dallas, Harris and Bexar. Thirty-nine of these delegates had been elected for the first time. In San Antonio only 4 of the 11 legislators present in the Sixty-Second Legislature returned in 1973. Matt Garcia's defeat of House Appropriations Committee chairman Bill Finck was especially significant. It cleared the way for the appointment of a liberal as chairman of the powerful Appropriations Committee who would support the bilingual education bill. It inadvertently brought another Mexican-American legislator to Austin who would also play a key role in the enactment of Truan's bilingual bill.

In Dallas county only four out of eighteen members of the Sixty-Second Legislature were re-elected. In Harris county, which had been redistricted before the court's decision, the effects were particularly noticeable. Eighteen of the twenty-four representatives had been elected for the first time. Of this group fourteen were liberal Democrats, three were moderates and seven were Republicans. The Harris county delegation was dominated by liberals (Deaton, 1973: 152-154; Pettus and Bland, 1976: 110).

A second development which may have had a contributing effect at this time was the decision of Bob Bulluck, Secretary of State, to change the residency voting requirement to thirty days. The invalidated Texas statute had required a one year residency in the state and six months in the county to qualify to vote. The Secretary's ruling was based on a Supreme Court decision, *Dunn* v. *Blumstein* in Tennessee, which implied that any such residency requirements beyond thirty days could be ruled unconstitutional ("Voting Residency Rule Cut to 30 Days in Texas," *New York Times,* 1 April 1972: 8).

The picture in the Senate was slightly different. The changes which occurred in the Senate were less affected by the political fiasco or the series of court challenges concerning voting rights and equal representation which were raised in 1972 (Maxwell, 1972). Most of the changes came as a result of ordinary reasons. Three senators voluntarily retired and eight had decided to run for other positions. Of the twenty incumbents left, nine ran unopposed. In eleven contests where incumbents were running for another term, four were defeated. Of all the senate races only three of the senators were ever questioned concerning their role in the Sharpstown affair.

Several reasons are offered to explain why senate members were less affected by the political scandal. The feud between the Speaker and the Dirty Thirty was centered in the House. Public attention was, therefore, focused on the governor, the speaker and the Dirty Thirty. Another reason given is the difference in size between House and Senatorial electoral districts.

The election of 1972 produced no extraordinary changes in the political orientation of the Senate. The four senators who were defeated were replaced by conservatives. The Senate in the Sixty-Third Legislature was tightly controlled by conservatives, "and was the 'death chamber' for lobby-opposed bills" (Deaton, 1973: 154-156). The mandatory bilingual education bill would not be opposed.

Four environmental changes have been described. The enactment of the federal Bilingual Education Act in 1967 provided the proponents of bilingual education in Texas with more federal money. The Act also legitimized the claims of bilingual education advocates, creating an even more cogent argument for eliminating restrictive language laws. The May 25th Memorandum provided bilingual education proponents with legal reasons for modifying the curricula of the Texas public schools. The two other developments which helped to shape the course of events during the Sixty-Third Legislature in 1973 were the Sharpstown Scandal and the intervention of the federal courts. Both events contributed to the rearrangement of old time political coalitions in Austin and enabled Texan voters to elect an urban, more liberal and reform minded legislature.

The political and social changes which altered the Texas political environment during this period account in part for the enactment of what can be considered landmark legislation in the area of state educational curriculum policy making. These environmental factors, however, only partially explain the enactment of bilingual education legislation in Texas. According to Meranto:

> External changes do not automatically bring about innovation in the system and in its policy outputs for the simple reason that the institutional structure of the system is rigged against producing change (Meranto, 1967: 110).

Explanations for new policy outcomes must also be sought within the framework of established customs and institutions. The objective of this part of the paper will be to describe the events and actions of the various actors which contributed to the successful passage of language related legislation in 1969 and 1973. In this study four variables were identified: two Mexican-American organizations, a statewide education association, the Texas Education Agency and the governor's office.

The League of United Latin-American Citizens

The League of United Latin-American Citizens (LULAC) was founded in 1929 by a group of urban, middle-class Mexican-Americans.The organization was formed to validate their newly formed middle-class status in the eyes of the dominant Anglo culture (Grebler, Moore, and Guzman, 1970: 542-555). LULAC was an apolitical, middle-class and assimilationist organization. It was opposed to radical or violent demonstrations which would "tend to create conflicts and disturb the peace and tranquility of" the country (Armando Navarro, "The Evolution of Chicano Politics," *Aztlan* 5 Spring and Fall, 1974: 63). The organizational aim was to maintain a low profile within the dominant society and to demonstrate their zealous patriotism as well as middle-class virtues.

During the period of increased Chicano protest, 1965 to 1972, LULAC continued its policy of accommodation, making steady gains for Mexican-Americans by appealing to the federal government for relief in the areas of health, education and employment. During the mid-1960s LULAC increased its interest and support of political candidates who supported Mexican-American interests. In 1967 Carlos F. Truan, a member of LULAC, was encouraged to run for the Texas legislature by LULAC and American G.I. Forum officials (Interview, Garza, 3/7/79).

According to Senator Yarborough, it was arranged to give Truan, as a promising LULAC leader, a chance to present testimony at the televised bilingual education hearings scheduled for Corpus Christi on May 26, 1967. These meetings would give Truan local visibility, helping him in the November 1968 election. When he won his bid for election on November 5th, he was the second Chicano to have ever been elected from this predominantly Mexican-American city (Interview, Truan, and Yarborough, 2/20/79; 3/27/79).

In spite of its early assimilationist aims LULAC's language position began to change during the mid 1960s. The organization began to support and call for the implementation of bilingual-bicultural education programs. It had successfully lobbied for the enactment of the federal Bilingual Education Act in 1967. Now it sought to do the same in Texas.

The increased militancy of Chicanos during the early 1970s was being assessed by state legislative leaders. They were faced with the choice of dealing with militant, leftist-leaning organizations such as La Raza Unida Party, and the Mexican-American Youth Organization, or, they could deal with the more moderate, conservative organizations such as LULAC and the American G.I. Forum. Legislators chose to deal with the older organizations.

Although both wings of the Chicano movement sought essentially the same material benefits—equal justice, equal educational opportunity, equal employment possibilities, more control over their own lives—their methods for achieving them differed. Although their methods differed, the effect of these differences was complementary. While one group demonstrated with boycotts, strikes and school walkouts, utilizing the tactics of confrontation and community organization, the other group continued to make increment gains within the system. One of these gains would be the enactment of the Bilingual Education and Training Act.

The American G.I. Forum

The American G.I. Forum was founded in 1948 by Dr. Hector P. Garcia in an effort to help Mexican-American veterans. However, ". . . the immediate cause of its formation was the refusal of a funeral home in Three Rivers, Texas, to bury a (Chicano) war veteran in 1948" (Navarro, 1974: 68). The Forum started out as a non-partisan civic organization. Today the Forum has taken a more active part in politics and in the state political arena. Although the organization has assumed more national visibility than LULAC, in Texas the name is synonymous with Dr. Hector P. Garcia. Between 1969 and 1973, Dr. Garcia actively supported the enactment of a state bilingual education law for Texas. In 1967 he had testified in support of Senator Yarborough's Bilingual Education Bill, S. 428. During the sixty-second and sixty-third legislative sessions Dr. Garcia continually visited Austin to testify and to lobby for the passage of a state bilingual education law (Interview, Garcia, 2/21/79).

After Dolph Briscoe had won the election in November, LULAC representatives and Dr. Garcia turned to him for the support of the adult and bilingual education bills which Carlos F. Truan was going to introduce to the legislature in January, 1973. Throughout the election year, however, the Mexican-American leadership approached all of the candidates who were running for governor and presented their demands for a fair share of the economic, political and social opportunities in Texas.

It is difficult to determine when particular events may have taken place, but the evidence does suggest that spokesmen of the two leading Mexican-American organizations frequently extracted promises of support for the bilingual bill from the various candidates.

During the campaign, for example, then Governor Preston Smith expressed his support for the enactment of a state bilingual education bill. Smith's credibility as a candidate was shattered when he stated that in his opinion there existed no discrimination in the state of Texas against any ethnic group in the areas of education, administration of justice and employment (Interview, Cárdenas, 2/28/79). The Mexican-American leadership abandoned any hope of supporting Preston Smith. Despite the falling out with Preston Smith, he still recommended the establishment of a new bilingual education program with a funding level of $6.4 million in his final address before the legislature in January, 1973 (*House Journal*, Volume I, 1973: 45).

The Texas Association for Continuing Adult Education

Controversial bills are seldom legislated without the support of an active lobbying group. In 1972 the advocates of bilingual education legislation in Texas were not well organized. The Texas Association for Bilingual Education was barely gaining the support of its few bilingual educators. The only consistent support which Carlos F. Truan could count on was from individuals like Dr. José A. Cárdenas, Dr. Theodore Andersson, and Dr. Hector P. Garcia. Although these individuals were well known and respected by many Texan legislators, what they could do to push for the bill's passage was very limited as their support seemed "special pleading." Truan realized that he needed more outside support in order to pass the bilingual bill during the Sixty-Third Legislature.

In the early part of 1972, Truan was approached by Harvey Owens, president of the Texas Association for Continuing Adult Education, and asked to sponsor a bill that would establish a state funded program of adult education in Texas. On the Senate side Mr. Owens had asked Senator Chet Brooks to carry the bill.

By the time the joint legislative committee on finance met in June, 1972 to consider the next year's budget, Representative Truan had devised a legislative strategy he hoped would insure the enactment of both bills. In a meeting with TEA Commissioner J. W. Edgar, Truan proposed to introduce the bilingual bill (H.B. 145) and the adult education bill (H.B. 147) as a package. Truan informed them that in order to get the votes they would have to support both bills. Bob Allen, director of the Adult Education Division at TEA, and his assistant, Manual Garza, were also present at this meeting. It was their suggestion that led Mr. Owens to ask for

Truan's sponsorship of the adult education bill (Interview, Owens, 1 April 1979).

The strategy served to bring the complete support of the Texas Association for Continuing Adult Education on behalf of both bills. The lobbying efforts of the association completely surprised the legislators. What could be wrong with a bilingual bill that was supported by Anglos? When Truan introduced his bills to the legislature in the winter of 1973 over half of the House membership signed on as co-authors. The lobbying efforts of the association had played a significant part in the enactment of the bilingual law (Interview, Camacho, 2/15/79).

The Texas Education Agency

Four months after President Johnson had signed the Bilingual Education Act, Commissioner J. W. Edgar was asking the twenty-four member State Board of Education for permission to develop a state plan of bilingual education for Texas public schools, and to set up a temporary Advisory Committee on Bilingual Education (*Official Agenda,* State Board of Education, April 6, 1968). On November 11th, Commissioner Edgar informed the Board that the Congress had appropriated $7.5 million dollars for bilingual education programs throughout the nation for the 1969 fiscal year. "Texas", he wrote, "should get a substantial share of the appropriation." In the same letter, he requested the Board to approve the Bilingual Advisory Committee's endorsement of the *Texas Statewide Design for Bilingual Education.* Lastly, he asked the Board to approve of the committee's recommendation that Article 288 of the Penal Code of Texas be amended to allow for the implementation of bilingual education programs (*Official Agenda,* State Board of Education, November 11, 1968).

Interest in the enactment of a state bilingual education law by Commissioner J. W. Edgar in 1968 can be attributed to several things. As early as 1964 several Texas school districts had been running experimental programs in bilingual instruction. Early evaluations of these programs were showing positive gains in achievement by many Chicano school children. The enactment of the federal bilingual law made available more money to increase the number of such programs. The federal initiative encouraged local advocates to push for the enactment of similar legislation. Such an early initiative was taken by Senator Joe J. Bernal.

By December of 1967 Bernal was fully convinced that the bilingual-bicultural approach to teaching Mexican-American students provided the best means for their educational success. As a former teacher he intuitively believed that this method of instruction would be far superior to what the educational system was offering. In a letter to Dr. J. W. Edgar he suggested that TEA draw up a bill that would amend the Texas language restriction, thus permitting the state to take full advantage of the money which the Congress had appropriated for bilingual education programs (Letter to Dr. J. W. Edgar, 1/29/79).

Dr. Edgar's response was assuring and supportive. He informed Senator Bernal that a state Task Force had been created to administer the program. In addition, he promised to prepare a bill that would amend the restrictive law (Letter to Bernal, 2/6/68). The momentum for the advocates of bilingual education in Texas quickly mounted. On April 6 the State Board of Education approved the agency's plan to develop a state plan for bilingual education and to establish an advisory committee. By August 24, fifteen appointees to the advisory committee had been confirmed. Both Senator Bernal and the newly elected House representative, Carlos F. Truan, were members of the committee (*Official Agenda,* State Board of Education, 4/6/68; 8/24/68).

In November 1968, TEA published its first recommendation on the subject of bilingual education to the state legislature. The document reflected the emerging interests in ethnic pride and the ideals of cultural pluralism, stressing the importance of becoming bilingual in Spanish and English for all the public school children in Texas. The Spanish-speaking population was described as a valuable resource which could contribute more than it had to the state's future development. The introduction also emphasized the promising research findings which had been made on the nature of language, language acquisition and on the psychological and cultural development of children. These new insights into language learning and early childhood development provided educators with more promise for educating both the English and Spanish monolingual child. Texas, it was hoped, would make all of its public school children bilingual in Spanish and English.

The agency then made three specific recommendations to the legislature:

1. English shall be the basic language of instruction in all schools.
2. The governing board of any school district and any private school may determine when and under what circumstances instruction may be given bilingually.
3. The policy of the state is to ensure the mastery of English by all pupils in the schools, provided that bilingual instruction may be offered in those situations when such instruction is educationally advantageous to the pupils. If bilingual instruction is authorized it should not interfere with the systematic, sequential, and regular instruction of all pupils in the English language. (*Recommendations for Legislative Consideration on Public Education in Texas,* November, 1968, 39)

The federal Bilingual Education Act was a year old when the Sixty-First Legislature convened in Austin on January 14 to consider the business of the state. Preston Smith, who had served as lieutenant governor during the previous six years, had been elected governor. Ben Barnes was elected lieutenant governor after having served as Speaker of the House for two terms. The powerful Speaker's position went to a newly elected House member from East Texas, Gus F. Mutscher. All three were conservative democrats who were not necessarily as interested in the economic and social problems of the Mexican-American as they were in protecting the corporate interests of the state. Nothing in their previous legislative records would necessarily attract them to the needs and demands which Texan Chicanos would bring to their attention. Yet, without their support or consent, the bilingual education bill which was proposed and passed during the Sixty-First Legislature would have had little success.

The bilingual education bill (H.B. 103) which was enacted in 1969 aroused very little public or legislative attention. The law was permissive, and its primary aim was to ensure that Mexican-American children were taught English. Very few legislators knew what the intent of the law was. The bill threatened no major business interests and it did not require state funding (*House Journal:* Volume I, 1969: 169-170; Interview, Truan, 2/20/79).

In 1970 TEA recommended a broadening of the bilingual law which had been passed the previous year. However, the Sharpstown Scandal, and Representative Truan's membership and activities in the Dirty Thirty, doomed the passage of House Bill 1024 (Interview, Truan, 2/20/79; *House Journal:* Volume II, 1971, 6431; *Recommendations for Legislative Consideration on Public Education in Texas,* November, 1970: 13-14).

In 1972 the State Board of Education once again requested the governor and the legislature to enact a bilingual education law that would benefit Mexican-Americans. The recommendations were essentially similar to the ones which had been made in 1970.

The legislators were informed that most of the bilingual education programs in Texas were federally funded. Consequently, only a small percentage of the children needing this kind of education were actually being served. Another problem mentioned was the need to train more teachers in the methods and philosophy of bilingual instruction. It was noted that while less than five percent of the teachers were capable of teaching in two languages, twenty-two percent of the school population was Spanish-speaking.

These were the conditions which were deemed unacceptable by the education agency. It was suggested that school districts with children who could not function effectively in the classroom because of language difference, should be helped with a bilingual instructional program. It was also suggested that the few bilingual teachers in existing programs should be given eleven and twelve month contracts so they could develop the badly needed curriculum materials. They also wanted the legislators to allow the agency to develop another method for obtaining the necessary bilingual textbooks, apart from the general textbook provisions provided in English (*Recommendations for Legislative Consideration on Public Education in Texas,* November, 1972: 3).

The agency also recommended the creation of a state funded adult education program. The report stated that there were many adults in Texas who were unable to obtain a high school education because there were no state funds. The money which was provided by the federal government was too limited to adequately finance the kind of program which was needed. Moreover, the federal Adult Education Act was restrictive in that it provided for educational activities up to the eighth grade level and limited its services to those persons who had had some schooling in Texas. Statistics compiled by TEA showed that 3 million adults over the age of 25 had not completed high school. Of this group over 1 million had not completed eight years of formal schooling, and 176 thousand had not completed one year of school. In order to meet this need the agency estimated that it would need about $5.1 million annually (*Recommendations. . . .,* November, 1972: 11).

From 1968 to 1972 the agency acted as a facilitator and responded to external demands for change that emanated from within the state or from Washington, D.C. The agency provided a formal, structural link between the demands of the Mexican-American community and the legislature.

The formal linkages, however, were not enough to assure the enactment of new and controversial education legislation. Between 1969 and 1973 the Texas Education Agency never actively lobbied for the enactment of its new educational proposals. The bilingual and adult education bills were no exception. The Agency's policy of political neutrality or noninvolvement in the legislative process dates back to 1949 when the superintendent, an elected official, was ousted from office by a hostile legislature and replaced by an appointed commissioner of education. Since then the agency has considered its role to be that of implementer of policy rather than as policy maker. Under Dr. Edgar's leadership the agency took on a new image of professionalism and expert objectivism. (Kirst, 1972: 24-243) The agency's input in 1969 and 1971 on behalf of bilingual education was limited to formal requests for new programs and to presentations at public hearings. In 1973 the agency's involvement in state education curriculum policy making had not changed. During the Sixty-Third Legislature it would be the realities of the legislative process, rather than the formal linkages, which would successfully articulate the demands of Mexican-Americans for a mandatory bilingual education law in Texas.

The Governor's Office and the Appropriations Process

Bilingual education advocates were hoping that the newly elected governor would support their bill in 1973. During the campaign, Briscoe had claimed that he was better acquainted with the needs and concerns of the Mexican-American community, because he was from South Texas. Briscoe appointed Rodolfo "Rudy" Flores, his friend and the vice-president of his bank in Uvalde, as his special administrative assistant to deal with the issues which the Mexican-American leadership considered to be important. Flores made it a point to emphasize that if Dolph Briscoe were elected, he had every intention of hiring more Mexican-Americans on his staff than any other previous Texas governor (Interview, Garza, 3/9/79). During the 1972 campaign, Briscoe had also promised to support the passage of bilingual education legislation (Interview, Flores, 3/21/79).

As he had promised, newly elected Governor Dolph Briscoe included adult and bilingual education in his recommended budget for the 1974-1975 biennium. For the bilingual program he recommended $1,622,000 for the first fiscal year, and $4,913,500 for the second. The adult education program was allotted $5 million for each fiscal year. Budgetary recommendation must also include the method of financing each line item. Money for the proposed bilingual program was to be funded through the general state revenues (Executive Budget, Governor Dolph Briscoe, Sixty-Third Legislature, 1974-1975 Biennium, IV-2 and IV-3).

The governor's budget, unlike the budget of the legislature, is influenced more strongly by his objectives, goals or campaign promises. Former Governor Smith's recommendation to the legislature that it consider the creation of a bilingual education program in no way obligated the legislature or the new governor, but the statement did strengthen the advocacy appeal of bilingual proponents.

In his inaugural address before the joint session of the Texas Legislature on January 16, 1973, Governor Briscoe further demonstrated his support for the bilingual bill. He stated that as part of his objective to create an environment in which every person had the "opportunity to rise to the maximum of his or her potential," he supported the enactment of "an adequate bilingual educational program" (*House Journal:* Volume I, 1973, 114-115). The next day the governor reiterated his position on bilingual education. In his statement the governor linked the need for bilingual education to the school finance case which at the time was being reviewed by the United States Supreme Court.

> I am concerned by the problems which the state will encounter in public education if the Rodriguez Case is upheld in the Supreme Court of the United States. I will consider carefully all of the reports and recommendations coming from the various study groups prompted by this case.
>
> Until the court acts, we cannot define the magnitude of these problems. It may well be that the case will not be settled until after adjournment of this Regular Session. But, regardless of the timing, and regardless of the outcome, I believe very strongly that the opportunity for a quality education must be available to every child, *including bilingual teaching where needed.* Quality should not be determined by where a child lives or the wealth of his community. By the same token, I also believe very strongly in local control and equitable local participation in the costs of public education (*House Journal:* Volume I, 1973, 140; Italics supplied).

Briscoe's statements in support of bilingual education were very brief and cautious. It seems quite likely that he was not entirely convinced about the merits of the bilingual bill which Truan and others wanted him to endorse. However, he had promised the Mexican-American leaders that he would endorse and work for the bill's enactment (Interview, Camacho, 2/15/79).

The governor's inclusion of line items for bilingual and adult education as a part of his budget was important, but it did not assure that the programs would be enacted or funded. Unlike most states where the budgetary preparation phase of the appropriations process is handled by the governor, in Texas this aspect of the budget is initiated and concluded by the legislature exclusively (Pettus and Bland, 1976: 322-333). The appropriations process in Texas involves the preparation of two budgets: the governor's executive budget and the budget which is recommended by the Legislative Budget Board. In 1973, although the governor included two new line items in his budget, these same items did not appear in the legislative budget because there was no prior legislation authorizing appropriations for bilingual and adult education. The availability of funds to pay for new programs and the political compromises which are agreed to among the various actors during and in the final days of the legislative session are among the two most important factors which determine the enactment of new legislation which is supported by the governor.

The appropriations process begins seven months before the legislature convenes on every odd-numbered year. Administrators of the various agencies submit their budget requests to the Legislative Budget Office and also the Governor's Budget Office between May and September of even-numbered years. Public hearings and analysis of the proposed two year budget are independently held by both offices. The analysis of budget requests and recommendations in the Legislative Budget Office is handled by a professional staff hired by the legislature. After all requests and recommendations are considered, the director of the office with the aid of his staff present the budget to the Legislative Budget Board. The Board, in turn, examines the budget and makes final last minute changes in the appropriations budget which it recommends to the legislature no later than December, several weeks before the beginning of the regular legislative session in January (Bowhay and Thrall, 1975: 213-216).

The Governor's Budget Office follows a similar procedure, with the governor playing the decisive role in the process. After the governor reviews, approves or disapproves of the recommendations and requests on the proposed budget, it is mailed to all the members of the legislature, state agencies and to the Legislative Budget Board by December 15. Seven days after the legislature convenes for the regular session, the Director of the Legislative Budget Office submits a copy of the budget prepared by the Legislative Budget Board to all legislators and to the governor (Bowhay and Thrall, 1975: 216).

The Legislative Budget Board is an especially powerful vehicle for determining what new demands for state funding are included or left out of the budget. By law the Board is composed of ten legislators. The lieutenant governor and the speaker of the house serve as the board's chairman and vice-chairman. The chairmen of the Senate Finance Committee, State Affairs Committee, the House Appropriations Committee, and the Committee on Taxation and Revenue are automatically members of the board. Two other members from each House are appointed by the speaker and the lieutenant governor (Bowhay and Thrall, 1975, 214).

Thus, legislators in Texas receive two budgetary documents, but work very closely with the budget recommendations which are prepared by the Legislative Budget Board. The governor's budget represents a revenue plan for funding old and new programs, while the legislature's budget represents a unified method of spending state funds (Pettus and Bland, 1976: 322-324).

After the initial budget has been submitted to the legislature at the beginning of the session the budgetary preparation is continued by the legislative leadership and the Senate and House financial committees. The negotiating process continues in both committees until very late in the session. The final task of forming an acceptable budget is done by the conference committee. This committee is tightly controlled by the speaker and the lieutenant governor and, to a lesser degree, the governor. The legislative leadership controls by appointing the membership of the committee. The governor's influence over the final product of the appropriations budget comes at the end of the session, when his power to line item veto increases his leverage over the process to some extent (Pettus and Bland, 1976: 325). In 1973 the proponents of the adult and bilingual education bills worked diligently in influencing the funding of both bills in the House Appropriations Committee and in the joint session of the conference committee.

Very early in the session Representative Neil Caldwell, chairman of the House Appropriations Committee, assured Representatives Matt Garcia and Bob Vale that they would be given an opportunity to present their request for funding the adult and bilingual education bills to the full committee. Committee members were not too receptive to the idea of providing funding for the bilingual and adult education bills, but Garcia and Vale continued to press for their inclusion. It was not until the very last days of the committee hearings that they were able to squeeze out a total of $7 million for both bills. Without the help of the committee chairman it is very doubtful that they could have obtained any funding for two bills which at the time had no legislative authorization. When the House budget was submitted for floor debate the funding level for both bills was not changed. It was not until the House budget was considered in the conference committee that the funding of the bills ran into serious problems. The House version of the budget included line items for adult and bilingual education, but the Senate version did not. According to the new rules which were adopted during the Sixty-Third Legislature to govern the function of the Conference Committee, the committee could not recommend a greater amount than that which had been recommended if the item appeared in only one version of the appropriations budget (Interview, Garcia, 6/5/79; Bowhay and Thrall, 1975: 218).

Towards the end of the Sixty-Third Legislative Session in late April the adult and bilingual education bills lost the funding which Matt Garcia and Bob Vale had worked so hard to include in the House version of the budget. The main objection raised by the conferees in the conference committee was that the bills had not been passed by the legislature and thus could not legally be appropriated funds (Interview, Garza, 3/7/79). Other opponents of the bills argued that the legislature would be funding programs which were not proven. This was especially the case regarding the bilingual education bill. The legislators were well aware that the major beneficiary of these bills would be the large Mexican-American population, and many of them made this fact the central argument against appropriating funds for such a program. Another argument which was used was that the legislature was dangerously close to expending monies which would not be certifiable by the state comptroller. Legislators who supported the bilingual bill looked upon this last argument as being a direct attack on the Mexican-American, since most of the funds would be utilized to help Mexican-American children. It was noted that the same argument was not used against funding highway construction, a bill to eliminate fire ants and other programs (Interview, Garcia, 6/5/79).

The Mexican-American legislative caucus and Bob Allen of the Adult Education Division of TEA wanted to ensure the passage of both bills with the funding which had been obtained in the House version of the appropriations budget. With the help of the Dental Association, Truan was able to organize a LULAC Legislative Seminar to which he invited the governor and his wife; Kelvin Guest, chairman of the state Democratic Committee, Rudy Flores, Manuel Garza, and the members of the Mexican-American caucus.

During the meeting Truan did most of the talking. He pleaded with the governor and his staff to lobby for the reinstatement of funding for both bills. He reminded him that LULAC had supported him in his campaign for governor, that they had stayed out of the primaries, and had supported him in the November elections. Moreover, he stressed that the Mexican-American caucus unanimously favored the bill. Briscoe agreed to push for the reinstatement of funds when the legislature reconvened that afternoon.

Kelvin Guest and Rudy Flores actively lobbied for the funding of both bills. By the end of the day the intense lobbying had succeeded. Funding for both bills was restored, but it was contingent upon their enactment by the Sixty-Third Legislature. The compromise which was worked out netted both bills a total of $7 million. The adult education bill was appropriated $4.3 million, evenly divided for the 1974 and 1975 biennium. The bilingual education bill was appropriated a mere $700,000 for the first year and $2 million for the next (Interview, Garza, 3/7/79 and *General and Special Laws of Texas,* Sixty-Third Legislature, 1973: 2065 and 2070).

The amount of money which was finally approved by the Conference Committee for the adult and bilingual education programs was not decided according to any predetermined formula. The funding which was approved was based on what money Garcia and Vale were able to extract out of the House Appropriations Committee. Funding also depended to a great extent on what the committee was willing or felt that it was able to provide for each program.

Another factor used to determine the amount of money which could be made available was the past history of each program. It was felt that the bilingual education program was a new, untested program, in contrast to the adult education program, and that therefore it would be best to start the program with seed money to prepare teachers and produce the necessary materials that would be used in the classroom. The following fiscal year the funding level would be increased to reflect the actual classroom instructional program.

At the time no one actually knew how much money it would take to fund a minimally acceptable bilingual program. There was very little data on how a bilingual program would differ from a regular monolingual program in terms of cost per child. The first attempt to empirically determine the cost of funding a bilingual education program was not undertaken until November, 1973, six months after the enactment of the Bilingual Education and Training Act (Cárdenas, Bernal, Kean, 1976; Interview, Garcia, 6/5/79).

Throughout the legislative session and even during the funding crisis TEA officials of the Office of International and Bilingual Education never actively intervened in the legislative process. Had it not been for the independent course of action which Truan, Garza, Garcia, Rudy Flores and others had taken in pushing for legislative authorization and appropriations for both bills, it is seriously questionable whether the bills could have been funded during that legislative session. With both bills assured of funding, the next step was to make sure both bills were enacted.

The Sixty-Third Legislative Session

The Sixty-Third Legislature is remembered in Texas legislative history as the "reform legislature." Practically all of the new legislators in the House had campaigned successfully on one issue: reform in state government. Governor Dolph Briscoe and Lieutenant Governor William P. Hobby had both campaigned against political malfeasance. Price Daniel, Jr. was elected as Speaker of the House on the strength of his reform platform. "All concerned had a vivid memory of the Sharpstown fiasco, and all wanted to be able to conclude the session with good, clean records of achievement" (*Accomplishments of the 63rd Legislature,* 1973: 1). Part of this record would include the enactment of the Bilingual Education and Training Act as well as the Adult Education Law.

When Representative Carlos F. Truan arrived in Austin for the new session, he was not only interested in correcting past legislative abuses, but he was already anticipating the strategy which he would employ in order to pass his bills. In the House Truan would carry the bill once again, but in the Senate it would be Senator Chet Brooks, a liberal Democrat from Pasadena, who would get the support of all of the senators for his version of the bilingual education bill.

On January 22, 1973, Representative Truan introduced House Bills 145, 146 and 147 as a package to the House. He then put an announcement on the desk of each of the 150 members inviting them to be co-sponsors of the bills. Seventy-seven House members responded by placing their signatures on all three bills. By obtaining the signatures of more than half of the House members on his bills, he had committed them to either supporting the bills to the very end of the enactment process or to support any other substitute bill. Truan's bilingual bill carried no mandatory provision, but the bill which Senator Chet Brooks would introduce later on in the session would carry mandatory requirements. Truan's bill still emphasized the local school district's option to implement a bilingual education program, mainly because Truan did not want to arouse undue suspicion about a bill whose primary beneficiary would be the Mexican-American. He was cautious and was not going to jeopardize the passage of the bilingual education bill in this session. Senator Chet Brook's sponsorship of the bilingual bill was very important, because it lessened the chances of it being labeled a Mexican bill. In Truan's opinion, former Senator Joe J. Bernal, as respected as he was in the Senate, could have never passed a mandatory bill in the Senate (Interview, Truan, 2/20/79).

One of the major changes which significantly contributed to the enactment of the bilingual bill during the Sixty-Third Legislature was the appointment of Carlos F. Truan as chairman of the twenty-one member Human Resources Committee on January 12. Truan had worked diligently to get Price Daniel, Jr. elected as Speaker. In exchange Price Daniel, Jr. appointed him chairman and promised to support the passage of his bills. On the other side of the Capitol rotunda Chet Brooks had also been appointed chairman of the eleven member Human Resources Committee in the Senate. The collaboration of both chairmen was a major force in the enactment of both bills (Interview, Camacho, 2/15/79).

Six days after Representative Truan had introduced his three bills, Senator Chet Brooks introduced Senate Bill 121, a bill related to bilingual education programs in the Texas public schools (*Senate Journal:* Volume I, 1973: 115). The bill was referred to the Committee on Education on the 30th of January, and was subsequently reported favorably out of committee on April 11 as Committee Substitute Senate Bill 121.

By April 30, when the bill came up for its second reading before the Senate, Senator Chet Brooks had obtained the co-operation of all thirty senators. As chairman of the Human Resources Committee, Brooks wielded considerable power. In addition, Senator Brooks was a very well known and highly respected member of the Senate. Despite his claims to the contrary, Brooks, who had made a commitment to pass the bilingual education bill, very probably used his position as Human Resources chairman to full advantage. Very few controversial bills ever get past the very close-knit senate without some kind of compromise or deals being made. In the course of this study, however, the author was unfortunately unable to ascertain the nature of the agreements, commitments or understandings which may have been reached at the time the bilingual bill was being considered (Interviews: Camacho, 2/15/79; Hooker, 6/7/79; Brooks, 6/5/79).

On the same day (April 30) Senate Bill 121 was read a third time and passed by a vote of thirty, with one senator counted absent. By this time Truan had decided to wait for Brook's bill to be introduced in the House. On May 3, three days after it had been introduced to the House, Truan made a motion to substitute his two bills for Senate Bill 121. The motion passed with no objections and with no points of order raised by any of the members of the Education Committee to which the bill had been assigned. The objections and tactics to delay the bill's passage, however, would come later when the bill was introduced for final floor action on May 15.

The supporters of the bill were anticipating the last minute objections which were raised by several House members when the bill was brought up for floor debate before the House. Had it not been for the support of the speaker the bill could very well have been defeated. The co-ordinated efforts of Truan, Garcia, Caldwell and the speaker successfully met the challenges of the few who were opposed to the bill's passage. On May 23, Senate Bill 121 was passed by a vote of 112 to 20, with 15 members noted absent (*House Journal:* Volume III, 1973: 4569). The Senate concurred with the amendments which had been added by Truan on the same day. On June 3, 1973 the Bilingual Education and Training Act was signed by Governor Dolph Briscoe.

To summarize, although the need, the interest, and much of the early expertise and support in the area of bilingual education came from Texas, it was not the first state to enact a mandated bilingual education law. The advocates of bilingual education legislation were successful in articulating their demands for educational change at the federal level before they were able to influence the passage of similar state legislation. This study was undertaken to identify the factors which may have contributed to the enactment of the Texas Bilingual Education and Training Act in 1973.

Meranto's model for explaining legislative outcomes was used to organize the study. The model called for an examination of the political changes which occurred within the legislature. It also stressed the importance of examining environmental changes which may have contributed to the legislative process and outcome.

The findings of this study seem to suggest that the election of a reform conscious legislative body in 1972 was a major factor in the enactment of the bilingual law during the Sixty-Third Legislature. The findings also demonstrated that a bill, regardless of how controversial, could be routinely passed through the legislature if it had the endorsement and support of the legislative leadership.

The link between the enactment of the federal Bilingual Education Act in 1967 and the subsequent enactment of similar state legislation in Texas two years later can be clearly demonstrated. However, the nature and the extent of the federal influence on the state legislative process in 1973 was less evident. In 1969 federal initiatives in this area were important because they accelerated the slower local pace. Increased federal funding provided the Texas Education Agency and local school districts with a major incentive to participate in new educational programs. The federal act also provided state advocates with legitimate reasons to ask for the elimination of restrictive language codes which prohibited the use of another language other than English as a legitimate medium of classroom instruction.

Another factor which contributed to the momentum for a state mandated bilingual education program was the release of the May 25, 1970 Memorandum by the Office for Civil Rights. The new guidelines for determining compliance with Section 601 of the Civil Rights Act of 1964 applied to all national origin minorities, but the Memorandum was principally concerned with rectifying local restrictions and procedures which affected a large percentage of Mexican-American school children. The criteria provided bilingual advocates with legal justification for supporting the enactment of a state mandated bilingual law.

It took four years to enact a mandatory bilingual education law in Texas. The evidence suggests that the gestation period was a reflection of how Mexican-American demands for change were influenced by the political culture of the state. In addition, the findings tended to confirm the subtle, but pervasive influence which Mexican-American leaders had on the political leadership of the state. The influence seemed to be based more on personal friendship and mutual understandings between ambitious Anglo politicos and Chicano leaders, than on any real electoral threat.

When Carlos F. Truan introduced his bill to the legislature in 1973, it carried no mandatory provisions. Conscious that the bill was already recognized as a "Mexican" demand, he did not want to jeopardize its chances of passing by attaching mandatory requirements. The willingness of Senator Chet Brooks to sponsor the bill in the Senate to some extent diffused the sensitive ethnic issue, contributing to the bill's enactment. It seems quite clear that Mexican-American legislators and leaders of the more prominent, recognized Chicano organizations could not have single-handedly pressed for change and been successful. Thus, it was very important for them to build coalitions with sympathetic Anglo leaders at every step of the enactment process.

Mexican-American leaders sought and received the support of the top legislative leadership. Speaker Daniel and Lieutenant Governor Hobby both supported the bilingual bill. Truan's appointment as chairman of the Human Resources Committee was especially important because it provided him with the necessary bargaining leverage in the House as well as in the Senate. Senator Brooks' collaboration with Representative Truan was also significant. As chairman of the Human Resources Committee, Brooks needed the co-operation of Truan to get his favorite bills passed, and thus assure his power base in the Senate.

The support of Governor Dolph Briscoe and House Appropriations Committee Chairman Neil Caldwell were also crucial. The newly elected governor delivered on his campaign promises by requesting over $16 million in new appropriations for the adult and bilingual bills. Without the support of the committee chairman and the intervention of the governor, last minute compromises in the Conference Committee on Appropriations to support the adult and bilingual education bills would not have succeeded.

Outside lobbying interests also played a major role in influencing the enactment process. The lobbying effectiveness of the Texas Association for Continuing Adult Education on Texan legislators cannot be underestimated. The ethnic overtones of Truan's bill were muffled somewhat when it became evident that Texan Anglos from northwest and southeast Texas also strongly favored the bilingual bill. On the other hand, the influence of the Texas Educational Agency on the legislative process was minimal. The Agency made its formal requests for legislative consideration of the adult and bilingual education bills as prescribed by law, but personnel in the bilingual division of the Agency did not actively push for their passage. With the exception of Bob Allen and Manuel Garza, TEA officials did not actively lobby for the enactment of either bill.

The historical evidence obtained in this study points to several conclusions. The success which bilingual advocates experienced at the federal level in 1967 increased the likelihood of similar state level legislation in 1969. Educational policy-making occurred incrementally rather than as a result of any single major event. The push for enacting a bilingual law was low-keyed. Advocates sought and received the support of the major educational associations during the process. Earlier successes in state bilingual legislation were used as precedents to broaden current demands for change. Finally, the study suggests that Mexican-American demands for educational reform could not have been achieved without the strategy of coalition building, bargaining, compromises, with the established Anglo political leadership.

BIBLIOGRAPHY

Accomplishments of the 63rd Legislature—Regular Session—January 9, 1973 to May 28, 1973. Austin: Texas Legislative Council, 1973.

A Study of State Programs in Bilingual Education. "A Final Report on Their Status." Supporting Volumes I-IV. Washington, D.C.: Development Associates, Inc., 1521 New Hampshire Avenue, N.W., (20036), March, 1977.

Bailey, Harry A., and Katz, Ellis, eds. *Ethnic Group Politics.* Columbus: Charles E. Merrill Publishing Company, 1969.

Bowhay, James H., and Thrall, Virginia D. *State Legislative Appropriations Process.* Lexington, Ky.: Council of State Governments and National Conference of State Legislatures, 1975.

Cárdenas, José A., Bernal, Joe J. and Kean, William. *Bilingual Education Cost Analysis.* San Antonio: Intercultural Development Research Association, 1976.

Carter, Thomas P. *Mexican Americans in School: A History of Educational Neglect.* New York: College Entrance Examination Board, 1970.

Clinchy, Jr., Everett Ross. *Equality of Opportunity for Latin-Americans in Texas.* New York: Arno Press, 1974.

Deaton, Charles. *The Year They Threw the Rascals Out.* Austin: Shoal Creek Publishers, Inc., 1973.

Easton, David. *A Framework for Political Analysis.* Englewood Cliffs: Prentice-Hall, Inc., 1965.

__________. *A Systems Analysis of Political Life.* New York: John Wiley and Sons, Inc., 1965.

Fishman, Joshua A. "The Social Science Perspective." In *Bilingual Education: Current Perspectives Volume I.* Arlington: Center for Applied Linguistics, 1977.

Gambone, James V. "Bilingual Bicultural Educational Civil Rights: The May 25th Memorandum and Oppressive School Practices." Ph.D. dissertation, The University of New Mexico, 1973.

Garcia, F.D., ed. *Chicano Politics.* New York: M.S.S. Information Corp., 1973.

General and Special Laws of Texas, Regular Session, 63rd Legislature, 1973.

Gerry, Martin H. "Cultural Freedom in the Schools: The Right of Mexican-American Children to Succeed." In *Mexican-Americans and Educational Change.* eds. Castaneda, Alfredo, et al. New York: Arno Press, 1974.

Grebler, Leo, Moore, Joan W., and Guzman, Ralph C. *The Mexican-American People.* New York: The Free Press, 1970.

Handlin, Oscar. "The Immigrant and American Politics." In *Foreign Influences in American Life.* Ed. David F. Bowers. Princeton: Princeton University, 1944.

Key, Jr., V.O. *Southern Politics in State and Nation.* New York: Alfred A. Knopf, 1949.

Kinch, Jr., Sam and Proctor, Ben. *Texas Under a Cloud: Story of the Texas Stock Fraud Scandal.* Austin: Jenkins Publishing Co., 1972.

Kirst, Michael W. "The Politics of Federal Aid to Education in Texas." In *Federal Aid to Education Who Benefits? Who Governs?,* pp. 235-275. Eds. Joel S. Berke and Michael W. Kirst. Lexington: D.C. Heath and Company, 1972.

Litt, Edgar. *Ethnic Politics in America.* Glenview: Scott, Foresman, 1970.

Maxwell, Jane Carlisle. *Litigation of Texas Election Laws: Toward Democratization of the Political Process.* Austin: The University of Texas at Austin, 1972.

Meranto, Philip. *The Politics of Federal Aid to Education in 1965: A Study in Political Innovation.* Syracuse: Syracuse University Press, 1967.

Mosher, Edith K., and Wagoner, Jr., Jennings L., eds. *The Changing Politics of Education.* Berkeley: McCutchan Publishing Corporation, 1978.

Navarro, Armando. "The Evolution of Chicano Politics." *Aztlan* 5 (Spring and Fall 1974): 57-83.

Official Agenda of State Board of Education. Austin: Texas Education Agency, 1968.

Pettus, Beryl E., and Bland, Randall W. *Texas Government Today.* Homewood: The Dorsey Press, 1976.

Rangel, Jorge C., and Alcala, Carlos M. "Project Report: De Jure Segregation of Chicanos in Texas." *Harvard Civil Rights-Civil Liberties Law Review* 7 (March 1972): 307-391.

Recommendations for Legislative Consideration on Public Education in Texas. Austin: Texas Education Agency, 1968, 1970, 1972.

Sanchez, Gilbert. "An Analysis of the Bilingual Education Act." Ed.D. dissertation, University of Massachusetts, 1973.

Schneider, Susan Gilbert. *Revolution, Reaction or Reform: The 1974 Bilingual Education Act.* New York: Las Americas, 1976.

Texas, *Executive Budget for 1974-1975 Biennium.* Austin: Legislative Budget Board, 1973.

Texas, Senate. *Journal of the Senate, Regular Session of the Sixty-First Legislature,* 1969.

Texas, House. *Journal of the House of Representatives of the Regular Session of the Sixty-Second Legislature,* 1971.

Texas, Senate. *Journal of the Senate, Regular Session of the Sixty-Third Legislature,* 1973.
Texas, House. *Journal of the House of Representatives of the Regular Session of the Sixty-First Legislature,* 1969.
Texas, House. *Journal of the House of Representatives of the Regular Session of the Sixty-Third Legislature,* 1973.
"U.S. Court Revises Texas Districts." *New York Times,* 23 January 1972: 30.
United States Commission on Civil Rights. *A Better Chance to Learn: Bilingual-Bicultural Education.* Publication Number 51. Washington, D.C.: Government Printing Office, 1975.
United States Commission on Civil Rights. *Hearings Held in San Antonio, December 9-14, 1968.* Washington, D.C.: Government Printing Office, 1968.
"Voting Residency Rule Cut to 30 Days in Texas." *New York Times,* 1 April 1972: 8.
Wirth, Louis. *The Ghetto.* Chicago: Chicago University Press, 1928.
Zamora, Jesus Ernesto. "A Survey of Texas' Bilingual-Bicultural Education Programs." Ph.D. dissertation. The University of Texas at Austin, 1977.

LIST OF PERSONS INTERVIEWED

Brooks, Chet, Texas State Senator, author of Bilingual Education Bill in 1973; telephone interview, 5 June, 1979.

Camacho, José E., Legislative Assistant for Representative Carlos F. Truan, 1970 to 1975. attorney with Juarez, Camcho, & Phillips, 1209 Parkway, Austin, Texas 78703; 15 February 1979.

Cárdenas, Dr. José A., Director of Intercultural Development Research Association, 2835 Callaghan Road, Suite 350, San Antonio, Texas 78228; 28 February 1979.

Flores, Rodolfo R. (Rudy), Special Administrative Assistant to Governor Dolph Briscoe during the Sixty-third Legislative Session, 1973. General Counsel and General Manager, Jimenez Food Products, Inc., 2620 Tillar Avenue, Fort Worth, Texas 76107, telephone interview, 21 March 1979.

Garcia, Dr. Hector P., founder of The American G.I. Forum in 1947; 1315 Bright Street, Corpus Christi, Texas 78405; 21 February 1979.

Garza, Manuel, LULAC Legislative Aide in Austin 1967 to 1969. Consultant for the Adult Education Division of the Texas Education Agency, 1967 to 1977. 1803 Fair Oaks, Austin, Texas 78745; telephone interview, 9 March 1979.

Hooker, Dr. Richard, Associate Executive Director of Texas School Boards Association, 1973; telephone interview, 7 June 1979.

Owens, Harvey, former President of Texas Association for Continuing Adult Education, 2013 13th Street, Lubbock, Texas 79401; telephone interview, 1 April 1979.

Truan, Carlos F., Texas State Senator, former member of the House of Representatives, 1969 to 1976. 230 Country Club Drive, Corpus Christi, Texas 78412; 20 February 1979.

Yarborough, Ralph, former United States Senator from Texas. 721 Brown Building, Austin, Texas 78701; telephone interview 27 March, 1979.

THE POLITICAL ECONOMY OF BILINGUAL BICULTURAL EDUCATION

John J. Halcón

The dominant controversy in bilingual educational policy making is whether or not bilingual programs meet the needs of the limited English proficiency (LEP) pupil; does bilingual instruction make a difference in the achievement of these pupils? Since the implementation of the federal Bilingual Education Act (1968), this has been the perennial question. After ten years of experimentation in the field and reported evaluations of achievement outcomes, the controversy has reached a new intensity with the publication of the Final Report of the Evaluation of the Impact of thirty-eight ESEA Title VII Spanish-English Bilingual Education Programs (1978), by the American Institutes for Research (AIR). The report essentially concludes that Title VII bilingual programs are ineffective and that the programs reviewed failed to significantly improve the academic achievement levels of participating students.

Opponents of bilingual education will no doubt use these findings to justify their abhorence of utilizing a language of instruction other than English in the classroom. Proponents of bilingual education, on the other hand, have begun to react in a predictably outraged and defensive manner. One proponent (Cervantes, 1978: 6-8) has attacked the findings of the report by citing everything from methodological inconsistencies, to irregularities in the awarding of the USOE contract to AIR, and a connection with the Watergate affair. Another, a project director, has contracted with an independent evaluator (Keleman, 1977: 1) to "study the Title VII versus non-Title VII students." This as a response in part to the AIR Report.

One has only to peruse individual program evaluation reports, professional journal articles, or the propaganda literature on bilingual education to realize the paradoxical nature of the controversy. Opponents can "prove" that bilingual education does not work by citing the AIR Report (1978). Proponents, on the other hand, can "prove" that students who are bilingual or limited speakers of English profit from instruction in their dominant language (Lambert, 1976: 39), and that bilinguals perform at a significantly higher level on measures of both verbal and non-verbal ability (Cummins and Gulatson, 1974). Proponents argue that if properly implemented, programs of bilingual instruction are the modus operandi that will guide the Spanish-speaking community towards equality of educational opportunity.

In the context of these arguments the development of bilingual education policy remains in a state of confusion about the effectiveness of current policy and about the direction of future policy.

I suggest that policy based solely on achievement scores without consideration of other possible factors, may be a narrow and inefficient perspective from which to derive bilingual program policy. Instead, I believe that additional information is needed concerning resources internal to the school district, upon which the impact of bilingual programs depend. There is no question that in bilingual education programs, achievement levels of program participants are not uniformly high. The AIR Report (1978) very clearly demonstrated this. Yet individual programs—Carpinteria (1977a; 1978b), Santa Barbara (1978), Goleta (1978) in California and Sante Fe (1978) in New Mexico, each report significant progress in achievement in their respective programs. Accordingly, the questions that need to be answered are: Which resources when delivered to LEP pupils account for achievement gains? What factors affect the delivery of these resources?

The main argument of this paper is the following: Between the legislation that mandates bilingual educational programs and the expected outcomes of these programs, there stands the complex organization of school districts which acts as a powerful intervening variable.

Rather than viewing achievement *outcomes* as the primary basis upon which bilingual educational policy is derived, I propose that we explore the *antecedents* to these achievement outcomes. By understanding which resources are most effective in producing learning gains among LEP pupils and by accounting for the conditions within the school district organization that affect the delivery of those resources, we may be in a position to develop more cogent policy for bilingual education. It is hoped, moreover, that the provision of information concerning the organizational factors which affect the flow of pertinent resources to LEP pupils may begin to dissipate the controversy surrounding the efficacy of bilingual instruction.

To focus more clearly and productively on the complex dynamics of the school district, I utilize Mayor Zald's political economy framework (Zald, 1970: 222). This framework for the study of change in complex organizations is a middle-range, integrative framework because it specifies the interrelation of a range of organizational dimensions. Moreover, it is a useful theoretical framework for comparative work.

In what follows, I shall review some literature that has pointed to particular resources as being important determinants of learning gains among LEP pupils. Then, I shall illustrate how particular organizational factors within school districts may operate to constrain the delivery of resources to these pupils.

REVIEW OF THE EFFECT OF CLASSROOM RESOURCES UPON PROGRAM IMPACTS

A review of the literature indicates that the allocation of some resources are highly correlated with positive achievement gains among LEP pupils.

Further, a review of various evaluation reports of successful* Title VII Bilingual Projects indicates that in their individual programs, there exists a high correlation between positive achievement gains and the utilization of these resources.

Teacher Competence

There have been many attempts to relate teacher process variables to pupil gain scores (Rosenshine and Furst, 1971; Medley and Mitzel, 1973; Brophy, 1975; and Calkins, et. al, 1976). In fact, Wideen, et. al (1977: 1) reports that there is a long history of studies attempting to identify characteristics of teachers whom students perceived as "good teachers." But in many cases, research on teacher effects have been inconsistent in their conclusions (Brophy, 1975; Calkins, et. al, 1976; Shavelson and Dempsey, 1977). There have been consistent results however, when pupil achievement has been related to teacher competency variables.

Calkins, et. al, (1976: 5) report that one line of research on teaching is the "effectiveness paradigm" which uses achievement outcomes as a measure of teacher effectiveness. Importantly, Burstein and Linn (1977: 2) specify that the effects of the school, the resources an individual receives, the individual's background and the influence of his community setting are phenomena which also effect pupil outcomes. Shavelson and Dempsey (1977: 5) suggest that under certain conditions some teachers may be more effective than others, and some teachers may also be more effective with particular groups of students. Cruickshank (1976: 59) and Brophy (1975: 11) both support these notions. By comparing task situations in both low and high socioeconomic status (SES) schools, they suggest that the teaching approach for either type of school may be vastly different. They found that successful teachers in high SES schools were task-oriented and had high expectations for their pupils, while in low SES schools, the successful teacher had to be more willing to take up personal matters with pupils and had to be more supportive of them. They were also found to have high expectations for their pupils.

Coupled with the trend for accountability in teaching and competency-based education programs, the relationship between effectiveness in teaching and achievement scores takes on a new significance for the classroom teacher. Cruickshank (1976: 59) argues that among the most promising variables related to reading and math achievement are: (1) use of small group interaction; (2) maximum direct interaction which includes monitoring and individual feedback; and, (3) the use of a variety of instructional materials.

Roberts and Becker (1976: 193) in a study of teaching effectiveness in industrial education suggest that measures of communication including dynamism, presentation skills, time spent interacting with students, and frequency of praise and banter are important variables. They find (p. 195)

---

*The following criteria were established by the California Title VII programs investigated as indicators of "success" in their respective programs:

1. The bilingual program is helping and/or at least not interfering with academic achievement.
2. The program is enhancing the achievement of all students, English dominant as well as Spanish dominant and bilingual.

that "effective teachers constantly moved from group to group, . . . the relationship between teachers and pupils is warm and supportive, . . . there is a great deal of positive reinforcement, . . . and, teachers tended to display confidence in the ability of their students."

Goodman and Hammond (1977: 208) in a study of learning-disabled children strongly imply that (special education) teachers need to be especially adept in their field in order to successfully teach academic skills. They argue that this cannot be done if the teacher does not have a thorough understanding of the skills they intend to teach. And Roberts and Becker (1976: 196) conclude that personal example is an important variable which modifies student behavior and influences their work. "Whether consciously or unconsciously, students tend to model themselves after the teacher, whether the teacher is good or bad."

Dual Language Competencies of the Staff

Consistent as a criterion of effectiveness among the Title VII Programs surveyed is the dual language competency of the staff. Each of the successful programs reported that the majority of their staff was bilingual, and either currently held a bilingual credential, a certificate of competency, or were enrolled in a program leading to that competency. In one case (Sante Fe, 1977-78), all staff, instructional aides, teachers, principals, the project director, the instructional materials coordinator and the project secretary were bilingual. The Goleta Project (1977-78) reports that all aides, with the exception of four pre-school teachers, are bilingual. Carpinteria (1976-77), reports that of eight teachers in the project, five were bilingual, and all eleven aides were bilingual. And, Santa Barbara (1978) reports that of the fifteen teachers in the program, nine are bilingual; of the sixteen instructional aides, fourteen are bilingual. A perusal of the AIR Project Descriptions (1977b) indicates that the majority of the staff in each program are reported to be either bilingual or of hispanic origin. Unfortunately, the programs fail (as does the AIR Report) to operationally define the extent of the "bilinguality" of the staff. Cervantes, (1978: 19) argues that a mere twenty-three percent of the programs' staff evaluated by AIR hold bilingual credentials.

Parent Involvement

The literature suggests that the active involvement of parents in the school district is highly correlated with the achievement outcome. Gillum, Schooley, and Novak (1977: 16) report that in districts where parents participated in deciding what was taught and also had the responsibility for working with the teachers and children, the achievement was higher than in those where parents were not involved. In particular, Fischer, Frederickson and Rosa (1976: 1) find that the active involvement of parents in the operation of bilingual education programs as teacher aides, school/community representatives, and members of advisory councils was one measure of the success of a bilingual program.

The Title VII projects reported a high degree of involvement of their "program" parents. Carpinteria (1976-77) reports that there is good community support for its program and that, generally, all the parents are very satisfied with it. The Goleta Project (1978) conducts a very active parent education program. This program consists of as many as twenty-seven different training sessions, which are all conducted bilingually. The remaining programs also report very active participation by their respective parent groups and community.

The majority of programs evaluated by AIR (February, 1977b) indicated that the involvement of project parents was minimal. In those programs where parents were involved, they were limited to participating in social activities and outings. A few programs reported that parents were involved in the decision-making process of the project, but most reported that the participation of parents did not affect the teachers and students in the classroom. One project did report that there is significant parent participation in school board and bilingual advisory committee meetings (No. 12: 12-10), and another reported that many of the parents are involved directly in the classroom (No. 14: 14-11).

Bilingual (Spanish English) As a Medium of Instruction

One of the most controversial issues encountered in education is a question of efficacy of a bilingual curriculum as a medium of instruction. The literature treats this resource both positively and negatively. However, there are indications that these apparent discrepancies may be due to considerations of assessment techniques or methodological inconsistencies. Cumins (1977: 5) finds that the "positive" studies take precautions to ensure that the subjects have similar degrees of competency in both languages, while "negative" studies fail to assess the relative degree of the bilingual competence of the subjects. Cumins and Gulatson (1974) report that bilinguals perform significantly higher on measures of both verbal and non-verbal intelligence. And, on tasks of concept formation, Liedke and Nelson (1968) found that bilingual children performed significantly better than unilingual children. She further suggests (1974) that children generally achieve high levels of competence in their dominant language when there is no danger of replacement by the second language. Her analysis (1977: 5) also suggests that a child's cognitive learning experiences are affected by the level of competency that the child achieves in both languages.

Ben-Zeev (1977: 94), in her studies of speech perception, concludes that the effort to become bilingual results in greater ability to process systemic structures and thus to re-organize incoming speech perception. Korn (1977: 40), during the development of instructional units correlating language and science instruction in a bilingual classroom, found that the language-science program enhanced the students' ability to deal with written English.

The Title VII projects surveyed report findings which coincide with the "positive" research studies. This suggests that a valuable insight can be gathered by analyzing the assessment techniques and methodological inconsistencies between programs which report negative impacts and those that report positive impacts. The Carpinteria Project (1977-78: 80) reports that achievement in reading of pupils is not suffering as a result of project participation and perhaps is being enhanced. The Santa Barbara Project (1977-78: 183) reports that the bilingual students performed better in English than both the Spanish dominant and the English dominant student, and they performed better in Spanish than the Spanish dominant student. The Golete Project (1977-78: 152) concludes that the results of its evaluation report tends to support the concept of developing the child's dominant language well before introducing the second language as a viable approach to educating their children. The Sante Fe Project (1978: 4) reports that the use of Spanish as a medium of instruction oscillated between thirty percent and fifty percent of the day. The strong correlation of the use of bilingual as a medium of instruction between the "positive" research findings and the evaluation reports of successful programs suggest that this particular variable may be one important indicator of the relative success or non-success of bilingual programs.

Classroom Methods and Structure

Nunney (1977: 1) comments that the lack of a systematic approach to determine the way in which students learn has been a major handicap for educators; he argues that the basic inability to clearly define those methods and techniques which are needed to deal with specific learner characteristics have only compounded the problem.

The relative value of certain classroom methods to the success of a program is highlighted by the Title VII Bilingual Projects. Carpinteria (1976-77: 19), Santa Barbara (1977-78: 27), and the Goleta Project (1977-78: 25) each report the development of domain referenced achievement tests which are specifically linked to their respective programs of instruction. These tests were especially useful because students in the respective projects were at different levels of development and thus they stressed individualized instruction.

The literature suggests that varying classroom strategies are necessary for different learning styles of individuals, and the literature also reports on the various impacts of classroom methods/structures on achievement. Lepke (1977: 16) suggests that selection of instructional strategies which offer maximum compatability with varying cognitive styles can be enhanced by analyzing the learning styles of the particular individuals involved, and Reinert (1977: 21) concludes that the magnitude of the diversity between individuals is so great that no single learning technique can be equally effective for every student. Giordano (1977: 39) argues that there are optimal methods of teaching bilingual children to read. Ideally, an "optimal" method would build on basic communicative strategies which are compatible with the major channel of language processing. Marshall (1977: 9) reports that the greatest growth in reading occurs in classrooms where students are involved in the learning task during the reading period. Marshall concludes that classroom structure and adequacy of implementation appear to be associated with reading scores.

Stability of Staff

An important indicator of a successful bilingual program, as suggested by the Title VII programs analyzed, is the stability of the staff, or the number of years the particular staff has worked with the respective programs. The Goleta Project (1976: v) reports that its director has been operating the program for the last seven years, while the Carpinteria Project (1976-77: 18) reports that the director has been with the project since the inception of its program. In turn, the Santa Barbara Project (1977-78: 25) felt that one of the weaknesses in the district's bilingual program was the lack of consistent leadership, while the Santa Fe Bilingual Program (1978: 3) reports that the year to year improvement of its project can be attributed to the great stability enjoyed by its staff. In this particular case, the director has been with the project for over six years, while all the teachers have been with the project since its inception (seven years).

AIR (1977b) reported that the overwhelming majority of teachers in the project evaluated had been with their respective projects three years or less. And a significant portion of those were in their first year of teaching in the bilingual program.

Number of Years the Student has been in the Bilingual Program

Another important resource or indicator of a "successful" program is the actual number of years that the pupil has been involved with the respective project. The conclusions reached by the Santa Fe Bilingual Project (1978: ii) indicate that over time, the Title VII students showed increasing capability in English language skills (particularly in reading) and in mathematics. The Title VII students over time also outperformed, in the majority of cases, the non-Title VII students in reading and math, and one group studied, surpassed and/or matched national norms in reading and in math. The Santa Barbara Project (1977-78: 154) reports that, after four years of bilingual instruction, test results show that the pupils appear to be meeting program expectations (p. 41) and that, as the grade level increases, more students in the programs are reading at higher levels as measured by the CLOZE tests (p. 80). Moreover, the third year Spanish-surnamed students seemed to do better than did first or second year students, and in a number of instances, the English-dominant students were performing at higher levels as the number of years in the program increased. The Carpinteria Project (1976-77: 51) reports that there is a slight increase in performance for numbers of years in the program. And, the Goleta Bilingual Project (1977-78: 89) reports that generally the third year pupils, in all comparison groups, achieved at a higher level than did the second year at the same grade level.

The review of the literature on classroom resources and their impact on program outcomes, suggests that strong relationships do exist. Achievement gains are influenced by the allocation and utilization of particular resources. A survey of several Title VII projects suggests that particular resources are effective indicators of successful programs. Specifically, the following resources appeared consistent in their association with program success as measured by individual student outcomes. Those resources indicated are:

1. teacher competence
2. dual-language competencies of the staff
3. parent involvement
4. bilingual (English/Spanish) as a medium of instruction
5. classroom methods and structure
6. stability of staff
7. numbers of years the student has been in the project

It is not my position that these resources are the only indicators of "successful" bilingual projects nor do I mean to imply that, in and by themselves, they will constitute a successful program. These are at best, some indicators of success, and it is reasonable to assume that there exists a universe of resources, as yet unexplored, that would serve a similar purpose. Granting that certain resources do affect achievement gains, let us now shift focus and explore how the school district organization affects the delivery of these resources to their clients. It is my hope that if we can understand the conditions under which an organization makes decisions to allocate or to utilize particular resources, then we can more clearly begin to understand the strengths and weaknesses of that organization when success of a program is measured by achievement outcomes.

The Political Economy of the Local School District

Of course, the local school district can be characterized as a complex organization. The political economy approach to the analysis of complex organizations leads us to focus on the school district as an organization in which change arises as a result of both internal and external processes (Wamsley and Zald, 1973: 16). The dominant concern of this model is with the political and economic processes of the organization. More traditional concerns of organizational analysis are subordinated and are only important in so far as they articulate with the political and economic processes (Zald, 1970: 225). Thus, the school district is conceptualized as consisting of an internal and external polity and of an internal and external economy.

It is important to clarify at this point that it is not my intent, nor is it necessary for my present purposes, to present an exhaustive theory about the political economy of the local school district. My purpose is a more limited one; it is to illustrate the pertinence of the mechanisms of this particular model for the study of bilingual educational programs.

Utilizing this model, I hope to illustrate how the political economy of local school districts affects the delivery of those resources within the school district that, in turn, determine the success or non-success of a bilingual instructional program. Since space does not permit a detailed illustration of how the political economy of local school districts affects the various resources I have previously discussed, I shall focus on one type of resource, namely staff competency.

Medley (1977: 6) suggests that observed measures of effectiveness are indicators of teacher competence, i.e., teachers who are more effective are also more competent. Therefore, a strong relationship between teacher effectiveness and a particular behavior can be interpreted as indicating that such behavior is characteristic of competent teachers. Shavelson and Dempsey (1977: 607) believe that certain teaching behaviors are more effective with certain groups of students; they suggest that teacher effectiveness, as measured by pupil outcomes, may depend on the luck of matching a teacher with a particular group of students.

Internal Polity and Bilingual Programs

The internal polity of an organization is defined as the internal power system of the organization (Zald, 1970: 237). It is the systematic manner in which power is distributed, mobilized, utilized, or limited in achieving or maintaining a set of goals or values.

When a bilingual program is introduced to a district, organizational elites oftentimes view it as a threat to the internal structure of the organization. In particular, when changes are advocated by minority groups, they are oftentimes perceived as politically motivated and institutionally threatening (Teitelbaum and Hiller, 1977: 11).

The threat to the internal structure of the organization posed by bilingual programs has two sources: first, there are the external sources such as community proponents of the program, state or federal agencies, and legislation (i.e., the external polity). Second, there are the internal sources. These include program proponents among the regular staff, the project director, teachers, aides and volunteer parents. The external sources limit the options of the executive elites and, in so doing, pose a threat to their autonomy. However, it is the internal sources that are the most politically threatening to the school district.

Organizational change is inevitable when bilingual programs are introduced to the school district. This change effects district policy, products, educational goals, existing technology and interunit relations.

One way in which district elites oppose change is through the process of succession in central positions. When changes in district policy by state and federal legislation are mandated, the district elite (though bound by the law) will interpret those mandates (as much as their power will allow) in favor of their own values and sentiments. This process of interpretation does not preclude attempts on their part to sabotage the spirit and intent of the legislation. In no place is this sabotage more apparent than in the structures and processes of the succession system.

The standard pattern of recruiting key personnel is determined both by the perceived requirements of top officers and the opportunities to develop those competencies provided in the organization (Zald, 1970: 247). District elites recruit both project directors and teachers whose values and inclinations most closely resemble their own. It is not surprising, therefore, that the State of California (State Board of Education, 1978: 27) reports that only thirty-seven percent of the bilingual classroom teachers were able to demonstrate skill awareness and applicability in the students' primary language.

Project directors are often brought up through the ranks into a directorship directly from the classroom with little or no administrative experience. Given this pattern of recruitment to decision-making positions in bilingual programs, a pattern that has its basis in the internal polity of school district organizations, it is clear that bilingual programs have, at least in this respect, been programmed to fail on the basis of administrative incompetence.

The Internal/External Economies and Bilingual Programs

Economies of an organization are systems for producing and exchanging goods. "Basic to any economy . . . , are considerations of specialization, role differentiation and divisions of labor. Specialization and differentiation within an organization . . . are largely functions of the state of the technology for producing a specific product, . . ." (Zald, 1970: 249). The internal economy of the school district is mainly concerned with the nature of the technical task, that is, with the raw materials to be processed, the divisions of labor and incentive systems necessary to task accomplishment, and the allocation of resources.

In an era of declining enrollment and teacher reduction, (Commission for Teacher Preparation and Licensing, 1978: 2) there is an increasing need for new and qualified bilingual teachers. McCurdy (1978) reports that the steady decline in overall enrollment will continue in California. The Office of the Superintendent of Public Instruction (1978: 10) estimates that while the Anglo student population is steadily declining, the LEP student population is gradually increasing. Moreover, with the recently proposed cutbacks in state spending caused by Proposition 13, the teachers' unions are increasingly pressuring the school districts not to release teachers who otherwise would be laid off. Instead there is pressure to place them in other programs.

The utilization of monolingual teachers for bilingual programs has been and continues to be a very real option for many school districts in California. Federal bilingual legislation makes no requirement that bilingual program teachers actually be "bilingual"; it does, however, recognize the lack of "adequately trained" professional personnel (Title VII ESEA, 1974). Schneider (1977: 184) has estimated from a sampling of Title VII projects across the country, a total need for roughly 35,000 trained bilingual teachers; there were approximately one-fourth that number of teachers in Title VII projects. Similarly, in the case of the State of California, there is a projected high level of demand for bilingual teachers and a projected substantial shortfall of such teachers (Commission for Teachers Preparation and Licensing, 1978: 27). California (Chacon-Moscone, 1976), does require that bilingual program teachers be "competent." However, in light of the teacher shortage, the law permits districts to waive the competency standard for a period of two years provided that non-qualified teachers are enrolled in programs of competency development.

The consequence of this situation is that in some districts choosing not to teach in the bilingual program is tantamount to not teaching at all. In at least one district of which I am aware, most monolingual teachers did not want to be in the bilingual program and were opposed to the concept of bilingual instruction. For the monolingual teacher, having to teach in a bilingual classroom may be a negative incentive which is also likely to be interpreted as a negative sanction. Given these conditions under which many monolingual teachers are transferred into bilingual programs, there appears to be operating, in effect, a system of negative incentives which may be importantly undermining the effectiveness of bilingual programs.

External Polity and Bilingual Programs

The external polity of an organization is defined as those groups or positions which have an active and somewhat organized influence on the process of decision making (Zald, 1970: 233). The relationship between "relevant others", (i.e., in this case proponents and opponents of bilingual instruction, who are effected by and interested in influencing the policies for which the district has primary responsibilities) form the basis for the external polity.

The introduction of bilingual programs into a school district effects the external political environment of the school district. Where once the amount and distribution of limited resources to district-approved and community sanctioned programs were the political norm, the imposition of mandated programs of instruction designed primarily for the non-typical pupil has upset the balance of the existing political relationships of the district. The "relevant others" that make up the policy subsystems are forced to reassess their political "niche" (Wamsley and Zald, 1973: 26). A case in point is the conflicting interests of the school district in relation to teachers' unions and bilingual proponents.

Whose interests take precedence: those of the mandated bilingual program, and the needs of its clients, or those of the powerful teacher union and its client, the classroom teacher? In this political question, there exists a dilemma.

I mentioned previously that the State Bilingual Education Act (Chacon-Moscone, 1976) stipulated that all teachers in bilingual educational programs in California must be "competent" and that Anglo student enrollments in California are declining significantly, while LEP students are increasing dramatically. In its relationship with the teachers' unions, this situation affects the school district in a most pernicious manner.

The district finds itself in the position of either violating a legal mandate or of violating a legitimate and legal contract with the teachers' unions. In its relationship to the external polity, the school district is under pressure to fulfill its primary mission, that of teaching the children, while trying to satisfy its political and legal responsibilities. Assuming that the district decides to hire additional competent teachers, the unions will balk at the possible release of member teachers who are not effective, but are tenured. If on the other hand, the district moves ineffective teachers into bilingual programs, it can expect the state or "relevant others" to raise questions of non-compliance. What options are left to the school district? Whose interests will the district serve? At what expense?

The previous discussion of the political economy of the local school district and bilingual programs is meant to illustrate the complexities of the effects of bilingual education on the school district. Clearly, this discussion is not meant to be an elaboration of the parameters of that complexity. The discussion only serves to highlight, from a complex organizational perspective, a limited number of potential processes and problems whose interrelationships must be understood if policy makers are to derive useful data from which to make clear decisions about bilingual policy. It is entirely too simplistic to look exclusively to educational program impact, as measured by achievement gains, as the single valid basis of policy decisions.

The political economy model of change in complex organizations provides a useful perspective because it allows a more "inclusive" perspective of the organizational dynamic which takes in raw material and is expected to produce an acceptable impact. Knowing that an impact has been positive only tells us that whatever we are doing may be working; if the impact is negative, we only know that what we are doing is not working. This is insufficient for the purpose of determining policy. The questions that need to be answered are: Why does a program work? What are the characteristics of a program that account for achievement gains? Under what conditions can we expect a program to "succeed"?

BIBLIOGRAPHY

American Institutes for Research (AIR), *Evaluation of the Impact of ESEA Title VII Spanish/English Bilingual Education Project.* Vol. 1: Study Design and Interim Findings. Palo Alto, California, February, 1977 (a)

American Institutes for Research (AIR), *Evaluation of the Impact of ESEA Title VII Spanish/English Bilingual Education Project.* Project Descriptions. Palo Alto, California, February 1977 (b)

American Institutes for Research (AIR), *Evaluation of the Impact of ESEA Title VII Spanish/English Bilingual Education Project.* Final Report Palo Alto, California, 1978

Anthony, B.C.M. The Identification and Measurement of Classroom Environment Process Variables Related to Academic Achievement. Unpublished doctoral dissertation. University of Chicago, 1977.

Ben-Zeev, Sandra, "The Effect of Bilingualism in Children From Spanish-English Low Economic Neighborhoods on Cognitive Development and Cognitive Strategy." *Working Papers on Bilingualism,* No. 14. Ontario Institute For Studies in Education, Toronto. Bilingual Education Project. October 1977: 94.

Brophy, Jere E., *Teacher Behaviors Related to Learning by Low vs. High Socio-economic Status Early Childhood Students.* Report No. 75-5. National Institute of Education (DHEW). Washington, D.C., d. 75. Paper presented at the Annual Meeting of the American Educational Research Association. Washington, D.C., April 1975.

Burstein, Leigh and Linn, Robert L. *The Identification of Teacher Effects in the Presence of Heterogenous Within-Class Relations of Input to Outcomes.* April, 1977. Paper presented at the 61st Annual Meeting of the American Educational Research Association. New York: April 4-8, 1977.

Calkins, Dick, Godbout, Robert, Lee, H. Poyner, and Kagle, C.L. *Relationships Between Pupil Achievement and Characteristics of Observed Teacher Behavior Distributions.* Research Report No. 6. Texas University, Austin. Research and Development Center for Teacher Education. January 6, 1976.

Carpinteria Unified School District, Carpinteria, California. *Evaluation of the Carpinteria Bilingual Project Funded Under ESEA Title VII,* PL-89-10. (Project Number 403 CH 70085) Final Report 1976-77. November 1977.

Cervantes, Robert, "An Exemplary Consafic Chingatropic Assessment: The AIR Report." Paper presented at Association of Mexican-American Educator's Conference. San Francisco, California. October 26-28, 1978.

Chacon-Moscone *Bilingual-Bicultural Education Act of 1976.* AB 1329. Section 1. Chapter 57.6 added to Division 6 of Education Code. Sub-Section 5757.10, State of California.

Commission for Teacher Preparation and Licensing, *Report of the Supply of and Demand for Bilingual Teachers in School Districts in California.* Presented to the California State Legislature. September 1, 1978: 2.

County Superintendent of Schools, Santa Barbara County, Santa Barbara, California. *Evaluation of the Goleta Bilingual Project Funded Under Title VII,* PL-89-10 (Project Number 403 CH 80031) Final Report 1977-78, November 1978.

Cruickshank, Donald R., "Synthesis of Selected Recent Research on Teacher

Effects," *Journal of Teacher Education*, Spring 1976, Vol. XXVII No. 1: 57-60.

Cumins, J. and Gulatson, M., "Some Effects on Bilingualism in Cognitive Functioning", in S. Carey (ed.) *Bilingualism, Biculturalism and Education*. Proceedings from the Conference at College Universitaire Saint Jean, The University of Alberta. 1974.

Cumins, J. and Gulatson, M., "Bilingual Education and Cognition", *Alberta Journal of Educational Research*, 1974, *20*: 259-266.

Cumins, Jane, *The Cognitive Development of Bilingual Children: A Review of Recent Research*. Center for the Study of Mental Retardation. The University of Alberta, Edmonton, Canada. 1977.

Fischer, Joseph, Frederickson, Charles, and Rosa, Carlos, *Parents Career Aspirations for Their Children Enrolled in Bilingual Programs*. Monograph No. 2. Chicago Board of Education, Illinois. Department of Research and Evaluation. March 1976.

Gillum, Ronald, Schooley, Daniel, and Novak, Paul D., *The Effects of Parental Involvement on Student Achievement in Three Michigan Performance Contracting Programs*. Paper presented at the Annual Meeting of the American Educational Research Association. New York: April 1977.

Giordano, Gerard, *Neurological Research on Language and the Implications for Teaching Bilingual Children to Read*. Occasional Papers on Linguistics No. 1. Southern Illinois University, Carbondale, Illinois, Department of Linguistics. Proceedings of the International Conference of Frontiers in Language Proficiency and Dominance Testing. April 13-21, 1977.

Goodman, Gay and Hammond, Brad, "An Assessment of Phonics Knowledge in Special Education Teachers", *Reading Horizons*, Vol. 17, No. 2, Winter 1977: 206-210.

Kelleman, Steven L., *Summary of the Final Evaluation Report, Proyecto de Culturas Unidas. ESEA Title VII*. Educational Consult Systems, Inc. Oxnard School District, 1977-78.

Korn, Caroline A., *Teaching Language Through Science in a Primary Bilingual Classroom*. Masters Thesis, University of San Francisco. August 1977.

Lambert, Wallace E., "The Effects of Bilingual Education on the Individual: Cognitive and Sociocultural Consequences", as cited in Korn, Caroline A., *Teaching Language Through Science in a Primary Bilingual Classroom*. Masters Thesis, University of San Francisco. 1977: 39.

Lepke, Helen S., "Discovering Student Learning Styles Through Cognitive Style Mapping", in Schulz, Renate A. (ed.) *Personalized Foreign Language Instruction: Learning Styled and Teaching Options*. Selected Readings from the 1977 Joint Meeting of the Central State Conference and the Ohio Modern Language Teacher's Association.

Liedke, W.W. and Nelson, L.D. "Concept Formation and Bilingualism", *Alberta* Journal of Educational Research, 1968, *14*: 225-232.

Marshall, Hermine E., *Variations in Classroom Structure and Growth in Reading*. Paper presented at the Annual Meeting of the American Psychological Association. San Francisco, California. August 1977.

McCurdy, Jack, "Segregation in Schools Grows, Survey Reveals", reported in *The Los Angeles Times*, October 19, 1978.

Medley, D.M. and Mitzel, H.E., "Some Behavioral Correlates of Teacher Effectiveness", *Journal of Educational Psychology,* 1959, *50:* 239-246.

Medley, D.M., "Closing the Gap Between Research in Teacher Effectiveness and the Teacher Education Curriculum". *Journal of Research and Development in Education,* Fall 1973: 39-46.

National Assessment and Dissemination Center, School of Education, California State University, Los Angeles. *Longitudinal Study Title VII Bilingual Program,* Santa Fe Public Schools, Sante Fe, New Mexico. June 9, 1978.

Medley, Donald M., *Teacher Competence and Teacher Effectiveness: A Review of Process-Product Research.* American Association of Colleges for Teacher Education. Washington, D.C., August 1977.

Nunney, Derek N., "Educational Cognitive Style: A Basis for Personalizing Foreign Language Instruction", in Schulz, Renate A. (ed.), *Personalizing Foreign Language Instruction: Learning Styles and Teaching Options.* Papers from the 1977 Joint Meeting of the Central States Conference and the Ohio Modern Language Teacher's Association.

Office of the Superintendent, Santa Barbara County Schools, Santa Barbara. *Planning and Implementing Bilingual/Bicultural Programs: A Handbook for School Administrators,* June 1976.

Public Law 90-247, Title VII ESEA, The Bilingual Education Act of 1968.

Reinert, Harry, "Elsie is No Bull! or: On Utilizing Information Concerning Student Learning Styles", in Schulz, Renate A., (ed.), *Personalizing Foreign Language Instruction: Learning Styles and Teaching Options.* Selected Papers from the 1977 Joint Meeting of the Central States Conference and the Ohio Modern Language Teacher's Association.

Roberts, Churchill L., and Becker, Samuel L., "Communication and Teaching Effectiveness in Industrial Education", *American Educational Research Journal,* Summer 1976, Vol. 13, No. 3: 181-197.

Rosenshine, B. and Furst, N., "The Use of Direct Observation to Study Teaching", *Second Handbook of Research in Teaching.* (ed. Travers) Chicago: Rand McNally and Company.

Santa Barbara School District, Santa Barbara, California. *Evaluation of the Santa Barbara Elementary Schools Bilingual Project Funded Under ESEA Title VII,* PL-89-10. (Project Number 403 DH 60186) Final Report 1977-78, November 1978.

Schneider, Susan G., *Revolution, Reaction or Reform 1974 Bilingual Education Act,* Las Americas. 1977.

Senate Report 93-763, Bilingual Education Act of 1968: Title VII ESEA and Education Amendments of 1974.

Shavelson, Richard and Dempsey, Nancy. *Generalizability of Measures of Teacher Effectiveness and Teaching Process.* Beginning Teacher Evaluation Process. Technical Series Reports No. 75-4-2. Far West Lab for Educational Research and Development, 1977, San Francisco, California.

Superintendent of Public Instruction, *Education for Limited English Speaking and Non-English Speaking Students.* Part II. Presented to State Board of Education, July 1978.

Tietelbaum, Herbert and Hiller, Richard J., "Bilingual Education: The Legal Perspective", in *Current Perspectives: Law.* Center for Applied Linguistics. Vol. 3, September 1977.

Torrance, E.P. and Parent, E., *Characteristics of Mathematics Teachers That*

Affect Student's Learning. U.S. Office of Education Cooperative Research Project No. 1020, Contract No. S.A.E.-8993. Minneapolis, Minnesota, 1966.

Walberg, H.J., "Predicting Class Learning". *American Educational Research Journal*, 1969, 6: 529-543.

Wamsley, Gary L. and Zald, Mayer N., *The Political Economy of Public Organizations: A Critique and Approach to the Study of Public Administration*. D.C. Heath and Company, Lexington, Massachusetts. 1973.

Wideen, Marvin F., Kennedy, Barry J., and Bettschen, Catherine, "The Identification of Teacher Process Variables Affecting Student Outcomes in Two Alternative Science Curriculum Treatment Settings". Paper presented at the Annual Meeting of the American Educational Research Association. New York: April 4-8, 1977.

Zald, Mayer N., "Political Economy: A Framework for Comparative Analysis", in *Power in Organizations*, Mayer N. Zald (ed.) Vanderbilt University. 1970: 222.

THE BILINGUAL EDUCATION ACT AND THE PUERTO RICAN COMMUNITY:

The Politics of Implementing Federal Policy at the Local Level

Lois Saxelby Steinberg

This paper is based on a four-year longitudinal study of the implementation of the federal Bilingual Education Act in New York City. The purpose of the study was two-fold: (1) to develop a theoretical framework for the sociological analysis of the integration of new groups based on changes in decision making and participation which reflect increased federal initiatives in local school problems, and (2) to apply this framework to an analysis of the participation of the Puerto Rican community in the implementation of the Bilingual Education Act.

The Theoretical Framework

For this analysis, integration is defined in terms of horizontal and vertical linkage. Horizontal linkage refers to the development of cohesive communities at the neighborhood level, including voluntary associations to promote group interests. Vertical linkage refers to relationships between local community members and host society representatives. This definition was derived from Warren's (1963) thesis on the "great change" in the American community, literature on the political machine and theory and research on community power. Application of network concepts to a comparison of the patterns of participation associated with the "old" political machine and those associated with the "new" bureaucratic machines provides a means to identify the requirements for the integration of new groups in the present urban context.

By network we mean a set of units—individuals, associations, ethnic groups—connected or linked to each other. The units to be studied here are individuals and groups that were involved in the visible activities to promote bilingual education in New York City.

The reason for employing the network concept in this analysis is that it provides a means to compare events that involve a variety of structural relationships (for example, negotiations between individuals acting as independent agents versus those between representatives of formal organizations), and patterns of participation at different points in time. More important, for our purposes, is the fact that we can study relationships between actors at different levels (e.g., the local community, the city, state or federal) of a policy system.

A number of studies which analyzed the effects of community action programs suggest that variations in local implementation of federal programs reflect contextual differences, such as the size of the "target" population, its pre-existing leadership and organizational development as well as existing power arrangements.

One way to study the effects of federal programs is in terms of the extent to which the resources were used to develop influence networks at the local level. A basic assumption underlying the network approach, consistent with the community action program evaluations, is that networks are largely determined by structural and environmental factors (Fischer et al., 1977; Kadushin, 1977; Laumann, 1976; Merton, 1957). These include the various institutionalized statuses occupied by an actor, the norms governing interaction within these statuses, as well as informal relationships developed in both institutionalized and non-institutionalized settings. To put it more simply, a person's social position has a strong influence on who he meets, where the interaction occurs and the incentives that will maintain the relationship.

To apply this line of thinking to the study of political participation, we would begin with the assumption that the basic reason for widespread political apathy within certain subgroups is primarily a function of structural and cultural rather than individual factors. These structural factors would include elements of the decision-making system such as the rules governing relationships between leaders and constituents (Pitkin, 1967; Peterson, 1979), opportunities for new groups to participate in the political organizations dominated by established groups, resources to develop independent organizations to articulate and mediate the group's interests and subgroup norms (e.g., cultural patterns may foster dense interpersonal relationships among family and friends rather than instrumental relationships outside the intimate circle).

When the participation of subgroups is restricted by the above and other circumstances, at least two types of resources are needed to promote change:

1. incentives to enable the group to develop a power base
2. machinery to mediate conflicting interests between old and new groups

The political machine is an example of a system which met the above conditions and thus was able to perform the integrative function for earlier immigrant groups. The machine generated horizontal integration in a period when a variety of institutions—the church, political parties, ethnic associations—promoted interaction at the neighborhood level (Clark, 1975).

As described in the literature, the networks associated with the political machine are similar to those characteristic of traditional society. They were primarily neighborhood based, homogeneous, informal and multistranded (Mitchell, 1969). Such networks tend to be found in small territorially bounded communities with relatively low levels of social differentiation where the same individuals have opportunities to interact in a variety of institutional contexts. Decisions related to the allocation of public goods and resources could, under this model, be controlled by decision centers close to the grass roots participants.

The political boss promoted and protected the ethnic community through vertical linkage to a city-level decision center which controlled the resources (incentives) distributed to the neighborhood. The machine accomplished this through its ability to create and provide jobs and other forms of patronage in exchange for votes (Clark, 1975). Thus it regulated two functions: the organization of political participation and the distribution of public goods and services.

The literature on collective decisions, participation, and social networks in contemporary American society suggests that changes in the urban decision making structure in many metropolitan areas, as well as small communities, have created conditions which make locality-based interpersonal networks ineffective mechanisms for influencing the policies related to the delivery of local services. Instead, political effectiveness for many issues is dependent on the linkage of professional or specialized networks with extra-local groups—or aspatial rather than horizontal networks (Greer, 1972; Litt, 1970; Craven and Wellman, 1973). Furthermore, in contrast to the earlier period where political effectiveness for ethnic minorities could rely on strong ties or group solidarity, there is evidence to suggest that access to decisions may require that some members of the network develop "weak ties" (Granovetter, 1973) at both the grass roots and extra-local levels.

Warren (1963) argued that the transfer of decision making from local to state and national levels had strengthened vertical linkage (between local and extra-local agencies) and fragmented horizontal linkage (or the integration of community based institutions and groups). Processes associated with modernization (social differentiation, industrialization, migration and so forth) tend to promote centralized and specialized decision centers. While some problems require national and/or regional solutions, others still require local solutions. However, many localities lack the resources to enable local residents to develop effective problem-solving or coping mechanisms (Warrne, 1973; O'Brien, 1975).

Some of the changes which eroded the influence of horizontal grass-roots groups began with the enactment of New Deal legislation and the institution of urban government reforms. The changes are related to at least five dimensions: (1) the base of power, (2) leadership recruitment, (3) the sources of rewards or incentives to induce participation, (4) criteria for allocating government jobs, and (5) decision centers.

The differences in these dimensions in traditional and contemporary communities stem from the increasing dependence of the local area on state and federal resources, the growth of large-scale service bureaucracies, government reforms, the creation of powerful occupational associations, and the erosion of community-based voluntary associations (including political parties). Whereas power was centralized informally by the political machine in the earlier period, in the present period it has been fragmented or dispersed by these trends. Decision-making has become specialized and the leadership which dominates decisions in a particular issue area is developed through the occupational or professional group rather than the geographically-based community (Iannaccone and Wiles, 1971; Gittell, 1967; Rogers, 1968; David and Peterson, 1973; Merton, 1957; Litt, 1971; Lamb, 1975).

In place of the dense, affective, and multi-stranded interpersonal networks characteristic of traditional society, the most effective networks for influencing the policy process today are likely to be diffuse, instrumental and single-stranded (Janowitz, 1967). A comparison of the characteristics of influence structures under the political machines and the new bureaucratic machines, shown in Table 1, illustrates these points. Besides being aspatial and specialized, participation is more sophisticated and formal. It is difficult for citizens at the community level to develop relationships that can link the grass roots to government structures (Litt, 1979; Lamb, 1975).

TABLE 1

COMPARISON OF THE INFLUENCE STRUCTURES UNDER THE POLITICAL MACHINES AND BUREAUCRATIC MACHINES

Characteristics	Political Machine	Bureaucratic Machine
Location of power base	Locality (neighborhood)	Aspatial (occupational group)
Sources of resources/ rewards	City levels	Federal, state level
Leadership	Generalist	Specialist
Scope of vertical linkage	Narrow	Broad
Horizontal linkage	Integrated	Fragmented
Interpersonal ties	Dense, affective, multi-stranded, homogeneous	Diffuse, instrumental, single-stranded, heterogeneous

Implications for the Integration of New Groups

It has been argued that under the conditions associated with the political machine, the integration of new groups began at the community level with the development of multi-stranded relationships between individuals and groups which supported the upward mobility of selected members of the group. These individuals created the linkage between the grass roots and the host society. The major factors contributing to the process were a stable and centralized decision-making structure and an expanding city economy.

In the contemporary period, the integration of new groups is impeded by changes in the economy and decision-making structure which have increased the scale of participation and promote extra-local or aspatial patterns of participation, dependence on federal and state authorities for additional resources, and occupational group control of the implementation process.

Given the above assumptions, a federal effort to create the functional equivalent to the political machine (e.g., a mechanism to integrate ethnic minorities) would require:

1. The activation of an aspatial ethnic network
2. Resources to create vertical linkage—or access to decision-makers to develop minority access to jobs
3. Vertical linkage between upwardly mobile members of the group and the grass roots community
4. Some degree of horizontal linkage between the ethnic group and other groups at the community level

This study examines the extent to which the federal Bilingual Education Act has provided resources for Puerto Ricans in New York City to create the linkages specified above.

Methods

The key concepts incorporated in the conceptual scheme are aspatial network, linkage, access and grass roots community.

Based on Schon's (1971) definition, the concept of network used here refers to a set of elements connected to each other.

"Aspatial network" refers to a set of individuals whose relationships are based on common bonds, commitment and interests which are not bound to a specific neighborhood or locality.

"Linkage" refers to "any current pattern of behavior which exists between two subsystems and is supported by both" (Aveni, 1977).

Two types of linkage were examined in this study: horizontal and vertical. Horizontal linkage refers to interrelationships between units at one level of a social system. The linkages we looked for were between Puerto Ricans at the neighborhood and city level (this included links between organizations and individuals).

Vertical linkages refers to connections between members of the network and individuals or groups at different levels of the system. These could include governmental and non-governmental groups.

Access refers to evidence of Puerto Rican influence in decision making in this case the educational system. It will be indicated by two factors:

1. A decision that increases the number of jobs for Puerto Rican teachers
2. A means to weaken the bureaucracy's control over implementation of the decision.

A comparative longitudinal design was employed, including data from 1967 through 1977. A variety of field and historical methods were used to identify: (1) pre-existing power arrangements, (2) the key decisions related to bilingual education policy in New York City, (3) the network of activists involved in these decisions, and (4) evidence indicating access to jobs in the school system.

Data sources included:

1. Interviews with participants and observers of key events; representatives of groups involved in federal hearings, nationally known bilingual education scholars, administrators in the New York City school system, the New York State Education Department and USOE, New York State legislators and legislative staff assistants, bilingual education teachers, and lawyers involved in the *Aspira* case. Almost 100 people were interviewed between 1973 and 1976.
2. Observation of national and New York City bilingual education conferences.
3. Analysis of federal laws, regulations and legislative hearings.
4. Reports on achievement of Puerto Rican students in the NYC schools.
5. U.S. Census Bureau reports.
6. Transcripts of hearings in the *Aspira* case.
7. Ethnic surveys of NYC school personnel.
8. Newspaper reports.

Identification of the Aspatial Network. Four approaches were used to identify network members and their relationships: (1) decisional—the visible participants in key decisions; (2) "snowball" technique—the visible participants were asked to identify others who participated in the events; (3) content analysis of documents to determine key participants in past events, and (4) observation of the behavior of network members at professional conferences and meetings.

Pre-existing Power Arrangements. A number of earlier studies identified several factors that restricted the ability of the Puerto Ricans to develop a community-level power base—or horizontal network—which could be used to promote access to the decision-making structure. Since this analysis is concerned with educational issues, we have looked for evidence of or access to *three* levels of decision-making relevant to the New York City situation: the state legislature, the New York City Board of Education, and, starting in 1970, community school boards.

Although Puerto Ricans, by 1970, constituted ten percent of the city's total population, its ability to achieve political representation proportionate to its size was impeded by its youthfulness, low educational levels, geographic dispersal, high levels of residential mobility and inability to speak English. Fitzpatrick (1971) observed that the adjustment or "assimilation" of the Puerto Ricans had been more difficult than for earlier groups because of their inability to concentrate or "cluster" in geographical areas or to use the Catholic Church as a basis for political mobilization and social support. Urban renewal and federally-imposed housing regulations have contributed to residential patterns which frequently place Puerto Ricans in close proximity to blacks, thus forcing them to compete with another disadvantaged minority for economic and political resources (Rosenberg and Beardon, 1974). These factors also affect their position in the Catholic parishes where they are usually a minority (Fitzpatrick, 1971).

These residential patterns limit opportunities for Puerto Ricans to form voluntary associations at the neighborhood level as well as the ability of city-level Puerto Rican organizations to promote grass-roots participation. This conclusion is based on the assumption that "social associations depend on opportunities for social contacts" (Blau, 1977).

Puerto Rican Voluntary Associations. Ethnic organizations, including self-help and religious groups, are regarded as an important factor in promoting the social, political and economic adjustment of earlier immigrant groups (Glazer and Moynihan, 1970). Other factors cited to explain the difficulty Puerto Ricans have experienced in developing strong community organizations related to differences between the Puerto Rican migration and earlier ethnic groups, including citizenship status, cultural diversity and changes in the urban context.

Puerto Ricans are the first non-English-speaking migrants to possess citizenship status on arrival. Cultural differences within the group are related to regional variations on the Island (Steward, 1957). The paternalistic Island culture did not promote participation in formal voluntary associations (Rogler, 1972). Their physical separation from the homeland is not as great as that for earlier groups and travel by air facilitates the maintenance of intimate ties to the Island (Fitzpatrick, 1971). The largest group to arrive in New York (between 1950 and 1960) came at a time when decision making was specialized or fragmented and more formal (Sayre and Kaufman, 1965). Finally, because of changes in the city's occupational structure (decline in unskilled jobs available to new groups), they are more dependent than earlier groups on the school system in order to attain the credentials required for upward mobility (Fitzpatrick, 1971).

A discussion of the failure of the Puerto Rican community to develop a political voice at a 1967 conference on group problems, stressed differences related to generational conflicts, leadership diversity and other internal sources of friction. Puerto Rican voluntary associations were described by Puerto Ricans as tending to be specialized, unconnected and dominated by professional rather than community-oriented interests. There was a need expressed for "true" leadership which could unify the various factions and develop consensus around specific issues.

There is little data available on community level Puerto Rican associations. At the 1967 conference representatives of the group reported that the associations that did exist at this level tended to be "home town groups" which were expressive rather than instrumental in nature. During the controversies over school decentralization, there were several sections of the city where Puerto Ricans were active but they were able to develop a stable organization in only one borough, the Bronx. This organization, United Bronx Parents, did not play a significant role in city level decisions related to bilingual education.

City level organizations. Beginning in the mid-1950s with the establishment of the Office of the Puerto Rican Commonwealth in New York City, designed to assist new migrants in their adjustment to city life, a variety of instrumental associations emerged. Groups like the Puerto Rican Merchants Association, the Puerto Rican Civil Service Employees Association and the Puerto Rican Forum, reflected the development of independent but "somewhat unconnected issue-oriented organizations" (Diaz, 1967).

There was a proliferation of independent and public-sponsored Puerto Rican groups in the 1960s such as the Puerto Rican Family Institute, Aspira, the Puerto Rican Community Development Project, the East Harlem Tenant Association, and the Puerto Rican Educators Association.

The School System. Prior to the decentralization of the New York City school system, education policy was formally vested in the Board of Education, a non-salaried, nine-member body appointed by the Mayor. The ability of the Board and its appointed superintendent to innovate was constrained by: (1) Board of Education by-laws, (2) the Board of Superintendents, (3) State Education Law, and (4) the professional groups representing teachers and administrators.

According to Sayre and Kaufman (1965), the supervisory group with the greatest influence was the Board of Superintendents whose ability to thwart change was facilitated by the Board of Examiners which devised procedures promoting "insiders." School officials, these authors found, yielded to four groups: the three major religious groups, the Board of Estimate, State Education Department and organized teachers.

Later and more detailed studies attributed the inability of the schools to meet the needs of the city's changing population to the closed nature of the decision-making system. One analyst, who favored decentralization as a means to broaden the base of participation and thereby promote innovation, warned that:

> Any effort to change the school system and expand civic participation must face the concentration of power in the professional bureaucracy and the resistance by the bureaucracy to any plan that would erode its power. Thus, any plan for change must have as its first objective the diminution of bureaucratic power. Meaningful plans for the reorganization of large city school systems must embody a formula for the decentralization of bureaucratic authority and the expansion of outside nonprofessional influences. (Gittell, 1967)

In 1969 the New York State Legislature passed the Decentralization Law which divided the City school system into thirty-one community school districts with their own elected boards (CSBs). (In 1973 the number of CSBs was increased to thirty-two.) District polciy was to be determined by a nine-member, elected, unsalaried board. However, few powers were transferred to the CSBs. The major power was the appointment of a community superintendent. Budget allocations were made by the central board and State Education Department mandates as well as teacher contracts negotiated by the central board. The central board, through the Board of Examiners, also maintained control over personnel policy. (The only exception pertained to schools with low reading levels where the school boards were permitted to appoint "off list" teachers.)

Data on turnout and outcomes in CSB elections raise serious questions about the effectiveness of this political restructing to promote parent participation. In the first 1970 election, 13.9 percent of those eligible voted. In 1977 this figure had dropped to about eight percent. More disturbing, was the success of the candidates supported by the teachers and supervisors unions. In 1975 union-backed candidates were a majority on twenty-seven of the thirty-two local boards. In 1977 they maintained majorities in two-thirds of the districts.

Statistics on the electoral participation of minority parents were especially disappointing. For example, of the 270 positions on CSBs in 1970, only thirty-eight (13.6 percent) were won by Puerto Ricans. Puerto Ricans were represented at the Central board, however, by Joseph Monserrat, who was elected president of the board in 1972 and since 1973, by Alfredo Mathew, Jr., who was made director of a new Office of Community School District Affairs.

The difficulty Puerto Ricans experience in achieving representation on CSBs reflect their inability to penetrate New York City politics generally. No study dealing with the role of Puerto Ricans in New York City politics has been concerned specifically with their participation in education issues. While many studies concerned with minority participation have included Puerto Ricans, the authors tend to combine this group with the black population. Political analysts have dwelt on the Puerto Ricans lack of political power—particularly when compared to earlier immigrant groups. At the time of this writing (1978), Puerto Ricans from New York city had won one Congressional seat (Herman Badillo), seven seats in the New York State Legislature, but at the city level, where one might expect the most representation (given their size of the total population), Puerto Ricans have made little impact. For example, as recently as November, 1977 Puerto Ricans held only three seats in the City Council.

All of the data reviewed for this study suggest that Puerto Ricans have limited resources to develop horizontal linkage—or a community level power base—to create access to any level of the educational decision-making structure. In addition, studies have documented

1. the domination of educational policies by bureaucrats—administrators and teacher groups
2. the superior strength of teacher groups and established interests at the community school district level

The Educational Problems of Puerto Rican Students and Teachers

The educational problems confronting Puerto Ricans in the New York City school system involve two issues: the achievement of Puerto Rican students enrolled in the system and the hiring of Puerto Rican teachers and administrators. Each will be discussed separately in this section.

"The most distressing incidence of academic failure . . . occurs among a group of children who are handicapped by a language barrier in the classroom—those 160,000 children whose native language is not English and whose difficulty comprehending English significantly impedes successful school performance." (New York State Commission, 1972)

Based on 1970 data, eighty-four percent of these children with English language difficulty were enrolled in the New York City public school system and a majority were Puerto Rican (State Education Department, 1972).

Puerto Ricans comprised almost one-fourth (259,879) of the New York City public school enrollment in 1970. One-third of the group (94,000) had difficulty speaking and understanding English. In 1970 English as a second language instruction was provided for one-fourth of these students (25,000). An additional 6,000 were enrolled in bilingual programs.

Data on achievement indicated that Puerto Rican students had the lowest reading scores, the highest drop out rates and the weakest academic preparation of all pupils in New York State. Based on the recommendations of a study conducted in the 1950s, most non-English-speaking Puerto Ricans, as other "new arrivals," were placed in "integrated" classes with mainland born children. A Board of Education policy specified that these students were to receive at least one-half hour of daily instruction in the English language, but the policy was never fully implemented. In 1970, for example, only one-fourth (25,000) of the students designated as having difficulty with English were receiving instruction in English as a second language. Another 6,000 were enrolled in bilingual programs (Steinberg, 1978).

Pressure to develop more services and more effective teaching methods for Puerto Rican students and to hire more Puerto Rican professionals emerged in the late 1960s, reflecting federal support of bilingual education and the mobilization of the Puerto Rican community around educational issues. Despite state legislation in 1970 which enabled local districts to implement bilingual programs and a 1972 Regents endorsement of bilingual methods, in 1973 only half (72,000) of the 143,000 students requiring a special language program received ESL or bilingual instruction. Of this group, approximately 14,000 were enrolled in bilingual programs. Central Board administrators had not developed a policy or issued guidelines related to bilingual and other language programs, viewing such issues as the province of community school boards.

Puerto Rican Teachers and Administrators

In 1969 there were only fourteen Puerto Rican supervisors, 464 teachers and no Puerto Rican directors or assistant directors employed in the school system. The largest number of Puerto Ricans were employed in positions with low prestige and low salaries (see Table 2).

Most studies which refer to the disproportionately low number of black and Puerto Rican professionals in the New York city schools, compared to their distribution in the total city population, blame the Board of Examiners for this state of affairs (Rogers, 1968: 285-294). The group, established by New York State law in 1898, was one of the earlier urban reformer's devices to institute a merit system and eliminate patronage in the city's schools. It is a division of the Board of Education which controls recruitment into and promotion within the system through its responsibility for examinations for teachers and supervisors and setting up eligibility lists for these positions.

The validity of the testing instruments developed by the Board of Examiners has been challenged in several studies. Critics have pointed out a number of formal and informal procedures, in addition to the tests, which favor the promotion of insiders and exclusion of innovators. Rogers refers to these procedures, which protect the interests of "whatever ethnic groups are in power," as "professional politics" (Rogers, 1968: 295).

Since the 1950s, Jews have held power in the professional associations and the Board of Examiners but by 1967 they had achieved only "middle and upper middle levels in the hierarchy" (Rogers, 1968: 295). Before the Jews, the Catholics were in control and in 1967 they still dominated the key administrative positions. As the Jews "move into greater power and prominence" Rogers predicted, "they will come into periodic conflict with emerging Negro and Puerto Rican groups who would like retribution for past discrimination and do not want to wait any longer for their turn" (Rogers, 1968: 296).

Two decisions which increased the number of blacks and Puerto Ricans hired in the school system were the Decentralization Law and the Mansfield Decision. Under the former, local districts could hire teachers who had passed the National Teacher Examination rather than the Boards' licensing examinations only if forty-five percent of the student body enrolled in a particular school was found to be reading below grade level. The Mansfield decision, a response to a 1970 lawsuit instituted by the NAACP on behalf of black and Puerto Rican candidates for supervisory positions, enabled community school districts to appoint principals and other supervisors without regard to the Board of Examiners' eligibility lists.

A comparison of white and minority (black and Hispanic) staff members hired by the community school districts and the Central Board between 1969 and 1972, provides data on the extent to which decentralization promoted the hiring of minorities (Bresnick, 1977). The author found the most "dramatic" gains for blacks and Hispanics at the decentralized level, with the greatest gains (on a percentage basis) for Hispanics, particularly in the category of school principal. Hispanics gained twenty-three principals, an increase of 287.5 percent. At the district level, Hispanics gained 470 teachers, a percentage increase of 78.2 percent. At the central level,

TABLE 2

ETHNIC DISTRIBUTION OF NEW YORK CITY BOARD OF EDUCATION PERSONNEL AS OF MARCH, 1969.

		Whites		*Blacks*		*Puerto Ricans*		*Spanish Speaking*	
	Total	No.	%	No.	%	No.	%	No.	%
DIRECTORS & ASS'T DIRECTORS									
Directors (Licensed & Acting)	38	36	94.7	2	5.3	—	—	—	—
Ass't. Dirs. & Ass't. Adm. Dirs. (Licensed & Acting)	121	106	87.6	15	12.4	—	—	—	—
PEDAGOGICAL PERSONNEL AND SUPPORTIVE STAFF									
Principals (Appointed & Acting)	969	923	95.3	37	3.8	4	0.4	—	—
Ass't. Principals (Apptd. & Acting)	2,039	1,781	87.3	239	11.7	10	0.5	2	0.1
Teachers in Charge	40	32	80.0	8	20.0	—	—	—	—
Dept. Chairman (Licensed & Acting)	1,192	1,128	94.6	57	4.8	4	0.3	1	**
Teachers (Regular & Substitutes)	59,108	52,827	89.4	5,395	9.1	464	0.8	181	0.3
Guidance Counselors (Reg. & Acting)	1,529	1,335	87.3	179	11.7	10	0.7	—	—
Bureau of Child Guidance (Regular, Acting, or Subs.)	605	491	81.2	104	17.2	3	0.5	2	0.3
Paraprofessionals	15,794	6,232	39.5	6,832	43.3	2,483	15.7	112	0.7
OTHERS									
Adm. Employees (Civil Service)	5,672	4,450	78.5	1,000	17.6	138	2.4	59	1.0
School Lunch Employees	9,226	5,496	59.6	3,109	33.7	584	6.3	21	0.2
TOTAL:	96,333	74,837	77.7	16,977	17.6	3,700	3.8	378	0.4

SOURCE: Office of Personnel, N.Y.C. Board of Education; table extracted from *Analysis of Puerto Rican and Black Employment in New York City Public Schools*
Richard Greenspan, 1970.

the comparable figure was 46.5 percent. There were 803 Hispanic teachers employed at the two levels in 1969. By 1972 the total was 1,367.

The results indicate that the community school boards have responded to ethnic group pressure whereas the central Board has continued to resist minority "inroads," probably due to the "persistence of the examination systems" at this level (Bresnic, 1977: 146).

Participation of Puerto Ricans in Title VII Legislation

The political strategy to promote federal support for bilingual education was devised by the National Education Association whose representatives worked with the staff of the Senate sponsor (Ralph Yarborough) of the Bilingual Education legislation which was initially intended to benefit Mexican-Americans. The decision to include Puerto Ricans was based on recognition that the participation of this group—primarily clustered in New York State—would create more broad-based support for the legislation.

Puerto Ricans were represented at hearings held in Washington by Joseph Monserrat, Director of the New York Office of the commonwealth of Puerto Rico, and Hernan LaFontaine, President of the Puerto Rican Educators Association (U.S. Congress Hearings, 1967). Subsequent hearings were held in New York City in June and July, 1967. Puerto Ricans who participated in the later hearings included political leaders and representatives from several Puerto Rican organizations. One of the participants criticized those responsible for the hearings for turning to Puerto Ricans from the "establishment" rather than the local communities:

> . . . I want to file a protest against the committee for coming into East Harlem, which is one of the most inadequate school systems in the whole city of New York, and coming here and not providing a chance and an opportunity and an honor to let the people from East Harlem express their views on the questions . . .
>
> . . . I have seen here, as I say, many people who are not residents of East Harlem and in the mind of the people . . . we thought you came here to listen to us, and not to have a show and bring in people from other places to express the kinds of things you wanted them to say. (hearings, p. 585).

According to the NEA representative who organized the hearings, the Puerto Ricans who participated volunteered. Yarborough's staff had not been in direct contact with New York City Puerto Ricans because of the rivalry between the Puerto Ricans and the Mexican-Americans. Some supporters of the bilingual legislation had wanted to involve Puerto Ricans as early as 1966, but that idea was discarded because of the "belligerency on both sides."

The data suggests that the vertical linkage of Puerto Ricans to the federal decision structure was tenuous and there is some question about the linkage between Puerto Rican leaders involved in the hearings and the grassroots community.

The Aspatial Network. The most visible actors in the events to promote bilingual education in New York City were Puerto Rican teachers and administrators who initially held overlapping memberships in the Puerto Rican Educators Association and Aspira. These educators formed the core of the aspatial network.

The network evolved from an informal clique of five Puerto Rican college students who met and worked together in a Spanish language program during the early 1960s. While attending college they also met Hernan LaFontaine and a few other Puerto Rican men who were among the first second generation Puerto Ricans to become professional educators. In 1965 LaFontaine brought these educators together to form the Puerto Rican Educators Association. When the women were recruited to the organization, the initial objective was to change the Board of Examiners' licensing procedures.

The bilingual education concept was introduced to the group through LaFontaine (in 1967) who had been asked by a superintendent to start a bilingual school in the Bronx. LaFontaine reported that his information about bilingual education came from the Dade County and Texas bilingual programs then in operation (LaFontaine, 1976). At first Puerto Rican Education Association members rejected bilingual education. According to one informant: "We thought it was a put-down. We said all the 'dumb' things most people say now if they are ignorant about bilingual education". (Perez, 1976).

LaFontaine reported that he went ahead with the idea. That led the others to think it might be a good idea and eventually they all became committed to bilingual education.

When Title VII funds became available to the city, the first proposals that were funded were written by network members. In addition to running these programs, they embarked on a series of negotiations with city and state officials which resulted in the establishment of an office of bilingual education at both levels of the system. However, the programs administered by these offices were limited to those funded by the state and Title VII. The network was also linked to a Puerto Rican State Senator who introduced, unsuccessfully, several bills in the state legislature that would mandate bilingual programs in the city system. Opposition came primarily from the United Federation of Teachers.

All of these activities—administering Title VII programs, attending bilingual education workshops related to Title VII programs, and promoting bilingual education locally—created numerous occasions for the network members to interact as a group, reinforcing what was described as a "tight knit" circle from the beginning.

When it became apparent that these traditional channels were not likely to result in additional funds for bilingual education, the group decided to support the *Aspira* lawsuit. This decision brought them into a city-level interorganizational network consisting of Aspira, The Puerto Rican Forum, the Puerto Rican Legal Defense and Education Fund. These three groups eventually developed a united front in support of bilingual education which included a variety of Puerto Rican organizations.

The inability of the activists to utilize these traditional channels to obtain additional support for bilingual education accounts for the group's endorsement of a coercive strategy: a lawsuit which would force the board of education to institute bilingual programs on a systemwide basis.

The Aspira lawsuit. Aspira is the organization exculsively concerned with Puerto Rican educational issues. When founded, in 1961, its primary purpose was to provide guidance and help to develop leadership among Puerto Rican youth. It is a national organization with affiliates in five states, and chapters in city high schools. In 1971, there were thirty-six clubs in New York City and a membership of 2,800. In 1975, the number had dropped to thirty-two with a membership of 1,199 (Aspira, 1975-76).

In 1971, Aspira and two other Puerto Rican groups sponsored a conference on Puerto Ricans in New York City schools and published ". . . And Others," which documented the failure of the city school system to respond to the needs of Puerto Ricans (Liem, 1971).

Following publication of ". . . And Others," the United States Civil Rights Commission came to New York to discuss with members of Aspira what avenues the federal government could use to assist Puerto Ricans in bringing about change (Santiago, 1973).

According to the recollection of one of the lawyers involved, the idea for the lawsuit began earlier. Around 1969, Antonia Pantoja, the founder of Aspira, consulted some civil rights lawyers about building a legal case that might change educational policy for Puerto Ricans. The lawsuit was filed in the spring of 1972 by the Puerto Rican Legal Defense and Education Fund and the Community Action Legal Services (Perales, 1975). Four groups were involved in the *Aspira* case: the Puerto Rican Educators Association, the Puerto Rican Educators Task Force, educators from Community School District No. 1 and the American Jewish Committee.

Members of PREA and the Task Force played a crucial role in the lawsuit serving as consultants to the lawyers. They were also involved in the recruitment of children to serve as plaintiffs, they did a large portion of the research and they recruited educators working in the system who could provide evidence to support the charges of discrimination against Puerto Rican students. The participation of these educators was equally crucial when Aspira filed a contempt charge against the Board of Education in 1975 for noncompliance with the consent decree.

The *Aspira* suit stated that:

> The individual plaintiffs are New York City public school children and their parents in families recently arrived from Puerto Rico for whom Spanish is their predominant or only language.

The suit was pleaded as a class action on behalf of 182,000 children said to be similarly situationed. The complaint alleged that:

> . . . the plaintiff children speak little or no English, that the schools they compulsorily attend offer instruction mainly or only in English; that the results for these children are inadequate learning, lowered educational achievement and test scores, a poor rate of promotion and graduation, and a train of attendant consequences for college entrance, employment, civic participation and the quality of life generally (*Aspira v. Board of Education of the City of New York*).

Although the *Aspira* suit was filed prior to the filing of the *Lau* suit, it was held in abeyance pending the decision in *Lau* since the latter was at the Supreme Court level and *Aspira* involved a lower court (Southern District).

Following the *Lau* decision, attorney for plaintiffs in Aspira moved for summary judgment. In April, 1974, Judge Marvin Frankel directed the defendants, with plaintiff participation, to prepare a survey to determine the number of "affected children" and the availability of programs to serve their needs. Both sides were directed to submit "detailed statements of the education programs they deem necessary to comply with the HEW regulations enforced in Lau" (72 Civ. 4002, 30 April 1974).

Under the terms of a consent decree, signed on August 29, 1974, the Board of Education agreed to provide three of the four elements requested in the plan requested by Aspira:

1. The introduction of reading in the Spanish language
2. Subject matter instruction in the child's home language
3. English as a second language, taught through a "sequentially structured program"

The fourth request, Puerto Rican culture, was rejected on the basis of insufficient evidence to justify the inclusion of culture as a separate element. This issue was resolved in a compromise—a provision in the decree that materials in the program "shall positively reflect, where appropriate, the culture of the children in the program. Additionally, any personnel training program shall continue to be sensitive to the cultural diversities of the children" (*Aspira v. Board of Education of the City of New York).*

There were other stipulations in the decree relating to the adequacy of the professional staff responsible for implementing the program, that plaintiffs believed would provide an effective substitute for the cultural element. These included that a "professional in the Program shall (a) be fluent in the Spanish language, and be able to fully comprehend and express himself in written Spanish." However, to fulfill this requirement the Board of Education was permitted to (1) develop and implement programs to retrain personnel, and (2) develop and implement an "intensive and on-going affirmative action program designed to recruit forthwith bilingual personnel in New York City and elsewhere". (Consent Decree, p. 6).

Implementation of the Consent Decree. Prior to the institution of the bilingual program on a system-wide basis by September 1975, the Board of Education had agreed to accomplish three tasks:

1. The designation of pilot schools to serve as a model for the system-wide implementation of the bilingual program mandated by the decree
2. The development of a language assessment instrument to identify students eligible for the program, and
3. The recruitment of bilingual teachers to implement the program for the designated students

A monitoring team composed of volunteers reported that the schools selected to serve as models were not likely to fulfill this function because they had been operating bilingual programs with special funds from federal and state programs, whereas the consent decree programs were to be set up without additional funds. Recommendations for improving bilingual programs, made by the monitoring team, were not acted on.

The Board and Aspira could not agree on the criteria for determining eligibility for the bilingual program. This dispute brought them back to the judge's chambers where the criteria were established by the Judge. Bilingual educators (including those who supported the Aspira lawsuit), linguistic scholars, and others familiar with events related to the LAB are highly critical of the test itself as well as the eligibility criteria.

Board of Education officials issued statements indicating that there would be no problem in recruiting teachers to implement the program.

Unanticipated Events. Two events which portended that the Board of Education might encounter serious obstacles in implementing the terms of the consent decree on a system-wide basis were the city's financial crisis and a teacher's strike. The financial crisis forced the Board of Education to eliminate 1,600 teaching positions and shut down several schools which resulted in an increase in class size. The increase in class size plus other issues that had created an impasse in the UFT's contract negotiations with the central board, provoked a teacher's strike three days after the schools opened in September, 1975.

Non-Compliance. In December 1975, Aspira filed a contempt suit based on numerous allegations of the Board's non-compliance with the provisions of the decree. The continued involvement of the court was one of the conditions of the agreement. The court was to mediate disputes which could not be resolved by the two parties and the board was required to submit monthly compliance reports to the court.

Plaintiffs charged that the board was not providing the program to thousands of entitled students, had failed to hire the necessary personnel and was using "unqualified personnel" in the program. Not surprisingly, the most frequently cited excuses by Board of Education administrators, to explain the failure to deliver the required program were the budget cuts and the teacher's strike. However, since the variations in levels of compliance were extreme, as indicated in Table 3, they were not acceptable to the Aspira lawyers.

In October 1976, the board was ruled in contempt and ordered to pay plaintiff's cost and attorneys' fees for the lawsuit plus the contempt proceedings which came to $130,000. The PRLDEF settled for $150,000 to avoid an appeal by the Board of Education.

The Number of Teachers Hired. "If the consent decree was effective at all," said one Aspira lawyer, "it was in keeping positions open to bilingual teachers who would have lost jobs because of low seniority (Teitelbaum, 1976).

The data indicate that the decree not only increased Puerto Rican access to teaching positions in the school system but was responsible for the maintenance of hundreds of Puerto Rican teachers who were already employed by the system before the decree was implemented when teachers from other groups were being laid off.

As the figures in Table 4 reveal, teachers with some form of bilingual license continued to be hired throughout the 1975-76 year. The Aspira lawyers attributed this to the continued involvement of the court and especially the contempt proceedings.

Staff members of the PRLDEF and Aspira, at the time they were interviewed, did not have data on the number of Puerto Rican teachers hired by the Board of Education to implement the decree, but estimated that the figure was around 3,000. Respondents who were queried on this issue noted that the data available from the Board of Education listed Puerto Rican teachers under a "Spanish surname" category which would include all Spanish surnamed teachers whether or not they were bilingual.

According to an attorney in the Board of Education's Division of Personnel, 2,300 licensed bilingual teachers had been hired between Septem-

TABLE 3

NUMBER AND PERCENTAGE OF ENTITLED STUDENTS RECEIVING ALL ELEMENTS OF THE CONSENT DECREE PROGRAM DECEMBER 1975, FEBRUARY, APRIL/MAY 1976

District	Number of Students Eligible	Percentage of Entitled Students Receiving all elements of Program		
		December	February	April/May
1	1,293	32%	78%	99%
2	952	41	55	86
3	1,950	30	90	92
4	3,095	28	67	90
5	654	35	37	79
6	4,930	77	85	87
7	4,580	28	69	93
8	2,483	44	81	95
9	4,776	73	81	98
10	2,253	36	60	93
11	313	47	14	96
12	4,181	68	80	98
13	1,249	44	87	90
14	2,188	56	83	99
15	2,224	75	96	96
16	338	60	98	95.6
17	889	67	99	99
18	272	67	96	100
19	2,221	30	83	95
20	1,242	46	93	96
21	842	35	37	88
22	121	31	93	100
23	1,237	65	70	70
24	1,933	77	84	91
25	370	15	32	81
26	63	100	100	100
27	873	19	94	100
28	639	49	63	77
29	242	23	31	98
30	N/A	0	—	N/A
31	291	8	71	88
32	2,950	59	94	98

SOURCE: Findings of Fact, August, 1976.

ber 1975 and June 1976, but the list he provided added up to only 1,588, as indicated in Table 4.

The charge that the Board had hired unqualified personnel for the program was based on an "ancillary certificate." This certificate was granted to teachers who had a monolingual teaching license who passed a test to demonstrate proficiency in Spanish. The allegation was dismissed by a bilingual Puerto Rican principal who was on the Board of Examiners when the consent decree was implemented (and also a supporter of the court action). He estimated that possibly one percent of the ancillary certificates

TABLE 4

NUMBER OF SPANISH/ENGLISH BILINGUAL TEACHERS HIRED BY NEW YORK CITY BOARD OF EDUCATION SEPTEMBER 1975-SEPTEMBER 1976

	Type of License	
Month	Bilingual Common Brach	Bilingual Early Childhood
September, 1975	240	51
October	65	6
November	32	1
December	59	3
January, 1976	93	20
February	138	24
March	57	6
April	32	27
May	27	2
June	5	—
TOTAL	748	140
OTHER LICENSES		
Bilingual Ancillary Certificates		290
National Teacher Exam Appointments		205[a]
Recertified[c]		198[b]
Bilingual School & Community Relations		7
TOTAL		700
TOTAL HIRED ALL CATEGORIES:		1,588

[a]Sept./Oct. '75:N=96; Sept. '76:N=109

[b]Sept./Oct. '75:N=79; Sept. '76:N=119

[c]The recertified teachers were those with temporary licenses who would have been laid off if it were not for the consent decree.

SOURCE: New York City Board of Education
Division of Personnel

might have gone to teachers who were not proficient in Spanish. He also stated that most of the bilingual teachers hired were Puerto Rican.

A look at the number of teachers hired in February 1976 (N + 162) two months after the contempt action was taken and the month that pre-trial hearings on the case began, suggests that the intervention of the court did have a positive impact on this factor.

In April, 1975, an administrator in the Office of Bilingual Education stated that 1,500 bilingual teachers were already employed by the school system. If this was correct, then the 1,588 teachers hired between September 1975 and June 1976 would have brought the total to 3,088, a little less than 500 from the estimated need of 3,500.

Possibly more important than the number of bilingual teachers hired to implement the consent decree, is the number of Puerto Rican teachers who were maintained despite the massive teacher lay-offs required by the budget cuts.

As shown in Table 5, between 1974-75 and 1975-76, the total number of teachers employed in the schools decreased by 7,368. There was a drop of only ten Spanish surnamed teachers between the two time periods contributing to a percent increase of teachers from this group from 3.1 percent to 3.6 percent. Comparable figures for blacks show a drop of 807 teachers and a drop in the percent of the total by 0.2 percentage points. Among white teachers ("other"), the change in absolute numbers—a decrease of 6,487 teachers—was more dramatic, but the percent decrease was relatively small—0.2 percent due to their larger share of the total to begin with.

Clearly the burden imposed by the lay-offs fell heaviest on white teachers and least on Spanish surnamed teachers. Despite the fact that the Spanish surname category includes non-Puerto Ricans, most observers agree that Puerto Ricans are the predominant group included in this category.

The Limitations of Litigation. Litigation proved to be an effective strategy for increasing Puerto Rican access to jobs in the school system, thus weakening the union's influence on the hiring and licensing of bilingual teachers. Nevertheless, there was evidence of five factors which may impede the Puerto Rican's ability to maintain the gains achieved by the consent decree or to promote future support for the innovation. These are: the nature of the program mandated by the court and manner in which it has been implemented, lack of leadership among bilingual educators, opposition of established educators and lack of sufficient resources to promote linkage between the activists and the grass-roots community.

The bilingual program mandated by the court is a transitional program. As soon as children can participate in instructional programs provided in English, they are to be transferred to those classes. Unless there is a stable stream of new migrants from Puerto Rico who are eligible for the bilingual program, the need for bilingual Puerto Rican teachers will decline.

Consent decree programs, like the programs funded under the BEA, tend to be isolated from other school programs. This isolation fosters and reinforces dense networks among bilingual teachers and Hispanic students, sometimes segregating them from their English dominant peers. This reduces the chances to diffuse the innovation through informal social ties.

The ability of the bilingual educators to promote strategies to institutionalize bilingual programs, by building support of both Spanish and English dominant parents is threatened by the erosion of program standards and the resistance of the teachers' union to policies that would help bilingual teachers maintain the job gains achieved by the lawsuit.

Failure of the bilingual educators to develop leadership within the occupational group, due to personal rivalries, conflict over strategies to promote the innovation and competition for federal funds, further weakens their chances to promote the innovation from within the bureaucracy. The focus of the educators on bureaucratic and pedagogical issues or a professional orientation, makes it unlikely that this group can be relied on to develop greater access to either the formal or informal decision-making structure.

While the opposition of the teacher's union was evident prior to the consent decree, resistance was increased at the time of its implementation which, because of the city's budget crisis, resulted in the displacement of English dominant teachers by bilingual teachers.

So far, the findings suggest, the potential of the activists to promote

TABLE 5

PROFILE: NEW YORK CITY SCHOOLS

FULL-TIME TEACHERS (EXCLUDING DISTRICT 75)*

	Total	Black		Spanish Surnamed		Oriental		Native American		Total Minority		Other	
1968-69**	51,832	4,079	7.9%	464	0.9%	137	0.3%	46	0.1%	4,726	9.1%	47,106	90.9%
1970-71	58,827	4,455	7.5%	798	1.4%	209	0.4%	10	0.0%	5,472	9.3%	53,355	90.7%
1971-72	54,889	4,426	8.1%	1,027	1.9%	214	0.4%	13	0.0%	5,680	10.3%	49,209	89.7%
1972-73	53,924	4,610	8.5%	1,154	2.1%	217	0.4%	12	0.0%	5,993	11.1%	47,931	88.9%
1973-74	54,726	4,746	8.7%	1,376	2.5%	288	0.5%	8	0.0%	6,418	11.7%	48,308	88.3%
1974-75	53,907	5,038	9.3%	1,688	3.1%	295	0.5%	10	0.0%	7,031	13.0%	46,876	87.0%
1975-76	46,539	4,231	9.1%	1,678	3.6%	233	0.5%	8	0.0%	6,150	13.2%	40,389	86.8%

STUDENTS (EXCLUDING DISTRICT 75)

	Total	Black		Spanish Surnamed		Oriental		Native American		Total Minority		Other	
1968-69**	1,063,587	334,641	31.5%	244,302	23.0%	15,753	1.5%	1,526	0.1%	596,222	56.1%	467,365	43.9%
1970-71**	1,140,359	393,516	34.5%	292,664	25.7%	17,115	1.5%	607	0.1%	703,902	61.7%	436,457	38.3%
1971-72	1,137,707	397,287	34.9%	301,380	26.5%	18,267	1.6%	308	0.0%	717,242	63.0%	420,465	37.0%
1972-73	1,113,601	399,804	35.9%	293,745	26.4%	20,146	1.8%	415	0.0%	714,110	64.1%	399,491	35.9%
1973-74	1,096,702	400,010	36.5%	296,589	27.0%	22,021	2.0%	613	0.1%	719,233	65.6%	377,469	34.4%
1974-75	1,094,609	398,572	36.4%	302,552	27.6%	23,088	2.1%	585	0.1%	724,797	66.2%	369,812	33.8%
1975-76	1,085,550	401,652	37.0%	308,551	28.4%	24,231	2.2%	727	0.1%	735,161	67.7%	350,389	32.3%

*All data from BEDS School Survey unless otherwise noted.

**Data from OCR Survey (101-102's)

SOURCE: U.S. Department of Health, Education, and Welfare, Office for Civil Rights. Letter to Chancellor Irving Anker from Martin H. Gerry, 9 November 1976, Appendix A.

linkage between the city-level group and the grass roots has been only partially realized and concentrated in districts with large Puerto Rican enrollments. Major problems in this regard are Aspira's limited and unstable funds which makes the group dependent on middle-class Puerto Ricans, many of whom, particularly educators, have a specialized and professional rather than a community-oriented perspective.

In conclusion, the theoretical framework suggested that an effort to create the functional equivalent to the political machine would require resources to activate an aspatial network, create vertical linkage to key decision centers, and linkage between the activists and the grass roots community.

The data reviewed here suggest that, at the time this study ended (1977), the federal support for bilingual education had provided resources to accomplish only the first two objectives. The most visible activists were members of a pre-existing aspatial interpersonal network. The decision which created access to jobs in the school system stemmed from a lawsuit sponsored by a city-level group, supported by the members of the aspatial network, with minimal grass-roots involvement. The lawsuit was resolved in a consent decree whereby the Board of Education agreed to provide bilingual education programs on a city-wide basis.

While the consent decree achieved a formal policy change, implementation was controlled by non-governmental groups—the administrators and teachers inside the school bureaucracy who perceived bilingual education as a threat to their professional interests. Their fears were compounded by the convergence of the city's financial crisis with the date for implementing the consent decree. Thousands of black and white teachers were laid off at the same time that the decree required the hiring of more Puerto Rican teachers. In addition the decree maintained the jobs of Puerto Rican teachers already working in the system. A total of 3,000 jobs was involved. However, mounting opposition to bilingual education by the teachers' union suggests that the Puerto Ricans in New York may have to seek other resources to create vertical linkage to the grass-roots community.

REFERENCES

Aspira, Inc. *Annual Report*. 1975-76.

Aspira of New York, Inc. v. Board of Education of the City of New York, 72 Civ. 4002 (S.D.N.Y., 29 Aug. 1974) unreported consent decree.

__________. 30 April 1974, Memorandum Decision.

__________. 29 August 1974, Court Memorandum.

Aveni, Adrian F. "Organizational Linkages and Resource Mobilization: The Significance of Linkage Strength and Breadth." Paper presented at the 72nd annual meeting of the American Sociological Association, Chicago, September 5-9, 1977.

Barnes, J.A. "Social Networks," Addison Wesley Module in Anthropology. 1972.

Blau, Peter M. "A Macrostructural Theory of Social Structure." *American Journal of Sociology* 83 (July 1974): 26-54.

Bresnick, David. "Blacks, Hispanics, and Others: Decentralization and Ethnic Succession." *Urban Education* 12 (July 1977): 129-153.

Clark, Terry N. *Community Structure and Decision-Making: Comparative Analysis*. San Francisco: Chandler, 1968.

__________. "The Irish Ethic and the Spirit of Patronage." *Ethnicity* 2 (December 1975): 305-359.

Craven, Paul and Wellman, Barry. "The Network City" in M. P. Effrat (ed.) *The Community*. New York: The Free Press, 1974.

David, Stephen M. and Peterson, Paul E. *Urban Politics and Public Policy*. New York: Praeger, 1973.

Diaz, Manuel. Proceedings of Conference "Puerto Ricans Confront Problems of the Complex Urban Society." New York, April 15-16, 1967.

Durkheim, Emil. *The Division of Labor in Society*. New York: The Free Press of Glencoe.

Fischer, Claude S.; Jackson, Robert Max; Stueve, C. Ann; Gerson, Kathleen; Jones, Lynne McCallister; with Baldassare, Mark. *Networks and Places*. New York: The Free Press. 1977.

Fitzpatrick, Joseph P. *Puerto Rican Americans*. Englewood-Cliffs: Prentice Hall, 1971.

Gittel, Marilyn. *Participants and Participation*. New York: Center for Urban Education, 1967.

Glazer, Nathan and Moynihan, Daniel P. *Beyond the Melting Pot*. Cambridge, Mass: MIT Press, 1970.

Granovetter, Mark. "The Strength of Weak Ties." *AJS* 78 (May 1973): 1360-1380.

Greenstone, J. David and Peterson, Paul E. *Race and Authority in Urban Politics*. Chicago: University of Chicago Press, 1976.

Greer, Scott. *The Emerging City: Myth and Reality*. New York: The Free Press of Glencoe, 1962.

Greer, Scott and Orleans, Peter. "The Mass Society and the Parapolitical Structure." *ASR* 27 (October 1962): 634-646.

Iannaccone, Laurence and Wiles, David K. "The Changing Politics of Urban Education." *Education and Urban Society* 3 (May 1971): 255-264.

Janowitz, Morris. *The Community Press in an Urban Setting*. Chicago: University of Chicago Press, 1967.

Kadushin, Charles. "On the Problem of Formalizing Emergent Networks Among Innovators in Education." Paper presented to School Capacity for Problem Solving Group, NIE, March, 1977.

Katz, Elihu and Lazarfeld, Paul F. *Personal Influence*. New York: The Free Press of Glencoe, 1955.

Katznelson, Ira. "Class Capacity and Social Cohesion in American Cities." In *The New Urban Politics*, Massotti, Louis H. and Lineberry, Robert L. (eds.) Cambridge, Mass: Ballinger. 1976: 19-36.

LaFontaine, Hernan. Executive Administrator, Office of Bilingual Education. New York City Board of Education, Brooklyn, New York. Interview, October 19, 1976.

Lamb, Curt. *Political Power in Poor Neighborhoods*. New York: John Wiley & Sons, 1975.

Laumann, Edward O. and Pappi, Franz U. *Networks of Collective Action*. New York: Academic Press, 1976.

Liem, G. Ramsay. ". . . and Others: A Report Card for the New York City Public Schools." New York: Aspira, Inc., 1971.

Litt, Edgar. Ethnic Politics in America. Glenview: Scott, Foresman, 1970.

Merton, Robert K. *Social Theory and Use of Social Structure.* New York: The Free Press of Glencoe, 1957.

Mitchell, J. Clyde. "The Concept and Use of Social Networks." In Social Networks in Urban Society. Mitchell, J.C. (ed.), Manchester, Manchester University Press, 1969.

New York State Commission on the Quality, Cost and Financing of Elementary and Secondary Education, 1972. Report, Vol. II.

New York State Education Department. "Bilingual Education: A Statement of Policy and Proposed Action by the Regents of the University of the State of New York," Albany, New York: 1972.

O'Brian, David J. *Neighborhood Organization and Interest-Group Processes.* Princeton: Princeton University Press, 1975.

Perales, Cesar A. Former Director, Puerto Rican Legal Defense and Education Fund, New York, New York. Interview, Brooklyn, New York October 29, 1975.

Perez, Carmen. Project Director, Bilingual Education. State University of New York, Albany, New York. Interview, September 3, 1976.

Perrucci, Robert and Pilisuk, Mark. "Leaders and Ruling Elites: The Interorganizational Basis of Community Power." *ASR* 35 (December 1970): 1040-1057.

Peterson, Paul E. "Forms of Representation: Participation of the Poor in the Community Action Program." *APSR* 64 (June 1970): 491-507.

Pitkin, Hanna F. *The Concept of Representation.* Berkeley: University of California Press. 1967.

Roger, Lloyd H. *Migrant in the City.* New York: Basic Books, 1972.

Rogers, David *110 Livingston Street.* New York: Random House, 1968.

Rosenberg, Terry J. and Beardon, James E. "Patterns of Residential Segregation and Change Among New York Puerto Ricans: 1960-1970." Paper presented at annual meeting of Population Association of American, 1974.

Sayre, Wallace S. and Kaufman, Herbert. *Governing New York City.* New York: W.W. Morton & Co., 1965.

Schon, Donald A. *Beyond the Stable State.* New York: Random House, 1971.

Steinberg, Lois. *Social Science Theory and Research on Participation and Voluntary Associations: A Bibliographic Essay.* Boston: The Institute for Responsive Education for the National Institute of Education. 1977.

__________. Report on Bilingual Education. New York: Community Service Society, 1974.

__________. "The Bilingual Education Act and The Puerto Rican Community: The Role of a Network in the Implementation of Federal Policy." Unpublished Ph.D. dissertation, Fordham University. 1978.

Steward, Julian. *People of Puerto Rico.* Champaign-Urbana: University of Illinois Press, 1957.

Teitlebaum, Herbert. Fifth International Bilingual/Bicultural Conference, San Antonio, 30 April-5 May 1976.

U.S. Congress. Senate. Committee on Labor and Public Welfare. *Bilingual Education.* Hearings before a subcommittee of the committee on Labor and Public Welfare on S. 428, 90th Congress, 1st session 1967.

Warren, Roland. *The Community in America.* Chicago: Rand McNally, 1963.

———. *Truth, Love and Social Change.* Chicago: Rand McNally, 1971.

THE ROLE OF THE MASS MEDIA IN THE PUBLIC DEBATE OVER BILINGUAL EDUCATION IN THE UNITED STATES

Armando Valdez

The media of mass communications are omnipresent and are a major force in the everyday life of the people in contemporary society. A massive constellation of images flow daily from media production centers and are readily consumed by the vast majority of the nation's inhabitants. The circulation of daily newspapers exceeds one per household while radios exceed four sets per household. Magazines reach an estimated sixty percent of the adult population; approximately twenty-five percent to thirty-five percent of adults read one book per month. It is estimated that fifty percent of all adults regularly attend movies and ninety-seven percent of all U.S. households have a television set. It is reported that we have more television sets than toilets in this country. Children spend more time watching television than sitting in school. Consumption of mass media transcends political, class, sex, age and racial boundaries. Constant exploration of new combinations of capital, organization and production techniques creates more effective modes of penetrating the mind and pocketbook. Consequently, the mass communications media have a significant influence on our conception of our social environment and social reality.

The public debate over bilingual education is occurring at different levels. The most visible and also audible debate is being waged in the mass media. This is not to say that it is the most important or influential forum; however, it is fair to say that the formulation of public policy cannot ignore this public debate occurring in the mass media.

A fundamental premise of this paper is that public policy is influenced by the climate of public opinion surrounding the issues under discussion; a corollary premise is that the mass media exerts a major influence in the public debate, both prior and subsequent to the promulgation of the public policy. This paper discusses the interaction between the mass media and the formulation of public policy on bilingual education.

Before proceeding, it is instructive to briefly sketch the characteristic function of the mass media in this nation to provide a context for addressing the impact of the mass media on the debate over bilingual education.

Our economic system, and that of all industrialized capitalist nations for that matter, requires a constant increase in production of goods and services to maintain its equilibrium. The aggregate value of all the goods and services produced annually by a nation is measured in terms of the gross national product (GNP). On the average, an annual increase in GNP of five to seven percent is required to maintain a stable economy in a capitalist economic system. Thus, the U.S. economy is organized around the principle of market expansion. As a technologically-based system of mass production and corresponding mass consumption, this economic system is unsurpassed in its capacity to supply an endless flow of commodities to an eager nation of consumers. It is a complex consumer-oriented market economy.[1]

THE FUNCTION AND STRUCTURE OF MASS MEDIA IN A MARKET ECONOMY

A requisite of a market economy is an efficient means of creating and stimulating mass consumer demand. Mass communications are structured as advertising channels and by virtue of their characteristic structure, they occupy a central role in a consumer-oriented society. In this economic context, the media of mass communication are the critical links in the system which bring the producers and consumers of goods and services together. The primary function of the mass media is to provide access for producers of commodities to a mass audience of consumers to whom advertising messages may be directed. The principal client relationship is between the advertisers and the media. In this economic arrangement, the audience becomes a salable entity; access to an audience of consumers is sold by the mass communication industry to the advertising industry who are acting on behalf of their client, the producers of consumer goods and services. First and foremost, the mass media are a marketing channel. Their primary source of support is advertising revenue.[2] One must keep in mind that the mass media are motivated primarily by economic considerations.[3]

Corporate conglomerate structure. The mass communication industry exhibits the same structural features of all major industries in this economic system. They are organized as corporate conglomerates in which a few dominate the entire industry—a characteristic pattern of this capitalist economy. This concentration is particulary apparent in the television industry. In the top fifty television markets, where seventy-five percent of the population lives, the three major networks—ABC, CBS, and NBC—have ninety-four percent of the audience (Bagdikian, 1971).[4] Eighty-two percent of all the commercial television stations in the nation are network affiliated. Of these, thirty-nine percent are affiliated with NBC, while thirty-four percent and twenty-eight percent are affiliated with CBS and ABC, respectively (Gerbner, 1972).

Economic concentration. In 1970, almost forty percent of the total television income went to the three networks and their fifteen owned and operated stations (Schramm and Alexander, 1973). By 1974, this amount increased to sixty percent (International Television Almanac, 1975). The remaining income went to the other 677 stations. The ownership pattern displays a comparable pattern of concentration. Seventy-four percent of all commercial television stations are controlled by chains (Bagdikian, 1971). Thirty-three percent of all the nation's broadcast stations are owned by groups or conglomerates (Gerbner, 1972). About twenty-five percent of all commercial television stations are owned in groups of five or more (Gerbner, 1972).

Advertising agency pattern. Television's allied advertising agencies and advertisers reflect a similar pattern of economic concentration.[5] A few of the top ad agencies handle a disproportionate share of the television billings, and the tendency toward greater concentration has increased in recent years. In 1960, the top ten agencies handled thirty-one percent of the national television billings; by 1972 this amount had increased to forty-one percent (Bogart, 1973).[6] It is estimated that in 1969, one ad agency, J. Walter Thompson, accounted for fifteen percent of all television time sales (Schramm and Alexander, 1973). Broadcast advertising in general represents over half of the agencies' accounts. The vast majority of the agencies' broadcast billings were for television time sales. One estimate indicates that two-thirds of the agencies' national broadcasting expenditures go to television (Schramm and Alexander, 1973).

Broadcast advertisers' pattern. The advertisers also mirror the concentration manifested by broadcasters and advertising agencies. The top 100 advertisers account for over twenty-seven percent of the national advertising expenditures and sixty-three percent of television's total income (Gerbner, 1972). The top fifteen advertisers provided about one-third of television's revenues in 1970 (Schramm and Alexander, 1973). In recent years, the top twenty-five network advertisers contributed fifty-four percent of the total television network revenues. In 1975 the top ten advertisers invested over twenty-five percent of the total national television advertising expenditures; the top five advertisers accounted for over seventeen percent of the total television advertising expenditures. The three major soap companies alone accounted for an estimated fourteen percent of the total network television billings (Gerbner, 1972). One advertiser, Procter & Gamble, has traditionally been the largest buyer of television advertising. In 1975, it again dominated the field, with expenditures about twice that of the second-ranked advertiser.[7]

MASS MEDIA AND PUBLIC OPINION

The wide spectrum of images and messages purveyed by the mass media have a correspondingly diverse spectrum of effects. However, all these messages convey values, beliefs and expectations. These symbolic messages are conveyed unobtrusively along with news, entertainment and advertising content. These strata of implicit messages symbolically mirror the order of things in that given society. However, beyond this implicit dimension of symbolic meaning, the mass media also provide explicit messages in the form of instruction about the social system. Gerbner (1967) argues that these messages "not only inform but form common images; they not only entertain but create publics, they not only satisfy but shape a range of attitudes, tastes (and) preferences."[8] It is through these implicit and explicit messages that the mass media shape public opinion.

Message redundancy. Careful analysis of the messages conveyed by the mass media shows that the basic themes presented are highly redundant. A market economy characterized by mass production of goods and services must have the means to foster a standardization of consumer values and tastes so that consumption of the mass produced consumer commodities is feasible. This means that a mass market with reasonably homogeneous consumer tastes is a requisite component of a market economy. This results in a socio-cultural hegemony in which the media portray only a limited set of values, beliefs and attitudes as representative norms for the social order. In this process, a standardization of formats, motifs and tastes are cultivated by the mass media. This leveling effect of media content is necessary for the media to effectively reach a mass, generally homogeneous audience. As a consequence, this mode of portrayal of information is characteristic of the mass media.

Socio-cultural maintenance. The mass media, like all other social institutions, embody and nurture the prevailing cultural beliefs, values and attitudes of the society in which they operate. Gerbner and Gross (1976) view the primary function of mass media as the reiteration of the established power and authority of the social system. They further argue that all the cultural devices that convey the prevailing definitions of reality "constantly cultivate and legitimize action along socially functional and conventionally accepted lines."[9] They conclude that this legitimation function of the mass media serves to sell us on the system, or simply stated, the system is the message.[10]

Media effects on public opinion. Irrespective of the specific content, this structural analysis of the mass media suggests three general effects on public opinion. They are the agenda-setting function, the trivialization effect and the crystalization effect.

Agenda-setting function. Due to its characteristic function in society, the mass media selectively report or ignore certain events or issues. In so doing, they focus public attention on a rather limited set of topics,[11] and these topics become the subject of public interest, scrutiny and debate. All others are ignored.

Trivialization effect. Due to its economic structure, the mass media tries to attract the largest possible audience and in so doing tend to highlight selected aspects of an event or issue; these treatments are often simplistic, uni-dimensional and often sensationalized to gain the attention of a large audience. Thus controversy and action take precedence over reason and deliberation.

Crystalization effect. The manner in which information is presented through the mass media particularly news content, tends to create polarizations on a linear value continuum. As a consequence of this mode of news presentation, audience opinions are often crystalized into judgments on issues which have been only superficially and simplistically presented. Nevertheless, public opinion is often crystalized by some catch words or sensational incidents reported which permit latent prejudices to surface. All too often, this is accompanied by identification of a scapegoat to blame for the problems at hand.

THE MASS MEDIA AND THE BILINGUAL EDUCATION DEBATE

The central thesis of this paper is that the public debate over bilingual education policy in the U.S. is a debate about cultural and linguistic pluralism. The basic issue being debated is the status of cultural and linguistic pluralism in this nation. The U.S. has historically exhibited an intolerance to linguistic and cultural diversity. The very nature of its capitalist economic and political structure, which stresses competition and domination, mitigate against pluralism. Bilingual education represents a minor yet fundamental departure from the one-dimensional language policy that dominated public education in this nation until recently. For this reason, bilingual education raises the spector of a national policy in which linguistic and cultural diversity are recongized and accepted as functional elements in the educational process. This perception of an imminent realignment in national policy is at the root of the public debate on bilingual education. Therefore, a socio-political dimension is superimposed on the pedagogical issues being debated.

Ideological Context of the Debate

From this perspective, the public debate over bilingual education is an ideological one. Bilingual education calls into question the conventional wisdom of the melting pot ideology, which regards culturally different traits as undesirable and insists that they be dissolved away in a melting pot. This melting pot intolerance to cultural and linguistic diversity is an innate feature of U.S. nationalism.

The ideology of forging a nation with a unified language, culture and religion was proclaimed by the U.S. Congress in 1792 in legislation authorizing the U.S. Mint to coin money. It required all coins to bear the Latin words, "*E Pluribus Unum,*" which conveys the national creed, "Out of Many, One."

Kohn (1961) has described U.S. nationalism as an extreme form of Western European nationalism, devoid of ethnic and cultural elements and essentially ideological. The components of this form of nationalism are abstract socio-political ideals embodied in the notion of the American Dream—democracy, personal freedom, equality and the pursuit of happiness. Yet, not only is U.S. nationalism devoid of ethnicity; it is fundamentally anti-ethnic. Fishman (1966) describes the U.S. as a supraethnic nation in which immigrant groups are expected to de-ethnicize themselves in order to emerge as Americans. This imposed metamorphosis from ethnic to national identity is the central premise of the melting pot ideology. Cordasco (1976) noted that immigrant groups are expected to "melt" their native cultural attributes as a precondition to share in the material and spiritual goods of American society (Cardasco, 1976). This is still the prevailing ideology and it finds expression in the current public debate over bilingual education.

Before examining the manifestations of this ideological debate in the mass media, it is important to understand the historical conditions that fostered present public opinion toward cultural diversity.

1880-1920: The Formative Years

The historical experience with the massive waves of European immigrants in the late nineteenth and early twentieth century shaped many of the present attitudes and policies regarding cultural and linguistic pluralism. The majority of the immigrants to the U.S. during the forty-year period from 1880 to 1920 were central and southeastern Europeans. Their arrival on these shores corresponded with the rapid industrial and territorial expansion in this nation. These immigrants provided the necessary pool of cheap and unskilled labor and were rapidly integrated into the labor market. Although their labor was welcome, their religion, language and cultural characteristics were not. These immigrants brought with them religious, linguistic and cultural patterns that were fundamentally different than those in the political social institution in the U.S. Hartman (1948) describes these immigrants as different in language, class and religion from prior immigrants and from nations with non-democratic political traditions. These immigrants possessed foreign and dissimilar traits and were regarded with suspicion, fear and ridicule. At the root of this reaction toward these immigrant traits was a basic fear that these traits, if permitted to survive, would undermine the nation's political and social institutions. Corvello (1967) notes that these:

> foreigners and foreign ideas and ways were a threat to American political, economic, social stability, and security. The infiltration of foreign culture, it was feared, would eventually bring about a deterioration of the American "way of life".[12]

A fear that these immigrants would harbor loyalties to a foreign nation led to the rise of major anti-ethnic movements: the American Protective Association (1887), the Immigration Restriction League (1894), the Gentleman's Agreement with Japan (1908) and the Ku Klux Klan (1920). These antiethnic Americanization activities culminated with the 1921 restrictive immigration laws that closed the doors to an era of open door immigration as embodied in the Statue of Liberty. The response to this perceived threat posed by immigrants was Americanization programs designed "... to supress or eliminate all that was conceived of as 'foreign' and to impose upon the immigrant a cultural uniformity with an American pattern."[13] Cubberly, that pillar of American education, urged educators to actively destroy foreign cultures through schools. He preached:

> our task is to breakup their groups and settlements, to assimilate or amalgamate these people as part of the American race (*sic.*), and to implant in their children, so far as can be done, the Anglo-Saxon conception of righteousness, law, order, and popular government, and to awaken in them reverence for those things which we as people hold to be of abiding worth.[14]

With the massive flow of immigrants curtailed by immigration quotas, the public fervor over cultural diversity ebbed; the task of promoting Americanization shifted and came to rest almost entirely on the public educational system. Recent legislation and court rulings on bilingual education have rekindled the antiethnic embers of the old melting pot and the public debate found its way into the mass media.

Bilingual Education Controversy

Public opinion toward bilingual education is polarized into camps of opponents and advocates. The opponents, on the one hand, favor English-only instruction—the traditional immersion approach. They share the widespread opinion that since this approach worked well for European immigrants, it should work equally well for other language minorities. The proponents, on the other hand, favor instruction in the child's native language. Yet even among those that accept the need for bilingual education, a polarization is manifested in the dichotomy between advocates of either a transitional or a maintenance approach. The advocates of the so-called transitional approach to bilingual education favor the use of bilingual instruction in the early grades to allow the child to function in English and thus more effectively mainstream the child into English-language instruction. Conversely, the advocates of the so-called maintenance approach propose instruction in the native language to allow the child to maintain and expand the use of the native-language while learning English.

At one end of the spectrum, opponents of bilingual education argue that it perpetuates diversity and retards or preempts the learning of English. The underlying ideological premise is that bilingual education runs contrary to the Americanization, and thus de-ethnization, of culturally and linguistically different populations. Examples of these cleavages in public opinion toward bilingual education are abundantly evident in the media coverage of the debate.

Media Coverage of the Current Bilingual Education Debate

Media coverage of bilingual education has been very sparse and uneven; mostly critical. The most attention to the subject has been given by political commentators, columnists and the like. Notably absent are education columnists and feature writers. The majority of the notwithstanding sparse coverage has been in the print media, and the majority of this coverage has been simplistic, and narrowly focused attention on some controversial aspect of bilingual education.

The following excerpts are taken from articles appearing in a wide variety of print media sources. They range from local newspaper articles and letters to the editor, to articles in major national newspapers and magazines, to articles in education magazines and newsletters. The sample is not drawn through random selection, nor is it intended to be an exhaustive and complete sampling of the media articles that debate the merits of bilingual education. These articles are merely those that the author randomly compiled in a brief period to examine the ideological themes expressed. The sample is admittedly laden with articles against bilingual education since the vast majority of the media coverage, both print and broadcast, present views in opposition to bilingual education.

The following articles presented herein all reflect their author's opposition to bilingual education; the underlying reason for this opposition is the perceived threat to the traditional assimilation of cultural and linguistic differences through a melting pot approach.

Steven Rosenfeld, reporting on bilingual education in the *Washington Post* in 1974 observed that:

> Congress had radically altered the traditional way by which immigrants become Americanized. No longer will the public schools be expected to serve largely as a "melting pot," assimilating foreigners to a common culture."[15]

Philip Quigg, a former editor of *Foreign Affairs* magazine, wrote an article on bilingual education for *Instructor,* a magazine for elementary school teachers. He warns that:

> As Hispanic Americans acquire political influence comparable to their

> numbers, it is only to be expected that they will try to make it more convenient for Latinos to live and work without knowledge of English.[16]

He further pleads:

> let us not run the risk of endangering national unity and permitting ignorance of a common language to be added to the difficulties of communicating with one another.[17]

This view of bilingual education is echoed in a letter to the editor of the *San Mateo Times* by G. K. Bruce, M.D. The letter, published on February 7, 1979 argues that:

> It is time for statesmen of courage to recognize that bilingual education does not represent an honest governmental effort to help non-English-speaking students to learn English, but is rather self-perpetuating, ever enlarging special interest groups of ethnic specialists, bureaucrats and closet racists who demand money government no longer has to institutionalize a Tower of Babel.[18]

This same insistence on linguistic and cultural conformity is again echoed in a letter to the editor of the May 14, 1976 *Register Pajaronian*, a Watsonville, California newspaper. Richard Crawford candidly expressed his views on the subject. He wrote:

> After all is this the United States of America, or Mexico? Sometimes I wonder.
>
> I feel that anyone who moves to this country to live and work should also speak the language and live by the customs of our country.[19]

This letter was apparently prompted by a plea by the Chicano community in Watsonville for more Spanish-language television programming. Another letter to the editor in the same issue of the newspapers sent by the La Rue family admonished that:

> This is America. It is made up of all nationalities living together as Americans. If Spanish [TV] programming is what some people desire, it is their privilege. But they should live in Mexico where it is produced.[20]

This nationlist fervor for U.S. cultural and linguistic homogeniety is not restricted to the middle-American. In a recent article in the *San Jose Mercury News*, California Senator S. I. Hayakawa warns that bilingual education programs may create a separatist movement among Chicanos similar to the "sometimes violent movement" among the French in Quebec. Hayakawa argues that bilingual education may foster cultural chauvinism and urges that the ". . . acquisition of American culture is the first necessity" for immigrants.[21]

The threat of separatism is a recurring theme in the bilingual education debate. In the concluding paragraph of a generally well written and balanced article in *Time*, Von Nieda Bebe, a bilingual specialist, poses the question:

> Does bilingualism lead to separatism? Is Dade county going to secede from the U.S. when all the English [sic] have moved out?[22]

In response to this rhetorical question, Beebe notes that in Miami, "Spanish is threatening to swamp English completely," and that ". . . native-born Americans, reacting against the *Spanish tide,* are abandoning Dade county."[23] This fear of separatism is born of a fear that bilingual education poses an imminent threat to the established political and economic order.

Philip W. Quigg, writing in *Instructor* describes bilingual education as ". . . a crutch permitting minorities to postpone their day of reckoning when they must—for their good and ours—be equipped to handle English." He continues, "it invites the fearsome dissension born of linguistic dualism and tends to perpetuate cultural separatism." He further argues that, "The notion that minorities have linguistic rights which the state must preserve seems totally alien to the Constitution."[24] In this reference to the Constitution, Quigg alludes to the threat that bilingual education supposedly poses to the nation's political stability. A comparable concern is voiced by Noel Epstein in a lengthy article in the *Washington Post* on June 5, 1977. The one and one-fourth page article is entitled "The Bilingual Battle" and is accompanied by a subhead that asks, "Should Washington Finance Ethnic Identities?" A broad panoramic exploration of issues in bilingual education, the article was written while Epstein was on leave from the *Washington Post* to attend the Institute for Educational Leadership at George Washington University. (The article is reportedly an adaptation of a policy paper written for the Institute.) Epstein quickly frames bilingual education as a political issue; his thesis is that:

> There is no question that bilingual-bicultural education policy has been governed in large measure by the Hispanic American quest for more political and economic power and prestige. The policy has, in fact, become perhaps the largest federally funded expression in this country of the ethnic political wave that has swept the globe over the past 20 years or so.[25]

Epstein's narrow and paranoic view represents a threat to the established political order rather than an incorporation of a formerly politically-alienated oppressed population. In an effort to infuse his simplistic and distorted view with authority and wisdom, he quotes extensively from the polemics of *Idols of the Tribe,* written by Harold D. Isaacs, an MIT political scientist:

> We are experiencing on a massively universal scale a convulsive ingathering of people in their numberless grouping of kinds—tribal, racial, linguistic, religious, national. It is a great clustering into separateness that will, it is thought, improve, assure or extend each group's power or place, or keep it safe or safer from the power, threat or hostility of others. This is obviously no new condition, only the latest and by far the most inclusive chapter of the old story in which, after failing again to find how they can co-exist in sight of each other without tearing each other limb from limb, Isaac and Ishmael clash and part in panic and retreat once more to their caves.[26]

Most recently, Tom Bethell writing in the February, 1979 issue of *Harper's* decries the decision of the U.S. Supreme Court in the *Lau* v. *Nichols* ruling as a further erosion of the established political order. He argues:

> In effect, the Office of Civil Rights has taken the position that the immigrants' tongue was to be regarded as a right, not an impediment, and the Supreme Court has meekly gone along with that argument.

He further deplores the "cultural revisionism that is the covert purpose of so much of the bilingual program."[27] Bethell is joined by Paul Copperman, author of *The Literacy Hoax,* who is quoted in the February 21, 1979 issue of the *Report on Education Research* attacking the Supreme Court's 1974 *Lau* v. *Nichols* decision as one of the most reckless decisions by the Court, since there is no evidence that there is a method of instruction better for foreign-speaking students than teaching them totally in English.[28] The need for these students to learn English is given a new twist by Congressman John Ashbrook of Ohio who is quoted by Bethell to have argued on the House floor that . . . "someday, somebody is going to have to teach those young people to speak English or else they are going to become public charges."[29]

Another prevailing theme in the media is the view of bilingual education as a necessary evil that must be tolerated as an intrim measure to assimilate the culturally and linguistically different child. Joseph Califano, HEW Secretary, is reported urging school districts administering bilingual education programs to have their project students "learn English as rapidly as possible" as the law mandates in the February 7, 1979 issue of *Report of Education Research.*[30] James Ward of AFT is quoted in the February 13, 1978 issue of *Time* as saying:

> "We fully recognize the benefits of cultural pluralism but we must be sure that the central effort is to bring students into the mainstream of American life."[31]

In an editorial favoring an increase in federal funds for bilingual education in California, the April 17, 1974 issue of the *San Jose Mercury* applauds the Supreme Court decision in *Lau* v. *Nichols* yet attests that ". . . proper assimilation of such children into the American scene is in the entire nation's interest—just as it is everyone's responsibility."[32]

Additional articles from a variety of sources reviewed by the author all repeat the two essential themes evident in these articles quoted. They are (1) the perception that bilingual education violates the norms and cultural assumptions under which ethnic and linguistic minority cultures have traditionally obtained an education in this nation and (2) the equating of bilingual education with the political ascendency of Hispanics in this decade. Nothing would be gained by citing additional examples.

To summarize, the significance of the public debate on bilingual education conducted through the mass media is that (1) this is the sole source of information on bilingual education that the majority of the citizens will receive and (2) the mass media characteristically simplifies, polarizes and distorts the issues and personalities involved. The sole-source effect of the mass media debate of bilingual education is that the general population forms an opinion and attitude toward bilingual education on the basis of very limited information. This problem is compounded by the manner in which the mass media presents the information. It is endemic that the mass circulation, commercial media simplify and highlight selected aspects of an issue or event. In this case, the mass media have cast bilingual education as a controversy pitting assimilationists against divisive separatists. Consequently, the most pronounced effect of the mass media on the public debate over bilingual education is the way that it has been able to define and limit the scope of the issues being discussed.

The implications of these media effects on the formulation of public policy are that the manner in which bilingual education is being presented through the mass media evokes racist fears and anxieties among the general population and thereby delimits the scope of legislation, court rulings and policy implementation. The current transitional orientation of bilingual education legislation (i.e., ESEA Title VII), and the Supreme Court ruling on the *Lau* v. *Nichols* case as a civil rights issue reflects the subtle impact of an antipluralistic public opinion that was crystalized and brought to the surface by the manner in which the mass media frames the issues surrounding bilingual education in the U.S.

REFERENCES

Advertising Age, August 5, 1974.

Advertising Age, May 24, 1976.

Bagdikian, Ben H. *The Information Machines.* New York: Harper & Row, 1971.

Bailey, G. "Bilingual Education draws Hayakawa ire: Quebec violence fear," *San Jose Mercury.*

Bethell, T. "Against Bilingual Education: Why Johnny Can't Speak English," *Harper's,* February, 1979, pp. 30-33.

Bogart, L. "As Media Change, How Will Advertisers?" *Journal of Advertising Research,* 13:5 (October, 1973), pp. 25-29.

Breed, Warren. *The Newspaperman, News and Society.* Columbia University, 1952, unpublished dissertation.

Breed, Warren. "Social Control in the Newsroom: A Descriptive Study." *Social Forces.* 33, (1955) pp. 326-35.

Bruce, G. K. Letter to the Editor, *The San Mateo Times,* February 7, 1979, p. 28.

"Budget Gives Bilingual Ed $174 Million for English Emphasis." *Report on Education Research.* February 7, 1979, p. 6.

Bunce, Richard. *Television in the Corporate Interest.* New York: Praeger, 1976.

Cordasco, Francesco. *Bilingual Schooling in the United States: A Sourcebook for Educational Personnel.* New York: McGraw-Hill, 1976.

Covello, Leonard. *The Social Background of the Italo-American Child: A Study of the Southern Italian Family Mores and their Effect on the School Situation in Italy and America.* Leiden, Netherlands: E.J. Brill, 1967.

Crawford, Richard. Letter to the Editor, *Register Pajaronian,* May 14, 1976.

Cubberly, Ellwood P. *Changing Conceptions of Education.* Boston, Houghton Mifflin, 1909.

Cutlip, Scott. "Content and Flow of AP News - From Trunk to TTS to Reader." *Journalism Quarterly.* Fall, 1954, pp. 434-446.

De Fleur, Melvin. *Theories of Mass Communication.* 2d ed. New York: David McKay Co., 1970.

Editorial. *San Jose Mercury,* April 17, 1974, p. 24.

Epstein, Noel. "The Bilingual Battle: Should Washington Finance Ethnic Identities?" *The Washington Post,* June 5, 1977, pp. C1 and C4.

"Feds Should Take Part of Blame for Poor Achievement, Panel Says." *Report on Education Research*, February 21, 1979, p. 5.

Fishman, Joshua A. "Language Maintenance in a supra-Ethnic Age: Summary and conclusions." In Francesco Cordasco. *Bilingual Schooling in the United States*. New York: McGraw-Hill, 1976. Reprinted from Joshua A. Fishman. *Language Loyalty in the United States: The Maintenance and Perpetuation of Non-English Mother Tongues by American Ethnic and Religious Groups*. The Hague: Mouton, 1966.

Gerbner, George. "An Institutional Approach to Mass Communications Research." In Lee Thayer (ed. and comp.), *Communication Theory and Research: Proceedings of the First International Symposium*. Springfield, Illinois: Charles C. Thomas Publishers, 1967.

__________. "The Structure and Process of Television Program Content Regulation in the United States." In *Television and Social Behavior*, Vol I. Washington, D.C.: U.S. Government Printing Office, 1972.

__________. "Cultural Indicators: The Third Voice." In George Gerbner, Larry P. Gross and William H. Melody, *Communications Technology and Social Policy*. New York: John Wiley and Sons, 1973.

Gerbner, George and Larry Gross. "Living with Television: The Violence Profile." *Journal of Communication*, 26:2 (Spring, 1976): 173-199.

Hartman, Edward G. *The Movement to Americanize the Immigrant*. New York: Columbia University Press, 1948.

International Television Almanac, 1975. New York: Quigley Publishing Co., 1975.

Kohn, H. *American Nationalism*. New York: Collier, 1961.

La Rue Family. Letter to the Editor, *Register Pajaronian*, May 14, 1976.

Rivers, William L. *The Opinion Makers: The Washington Press Corp*. Boston: Beacon Press, 1965.

Rucker, Bryce W. *The First Freedom*. Carbondale: Southern Illinois University Press, 1968.

Schramm, Wilbur, and J. Alexander. "Broadcasting." In Ithiel de Sola Pool, Fredrick W. Frey, Wilbur Schramm, Nathan Maccoby and Edwin B. Parker (eds.), *Handbook of Communication*. Chicago: Rand McNally, 1973.

"The Three Rs in 70 Tongues: Debating the Uses of Bilingual Instruction." *Time*, February 13, 1978, p. 65.

White, David Manning. "The Gatekeeper: A Case Study in the Selection of News." *Journalism Quarterly*. Fall 1950 pp. 383-390.

NOTES

1. In the past two decades, it has shifted from a system of production oriented to provide the heavy equipment and machinery required for industrial development, to one oriented to the production of consumer goods and services. This change is reflected in the growth of personal consumption expenditures (PCE) for services. In 1950, thirty-three percent of all the nation's PCE were for consumer services. Two decades later, by 1972, the PCE for consumer services had increased to forty-two percent (Bogart, 1973). The incessant supply of these con-

sumer products and services requires a comparably incessant consumption.

2. In 1970, the U.S. expenditure for advertising was almost $20 billion, or $96 per capita, the largest proportion of GNP spent on advertising of any nation. Two percent of the U.S. GNP for 1975 was spent on advertising; in fact, advertising expenditures in the U.S. have run at around two percent of the GNP fairly consistently since 1940. The advertising support of commercial broadcasting in the U.S. amounts to more than $4.5 billion a year of which a vast majority goes to television. Advertising revenues provide eighty-three percent of television broadcasting's total income. It is indeed symbolic that the first test pattern broadcast in an early experiment of television was a dollar bill (Rucker, 1968).
3. In contrast to commercial media, non-commercial or public media reaches only a very small, generally elite segment of the population. Therefore, in this paper, the term mass media is used synonymously with commercial media.
4. When only those radio and television stations owned and operated by the three major networks are taken into account, their coverage of the national audience is 67.5% of the total, according to data cited in Richard Bunce. *Television in the Corporate Interest.* New York: Praeger, 1976.
5. Concentration of ownership and economic activity is not unique to these industries; rather, it is increasingly a characteristic feature of the nation's economy. For example, in 1950, fifty-four percent of all general retail stores were chain owned. By 1972, this had increased to seventy-eight percent of all general retail stores. Comparable concentration is also evident in food retailing. Chain ownership increased from thirty-eight percent in 1950 to fifty-six percent in 1972 (Bogart, 1973).
6. This alliance with television has meant lucrative gains for the advertising agencies; for at least the last decade, their profit margins have been averaging around eight percent (*Advertising Age,* August 5, 1974).
7. Procter & Gamble's dominance as the nation's largest advertiser is unrivaled. It projected ad expenditures in 1976 for one product alone, Charmin bathroom tissue, of $250 million, compared to General Motor's total advertising budget for 1975 of $261 million (*Advertising Age,* December 15, 1975).
8. Gerbner, 1967:429.
9. Gerbner and Gross, 1976:176.
10. Elsewhere, Gerbner (1973) argues that, "Studies demonstrate that the mass cultural presentation of many aspects of life and types of action teach lessons that serve institutional purposes. People do not have to accept these lessons but cannot escape having to deal with the social norms, the agenda of issues, and the calculus of life's changes implicit in them."

    Defleur (1971) regards the function of media programming as eliciting the attention of the largest audience and persuading them to purchase goods, while remaining sufficiently within the bounds of moral norms and standards of taste. This orientation of mass media stems from the functional imperative of a social system: to motivate the audience to carry out roles to satisfy the needs of the system.

11. The process by which certain items are either selected or ignored is guided by prevailing assumption of newsworthiness. This selection process, commonly termed gatekeeping, has been the subject of numerous studies. For a discussion of this process, consult B. H. Bagdikian, *The Information Machines* (1971); D. M. White, "The Gatekeeper or A Case Study in the Selection of News," *Journalism Quarterly,* Fall, 1950; S. M. Cutlip, "Content and Flow of AP News—from Trunk to TTS to Reader," *Journalism Quarterly,* Fall, 1954; W. L. Rivers, *The Opinion Makers; The Washington Press Corps* (1965); W. Breed, "The Newspaperman, News and Society," (1952); and W. Breed, "Social Control in the Newsroom: A Descriptive Study," *Social Forces* (1955) among others.
12. Corvello, 1967:411
13. Corvello, ibid.
14. Cubberly, 1909: 16
15. Quoted in Bethell, 1979.
16. Quigg, 1978. This article was run as a point-counterpoint feature in a number of Ridder-Knight newspapers around the country in early January, 1979. The counterpoint to Quigg's views was expressed by María Medina Swanson, formerly the president of the National Association of Bilingual Education and presently, Chairperson of the HEW National Advisory Council for Bilingual Education.
17. Quigg, ibid.
18. Bruce, 1979
19. Crawford, 1976.
20. LaRue, 1976.
21. Bailey, 1979.
22. *Time,* February 13, 1978.
23. *Time,* ibid., emphasis mine.
24. Quigg, ibid.
25. Epstein, 1977
26. Quoted in Epstein, ibid.
27. Bethell, 1979
28. *Report on Education Research,* February 21, 1979
29. Bethell, *loc. cit.*
30. *Report,* February 7, 1979
31. *Time,* February 13, 1978
32. Editorial, *San Jose Mercury,* April 17, 1974.

DEVELOPING AN ADVOCACY MODEL IN BILINGUAL EDUCATION: A STRATEGY FOR PROGRAM IMPLEMENTATION

Rodolfo Martinez

This is an essay on the politics of bilingual education. It is suggested as an attempt to focus attention on the need for the study of politics and its relationship to the formulation of educational policy.

It is also intended to underscore the need to develop an awareness that bilingual education, at the present, is a political program dependent on political support for its continued existence. The present status of countermoves in some states to weaken the foothold of bilingual education is symptomatic of the failure of practitioners to develop the area of educational political gamesmanship. This evidence is further reinforced by the fact that in the ten years of the existence of Title VII-ESEA programs, the literature in the field of politics in bilingual education is virtually nonexistent.

One of the reasons for this dearth of research is that American educators traditionally maintain the concept that politics and education do not mix. For the most part, they feel that for them to participate in politics demeans their stature and dilutes their professional standing.

Iannaccone (1967) suggests that those who believe education and politics should be kept separate, ignore the fact that they have *never* been separated. One has only to examine the transformation of the U.S. Office of Education from a "consumer-oriented" delivery system (Mosher, 1977); established in 1867, the federal education agency was primarily used to gather educational statistics and to disseminate information. However, with the growth of educational professions and their increasing influence in the policy-making processes of government, the office was soon transformed into a vital force in the educational enterprise of the nation. The rapid increase in the funding policies has enabled vested interest groups to become more articulate in maintaining productive lines of communication with the federal government.

For the bilingual program educator, the primary task is to understand the political process and to work through it in order to accomplish the goals of the program. Martinez has hypothesized that personnel in bilingual education programs should understand the political process, not only for the adoption of the bilingual education innovative enterprise, but also to help bring about the adoption and implementation of the innovation in the school system, after outside funding stops.

The recent revival of the bilingual education movement in the late 1960s often catapulted into administrative and teaching positions Latino educators who found themselves outsiders on an all-Anglo staff. Because of their rapid hiring into the system, these educators often found themselves without the benefit of an established set of interrelationships (network) in the educational system which they could rely on for support in the competitive struggle which invariably accompanies the adoption of an innovative enterprise or the formulation of educational policy. To compound the situation, they often came to their positions because of the community pressures that prompted many school districts to apply for federal funding in order to establish bilingual education programs. Frequently, community input was given in the selection of personnel for the administrative and teaching staff. This often made the newly employed personnel suspect, because the educational establishment jealously guards this function as one of its prerogatives.

The catalytic function of bilingual education personnel in the implementation of bilingual education programs frequently met stiff resistance from central office staffs (COS) who generally are not noted for their willingness to bring about change or to adopt educational innovative enterprises (House, 1974). They often devised ways of ensuring that bilingual personnel did not upset the equilibrium in the system by placing bureaucratic obstacles before them such as holding audit evaluations, or establishing a peer group panel (usually made up of Anglos) to determine salary increases, and the like (Martinez, 1977a). Often, the bilingual program personnel encountered "foot dragging" in the delivery of supportive services such as supplies and materials through regular channels. Other "gatekeeping" tactics and maneuvers were generally employed in order to soon delimit the "territory" of the bilingual program personnel. In addition, tactics such as employing "safe" Latino educators were often used by school districts and these newly employed persons were watched closely by the COS administrators so that they kept their place.

To fully understand these forces at work, it is necessary to first understand the bureaucratic environment in which they operate, discern the inter-workings of the various groupings which make up the bureaucracy, and view the impact on the bilingual education program personnel.

The School District Bureaucratic Setting

It can be generalized that the initial implementation point for bilingual education programs takes place at the school district central administration office. It is at this nerve center that the various interest group pressures come to bear on those officers who will not only make final decisions about programmatic design, but also about the staffing of the project. Because these two functions are vital in helping to safeguard their territory, the regular COS must ensure that the final policy decisions do not threaten their status. As a way of protecting their defined territory, the various groups usually begin to competitively struggle to maintain the upper hand.

This view is not usually understood by the general public because it is generally assumed that the school system is a deliberate, integrated, problem-solving institution which assesses all of the strong points and weaknesses of any proposed program or policy. In reality, the school central administration is made up of various departments and units engaged in a competitive struggle for scarce resources. The final outcome depends on which group, or coalition of groups, is on the rise at the moment (House, 1974).

The COS, according to McGivney and Haught (1972), perceives itself to be in control of the educational process because it is made up of professional educators who know the craft of education. They would rather play the political game within the "privileged sanctuary of its private preserves" (Iannaccone, 1967). These educators, called "pedagogues" by Iannaccone, participate in the political "pedagogics" exercised by the select few who have "mastered the mysteries of education expertise."

To effectively exercise mastery over this process, the COS employs techniques such as "stacking the deck," which involves including two or more of its own members in the recruitment of new teachers to ensure that the "right" persons are employed. Another technique involves "lining up the ducks," which means that administrative positions are advertised *only* after the COS has lined up a candidate for the position (McGiveny and Haught, 1972).

McGivney and Haught also suggest that the COS is made up of several groups, with two major ones interacting daily. One of these interacts at the superintendent's weekly administrative staff meeting. It also has "gatekeeping" functions which control the flow of information to the superintendent and to the elected board of education members.

The other major group is generally made up of members of the "old guard" who have more tenure in the district and still show an orientation towards the leadership of the former superintendent. The members of this group enjoy a greater rapport with the building principals and teachers.

Each of the major groups is divided into subgroups which interact with the major group in official and social capacities. It soon becomes apparent that each new idea has to earn a consensus in both the minor and major subgroups before it can pass to the larger group for official sanction. Outside proposals presented to the school board are referred to the COS for consideration. Failure to receive a consensus for approval from the COS means complete rejection. However, the COS tries to intercept all outside proposals before they get to the school board. Whenever outside proposals are made at public meetings, the COS tries to undermine the credibility of outside groups by questioning their sources of information (McGivney and Haught, 1972), thereby impugning their validity.

It should be noted that these groups are conditional in nature and happened to be temporary coalitions which may be on the ascendancy at a particular point in time. Rather than being enduring work compacts, they are more like "uneasy truces" (Briner and Iannaccone, 1971). Because of this provisional character, advocacy groups can frequently muster enough strength to obtain program approval though some COS groups may be reluctant to give it.

Infighting continues at another administrative level which can spell a deathblow to the implementation of a bilingual-bicultural education program if the political process is not effectively handled. This action takes place at the building level where the interests of the school system, the community, and the teachers come into sharp focus.

The school district's representative at the building level is the principal, the central administration's "middle-man" who implements school district policy and ideology at the local level (Spindler, 1963). He presides at the nerve center of his outpost, transmitting to the central administration sentiments, feelings, and reactions from pupils, parents, and classroom teachers.

When confrontations take place between the various interest groups in his domain, he transmits information to the central administration office. He also attempts to mediate the struggle in order to maintain continuity and stability in the system.

The principal's role, then, becomes one of "balancer of forces" to produce order, and is less apt to bring about innovative changes. Thus, as an officer of the organization, he becomes one of the most important socializing agents in the system.

The main interests of the teacher lie in job security and job protection, particularly in an era of declining enrollments and in the face of teacher lay-offs. For bilingual education programs already in operation, this presents a potential conflict because teachers feel their "territory" is invaded with bilingual-bicultural teachers who report to their buildings. For some, social action programs which seem to favor the minorities also constitute a threat to them. Many try to find subtle ways to impugn the credibility of the program by their view that the learning of English is the most important objective.

The community's and the parents' interests become visible at the building level because they can identify with the system through the neighborhood school. Its location is in the proximity and represents the education process to them. The central administration office seems so distant, particularly in the large urban school systems.

It is the community which can ultimately bring about change in the system. The process through which this is accomplished is politics. Cistone (1972) maintains that the political process determines the scope and character of education by allocating costs and benefits. He further suggests that there is an interdependence between the schools and the political system. If one accepts this, then one must recognize the vital role played by the community in the educational process.

The Community's Role in Bilingual-Bicultural Education

Educators, generally, have not yet learned to fully appreciate the vital role which the community can play in the educational process. For bilingual-bicultural education, community resources constitute the very foundation of its vitality and strength. For it is only through effective community utilization of the political system that any hope can be generated for the institutionalization and adoption of bilingual-bicultural education programs into the regular school curriculum. Evidence is overwhelming that school districts are slow to change; however, in places where the community has utilized the political process, bilingual education programs have been adopted by the school system.

For the effective implementation of bilingual education programs, the most important task is for the personnel in bilingual education programs to learn to effectively use the commmunity. To this end, one must first learn about the community and the various functions and roles it can play.

In another study (Martinez, 1977a), it has been suggested that although there are several communities involved in the educational process, there are two which are most important to the educator. One of these is the Education Political Action Community (EPAC) and the other is the Education Action Community (EAC). The EPAC, it is suggested, is the community most closely involved in the political process. It provides militancy when needed, and applies pressure to the sensitive school administration pressure points when essential. By the nature of its role, it provides the thrust that can bring about change because of its political clout developed by the broad base of support from the target minority, as well as from the leadership style of its charismatic leaders.

On the other hand, the EAC's main functions are more academically oriented and generally deal with those roles that are advisory in nature. When the EAC functions as a bilingual education program advisory committee, it gives the central administration office perceptions about the program in order to enable the staff of the program to determine whether the program is able to meet the needs of students. This advisory function also enables the committee to make recommendations for program modification; give inputs for the proposal; provide on-going monitoring and evaluation; give inputs on programmatic content; and help identify the cultural content which should be included in the program.

These different functions and roles exercised by both communities are essential to the effective implementation of bilingual-bicultural education programs in the school system. The important charge becomes for the program staff to distinguish which functions can be best performed by either of the two communities to ensure program survival. It is unfortunate that many bilingual program personnel fail to distinguish between the two communities and expect them to perform those roles which the community may not be prepared to exercise. The EPAC, for instance, can play four vital and significant roles: (1) it gives political support to the bilingual education program, helping to assure the continuation of the program; (2) it helps to sensitize old-line administrators to the needs of bilingual children; (3) it helps to expand the program to other buildings and grade levels once it has attained success in its initial implementation; and (4) it assesses community needs and provides the political resources to pressure the school districts into responding.

The EAC has functions which are also necessary to make the program successful. They are as follows: (1) it makes the program accountable to federal and state education officials by monitoring the project to ensure that the objectives are being met; (2) it assists the school district by making the bilingual education program responsive to specific cultural and educational needs; and (3) it provides flexibility to the program by making it adapt to change with its on-going feedback mechanism which provides input to the program on the changing needs of the students.

The responsibility now becomes for the program staff personnel to mobilize the two communities so that they can assume an advocacy role. It must be remembered that the superintendent, in order to function effectively, must have community support for the educational management and programming of the school system and must have stability and flexibility in the organization in order to function effectively (Walker, 1968). An adroit superintendent is successful in maintaining a balance between the external pressures which resist the change and those who demand it so that the needs of children can be met. He is also dependent on the community for the political support necessary to fund the normal activities of the school educational enterprise, particularly at bond elections. It behooves the constituent communities in bilingual education to determine a propitious time to pressure the sensitive central administration pressure points, thereby serving notice that they have assumed advocacy functions.

It would seem reasonable to assume that the most auspicious time could be determined by those who know the program well and who have knowledge of the inner-workings of the central administration system. Thus, the bilingual education program personnel would play a key role.

The Political Role of Bilingual Education Program Personnel

It is suggested that staff personnel involved in bilingual education programs must appreciate the fact that one of their most important functions is to serve as a vital link between the community and the school system. Current federal guidelines mandate that bilingual-bicultural education programs have advisory committees made up of parents and students in the program which give programmatic inputs as well as exercise all of the functions which have been outlined above for the EAC communities. This institutionalized method of involving parents and community, mandates that bilingual program personnel establish a relationship with them. This, therefore, gives the staff an excellent opportunity to establish a community advocacy group for purposes of sustaining the program.

This vital linkage function can be seen in the Rand Corporation study made by Berman and McLaughlin (1975) for the US Department of Health, Education, and Welfare, in which they conclude that in the federally funded programs studied, federal policy had little influence on the project outcome and that program adoption, once federal funds were no longer available, depended on the ground work established by the local project personnel. It was further concluded that federal money in itself did not provide the necessary stimulus for the school districts to adopt the program once funds were no longer available. Even though most school systems promised to continue the programs, they only made the promises in order to obtain funding. Program adoption through local funding really depended on the relationship established with the community.

In another Rand Corporation study, Sumner and others (1975) point out that all of the bilingual education projects visited exhibited almost the same level of success because the project personnel had established linkages with the community. What is meant by this is that the programs had reached a high degree of achievement because they had community support (see Martinez, 1977a). In addition, Sumner, et al found that project personnel had extended this community support to develop the political clout necessary to assist in the passage of state bilingual legislation. It would appear that the project personnel involved were successful in developing the necessary skills to use the appropriate communities in an advocacy role when necessary.

Role of Godfather-Patron and Power Broker

It was suggested in another study (Martinez, 1977a) that the bilingual education program personnel must cultivate the skills necessary to deal with the community. It was proposed that the staff should learn the functions and roles of godfather-patrons and power brokers, and they should articulate them so that they can develop those political skills necessary for program survival. The functions of the godfather-patron are as follows:

1. *Voluntary.* The patron-client relation in the social network context is voluntary on the part of the actors in which said association is based on mutual obligations and expectations. Each has needs which the other can fill, and once service was performed, it established an obligation for a reciprocal service on a *quid pro quo* basis (Foster, 1969).
2. *Personalized.* This relationship is a personalized, affective relationship in which one has a superior position in the social network because of the resources at his command. It becomes "binding" and "adhesive" because of its affective character (Lemarchand and Legg, 1972).
3. *Mediation.* In the social network where mobility is limited, the patron is able to perform mediation services, particularly in societies in which the bureaucratic infrastructure has developed. Thus, he is able to speak to bureaucrats in behalf of his client (Silverman, 1965).
4. *Linkages.* Because of the resources at his command, the godfather-patron is able to establish linkages at all levels of the social network. This function becomes important for bilingual education program staff personnel in that they are able to move through the various bureaucratic levels, serving as a link between the community and the school district administration.
5. *Communications.* Patron-client relationships provide for the development of a communications system in which clients rely on their patrons for information because of the social distance between them and their social betters. Patrons facilitate access to them particularly in official capacities in which they are seeking services (Boissenvain, 1966).
6. *Mutual Benefits.* The patronage system is mutually beneficial to all parties. On the one hand, the client receives the necessary services requested, while on the other the patron benefits by the information provided on the activities of the patron's enemies. Armed with this information, the patron's power is increased. The more power he has, the more he is able to serve the client's needs, thereby increasing his power. Power begets power.

The godfather-patron roles can assist bilingual education staff personnel in cultivating political skills to ensure not only program survival, but also the survival of the staff personnel. The program administrators, for example, can provide employment opportunities for community people at the paraprofessional level so that the community's interest and stake in program survival increases. In those school districts where there are few or no bilingual-bicultural teachers employed, the Project offers professional opportunities to bring into the system professionally trained teachers from the target linguistic group.

In addition, the godfather-patronage system can be extended to bring regular school teachers and administrators into this social network. Regular teachers in the building, for example, can be invited to attend bilingual education conferences and seminars to increase their awareness and understanding of the needs of bilingual children. The bilingual program staff person can also make conference attendance available to building administrators as well as to supplement his usually meager resources such as paper supplies, materials, ditto fluid, and the like. Co-optation of the principal is crucial because the success or failure of the program rests, in large measure, with the support he gives to it (Martinez, 1977a).

It can be concluded that if this godfather-patron role is played with articulate boldness, the program staff personnel and administrators will succeed in obtaining vital community support which will give them maneuvering room when dealing with hard-core bureaucrats who feel threatened by an invasion of their "territory." This community support can also protect bilingual administrators in the school system. It must be noted that they are probably new in the central administration which is overwhelmingly staffed by Anglo administrators who have been in the district for a period of time and came up the bureaucratic ladder through a series of linkages and friendships. In the process of continuous jockeying and maneuvering for membership in the "in-group" close to the superintendent, an outsider, who in all likelihood is a minority person, is hired to administer the bilingual program. The COS's immediate reaction is to keep a watchful eye to see that he does not gain power within the administrative hierarchy with such techniques as "double-teaming" him to see that all decisions such as hiring of personnel, purchase of supplies and equipment, and the like, are "safe" decisions and do not "rock the boat."

This condition places the bilingual program staff person in a vulnerable position, leaving him at the mercy of the Anglo COS. Being new in the system, or at least in that position, he has not yet built a network of social relationships with the COS network. It is almost certain that he does not have linkages with "in-group" members. This places the program staff in possible jeopardy and makes program survival uncertain.

In addition to the role of godfather-patron, the program staff personnel (particularly the director) must develop the ability to function as a power broker because he has at his disposal more than the normal share of resources such as the fifteen percent of the total bilingual education program budget which is earmarked for training.

A prototype project training program might include a variety of activities such as conference attendance and enrollment at a local college or university to take courses in bilingual education. For those teachers and administrators who are trying to upgrade their skills, an opportunity to get additional college credit which can be translated into an increase in the pay increment is an opportunity which will be cherished by all recipients. This gives the bilingual program staff person power.

It is the effective use of power which helps the staff personnel to develop skills of power brokerage. It requires that the person cultivate the talent for adroit maneuvering and the capacity to take risks without fear of failure. This role, tenuous though it may be, will enable the staff person to complement his role of godfather-patron. It has several characteristics:

1. *Personal Influence.* The broker has the skill and ability to link units and persons at different levels in a social network which makes access to higher status persons difficult for those of inferior positions (Adams, 1970). It is almost certain that in communities with bilingual programs, parents and community leaders do not have access to COS personnel who make decisions which affect their children.
2. *Man-in-the-Middle.* The brokerage system suggests that the social

network is static and that there is little upward mobility (Adams, 1970). For the parents of bilingual children, it would seem that the system remains static because minorities do not have the education, economic status, or social position as the Anglos. Thus, the power broker fulfills a vital function by assisting minority members in confronting those in superior status positions. The broker is able to place those persons in an inferior status in contact with those of a superior station. The broker gains power every time such a transaction is completed.

3. *Resource Information.* The power broker has power because he possesses information (Paine, 1971). This information may not necessarily be used in his brokerage role, but the fact that he has knowlege of the various roles and functions of various departments enhances that power. The bilingual program staff person derives power from the fact that he possesses information about the various functions of the influential COS persons in school departments. Thus, this capacity to determine the real wielders of power in the central administration office offers the broker the opportunity to bring the influential person together with the community person or parent. The broker knows where the power lies.

The calculated development and exercise of the godfather-patron and power broker roles by the program staff person will not only help assure program survival, but that of the bilingual personnel as well. The articulation of these functions requires that the program staff kindle the political process necessary for the formation of an advocacy group.

The "Inside-Outside" Advocacy Model

It is suggested that one of the most important factors in ensuring the adoption of an educational enterprise is the formation of an advocacy group which will become one of the strongest elements in seeking resources for implementation (House, 1974). Usually advocates, led by a charismatic leader, will seek all resources possible to ensure survival of the program. The advocacy leader may be a school administrator or an outsider, but all energies have to be exerted within the administrative structure for it is there that educational enterprises succeed or fail.

To obtain adoption and institutionalization of bilingual-bicultural education programs in a school district, the project personnel (particularly the director) must assume an advocate's role. He can organize human and financial resources at his disposal to assist in the institutionalization process. As a leader, his success depends on his willingness to boldly and calculatedly take the necessary risks to impact the system. Thus, he becomes an *inside* advocate.

It is also postulated that an advocacy group must be established *outside* of the school administrative establishment. This group should be community-based and politically oriented so that it can provide the necessary pressures which cannot be exerted from the inside because the bilingual education program personnel are part of the system and must give loyalty and faithful service to the system or they will be dealt with accordingly. This is not to imply that the activities of the program personnel may be in contradiction to the philosophy of the school district. It merely means that the actions of the program staff may be misinterpreted by bigoted administrators who do not have an understanding of bilingual education and see it as "un-American."

The *outside* advocacy group should be led by a community person with strong political leanings accentuated by a mixture of militancy and charisma which will enable him to mobilize community resources. He stands to gain from this role because his political power is enhanced by his ability to meet the needs of the community.

The fusion of these two advocates into a meaningful partnership based on mutual commitment and trust is the basis of the proposed "Inside-Outside" Advocacy Model which can be seen diagrammed in Figure 1. The hierarchial positions in the pyramid show the various levels of responsibility ranging from superintendent (at the apex) to supervisors and department heads. The circles represent the various informal groupings which form in the bureaucracy and in which some administrators may have overlapping membership. The bilingual education program administrator is shown in a lone square, denoting an almost certain lack of membership in the various groupings.

The rectangle to the right of the pyramid suggests the two communities which have been discussed above. However, it should be noted that in all probability, the leadership comes from the EPAC.

The success of the model depends on the relationship established between the "inside" and the "outside" advocates. This relationship implies the sharing of philosophy and commitment to the bilingual education concept which is followed by the school district. In fact, this team can exert the necessary pressure to cause the system to adopt the bilingual concept shared by the advocates. For example, given the community support for a maintenance type of bilingual education program, the school system will be hard pressed to adopt it.

The "inside" advocate possesses certain characteristics which are essential for the effective functioning of the partnership. They are as follows:

1. *Technical Knowledge.* Because of professional training, the advocate possesses the pedagogical and methodological background for utilization of bilingual education for the training of children of limited-English-speaking ability. In addition, he is knowledgeable about the research and literature in the field which he can use to convince a skeptical administrator or parent about the benefits of bilingual education programs.
2. *Information Sharing.* The advocate has much information regarding the technical aspects of the program as well as information of the political climate in the central administration office. As a member of the COS, he should have an accurate picture of the *real* power wielders in the office and who has the ear of the superintendent. Sharing this information with the "outside" advocate will give the latter the information on whom to "hit" with political pressure. It would be ineffectual if the pressure is applied to someone who cannot make decisions or does not have credibility among colleagues.
3. *Educational Concept.* The advocate must have knowledge of the concept of bilingual education which is to be implemented in the district. Of particular importance is knowledge of the relationship of bilingual education to the regular school curriculum, because it becomes paramount in the institutionalization process.
4. *Professional Competence.* The advocate must be an effective administrator and have the credentials necessary to build up a credibility among COS colleagues. Once this credibility is built, he will

FIG. 1: The "Inside-Outside" Advocacy Model

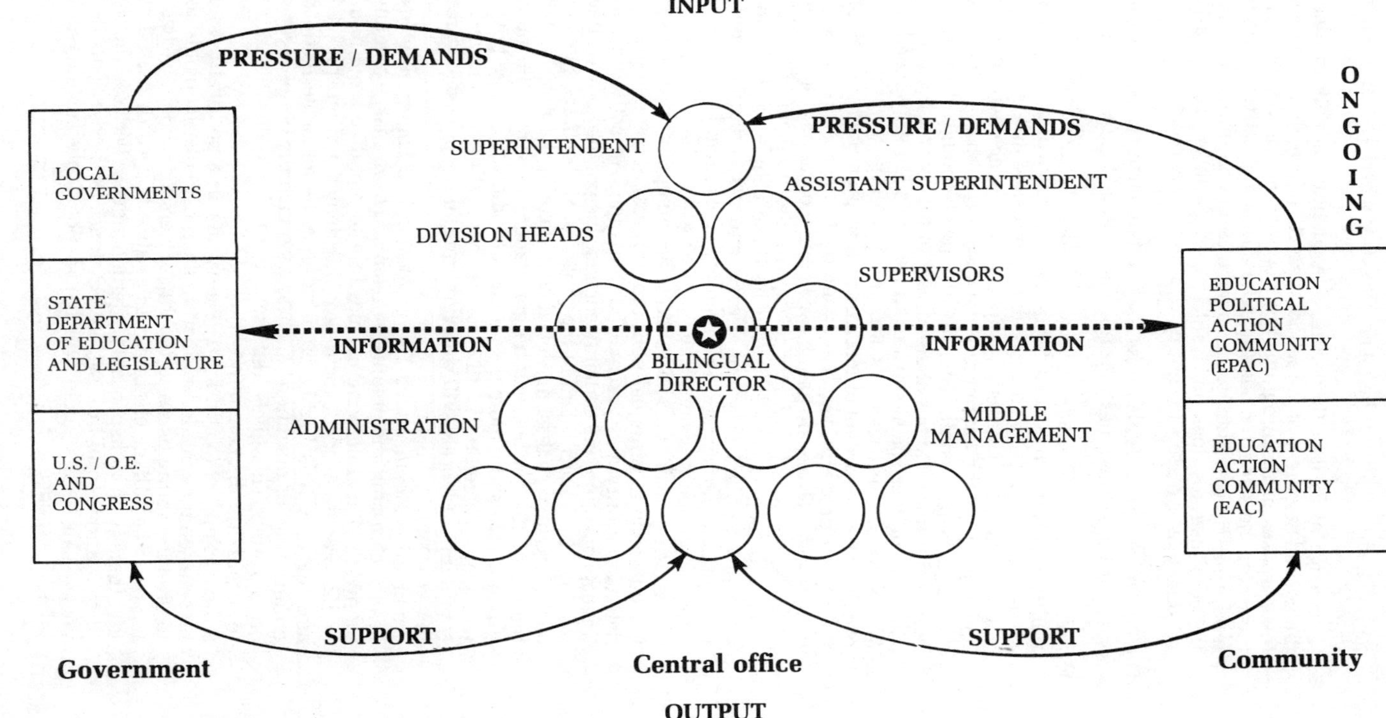

be listened to and will be taken seriously whenever an opinion is voiced.

5. *Knowledge of District Resources.* The advocate is able to identify the needed resources of the school district and use them to advance the purposes of the program. For example, he knows that school buses can be used for certain extra-curricular activities such as field trips. He can identify the person in charge in the event that the administrator does not want to provide buses and gives lack of money as a reason for not providing transportation.

The "outside" advocate also possesses certain characteristics which are necessary for the success of the team. They are as follows:

1. *Political Power.* The advocate, as a leader in the community, has political power which can be translated into votes. Local politicians court his favor and he is able to translate this courtship into voting lists which he is able to produce at election time. As a spokesman for the community, he speaks out on the social issues of the day and people listen to him (even though they may not agree with him). He has attained part of this power because of his ability to deliver social services to needy community members.
2. *Militancy.* The advocate is vocal and is willing to publicly attack or criticize city or state officials as well as prominent businessmen for alleged practices which are contrary to the best interests of the community. These allegations may be accusations of racism, or other issues which are sure to capture the newspaper headlines. Such a person is usually feared by these people for they do not want any publicity. School superintendents certainly avoid adverse publicity, therefore, a community spokesman is usually given a hearing when he wants one.
3. *Constituent-Consumer.* The advocate has an opportunity to exercise his influence in bilingual education programs because they mandate community and parental participation. An active role in bilingual education will certainly enhance his political power, thereby making him a constituent of the program. He becomes a consumer of the product, that is, he develops a stake in the project. This is important to him because he gains more power as the program expands. Thus, the more the program expands, the more power he will gain. Therefore, in this role as a constituent-consumer, the community advocate will do everything in his power to "protect" the program.
4. *Community Mobilization.* The advocate, as a community leader, has the charisma and organizing talents to have a large community following. This following enables him to mobilize large numbers of persons, as needed, for a peaceful demonstration, picket line, and the like. It is highly probable that the advocate has a community base of operations such as a community action agency or organization. This gives him the opportunity to devote more time to organizing the community.
5. *Political Support to District.* The advocate, as a politically oriented person, can give needed support to the school district by his ability to produce voting lists and mobilize voters for school districts during bond or millage elections. It has already been discussed above that there is an indispensable interdependence between the school district and the political system. (Cistone, 1972); the "outside" advocate can be a vehicle which can positively sustain such an interdependence.

The establishment of an "Inside-Outside" Advocacy Model can assure that the school system is impacted and that it is placed into a posture which will lead to change. It is recommended that such a model be developed for the purpose of implementing bilingual education programs.

In conclusion, it has been demonstrated in this paper that the staff personnel in bilingual-bicultural education programs must cultivate political skills which will enable them to bring about the change of attitudes among school district decision makers so that programs will be implemented as part of the regular school curricula. It can be postulated that such an environment will not be established without the political support of the community. Indeed, it can be further stated that without community backing, the bilingual education programs will falter and not be successful.

The "Inside-Outside" Advocacy Model has been presented as a vehicle which enables the project staff personnel to assist in the institutionalization of the program. This model, if implemented as intended, will produce positive results for both the school district and the community. Politics has not been completely accepted by most educators as a viable process to bring about educational change. This is a failure on their part, because education cannot exist without politics. In the final analysis, however, the prime beneficiaries will be the school children who have a limited knowledge of English. This, then, makes all efforts worthwhile.

BIBLIOGRAPHY

Adams, Richard N. "Brokers and Career Mobility Systems in the Structure of Complex Societies," *Southwestern Journal of Anthropology,* XXVI (Winter, 7970): 315-327.

Berman, Paul and McLaughlin, Milbrey W. *Federal Programs Supporting Educational Change.* Vol IV. *The Findings in Review.* R-1589/4 - HEW. Santa Monica: Rand Corporation, 1975.

Boissevain, Jeremy. "Patronage in Sicily," *Man: The Journal of the Royal Anthropological Institute,* I, n.s. (March, 1966): 18-33.

Briner, Conard and Iannaccone, Laurence. "Selected Social Power Relationships in Education," *Educational Administration: Selected Readings.* Edited by Walter G. Hack, John A. Ramseyer, and James B. Heck. Boston: Allyn and Bacon, Inc., 1971.

Cistone, Peter J. "The Politics of Education: Some Main Themes and Issues," *School Boards and the Political Fact.* Edited by Peter J. Cistone. Toronto: The Ontario Institute for Studies in Education, 1972.

Engel, Martin. "Politics and the Requisites in Educational Change," *Phi Delta Kappan* (March, 1974).

Foster, George M. "Godparents and Social Networks in Tzintzuntzan," *Southwestern Journal of Anthropology,* XV (Autumn, 1969): 261-278.

House, Ernest R. *The Politics of Educational Innovation.* Berkely: McCutchan Publishing Co., 1974.

Iannaccone, Laurence. *Politics in Education.* New York: The Center for Applied Research in Education, Inc., 1967.

Lemarchand, Rene and Legg, Keith. "Political Clientelism and Development," *Comparative Politics,* IV (January, 1972): 149-178.

Martinez, Rodolfo. "Bilingual/Bicultural Education: Innovation in a Political Setting." Grad. Bilingual Education Program. College of Education, University of Illinois. Urbana: 1977. Forthcoming. (Mimeographed).

Mosher, Edith K., "Education and American Federalism: Intergovernmental and National Policy Influences," *The Politics of Education* Chicago: The Seventy-six yearbook of the National Society for the Study of Education, 1977.

McGivney, Joseph H. and Haught, James M. "The Politics of Education: A View From the Perspective of the Central Office Staff," *Educational Administration Quarterly* (Autumn, 1972): 18-38.

Paine, Robert. "A Theory of Patronage and Brokerage," *Patrons and Brokers in East Artic.* Edited by Robert Paine. Memorial University: Newfoundland Sociological and Economic Papers, 1971.

Silverman, Sydel F. "Patronage and Community-Nation Relationships in Central Italy," *Ethnology*, IV (April, 1965): 172-189.

Spindler, George D. "The Role of the School Administrator," *Education and Culture.* Edited by George D. Spindler. New York: Holt, Rinehart, and Winston, 1963.

Sumner, Gerald C., et al. *Federal Programs Supporting Educational Change.* Vol. III. *The Process of Change.* R-1589/3-HEW. Santa Monica: Rand Corporation, 1975.

Walker, Hill M. "The Superintendent's Use of Cooptation in Handling Internal Interest and Pressure Groups: Its Effects and Consequences," *Educational Administration Quarterly*, IV (Winter, 1968), 32-44.

Part III

LA COMUNIDAD/THE COMMUNITY

TOWARD A LANGUAGE POLICY FOR PUERTO RICANS IN THE UNITED STATES: AN AGENDA FOR A COMMUNITY IN MOVEMENT*

National Puerto Rican Task Force on Educational Policy, 1977: A Summary and Comment by Frank Bonilla

Before getting into the summary of this tentative policy statement, there are a few points concerning its origins and scope that should be made explicit.

1. This is not my document or that of any individual or a single institution. It reflects a consensus achieved over nearly two years of discussion among a group with wide-ranging backgrounds, interests and political perspectives. The group includes educators, social scientists, lawyers and community activists from Puerto Rican communities widely scattered around the U.S. and Puerto Rico.
2. The group was united by a common reaction to the experience of highhandedness, tokenism, indifference and resistance to reasoned argument among federal officials and agencies charged with formulating educational policy and supportive research affecting our communities. The common elements in that reaction were the determination to maintain a united front in rejecting externally imposed, short-run agendas and to take the time necessary to thoroughly think through alternatives flowing from a sense of direction, needs, and priorities rooted in knowledge of ourselves. The group worked closely over a half-dozen intensive weekends with a part-time coordinator keeping things in motion between sessions.
3. The statement speaks to a situation that we expect will be essentially with us for at least two decades or so—that is, we are talking about middle-run planning for a fifteen to twenty year period. We have projected ambitious, but, we feel, realizable, minimal goals. The document addresses in the first instance, Puerto Ricans in the United States, inviting discussion and counter argument. We are also reaching out to other Hispanics and other groups concerned with language. We regard a substantial consensus within Hispanic ranks as a basic precondition to obtaining a fair hearing among a larger public.
4. It is important to make clear that we do not approach this task from what have been advanced in the planning literature as the main concerns of language planners. That is, we are not intent on establishing or protecting the primacy, integrity or purity, of any language or dialect, qua language. We do not suppose that there are some suprapolitical definitions and solutions to language problems. Our

*Copies of the full document are available through ERIC ED 164 69D.

concern is with language as an essential tool and expression of a particular people's being and capacity for action in a given historical circumstance. Since those historical circumstances are only partially known and changing, our goals and strategies must also be tentative and flexible.

5. Finally, this policy statement needs to be seen in tandem with a larger set of documents—an earlier historical overview of the Puerto Rican language issue (*Bilingual Review,* 1978, Nos. 1 and 2), two key appendices to the document itself (one on data needs and research, the second on a program of action), and lastly the community manual for litigation on language rights presented in this volume by Manuel del Valle as well as Attinasi's report on related ethnolinguistic and attitudinal research.

Our conviction that it is now both necessary and possible to formulate language goals and map some related actions is based on the following general considerations. First, by all indications, the movement of Puerto Ricans to the United States will continue at substantial levels over the coming decades. This migration is increasingly dispersed over the United States. Migration is now a way of life for many Puerto Ricans rather than a single life-transforming experience. More and more Puerto Ricans alternate periods of residence in various parts of the U.S. with stays of varying duration in Puerto Rico. These patterns of alternation and circulation have yet to be closely studied. In point of fact, natural increase now adds more to the Puerto Rican population living in the U.S. than does migration, but those born here are also part of the complex migration flows. Thus, the language needs and preferences of this growing community are increasingly projected to the *national* level as a distinct dimension within a complex of policy issues related to education, work, social planning and political action.

Secondly, the vigor of Spanish as a major first or second language among U.S. residents is evidenced in many ways. Spanish is the principal language other than English learned and spoken in the home; the Hispanic-origin community is the fastest growing minority in the country with an increasing number of important regional concentrations. The reaffirmation of national identity by Hispanics lends an unparalleled thrust to the current movement for bilingual education which is flowing over into the affirmation of language rights in politics (voter registration and balloting), demands for government services and employment in both the public and private sector, as well as the mass media and entertainment. The legal and institutional base of this linguistic affirmation is gradually being consolidated. Increasingly, knowledge of Spanish is a practical necessity in effective organizational and institutional activity at every level and it is a concrete link to a richly creative intellectual and political tradition that is world-wide in scope. The number of young, college-trained professionals, business, government and service workers whose command of Spanish is an essential qualification for employment and job advancement is also growing. Spanish competence will remain a vital feature of life in U.S. communities for decades to come.

Third, throughout its history in the U.S., the Puerto Rican community has asserted its collective identity and sought to build and control its own institutions locally. Thus as the issues affecting Puerto Ricans are thrust into the national policy arena, we can expect that appropriate organizational bases will be constructed. Seen in this light, the task force producing this document is only one of many improvised structures meeting this need in an interim way.

Fourth, at stake are not merely the educational or language rights of Puerto Ricans, but also the very fiber and legal foundations of political association in the U.S., and especially the role of the federal government and courts in protecting the rights of minority peoples. More specifically, what is at issue is the content that can be given to such concepts as "linguistic or cultural pluralism" with reference to those minorities that are racially stigmatized, overwhelmingly working-class in composition, and have a common experience of colonial domination by the U.S.

Fifth, mass bilingualism as a late feature of advanced colonialism, the transnational movement of investment, and the massive migration of workers from formerly colonized regions to metropolitan centers emerges in the last two decades as a new historical phenomenon of global import. The Puerto Rican case thus acquires added significance as a particularly developed instance of prolonged language interaction and struggle within an evolving and conflictful socio-economic and political framework.

Finally, the particular colonial situation of Puerto Rico and the structural forces that compel not only migration or resettlement but a continuous circulation of population to the United States further complicates language options. Despite prolonged attempts, the U.S. has not succeeded in displacing Spanish in Puerto Rico. Since 1947, Spanish has been the first language of instruction, and there has been de facto acquiescence in this policy by the U.S. When Puerto Ricans come to the U.S, however, they must submit to English-only schooling. The denial of Spanish schooling that has been successfully resisted in Puerto Rico is readily accomplished in the U.S. Many adolescents or young adults return to the Island as linguistic aliens in their own country. Manuel del Valle and his colleagues raise in their litigation manual some interesting questions about the obligations of the dominant nation to the language and culture of the colonized in a situation of this kind. In any case, it is important to understand that in Puerto Rico, bilingualism or language parity is clearly understood as a code word for the imposition of English.

What we are saying, in brief, is that our knowledge of demographic trends, the history of Puerto Rico and our community in the United States, the constitutional and legal issues raised by the thrust of linguistic or ethnic claims in this country, as well as the changing configuration of capitalist production on a world scale, all lead us to believe that language issues will constitute a primary focus of policy contention in the next few decades. As a community whose survival may hang in the balance, we must strive for a realistic sense of the full complexity of the processes involved, and for reasoned judgments about desired outcomes and lines of action within our reach.

Having brought into view this larger context, we come back to the school, the institutional site in which the evidence of society's failure with respect to basic needs is most compelling. The discouraging figures on school achievement, delayed education and dropout rates are recapitulated in the report. The presumption that language is the primary factor behind this failure has gained easy currency both outside and within our communities. However, recent comparative analyses of Puerto Rican communities around the country suggest that economic and class factors, recency of migration and level of political mobilization are closely linked to what our young people get from schooling in a particular locality. In giving a high priority to the definition of language goals we by no means discount the importance of other factors nor do we claim primacy for language as a solution to educational problems. But it is also clear to Puerto Ricans that the languages they bring to the school are looked down upon, shunted aside and repressed or simply excluded from the teaching process. This reality is coupled to the widespread recognition that language proficiency is not only critical to school success but decisively shapes our individuality and commonality as a people. This helps to explain why language has been at the heart of the Puerto Rican response to the educational crisis and became the central focus of this committee's reflections.

There was considerable soul-searching among us as to whether it made any sense at all to formulate language goals, however tentative, given the magnitude of the uncertainties concerning crucial questions and the precariousness of the means at our disposal. The path chosen, which I believe is a sensible one, was to be meticulous about mapping areas of ignorance. The long section between pages nine and twenty-eight is largely a catalogue of unanswered questions, a proto-research agenda which may seem ingenuous and pretentious in its sweep, ranging as it does from the most basic queries about the current speech of Puerto Ricans, through a complex chain of questions about bilingualism and learning as well as language and identity, and on to a review of the legal grounding of language and educational rights. The best reply we can make to skeptics is, of course, that in the brief span since the document was written a fair start has been made in obtaining some initial, empirically grounded answers to some of these questions. As the other presentations and related publications demonstrate, we do know more about the Spanish and English that Puerto Ricans speak, about the nature of code-switching, about the practical and symbolic uses of Spanish in the formation and projection of self and group identity, and about the possibilities and limitations of litigation in advancing language objectives.

The following four items constitute the statement of language goals proposed in the document we have been discussing:

1. We propose that bilinguality should become a selfconsciously articulated goal for our community in the U.S. By this we do not mean a community with a mix of English and Spanish speakers but a community in which as many as possible acquire competence in both languages. Implicit in this idea of bilinguality is the ideal of mother tongue retention. This means not merely "maintenance" of Spanish for native speakers but the passing along of both languages to their offspring by bilinguals.
2. To frame a policy means not just to choose a language but also some language standard. Educationally, our goal should be the spoken and written command of the standard dialect in Spanish and English. This does not mean a downgrading or rejection of other dialects, vernaculars or linguistic combinations in education or other settings.

3. Framing a policy also means defining educational strategies, especially languages of instruction. It is here that we see the necessity for the greatest flexibility, openness and sensitivity to local needs. It is at this level that constructive solutions must appear in terms of the schools' use *(aprovechamiento)* of the language resources the community brings to it and the returns in language growth and vitalization the community can draw from the school.
4. Such a policy must project action in extra-school contexts and institutions in ways that are responsive to the richness of language events and combinations already perceptible in expanding areas of Puerto Rican life (poetry, theater, professional and organizational arenas).

A number of questions to which we do not have satisfying answers commonly crop up in discussions of these goals. It is important to clarify first some of our ideas about bilinguality. In present conditions, bilinguality is needed not only for effective communication between members of the community and "the outside world," but also for communication *within* the community itself. Since our children are already communicating in multiple language forms (however misunderstood, unrecognized or utilized by the schools), we have good reason to be fully confident about their ability to acquire a full command of two languages. In addition, we are not only interested in achieving bilinguality (that is, schooling toward the successful acquisition of a second language), but with mother tongue retention the transmission from one generation to another of the first language of parents. The factors associated with these two processes seem to be different but both are necessary to an eventual stabilization of bilinguality. Some of the structural conditions that support the expectation that Spanish will show such staying power in the U.S. over the next two or three decades have already been mentioned.

As regards the "standard dialects" of English and Spanish mentioned as educational goals in item two, there is also some fuzziness. Clearly, even if this were possible, we do not have in mind the abandonment or downgrading, in our own speech or in the school, of all variants marked by class, nationality or region. We do recognize the need for the school to extend that repertoire of dialects to a common form appropriate for more generalized or formal contexts. Since historically this has meant the dogmatic imposition of the standard dialect of a particular class in the school, there is naturally some apprehension about how the linguistic variety and distinctiveness of the community will fare under any standard, however formulated.

This brings us back to the further question, related to item four, of whether it is possible to have a language policy in the absence of a cultural policy or at least a clear understanding of the cultural processes that will be building on and revitalizing the linguistic practice of a community. Once again we have to confess to having only hazy notions about these connections, but we have been heartened by the modest research now going on into the history of our popular music and its present place in our communities, by the vigor, thoughtfulness and principled awareness of Puerto Rican cultural workers (poets, playwrights, painters, musicians) and their ideas about language, and particularly by their readiness to reach out to young people and children.

Merely posing the idea of bilinguality as a sustained goal for our community in the U.S. has raised an unprecedented order of questions. Are these goals real; that is, practical and functional, or merely symbolic? I am personally inclined to regard them as in large part realizable, and in any case, a clear ground for class and national struggle for many years to come. They encompass, moreover, some of the most challenging intellectual problems of our time. Approaching them with some seriousness at least exposes the sterility and shallowness of the formulas proferred to us under the banners of the bicultural and the pluralistic.

Much of the remainder of the document is taken up with sketches of lines of action and the spelling out of minimal data, research and organizational requirements to move forward with goals of this kind. The appendix in the data base, prepared principally by José Hernández of the University of Wisconsin, is a compact assessment of national data on Hispanics, from the census and current population surveys to vital statistics and local school system records. The obstacles, political and other, that stand in the way of an accurate and universal count even in the forthcoming 1980 census are such that Hernández includes methods for locally estimating undercounts and a design for self-enumeration.

The document, along with some of its companion pieces, has now circulated fairly widely. In a few communities (Boston, San Jose, Milwaukee) there have been group discussions and questions raised which have in part informed this presentation. Our principal preoccupation has been to devise and begin to put into place some mechanism for coordinated grassroots discussion of the language options before us. Much of what we have heard at this conference suggests that the moment is not propitious. Over and above the ambivalence about English, fear of Spanish has been instilled among some parents. Parental involvement in defining bilingual programs, we are told on hard evidence, is no more than ornamental. Limited enforcement of court and legislatively prescribed programs is the rule while the media announce that the republic is about to crumble under the weight of language separatism. According to a thoughtful and informed linguist, Roger Shuy, in remarks at a recent conference on language planning, "there is no challenge to the single language idea in the U.S. today."

In these circumstances there would hardly seem to be much room for "ethnoperspectives" on the question, especially any in which language figures as only one component in a process of social transformation. In a recent discussion of this document, Camille Rodríguez García, of the task force, was pressed to pinpoint what is new or radical about the proposed goals and approach. She alluded first to the groups' commitment to extensive community involvement in the working out of a fully-stated policy and program. More importantly, she noted, that the proposals are radical because they reject language oppression of every kind, whether in English or Spanish. "We have been colonized in both English and Spanish," she said. In other words, the classes that have dominated us, some of whom press monolinguality in Spanish or English on us, have no problems with bilinguality for themselves, and part of their power over us rests on their command of language. She also stressed that we bring no hangups about language primacy or purity to this work; code-switching, class or racially-marked speech raise no hackles in our midst. Furthermore, we see bilinguality as a key to sustained unity as a group, as a means for reaching out to others who are similiarly situated, and as a means for a principled reaching beyond narrow nationalisms.

In closing, I will say then, that if "ethnosperspective" conveys to some of you as it does to me the notion of a view "from the bottom" or from the restricting confines of an ethnically delimited world, I can only hope that this *compañero's* breadth of vision may be matched by those with more privileged vantage points of observation.

A MIDWESTERN COMMUNITY AND ITS SCHOOLS: AN ANALYSIS OF MUTUAL IMAGES AND INTERACTIONS

Alfredo H. Benavides

The focal point of the study from which this paper is derived is the interaction between a metropolitan Mexican-American Michigan community and the educational, public, and welfare institutions which serve it.[1] Within this context, this paper will focus on the relationship between formal educational institutions and the small Mexican-American population within the city. More precisely this paper will examine the quality of relationships which schools have developed with the Mexican-American community; how school policy affecting the Mexican-American is determined by school administrators; and the attitudes expressed by the community and school personnel toward each other.

Importance and Significance

The importance and significance of this type of research is two-fold. First, it is the author's thesis that the quality of the existing school-community relationship in any given community directly affects the quality of services provided to that community by its school system. Second, the author also contends that this type of descriptive research is basic and necessary if educators are going to be able to identify and understand the nature of the particular educational needs and problems of a given community. Given this understanding, educators can begin to address the needed issues and ultimate changes which must occur in order to benefit the community as well as the educational system which services it.

Methodology

The approach to this study of Mexican-Americans is both descriptive and anthropological in nature. Lindquist (1970, pp. xiii-xiv), states:

> The role of the anthropologist in studying education is partially the application of ethnographic fieldwork methods and cross-cultural reference points to some aspect of education. Basic fieldwork methods, in summary, include (1) the need for participation and observation; (2) maintenance of as value-free and "objective" an attitude as possible toward the group being studied; (3) constant attempts to place the data being collected into a holistic conception of the culture and society of the group or groups involved; (4) gaining an understanding, even in the absence of agreement, of the goals of the superordinate

group, if there is one; (5) grasping the variant meanings of symbols which the groups involved are using, both within each group and in communication between groups.[2]

Within this framework, three principal methods of investigation were employed in this study: participant-observer, key informant, and survey—open-ended questionnaire.

As a participant observer, the investigator actually participated in and observed the events described in the study, since only through this method can one gain the insight necessary to the understanding of community composition as well as the population's basic needs and problems. In order to maintain proper perspective and objectivity in conducting the research, the investigator declined several attempts by community members and leaders, as well as school administrators, to act as spokesperson for any one group. Nevertheless, the investigator was allowed to participate in and observe all meetings and communicative interactions between the community and the school system.

A second feature of the methodology employed was the key informant method of investigation. Key informants were defined as those community leaders or members, school personnel, or social and public welfare agency personnel who, in the course of daily affairs, possessed knowledge of the community or its local institutions.

The enlistment of key informants was a slow process. However, this was accomplished in several ways. First, the investigator spent two days per week during the initial phase of the study (June 1974 to September 1974) interviewing directors of social service agencies within the community. Through the Mexican-American personnel in some of these agencies, the investigator began to discover who the community leaders were, the social point of community interaction, and other general information about the community.

Second, after the investigator became known in the community, he was asked to become a member of the Latin American Club, the community's social organization. This opportunity was quickly accepted since the investigator felt that through such membership he could acquire more specific knowledge of the Mexican-American community.

Another means of establishing key informants came about through a fortuitous circumstance. In March of 1975, the investigator was offered a research position within a community agency whose main function was to aid the Mexican-American community. Through the auspices of this agency the investigator eventually came to know well all community leaders, many key school administrators and teachers, and many agency directors and personnel. This agency also brought the investigator into close proximity to the Mexican-American community.

Field notes were a great asset to the research endeavor. Notes of all interviews, meetings, and significant observations and encounters were kept from the very beginning of the study. When note-taking was not possible, it was necessary to rely on memory with notes being recorded as soon as possible. With time and successive interaction, it was possible to achieve acceptance as a "semi-resident" of the community. This acceptance aided in the enlistment of key informants.

All information provided by informants was checked with other informants when possible. There was no evidence of having been given intentionally misleading information during the period of study. The confidentiality of informants was protected at all times. All names and places appearing in this study have been changed to maintain confidentiality. The people and events, however, represent real people and circumstances.

The third and final method of investigation employed is that of the open-ended survey questionnaire. The questionnaire was administered to 364 Mexican-American heads of households, by specially trained interviewers from the community. The interviewers averaged twenty-one years of age and were bilingual (Spanish-English).

The survey questionnaire was especially devised by the investigator for the Spanish-speaking population. No attempt was made to obtain similar information from the non-Spanish-speaking population. The survey questionnaire was aimed at obtaining specific demographic data and other relevant characteristics about the Mexican-American community. Specific information was obtained in the following areas:

1. housing
2. income and employment status
3. formal education and skill training
4. place of prior residence and length of present residency
5. need and use of social and public welfare agencies
6. attitudes toward education, community schools, and social service agencies

Specific questions such as place of birth or any question pertaining to the citizenship status of individuals were purposely omitted. This was done in order that community members who might have been illegal residents or undocumented workers would cooperate willingly. In all but a few cases, information was readily given and recorded. The collection of this data required five and one-half months, from April 1975 to September 1975.

Limitations of the Study

There were several factors which limited the scope and intensity of the study. One such factor was that a similar study was not conducted with the non-Mexican-American community. This tends to limit the study in generalizability. The findings cannot be adequately compared to non-Mexican-Americans in terms of problems and attitudes. This limitation, however, may be better explained and perhaps justified by other factors which defined the scope of the study. These factors were time, a lack of money, and also the lack of qualified personnel to help in data retrieval.

Even with these limitations, it is the investigator's opinion that the information derived from this study is representative of the problems and attitudes among the Mexican-Americans of this community and perhaps others like it. This type of research will hopefully show the need for more in-depth study within similar communities and also be of practical value to community people, educators, social and public welfare agency personnel, and others who come into contact with Mexican-American communities. Whatever the limitations and weaknesses of this study may eventually prove to be, one should not deny its value as a practical attempt to serve as one model for further research of this nature.

Community History and Diversity

Port City, Michigan (pseudonym) is a community of approximately 62,000 people. Mexican-Americans comprise approximately 3,700 of this total.[3] This study is based on data collected from 1,537 community Mexican-Americans.

Although Port City is essentially an industrial community, it is surrounded by counties which are heavily dependent upon agriculture as an economic base. This in itself presents a paradoxical view of the existing Mexican-American community. While many residents of Port City are of the opinion that all Mexican-American residents arrived in Port City as a result of the agricultural migrant stream, this is not the case.

According to Port City voter registration files, there were "voting-age" Spanish-surnamed individuals in Port City as early as the 1890s. However, the first substantive movement of Mexican-Americans into Port City came just prior to and during World War II. Contrary to the belief that these early settlers were agricultural fieldworkers, these first Mexican-Americans were skilled and semi-skilled industrial workers coming from a variety of places such as Monterrey and Torreon, Mexico; Texas, and New Mexico. These "first" Mexican-Americans gained employment in factories and foundries in or within the vicinity of Port City.

According to community sources, many of these original Mexican-Americans were recruited and hired by the factories themselves. During the manpower shortage of World War II, many companies hired bilingual recruiters to attract able-bodied men to work for them. These workers were many times hired in Texas, Mexico, or elsewhere and brought to Michigan (with their families) at company expense. Originally, many of these workers were housed in company housing projects.

The importance of bilinguality in the industrial job market must be noted here. According to Jesus Garcia, a retired factory worker and community resident for over forty-five years, being bilingual was a definite asset during this time. By hiring bilinguals who were highly skilled at their jobs, the company could promote them to foremen, and assign monolingual Spanish-speaking workers to them. In this manner, the company was able to meet its labor demands.

As previously stated, Port City is surrounded by counties which are heavily dependent upon agriculture. During the early 1900s and continuing to the present, agricultural fieldworkers have always made their way to this area for the annual harvesting. Some of these migrant families were also able to secure factory employment on a permanent basis.

More significant, however, is the fact that a significant number of migrants began settling out of the migrant stream in non-industry related employment. This settling out process was hastened during the 1950s as more farmers began using mechanical devices instead of fieldworkers. By the mid-sixties several federal and state agencies such as United Migrants for Opportunity, Incorporated, began to make concerted efforts to settle-out families. According to present and former U.M.O.I. officials, these settling-out efforts were conducted in order to provide more stability within the migrants' lives, and also to decrease their numbers. This influx of Mexican-Americans into Port City created a need for more jobs and/or social service agencies to care for jobless families. It also created a division within the Mexican-American community.

The divisions created within the Mexican-American community were ultimately felt at the social, political, and economic levels. This division was due directly to two differing groups of people being thrust together and looked upon as one and the same.

One must keep in mind that the original Mexican-Americans in Port City were skilled workers. As such they were able to secure factory employment and some measure of economic stability. This group manifested a high degree of assimilation and later, acculturation, into the mainstream of Port City society. Many of the second and third generations of this older group of residents adapted quite readily to Anglo-American norms and customs. There is evidence of a high degree of intermarriage.

By contrast, the settled-out migrant population was largely unskilled and took lower paying jobs. They seemed to cluster in a dilapidated area of town later to be known as *"el barrio"*. This group also manifested a high incidence of welfare recipiency. The migrant problem was compounded annually as more and more migrants were settled-out.

Socially, the "older" population of Mexican-Americans looked upon this "younger" population as somewhat inferior. Typical comments were made about "*esa gente corriente*". The investigator also heard comments about the ex-migrants' gruff and often non-standard Spanish.

Although some of these feelings still persist today, the animosity between the two groups has dissipated to a great extent. The investigator speculates that two reasons exist for the reduction of anxieties. One is the overall impact which the Chicano movement of the sixties and early seventies had on the community as a whole. It seems that this political movement raised the socio-political awareness level in many Mexican-Americans. In a sense, they began to see that the Anglo treated them the same regardless of group affiliation. They still had no political power. Economically they were still at the lower levels. Furthermore, educationally they were still fighting an up-hill battle.

The second reason for the easing of anxieties was the creation of the Latin-American Club in the community. The Latin-American Club became the focal point of community interaction. Established in 1952, the Latin-American Club was first a social organization. Later, in the sixties and seventies, it became the focal point of not only social organization and enjoyment but political and economic as well. The club served as a political sounding board for community members who desired an active role in up-grading and changing the Mexican-American community.

General Characteristics

It is indeed necessary to familiarize oneself with the general characteristics of a given community under study. Such information as housing, income, employment, and educational data can help us understand the community at hand. As pointed out earlier, the gathering of this type of data was essential to this investigator's study. The following five tables provide a representative view of Mexican-American life in Port City.

From this data it is difficult to make definitive statements about Mexican-Americans in Port City. At best, one can point to patterns and tendencies with the community. It is these patterns and tendencies, however,

TABLE 1

ANNUAL INCOME AMONG MEXICAN-AMERICANS IN PORT CITY

Number of Respondents	334
$5,900 or less	34.4%
$6,000-$7,900	17.9%
$8,000-$10,000	14.1%
Above $10,000	33.5%

TABLE 2

EMPLOYMENT STATUS OF MEXICAN-AMERICAN MALE HEADS OF HOUSEHOLD

Number Employable	238
Number Employed	175
Number Unemployed	63
Percent Employed	73.5
Percent Unemployed	26.5

TABLE 3

MEXICAN-AMERICAN HOUSEHOLDS RECEIVING PUBLIC SERVICES IN PORT CITY

Number Respondents	356
Number Unknown	8
Number Receiving	216
Percent Receiving Aid	60.6

that give us the latitude for more ethnographic research. Also, these preliminary findings help us acquaint ourselves with the nature of community life.

The nature of Mexican-American life in Port City is one of heterogeneity. Although data is sketchy, there is a definite sign of heterogeneity in the Mexican-American community. One indication of this is the annual income for Mexican-Americans. If one were to divide the income categories into low, middle, and high, the results show that approximately one-third of the population fits into each category. Similarly, the table showing the types of social services utilized by Mexican-Americans in Port City shows a variety of services being used.

This and similar attitudinal data collected by the investigator tends to point to problems in the community which are varied in nature. This

TABLE 4

TYPES OF SERVICES AND WELFARE RECEIVED BY MEXICAN-AMERICAN HOUSEHOLDS IN PORT CITY

Type of Service	Number Utilizing	Total Percent
Food Stamps	82	22.5
Aid to Dependent Children	52	14.2
Social Security	45	12.4
Direct Aid	8	2.2
Unemployment Compensation	59	16
Nutrition Services	5	1.3
Health Services	36	9.9
Counseling	11	3
Special Education	11	3
Adoption Services	3	.8
Family Planning Services	23	6.9
Totals	335	92%

TABLE 5

ESTIMATED VALUE OF MEXICAN-AMERICAN HOMES IN PORT CITY

Average Home Value	$15,868
Number Above Average	68
Number Below Average	111
Number Respondents	179

point, in the opinion of this investigator, cannot be stressed enough in terms of understanding the general nature of the Mexican-American community. Often, Mexican-Americans are viewed as a homogeneous population with homogeneous problems. This many times leads to very narrow and homogeneous solutions to community problems. Although the survey data, as previously stated, are not definitive, when combined with the other methods of investigation utilized in this study, the data tend to point to a relatively high degree of heterogeneity within the Mexican-American population of Port City. Therefore, not all Mexican-Americans in Port City are economically poor, on direct welfare payments, or chronically unemployed.

The issue of heterogeneity becomes critical in the study of school and community relations in Port City. In order to maximize efforts at viewing interaction between school officials and community members the investigator felt that an issue was needed—an issue which would result in conflicting points of view taken by the community and the local school hierarchy. This issue arose quickly in the form of bilingual education. What follows is a description of the opposing forces—the school and the community—as they clashed head-on in what became an extremely volatile issue.

Community Organization and Perspective

Before bilingual education became an issue in Port City, it was generally felt that Mexican-American children fared badly in the community's schools. One school in particular—King Elementary—had a sizable Mexican-American student population. King was located in the heart of "*el barrio*." Although other schools had Mexican-American students, King Elementary had the greatest number, approximately twenty-five percent of the total school population.

King Elementary had been a source of discomfort among Mexican-American parents for many years. The parents, however, felt powerless to make the changes they felt were needed. These changes did not necessarily mean bilingual education. Rather, they were more interested in making the school an attractive and enjoyable experience for their children. Among the desired changes the parents wanted were:

1. more Mexican-American teachers
2. the removal or dismissal of the school principal
3. the removal of some teachers and school personnel
4. a general acknowledgement from the central administration that they as parents did matter and could have input into their children's school

The reasons for the desired changes were obvious to many parents. First and foremost, their children were not doing well in school. Second, many parents had been themselves the victims of discriminatory practices when they had attended school at King, and they had seen no progress made in the school personnel's treatment of their children. Third, the only Mexican-American teacher ever employed at King had been denied tenure and dismissed from the district in 1973. All of these negative factors helped parents solidify their attitudes towards King Elementary. These attitudes only needed a spark to ignite them.

The spark finally came in April of 1975. Gloria Steiner [pseud.], the director of the Mexican-American agency for which this investigator was conducting research, took it upon herself to inquire about the possibilities of bilingual education in the Port City School District. She was fully aware that the Michigan legislature had recently passed a bilingual education bill mandating bilingual instruction in schools which had at least twenty limited-English-speaking students. Middle-level school administrators assured her that it would be considered.

Months passed without any response from the school district. When by August, Steiner had not received a response from the district, she began to mobilize community leaders and members for a direct confrontation with the school district.

Community leadership at this time was composed of "older generation" Mexican-Americans. This leadership had been active in the Latin-American Club and the community in general. It was not, however, representative of the heterogeneous population of Port City. This would later appear to stifle community participation in the bilingual movement.

The leadership called a general community meeting for the middle of August. State Department of Education officials were invited to address the group on matters relating to bilingual education. This first community meeting was successful from the community's point of view, yet unsuccessful from the state officials' viewpoint.

The differences were due mainly to differing expectations. The community took the opportunity to socialize and rehash stories of historical cases of discrimination with each other and the state officials. The state officials appeared to be more intent on full-scale instruction than on storytelling. However, the meeting was beneficial. The community was able to vent some of its frustration and state officials were able to instruct, advise, and inform the community. Also, this meeting resulted in the formulation of several committees whose overall purposes were to gather more community support and devise a means by which to formally approach the school board. From this meeting, there also resulted a Parents' Advisory Council, self-elected, and composed mainly of the "older" leadership.

The second meeting took place two weeks later and the community response was significantly smaller. Whereas the first meeting had been attended by approximately fifty people, this second meeting drew only about thirty. The chief accomplishment at this meeting was the drafting of a letter to the local school superintendent requesting that something be done to ameliorate the education of Mexican-American children in the district. The text of the letter is as follows:

> Dear Sir:
>
> We are writing this letter in hopes that perhaps you will take the initiative in what we consider a very grave matter. We have united as a concerned organization of Spanish-speaking parents to specifically deal with the issue of bilingual-bicultural education within the Port City public schools.
>
> Historically, the Spanish-speaking children of Port City have been either ignored or completely disillusioned by the educational establishment. We are also extremely concerned about the lackadaisical attitude taken by the schools whenever it concerns our children. This lack of concern and ineptitude on behalf of the schools is evidenced by an extremely high dropout rate, and an inexcusable general state of academic unpreparedness among Spanish-speaking students who are in or have been in the Port City public school system.
>
> We feel that the above situation is caused in part by the lack of adult role models for Spanish-speaking children to identify with. According to Mr. Roy Hart, Assistant Director of Personnel, there are only two Latino teachers out of a total teaching staff of over 570 in Port City alone. We feel that this is a totally unjust and unacceptable situation. In a time when bilingual and bicultural teachers are in plentiful supply, your failure to hire them is taken by the Spanish-speaking community as an act of bad faith.
>
> Furthermore, we feel that these problems can be alleviated by a strong bilingual and bicultural education program. This program must, if it is to succeed, be directed and staffed by qualified bilingual and bicultural personnel. This we feel is extremely important due to the cultural values which our children possess upon entering the edu-

cational system for the first time. For too long a period of time, these values have been systematically and consciously erased from their minds. We will no longer passively accept this form of cultural and educational rape.

We hope you will take this matter into serious and quick consideration. As a Parent's Advisory Council we will do all we can to help in the creation of a program such as the aforementioned. We have at our disposal professional consultants to advise us, a list of over 300 recent bilingual and bicultural graduates of several colleges and universities, and a great desire to better our children's education. We are well aware of House Bill 4750, and of its implications for the Port City Public Schools.

The time has come for Port City school officials to act diligently in accordance with the law, in creating a viable instructional tool for our children. We urge you to contact us quickly so that we may begin the basic groundwork that needs to be done.

Sincerely,

Alicia Alvarez, Chairperson
Parent's Advisory Council

It is important to note that although the letter is strongly worded, it is written in such a manner that it seeks cooperation. The parents did not wish a confrontation with school officials. Instead, they wanted the schools to begin preliminary assessment for the following school years. In essence, the newly-formed Parents' Advisory Council was letting the school system "off the hook" for the 1975-76 school year, yet serving notice that community action would follow if positive steps were not taken.

Community reaction to the letter was quick to surface because copies had also been sent to the local media. Several community members called the local Mexican-American agency to inquire about the bilingual issue. One Mexican-American woman wrote to the editor of the local newspaper and said she was totally against bilingual instruction in Port City schools. The school system, however, did not respond.

The parents' group met a third time, again drawing fewer people than at the previous meetings. This meeting resulted in a decision to formally confront the school board at its next meeting. This was in September and classes had resumed.

The dwindling numbers of parents showing up for the Parents' Advisory Council meetings had begun to worry the group leadership. They realized that their confrontation with the school board must prove successful. In light of this, the leadership again invited state department officials, civil rights officials, and agency personnel to attend. They also made an effort to attract more community people to the meeting. Their strategy for confrontation was also decided at this time. It was basically very simple—speak only in Spanish to the board members and have all communication from them translated by an interpreter.

The confrontation was successful. Board members were amazed at the manner in which the community had communicated with them. Only two factors spoiled an otherwise perfect confrontation. One, unnoticed by the board, was that very few parents were in attendance. Although there were approximately fifty Mexican-Americans at the meeting, more than half were agency personnel and students, state department, and civil rights officials. At most there were perhaps ten parents in attendance.

The second factor was Ben Garza [pseud.], one of the community leaders. The board directed that the assistant superintendent take the issue of bilingual education and give it serious consideration. The community members present saw this as a victory. Garza, on the other hand, did not. Taking the floor, Garza threatened that either bilingual education was instituted at once or Chicano children would immediately boycott classes. Garza was ignored both by the board and by parents and community leaders in attendance. Parents felt that this type of intimidation had not been part of the strategy, and if Garza had bothered to attend the community meetings he would have known this.

After this board meeting the issue of bilingual education seemed to die. There was no response from the school administration. Supposedly, the issue was being "considered." The Parents' Advisory Council informally disbanded; that is to say, they discontinued their meetings. For all intents and purposes it seemed as if school administrators were ignoring the issue and that bilingual education had been placed on the back burner.

This, however, was not the case. Community leaders, state department officials, and Port City school administrators held several meetings that fall, on the feasibility of implementing bilingual education. Often these meetings were heated exchanges of dialogue between the parties involved. The bilingual issue appeared deadlocked. Community leaders wanted nothing less than full scale implementation. School administrators argued that they had no money, personnel, or facilities.

Institutional Perspective

Of primary importance at this point were the attitudes and perceptions of Port City school administrators. The community had made its demands. The law dealing with bilingual education was explicit. Could Port City school officials ignore the community? Indeed, would they ignore the community? Also, how did school administrators view the problem and its possible solution?

These questions are necessary if one is to understand the basic premise from which Port City school officials were operating. Basically, school officials were ignorant of the Mexican-American school population within their system. This ignorance came to light in several significant ways.

According to sources within the school administration, Mexican-American children were not thought of as limited-English-speaking. They were not considered to have problems at all. The principal of King Elementary told the investigator that any problems his school had could be directly attributed to "lower socio-economic class whites". He felt that the high incidence of poverty and divorce among "whites" made it difficult for their children to succeed in school. He added, "since most Mexican-American homes are rarely broken, then most Mexican-American children are very successful at King."

The principal told the investigator that King had only thirty to forty Spanish-surnamed students at King, although the investigator's survey showed sixty-two. He continued (Benavides, 1978: 160-161):

> Only one or two have problems with English. We used to pair these non-English speakers with children that were bilingual. This is the only thing we ever did. Eventually the kids did very well and caught

> on to everything. The Spanish-speaking students here have always done well. They score in the top one-half of the class on aptitude tests. We had one other program here about six or seven years ago—the Miami Linguistic Program. It failed miserably because none of the children really need the program.

The principal went on to state that bilingual education was not needed at King Elementary. Stressing that he had always had great cooperation from the Mexican-American community, (he neglected the community picket line thrown up around King when the only Mexican-American teacher was denied tenure) he stated (Benavides, 1978: 161):

> It (bilingual education) is simply not needed here. As I understand it, the woman who is chairing the bilingual committee, or spearheading the drive for it, is not even Mexican—by any means! She doesn't even live in this area. I think that bilingual education is only an excuse to hire people from the outside because currently there is no teacher in Port City who is certified as a bilingual teacher.

The principal's views were not without support from teachers and central administration. Several teachers felt that bilingual instruction was not needed. One teacher, however, did support bilingual education and blamed teachers' attitudes as well as the principal's attitude on negative experiences with Mexican-Americans in the community. This teacher also said that most Mexican-American children at King Elementary did have problems with English and could use some form of help. This teacher, who was responsible for tutoring Mexican-American children, stated that she was not allowed to work with children who had a C average or better academically or who were not discipline problems.

In central administration the attitudes of many were similar. The district superintendent never met with parents, community leaders, or anyone having to do with bilingual education. The assistant superintendent who was asked by the school board to take the issue of bilingual instruction into consideration, delegated authority to the director of instruction.

This person did meet with community leaders and state department officials several times. These meetings were strenuous discussions on the feasibility of bilingual education in Port City. His position never varied. He stated over and over that the monies simply did not exist. At the last meeting, over which he presided, he was harangued by state department officials until he was visibly upset. According to other sources in central administration, at this point he delegated responsibility to the director of compensatory education and special programs. He was in effect "washing his hands" of bilingual education.

The person inheriting the school district's "burden" for bilingual education was Don Wrigley. In all of the prior discussions and negotiations dealing with bilingual education Wrigley had never been a direct participant. Wrigley, however, became this investigator's best source of information about policy and decision making within the Port City school administration. This relationship developed largely because Wrigley asked the investigator's help in securing data on Mexican-American children in the Port City School District.

As previously stated, the bilingual issue appeared deadlocked and not progressing at all in the fall of 1975. During the Christmas break, the investigator received a call from Don Wrigley. Wrigley in effect was soliciting any kind of data obtained from the investigator's survey which might prove useful in implementing bilingual education or at a minimum showing that a need existed. The investigator agreed and a meeting was arranged for January.

The January meeting was attended by Wrigley and the investigator only. At this meeting the investigator presented the following table on age-grade retardation among Mexican-American children at King Elementary.

TABLE 6 AGE-GRADE RETARDATION AMONG MEXICAN-AMERICAN CHILDREN (King Elementary School)

Age / Grade	Pre-	K	1	2	3	4	5	6
5	m=0 f=1	m=1 f=1	m=0 f=1					
6		m=4 f=1						
7		m=1 f=2 **	m=3 f=2		m=1 f=0			
8		m=1 f=0 **	m=0 f=3 **	m=2 f=4	m=0 f=1			
9				m=1 f=2 **	m=5 f=0	m=0 f=1		
10					m=0 f=1 **	m=3 f=0	m=2 f=1	
11						m=1 f=3 **	m=1 f=0	
12						m=0 f=1 **	m=2 f=3 **	
13							m=1 f=0 **	m=2 f=3 **

Total Population=62 m=male f=female

**=Age-grade retardation 9 males and 18 females manifest age-grade retardation—42.8%

In his own words, Wrigley was "shocked" at the figures on age-grade retardation. According to Wrigley, it was at this point that he decided something had to be done. He had already looked through his lists of students in compensatory and special education programs and "found too many Latin names". His information and the 42.8% age-grade retardation figure were apparently the turning point for bilingual education in Port City.

This does not mean to imply that all was well in the school district. Wrigley acknowledged that there was still much opposition and many hurdles to the implementation of bilingual education. Although Wrigley, a key figure in central administration, had been won over to the side of the community, he remained very pessimistic as to the final outcome.

In the many discussions and talks which the investigator held with Wrigley, the administrator came across as honest and sincere. Wrigley revealed himself and his colleagues as very fallible human beings. He expressed concern that the Mexican-American community felt that the district had never tried to help their children. He specifically pointed out that the district had hired a Mexican-American aide at King Elementary in 1970. He also pointed out that he and another previous administrator had been responsible for the Miami Linguistic Program at King. The fact that this program had failed he attributed directly to the teachers and principal at King. Wrigley acknowledged that the problems at King Elementary were directly caused by teachers who "shirked their responsibilities" and a principal with "no guts in controlling his teachers". He went on to say that he felt that there had been a total administrative breakdown with regards to King Elementary.

Wrigley revealed another interesting side to decision making among himself and his peers. Wrigley's initial non-involvement in bilingual education meetings and his reluctance to join the discussion, stemmed mainly from a state of unawareness as to the severity of the problems and fear. His feeling was that if he took the responsibility for bilingual education and failed, it would in essence reflect badly upon him—both from the point of view of his superiors and the Mexican-American community. However, after studying the information presented to him, he felt that "something had to be done."

Wrigley did receive criticism from his administrative peers. At one meeting of elementary school principals he was accused of "giving everything away." His response was that he was concerned with kids and their education. It was at this time that Wrigley was told by the assistant superintendent in charge of federal programming that he had a friend in Washington, D.C. who read bilingual proposals. He urged him to apply for Title VII monies.

Wrigley then used the investigator's knowledge of the community to identify Mexican-American parents who had children at King Elementary. These parents were contacted and meeting times were arranged. None of these parents had been members of the original Parents' Advisory Council—another indication of the lack of heterogeneous leadership in the community.

Throughout this series of meetings Wrigley's pessimism was still evident. He emphasized to parents that no guarantees could be made concerning bilingual education. Privately to the investigator Wrigley confided that he did not feel the proposal had a chance. "We are not in a high density area," he would say. Then he would add, "but I want the record to show that we are doing something for this community."

In May of 1976, the investigator left Port City, having concluded his basic study. The Port City School District continued to call the investigator for demographic data into the fall of that year. The investigator learned much later that the data he had supplied to school officials—in raw form—had been utilized in their initial Title VII proposal. This proposal was accepted and approved and bilingual education became a reality in Port City. The community's efforts had taken more than two years before the results were realized.

In summary, it is important to point out that there appear to be several distinct tendencies and patterns which emerge from the school-community relationship. These tendencies and patterns can be directly drawn from the interviews with school officials, their meetings with community members and leaders, and the behavior and reaction of both groups when confronted with similar problems.

First, it appears that schools and school administrators have been unable to identify specific educational problems among Mexican-American children in Port City. This gives the school system the label of being "unaware." Also, school officials do not use the institutional research capability within their own system. They had to rely on this investigator's survey data for information concerning Mexican-American children. In this same vein, the schools also rely heavily upon community leaders who more than likely are not qualified to make professional educational needs assessments.

Second, there is a strong tendency exhibited by Port City school administrators to react to Mexican-American community political pressure rather than planning ahead in a proactive manner. This reaction can be viewed as detrimental because many times the schools are reacting to individual community leaders who may not accurately represent the problems, perceptions, or attitudes of the community. As pointed out earlier, Mexican-Americans in Port City are diverse and heterogeneous in composition. The community leadership, however, is homogeneous in composition. Therefore, it would be difficult for a few leaders to represent the diversity of community sentiments. This severely limits school administrators in that their solutions to Mexican-American educational problems become in and of themselves homogeneous.

An excellent example of this was the issue of bilingual education in Port City. School officials decided to attempt implementation based on what community leaders demanded and articulated as being needed. No attempt was made by school officials to determine the children's educational needs based on expert or professional judgment. Bilingual education became an expedient and inexpensive political tool to utilize in stabilizing a troublesome community. However, one must remember that before a specific solution to a problem can be decided upon, one must acknowledge that a problem exists. This was something which Port City school officials never formally acknowledged.

Three other important variables must be examined by this summary. One is the human variable as it pertained to Port City school administrators and community members. A second variable is that of homogeneous community leadership as it affects policy making and community life in general. Third is the role of federal money at the local level in bilingual education. These variables appear to be independent of each other; however, many times they indeed become interdependent thus creating more confusion as to the nature and solution to community and school relations.

As previously stated, several key administrators proved to be very fallible human beings. In essence they were afraid. Intimidated by a group of angry parents and community leaders, they chose to ignore the problem, procrastinate, refuse to accept responsibility, and finally, acquiesce. These actions viewed from a humanistic point are not totally incomprehensible. Rather, they point to a severe shortcoming on the part of the school administration and staff. "Why are they afraid?" we must ask. Could it be that they realize that they do not understand Mexican-Americans at all? Could part of this fear stem from the notion that the schools have not really tried to communicate with the Mexican-American community?

On the other hand, community members can also be accused of being human. They care about their children and attempt to articulate unmet needs as best they can. The fact that they are many times unrepresented in school affairs is not the total fault of the community. For community leadership to be truly representative it must be allowed access to the mainstream of community life and organization. This is something which rarely occurs in minority communities and certainly was not the case in Port City.

Community leadership in Port City is homogeneous due to the lack of mainstream opportunities. Leadership is mainly comprised of older citizens who have long and established roots in the community. In a sense, mainstream leadership is a closed society. Younger leadership thus cannot be developed, or they abandon Port City at the first opportune moment.

The third major factor is the role of federal money at the local level. In the final analysis it became apparent that Port City school officials were willing to commit nothing to bilingual education. In essence, all funding had to be external. How convenient for Port City to be able to receive federal money to alleviate a social and educational problem which they were chiefly responsible for in the first place. With no sense of internal "ownership" of an existing educational problem, federal funds allowed Port City to continue its non-proprietorship and provided an expedient means by which to divest themselves of any responsibility. After all, these administrators were scared and fallible human beings. They can always point to Washington and relieve themselves of any guilt.

Another interesting side to local federal funding is the ultimate impact it has on community leadership and interests. Federal monies can and do alleviate some negative social conditions. However, they also create a weak, uninspired, and economically and politically dependent leadership. Although data was not presented relevant to this specific conclusion (Benavides, 1978: 65-67) it can be said that persons employed in communities by federal money are at best marginal members of the economic and political mainstream. In case after case, social and public welfare employees whose agency was heavily federally funded, experienced a feeling of not belonging. Many times these employees (who often represent community leadership) found themselves switching from job to job and program to program. The impact this has on the community as a whole is to create a great amount of skepticism (Benavides, 1978: 67).

In conclusion, one can make the following observations about Port City:

1. The relationship between Mexican-Americans and the Port City School District is primarily negative.

2. There is a lack of understanding among educators about Mexican-Americans in general and a specific lack of knowledge with regard to educational problems.
3. That policy decisions arrived at by school administrators are often motivated more by federal money and politics than the desire to correct educational disadvantage.
4. Mexican-American leadership is often more concerned with the immediate employment impact federal monies have rather than the long-term benefits hard commitments may bring.
5. Academic failure, as well as failure later on in life, cannot be totally blamed on schools—it must be shared by schools and community alike.

This last point is perhaps in need of explanation. While this study may be flawed in many ways, the one consistent point that surfaces is the lack of understanding displayed by both sides in the school-community struggle. The community must develop a more informed, more articulate, and more heterogeneous leadership. This leadership must be able to understand education and all its benefits and shortcomings. Above all, however, this leadership must be able to work with—not against—its local school system. It must be able to make the system work for them. After all, it is the only system presently available.

School administrators must also begin to face reality. They must understand that what Mexican-American parents desire for their children is success—just like any other well-intentioned parents. Schools and school administrators must realize that a common denominator solution does not exist for Mexican-American children. Like any other children, their problems are also diverse and require diverse solutions. To believe that one approach—bilingual education—can be a cure-all is being extremely narrow and myopic.

The ultimate benefits to both community and schools rests with a common purpose. School administrators must realize that a great part of this purpose is to attempt to ensure success among all children—by whatever means. Similarly, communities must realize that education per se is not a panacea. It is an essential ingredient in the recipe for success. This success, however, will ultimately depend on the harmonious working relationship established by them and the school system.

REFERENCES

1. Benavides, Alfredo H. *Mexican-Americans and Public Service Institutions in a Midwestern Community: An Analysis of Mutual Images and Interactions.* Michigan State University, unpublished dissertation, 1978.
2. Lindquist, Harry, ed. *Education: Readings in the Process of Cultural Transmission.* Houghton Mifflin Company, Boston, 1970.
3. U.S. Bureau of the Census, Census of Population and Housing: 1970 Census Tracts. Final Report PHC (1)-138 Port City, Michigan SMSA, U.S. Government Printing Office, Washington, D.C., 1972.

BILINGUAL EDUCATION PROGRAM FISCAL ACCOUNTABILITY

Joseph O. García

The purpose of this paper is threefold. First, it presents the results of an empirical study which assesses the impact of the California School Finance Reform Act (AB 65) on bilingual education. Second, it documents the need and establishes the rationale for a sound monitoring and accountability system to assure that school districts comply with the legislative provisions in meeting the educational needs of limited- and non-English-speaking (LES/NES) students. Third, this paper proposes a system which allows community members to hold school district officials and legislators fiscally accountable for funds appropriated for bilingual education.

Bilingual Education Prior to AB65

The first successful legislative efforts in California to enact bilingual education programs began with the enactment of AB 2284 in 1972. The legislature appropriated approximately $5 million to implement the new Bilingual Education Act with the expressed purpose of allowing California public schools the opportunity to establish bilingual programs.[1]

With the enactment of AB 1329 in 1976 bilingual education became more specific and demanding. Whereas in AB 2284 bilingual education was optional for districts to participate; in AB 1329 bilingual education was mandated in school districts where more than the minimal number of limited- and non-English-speaking students existed. Specifically AB 1329 required California school districts to offer bilingual learning opportunities to each limited-English-speaking pupil enrolled in the public schools and to provide adequate supplemental financial support to achieve such purpose.[2] Under AB 1329 bilingual education programs are required where ten or more non-English-speaking pupils or fifteen or more limited-English-speaking pupils are located.[3]

In 1977-78 bilingual programs pursuant to the provisions of AB 2284 were repealed and the programs operating pursuant to that act with a funding level of approximately $8.6 million were subject to the programmatic provisions of AB 1329. Those districts currently providing bilingual education programs under the provision of AB 2284 will continue to receive the same level of funding in 1977-78 as they were receiving previously. In addition, three million dollars were made available to schools via AB 1329 and allocated pursuant to the funding provisions of that bill.

In 1978-79, for grades K-6, the funding of both programs will combine and allocate on the basis of the provisions of AB 1329. For grades 7-12, funding will continue to be allocated as it was under AB 2284. Approximately $12.3 million are available for grades K-12 in 1978-79 for the purpose of providing bilingual education to LES/NES students.

There are approximately 233,000 limited- and non-English-speaking students who have been identified in the California public schools for 1978-79. This is a most conservative count of the targeted population requiring bilingual education services.

Approximately $12.3 million of state bilingual funds were allotted for providing bilingual education programs to an estimated 41,000 plus LES/NES students who were served during 1978-79. On the average, approximately $300 was made available per LES/NES student served during 1978-79. If all 233,000 identified LES/NES students were to be served with the $12.3 million, then only $53 per pupil could have been spent. The $12.3 million represents only AB 2284 and AB 1329 legislative appropriations.

Studies on the costs of providing bilingual education programs in New Mexico[4] and Texas[5] show that extra costs for providing bilingual education programs are approximately thirty percent above the costs incurred in providing regular educational programs. If the average cost of providing regular educational programs in grades 1 through 6 is approximately $1,300 per pupil, then the added costs for providing bilingual programs to LES/NES students should be approximately $390 per pupil. Given that the most recent count of LES/NES pupils is 233,000 then the legislative appropriation for funding 100 percent of identified need at $390 per LES/NES pupil is $90,870,000. The current state legislative appropriation earmarked for bilingual education programs is at thirteen percent[6] of funding total identified LES/NES student's need.

Given the judicial mandate stipulated in the *Lau* v. *Nichols* decision the current legislative appropriation for bilingual education programs in meeting the needs of LES/NES students is inadequate. The Supreme Court in *Lau* v. *Nichols* found that a school district's failure to provide non-English-speaking students with a program to deal with their language needs is a violation of Title VI of the Civil Rights Act of 1964. To comply with the *Lau* v. *Nichols* decision school districts should make provisions for instructional programs in a language understandable to each non- and limited-English-speaking student. Substantial increases in state appropriations are required in order to comply with the *Lau* mandate.

Impact of AB65 on Bilingual Education

In 1976 Governor Brown recommended to the legislature that two state funded categorical programs, Bilingual Education and Educationally Disadvantaged Youth (EDY), be combined under a new program entitled Economic Impact Aid as part of AB65. Governor Brown signed AB65 into law on September 17, 1977. Prior to that time state funds for bilingual education were appropriated through two specific bilingual education bills (AB 2284 and AB 1329). With the enactment of the new School Finance Reform Act of 1977 (AB 65), Governor Brown's recommendation was adopted and bilingual education appropriations became a part of the state general aid funding system for the support of public schools.

Funds for bilingual education as of July 1, 1979 are to be allocated to school districts under the Economic Impact Aid (EIA) formula. Even though the EIA appropriation formula is an improvement over the current Educationally Disadvantaged Youth (EDY) formula, substantial room for improvement remains relative to achieving an equitable funding level to meet the needs of LES/NES students. (See Appendix A for a description of the EDY and EIA formulas.)

A basic problem with the EIA formula is the use of economic criteria (number of AFDC[7] and Orshansky[8] students). Educational criteria such as number of LES/NES students, percent students reading below grade level, or students cumulative scores on standardized tests in the bottom twentieth percentile are better criteria and should replace the current economic drivers in the EIA formula.

The current EIA formula favors school districts with high concentration of poverty children as defined by AFDC students (students whose parents are receiving welfare payments) and Orshansky students. The EIA formula assumes that LES/NES students are adequately taken care of within the poverty provisions for additional educational services. This is not the case, since LES/NES students whose parents are not receiving welfare payments would not attract EIA funds to their district. This inequity is obvious since the need for those funds has been established by the number of LES/NES students in the state. Economically disadvantaged bilingual students are being discriminated against by the inequitable method of allocating state funds in meeting the needs of LES/NES students.

State funds specifically earmarked for bilingual education, e.g. AB 2284 and AB 1329 have not been increased under AB 65. However, major revisions in AB 65 (to be discussed later) do allow districts to utilize funds under the School Improvement Plan (SIP) and EDY programs to meet the needs of LES/NES students. School districts requesting SIP and/or EDY funds must submit a plan to the superintendent of public instruction. These in turn must be approved by the State Board of Education.

If one were to compare the current state public school finance legislation with former school finance legislation relative to bilingual education, a major difference is noted in the inclusion of provisions for the financial and programmatic needs of limited- and non-English-speaking students; these provisions are contained in AB 65 under three components; (1) School Improvement Plan (SIP), (2) Educationally Disadvantaged Youth (EDY), and (3) Economic Impact Aid (EIA).

A discussion follows providing a brief description and implementing guidelines for each of these three provisions and their impact on LES/NES students.

School Improvement Plan

The School Improvement Plan is a plan developed at an individual school which is based on an assessment of school capability to: (1) meet the educational needs of each pupil, (2) specify improvement objectives, and (3) indicate steps necessary to achieve such objectives, including intended outcomes. The legislative appropriation for implementing this program was $128 million for 1978-79. School district applications for SIP allocations shall assure that they are providing each limited-English-speaking pupil with an educational opportunity equal to that available to English-speaking pupils; and recommend acceptable projects for approval by the school board.[9] Furthermore, the State Superintendent of Public Instruction shall ensure that funds appropriated pursuant to this article supplement and do not supplant categorical funds allocated from other local and state sources in meeting the needs of limited-English-speaking pupils.[10]

Funds claimed by school districts for purposes of implementing their proposed School Improvement Plan may be expanded for the employment of bilingual/cross-cultural teachers and aides.

School districts must prepare and submit to the superintendent of public instruction an assessment of the needs of the limited-English-speaking pupils in attendance in the school. Based on the needs assessed, the district shall prepare an application on forms provided by the State Department of Education. The state superintendent will in turn recommend acceptable projects for approval by the State Board of Education.

In allocating funds pursuant to this article, priority is given to districts with high concentrations of LES/NES pupils in kindergarten through grade 6. The state superintendent shall rank all school districts with LES/NES pupils in grades K-6 in order of the ratio of such pupils to all pupils in grades K-6 in the district. As additional funds become available, districts shall become eligible for funds based on their ranking percentage of LES/NES students. However, once these districts have been funded, districts with high concentrations of LES/NES students in grades 7-12 are eligible for funds based on a similar ratio.

The state superintendent is responsible for the administration, review, *monitoring,* and *evaluation* of this program. A responsibility of the superintendent that is of particular importance to language minority groups, is a provision which requests that a "*plan be developed to provide for an adequate monitoring of school and school district compliance with the provisions of this article.*"[11] In the absence of an adequate plan and systematic monitoring, the legislative intent will fail to be implemented. Consequently, LES/NES students will not be provided the educational opportunities stipulated in AB 65.

Educationally Disadvantaged Youth

Provisions for bilingual education under AB 65's Educationally Disadvantaged Youth component are contained in Section 54004.7 which stipulated that the intradistrict allocation plan shall assure adequate support to any school to provide programs appropriate to the educational needs of limited- and non-English-speaking pupils as required by the Chacon-Moscone Bilingual Bicultural Education Act of 1976.[12] The legislative appropriation for implementing this program was $118 million for 1978-79.

One of the factors to be considered in determining the eligibility of school districts to receive EDY funds is the ratio of "potential impact of bilingual-bicultural pupils." This bilingual-bicultural index is determined by dividing the percent of pupils based on the 1973-74 ethnic survey by the state-wide average percentage of such pupils for unified, elementary, or high school districts, as appropriate.[13] This factor is insignificant when compared to other factors in the EDY funding formula. Specifically, the bilingual-bicultural index is used to determine district *eligibility* for EDY funds but does not determine the *amount* of EDY funds a district will receive. The amount of money a district receives is primarily based on the number of AFDC students times a constant ($128 for 1975-76).

School districts must submit a plan to the superintendent of public instruction to receive funds for implementing their EDY programs. AB 65 is very specific on the particulars of the plan. The plan is to include an explicit statement on what the district proposes to accomplish; a description of the program and activities designed to achieve these purposes; and a planned program of annual evaluation, including the criteria to be used to measure the effectiveness of the program.

Section 54005 of AB 65 stipulates that "The State Board of Education shall adopt regulations setting forth the standards and criteria to be used in the administration, *monitoring*, evaluation, and dissemination of programs submitted for consideration."[14] This program will become inoperative as of July 1, 1979 at which time it will become part of the Economic Impact Aid program.

Economic Impact Aid

The Economic Impact Aid component of AB 65 combines bilingual education programs and funding with EDY programs and funding as of July 1, 1979. The purpose of this program is to provide a method of impact aid allocation which will allow efforts initiated under the Bilingual Education and EDY programs to continue and expand so long as need exists while previously unserved and underserved populations are provided with adequate aid. Most of the programmatic requirements of the Chacon-Moscone Bilingual-Bicultural Education Act of 1976 are contained in the EIA program.

It is the legislative intent to provide those districts receiving EIA allocations with "sufficient flexibility to design and administer an intra-district allocation system which reflects the distribution and the needs of the needy population and assures the provision of services to students traditionally served by the educationally disadvantaged youth programs and bilingual education programs."[15] The legislative intent allows for local district autonomy in meeting its unique educational needs. Of concern to the language minority community is the extent to which the district is exercising the desired flexibility in meeting the needs of LES/NES students.

It is evident by the above that AB 65 contains major provisions on bilingual education. However, it is important to note that the provisions are statutory in nature and at best reflect the intent of the legislature. To assume that the intent of the legislature will be carried out to the letter of the law is an unwarranted assumption and one that needs to be empirically tested. Principle reasons for the expressed concerns about the implementation of the bilingual education provisions will be discussed in the following sections.

It is of utmost importance that a sound monitoring system be developed by the State Board of Education; and that such a plan be rigorously enforced by the superintendent of public instruction.

Rationale for a Sound Monitoring and Accountability System of Bilingual Education Legislation

Given the potential impact of AB 65 on bilingual education as discussed above, it becomes imperative that AB 65 be closely monitored. However, one is not to assume that AB 65 is a comprehensive, all inclusive piece of legislation that adequately addresses the needs of LES/NES students; nor does it propose a model bilingual education program. On the other hand,

AB 65 contains certain assurances and provisions for meeting the needs of LES/NES students.

AB 65 via the School Improvement Plan and Educationally Disadvantaged Youth Program has appropriated approximately $246,539,000 which may be utilized in meeting the needs of LES/NES students during 1978-79. Of significant importance is the fact that a large amount of state funds are available to districts to implement programs essential in meeting the needs of LES/NES students. A major accomplishment of AB 65 relative to bilingual education is the provision for LES/NES students. These provisions are totally unknown in previous major school finance legislation.

Apart from the $246 million, the Legislature has also appropriated $12 million earmarked specifically for bilingual education via AB 2284 and AB 1329 during 1978-79.

The State Board of Education has been charged by the legislature with the responsibility of adopting rules and regulations and setting forth standards and criteria to be used in the administration, monitoring, and evaluation of such programs. In adopting such rules and regulations it is imperative that the intent of the legislature be met.

Three factors are essential in the development of a sound monitoring system for the implementation of quality bilingual programs for LES/NES students. First, a community network of parents must be established to see that the quality of bilingual programs are consistent with the rules and regulations adopted by the State Board. Second, adopted state rules and regulations must be based on model bilingual education program guidelines. Third, access to legal interpretation and analysis of state statutes, state policies, rules and regulations is essential to permit maximum effectiveness in the monitoring process. Language minorities and bilingual members from the broader community must take the responsibility in assuring that the highest standards and best criteria be developed, and that such standards and criteria be sensitive to the cultural, linguistic, and educational needs and conditions of the targeted populations the programs are designed to serve.

Ensuring that school districts receive the required state funds to adequately implement bilingual education programs essential in meeting the needs of LES/NES students is only one of many major problems language minority group members have to contend with. The other major problem faced by language minority groups is the development and implementation of a monitoring system to assure that school districts are spending the appropriated funds in providing adequate, high quality programs for LES/NES students.

The State Board of Education's rules and regulations should require the implementation of only those programs which have proven successful in providing quality programs to LES/NES students. To allow school districts the "flexibility" to design their own programs—given the history of districts' reluctance, and in some cases outright refusal, to meet the needs of LES/NES students by implementing quality bilingual programs—is for the most part very dangerous in that it provides certain districts with the loophole to subvert the law, and unfortunately for LES/NES students, get away with it.

The rules and regulations should also require that the best qualified staff, using the best materials available be utilized in providing *quality* programs to LES/NES students. Techniques for implementing a sound monitoring system are also required of the regulations. Unless the Board's rules and regulations require the implementation of quality educational programs by applying the highest standards to all districts, then the availability of millions of dollars for meeting the needs of LES/NES students is at best, symbolic and at worst, fraudulent.

The superintendent of public instruction is responsibile for the administration, implementation, and *monitoring* of such educational programs in accordance with the rules and regulations adopted by the State Board of Education. AB 65 also stipulates certain responsibilities for the state superintendent relative to educational programs designed for LES/NES students.

A number of the responsibilities require that the superintendent of public instruction ensure that: (1) sufficient bilingual personnel are available within the Department of Education who are familiar, competent, and proficient in bilingual-crosscultural instruction, (2) the Department of Education personnel be sufficiently trained to carry out the legislative intent in meeting the needs of LES/NES students, (3) an administrative unit with the Department of Education be established which is responsible for bilingual-bicultural educational programs and policies, (4) an annual evaluation of bilingual needs and programs within the State be developed for submission to the legislature and the governor, and (5) *a plan be developed to provide for adequate monitoring* of school and school district compliance with the provisions of said article.

The strictest adherence to and successful implementation of an adequate monitoring plan by the state superintendent is of utmost concern to language minority groups. The importance of this legislative mandate cannot be over-emphasized. If the state superintendent fails to adequately *monitor*, review, and evaluate the school districts' performance and programs designed for LES/NES students, then the state appropriated funds combined with the State Board of Education rules and regulations have no significance or impact.

Language minority groups and advocates of bilingual education must take the responsibility for holding the State Board of Education accountable for the adoption of rules and regulations which assure quality educational opportunities for LES/NES students, and maintain fiscal integrity.

Furthermore, language minority groups and advocates of bilingual education must take the responsibility for holding the state superintendent of public instruction accountable for all of the responsibilities stipulated in AB 65 for those educational programs designed for LES/NES students. Foremost of those responsibilities is not only the development of a plan for an adequate monitoring system, but the successful implementation and enforcement of such a system.

The urgency for this matter is demonstrated by *Flores* v. *El Centro School District, et al,*[16] a class action suit which alleges that the state defendants[17] continued to allow El Centro School District to deny the plaintiffs an equal educational opportunity. Specifically the case states that:

> Defendant Riles has a duty under the California and United States Constitution to ensure that all students in California school districts receive an equal educational opportunity, regardless of their race, ethnic origin, cultural background, or primary language. State defendants know

or should know that local defendants have denied an equal educational opportunity to plaintiffs.[18]

The implications of this suit strongly suggest that the State Department of Education and the superintendent of public instruction have failed to develop and implement a monitoring system to account for the fiscal and programmatic provisions in assuring equal educational opportunity to the plaintiffs.

In large part, the key factor in assuring that the needs of LES/NES students be adequately met and that quality educational programs be provided to them, is the extent to which language minority groups can hold the state superintendent of public instruction accountable for assuring that school districts are in compliance with the State Board of Education's rules and regulations via a strict monitoring system.

Community Participation in Monitoring and Fiscal Accountability of Bilingual Education Programs

A commonly held misconception by the public at large consists of the fact that enacted legislation along with the required funding suffice for the successful implementation of that enactment. With particular reference to bilingual education in California, there exist a number of bilingual education legislations (AB 1329 and parts of AB 65) with up to $258 million to implement bilingual education programs.

Visits to school districts with concentrations of LES/NES students reveal that irrespective of the laws and funds available for bilingual education, there are many LES/NES students whose educational needs are not being met. Therefore, one cannot assume that bilingual education legislation and funding as such provide the necessary assurances that the needs of LES/NES students will be adequately met by school districts.

Assurances that adequate programs for LES/NES students will be implemented by school districts officials can only be made by the communities in the respective school districts. Parents of LES/NES students, community members, and bilingual education advocates must take the primary responsibility of monitoring bilingual education programs and holding school district officials fiscally accountable for funds earmarked for such programs.

Often school district officials tend to ignore the fact that parents, in essence the community, are taxpayers. As taxpayers they are directly responsible for financing public education. As taxpayers, community members have the right to know how their money is being spent by school district officials in providing educational services to their youth. In essence, the community can have a significant impact on how their taxes are being spent in the public schools. Unfortunately, they are unaware of the power they possess as taxpayers.

Traditionally, community group efforts have failed to ensure that adequate bilingual education programs for LES/NES students are provided for them and that funds be expended in an efficient and effective manner due to the following four primary reasons:

First, community groups have failed to be in a bargaining position with the school district. For example, if parents of LES/NES students request/demand a maintenance type of bilingual education program be taught with a particular curriculum by bilingual/bicultural teachers; and school district officials say no for whatever reasons, such parents have no real recourse. There is little if anything they can do about it in effectively implementing their demand.

If community groups are to be effective in working with school districts, they must be able to exercise the power necessary for school district officials to respond to their needs. Primary sources of power for community groups are *information,* training, and access to the news media and legal advice.

Community groups should secure the services of professionals in the field of education, particularly college professors, teachers, and program coordinators. These people should act as technical advisors and leave all decision making to the community. They should remain in this advisory position for as long as the community feels it is necessary.

Second, community groups have usually responded to crises situations. Almost always community groups are forced to respond to problematic situations that require an immediate solution. Due to the urgency of the matter and consequent pressure involved, the solutions in most instances result in a "band-aid" approach. The problem is remedied temporarily until the next time.

Power in the form of political clout and legal muscle cannot be acquired through sporadic responses to crises situations, but must be developed through a well-organized, well-conceived program of attack on clearly defined issues.

Third, community groups have not had data/facts on which to base their decisions and make sound evaluations. By and large school districts have mastered the art of not making public information readily available to the public and in particular, to interest groups. School district officials know quite well that *information is power;* something they are not willing to share but keep almost at all cost. Consequently, community groups attend school board meetings and/or approach district officials with "I think's" and "I feel's" rather than "I know's." When asked to provide specific documentation or evidence relative to a particular inequity or problem, they have none.

It is imperative that community groups, with the assistance of their technical advisors, develop a systematic and accurate method of data collecting and record keeping which parents can understand and control.

Every charge must be backed by researchable and documented evidence which indicate that an improper and/or illegal misuse of funds earmarked for bilingual education programs has occurred.

Fourth, community groups have failed to systematically and comprehensively plan. Due to the fact that community groups have mostly been put in a position to react to crises situations, such groups have lost sight of the so-called "big picture." They are too busy (by design) winning individual battles while simultaneously losing the war. Community groups would be wise to engage in a systematic and comprehensive plan that would put them in control of the situation, in essence, to be on the offensive rather than on the defensive.

In the development of a systematic and comprehensive plan, a community awareness program must be established so that parents and other interested community members can take an aggressive stand on any issues which may occur and be in a position to provide viable solutions to documented inequities. A training program should be established to educate the community in terms of their rights and how they can make school district officials accountable to them. The school district's hierarchy of power must be clearly defined for the parents so that when they've obtained the necessary facts and data to challenge the school district, they will be familiar not only with the most effective procedures, but also, they will know where to apply the most legal and political pressure in order to gain the most effective results.

A training program for the community should include but not be limited to: (1) establishing a task force or committee, (2) defining the committee's policies, goals and objectives, (3) identifying what data sources the school district has and how to obtain them and use them, (4) defining the procedures necessary to adequately research and document the inequities existing within the district, (5) defining a method whereby the community can present their concerns and/or problems to the appropriate school district official(s) and be successful, and (6) defining what political and legal courses of action are available to them as alternate options.

In order to assist efforts of community groups to provide assurances for adequate bilingual education programs and fiscal accountability, the California School Finance Reform Project has developed a computer printout which lists crucial data relative to bilingual education by school district for each legislative district. (See Appendix B).

Community groups of the respective school districts can hold their school district officials accountable for the total amount of earmarked funds received for bilingual education. The figures provided are official and were obtained from the California State Department of Education. This type of information is hardly ever provided to community groups by school district officials.

Once community groups know specifically how much money, by categorical program, was allocated to the district, they are then in a position to ask such particulars as "How much was expended for teachers, aides, materials, etc?" The district's line-item subtotals must equal the grant total provided in the printout. If per chance the district's total is less than the total in the printout, school district officials will be hard pressed to explain the discrepency.

Summary

Based on the results of this study, the California School Finance Reform Act has had a major impact on bilingual education. Provisions for meeting the needs of limited- and non-English-speaking students are contained in AB 65 under three different educational programs. For 1978-79 legislative appropriations approximating $246 million are available through provisions contained in the School Improvement Plan and Educationally Disadvantaged Youth Programs for meeting the needs of LES/NES students.

The State Department of Education must develop rules and regulations to assure that the needs of LES/NES students are met in accordance with the legislative provisions. The superintendent of public instruction must be held accountable for the administration, implementation, and monitoring of such educational programs in accordance with the rules and regulations adopted by the State Board of Education. Furthermore, the superintendent must comply with the responsibilities stipulated in AB 65 regarding educational programs designed to meet the needs of LES/NES students.

Public school officials must likewise be held fiscally accountable for funds they receive earmarked for bilingual education. Parents of LES/NES students and community groups must take the primary responsibility for monitoring such programs and holding district officials accountable for the right expenditure of such funds. Such groups are most effective when they possess the necessary data and engage in a systematic and comprehensive plan. The quality of education will improve only with a well-organized, knowledgeable, and powerful local community constantly observing and monitoring the individuals and agencies which decide the policy and practice which take place in the schools both now and in the future.

NOTES

1. *Education Code*, Chapter 1010 Statutes of 1976, Part 28. General Instructional Programs, Chapter 7, Bilingual Education, p. 1290.
2. Assembly Bill No. 1329, California State Legislature, Chapter 978, September 1976, p. 3.
3. *Ibid.*, p. 61.
4. Garcia, Joseph O., "Cost Analysis of Bilingual, Special, and Vocational Public School Programs in New Mexico," Unpublished Ph.D. dissertation, University of New Mexico, 1976.
5. Cardenas, Jose A., Bernal, Joe L., and Kean, William. "Bilingual Education Cost Analysis". Intercultural Development Research Association, 1976.
6. The thirteen percent figure is determined by dividing the 12.3 million combined appropriations in AB 2284 and AB 1329 by $90,870,000, the amount required to fund 100 percent of identified need.
7. AFDC - Aid to families with dependent children is an indicator of poverty as determined by the number of children (ages 5 - 17) from families receiving welfare payments.
8. Orshansky is a measure of poverty as determined by the number of children (birth - 18 years) falling below the Orshansky poverty level. The Orshansky poverty level is determined on the basis of the cost of food for farm and non-farm families of various sizes.
9. *Assembly Bill No. 65*, California State Legislature, Chapter 6, Improvement of Elementary and Secondary Education, Section 52117 (5), p. 49.
10. *Ibid.*, Section 52168 (a), p. 46.
11. *Ibid.*, Section 52177 (6), p. 49.
12. *Ibid.*, Section 54004.7, p. 53.
13. *Ibid.*, Section 54002 (a) p. 51.
14. *Ibid.*, Section 54005, p. 53.
15. *Ibid.*, Section 54005.3, p. 53.
16. *Flores* v. *El Centro School District, et al.* Originally filed on October 10, 1975 at the Los Angeles Superior Court, Case #C13811.
17. State defendants refers to the superintendent of public instruction and State Board of Education.
18. *Flores* v. *El Centro School District, et. al.*, op. cit., p. 9.

ADDENDUM A

The following equation illustrates the components in the Educationally Disadvantaged Youth (EDY) Program formula:

$$EDY_d = \frac{BB + FP + PT}{3} \times AFDC \times c$$

Where:

EDY_d = EDY entitlements to a district
BB = Index of bilingual-bicultural pupils
FP = Index of family poverty
PT = Index of pupil transiency
AFDC = Number of AFDC students
c = constant (in 1975-76, c = $128)

NOTE: $2 > \frac{BB + FP + PT}{3} \geqslant 1$

The following equation illustrates the components in the Economic Impact Aid (EIA) formula:

$$EIA_d = \frac{BB + FP + PT}{3} \times \frac{AFDC + OSKY}{2} \times c$$

Where:

EIA_d = EIA entitlement to a district
BB = Index of bilingual-bicultural pupils
FP = Index of family poverty
PT = Index of pupil transiency
AFDC = Number of AFDC students
OSKY = Number of Orshansky students
c = constant (1979-80, c = $440)

NOTE: $2 > \frac{BB + FP + PT}{3} \geqslant .35$

The Economic Impact Aid formula combines the state allocations for EDY and Bilingual-Bicultural Programs (AB 1329). Besides the obvious semantic change in the names of the allocation systems from EDY to EIA there are three important changes.

Change #1

The first change is the inclusion of the Orshansky measure in the driver of the EIA equation. The drivers for the two formulas are:

Formula	*Driver*
EDY (old)	AFDC
EIA (new)	$\frac{AFDC + OSKY}{2}$

Under the EDY formula only those districts with students whose parents are receiving public welfare assistance (AFDC students) are able to generate entitlements. The more AFDC students, the more entitlements the districts are eligible to receive.

By including the Orshansky measure in the EIA formula, districts with students who are economically disadvantaged but whose parents are not necessarily receiving public welfare assistance are eligible to receive entitlements. A significant advantage of the EIA formula over the EDY formula is that, in the EIA formula parents of students in need of special educational services, i.e., bilingual education, and who are economically disadvantaged, need not be receiving public welfare assistance in order to qualify for state categorical entitlements.

Change #2

The second important change is the reduction of the lower limit of the average of the three indices from 1.0 to .35.

Formula	*Indices*
EDY (old)	Note: $2 > \frac{BB + FP + PT}{3} \geqslant 1.0$
EIA (new)	Note: $2 > \frac{BB + FP + PT}{3} \geqslant .35$

The sum of the three indexes (bilingual-bicultural pupils, family poverty, and pupil transiency) represents a measure of the district's educational need. There is a formula to calculate each of the three indexes. Under the EDY formula with a lower limit of 1.0 a total of 426 school districts received EDY entitlements. Under the EIA formula with a lower limit of .35 a total of 888 districts will receive EIA entitlements. The lowering of the lower limit by .65 resulted in an increase of 462 school districts eligible for compensatory education funding.

Change #3

The third change is the increase in the constant from $128 (1975-76) to $440 (1979-80).

Formula	*Constant*
EDY (1975-76)	$128
EIA (1979-80)	$440

The $312 increase is significant because it goes well beyond the average six percent annual increase in all the other funding categories.

ADDENDUM B

CATEGORICAL FUNDS FOR LES/NES STUDENTS, LISTED BY CALIFORNIA STATE ASSEMBLY AND SENATE DISTRICTS

MARCH 1979

California School Finance Reform Project   Tel: (714) 286-6692
San Diego State University
San Diego, California 92182

Purpose: In light of complaints that money appropriated for Limited-English-Speaking/Non-English-Speaking (LES/NES) students is not yielding the intended quantity or quality of needed services, we compiled the following. We designed this report specifically to aid other researchers, educators, community leaders, parents and anyone else who is genuinely eager to act in assuring that money alloted to help LES/NES students in fact does so in the manner intended. If we can do anything more to help, please let us know.

Legislative District headings: For each of California's legislative districts (eighty assembly and forty senate) we print the following:

1. Official number of the legislative district,
2. Name of legislator,
3. Political party affiliation of that legislator, and,
4. Full address and telephone of that legislator's district office.

Body of the report for each legislative district: Within each legislative district we list school districts alphabetically by county, and for each school district we provide the following:

1. ADA — Average daily attendance, i.e. the average number of students attending that school district for that year. The total ADA for 1977-78 was 4,400,608.
2. LES/NES — The number of Limited- and Non-English-Speaking students identified in that school district for that year. The total LES/NES students for 1977-78 was 233,074.
3. AB 2284 — Total funds allocated to the school district under AB 2284 (a state assembly bill) earmarked specifically for bilingual education. Total state appropriation for this bill in 1978-79 was $8,231,882.
4. AB 1329 — Total funds allocated to the school district under AB 1329 (a state assembly bill), earmarked specifically for bilingual education. Total state appropriation for this bill in 1978-79 was $2,861,854.

5. SB 1641 — Total funds allocated to the school district under SB 1641 (a state senate bill), earmarked specifically for bilingual education. Total state appropriation for this bill in 1978-79 was $20,156,627.
6. Title 7 — Total grants to the school district under the Title VII bilingual education act (a federal act) specifically for bilingual education. Total appropriations to California under this title in 1978-79 were $25,928,872.
7. Total B.E. Funds — Total state plus federal funds allocated to the district, earmarked specifically for bilingual education. State plus federal appropriations within California for 1978-79 total $57,179,235.
8. EDY — Total funds allocated to the school district under AB 65 (a state assembly bill) that may, at the district's option, be spent in meeting the special needs of LES/NES students.
9. Title 1 — Funds allocated to the school district under Title I of the elementary and secondary education act (ESEA—a federal act) that may, at the district's option, be spent in meeting the special needs of LES/NES students.

At the end of a given legislative district's section, totals for that district appear for each of the above nine categories. The amount labeled "Total Categorical $" represents the total funds, received by all school districts in the given legislative district, which may be spent in meeting the needs of LES/NES students.

California School Finance Reform Project Date: June 1979 Page: 82
Assembly District 67 Legislator: William Leonard (Republican)
District Address: 405 E. Citrus Ave.
Redlands 92373 Dist. Phone: (714) 793-7674

County	School District	ADA 77/78	LES/NES 78/79	AB 2284 78/79	AB 1329 78/79	SB 1641 78/79	Title 7 78/79	Total B.E. Funds	EDY 77/78	Title 1 77/78
Riverside	Alvord Unif.	9,566	218	0	0	50,321	0	50,321	272,571	343,053
Riverside	Banning Unif.	2,840	15	0	0	30,291	0	30,291	193,095	164,509
Riverside	Beaumont Unif.	2,524	53	0	0	16,813	0	16,813	109,014	102,347
Riverside	Corona-Norco Unif.	18,478	855	102,178	12,593	173,939	242,669	531,379	182,729	299,797
Riverside	Elsinore Union Elem.	2,245	51	0	0	11,937	0	11,937	64,656	89,502
Riverside	Elsinore Union High	1,255	15	0	0	10,556	0	10,556	57,177	59,591
Riverside	Hemet Unif.	7,419	0	0	0	0	0	0	0	136,899
Riverside	Jupupa Unif. Co. 36	9,390	269	0	0	70,359	0	70,359	381,118	458,094
Riverside	Menifee Union Elem.	241	0	0	0	0	0	0	0	0
Riverside	Moreno Valley Unif.	6,713	139	0	0	18,505	0	18,505	100,236	189,128
Riverside	Nuview Union Elem.	411	9	0	0	889	0	889	4,816	8,973

ADDENDUM B continued

Riverside	Palm Springs Unif.	7,802	288	0	3,693	25,723	127,773	157,189	139,332	204,543
Riverside	Perris Elem.	1,466	132	0	2,378	15,303	0	17,681	95,321	80,989
Riverside	Perris Union High	1,349	28	0	0	17,233	0	17,233	93,344	112,970
Riverside	Riverside Unif.	24,881	1,301	70,271	16,700	443,470	235,330	765,771	465,881	728,671
Riverside	Romeland Elem.	300	12	0	0	1,918	0	1,918	10,389	12,655
Riverside	San Jacinto Unif.	2,003	111	0	1,243	15,438	60,885	77,566	83,600	80,299
Riverside	Val Verde Elem.	862	58	0	1,044	6,593	0	7,637	42,510	56,830
San Bernardino	Barstow Unif.	7,816	35	0	0	125,722	0	125,722	132,076	227,045
San Bernardino	Bear Valley Unif.	2,167	1	0	0	5,193	0	5,193	28,130	47,054
San Bernardino	Golton Joint Unif. Co. 33	10,839	376	54,761	5,080	89,415	0	149,256	484,334	441,071
San Bernardino	Los Flores Elem.	23	0	0	0	0	0	0	0	0
San Bernardino	Lucerne Valley Union Elem.	435	20	0	360	2,926	0	3,286	3,074	8,451
San Bernardino	Morongo Unif.	5,024	0	0	0	0	0	0	0	85,427
San Bernardino	Needles Unif.	1,198	2	0	0	7,111	0	7,111	38,517	39,423
San Bernardino	Redlands Unif.	10,489	479	41,893	5,026	35,501	100,729	183,149	192,300	284,605
San Bernardino	Rim of the World Unif.	4,092	0	0	0	0	0	0	0	48,652
San Bernardino	San Bernardin City Unif.	30,881	2,147	139,579	23,222	262,210	105,157	530,168	1,730,680	1,746,006
San Bernardino	Victor Valley Jt. Un. Hi	4,190	0	0	0	0	0	0	0	97,533
San Bernardino	Yucaipa Joint Unif. Co. 3	5,063	0	0	0	0	0	0	0	85,038
Totals All Districts		181,962	6,614	408,682	71,339	1,437,366	872,543	2,789,930	4,904,900	6,239,155

Total Categorical $13,933,985

BILINGUAL EDUCATION FOR A BILINGUAL COMMUNITY: SOME INSIGHTS GAINED FROM RESEARCH[1]

Andrew D. Cohen

This paper deals with insights gained and lessons learned from researching or not researching the bilingual community that hosts a particular bilingual education program. The writing of such a paper provides an opportunity to call attention to research documents which in some cases have had only minimal circulation. The paper will deal especially with research on parental involvement in bilingual education. In actuality, there have been few studies which have compared parents of children in a bilingual program with parents of similar children in a conventional program on one or more dimensions such as language use and attitudes toward language, over time. In fact, a leading scholar in the field was hard put to find research on parental attitudes and interest to cite in a recent review of literature on the social context of bilingual education. This state of affairs prompted him to make the following comment, "The area of parental involvement in bilingual education is far too crucial to the direction and success of such education to remain as little explored as it is at the moment" (Fishman, 1977: 45).

Actually, while there is some research on what a bilingual community hosting a bilingual program knows about itself—i.e., empirical data on bilingual language proficiency, language use, and attitudes toward language—there is hardly anything on what the bilingual community knows about billingual schooling at the outset or while the program is in operation, beyond certain global pronouncements. In reality, parents may well know something about the characteristics of their bilingual community and may well be aware of certain features of ongoing bilingual education programs. However researchers have not systematically documented such knowledge, so that much of what is said about community participation in bilingual programs is anecdotal in nature. Anecdotes are without doubt important, and need to be collected, but they may well be unrepresentative and thus do not provide a sound basis for generalization.

This paper will deal with the research that I am aware of concerning the relationship between parents and bilingual programs. The main purpose is to see what the research would suggest about the role of parents in formulating public policy on bilingual schooling. Behind the question, "What can research findings contribute to parental role in shaping public policy in bilingual education?" is the question, "What research are we willing to conduct and then publicly report?"

Before getting into particulars, it is important to point out that there may be a temptation to criticize past research or the lack of it too harshly. It is always easy to indulge in hindsight and to suggest what bilingual education programs should have researched. It is certain that not only were research tools themselves in an early stage of development, but there were real politico-emotional reasons for *not* delving too deeply into details. For example, to obtain federal Title VII funds, it was imperative to stipulate certain things about the target population; for example, that they were dominant speakers of a language other than English. If the facts were otherwise, chances of funding seemed limited.

Researching Language Proficiency and Language Use in the Bilingual Community

In the early 1970s, the New York City Bilingual Consortium conducted a data-gathering operation, referred to as Project BEST, which had as one major goal the collection of detailed information about federally funded bilingual education programs. The Project BEST staff first gleaned as much information as they could from the project documents (mostly proposals, and a few interim and final yearly evaluation reports) for 125 Title VII programs for 1969 and 1970. They sent these partly-filled-out questionnaires to the project directors for verification by the local staff. Only fifty-eight projects (forty-six percent) verified the questionnaires by adding and correcting information. This already says something about the reluctance to share information in those early years of federally funded bilingual education. Among other things, there was a fear that funds would be prematurely cut off.

Among the questions that were asked of bilingual programs was how the language dominance of participants was determined. A full twenty percent reported inferring dominance from surname, fifty-one percent reported using formal testing, and twenty-nine percent said they used informal measures. With regard to the use of surname, the Project BEST staff noted: "Since a curriculum designed for a Spanish-dominant child would be inappropriate for an English-dominant child, it is surprising that so many projects (twenty percent) used a child's surname to infer his language dominance" (Shore, 1974: 72). Project BEST also found that fewer than half of the verified programs were even planning on conducting a sociolinguistic survey to find out what languages were spoken at home and the language proficiency of the speakers. Whether these surveys were, in fact, carried out is another issue.

Given this background, it is perhaps not surprising that there should be cases of mismatch between the curriculum and the students. In 1974, I was asked to conduct a comparative summary of the evaluation of Title VII projects in one urban and two rural school districts in Northern California, all three evaluated by the same set of research associates. This survey was conducted at the request of Consultants in Total Education, the curriculum company that was supplying these programs with all curriculum materials, except for English reading. One of the first things that I learned upon making a site visit to the program in the urban school district was that the supposedly Spanish-dominant students were unable to cope with the math curriculum because it had been written for native Spanish-speakers. As I checked through the actual evaluation data, the fact emerged that the majority of these students were English dominant. The way the evaluation reports were written up, this fact was somewhat obscured and in the interpretation of the statistical findings, the matter was all but finessed.

Yet the reality was that across grade levels (one to three) and across tests (the Inter-American Listening Comprehension Test, the Moreno Speaking Test, the Peabody Picture Vocabulary Test), the urban district students performed much lower on the Spanish language version than on the English language version (Cohen, 1974b). These children lived in a downtown environment, and English was apparently spoken extensively in the home. The other bilingual programs were located in rural farming areas where more Spanish was spoken. As can be seen in Table I, the students in the two rural districts also performed better on the English version of the tests than on the Spanish version, but their Spanish scores were considerably higher than those of the urban district children.

The phenomenon of lower-than-expected performance on Spanish language tests at school occurs time and again, and probably results from a variety of factors, such as (1) a desire to do better in English due to an attitude that English is more prestigious, (2) a feeling that it is unnatural to do such tests in Spanish, (3) a lack of proper training in how to take such tests in Spanish, and (4) the fact that in all three cases, the Spanish version was a direct translation from the English test, with its cultural and cognitive biases.

There are, of course, other reasons for collecting language proficiency and language use data from children in bilingual programs and from their parents, besides the concern for providing the appropriate school curriculum. One major reason is to determine how participation in a bilingual program may effect not only the language use patterns of the children, but of their parents as well. If, for example, a bilingual program is designed to help maintain a minority language, it is possible to assess whether, in fact, the language is being used regularly. Language use patterns in a *language maintenance* oriented bilingual program were researched over

TABLE 1

PERFORMANCE IN SPANISH BY SCHOOL DISTRICT

	Inter-American Listening Comprehension Test		*Moreno Speaking Test*						*Peabody Picture Vocabulary Test*					
	1st Grade		1st		2nd		3rd		1st		2nd		3rd	
	English	Spanish	E	S	E	S	E	S	E	S	E	S	E	S
Urban-District Program	27.7[a]	15.9	75.8	11.1	93.6	23.4	92.6	19.5	57.6	14.8	61.9	22.9	66.8	21.5
Rural-District # 1 Program	27.7	20.3	66.5	29.3	85.9	52.9	94.3	71.9	53.0	32.8	59.4	43.7	63.5	48.0
Rural-District #2 Program	27.4	21.6	64.4	33.3	90.6	51.9	90.5	41.6	54.8	33.4	60.3	38.0	63.6	41.8

a. Data expressed as mean raw scores. There were approximately forty students tested at each grade level for each program.

time in Redwood City, California (Cohen, 1975, ch.9). The question was asked whether children in the program would use Spanish as much several years after being in the program as they did at the outset, and whether this use of Spanish would be greater than that of comparable non-project participants.

The issue was researched in the following way. Forty-five Mexican-American children at three grade levels (one to three) were studied over a two-year period, as was a comparable group of forty-five Mexican-American children receiving conventional English-only schooling at a nearby school. Student language use patterns were measured in three ways. Children were asked to report their own language use by domain and by interlocutor, at the same time that their parents were also asked to report on the students' language use patterns. These data were collected both at the beginning of the two-year period, and at the end. Furthermore, toward the end of the period, direct observations of the students' language use were obtained in four different contexts at school, two within the classroom setting (math and social studies/science) and two outside the classroom (lunch and playground).

In general, the three separate measures of language use (student report, parent report, and direct observation) all showed children in the bilingual program for several years to be using Spanish more than children not participating in the program, and that the students in the bilingual program were continuing to use Spanish more than English, whereas children in the comparison group were using English more than Spanish. This finding illustrates how language use data can speak to the effects of bilingual schooling with regard to minority language maintenance.

Another way of looking at language use is through the effects that a bilingual project may have on *family* language use patterns. In the Redwood City study, the children who had been in the program for three years (the pilot group) reported that other family members (parents and siblings) used significantly more Spanish with them than comparison students reported their families doing (even after adjusting statistically for initial differences between the bilingual and comparison students) (Cohen, 1975: 221). As participation in the program seems to have stimulated students to use more Spanish at home, family members responded to them more frequently in Spanish.

Finally, just as a bilingual program can influence language use patterns, so language use patterns can influence language achievement at school. As part of an evaluation of bilingual programs in downstate Illinois, parental reports of language use patterns of 140 third graders were related to the students' Spanish and English language achievement (the Test of Basic Experiences), using the statistical procedure of analysis of covariance. It was found that students who spoke Spanish at home also did *better* on the Spanish version of the test and that students who did *not* speak Spanish to their mother performed *poorly* on this Spanish version (Cohen & Rodríguez-Brown, 1977; in press). In this analysis, there were no data available from children in a comparison group to permit even tentative statements concerning the role of bilingual schooling in language use patterns. Such a research design would have been particularly relevant in Illinois since at the time of the study, the state endorsed a *transitional*, rather than a maintenance oriented approach to bilingual education.

The emphasis was on giving the students only enough bilingual schooling (maximum three years) so that they could function in English. Such an approach might be expected to explicitly or implicitly encourage the spread of the use of English within many, if not all domains of language use.[2]

Researching Parental Support for Bilingual Schooling

In the early years of U.S. bilingual programs, it may have seemed to some proponents of such programs that parental support for bilingual education was, in fact, a "given." The reality is that there may *not* have been support for public-school bilingual education in certain bilingual communities, just as there still may not be support in some places today. Again referring to the Project BEST survey, it was found that only thirty-one percent of the verified projects asked minority-group parents what they thought about their children using the minority language as a medium for learning subject matter at school (Shore, 1974).

It is possible that even if bilingual program administrators sensed some parental reticence, they were convinced that parents' attitudes could be positively influenced by the success of such a program—that "seeing is believing." Thus, they would feel it crucial to get the program going, regardless of whether the parents felt it was "anti-intuitional"[3] to have their children exposed to exclusive or extensive use of the first language as a medium for instruction at the outset. However, such an approach could be construed as one of unethical coercion, particularly if the parents are not adequately informed as to the nature of the bilingual program. John Halcón (personal communication) suggests that in some cases, parents are not so much *educated* regarding a bilingual program as they are *indoctrinated*.

At least one U.S. study of parents in a bilingual community found that they preferred instruction in the early grades to be exclusively in English (Manna, 1975). It would even be fair to say that this finding came as a surprise to the researcher. One special feature of the study was that the investigator asked a series of specific questions about parental preferences regarding actual aspects of the bilingual schooling model, and did not deal with bilingual education simply as an abstraction.

The subjects were fifty-eight adults and fifty-seven teenagers (ranging in age from thirteen to eighteen) from the Spanish-speaking community in the Pico-Union neighborhood of Los Angeles. These Spanish speakers, mostly from Mexico and other Central American countries, constituted fifty-three percent of the neighborhood population of 10,000. The adult sample was obtained by interviewing adults in every fifth household. A member of the community went along to help explain the purpose of the study and to help ensure the cooperation of the community members. The teenage sample was obtained by stopping every fifth student who walked by outside the school.

Among a series of questions regarding the language of instruction, the adults and teenagers were asked the following:

> ¿En qué año de la escuela elemental piensa Usted que el español debería usarse exclusivamente como medio de instrucción para alumnos en todas las materias?
> Grados 1 2 3 4 5 6

(In which grade of elementary school do you think Spanish should be used exclusively as the medium of instruction to teach all subjects to school children?)

Clearly this item forced a choice, but respondents were not obliged to answer, and in fact, fifteen of the fifty-eight adults and four of the fifty-seven teenagers chose not to. Most of the adults responding (fifty-three percent) chose grades four to six. Most of the teenagers (fifty-seven percent) chose grades one to three (Table 2). The investigator interpreted this finding as suggesting that parents wanted to give their children an early start with English for several reasons: to help get them acquainted with English as a learning instrument, to help them adapt to the life style in America, and to help them get a better job. The investigator noted that while the teenagers' views about use of vernacular first were consonant with the view of a number of educators who had implemented bilingual programs, the adults' view "runs somewhat counter to this approach." The issue then becomes whether to follow the wishes of the parents or of the teenagers (Manna, 1975: 68). The researcher pointed out that educators would hope the bilingual schooling experience itself might prove to Spanish-speaking adults that initial use of Spanish at school may actually facilitate subsequent acquisition of English.

In support of the position that a bilingual education program itself can positively influence parental attitudes toward such a program, I draw on more data from the Redwood City study. Through personal visits to the homes of parents in the Redwood City study, I learned of initial misgivings with regard to using Spanish as a medium of instruction at school. As I have pointed out elsewhere (Cohen, in press), I found that some Mexican-American mothers in particular wanted their children schooled almost exclusively in English. It was the fathers who seemed to be more concerned about preserving Spanish skills. Arguments given for teaching English fast and effectively were that English was needed for getting ahead economically and for purposes of social interaction. Fathers who were more concerned about Spanish maintenance, in some cases were thinking of returning with their families to Mexico for visits or to stay, while others just seemed more optimistic than their wives about the potentially beneficial effects of bilingual schooling. Since mothers were the most frequent

TABLE 2

COMMUNITY SURVEY DATA ON EXCLUSIVE USE OF SPANISH AS THE MEDIUM OF INSTRUCTION

	Adults	Teenagers
Grades	% (n)	% (n)
1 - 3	26 (11)	57 (30)
4 - 6	53 (23)	39 (21)
1 - 6	21 (9)	4 (2)
	100 (43)	100 (53)

respondents because they were more readily available for home interviews,[4] changes in attitudes toward Spanish language primarily reflects shifts in the mothers' attitudes toward bilingual schooling.

In order to systematically assess parental attitude toward instruction through two languages, a language orientation questionnaire was developed.[5] This instrument assessed parental reaction to reasons for their children to learn Spanish and English at school. Parents of students in the bilingual and comparison groups were asked to fill out the questionnaire at the start of the study and again two years later. The aspect of longitudinality and that of a comparison group of parents whose children were not in a bilingual program provided the opportunity to determine if "seeing is believing." There were, in fact, several findings supportive of this position.

Two of the reasons given for learning Spanish were the following:

> Nadie está completamente educado si no puede hablar el español correctamente.
> (No one is really educated unless he is fluent in Spanish.)
>
> Les ayudará a preservar su idioma y su cultura.
> (It will help them to preserve their own native language and culture.)

Parents of children in the Pilot and Follow Up I groups[6] increased their rating of this first reason for learning Spanish, that is, completing their education, while parents in the comparison group lowered their rating, producing significant differences. Follow Up I parents also maintained a high rating for the second reason, preserving native language and culture, while comparison group parents lowered their rating, producing significant differences. Parents were also asked to select the two best reasons for their children to learn Spanish and English. The bilingual group parents rated the following reason among the best reasons, while the comparison group parents did not:

> Les ayudará a encontrar un buen trabajo.
> (It will be useful to them in getting a good job.)

I concluded from these findings that parents who had their children in the bilingual program for several years were more positive than comparison group parents about the virtues of Spanish for not only integrative reasons, such as to preserve language and culture, but also for instrumental reasons, such as to become better educated and to get a job. The results suggested the possible effects of the program upon the parents' langauge attitudes (Cohen, 1975: ch. 11).

Researching Parental Knowledge about Bilingual Programs

What little there is in the research literature on parental involvement in bilingual education suggests that parents may too frequently simply be endorsing an abstraction. Clearly, the success of any given bilingual program would depend on the level of training of the teachers and teacher aides; selection, sequencing and pacing of materials; and choices as to use of languages for instruction by teacher, by subject matter, and by classroom. Whereas bilingual education specialists have always been aware that bilingual schooling is a whole variety of options, it is likely that many parents have not had this awareness. Of course this is a generalization. Many parents have spent time in the bilingual classroom as volunteer aides or have served on parent advisory councils. The real issue is how parents have exercised their awareness of what does or can go on in a bilingual classroom.

As part of a study of the role of parent advisory councils serving federal Spanish-English bilingual education programs, Cruz (1979) had parent council members rank order possible tasks that parents would perform at the planning, implementation, and evaluation stages. Whether parents actually performed these tasks is another issue. In an effort to determine how parent advisory councils actually do function, Rodríguez (1979) utilized a typology of five levels of formal citizen participation—placation, sanctions, information, checks and balances, and change agent. In applying this typology to sixteen advisory committees in federal bilingual programs in Texas, he found that the parent committees did not function at the "checks and balances" or "change agent" levels at all, but rather at the lower levels—thus essentially performing the function of endorsing the programs.

It was noted earlier that questionnaires about bilingual education have tended not to include detailed questions about the make up of a particular bilingual program. Rather, the questions have been of a more general nature. One questionnaire of 1973 vintage, entitled *Questionnaire: Parent Attitude toward Bilingual Education,* perhaps serves as a model for the more typical questionnaire to which parents have been asked to respond. Five questions are not specific to bilingual education at all—questions concerning the eagerness of the teacher to talk to the parent, the frequency of parent visits to school, parent interest in hearing about the program, parent feelings about being informed, and parent involvement in decision making. With respect to what could be considered bilingual-program-specific questions, the parents are asked to indicate: whether the student's education was better before or after the program started, the school's influence on the child's self-concept, whether the child seems happy, whether the child is learning about his own heritage and culture, and whether school is encouraging him to make friendships with children from other cultures. The parents are also asked to indicate whether having bilingual skills is advantageous, and to specify whether such skills will help obtain a good job with a high salary. Finally, parents are asked to indicate how well they understand what the school is trying to do for their child.

The directions to administrators include a list of uses for the information gathered: to see how well project personnel have communicated with parents about the program, to identify specific children who are having problems of emotional adjustment to the program, and to indicate ways to modify the parental involvement component, such as by involving certain parents to a greater extent. Further, the instrument was intended to provide information having implications for modifying the instructional program. We see, particularly in this last suggested use, that parental input was conceived at a level substantially removed from the particulars of a given program.

The Pico-Union-Spanish-speaking community study (Manna, 1975) was different in that there were detailed questions about bilingual education. And it is noteworthy that the researcher did not ask respondents to rate how much they knew about bilingual education until the end of the questionnaire. Rather, the respondents were first asked specific questions about their attitudes toward the workings of a bilingual program and then they were asked the general question:

> ¿Cuánto sabe Usted acerca del programa de educación bilingüe?
> (How much do you know about the bilingual education program?)

As it turned out, of the fifty parents (out of fifty-eight) who responded to the question, only sixteen percent indicated that they knew what bilingual education was about, thirty-two percent said they knew a little, and fifty-two percent indicated that they knew very little or nothing at all. In other words, once bilingual education is *not* presented as an abstraction, but rather as a set of specific options, it clearly becomes more difficult to "know about" such a program. It might also have been interesting to ask this question at the outset as well, to see whether, in fact, such specific questions actually influenced the parents' views of their general knowledge. On the other hand, it may be best to avoid general questions of this kind altogether.

There was an interesting sidelight to the Redwood City study that is now appropriate to this topic of parental knowledge about bilingual education. The Home Interview Questionnaire administered to parents as an after-measure included the question:

> ¿Qué es el idioma de instrucción en la escuela de ________ ?
> (What is the language of instruction in ________'s school?)

The question was asked primarily to see if children other than those in the bilingual or comparison groups were receiving bilingual instruction somewhere. An unexpected result was that some of the comparison group parents, perhaps five, indicated that a child of theirs in the comparison group, was receiving his instruction in Spanish and English. At the time, I dismissed this finding as irrelevant, as well as embarrassing. There may actually have been some confusion as to the language of the classroom at the comparison school, since the principal for the second year of the study was a native Spanish speaker from Guatemala. Consequently, he personally conversed with these parents in Spanish. Yet the team of Mexican-American research assistants who collected language use observations at the comparison school confirmed that the teachers did not use any Spanish in the classroom (Cohen, 1975c: ch.9), so these parents had a misconception about the nature of their children's school program.

There appears to be research-based justification for concerning ourselves with parental knowledge about the working of bilingual education programs. There is some evidence that the model for schooling may make a difference, and there is also evidence that parents' ability to deal in specifics has an important effect at the planning stages.

As for the bilingual model making a difference, let me refer to two pieces of research. First, as part of the Redwood City study, the oral language of bilingual group and comparison group students was submitted to error analysis on a pre- and posttest basis. The findings showed that whereas the comparison group students had proportionately fewer deviant forms in their spoken Spanish attributable to interference from English (pretest: fifty percent, posttest: forty-one percent), the bilingual group students maintained roughly the same proportion of deviant forms in spoken Spanish attributable to interference from English (pretest: forty-four percent, posttest: forty-five percent) over a two-year period (Cohen, 1975: ch. 8).

The model used for bilingual instruction in Redwood City was primarily that of "simultaneous translation"—i.e., a bilingual teacher gave a lesson in both languages simultaneously by translating word by word, sentence by sentence, or paragraph by paragraph. The finding here suggests a linguistic spin-off from such a model, namely increased interference from English in speaking Spanish. While the comparison group students were learning and using their Spanish in domains largely non overlapping with those in which English was used (e.g., at home, on the playground, or at school), the bilingual group students were not only constantly in a two language environment but also in an environment where they had Spanish and English forms quite frequently juxtaposed.

The second piece of research was conducted by the Department of Research and Evaluation for the Chicago schools (Chicago Board of Education, 1977). They were interested in comparing the effects of different models of bilingual schooling on achievement. The five models were: the self-contained classroom (a teacher and an aide), team teaching/separate rooms, team teaching/same room, team teaching/half day, and integrated (a euphemism for "pull out"). The effects of these five bilingual schooling models on English, Spanish, and math achievement in the elementary grades (one to six) was determined for a sample of over 550 children, using the vocabulary, English reading, and math subtests of the Iowa Test of Basic Skills, and the Inter-American Spanish Reading Test (the *Prueba de Lectura*).

It was found that the team teaching/separate-room model proved most conducive to high achievement in English and Spanish reading and in math, while the team teaching/half-day model was most conducive to high achievement in English vocabulary. It was also found that the self-contained and team teaching/same-room models were least conducive to achievement in English reading. The team teaching/same-room model was also least conducive to achievement in math. The team teaching/separate-room model was least conducive to achievement in English vocabulary, while the integrated model produced the lowest results in Spanish reading.

Findings such as those from Chicago seem to dramatize the importance of comparing *different* approaches to bilingual education, rather than simply evaluating bilingual education itself as a single entity that is or is not successful. For example, such an analysis may help us decide which approach to use if we wish students to demonstrate high achievement in Spanish reading. The Chicago results indicate that the highest mean on the *Prueba de Lectura* was obtained through team teaching/separate rooms (18.78, n = 60), then through self-contained instruction 13.18, n = 117), then through team teaching/half day (12.14, n = 115), then through team teaching/same room (9.81, n = 145), and then through the integrated approach (9.65, n = 119) (Chicago Board of Education, 1977: Table 20).

This is not to say that the models as delineated in the Chicago research are necessarily at a level of specificity which is adequate for the given needs of administrators and parents of bilingual education programs. It would depend on the issues of local relevance. There is work being done to further clarify certain approaches to bilingual instruction. For example, it was noted above that the "simultaneous translation" approach, also referred to as the "concurrent" method, seemed to encourage interference from English in spoken Spanish. Recently, an effort has been made to spell out with precision just what a *successful* "concurrent" approach would consist of—so that the switching from one language to the other is properly strategized by the teacher and implemented in accordance with certain learning objectives that are linguistically and culturally relevant (Jacobson & Rubio, in press; Jacobson, 1979). In effect, Jacobson has worked out a system of cues for teachers as to choice of language so that each of the child's languages is offered equal prestige. A particular language is selected as a deliberate teacher strategy, as the natural vehicle for certain curriculum materials, as a stimulus to language development, or as an aid to interpersonal relationships.

This discussion of program models making a difference leads us into the second point, that the impact of parent input regarding the planning and continuation of bilingual programs is enhanced if it is specific. I witnessed one instance of how parents convinced a school board about the importance of maintaining immersion education (i.e., Spanish-only instruction) through their informed, detailed arguments. In the summer and fall of 1972, there was a major controversy over whether the Spanish-language-only kindergarten program could continue. At a Culver City board meeting, a parent in the Culver City community publicly read a section of the Education Code of the State of California (Section 71), which required that the basic language of instruction in all schools in the state be English, and that only after a child became fluent in a foreign language could he be instructed in that language.

Parents of children in the Spanish immersion program spoke out at a Culver City School Board meeting, emphasizing the need to keep the program as monolingually Spanish as possible. Their argument was that introduction of English in the classroom would simply lessen the children's need to communicate through Spanish. What probably helped to convince the school board members was the specific nature of parents' comments.[7] Willing to test the matter in court, if necessary, the Culver City board voted to initiate a second immersion kindergarten class. Then, at its January 1972 meeting, the California State Board of Education unanimously approved the Culver City decision to establish a new Spanish-only kindergarten class (Cohen, 1974a).

It is true that parents who spoke out at the School Board did not necessarily represent the views of *all* the parents. When twenty-nine parents of immersion-program children were interviewed as to their views about maintaining the bulk of instruction in Spanish, rather than increasing English, about half said that they did not want to increase English, about a quarter said they did, and another quarter did not wish to comment (Cohen & Lebach, 1974). The important point is that parents should be equipped to express informed views on a subject such as the percent of time devoted to instruction through one language or another at school.

This paper has dealt with research on the relation between parents and bilingual programs. We have looked for guidelines from this research concerning the parental role in formulating public policy on bilingual schooling. The following points have been made either explicitly or implicitly:

1. Knowledge about the language proficiency and language use patterns of children and their parents is most useful in developing bilingual curriculum materials and in determining how to use these materials most appropriately.

2. Research on language use patterns of bilingual program children and of their families can indicate to program administrators whether a goal such as minority language maintenance is actually being met.

3. It is not a "given" that bilingual parents support a bilingual program. Yet initial parental misgivings about bilingual schooling may well be replaced by more positive feelings as they see the results of the program. If the results are not very satisfactory, then the fault may well lie in the choice of bilingual schooling model and/or in its execution, rather than in bilingual education.

4. If parents are to make genuine choices about the bilingual schooling of their child, then they may need to be involved in program specifics, rather than endorsing an abstraction.

5. Parents who can deal in specifics can be in a better, perhaps more powerful role with respect to shaping bilingual education policy at whatever level within the system.

This paper has primarily been reflective in nature—looking back over insights gained both from past research on bilingual schooling and from the lack of such research. The next step is to reflect on current efforts being undertaken in the area of parental involvement. Then the third step is to see what kinds of research can and should be carried out in the future. For example, there is clearly a need to improve questioning procedures in order to tap parental knowledge and opinions about bilingual schooling. José Rosario (personal communication) suggests encouraging parents to explain their answers to interview questions about bilingual education in an informal, open-ended way, so as to encourage more natural and more truthful statements. Matute-Bianchi (1979) conducted a study employing a series of methodological tools, such as participant observation, structured and open-ended interviews, and analysis of documents.

Beyond the question as to means of assessment, there is the issue of who the respondents should be. Throughout this paper, reference has been made to "parents." It may also be crucial to tap the views of *grandparents* as well, particularly in bilingual communities where their views have great importance in the education of their grandchildren, such as among the Navajo Indians (Bea Medicine, personal communication). It may be, for example, that transmission of the native culture is to be left to the older members of the community and not to be brought into the school program.

What seems to me perhaps the most fascinating aspect of the parent-child relationship with regard to bilingual schooling is the *two-way* dynamics at work in the areas of language use and language attitudes. In other words, it is not simply that parents' bilingual language behavior influences that of their children, but also that the bilingual language experiences that the children have within a bilingual program may have a measurable, and sometimes even striking effect on the parents both in terms of their language use patterns and their attitudes toward these languages.

BIBLIOGRAPHY

Chicago Board of Education. *Chicago's Bilingual Programs Evaluation Report 1975-76.* Department of Research and Evaluation, 1977.

Cohen, Andrew D. "The Culver City Spanish Immersion Program: The First Two Years." *The Modern Language Journal,* 1974a, *58* (3-4): 95-103.

Cohen, Andrew D. "Evaluation of the CITE Curriculum 1970-1973. Part II: Mexican Americans in Northern California." Report submitted to Consultants in Total Education, Los Angeles. Los Angeles: Department of English, University of California at Los Angeles, 1974b.

Cohen, Andrew D. "Mexican American Evaluational Judgments about Language Varieties." *International Journal of the Sociology of Language,* 1974c, *3:* 33-51.

Cohen, Andrew D. *A Sociolinguistic Approach to Bilingual Education: Experiments in the American Southwest.* Rowley, Mass.: Newbury House, 1975.

Cohen, Andrew D. "Bilingual Education." In M. Celce-Murcia, ed. *Essays on Selected ESL Research Areas.* Rowley, Mass.: Newbury House, in press.

Cohen, Andrew D. & Lebach, Susan M. "A Language Experiment in California: Student, Teacher, Parent and Community Reactions After Three Years." *Workpapers in Teaching English as a Second Language,* 1974, *8,* University of California, Los Angeles: 33-46.

Cohen, Andrew D. & Laosa, Luis M. "Second Language Instruction: Some Research Considerations." *Journal of Curriculum Studies,* 1976, *8* (2): 149-165. (Reprinted in H. T. Trueba & C. Barnett-Mizrahi, eds. *Bilingual Multicultural Education and the Professional: From Theory to Practice.* Rowley, Mass.: Newbury House, in press.)

Cohen, Andrew D. & Rodríguez-Brown, Flora V. *Evaluation in Moderate-to-Small School Districts; Downstate Illinois.* 500 S. Dwyer Ave., Arlington Heights, III.60005: Bilingual Education Service Center, 1977.

Cohen, Andrew D. & Rodríguez-Brown, Flora V. "Methodological Considerations in Large-Scale Research." In A.D. Cohen, M. Bruck, & F.V. Rodríguez-Brown *Bilingual Education: Evaluating Evaluation.* Arlington Va.: Center for Applied Linguistics, in press.

Cruz, Norberto, Jr. "Roles, Functions and Compliance of Parent Advisory Councils Serving Spanish-English Bilingual Programs Funded under ESEA Title VII." 1979, this volume.

Fishman, Joshua A. "The Social Science Perspective. In *Bilingual Education: Current Perspectives/Social Science.* Arlington, Va.: Center for Applied Linguistics (1977): 1-49.

Giles, Howard; Baker, Susan, and Fielding, Guy. "Communication Length as a Behavioral Index of Accent Prejudice." *International Journal of the Sociology of Language,* 1975, *6:* 73-81.

Jacobson, Rodolfo. "Can Bilingual Teaching Techniques Reflect Bilingual Community Behavior?—A Study in Ethnoculture and its Relationship to Some Amendments Contained in the New Bilingual Education Act." 1979, this volume.

Jacobson, Rodolfo & Rubio, Olga. "Code-Switching in Community and School: Community-Relevant Teaching Techniques for Bilingual Students." In R. Duran, ed. *Latino Language and Communicative Behavior.* Norwood, N.J.: Ablex Publishing Co., in press.

Las Cruces Public Schools. *Questionnaire: Parent Attitude toward Bilingual Education.* Austin, Texas: Dissemination Center for Bilingual Bicultural Education, 1973.

Manna, Samuel Y. "An Inquiry into Community Attitudes towards Bilingual-Bicultural Education." M.A. Thesis, University of California, Los Angeles: 1975.

Matute-Bianchi, María. "The Federal Mandate for Bilingual Education." 1979, this volume.

Rodríguez, Rodolfo. "Community Client Participation in ESEA Title VII Programs: An Inquiry into the Impact of a Federal Mandate." 1979, this volume.

Shore, Marietta Saravia. *The Content Analysis of 125 Title VII Bilingual Programs Funded in 1969 and 1970.* New York: Bilingual Education Applied Research Unit, Project BEST, New York City Bilingual Consortium, Hunter College Division, 1974.

Swain, Merrill. "Bilingual Education: Research and its Implications." Toronto: Ontario Institute for Studies in Education, 1979.

NOTES

1. I wish to thank José Rosario, John Halcón, María Matute-Bianchi, Donald Solá, Bea Medicine, and John Attinasi for constructive comments which I have incorporated in this revised version of the paper.
2. It *was* found that attitudes toward self, toward school, and toward community were negatively influenced by incremental years of bilingual schooling at the elementary school level in these transitional programs (Cohen & Rodríguez-Brown, 1977; in press, Ch. 5).
3. I borrow this notion from Swain (1979) who warns that bilingual education should not be imposed upon parents who want their children to learn English.
4. In pre-testing, fifty-six mothers were interviewed alone, twenty-two fathers were interviewed alone, and there were three instances of parents interviewed jointly. (Cohen, 1974c).
5. The method used here—a questionnaire within an interview—was only assessing parental *beliefs* about the reasons for learning Spanish and English. It is also possible to assess attitudes through other means, such as through obtaining gut (stereotypic) reactions to speakers of the languages (referred to as the "matched-guise" technique) and through behavioral indices of attitude (i.e., how emotional reaction to a language influences the carrying out of some activity. See, for example, Giles, et al, 1975).
6. There were three groups: the Pilot group starting in grade two and ending in grade three, the Follow Up I group starting in grade one and ending in grade two, and the Follow Up II group starting in kindergarten and ending in grade one.

7. It is important to point out that this program of Spanish immersion was for middle-class Anglo children and that their parents were consequently well educated and rather actively involved in the program. It is important to distinguish these parents from the Mexican-American parents in, say, the Redwood City program, who worked long hours, had large families to care for, and were probably more unsure of their attitudes about what specifics they wanted in their children's program than were the Culver City parents. (For a detailed contrast of Redwood City and Culver City program variables, see Cohen & Laosa, 1976).

CITIZEN PARTICIPATION IN ESEA TITLE VII PROGRAMS: AN INQUIRY INTO THE IMPACT OF A FEDERAL MANDATE

Rodolfo Rodríguez

The history of citizen participation in the management of education in the United States is characterized by cyclical fluctuations in the extent and significance of this activity. Early colonial schools were governed directly by local citizenry. Direct citizen influence was gradually relinquished in favor of elected boards of education.

By 1900, schools were staffed by a new class of professionals who claimed exclusive right to the governance of public education. The emergence of what Weber[1] called a "specialized bureaucracy" effectively excluded the political participation of the lay public, and to a larger degree, the low income and minority citizen.

Several factors which had their primary locus in the economic and political environment of the early 1900s precipitated the emphasis on professionalization. Theories of efficiency in industry and a general disenchantment with the politics of the time were especially vital in providing the impetus. This movement for school reform culminated in the centralization of school administration, increased administrative autonomy (predicated on professional expertise), and separation of schools from overt politics.[2]

Underlying much of this apolitical doctrine was a determination by educators to emancipate schools from the unscrupulous schemes of political parties, payoffs, patronage, and spoils. According to Scribner and Englert, "the spoils system abuses and corruption of the early 1900s were genuinely feared (by educators), and many associated them with politics."[3] In the opinion of some observers the decentralized, ward-based system for administering public education and the exceedingly large governing boards were the source of much that was wrong with education.[4]

In this attitudinal environment, professional school people worked diligently to maintain the autonomy of public education. According to Wirt and Kirst, the reform movement of the period established "the basic administrative structure and patterns of school policy making we have today."[5]

Several important national developments in the past decade have made the public schools more overtly political, defying traditional school administrative principles of political separation and professionalization. The enactment of the Elementary and Secondary Education Act (ESEA) of 1965, precipitated largely by the political activity of low income and minority citizens during the late 1950s and early 1960s, contributed markedly to the new politicization of public education. In response to the needs of impoverished segments of the population, ESEA was

> . . . heralded as a way of raising school achievement levels of children from low income (and usually minority-group) families (thereby) allowing them to break out of the cycle of poverty through education.[6]

Title I of the legislation which accounted for about $1.1 billion of the approximately $1.3 billion authorized for ESEA in 1966, became the chief source of support for programs designed for the so-called "disadvantaged student." In 1968, ESEA was amended to include Title VII (also known as the Bilingual Education Act) thereby sharpening the focus of the legislation on the educational needs of limited-English-speaking ability children. The series of events which ultimately led to the passage of Title VII were expectedly rooted in politics and represented the abiding struggle of Chicanos, Puerto Ricans and other language minorities for improved educational opportunities for linguistically and culturally different learners. The political reality of education and indeed its inextricable relation to local district policy-making structures have become even more apparent in recent years as a result of the *Lau* v. *Nichols* Supreme Court decision and subsequent administrative policies promulgated by the U.S. Office of Civil Rights supporting the school reform posture of language minority groups.

An important requirement associated with the ESEA legislation (including Title VII) which had its origin in the social action programs institutionalized by the Economic Opportunity Act of 1964 was the involvement of citizen-clients in program development activities. This outreach of the schools into the community as mandated by the ESEA legislation challenged even more severely the apolitical tenets of professional educators established by the early twentieth century reformers. In effect, school officials with ESEA programs were being required to open up traditionally "closed" decision-making systems and to allow low income and minority parents to bring their life styles and customs, which they shared at home with their children, into the classroom.

It is interesting to note that the federal commitment to and mechanisms for citizen involvement in ESEA programs have emerged rather slowly and have undergone frequent changes since the inception of the ESEA law in 1965. Increasingly, the emphasis of the federal requirements for citizen participation has been on programmatic decision making as discussed later in this paper. In this connection, citizen advisory committees have been installed in school districts (pursuant to ESEA requirements) as the primary devise for facilitating the school-community collaboration intended in the federal regulations. As there are very little research data which define the myriad forms and characteristics of these advisory committees, questions relating to the operation of these groups (and indeed their effectiveness in complying with federal requirements) can be answered only in a tentative and highly speculative manner.

Purpose of the Inquiry

A principal interest of the research discussed in this paper was to provide descriptive data on the decision-making characteristics of ESEA Title VII Advisory Committees.[7] Specifically, the study was concerned with comparing levels of citizen participation[8] planned by school officials with those expected by the federal government—and, more particularly, the U.S. Office of Education (USOE)—and other political institutions surrounding the school system, e.g., the courts.

A five level typology posited by the Recruitment and Leadership Training Institute (RLTI) at Temple University was adopted as the basic analytical tool for making distinctions among levels of formal citizen participation.[9] The RLTI typology was applied in the research in order to test whether significant variations in formal participation occurred and whether these variations would be associated with different program outputs. According to RLTI definitions:

1. *The Placation (Role)*—School officials and school boards allow community persons and parents to . . . make whatever minimum decisions (are) necessary to keep the noise level down. The "noise" may be generated from various sources—the federal government, state level agencies . . .
2. *The Sanctions (Role)*—The major purpose is to find persons, preferably highly visible to the widest community, who will give sanction to already established or newly developed school goals. The choice of citizens who . . . participate is left solely to . . . school officials or board members . . . participants are selected to serve various predetermined ends, in general to spread the word of approval concerning goals which remain largely shaped by school officials themselves.
3. *The Information (Role)*—The major purpose is to bring together a group of persons who have information which school officials have decided they need or which they have been directed to obtain by, e.g., the federal government or their own board. The . . . school officials maintain control over the choice of persons who will participate . . . When programs are involved, the school officials must locate and bring together persons whom the programs are designed to serve. It is assumed that the participants have information (which the school officials lack in some measure) about what needs those programs should be designed to meet, services those programs should offer, and what features should be avoided.
4. *The Checks and Balances (Role)*—The major purpose of this (role) is to provide citizens or some segment of them with some inquiry, veto and "checkmate" powers . . . The model necessitates a two-way exchange of information between citizens and school officials, and citizens must approve or disapprove certain decisions regarding programs they have been gathered together to protect and foster in their own interest.
5. *The Change-Agent (Role)*—. . . The major purpose is to set in motion a series of events that will assure that the group, as individuals and as a collective, and the substance with which they are dealing, will change over a period of time. The changes must be goal-oriented in terms developed by the participants . . . In this model citizens have what might be called "negative power" (to prevent things) but they also have "forward motion power" through the new roles they develop.[10]

The RLTI typology juxtaposes community citizens (the powerless) with school authorities (the power holders) in order to highlight the fundamental divisions between them in a formal participatory structure, e.g., the Title VII Advisory Committee. As shown in the study findings discussed later in the paper, divisions between the various stages of the typology are blurred rather than sharp. Also, the various levels of the typology should not be viewed as strictly sequential and/or developmental in their application. Thus, citizen committees may experience the stages of the typology upward or downward. (See Figure 1.) Under certain conditions, for example, the Placation (Level 1) committee may escalate to Information (Level 3) or the Checks and Balances (Level 4) committee may decline to Sanctions (Level 2).

Finally, it should be noted that the typology does not allow for an analysis of the primary determinants of political behavior—cultural values and attitudes of participants in a political process. As shown above, the RLTI typology focuses only on the characteristics of power and authority in a formal school-community participatory structure. The application of selected concepts from Easton's analysis of political systems in the investigation allowed the examination of particular behavioral/attitudinal features which gave that power and authority its legitimizing force. This offered cultural as well as socio-political insight to the power relationship analyzed in the research.

Figure 1:
Five-Level Typology of Citizen Participation

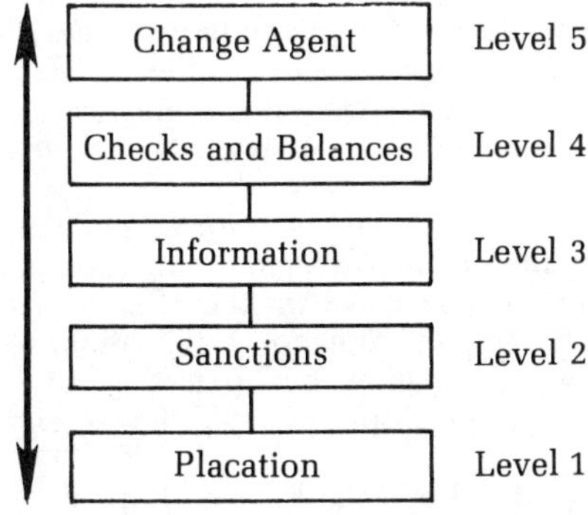

Conceptual Considerations in Political Systems Analysis

The concepts of power and decision making which explicitly undergird the RLTI typology have inspired much of the current research on the politics of education. According to Rosenthal, politics, power, and decision making are inextricably related. He further maintains that the investigation of educational decision making is the means for locating educational power. In this perspective, power is defined

> . . . as the relative ascendency or predominance of one individual or group over others, with regard to particular values, resources, or objectives.[11]

Easton (in his analysis of political systems) referred to these values as cultural mechanisms which regulate whether citizen wants will be converted into demands in a political system, e.g., the school system.[12] More specifically, Minar viewed citizen participation as a quality of the political culture (or ethos) "... as emerging in the first instance from the values and attitudes citizens have concerning how politics ought to be conducted."[13] This perspective has found support in several studies on school-community relations.[14] Ethnicity, sex, and wealth of a community, i.e., socioeconomic status, are factors frequently mentioned in the pertinent research which can influence the character of community demands made toward school authorities and the way these authorities respond. Similarly, the socioeconomic status of a community influences its organizational resources, and its ability to mobilize demands.

In contrast to citizen attitudes toward political participation, Easton believed that the extent to which governmental structures, i.e., the authorities, embrace citizen participation influences the character and quantity of demands flowing into the political system.[15] Racism, paternalism, chauvinism, and resistance by school officials to power redistribution are cultural mechanisms (as defined by Easton) which can deter citizen groups from achieving genuine levels of participation.

The concept of administrative representation has evolved in recent years to describe behavioral styles of school administrators in relating to community-clients in decision-making processes. According to Mann, administrators generally select from three styles of representation in professional decision making. The *trustee representative* is someone whose decisions are based on his/her own values, even though those values may contradict those of the community. A *delegate representative* reverses the priority and is guided by expressed citizen preferences in his/her decision-making activity. The *politico representative* vacillates between the previous two role orientations.[16]

Levels of citizen power in government subsidized programs were a pivotal feature of a typology devised by Arnstein. Using examples from urban renewal, antipoverty, and Model Cities, Arnstein described eight levels of community participation ranging from no participation, i.e., manipulation, therapy, informing, consultation, and placation; to high levels of decisional participation—partnership, delegated power, and citizen control.[17] (See Figure 2.)

Arnstein's typology was used by Cibulka in a study of citizen involvement in federally funded education programs in Chicago between 1965 and 1970. Cibulka was interested in comparing the level of community client participation planned by school officials with the level expected by the federal government, city hall, and other institutional actors surrounding the school system. It was reported by the same researcher that school authorities would develop low steps of formal participation, e.g., therapy, consultation, placation, employing Arnstein's scale, where the environmental pressures were low. In contrast, an escalation in the administrative plans for participation was recorded where the participation step envisioned by the same external political forces was high, e.g., partnership. Cibulka was able to demonstrate through the Arnstein model that at no point in the research was a high level of citizen participation fully accomplished.[18]

Political scientists have defined politics as "the struggle of men and groups to secure the authoritative support of government for their values."[19] García has further conceded that:

> Groups and organizations, constructed along economic, social occupational, religious, and cultural lines are the primary actors in the political system.[20]

This contemporary view of politics has helped to provide a more realistic approach to the study of political influences in education. Studies on the policy-making structures of educational systems may thus consider questions that could not be analyzed usefully with conventional concepts of politics, i.e., partisanship and elections.

Figure 2.
Arnstein's Eight Step Ladder of Citizen Participation

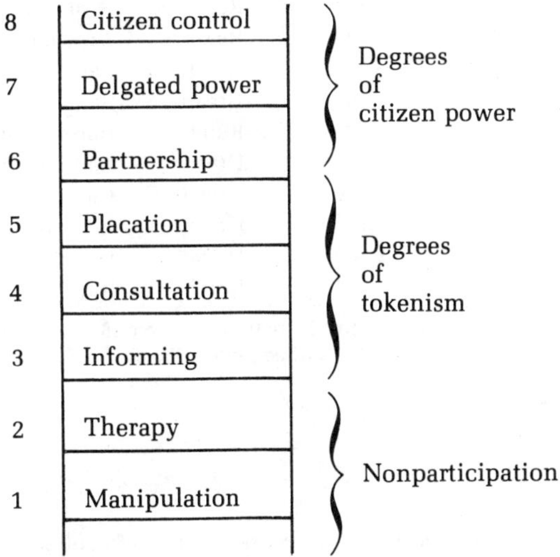

Source: Sherry R. Arnstein, "A Ladder of Citizen Participation," American Institute of Planners Journal, *XXV (July, 1969): 217.*

The Research Procedures

Fifteen ESEA Title VII Advisory Committees in Texas public schools were scrutinized to determine the extent and significance of community client participation in programmatic decision making. (See Table I for descriptive characteristics of study sample school districts.) A self-selected sample of twenty-eight school districts originally identified for the study was further reduced to the aforementioned fifteen districts in an attempt to generate a sample which would closely resemble the larger aggregate of Texas Title VII Advisory Committees (n=42). The fifteen study sample committees were compared to the state population of committees on three important characteristics of committees: ethnicity of committee members, type of committee membership, e.g., parent/non-parent characteristic of members, and sex.

TABLE 1

DESCRIPTIVE CHARACTERISTICS OF STUDY SAMPLE TITLE VII PROGRAMS AND COMMITTEES

School District	FY 1976 Title VII Level of Funding	Number of Years in Force	Title VII Student Enrollment	Demographic Characteristics	RLTI Committee Role
A	$135,495	2	1,650	Urban	Placation
B	82,754	5	290	Rural	Placation
C	88,748	7	460	Urban	Placation
D	117,187	6	250	Rural	Placation
E	152,635	3	425	Rural	Sanctions
F	102,528	2	410	Rural	Sanctions
G	151,848	7	1,030	Rural	Sanctions
H	84,167	3	343	Rural	Sanctions
I	400,000	7	2,900	Urban	Sanctions
J	201,053	7	833	Rural	Information
K	143,543	6	675	Urban	Information
L	468,291	8	1,756	Urban	Information
M	425,916	7	2,104	Urban	Information
N	400,000	6	1,203	Urban	Information
O	159,915	3	615	Rural	Information

Source of Data: Dissemination Center for Bilingual Bicultural Education, *Guide to Title VII ESEA Bilingual Bicultural Projects in the United States.* Austin, Tx.: DCBBE, 1976.

The exploratory nature of the investigation necessitated a data collection plan that was structured enough to direct the study toward accomplishing its goals but flexible enough to allow for the inclusion of other pertinent data. To meet these specifications, four data collection techniques were employed as part of a convergence of evidence strategy, i.e., confidence was placed on those findings which were identified in two or more data sources. The data collection instruments used in the study were tested for content validity and reliability and found to be adequate for the purpose of the study. The acquisition of the relevant data was accomplished through a two-phase design.

Phase I data were obtained directly from members of study sample committees (n=263) through a mail survey conducted during the spring semester of the 1976-77 school year. Based on a 46.7 percent average return rate from each study sample district, the fifteen Title VII committees were classified in relationship to the five levels of citizen participation described by RLTI.

Phase II data were acquired through a review of records of Title VII programs in the study, e.g., federal proposals, interim and final evaluation reports, and on-site interviews with the Title VII project directors and randomly selected committee members. Materials examined as part of the records review process covered a time span of eight years. A total of sixty committee members (an average of four members per district) and thirteen project directors were interviewed during the on-site visitations. The interview survey of committee members yielded an eighty percent response rate as seventy-five members were originally scheduled for this part of the study. Two of the fifteen Title VII project directors were not available for the interview as they had resigned their position with the district.

Phase II of the study had a two-fold purpose; to verify the accuracy of data collected in Phase I, and to acquire other data relevant to the problem of the study not included in the preliminary phase of the investigation.

An Analysis of the Federal Requirements for Citizen Participation in ESEA Title VII Programs

Before discussing the findings of the study and, in particular, the way administrators put the concept of citizen participation in the ESEA Title VII legislation into operation, it is important to develop first an understanding of the objectives of the legislation. Once this conceptual background and political context are known, it becomes easier to understand how and why local administrators acted as they did.

The evolution of formal citizen participation in the Title VII programs can be conceptualized as having occurred in three major stages in accordance with the RLTI typology: Placation/Sanctions, Information, and Checks and Balances. (See Figure 3.) It should be recalled that much of the original social and education legislation enacted during the 1960s coincided with the larger emphasis on poverty and civil rights—two issues which were particularly popular during President Johnson's administration. Consequently, citizen participation as it evolved in the federal programs of the 1960s was seen "as merely one aspect of the broader need for improving the livelihood of . . . the poor, the less educated, and racial and ethnic minorities."[21] More ominously, "culturally disadvantaged" groups were viewed by the early program planners as individuals with little education and skills who presumably had little to offer their children. As for the children, they were ". . . lacking motivation for school and were products of limited backgrounds."[22]

Implicitly, these early attempts to involve "have-not" Chicanos, blacks, Puerto Ricans, and other disenfranchised American minorities were not intended to enable people to participate in planning or conducting programs, "but to enable powerholders to educate or cure the participants."[23] A statement contained in the Metropolis Public Schools' (a pseudonym for the school district) 1968 Title I proposal epitomized this "therapeutic" involvement of the poor:

> . . . it is hoped that (the parent involvement program) may instill in parents a more positive attitude toward education and evoke in them a healthy and worthwhile attitude toward increased motivation, help, interest, attention, and supervision of children.[24]

Inasmuch as the original federal regulations for parental involvement issued by the newly formed division of bilingual education in 1968 called for the installation of advisory committees in school districts with Title VII programs, at the heart of these directives was an interest to promote

Figure 3.

Stages of Citizen Participation Based on Administrative Regulations and Guidelines for ESEA Title VII Programs Between 1968 and 1978 As Defined in the RLTI Typology

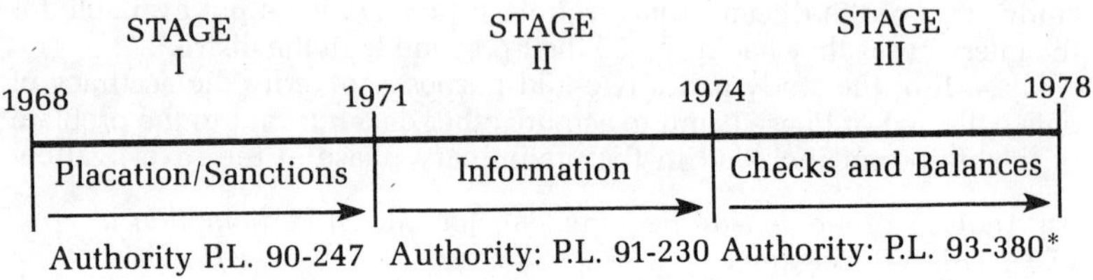

**Requirements for community involvement were not officially mandated by the U.S. Congress until 1974 through P.L. 93-380. Previous directives for formal participation issued by USOE through its administrative regulations and guidelines did not carry the power of law.*

a compensatory model of education (as described in the Metropolis Schools' Title I proposal). It should also be mentioned that, while the advocacy efforts of bilingual education proponents for significant levels of community involvement during the early years of the Title VII legislation were laudable, the obsessive mood of the country during the 1960s to eliminate poverty, predominated in shaping the goals and objectives of programs designed for the so-called "disadvantaged" citizenry. The requirements for parent and community advisory committees in Title VII issued by USOE during the time did not only fail to provide a clear definition of purpose and relation of these groups to the ESEA programs but, more significantly, were lacking in a solid legal base. This apparent impotence of the federal directives combined with the strong anti-poverty mood of the country suggested that federal officials may have expected a placation or sanctions level of community involvement in advisory committees.

In the April 1971, guidelines for Title VII, school authorities were required to consult with parents and other community members in planning the bilingual program. For example, it was stated in these guidelines that:

> Needs cannot be adequately assessed without consultation with the parents and community representatives, the people who have "been there" and who live with first-hand knowledge of their children's problems in an English-speaking environment. Nor can long range goals be postulated without the knowledge of parents' aspirations for their children. Without the active support of the parents and the community, the goals will be inadequately achieved and plans will contain hidden pitfalls.[25]

Ostensibly, an escalation in the level of community participation in bilingual programs was envisioned by USOE in comparison to earlier requirements. The new posture by USOE suggested that community advisory committees were expected to function in accordance with the information participatory model described by RLTI.

The same guidelines also placed emphasis on involvement which reflected and strengthened parent and community support for bilingual education. Dr. Albar Peña, director of Title VII programs during the early years of the Title VII legislation, pointed out the significance of this objective in a talk delivered at the "Symposium on the Mexican-American and Educational Change."

> The community, both majority and minority representatives, must be made aware of what bilingual-bicultural really is, how it works, and how the school district plans to translate this philosophy into a workable plan . . . the community must be aware of the true benefits of such a program to insure their full support, which is needed for success.[26]

The law passed by the U.S. Congress in 1974, (Public Law 93-380), suggested an increased level of participation by community clients in bilingual education. Inasmuch as this law and the subsequent administrative regulations issued by USOE mildly encouraged parent-citizen participation in many roles, e.g., paid paraprofessional and volunteer aide, government officials emphasized involvement in decision making. Prompted by a major interest at the federal level "to combat the ills of overly centralized decision making," USOE, through the authorization contained in P.L. 93-380, issued regulations which required school districts applying for ESEA funds (including Title VII) to "establish an advisory committee for the entire district." In addition, the mandate required that these committees:

a. (have) a majority of its members parents of children to be served;
b. (be) composed of members selected by parents in each school district;
c. (be) given responsibility by (the district), for advising it in the planning for, and the implementation and evaluation of such programs and projects . . .
d. (be) provided by such agency (the district) with access to appropriate information concerning such programs . . .[27]

School officials were further obligated to hold public hearings on applications for federal assistance prior to their submission to USOE. Funds were also made available for parent-clients to attend national, state, and local workshops and conferences. It was apparently felt that community impact on decisions would be strengthened if community people were properly informed of the nature of federally funded programs and related requirements governing their operation.

The amended requirements for ESEA programs, including Title VII, broadened the concept of community participation to bring it closer to involvement strategies found in Head Start, Model Cities, and other federal programs. The new posture assumed by the U.S. Congress in 1974 through P. L. 93-380 reflected the government's intent to endow citizens with power over federally funded programs. While the advisory relationship to administrators described in the 1974 government mandate displayed features of token community representation, it was nevertheless much more specific in the expectations and standards it placed on local administrators for compliance. This change in legislative policy further suggested that government officials may have envisioned community group participation in ESEA programs in accordance with the checks and balances role model defined by RLTI.

The Study Findings

The foregoing discussion provides a good backdrop for understanding the actions of school officials toward formal citizen participation as analyzed in this section. Data for the study sample are analyzed and presented in relation to the three stages of citizen participation suggested in the ESEA Title VII program requirements. (See Figure 3.)

Beginning with the first federal proposals filed by school districts in 1969, local program planners were required to specify how parental and community involvement would be achieved in Title VII programs. In reviewing the early proposals for the bilingual programs of the study sample which were funded under the original ESEA Title VII legislation (n=6), it was suggested that federal officials may have seen community involvement in a limited way. There appeared to be little demonstrable community involvement activity in existing programs. Evidence of citizen participation was primarily limited to a display of lists of community "representatives" attending bilingual program meetings called by school officials. These meetings were generally held to inform the community of the bilingual program. Although these data were sketchy, the evidence did tend to suggest that the local district plans for formal participation in the early Title VII programs were in accord with federal expectations, i.e., placation/sanctions level of citizen participation as defined by RLTI.

The extent to which community involvement in bilingual programs was achieved pursuant to the requirements issued by USOE in 1971 was not altogether clear. Data sources other than written records, e.g., interview data with personnel serving in the Title VII programs during the period, would have helped to provide more descriptive data of actual participation.

Through the application of the RLTI typology, fluctuations in citizen participation were recorded, however, in districts with court-ordered desegregation plans. Five urban districts were identified in the study with desegregation programs mandated by the courts (during the years 1971-1974). These district plans also included provisions for bilingual education. In connection with these programs of desegregation, federal funds were made available to the five urban districts under the Emergency School Assistance Act (ESAA) to support administrative efforts in implementing desegregation plans including bilingual education. Like ESEA Title VII, ESAA required community involvement in program development and implementation. The intensity of the combined pressures of ESEA, ESAA, and the federal courts for meaningful levels of community involvement were clearly evident in the evaluation reports of the study sample districts affected by desegregation. The evaluation reports for a district in east Texas revealed evidence that community client members of ESEA-ESAA Bilingual Advisory Committees were "actively" involved in determining school assignments of Chicano and black children (for purposes of desegregation). In a northcentral Texas school district, members of Bilingual Advisory Committees were selected to serve in a "Tri-Ethnic" Committee appointed by the district federal court to assist in drawing up the desegregation plan for the school system. Another committee of a district affected by court ordered desegregation assisted in determining the eligibility of schools for bilingual education programs.

The above descriptive data suggested that the level of citizen participation planned by local district officials may have escalated to information or checks and balances according to the RLTI typology. It was strongly indicated, furthermore, that administrative officials may have scaled up their plans for citizen participation to comply with the participatory step envisioned by both the courts and USOE.

As the major thrust of the present study was on reviewing the Title VII committees operating during the 1976-77 school year, a more precise assessment of the participatory levels of these groups was possible due to the comprehensive nature of the data collection design. As previously indicated, the legal basis for these committees was contained in P. L. 93-380 as enacted by the U. S. Congress in 1974. According to Phase I and II study findings, four school districts had committees operating at the placation level; five districts at the sanctions level; and six districts at the information level. (See Table 1.) At the time of the present investigation no committees are functioning at the level intended by the 1974 federal law and subsequent related regulations, i.e., checks and balances as categorized by RLTI.

Typically members of the Title VII committees (in the study sample) were of Mexican-American origin, female, and parent of a child in bilingual education. (Other descriptive characteristics of the study sample are shown in Table 1.) The level of responsibility considered appropriate for parent-clients in the study sample programs, including the mechanisms established by school officials for participation, did suggest basic differences in the philosophies under which the different programs operated. It was found, for example, that Title VII programs with placation or sanctions type committees tended to emphasize community involvement activities that would help the community client assimilate new knowledge and attitudes. This involvement of minority group communities was demonstrated in a statement filed by School District C as part of their 1976 interim evaluation report. The statement read:

> While the efforts of this group (volunteer parent aides) are highly appreciated, they do need definite training in lettering, coloring, operating the duplicating and laminating machines and on techniques on how to work with children. In an effort to solve this, the bilingual-bicultural professional staff plans to help these volunteers improve their skills, techniques and self-confidence.

In District B's Title VII proposal it was stated that:

> . . . the bilingual program seeks to develop parents to the end that they become better parents, effective teachers of their own children, and supportive resources of the school.

The foregoing objectives for client involvement affected the types of parental roles encouraged by school officials including the degree of participation elicited. For example, when asked in the Phase II interview, "What, in your opinion, is the most important contribution your committee has made to the bilingual program?" typical responses from citizen members of the placation and sanctions committees were: judging of a holiday spirit contest; making Christmas decorations; to make parents turn negative feelings about the program into positive feelings; trying to help children get home assistance; to assist in the classroom.

Of the five proposals reviewed for the Title VII programs with sanctions committees, all but one of the plans for parent involvement placed emphasis on imparting something to parents so that they would become supportive of the bilingual program. District E's proposal showed that a primary function of the advisory committee was

> ...to make the parents and community aware of the existence of the bilingual program.

The director of District G's bilingual program reported in the interview that a purpose of his committee was "to make the community aware of the advantages of bilingual education." A parent from the same district responding to the question "What is the major function of your advisory committee?" indicated:

> ...to find out what is going on and to tell other parents what the program is all about.

A teacher in the District G bilingual program responded as follows:

> The committee is the parents' voice—to report to the rest of the people what is going on.

It was suggested therefore that the function of the advisory committees classified as placation and sanctions was not to advise on the direction of the bilingual program per se. The focus was on improving or changing parental behavior. Moreover, the extent to which the community resources were to play a role in the schools was not the prerogative of parent-clients. This was decided by the professionals. This suggested that as formal mechanisms for citizen involvement, placation and sanctions type committees were amenable to control by administrators.

Compliance with the community involvement requirements contained in P. L. 93-380 was most nearly achieved by school districts with information type committees. Citizen participation activities originating from the information model tended not to assume deficiencies on the part of the community clients comprising the target population of Title VII programs. It was assumed rather, that culturally different clients possessed special knowledge and skills which could effectively be used in the development of the bilingual program. For instance, when asked, "What, in your opinion, is the most important contribution your committee has made to the bilingual program?" a District L committee member remarked:

> One thing that has come about because of a committee suggestion is *La Feria Estudiantil* (the Student Fair) which will be completely bilingual next year. It will involve spelling, art and music and it will be district-wide.

Another member of the same committee who taught in the bilingual program discussed the work of the parents in evaluating Spanish language materials for relevancy of vocabulary to the local community.

In School Districts J, K, N, and O, community rooms having names of special cultural appeal, e.g., *El Quiosco* and *Casa Amigo,* were designated in school buildings as a meeting place for parent-clients. These community rooms also served as a work area for parents to make piñatas, cultural costumes for the children and teaching aids for the classroom.

A major accomplishment of the District J Committee, according to the community liaison officer was

> the three cultural centers which provide art, music, dance and dramatics for students. The parents also teach folk dances in these centers.

In a newspaper article included in the 1976 evaluation report, District O proudly announced "Parents Consulted about Library Decisions: Parental Involvement in Action." The same article reported:

> Parents assist with the ordering of educational toys for the "Casa Amigo" toy lending library. Parents know what works and what other parents prefer to use with their children, so they were consulted in this decision-making project. This is an example of parental involvement in action.

At this third level of client participation it appeared that program planners did listen to citizen insights and altered their plans accordingly—which, in relation to RLTI, is the primary merit of the information role model. Moreover, the results of promotional efforts by the advisory committees, including staff members of the bilingual program, were especially noticeable among all information level projects as illustrated below. These are selected comments (from the interview survey) by parents and bilingual program personnel in School District, J, L. M, and O:

> The advisory committee has brought a much greater knowledge (to the general community) of the bilingual program, the workings of it, and its goals and objectives.
>
> I have said before, but this bears repeating—I consider bilingual education to be an elite part of public education.
>
> Two years ago people did not know why children were learning Spanish. The council helped in spreading the word.
>
> Lack of communication between school and community is getting to be more a thing of the past.

In sum, it can be noted from the above discussion that as federal mandates increased the demands for meaningful participation, school districts become less and less willing to write these mandates into their plan. (This was especially evident in districts with placation and sanctions type committees). It was further apparent that school authorities tended to resist implementation of the formal plans for citizen participation unless external political pressures were sufficiently strong to alter or overcome bureaucratic objections or delays. The pressure exerted by the courts and USOE for a greater degree of formal participation in connection with issues of desegregation, for example, effected a higher stage of citizen involvement according to the RLTI typology. A correspondence was suggested, therefore, between the formal participatory role planned by local school authorities and what they were forced to do by outside pressures. The greater the pressure, the higher the levels of participation planned. Based on this rationale, it can be argued that a decrease in the intensity of the same outside pressures, i.e., from the federal courts and USOE, resulted in the scaling down of formal participatory plans by local school officials. Consequently, by 1976, four of the five districts affected by the desegregation mandate (initially ordered by the courts in 1971-72) were operating their committees at the information level. One district (District I) had scaled down its participatory plans to the sanctions level. These data further suggested that school authorities may have been ignoring or minimizing their school-community relations program in favor of relationships with broader constituencies, i.e., the federal government.

A corollary facet of the inquiry included an examination of the administrative representational style of ESEA Title VII directors, i.e., the extent to which these administrators were committed to honoring expressed community interests in their professional decision-making activity. In this regard, Title VII directors were expected by federal regulations to represent the community in a responsive manner. Initial interview data acquired from the directors with the three types of RLTI committees tended to bear out this expectation. These data indicated that the directors (in the study sample) were receptive to community input in administrative matters and were willing to implement community requests for changes in the bilingual program. In accordance with Mann's three-level interpretation of administrative representation, the representational role orientation of the ESEA Title VII directors appeared, at first glance, to be consistent with the primary characterization of the delegate representative. Further probing in the interviews combined with data acquired in the records review and interviews with parent-clients suggested that the directors were relatively powerless in dealing with the community despite their claim to have "a great deal" of authority over community matters related to the bilingual program. In a school district in central Texas, for example, the project director talked about the "ingenious protections in his programs against militants." According to the director, these provisions had been built into the bilingual program by the area superintendents who wanted the bilingual committee to be composed of citizens supportive of the school programs. Further probing in the interview prompted information from the director which suggested that school administrators were fearful that members of a so-called "militant" community organization might "infiltrate" the schools. This community group, consisting mainly of Chicanos, had achieved a negative reputation among both city government and school officials for their unconventional pressure-type politics. School officials had expertly devised a checks and balances system in the selection of candidates for the advisory committee involving the building principals, the project directors, and finally the area superintendents. The director whose committee was classified as information confided that:

> Advisory committees will never be effective in any school program unless they become autonomous. As long as the school district controls their composition and functions, they will never be autonomous.

There were other instances cited in the investigation which suggested that the principal's authority exceeded that of the Title VII directors. In a south Texas school district, the project director and advisory committee members talked about their problem with one of the bilingual school principals and her lack of cooperation. A committee member expressed her discontent as follows:

> We always went to the (elementary school) principal (of School X) for approval of our projects, but she said no to a lot of things. The parents wanted a graduation for the little kids and she said no. They asked for a field trip for the sixth graders to acquaint themselves with junior high and she said no. The community specialist had to take the volunteer parents to another school because the principal didn't want them there. Mrs. Garza (a pseudonym) had to take the volunteer parents to (School Y) to help because the principal of (School X) doesn't like for parents to help, even with the backing of Mr. López (a pseudonym for the project director).

It was suggested in the data, therefore, that despite a basic inclination among the directors to honor community interests in their decision-making activity, control by their bureaucratic superiors prevented them from adequately responding to community interests. A second factor which prevented effective administrative representation of community interests was the socioeconomic background of the communities served by the Title VII programs. In three rural school districts, the project directors complained of the poor attendance and/or inactivity of low-income parent-clients in Title VII committee meetings. In these districts, the project directors had no choice but to use their own ideas about community needs and interests in programmatic decision. Thus, the Title VII directors reluctantly assumed a trustee representational role according to Mann's definition.

It appeared therefore that the extent to which project directors came to accept a formal role for communities in the decision-making process was a relatively weak one (especially in placation and sanctions type programs.) This left local communities dependent on administrative good will. It should also be mentioned that data in the exploratory study did not make it altogether clear why administrative officials in study sample districts tended to regulate the community activities of Title VII project directors. It can only be speculated that it was not in the best interest of the administration to encourage too strong an accountability relationship between the director and the local community since this could reduce the project director's accountability to the administration itself. It is further possible that school authorities viewed communities engaged in meaningful participatory activities as a threat to the professional control of the schools. It appeared, therefore, that the conservation posture of school administrators of study sample districts posed a crucial barrier to Title VII advisory committees achieving the participatory level envisioned by federal officials in the 1974 ESEA mandate, i.e., checks and balances employing RLTI.

Discussion of Findings in Relation to Easton's Political Systems Analysis

The conceptual framework which was used in the study to integrate the study data was Easton's political systems analysis. According to Easton, a basic characteristic of a political system is its openness; that is, its responsiveness to conditions existing in its environment which have been converted to political demands by members within the system:

> Thus, phenomena, both physical and social, that occur outside the boundaries of a political system may play . . . a crucial role in influencing the manner of interaction within the system and the consequent outputs.[28]

Findings in the research study tended to support this basic characterization of Easton's model. It was found, for example, that environmental factors such as federal court decisions and grants-in-aid programs, e.g., ESEA and ESAA, yield important input affecting local district policies (or output). Some of the most obvious system changes resulting from the influence of these outside forces (as shown in the research study) included a new awareness of the needs of linguistically and culturally different children and the implementation of appropriate programs, i.e., bilingual education, to meet their educational needs. Of special interest to the study was the effect of federal requirements on bringing about the formation of advisory committees consisting of community citizens who traditionally had been denied meaningful access to decision-making processes in education, i.e., the poor and culturally different.

A key question emerging from the investigation was why the stress (or environmental pressure) placed on school systems with Title VII programs through P. L. 93-380, did not eventuate in a high degree of citizen participation, i.e., checks and balances level as envisioned by federal officials? This level was temporarily accomplished only when this pressure from USOE was combined with court-mandated requirements for citizen participation in conjunction with school desegregation policies. Thus it was seen that school authorities were not inclined to raise the level of citizen participation merely on the intensity of pressure they felt from the ESEA Title VII mandate. They altered their behavior only after they were subjected to pressures from the courts, and the combined Title VII and ESAA mandates for citizen participation. In view of this finding, one was forced to focus on the *character* of the stress, which was influenced in Easton's parlance by two factors; the support system for the authorities and the support system for the regime. Borrowing from similar findings by Cibulka,

> This distinction between the character of stress and its intensity is significant because it helps us understand the support structures . . . support for the authorities and for the regime . . . which affected the propensity of the (school) system to achieve accountability representation toward local communities.[29]

It was further suggested in the study, since citizen participation did not achieve the RLTI checks and balances participatory level intended in the ESEA law, that perhaps the no-politics doctrine promulgated by the turn-of-the-century professional elites may have influenced the attitudes, i.e., the political culture, of school administrators toward the involvement of "non-elites" in school affairs. Thompson elaborates lucidly and succinctly:

> Educators have been notably successful in developing and conveying to others a set of ideological doctrines indicating that education is a unique governmental service that must be "kept out of politics." These beliefs have given them considerable autonomy and insulation from public pressures . . . As a result, the policy-making processes in school systems are relatively closed to many of the demands of the community.[30]

Findings in the study also suggested a distinct political culture (or ethos) for citizen-clients involved in the committees. It appeared that advisory committee members involved in the research study favored the use of persuasive deliberations in the articulation of demands upon authorities rather than use of conflict techniques. Generally, citizens demonstrated their influence by working cooperatively with professionals, i.e., the Title VII project directors and their staff, who, for the most part, shared a common ethnic background, philosophy, and priorities with the community.

A correspondence was further suggested between the low socioeconomic status of communities and quality of citizen participation in the Title VII committee deliberations. Three districts were cited in the study where the directors were unable to encourage the effective involvement of their low income parents in activities of the Title VII bilingual programs and, more particularly, the Title VII advisory committee.

The Study Recommendations

The research was built on the assumption that increased power for citizens in the governance of the schools can help create more effective, responsive schools. In view of this consideration, an overriding recommendation of the study was that objectives for community involvement programs in Title VII programs recognize that parent-clients have special knowledge of their children's cultural and academic needs. In this way, citizen advisory committees can be seen as a means for creating meaningful changes and/or improvements in school programs designed particularly for linguistically and culturally different learners. Findings in the study relative to programs with information committees tended to support this recommendation.

While a need to involve poor and minority parent clients in activities designed to develop their self-esteem and skills in working with their children is recognized, program administrators promoting an exclusive therapeutic approach may find it difficult to experience success in their community involvement efforts. The study data presented for bilingual programs with placation and sanctions type committees tended to support this assertion. In the same regard, the Stanford Research Institute averred:

> Participation may be limited in programs (which employ the therapeutic approach) because many parents feel that school personnel perceive them as ignorant . . . they feel they do not belong, and are looked down on. No person eagerly participates in a program which communicates his deficiencies to him.[31]

There was little evidence found in the research data which indicated that attempts were being made by school districts to train community people to be effective collaborators in educational decision making. It was recommended therefore that training programs such as the one developed by the Leadership Training Institute of the Urban/Rural School Development Project be implemented in school districts interested in involving community groups in programmatic decision making. This training program involves both professional educators and lay citizens in the process. In general terms, the Leadership Training Institute's Program:

> . . . utilizes the educational resources available in both the school and the community. (An example might be the employment of local citizens to provide school staff members with information about the community and its unique qualities.) . . . The total training package includes activities that help professional staff members and commu-

> nity people develop techniques designed . . . to translate the local situation into educationally relevant programs, i.e., black studies, Indian education, bicultural education.[32]

A major goal of the training model according to Terry and Hess is to promote: ". . . mutual collaborative planning and decision making on the part of those giving the (educational) service as well as those receiving the service."[33]

Further research was recommended which employs the RLTI typology. The investigation suggested that the typology can serve as a viable analytical tool for assessing levels of citizen participation in education programs. It was therefore recommended that a comparative study be conducted of citizen participation in programs funded by the federal government, e.g., ESEA Title I, Head Start ESAA, Follow Through. This study should be designed to analyze relationships between advisory committees operating at the various levels of the RLTI typology and their subsequent impact on the quality of programs. Attitudinal surveys should be employed to determine the influence of differentiated levels of participation on the behavior of the lay participants, i.e., to what extent does participation in advisory committees reduce feelings of powerlessness and/or alienation among low income and minority clients? Such a study might also examine particular cultural orientations of minority group citizens and the extent to which these orientations influence the political participation of this group. There were a number of threads running through the data which suggested that the socio-cultural experience of the Mexican-American can influence the character of his/her political participation.

Finally, since the concept of administrative representation has been applied on a very limited basis to educational administration, more research is needed in order to make it a useful analytical tool for practicing administrators. (The study findings suggested possible variations in the representational role orientations of Title VII project directors.) It is recommended, moreover, that the proposed study be conducted across various school systems and/or federally funded programs. A research focus on the similarities and differences of representational styles of minority and majority group administrators would yield data which could improve the training of administrators for multicultural communities.

In conclusion, the generalizability of the exploratory study data presented in this paper may be assessed on the basis of the representativeness of the study sample to the larger aggregate of Texas Title VII advisory committees. In this regard, it should be emphasized that a special effort was made to maximize the comparability level of the study sample to the general population of Texas committees. As previously indicated, three characteristics—ethnicity, sex, and parent/non-parent committee membership characteristic—were selected as the basis for this comparative analysis. These three characteristics were chosen due to their particular importance and relevance to the study of parent and community participation in programmatic decision making. In judging the applicability of the study results to states outside Texas, one should exercise caution. In this respect, it should be mentioned that there seemed to be a number of characteristics in the Title VII programs and advisory committees in the sample, e.g., funding level and socioeconomic characteristics of community, which might also be operative in similar programs and committees in other state settings.

While there were some inherent limitations to the study due primarily to its exploratory design, it supported the value and utility of theoretical application to data acquisition and analyses. Easton's analysis of political systems, with its sensitivity to the interactions of political systems with the environment, was especially useful in the analyses and organization of the study data. For this writer, as for Wirt and Kirst,

> The utility of systems theory is that, of all heuristic schemes, it enables us at least to order existing knowledge or hunches and thereby to determine what portions of the scheme are clearly untenable, which ones have at least some support, and which need to be further studied.[34]

Lastly, the increasing trend toward citizen participation in governmental programs presents a need for research tools which are capable of assessing the extent and significance of this participation. The RLTI typology, which focuses on the power relationships between citizens and authorities, may prove useful in this assessment process.

NOTES

1. For a discussion on Weberian theory see Amitai Etzioni, *Modern Organizations* Englewood Cliffs, New Jersey: Prentice-Hall Inc., 1964.
2. Frederick M. Wirt and Michael W. Kirst, *Political and Social Foundations of Education.* Berkeley, California: McCutchan Publishing Corporation, 1975.
3. J. D. Scribner and Richard Englert, "The Politics of Education: An Introduction." *The Politics of Education,* 76th Yearbook of the National Society for the Study of Education, Part III ed, J.D. Scribner Chicago, Illinois: University of Chicago Press, 1977: 4-5.
4. Writ and Kirst, loc. cit.
5. Ibid., p. 5.
6. Stanford Research Institute, *Parent Involvement in Compensatory Education Programs.* Menlo Park, California: Stanford Research Institute, 1973: 1.
7. A more detailed description and analysis of the research can be found in Rodolfo Rodríguez, "Citizen Participation in Selected ESEA Title VII Advisory Committees: An Exploratory Study of Power Relationships Between Community Clients and School Authorities." Unpublished Ph.D. dissertation, University of New Mexico, 1979.
8. For the purpose of the study, citizen participation was used as a categorical term for citizen power.
9. Recruitment and Leadership Training Institute, *Community Parity in Federally Funded Programs,* a report prepared for the U.S. Office of Education National Center for the Improvement of Educational Systems, Philadelphia, Pennsylvania: Temple University, 1971.
10. Ibid., pp. 29-30.
11. Alan Rosenthal, Introduction to *Governing Education: A Reader on Politics, Power, and Public School Policy.* ed. Alan Rosenthal, Garden City, New York: Anchor Books, 1969: x.

12. David Easton, *A Systems Analysis of Political Life* New York, New York: John Wiley and Sons, Inc., 1965: 86. Citizen "wants" Easton defines as expressions of interests, opinions, expectations, and preferences. "Demands" are wants which constituent groups, e.g., community clients and the federal government, express toward administrators for authoritative action.
13. David W. Minar, "The Community of Conflict in School System Politics." *American Sociological Review,* XXXI December, 1966: 9822-34.
14. See, for example, Stanford Research Institute, op. cit.
15. Easton, loc. cit.
16. Dale Mann, *The Politics of Administrative Representation* Lexington, Massachusetts: Lexington Books, 1976.
17. Sherry R. Arnstein, "A Ladder of Citizen Participation." *American Institute of Planners Journal,* XXV July, 1969.
18. James G. Cibulka, "Administrators as Representatives: The Role of Local Communities in an Urban School Systems." unpublished Ph.D. dissertation, University of Chicago, 1973.
19. Writ and Kirst, op. cit., p. 4.
20. F. Chris García, "Politics and Multicultural Education do Mix," *Journal of Teacher Education.* XXVIII May-June, 1977: 25.
21. Robert K. Yin, et al., *Citizen Organizations: Increasing Client Control over Services.* Santa Monica, California: Rand Corporation. 1973: v.
22. Ibid.
23. Arnstein, op. cit., p. 217.
24. Statement taken from Cibulka, op. cit., p. 227.
25. United States Department of Health, Education, and Welfare, *Programs under Bilingual Education Act (Title VII, ESEA) Manual for Project Applicants and Grantees.* Washington, D.C.: Government Printing Office, 1971: 1.
26. Dr. Albar A. Peña. "Creating Positive Attitudes Towards Bilingual Bicultural Education." in Alfredo Castañeda et al., *Mexican American and Educational Change.* Riverside, Califronia: University of California, 1971: 14.
27. United States Congress, *Public Law 93-380,* 93rd Congress, H.R. 69, August 21, 1974 Washington, D.C.: Government Printing Office, 1974: 14.
28. Easton, op. cit., p. 121.
29. Cibulka, op. cit., p. 198. Support for the regime focuses on the roles, offices, norms, and rules which govern the authorities.
30. John T. Thompson, *Policymaking in American Education: A Framework for Analysis.* Englewood Cliffs, New Jersey: Prentice-Hall Inc., 1976: 46.
31. Stanford Research Institute, *Parent Involvement in Compensatory Education Programs.* Menlo Park, California: Stanford Research Institute, 1973: 42.
32. James V. Terry and Robert D. Hess, *The Urban/Rural School Development Program: An Examination of a Federal Model for Achieving Parity Between Schools and Communities.* Stanford, California: Stanford University, 1975: 52-54.
33. Ibid.
34. Wirt and Kirst, op. cit., p. 14.

ROLES, FUNCTIONS AND COMPLIANCE OF PARENT ADVISORY COUNCILS SERVING SPANISH-ENGLISH BILINGUAL PROJECTS FUNDED UNDER ESEA TITLE VII

Norberto Cruz, Jr.

In recent years there has been a concerted national effort to provide equal educational opportunities for all children in public schools. Because of the failure of some local and state governments to produce needed monies to effectively accommodate the rise in selected student populations and meet certain educational needs, the Congress has intervened with federal grants.

With the passage of the Elementary and Secondary Education Act of 1965 (ESEA), Congress continued the precedent set by the Smith-Hughes Act of 1917 and authorized grants to be paid directly to local school systems to improve the school program for all children. The ESEA was intended to expand and improve the quality of selected educational programs.

Originally the Elementary and Secondary Education Act was aimed at bringing better educational opportunities to the children who were disadvantaged because of poverty conditions in the United States. Congress further defined the term "disadvantaged" when it recognized the needs of linguistic minorities and amended the ESEA of 1965 by passing Title VII, better known as the Bilingual Education Act of 1968.

Important to linguistic minorities, as well as to other minorities, were the mandates on citizen participation in federal programs which Congress legislated. The term "participation" was first widely used in the Economic Opportunity Act of 1964. This act made provisions for maximum participation by all citizens whenever feasible. Citizens now had a voice in some of the policies which directly affected their lives.

The key sections of the Economic Opportunity Act of 1964 provided for Job Corps, Community Action Programs, Special Programs to Combat Poverty in Rural Areas, Employment and Investment Incentives, and Work Experience Programs. The word "participation" can be found throughout the EOA of 1964, but nowhere is the word used with more emphasis than in the section defining the Community Action Program: "The term Community Action Program means a program . . . which is developed, conducted and administered with the maximum feasible participation of residents of the areas and members of the groups served."[1]

Citizen participation in educational programs had its major inception with federal programs like ESEA Title I and Headstart. Local school districts had to create parent advisory councils which were to assist local school officials in the planning, implementation and evaluation of the specific federally funded program. The following section describes the specifics of parental involvement in federally funded bilingual projects.

Regulation of Parental Involvement Under Title VII

Bilingual Education funded under ESEA Title VII provides for parent and community involvement in "all" aspects of program planning, implementation and evaluation. Parent advisory councils have been the vehicles for this involvement in bilingual programs. A year long research project identifying roles and functions of parent advisory councils serving Spanish-English bilingual projects funded under ESEA Title VII was recently completed by the author. From the literature reviewed in preparation for the study, it was evident that roles and functions of parent advisory councils serving bilingual projects funded under ESEA Title VII have never been adequately specified nor have all the rules and regulations been strictly followed by some local education agencies receiving Title VII monies.

In the Bilingual Education Act of 1968, there is no language which mandates parent/community participation through an advisory council, committee or other group. It does, however, state:

> Applications for grants under title may be approved by the Commissioner only if . . . the program set forth in the application is consistent, with criteria established by the Commissioner.[2]

This provision gave the Commissioner the right to develop criteria which local and state educational agencies were required to meet in order to qualify for Title VII funds. In 1971, criteria for eligibility of Title VII funds were printed in the *Manual for Project Applicants and Grantees*. The *Manual* did not mandate parent advisory councils, which is evident by the word "should." Such wording is a suggestion rather than a regulation. The *Manual* states:

> A project advisory group consisting of parents and community representatives should be formed before the project proposed is prepared and should continue to be involved at all stages of the project's development and operation.[3]

In May of 1974, hearings were held in Washington, D.C. and in New York City before the General Subcommittee On Education of the Committee on Education and Labor. Hearings were held on H.R. 1085, H.R. 2490, and H.R. 11464 which were bills proposed to amend ESEA Title VII. The testimony at the hearings revealed the importance of parent/community involvement in bilingual programs. Recommendeations for revisions of regulations by the National Advisory Committee on the Education of Bilingual Children reflected the views of witnesses giving testimony, as well as the views of committee members.

The Bilingual Education Act of 1974, in part because of recommendations by the National Advisory Committee on the Education of Bilingual Education, mandated participation by parents of children enrolled in bilingual programs. Specifically, the law reads as follows:

> An application for a program of bilingual education shall be developed in consultation with parents of children of limited English-speaking ability, teachers, and, where applicable, secondary school

> students, in the areas to be served, and assurances shall be given in the application that, after the application has been approved under this title, the applicant will provide for participation by a committee composed of, and selected by, such parents and, in the case of secondary schools, representatives of secondary school students to be served.[4]

The Bilingual Education Act which now mandated parental involvement made it possible for new rules and regulations to be written for those agencies applying for Title VII funds. Rules and regulations which reflected the language of the new act were incorporated into the "Criteria for Governing Grants Awards" which appeared in the *Federal Register* on June 11, 1976.

Even with the legislation mandating participation by a "committee" (known as an "advisory group" in the rules and regulations), the quantity and quality of participation has been a concern to school officials and citizens. The functions of parent advisory councils vary from project to project, a fact revealed in a report entitled *Federal Programs Supporting Educational Change*. The report stated: ". . . some councils' functions are purely ceremonial whereas others seem to actually contribute to policy."[5] Even with parental involvement being mandated through advisory councils, there is no assurance that they will function properly. The following section focuses on why councils may not operate effectively.

Lack of Specific Functions for Advisory Councils

According to Clasby, the goal of "maximum feasible participation" was not clearly stated in the educational legislation. The exceptions, of course, were some of the provisions in Title I which provided for citizen involvement. Clasby criticizes the regulations developed by the federal government for advisory councils because "a commitment was announced without attention to implementation, followthrough, or documentation of results."[6] Clasby clarified this by the statement:

> Federal regulations for councils, with precise requirements for membership emphasize structure rather than function. Councils have the right to convene, to receive information and to sign off on proposals for funding. There are few, if any, provisions for technical assistance, for monitoring or evaluating the activities, or for funding.[7]

With citizen participation widespread in the United States, there is evident variety in the quality of participation. A three-year National Institute of Education study of citizen participation revealed key factors which undermined the quality of citizen participation. One particular weakness, according to the study, was that officials:

> concentrate on structures and ignore functions. Create new groups and focus attention on numbers: how many members, how often they meet, etc. Never clarify roles, rights, responsibilities. Give these groups no power.[8]

Davies best relates the importance of power to citizen participation by stating:

> Participation without power is demoralizing for an informed constituency, leading to cynicism and public mistrust of the education

> establishment. Without adopting a coherent policy for participation with incentives for local professionals to comply with it, state and federal policy makers will be embarking on a venture producing more harm than good.[9]

Davies further emphasized the importance of this concept by saying that participation:

> . . . is particularly significant when applied to those who are often badly served by the school—the urban and rural poor, minorities, and working class white—who now have the least power in shaping school policies.[10]

Even though the Civil Rights Act of 1964 did not allow discrimination in federally assisted programs, improprieties did continue in education. Weinberg feels that minorities have never truly had complete educational opportunities. He further feels that "racial and ethnic barriers were accepted by school people as inevitable limitations on educational opportunity."[11] Minority groups have had difficulty entering the democratic process in general but, in the educational process specifically, supporting Weinberg, Lapote states:

> Minority children and their parents have been progressively isolated from decision-making levels in schools through consolidation and centralization. These children and their parents have had little identification and only modest involvement in the educational process; they have not participated in education or in the social-political life of their nation.[12]

Educators can benefit from the involvement of citizens by becoming more familiar with the attitudes and the aspirations that the community has for its children. With respect to bilingual education, Ulibarri feels that the program must be completely in tune with the community it serves. He points out that:

> A program that does not take into account the problems of the community, the needs of the individuals, and the aspirations of the people cannot hope to be anything more than a veneer that helps to hide the anomalies of the community and to engender helplessness in the individual. Such a program will never have the support of the community nor the enthusiasm of the individual.[13]

Community involvement in bilingual education has been of major concern to both school systems and communities. John and Horner agree with Ulibarri by emphasizing the importance of community involvement when they state:

> The participation of parents is a critical aspect of bilingual education. Although many bilingual educators support this view, they fail to implement it. When programs are planned in isolation from the community, parents' contributions become merely incidental. Parental participation and community control do not guarantee relief from the shortage of qualified teachers, the lack of curriculum materials, limited funds, or from any other of the problems in bilingual education. Such participation and control do, however, provide support for the continuity to the schools' efforts.[14]

Roles and Functions of Parent Advisory Councils

It is assumed that if parent advisory councils in bilingual education are to function properly and to contribute to the program, roles and functions of the councils should be clearly defined in order for all parties to adequately fulfill their respective responsibilities. The author, being aware of the lack of direction for advisory councils, decided to do research with respect to roles and functions of advisory councils on bilingual education. The research study previously mentioned was a dissertation entitled, *An Investigation of the Roles and Functions of Parent Advisory Councils Serving Spanish-English Bilingual Projects Funded under ESEA Title VII.*

The author's primary purpose in the study was to identify and examine the roles and functions of parent advisory councils in bilingual education programs. In order to accomplish this purpose, it seemed appropriate to investigate the perceptions of project directors, school principals and parent advisory council chairpersons regarding the operation of advisory councils. Twenty-one Spanish-English bilingual projects funded under Title VII were randomly selected for the study. A project director, principal and advisory council chairperson from each of the twenty-one projects were chosen to be participants in the nationwide research study. The aforementioned participants were chosen for the study because of their working relationship with the parent advisory council.

The literature search revealed four basic roles assumed by advisory councils. Cronin and Thomas felt that the roles of advisor, director, and supporter generally characterize councils.[15] Information found in the report entitled *Federal Programs Supporting Education Change* supported a fourth role: that of non-supporter.[16]

The literature revealed that advisory councils were generally characterized as advisory in nature, but there were indications that some councils desired more than just an advisory role. Councils wanting more involvement in the decision-making process appeared to be demanding a role characterized as director. Other councils were termed as supporters and their activities did not usually deal with recommendations and never dealt with the development of directives but almost always dealt with support for school officials on attaining goals. The non-supporter role chosen by some advisory councils appeared to be based on council reactions against the program in question and is characterized by an almost total lack of support of school officials in achieving program goals. It was recognized by the author that all four roles can be present in any one advisory council but that a council usually associates itself with one major role.

The four roles for advisory councils were defined in the research instrument and randomly listed. The instructions requested that the defined roles be ranked by the participants according to primacy. The functions of advisory councils that were used as items on the research instruments were selected from Caldwell,[17] Linscomb,[18] Kindred,[19] Marlow,[20] Pumphrey,[21] and Woons.[22] The researcher also included some functions which were not generally found to be performed by the advisory council, but were almost always reserved for the Board of Education, i.e., budget planning, personnel policies, planning of school facilities, and evaluation of students, teachers and administrators.

The various functions were identified under the three program areas of planning, implementation and evaluation. The functions listed under program planning were: textbook selection, course selection, budget planning, development of objectives, identification of needs and planning of school facilities. Under program implementation there were five functions: identifying community resources and public relations, interpretation of the bilingual program to the community, curriculum support, personnel policies and inservice training. The third area of program evaluation had the following functions: evaluation of students, teachers, administrators, program, parent advisory council, community and objectives. The role and function descriptors were incorporated into a questionnaire where the participants were asked to rank the roles and functions under each program area according to primacy. The sixty-three participants surveyed in the research study were also asked to answer questions concerning the organizational format, procedures and composition of the advisory councils they represented. Responses were received from sixty-seven percent of the chairpersons, seventy-one percent of the principals and ninety-five percent of the project directors. Combined responses from the three groups of participants equaled seventy-seven percent.

There was significant agreement within each group of chairpersons, principals and project directors in regard to the ranking by importance of the roles and functions of parent advisory councils. The analysis of the data indicated that the role of advisor was ranked first, followed by the roles of supporter, director and non-supporter, in that sequence. This is in accordance with the review of literature which indicated that most advisory councils acted in an advisory capacity and supported the efforts of the school administration in the development and implementation of goals.

The analysis of the data concerning the ranking of functions under the three areas of program planning, implementation and evaluation indicated that there was significant agreement among the three groups of participants surveyed. Under program planning there were six functions ranked. The primary and secondary functions under planning were identification of needs and development of objectives, respectively. This indicated that the parent advisory council should be involved in the identification of needs with respect to bilingual education and, once those needs were identified, the involvement of the council in the development of objectives to meet those needs was desirable. Under program planning, course selection was ranked third, followed by budget planning, textbook selection and planning of school facilities, in that order.

The second set of functions were under the program heading of implementation. The five functions were those which advisory councils would be able to perform after the bilingual program was planned. The functions ranked first and second were interpretation of the bilingual program to the community and public relations, respectively. The remaining three functions under implementation were ranked in this order: curriculum support, inservice training and development of personnel policies. This indicates that the respondents felt that an advisory council should be more involved with interpretation of the program and with public relations and not so involved with administrative responsibilities such as inservice training and personnel policies.

Program evaluation was the third area and included seven functions to be ranked by participants. Evaluation of the program and evaluation of objectives for the curriculum were ranked first and second, respectively. The ranking of evaluation of the program and evaluation of objectives for curriculum is in harmony with the needs and development of objectives ranked first and second under planning and with the interpretation of the bilingual program ranked first under implementation. If the advisory councils are indeed involved in the development of objectives, then the councils should also be involved in the interpretation of the bilingual program to the community. The next appropriate functions for the advisory council should then be an evaluation of the program and objectives for curriculum. The function ranked third was the evaluation of the community. The three other functions, that of evaluation of students, teachers and administrators were ranked fifth, sixth and seventh, respectively.

The participants were also asked to answer questions relating to the format of their respective councils. The study revealed that parent advisory councils serving Spanish-English bilingual projects are similar to advisory councils described by the literature with respect to the organizational format of councils, the method of choosing chairpersons, the time, place and frequency of meetings, the term of membership, and the method of making decisions. The majority of councils represented had organizational formats with rules that were either written or understood. Chairpersons were generally elected by the entire council. The majority of councils had meetings in the schools, once a month and in the evenings when the rate of attendance is higher. A one-year term of membership was specified in 65.3 percent of all responses. The method of making decisions by simple majority (fifty-one percent) was the most prevalent, according to the responses received. The major differences relating to the mechanics of organization in councils were how the general membership is chosen and the number of members on a council. The literature indicated that general membership is most often attained by an election. However, in the councils surveyed in this study, general membership was most often achieved by volunteering one's services. The councils represented were comprised of ten to fifteen, or more than twenty members, which differs slightly from the recommended number of fifteen to twenty members. A large majority, 77.1 percent of the respondents, were Spanish-English bilinguals. This large percentage was a positive response in that many, if not most, dealings with the community should be conducted in the language familiar to the parents.

The following conclusions from the study are based on several activities or situations which are not desirable and probably have a negative effect on bilingual programs. Over one-third of the respondents indicated that the board of education or the superintendent had not developed a formal plan or statement giving recognition to the council. Also, over half of the respondents stated that limits of authority were not specified by either the board of education or the superintendent. It is not known why most of the councils represented did not have the formal recognition of the board or the superintendent. With respect to limits of authority, an advisory council needs to be cognizant of what it can do and also know the acceptable procedures for successful accomplishment of duties. The literature reviewed for this study was explicit in regard to the limits of authority by emphasizing that councils were more efficient when limits were specified.

The instances of noncompliance by some councils not having at least half of the membership comprised of parents with children enrolled in the bilingual program was very small, with only 6.1 percent of the respondents indicating this to be the situation in the councils they represented. However, the instances of noncompliance by some councils not existing prior to the preparation of the proposal submitted to the Office of Bilingual Education was unusually high, with 34.1 percent of the respondents indicating this to be the case. This item on the questionnaire had a non-response rate of 10.2 percent, which was the highest non-response rate on the entire questionnaire. The 10.2 percent of non-respondents to the question of parent advisory councils existing prior to the preparation of the proposal submitted to the Office of Bilingual Education was alarming. If the non-respondents did not know whether or not their respective councils existed prior to the preparation of the proposal, they were derelict in their responsibility to know the Bilingual Education Acts and the rules developed by the U.S. Office of Education with respect to Bilingual Education and parent advisory councils. If, on the other hand, the non-respondents did not wish to answer in the negative when, in fact, they were aware that their respective councils had not existed prior to the preparation of the proposal, these participants were concealing a violation by local school administrators and/or local school boards.

The 34.1 percent of respondents who indicated that their respective local education agencies were in noncompliance with the existence of parent advisory councils prior to the preparation of the proposal are to be commended for revealing those conditions which definitely need investigation. Several questions come to mind when reviewing the fact that a little over one-third of bilingual projects do not have existing parent advisory councils prior to the preparation of the proposal. One, do these local education agencies in noncompliance ever convene an advisory group after the project is funded? Two, if, in fact, an advisory council is formed, is it just a rubber stamp for what has already been developed by the local school board and/or school administrators? Three, are the local education agencies in noncompliance only interested in federal funds without affording the parents of bilingual children an opportunity to participate in the development of the bilingual education program which will directly affect their children? Four, why has there not been closer scrutiny by the Office of Bilingual Education with respect to parent advisory councils? Five, why has there not been a booklet developed with general and specific guidelines (roles and functions) for parent advisory councils funded under Title VII? These questions are indeed very difficult to answer without doing objective research. Hopefully, if research is done to answer these aforementioned questions, solutions will be developed to remedy the problems caused by these unanswered questions.

The purpose of the study was to identify roles and functions of advisory councils and to have advisory council chairpersons, principals and project directors rank these roles and functions according to their perceptions with respect to bilingual projects. Identifying the roles and functions of parent advisory councils serving Spanish-English bilingual projects funded under ESEA Title VII is the first study of this type according to the extensive review of literature conducted by the researcher. The study revealed that the roles and functions identified in the literature do exist in bilingual projects. The relationship between the school boards and the parent advisory councils is new and at times there does appear to be confusion with respect to what councils should do. There are some school boards and superintendents that have not recognized or specified the limits within which these councils may operate. Councils not knowing their limits of authority have difficulty in fulfilling roles and executing functions. The respondents in this study have indicated, through their perceptions, that parent advisory councils in bilingual education should fulfill specified roles and functions. These roles and functions should be allowed to be undertaken by parent advisory councils in bilingual projects. These parent advisory councils should not, however, operate unchecked. They should be evaluated by several measurements: first, to evaluate if the educational standards of linguistic minority children are on an equal basis with other children; and, secondly, to evaluate the operation of the council and involvement of parents. It is imperative to point out that before councils are evaluated the researcher feels that a complete program to familiarize the council members with their responsibilities be initiated, that roles and functions be specified, that goals and objectives for the councils be developed. Only then, can objective evaluations of parent advisory councils take place.

Recently Proposed Regulations

During the preparation of this paper, information was obtained from the Office of Bilingual Education which indicates an effort to insure compliance by local education agencies with respect to parent advisory councils. Interim regulations have been developed in accordance with the Bilingual Education Act of 1978. The Office of Bilingual Education will use the interim regulations for the awarding of the 1979-1980 grants.

The interim regulations have points which have been long overdue. Following are some of the highlights. Before the application is prepared, the applicant agency must form an advisory council with at least seven members. The majority of the advisory council must be composed of parents of children with limited-English-speaking proficiency. Other members on the advisory council may be persons interested in bilingual education. The regulations now require that the advisory council participate in three ways: assist in the planning of the project, review drafts for the applicant agency, and prepare comments on the application submitted to the Office of Bilingual Education.

The significant change in these proposed regulations is that the applicant agencies must allow the advisory council to participate. The regulations also state that the applicant agency shall produce documentation that the advisory council did, in fact, participate in the development of the proposal. The applicant agency must also include comments on the application made by the advisory council with respect to the proposal. After the proposal has been reviewed by the Office of Bilingual Education and approved for funding, the regulations state that an advisory committee must continue participation in the bilingual program. The advisory committee, like the advisory council, must be composed of and selected by the parents of children with limited-English-speaking proficiency. In bilingual projects that serve secondary school students, the regulations provide for secondary school students on the advisory committee. An advisory council member may also be a member on the advisory committee. This is specified in the regulations because prior to these regulations, the language had not differentiated between an advisory council and an advisory committee. The difference now is that the advisory council participates in the development of the proposal and the advisory committee participates after the proposal has been accepted. Finally, assurances must be given by the applicant agency that after the application has been approved, the applicant agency shall provide for continuing consultation with and participation by the advisory committee.

These new regulations for applicant agencies with respect to parent advisory councils (committees) indicates an effort by the Office of Bilingual Education to assure parent/community involvement in bilingual programs. The point must be made, however, that even though Congress has, for a second time, mandated parental involvement in bilingual programs and the Office of Bilingual Education has written proposed regulations for applicant agencies insuring parental involvement, there still exists a lack of specific roles and functions for parent advisory councils (committees), and virtually no monitoring system.

In summary, as revealed by the study, councils not knowing their limits of authority have difficulty in fulfilling roles and in executing functions. Advisory councils, therefore, must know their specific roles and functions. Parent advisory councils should not, however, operate unchecked. They should be evaluated on a continual basis with specified performance indicators. It is imperative to point out that before advisory councils are evaluated, a complete program to familiarize the council members with their responsibilities be initiated, that roles and functions be specified and that goals and objectives be developed. Only then can objective evaluations of parent advisory councils take place.

Recommendations

It is the recommendation of the author that the interim final regulations written by the U. S. Office of Education for the Office of Bilingual Education be implemented. The Office of Bilingual Education should scrutinize the compliance of local education agencies regarding parent advisory councils. The Office of Bilingual Education has made an effort in the right direction but has still fallen short in requiring such things as formal recognition of the parent advisory council by the local school board, specified limits of authority by the local boards for effective operation of the advisory councils, and periodic evaluation of the effectiveness of the parent advisory councils.

There should be a manual developed for dissemination to all parent advisory councils which includes specific roles and functions. Consideration of the community is important when assigning functions. Size of the community and resources available should be taken into account when parent advisory councils undertake specified functions. Parent advisory councils should be made aware of the responsibilities they possess and given the proper training, technical assistance and funding to successfully operate the planning, implementation and evaluation of bilingual projects.

One of the most important recommendations is a national conference for members of parent advisory councils working with bilingual projects funded under Title VII. At this conference, hearings should be held to identify the concerns of bilingual communities through testimony of council members. Time should be dedicated for training of council members in all program areas. Resource and training centers should be developed so that parent advisory council members can get assistance on a regional basis. Funds must be appropriated for the continual training of new advisory council members.

Research must be funded so that successful organizational formats and innovative ideas for parent advisory councils can foster knowledgeable and informative parental involvement. Parents can be positive influences on their children at home and school, but must be afforded the opportunity to enter the democratic process. At all cost, assurances must be made that linguistic minorities are never denied the right to participate in governmental affairs.

NOTES

1. *United States Code Congressional and Administrative News:* 88th Cong., 2nd Sess., 1964, I, St. Paul, Minnesota: West Publishing Company, 1965: 595.
2. *Elementary and Secondary Education Amendments of 1965, Statutes at Large* 81, (1968): 786.
3. United States Office of Education. *Manual for Project Applicants and Grantees.* Washington, D.C.: Department of Health, Education and Welfare, 1971: 67.
4. *United States Code Congressional and Administrative News:* 90th Cong., 2nd Sess., 1974, I, St. Paul, Minnesota: West Publishing Company, 1975.
5. Gerald C. Sumner and others, *Federal Programs Supporting Educational Change.* Santa Monica, Ca.: The Rand Corporation, 1975: III-4.
6. Miriam Clasby. "The Community Voice In Public Education." *Social Policy.* November/December 1977: 74.
7. Ibid.
8. Don Davies, Miriam Clasby and Brian Powers, "The Plight of Citizens." *Compact,* Autumn, 1977: 17.
9. Ibid.
10. Don Davies. "Citizen participation in schools: a network of illusions." *Citizen Action in Education,* V, No. 1 (January, 1978): 1.
11. Meyer Weinberg, ed., *A Chance to Learn.* Cambridge: Cambridge University Press, 1977: 2.
12. Carole Lapote. *Some Effects of Parent and Community Participation on Public Education.* New York: Columbia University, 1969: 36.
13. Horacio Ulibarrí. *Bilingual Education: A Handbook for Educators.* Albuquerque: University of New Mexico Press, 1970: 1.
14. Vera P. John and Vivian M. Horner. *Early Childhood Bilingual Education.* New York: The Modern Language Association of America, 1971: xxii.

15. Thomas E. Cronin and Norman C. Thomas. "Federal Advisory Processes: Advice and Discontent." *Science*, CLXXI (February, 1971), 771.
16. Sumner, op. cit.
17. T. P. Caldwell. "An Assessment of Arizona Community School Administrators Concerning School-Community Advisory Councils in Educational Decision-Making." (unpublished PhD dissertation, The University of Michigan, 1974), p. 67.
18. J. P. Linscomb. "The Structure and Organization of Successful Community Advisory Councils in an Inner-City Area of Los Angeles City Unified School District." (unpublished PhD dissertation, Brigham Young University, 1972: 81.
19. Leslie Kindred, Hubert M. Hamlin. *Citizens' Committees in the Public School.* Danville, Ill.: Interstate Printing Company, 1952: 174.
20. Frank M. Marlow. *Putting Citizen Advisory Committees to Work in Your School.* New Jersey: Prentice-Hall, Inc., 1969: 12.
21. W. S. Pumphrey. "The Structure and Organization of Successful Community Advisory Councils in an Emerging Middle-Class Area in the Los Angeles City School Districts." (unpublished PhD dissertation, Brigham Young University, 1971).
22. G. J. Woons. "The Community School Council: Functions, Characteristics, and Issues." (unpublished PhD dissertation, Michigan State University, 1972).

Part IV

MODELOS Y PROBLEMATICA/MODELS AND ISSUES

A FLEXIBLE-TECHNOLOGY MODEL FOR BILINGUAL EDUCATION

Donald F. Solá

This paper is essentially a "think-piece," an exploration of some ideas that seem promising rather than a report on completed empirical research or practical work. The ideas did grow out of experience in the real world, especially from several years of experimental research in Quechua-Spanish bilingual education in highland Peru. But they need more thought and criticism before they can be applied, a good deal of testing before they can be used reliably.

A brief orienting comment may give some sense of the motives behind this paper. In general we can be skeptical about approaches to bilingual education that look for the *best* policy, or the *right* program, or the *just* solution. There may turn out to be some generally applicable notions in the end but, as we seek them, we should be more interested in knowing the direction in which programs, given their circumstances, are going, how fast they are moving, what dimensions of change are involved, which factors influence most their direction and velocity, and how aware all parties—teachers, parents, community leaders, policy makers—may be of their options and the variables on which their options lie. We therefore need a model that will deal with these questions, a model that permits us to say to a teacher or policy maker, "In your situation, with your goals, you are headed in the right direction at an admirable velocity," and show them, in the terms of the model, why we believe this to be true. At present, there are few grounds for confidence that we can soon say to such persons, "You've found the right solution." So this paper has more to say about directions on dimensions than about criteria for excellence or justice.

The Model

The *flexible-technology* (F-T) model proposed here may respond to the need for a dynamic descriptive typology for bilingual education programs. The name is chosen, first, to call attention to variation among programs and within programs and to the dimensions of variation; and, second, to suggest that if more flexibility is introduced into programs, on dimensions we all perceive as significant, we may make programs more resilient, less brittle and fragile, more likely to improve steadily, and more capable of coping with regressive pressures when these appear. The frame of reference for the F-T model is bicultural education generally, rather than bilingual education in a selective or contrastive sense. Societal bilingualism, nowadays often called *diglossia* (Ferguson, 1959; Fishman, 1967), always coincides with diversity of culture, and, conversely, cultural differences are always faithfully reflected in linguistic usage in some way, even when two groups may be said to use the same language (Hymes, 1962). *Bicultural education* is then defined as any instance of formal education in a bicultural zone, that is, in any area in which two or more cultures, languages, or dialects are in social interaction, and the F-T model is pertinent to all such situations, not just to those programs we may perceive as having adopted a bicultural or bilingual policy. In other words, the model is capable of locating within its typology even the null case, the program that makes no response at all to bicultural conditions. This generality contributes greatly to the model's power; it systematizes the relationship between bicultural education policy and education policy in general. However, given the particular experiences that suggested the model, this paper focuses most on language education in primary school, in cases where a minority language group is expected, through formal education, to extend its linguistic repertoire (Gumperz, 1968) to include a second language of wider use in the society.

The F-T model incorporates *institutional* (including social) variables as well as *technological* (some prefer the term methodological) variables and relates the two types, and reduces to three basic quantitative dimensions the complexity we see in bilingual education programs. The basic dimensions form a cube (Figure A), a tridimensional space within which we can locate programs relative to each other and interpret their movement and their potential for change. The first dimension, *heterogeneity,* describes the relative degree of differentiation in the sociocultural context of the program. The second dimension, *efficiency,* describes the properties of the educational delivery system considered as a communications device. The third dimension, *pluralism,* describes the relative degree of support for the maintenance of sociocultural differences. To repeat this in another way, *I* is the context, *II* is how we deliver education in that context, and *III* is what we intend to deliver, what behavior we want to induce in the society. Policy makers have some direct control over the second and third dimensions: the delivery system and cultural policy. The first dimension, social context, is the one policy makers respond to and hope to have some impact on.

Locating a program in the cube involves relative rather than objective judgements. We will be able to say that one program, in comparison with another one, operates in a more (or perhaps less) heterogeneous situation, that it uses a more (or perhaps less) efficient delivery system, and that is has a more (or perhaps less) pluralistic policy. These relative judgements will be reasonably reliable if we are satisfied that certain manifestations in programs—let us call them *events*—are in fact variations along a continuum, that the differences among them are just matters of degree on a particular variable rather than qualitative differences. The possibility of identifying events that can be related to each other in a reasonably honest way depends on another feature of the model. Each of the three dimensions is componentialized, broken down into components or factors—let us call them *scales*—that refer to reality directly and as a set account for the dimension in some reasonably complete way. Actual judgements about

Figure A

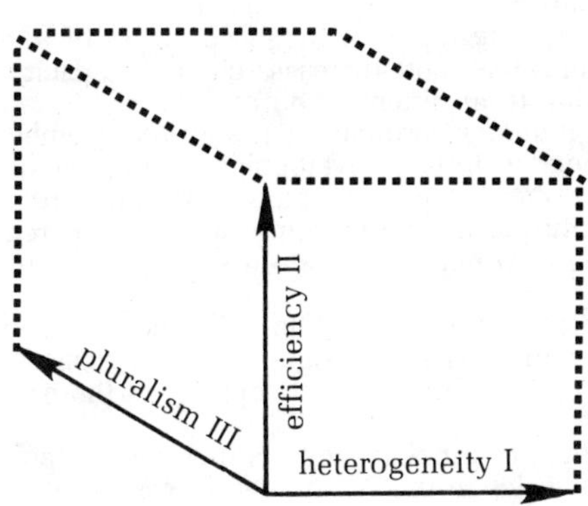

relative locations of programs are then made on these component scales. Ultimately we will seek to integrate judgements on the various scales, in order to locate programs, relative to others, on the main dimension itself. This process, carried out on all three dimensions, will locate programs relative to each other in the cube.

Componentialization of Dimension II

efficiency
low ——————→ high

E1. *Technological scales.*
E1.1. *Content:* educational content that approximates the learner's previous linguistic and cultural experience increases redundancy.
E1.2. *Structure:* instruction that uses the learner's natural units of expression and perception as the point of departure increases redundancy.
E1.3. *Configuration:* a teacher-learner relationship that resembles social interaction patterns outside the school increases redundancy.
E2. *Institutional Scales.*
E2.1. *Sociolinguistic research:* channel capacity is increased by decentralization of sociolinguistic research.
E2.2. *Recruitment:* when teachers and other implementing personnel share the learner's language and culture much more information becomes available for improvement in degree of redundancy.
E2.3. *Materials development:* channel capacity is increased by decentralization of materials development.
E2.4. *Teacher training:* development of teacher skills for participation in such tasks as sociolinguistic research, materials preparation, and curriculum planning, rationalizes and integrates information from different sources.
E2.5. *Technical support.*
E2.51. *Organization:* decentralized decision making makes better use of the full channel capacity of the delivery system.

E2.52. *Information flow:* high bidirectional information flow between hierarchical levels improves rationalization of information from different sources.
E2.53. *Disciplinary integration:* a broad spectrum of integrated scientific and technical support increases channel capacity and rationalizes information from different sources.
E2.54. *Task integration:* Coordinating and mutually embedding such tasks as training, materials development, and sociolinguistic research rationalizes and integrates information from different sources.
E2.6. *Community participation:* community and parental participation increases channel capacity and further decentralizes decision making.
E2.7. *Public attitudes:* as the public is better informed about sociolinguistic conditions and program policy, decision making makes better use of the full channel capacity of the program.
E2.8. *Policy.*
E2.81. *Formulation:* channel capacity is increased as policy takes into account all scales in the F-T model or one like it.
E2.82. *Implementation:* financing and administrative arrangements that provide effective articulation among program components increase information flow.

We must then be more explicit about the kinds of events to be related to each other, about the component scales of each dimension, and about the means of integrating the scales. For the sake of brevity we forego this exercise for the first dimension. Let us agree that some bilingual contexts are more heterogeneous, more differentiated, than others, and that if we take into account the diversity of language, culture, social structure, ecology, technology, and the institutions in the social context, we will doubtless be able to come up with a set of scales that permit us to rate programs, relative to each other, as to degree of heterogeneity. The typology suggested by Stewart (1972) is, in any case, a convenient first approach; it allowed him to demonstrate easily that, in Netherlands America, Surinam is far more heterogeneous sociolinguistically than the Netherlands Antilles, and that among the Antilles the Curacao Island Group is more heterogeneous that the Leeward Island group.

Let us also, before attempting greater specificity, take note of some limitations in the model; these can be explained by reference to Figure B, which represents conventionally the paradigm for a research design that would serve for testing policy options in bilingual education. The paradigm provides the terms we normally use to hypothesize that certain outcomes (specifiable on dependent variables) will result from the application of certain programs (describable in terms of a complex of independent variables). The first and most significant limitation of the F-T model is that it incorporates no predictions of this kind; it includes no dependent variables, only independent variables. This being the case the model avoids value judgements; it does not pretend to say that one configuration of locations on independent variables will be better or in any way more cost-effective than another in producing an educational product. The model's only purpose is to describe the independent variables at work in bilingual education in a systematic, comprehensive, and quantitative manner, so that those of us who engage in hypothesis and experimentation may do so more effectively and convincingly. There is a minor exception to this limitation: if in fact the model's capacity to describe internal variation within programs tended to promote experimentation with more flexible options, we might predict a higher *survival rate* for flexible-technology programs, since their resilience should protect them against shocks in the name of progress and regressive pressures; but there is no guarantee that a program that simply survives is producing cost-effective education.

Thus the model is not offered as an educational solution for heterogeneous sociocultural conditions; it claims only the capacity to describe all possible program responses to such conditions. Despite this disclaimer of prejudice in the model, the author of this paper does indeed hold some strong convictions as to good education under bilingual conditions, and they doubtless show through at various points in what is intended to be a neutral discussion. Other writers have proposed essentially neutral typologies for bicultural education, more or less as it is defined here. Each of them, whether addressing the question partially or comprehensively, makes the point that our *understanding* of the phenomenon will be increased by viewing it through the categories of his model; some, with every right, then state personal preferences among the options established. Fishman (1972) clarifies the relationship between bilingual and bidialectal education; Brudner, White, and Walters (1976) suggest quantifying improvements; Spolsky, Green, and Read (1976) and, in a brilliant book, Beeby (1966) call attention to pertinent social and institutional variables. Craig (to appear) shares the present writer's interest in a typology that takes account of the null response to heterogeneity and the nature of internal variation in programs.

Figure B

Independent variables:			
Primary (stable):		Policy	first level
Mediating (unstable):		Public attitudes Support units Development projects	
		Classroom technology	second level
Dependent variable:		Cost-effectiveness of education product	

A second limitation is selective rather than general. The policy variable, identified in the paradigm as primary, will of course appear in different degrees in different programs, but within a single program we expect policy to be quite stable. It is after all recorded in laws, regulations, budgets, and other documents that are fixed for some period of time. But implementation of policy involves individual human attitudes and reactions—in the community, among teachers, in technical assistance agencies, in development projects. So internally in programs we expect to observe normal, and even abnormal, individual variation on all policy mediating variables. What happens in a program on a particular implementing scale is then not a single event but a *range* of events. Finally, classroom technology—that aspect of a program that impinges directly on the student—is a second-level variable, derivative of social and institutional circumstances, determined by conditions prevailing in policy, public attitudes, support units and development projects. This implicational correlation is thus a guide for calibrating the two levels.

Efficiency

The ideas discussed in this paper began to take form in the course of recent experimental research in Quechua-Spanish bilingual education in highland Peru. As our interdisciplinary research team from Cornell University and Peru sought a research design for comparative evaluation of program options, we faced the question of what and how many "methods" to test, and in what form, and how to relate these options on independent variables. We came to the conclusion that available options could all be related in a systematic way to a *formal-informal* continuum based on the Peruvian reform policy of adjusting educational technology and objectives to the country's social reality. The project also involved institutional components such as teacher training and development of decentralized technical units for sociolinguistic research and materials development. As the work evolved these also were seen to be susceptible to description in relation to the formal-informal continuum, in the sense that different methodological options tended to prosper, i.e, have more acceptance, under different institutional conditions. Ultimately then, the research design incorporated both institutional and technological components and related both to the continuum, which was described as follows:

> In education, delivery systems are distributed on a continuum from a formal pole, at which are found those that accommodate least to the individual learner and generally impose unfamiliar experiences on him, to an informal pole, at which are located systems that accommodate most to the individual learner and give him a familiar experience.

Formal—————————————— Informal

Unfamiliar experience   Familiar experience

The inductive history just given is complemented by a deductive thrust that leads to the same conclusion and did in fact, contribute to our reasoning. Formal education, anthropologists tell us, is one part of the socialization process that each generation provides for the next. In part through formal education, a communicative process, children learn the culture of their parents—their knowledge, habits, skills, and aspirations—and the norms of their society. Such important figures in science as Wiener (1950) and Deutsch (1953) long ago pointed out that formal education shares the properties of all communication systems; we can use two of these properties, *redundancy* and *channel capacity* to characterize the efficiency dimension of the F-T model and show its correspondence to the formal-informal continuum. To begin with we interpret redundancy as it applies to the efficiency dimension's technological scales.

Redundancy

Communicative codes differ in their degree of redundancy; that is, with respect to the percentage of new information, as compared with old familiar information, they allow in each message. A low-redundancy code yields messages containing much unfamiliar information, with little familiar context to aid in interpreting it; a high-redundancy code yields messages containing relatively little unfamiliar information, which is embedded in ample helpful context. Applying this distinction to the first efficiency scale (E1.1) which has to do with the *content* of classroom material, we can readily locate three different programs relative to each other in the event that one uses the child's own local language or dialect for classroom material, another uses a standardized form of his language that he has little experience with, and the third uses a second language completely strange to him. In the teaching of initial reading skills—let us say in the first grade—the skills components to be communicated to the child will be bathed in far more familiar material, as compared with the other cases, if taught in his own local dialect. Thus the first option is most redundant, the second less so, and the third least redundant of the three.

It is not difficult, in particular cases, to establish a finer-grained progression on this scale. For example, some years ago the Peruvian Ministry of Education produced a Spanish language first reader whose cultural content was oriented much less to urban Hispanic culture than those in use earlier; it reflected better the rural experience of many school children. In our terms the reader was a deliberate attempt to make the teaching of reading more redundant, more familiar in its content. But not much more; initial reading was still in Spanish, a language not understood at all by many rural Indian children.

In 1975 the Peruvian Educational Reform took a more significant step by approving a new official alphabet for Quechua, the most important minority language in Peru, with several million speakers (Ministerio de Educación, 1977). The alphabet was structured as a panalphabet, with provision within it for writing six regional dialects of Quechua, thus laying a foundation for reading materials that came closer to each Quechua-speaking child's own linguistic experience. Finally, in one of our experimental options in Peru, children themselves suggested the Quechua expressions they would learn to read and write, thus guaranteeing absolutely the high redundancy of communication intended for teaching the necessary reading skills. In the F-T model these are all different objective events we can locate relative to each other on the content scale by the redundancy criterion, setting up as many different points on the scale as we may need for the purpose.

Similarly, the sequencing or *structure* of classroom materials (Scale E1.2), in different programs can be compared for relative redundancy. In the Peru project we considered as our highest redundancy structural option in teaching reading skills, the case where each new structural element was presented in a familiar, already known or learned, structural context. The most familiar context for the beginning reader is the natural language he uses in conversing with family and friends; our informal option therefore used conversational expressions or very short natural dialogues as the point of departure for reading instruction. After sufficient exercise in reading recognition, and writing, at this level, children were taught to read and write separately the individual words that had occurred in the sentences already learned, and subsequently to shift the order of familiar words and introduce them to other already learned structural contexts.

And so on, subsequently, with syllables and letters. Obviously the most severely nonredundant sequencing option in reading would begin with the teaching of letters bereft even of mnemonic words, an option that the project did not consider worth testing.

About twenty years ago Olive Shell (Gudschinsky, 1959) talked about trends at that time in first readers prepared by members of the Summer Institute of Linguistics. She said, "There are two extremes in methods of primer making. At one extreme are methods such as the alphabet, syllable, and phonic methods where the components of words, often unmeaningful in themselves, are taught first, and then words are figured out from them. At the other extreme are methods such as the story or sentence methods, where the whole 'story' is presented first, and little by little it is broken down into words, and finally perhaps into their component parts. The psychophonemic method takes one to neither of these extremes. Rather, from its central position it works out both ways, eventually covering the areas of both of the extreme method groups. By working from meaningful word units, by repetition and association it focuses attention on word parts which serve as tools for attacking new words; by presenting words with interesting content and sentences, and stories as soon as possible, pupils are provided with interesting thought content from the first." Olive Shell was obviously using something like our structure scale as a frame of reference, and recommending that programs adopt a middle location.

Finally, programs can be compared for relative degree of conformity of their classroom *configuration* (Scale E1.3) with the experience of the child outside the classroom and at home. Let us assume, for the sake of initial simplicity, that the child's experience, before he begins his education, is essentially interactive, by contrast with the rigid vertical classroom discipline derived from elitist tradition. Outside of school the child has relative freedom, opportunity for self-expression, a chance to reveal aspects of his individual personality and experience. In a similarly configured school situation the teacher becomes better informed about individual children and can adjust to them. At the opposite pole, where a formal vertical configuration has the teacher working with all of the class at the same time, all students work from the same material, which thus tends to be paler in interest and meaning for some children, at best a reflection of their common social experience rather than individual personal experience.

Cultural norms differ, so that comparisons between programs must be cautious. For example, Quechua children, from infancy to early childhood, go everywhere with their parents or older siblings, being carried or tagging along as their elders perform tasks. Teaching these tasks to youngsters seems to depend relatively little on verbal communication, much more on setting an example and depending on the natural tendency of the child to imitate and participate. In the United States we see something like this happening when a four year old wants to "drive" the family automobile. But, at an age that seems tender by our standards, small Quechua children are sent to perform tasks involving considerable responsibility, without ever having received what we might consider explicit instruction in those tasks. We might conclude that, outside of school, Quechua culture tends to emphasize socialization by example more than by verbal interaction, whereas in the United States this emphasis is reversed. Comparisons between the two situations must take this into account; the scale cannot be viewed as measuring distance from one particular communicative style.

Channel capacity

The concept of channel capacity in communication theory refers to the amount of information the system has available to manipulate, and the number of distinctions it can make. This amount obviously differs from code to code; for example, the red/green traffic signal commonly used in New York City has less channel capacity than the red/yellow/green signal installed in many other places. In the F-T model we expect that bilingual programs higher in redundancy will probably also be higher in channel capacity. In the Peruvian case, the policy decision (Ministerio de Educación, 1972) to begin instruction in the mother tongue for monolinguals in Quechua and other so-called vernaculars, required (and still requires) a large increase in the channel capacity of the educational delivery system; under the new dispensation, the system has to be able to manipulate information about vernacular languages and cultures *in addition to* all of the information it formerly had available concerning Hispanic language and culture. This concept of channel capacity provides the fundamental link between technological and institutional scales in the F-T model; we can demonstrate that changes in channel capacity, and therefore potentially in redundancy, are a result of various kinds of *information management* by institutional means. The institutional scales of Dimension II represent, tentatively, those areas of institutional activity in which by some criterion (in effect, a variable) we can locate programs relative to each other with respect to aspects of information management as these correlate with increasing Dimension II. It may be helpful to give an account of the Peru experience in these terms.

The current period of Peruvian Reform dates from a military coup in 1968 by officers who, for the first time in Peruvian history, did not identify with the interests of the traditional socioeconomic oligarchy. Perhaps for this reason, and because authoritarian sanctions were mainly directed at the formerly privileged and extreme left, an informal working relationship developed between the generals who took power and some progressive intellectuals. Reformist rhetoric, as it developed during what has been called the "first phase" of the Reform, declared that the military government would pursue an independent middle course between the great competing ideologies, that this course would take into account the country's cultural and regional diversity and its great traditions, and be guided by a heavy measure of participation from all levels and sectors in Peruvian society. The institutional apparatus of the state was to be put to work in what was called the Peruvian Process, intended to produce a new Peruvian Man, conscious and proud of his particular cultural origins, but able to cooperate with his fellow citizens in the interest of national solidarity. In applying these notions to education, the obvious consequence was a policy that favored high redundancy technology for vernacular speaking minorities. Even more important, the nationalistic mood required that this technology be a product of institutional processes that were highly participatory and *netamente peruanos*, that is, distinctively Peruvian in sociocultural redundancy in the classroom. For each component scale, we have attempted a brief and necessarily primitive formulation of the nature of the correlation in that area of activity, making use informally of processes that seem to be involved in information management: (1) production of new information; (2) the means by which it is inserted into the system; (3) the rationalization and integration of information from different sources; (4) the improvement of information flow and the articulation of different information management tasks; and (5) the organization of decision making, essentially a process of selecting appropriate information for use in particular situations.

Before proceeding, we must, as a matter of unfinished business, provide a more precise definition of Dimension II. The critical variable is clearly degree of redundancy in messages, i.e., experiences, given to the learner by the classroom technology, and, we have argued, this degree, in a given program, reflects institutional management of information in the delivery system. Efficiency, then, is a measure of the degree to which information management copes with the redundancy needs of the diverse groups in the community. We emphasize that judgements about relative efficiency are made without considering relative cost. As a concept in the F-T model, efficiency is not to be confused with cost-effectiveness; cost as an independent variable is added to the model only when it is used to predict an optimal product, as in the research paradigm in Figure B. At this point, to aid in understanding the logic of componentialization of Dimension II, it may be helpful to give an account of the Peru experience in these terms.

The present author, though not Peruvian, had for many years been involved in Quechua language research and institutional development projects in the country, and was invited to join in designing and implementing experimental research to serve Reform objectives in Quechua-Spanish bilingual education. The independent variables in the design which emerged can be described conveniently by the F-T model. The design would be located relatively high on efficiency in technology: consideration was given to first literacy in Quechua for the monolingual child, to the structure of Quechua, and to the nature of the child's social and individual experience outside of school. Institutionally the work was greatly decentralized, sociolinguistic research, materials preparation, and teacher training took place close to the community and the classroom. Arrangements were developed for participation in project decisions and development tasks by teachers, district-level supervisors, and technical personnel. All project personnel and experimental teachers were fluent Quechua-Spanish bilinguals. A regional interdisciplinary technical unit included anthropologists, sociologists, psychologists, linguists, and educators, in an attempt to shed light on all aspects of Quechua children's experience. The members of the unit engaged in sociolinguistic field research and also gave training to bilingual teachers and supervisors. Institutional measures were undertaken to speed the flow of information among project personnel trained in different disciplines, and to enhance interaction between levels in the project hierarchy.

The project's mission went beyond the conventional question of whether first literacy in the mother tongue is or is not good for the child and his community. That had been decided as a matter of policy: Children monolingual in a vernacular, or limited in Spanish skills, would begin formal education in their first language. The major hypothesis had to do with participation; the prediction that cost-effective results would come from education carried out under highly participatory institutional conditions.

At the same time, the project design recognized that participation, as contrasted with nonparticipation, is not a qualitatively discrete phenomenon but rather a matter of degree, so that subsidiary hypotheses would be needed to predict the cost-effectiveness of different degrees of participation under the diverse conditions we would find in twenty experimental school districts (of a total of ninety-three in the Fifth Education Region, whose seat is in the highland city of Cuzco).

We expected, in other words, to characterize each experimental option by its relative amount of efficiency and by analyzing local school and community reactions to assess the compatibility of each option to the local bias in each case. We constructed two classroom *strategies* (Solá and Weber, 1978. Appendix G), contrastive as to degree of redundancy in content and structure of materials, and in classroom configuration. Our *formal* strategy was not excessively so, certainly not identical with traditional practice because the Reform would not have permitted this. Our *informal* strategy incorporated many elements of the "language experience method" and Sylvia Ashton-Warner's (1963) "organic" method, and was, in rural Peru, somewhat venturesome. Neither strategy violated Reform policy in education and none of the students involved were exempted from the system's achievement expectations, i.e., curriculum objectives were the same for both strategies and identical (in terms of skills and cognitive development) with mandated Ministry standards, and achievement testing in the two strategies was to be uniform. We did not expect the two strategies to remain objectively stable during the experiment, but rather that shift would occur in one or the other direction on the continuum as local conditions exerted their influence. We thought our formal strategy would be acceptable to many teachers and parents; their rather formal past experience of education would tend to condition their preferences. But teachers not sensitive to Reform goals, or not informed about them, might push even the formal strategy to an even more formal location on the continuum. Contrastively, some teachers in both strategies might perceive higher redundancy in the classroom as more interesting and productive, derive enough satisfaction from this to become defenders and practitioners of more informal methods, and perhaps receive encouragement in this from their communities.

The experimental design was itself the product of an extended participatory exercise in 1976. The interdisciplinary Peruvian staff of the regional technical unit in Cuzco taught an eight month course of their own design to a first group of bilingual supervisor trainees. During the course all members of the project "family," including foreign advisers, worked together to determine their respective roles and obligations in the implementation phase and to prepare materials. The design held through 1977, during which the newly trained supervisors guided bilingual first grade teachers in the use of the experimental materials and methods the supervisors themselves had helped to develop. Unfortunately, at this point, as a consequence of personnel and policy changes at top levels in the Peruvian government and the international development agency supporting the work, the participatory approach was nullified. By 1978 a "second phase" of the Reform, under more conservative and elitist leadership, had taken over; it was now politically disadvantageous for any Peruvian official or social scientist to be associated with the concept of participation. The project changed its character entirely and Cornell University is no longer involved.

But there were some profits. During the years of project development we gained more explicit understanding of the nature of the institutional apparatus required to deal with great diversity at the community level. And specific experiences buttressed the insight that relative formality was a powerful predictor of institutional behavior. Some structural decentralization had been carried out by the Ministry in order to facilitate the "first phase" policy of participation. But many lower level administrators and technical personnel did not believe that rural teachers could be trained to make a useful contribution to such tasks as materials development and sociolinguistic research, and were reluctant to use the new structure to this purpose. Fortunately, some key officials were optimistic enough so that we could proceed on this tack for some time, but this did not relieve us of the obligation to work out compromises with others of more conservative opinion.

A similar range of attitudes existed in Cuzco. The supervisor trainees, toward the end of their course, were given the choice individually of working in either the formal or informal strategy. Those who opted for informality seemed, during the implementation phase, to have greater vocation for their profession, to be less opportunistic and cynical as members of the educational establishment, and to be more willing to work overtime and otherwise to take initiatives toward integrating language objectives with other curriculum goals. Trainees opting for the formal strategy seemed more sensitive to the risks of departing from traditional norms, more dependent on identification with outside groups, particularly teachers unions, and, though not at all less intelligent, they were as a group not energetic. Subsequently, the informal supervisors were strikingly successful in some cases in training bilingual teachers in novel techniques; we have videotapes to prove this. The formal supervisors, on the other hand, were reluctant to be identified with some deformalizing innovations built into their strategy, but said this was because "teachers and parents won't accept them" rather than because "children won't learn." This kind of variation is of course, inevitable in any large teachers corps and is reflected even in small groups screened for special training; the project had to respond to it by making adjustments when rejection was threatened.

But it was the range of these reactions, (and the fact that, as technological and institutional adjustments were made, all parties could discuss them in relation to the formality continuum), that constituted the major lesson and led to the F-T model, a more rigorous attempt to describe the phenomenon of bilingual education in its many manifestations.

These experiences lent weight to Beeby's (1966) hypothesis. He had argued that beyond the economist's quantitative approach to educational development in the Third World—more students, more teachers, more books, and more classrooms—educators must be equally concerned with differences between "stages" of institutional growth in educational systems. The Peruvian lesson suggested that we might consider quantifying these differences more explicitly, in relation to the formal-informal continuum, and in this way gain better control over the management of flexible response to differing local situations. We could envision systematizing and quantifying the independent variables that shape programs. Not long ago, John Macnamara (1974) concluded that "people who propose to launch, extend, or revitalize a project in bilingual education would be better advised to concentrate their energy on their own operation, rather than dissipate it by examining a thousand others."

In other words, we are poorly equipped theoretically, in spite of the many bicultural programs in existence, to make generalizations about them and perceive their similarities and differences. Entirely aside from the question of evaluating product quality, we have a poor sense of the independent variables: Even if we do achieve a satisfactory product, under whatever policy criteria we may invoke, we may fail to conceptualize very well the conditions that produced it. The F-T model responds to these deficiencies.

Let us assume we have applied the model to a sample of programs, and made enough relative judgements about them on the scales to result in an intuitively satisfactory efficiency measure, capable of distinguishing differences between programs as matters of degree along Dimension II. Let us assume further that we possess equally satisfying measures for relative degree of heterogeneity in the community, on Dimension I. An application of these measures to *perfect* programs, that is, programs whose efficiency does indeed cope with the actual degree of heterogeneity in the communities they serve, will yield Figure C. All these perfect programs will lie on the straight program line. Of course, if program x is, for lack of efficiency, not perfect, because it lives in community *d* rather than *c*, we know that it must become like program *b*, increase its efficiency from *f* to g, in order to achieve perfection in this regard.

Figure C also represents a fact we already know from communication theory and empirically from our experience in education. The theory implies that no education program can ever be completely redundant or completely nonredundant. If education were a completely familiar experience for the learner no new information would be passed, nothing educational would happen. At the other extreme, communication in which there is no redundancy, in which all is unfamiliar and new, provides no

Figure C

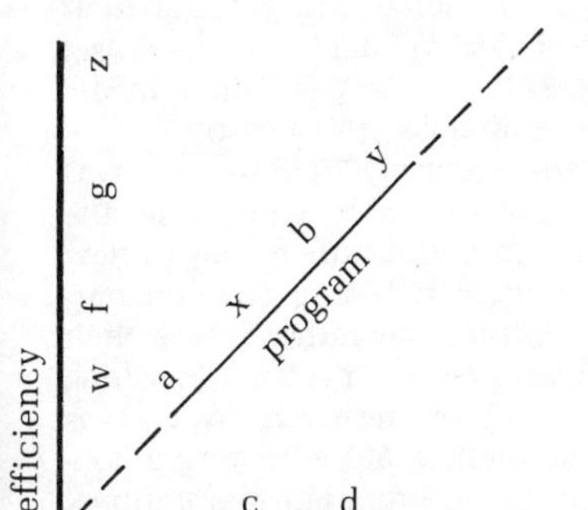

Figure D

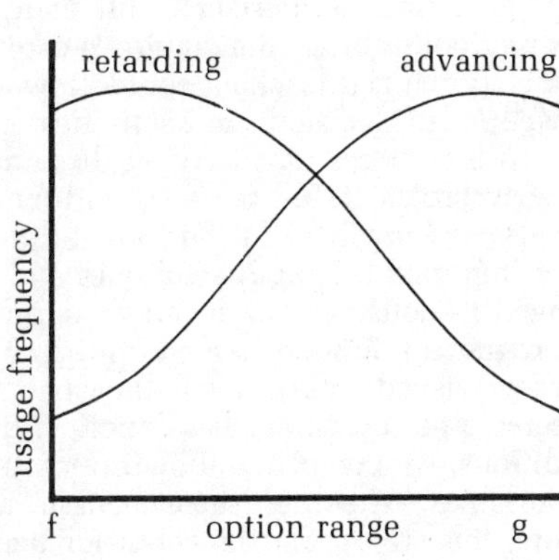

anchors, no points of orientation to interpret the new information transmitted. This produces paralysis and alienation. Again, no communication. The two broken ends of the program line in Figure C represent these vacancies. As a practical matter we can accept this because no education program worthy of the name will, on the one hand, completely ignore heterogeneity or allow education to be devoid of context, or, on the other, individualize its pedagogy literally or leave it devoid of content. The solid line *a–y* therefore represents the range of actual or hypothetical perfect programs we might compare on our scales. The range *w–z* sets the limits on the degrees of efficiency we expect to observe in actual programs or might want to test experimentally.

Let us assume further that, in our sampling, we have paid attention to the correlation, within programs, between the *option range* of the program, i.e., that range of implementing events mandated by policy, and the *usage range,* i.e., that range of behavior actually exhibited by program personnel in the classroom and in institutional processes. If the two ranges coincide or greatly overlap, the program should survive, though perhaps somewhat complacently. Disjunctions are the source of failure; an experimental program that asks for adherence to an option range *g–z,* from teachers, administrators, and technicians only capable of executing in the usage range *w–f,* generates serious internal anxieties, aside from the fact that it cannot achieve its objectives. On the other hand an option range that overlaps with expectations, but also extends beyond these in the direction of development policy, may encourage a comfortable but noncomplacent working environment in which some program participants may respond to new options.

In Peru, the "first phase" policy rather brusquely shifted the efficiency option range from, let us say, *w–f* to *f–g.* In at least one respect this improved coincidence with usage range: Many bilingual teachers had for years taught children in Quechua (though not to read Quechua), ignoring earlier Ministry norms that restricted the language of instruction to Spanish. At institutional levels the shift was a great shock; the new participatory policy went completely counter to traditional Peruvian norms of highly centralized, vertical, status and power relationships. Thus initially our experiment was received sympathetically by educators in Cuzco, virtually all bilingual in Quechua, who saw that finally the language was to be given its due importance. But many of them, along with most of their superiors in Lima, the country's capital, had extreme doubts at the outset that provincial teachers could or would be allowed to participate in development decisions and activities or were trainable in this respect.

In the interest of surviving these doubts the project's option range was fairly broad, let us say *f–z,* and emphasis was given to explicating the variables involved in the formal-informal continuum rather than to new or imported teaching techniques and materials. Participants were encouraged to consider not so much particular options but rather where their programs might be located on the continuum and the direction in which they wished to go or felt they had to go. But the research design was foreclosed, by "first phase" policy, from nonparticipatory operating conditions; we could not allow option range *w–f* on important institutional variables. When the "second phase" abruptly declared participation a failure, the project had no room for temporary retreat, keeping available as many participatory options as it could. There was no doubt that slowly but surely project personnel were learning to participate and saw resulting benefits. They knew that, as they helped to review and revise instructional materials and methods, they played a vital role in making progress along the formal-informal continuum or at times in making a tactical withdrawal. They were stimulated intellectually and many worked diligently and creatively. Gradually they were perceiving, through much institutional fog, that participation itself, not bilingual education, was being put to an experimental test. These examples suggest a further quantifying elaboration of the F-T model.

Let us plot, as in Figure D, the option range $f-g$ against *usage frequency*, in a particular program under a policy favoring high redundancy. Scale E2.2 makes the claim that channel capacity is increased by recruitment of bilingual teachers, supervisors, and other personnel in the system. The program actually recruits over the whole range of subordinate to coordinate bilinguals but gives heavy preference to the latter, so that recruitment can be seen as an *advancing* factor. These are approximately the normal conditions in the Cuzco area and were intensified in our project; experimental teachers and supervisors were screened for their Quechua speaking minority, recruitment under the same policy conditions language skills. In Ecuador, another Andean nation with a Quechua speaking minority, recruitment under the same policy conditions would be a *retarding* factor. Unlike the Cuzco case, rural teachers in Ecuadorian Quechua communities are almost all monolinguals drawn from Spanish-speaking areas. A large experimental program in bilingual education in Ecuador would find this a major initial obstacle in the path toward higher efficiency. In Peru, "first phase" policy makers saw institutional and social factors as monumentally retarding, as indeed they turned out to be. The "first phase" leaders were themselves undone, in an arbitrary though fortunately bloodless change of government that installed generals of, in F-T model terms, less "efficient" persuasion.

In our project some steps were taken that resulted in more teachers, more of the time, breaking away from vertical dependency relationships, participating more fully in shaping the program, and increasing the system's channel capacity by providing accurate information about language and life in the Quechua communities they served. "Second phase" policy halted systematic research on this process under the participatory hypothesis. There may nevertheless have been some unmeasured net practical gain for the Cuzco region on the institutional scales of Dimension II—once teachers have learned to participate and found satisfaction in it, they may continue to seek new opportunities to apply this valuable skill.

Pluralism

Bilingual education programs can be compared as to their relative degree of commitment to a policy favoring stable cultural plurality in the community. Theoretically, the absence of such a policy in a culturally heterogeneous community will lead to cultural homogeneity. We expect to observe internal variation in programs, as on Dimension II; thus the concepts of event range and event frequency will continue to be useful, but in the interest of brevity will not be further explored in this paper. We must again componentialize, in pursuit of objective relative measurement:

we want to locate objective events relative to each other on specific scales that refer to a comprehensive set of recognizable areas of program activity. The minimal set given for Dimension III clearly requires elaboration, but let us assume that in the two technological scales and one institutional scale we have succeeded in identifying major areas of activity that subsume all others we may eventually wish to describe.

Componentialization of Dimension III

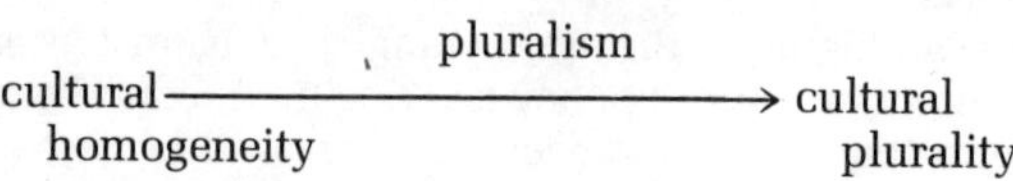

P1. *Technological Scales.*
P1.1. *Maintenance curriculum:* all-skills training in first language and culture, through successive stages of cognitive growth, favors plurality.
P1.2. *Transition curriculum:* all-skills training in second language and culture, through successive stages of cognitive growth, favors plurality.
P2. *Institutional Scales.*
P2.1. *Compatibility:* institutional reinforcement of non-conflicting roles for first and second languages and cultures, favors plurality.

The technological scales deal with curriculum, the educational structure of the child's experience in school. The F-T model assumes that achievement and maintenance of maximum cultural plurality in the community requires achievement of bilingualism in each individual. A maximum technological response on the pluralism dimension provides full curricular extension and development throughout the formal education program, for *maintenance* (Scale P1.1) of the first language and *transition* (Scale P1.2) to a second language. We remind ourselves at this point that communication theory would identify curriculum as new information only, the new or modified or further developed behavior the program wishes to inculcate in the child. Curriculum is not pedagogy, the communication process used to achieve curriculum objectives. We have already gone to some length to characterize that process in terms of management and manipulation of both old and new information. The model claims that a highly pluralistic program will seek to produce bilingual individuals with well developed skills in two languages and cultures, accomplishing this with a degree of communicative "efficiency" more or less appropriate to the circumstances of heterogeneity in the community.

For a given program there is clearly a substantive cultural link between pluralism and efficiency; increases on both dimensions share the property of increasing recognition of a particular form of cultural behavior, for example a particular minority language. But the F-T model insists that this cultural manifestation be thought of in two distinguishable contexts: its role in increasing efficiency in classroom pedagogy, and its separate role in reinforcing cultural pluralism. The link nevertheless implies that some institutional strategies of information management, devised to increase channel capacity on Dimension II, may have an additional payoff on Dimension III. For example, in Peru we sought, through sociolinguistic research and the various participatory exercises with bilingual teachers, to introduce new information about Quechua and its structure into the system with the immediate purpose of increasing the degree of redundancy in classroom technology. But the same research and consultative process would have yielded information also about the way Quechua is used creatively and expressively by mature persons: this kind of information would then have helped to formulate skills development curriculum objectives on the maintenance scale.

A high commitment to individual bilingualism is a necessary but not sufficient condition for maintaining cultural plurality. One generation of bilinguals does not guarantee a second generation of bilinguals. Stewart (1972) provides the essential criterion: "Multilingual situations may be considered stable when the different linguistic systems are geographically, socially, and functionally non-competitive." In other words, stable cultural plurality depends on social and institutional circumstances outside the bilingual classroom. The F-T model expresses this criterion in a *compatibility* scale (P2.1), and we can consider its relationship to curriculum.

Figure E locates three programs relative to each other on the dimensions of pluralism and efficiency. All three, let us assume, are operating under conditions of high heterogeneity. Figure F shows how we might expect these programs to score on the three pluralism scales. Program *a* must certainly be low on maintenance because it is not efficient enough for speakers of the minority languages present in a heterogeneous situation. It may be high on transition, and compatibility is high because the child's first language will never have a chance to compete in the wider society, but the final outcome will be cultural homogeneity not plurality.

Program *b* gives two possibilities, in both of which it must be high on maintenance because of its high efficiency. But if it is low on transition, the first case, the student will never come to participate in a stable cultural plurality; he will simply remain monolingual, outside of that plurality. In the second case, there is a strong policy commitment to both languages but the two are competitive in social use. Stewart's criterion is not met, the weaker language with no domain of its own will yield, and we cannot expect stable bilingualism to result.

Program *c* is high on cultural pluralism; looking back to the cube, in Figure A, it would be near the top at the rear right hand corner. Full curriculum attention has been given to both languages and in addition some way has been found to keep them from being competitive in social use. Let us say that program *c* policy is to produce *culturally bifocal* citizens, competent in two languages and finding pleasure and profit in using both of them in their respective sociocultural domains.

A Policy Interpretation for the United States

The laws, policy declarations, and regulations for bilingual education in Peru are still those of the "first phase" of the Reform, and they rather emphatically endorse the concepts involved in program *c*. Present implementation, however, especially since the advent of the "second phase," has managed, through the use of Quechua, just a minor technological improvement over program *a* on the efficiency dimension, with no perceivable improvement over *a* on the pluralism dimension. In comparison,

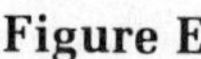

Figure E

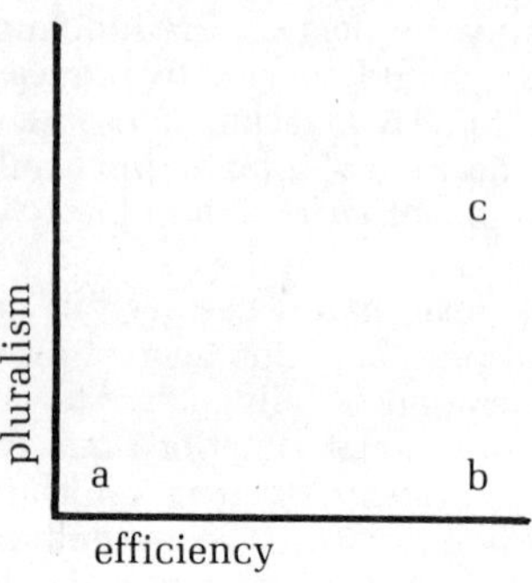

Figure F

PROGRAM		SCALE		
		maintenance	transition	compatibility
a		low	high	high
b	1	high	low	high
	2	high	high	low
c		high	high	high

in the United States, federal policy seems to envision program *b*, although, if we evaluate actual programs on the technological and institutional scales of Dimension II, most seem to operate at levels of efficiency much closer to program *a*. As to Dimension III, in spite of a traditional American belief that the will of the majority must respect the rights of the minority, there is no vestige of pluralism as a stated policy in federal legislation. Certain communities, the Navajo for example, reinforced by a long and distinctive cultural tradition that is still highly functional, do sponsor some programs resembling *c*.

We said earlier that policy makers have some direct influence on both efficiency and pluralism dimensions in bilingual education. Now at the end we must distinguish the two cases more clearly. Program policy on efficiency has most to do with determining what happens in the classroom and in formal agencies and institutions structurally related to the classroom within the educational system. To achieve high efficiency in a program, the community, by the argument of the F-T model, will have to participate of course, but policy analysis and policy control will largely be the business of education authorities. Program policy on pluralism differs from this. Although in order to score high on pluralism, policy makers must have strong curricular commitment to both languages, the possibility of eventual stable pluralism depends crucially on social and institutional arrangements that are not entirely within the policy domain of political authorities of any kind. Minority groups themselves will have to define the kind of complementary relationship between the two languages and cultures that they prefer, develop the policy analysis, and mobilize the institutional means needed to establish and maintain this relationship. Political authorities can no doubt be protective and helpful to minorities as they do this, even promoting pluralistic values through formal education, and to that extent adopt a pluralistic policy, but the eventual form that bifocal cultural pluralism may take in any particular community is largely in the hands of the minority groups themselves.

Finally, to return to the main theme of this paper, a peaceful and profitable outcome in bilingual education may depend most on our success in developing flexible options on many technological and institutional variables, so that we can respond in a resilient fashion to pressures for change, and move around temporary obstacles, as we seek cost-effective educational solutions. There is every reason to be confident that cultural bifocality will turn out to be an important component of education in the United States, both because of our numerous and in some cases large and culturally mobilized ethnic minorities, and because of our strong ties with other nations in a multilingual world. Walker Connor (1973) explains the worldwide rise of ethnicity as the natural consequence of "popular sovereignty," or, in a loose translation, participatory democracy. We can believe, on these grounds, that, at least while democracy lives, and perhaps even, as in Peru, when it is temporarily suspended, cultural pluralism is inevitable, and we can give our attention to the more serious question of just what form a culturally plural society's educational system should take.*

BIBLIOGRAPHY

Ashton-Warner, Sylvia. *Teacher*. New York: Simon and Schuster, 1963.

Beeby, C. E. *The Quality of Education in Developing Countries*. Harvard University Press, 1966.

Brudner, Lilyan A., White, Douglas R., and Walters, Anthony S. "National Policy Programming: A Prototype Model from Language Planning." In *Anthropology and the Public Interest*. Ed. by Peggy Reeves Sanday. Academic Press, 1976.

---

*This work was carried out in part under Cornell Contract No. AID-1a-C-1096. The views expressed herein do not necessarily represent those of AID or the U.S. Government.

Connor, Walker. "The Politics of Ethnonationalism." *Journal of International Affairs.* Vol. 21. No. 1. 1973.

Craig, Dennis R. "Models for Educational Policy in Creole-speaking Communities." In position papers, Conference on theoretical orientations in creole studies. St. Thomas, U.S.V.I. 1979. Sponsored by U.S. National Science Foundation, Indiana University and College of the Virgin Islands, in press.

Deutsch, Karl W. *Nationalism and Social Communication.* New York, 1953.

Ferguson, Charles A. "Diglossia" *Word.* Vol. 15. 1959.

Fishman, Joshua A. "Bilingualism With and Without Diglossia; Diglossia With and Without Bilingualism." *Journal of Social Issues* 23:2. (1967) 29-38.

__________. "Bilingual and Bidialectal Education: An Attempt at a Joint Model for Policy Description." In *Language in sociocultural change.* Ed. by Anwar S. Dil. Stanford University Press, 1972.

Gudschinsky, Sarah C. "Recent Trends in Primer Construction." In *Fundamental and Adult Education.* Vol. XI. No. 2. Unesco, 1959.

Gumperz, John J. "The Speech Community." In *International Encyclopedia of the Social Sciences.* New York. Macmillan, 1968.

Hymes, Dell H. "The Ethnography of Speaking." In *Anthropology and human behavior.* ed. by T. Gladwin and Wm. C. Sturtevant. Washington D.C. Anthropological Society of Washington, 1962. Reprinted in *Readings in the Sociology of Language.* Ed. by Joshua A. Fishman. Mouton 1968.

Macnamara, John. "The Generalizability of Results of Studies of Bilingual Education." In *Bilingualism, Biculturalism, and Education,* ed. Stephen T. Carey. Edmonton, Alberta. University of Alberta, 1974.

Ministerio de Educación. *Política nacional de educación bilingüe.* Lima, 1972.

__________. *Educación bilingüe: marcos legales.* Dirección general de educación básica regular. Unidad de educación bilingue. Lima, 1977.

Solá, Donald F. and Rose-Marie Weber. *Educational Planning in Multilingual Countries: A report on a working conference.* Language policy research program. Cornell University, 1978.

Spolsky, Bernard, Green, Joanna B., and Read, John. "A Model for the Description, Analysis, and Perhaps Evaluation of Bilingual Education" In *Language in sociology.* ed. by Albert Verdoodt and Rolf Kjolseth. Institut de Linguistique de Louvain, 1976.

Stewart, William A. "A Sociolinguistic Typology for Describing National Multilingualism." In *Readings in the Sociology of Language.* Ed. by Joshua A. Fishman, 1972.

Wiener, Norbert. *The Human Use of Human Beings: Cybernetics and Society.* Boston, 1950.

ON THE REPRODUCTIVE FUNCTION OF EVALUATIVE RESEARCH: A CASE STUDY IN THE USE OF EVALUATIONS FOR SHAPING PUBLIC POLICY

José Rosario and John M. Love

There are currently eleven major national evaluation studies of Head Start services underway. These evaluations "are designed to improve the quality and delivery of local Head Start services in the areas of education, parent involvement, social services, health (including medical, dental, mental health and nutrition), and services for children with special needs—handicapped, Spanish-speaking, Indian and migrant."[1] One of these eleven major studies is the Juárez and Associates evaluation of the Head Start Bilingual-Bicultural Curriculum Project.

This *is* a major evaluation, and it should not be taken lightly by those with an interest in bilingual education. Although it has a different purpose and audience, given its scope and design, the impact of this evaluation may very well make the American Institutes for Research (AIR) evaluation of Title VII programs pale in comparison. As such, it deserves close attention. The general purpose of this paper is to present this evaluation in an open forum to allow greater discussion of its potential impact on bilingual education than has occurred up to now. The Juárez evaluation also offers the attractive opportunity of specifically looking at the *reproductive function* of evaluative research, a topic which should be of greater interest to bilingual education researchers than it currently is. This is the more specific purpose of this paper.

In this paper we argue that evaluative research can and many times does serve a reproductive function and that the Juárez evaluation of the Head Start Bilingual-Bicultural Curriculum Development Project can and probably will serve that function rather well. The argument will proceed as follows. First, in order to shape a context for the discussion, we provide a brief description of the Head Start Strategy for Spanish-Speaking Children and discuss generally the plans for evaluating its curriculum development component. Second, we will discuss in some detail the purposes and design of the Juárez evaluation. Third, we will point to the reproductive function the Juárez evaluation is likely to serve by drawing attention to how evaluative research can be used to legitimate social action programs. The Westinghouse/Ohio evaluation of Head Start will serve as an example. Finally, we will conclude by trying to carve out some direction for this kind of work.

The Head Start Strategy for Spanish-Speaking Children

It is estimated that approximately fifteen percent of the total child population currently served by Head Start is Spanish surnamed. This is a subpopulation of children with known variation along the dimensions of language use and place of origin. That is, these children come from families that are Mexican, Puerto Rican, Cuban or Latin American in origin. And while some speak limited English, many others speak only Spanish.

In 1975, the Office of Child Development—now the Administration for Children, Youth and Families (ACYF)—initiated a major program to address the specific needs of these children. This new comprehensive program was christened the Head Start Strategy for Spanish-Speaking Children. This strategy consists of carrying out substantial work in four relatively undeveloped areas in the field of bilingual early childhood education: staff training, bilingual-bicultural resource networks, research and curriculum development (contracting Corporation of America, 1977). The current work in basic research, for example, covers such areas as early childhood bilingualism, heart murmurs among Mexican-American children and parental resistance to diagnostic and remedial heart care. The work in the area of staff training, on the other hand, reduces to the development of four bilingual-bicultural staff training models following the competency-based framework set forth in the Child Development Associate (CDA) program. There is concurrent development of two additional models being specifically designed to include procedures for training bilingual-bicultural CDA trainers. To remedy the lack of bilingual-bicultural resource networks, a prototype network was set up in Denver, Colorado to provide Head Start agencies in Region VIII with inservice training, bilingual-bicultural materials, and technical assistance in the implementation of bilingual-bicultural programs. This prototype network was designed and established with the idea that it would later serve as a replicable model for other regions. The network is now functioning and the nationwide replication is in process.

Finally, the work in the area of curriculum development focused specifically on the design of bilingual-bicultural curricula for preschool children. In 1976, ACYF contracted with four institutions—Columbia Teachers College, the High/Scope Educational Research Foundation, Inter-Cultural Development Research Associates and the University of California at Santa Cruz—to take on the task of developing four early childhood bilingual-bicultural curriculum models. The contractors were expected to work closely with local Head Start centers in a four-year development process. The work plan for the first year (1976-77) consisted of model development and preparation for training Head Start staff and parents to carry out implementation of the model which was expected to occur during the second year (1977-78) at the participating Head Start centers in the communities where model development was occurring: New York, New York; Detroit, Michigan; San Antonio, Texas; and Watsonville, California. The third year (1978-79) called for model replication in Head Start centers at two additional sites, and the fourth year (1979-80) is to be devoted to the provision of continuing supervision and technical assistance to the Head Start centers at the replication sites.

Thus far, the development of the models shows them to be fundamentally similar in principle but dissimilar in educational approach. All the models explicitly acknowledge the importance of attending to child development and the language and cultural needs of Spanish-speaking children as bases for program design, but each model calls for a different programmatic approach to the education of bilingual children. These differences are to be expected, for the pedagogical principle structuring the efforts behind Head Start's bilingual-bicultural curriculum project is the "no single best approach." The director of the Head Start Strategy for Spanish-Speaking Children describes the principle as follows:

> There is no single "best" bilingual-bicultural preschool function of the group it serves. The cultural and linguistic differences among Chinese, Native American, Spanish, Filipino and other groups are wide, and there are differences even within each group. A preschool program serving Chinese-American children in San Francisco, for example, may not be appropriate for a Chinese-American group in New York. Furthermore, several racial and ethnic groups, with or without a different language or dialect, may be represented in a particular community. Often the reality of a preschool program is that it is bilingual and multicultural. The specific style and content of each program must be tailored to the needs of the community and the groups within it (Arenas, 1978, p. 1).

Of the four components in the Head Start Strategy for Spanish-Speaking Children, the curriculum development project is the only one being evaluated, and plans for evaluating the products of this "no single best approach" principle were recently put in motion. In 1977, ACYF contracted with Juárez and Associates, a consulting firm based in Los Angeles, California, to conduct an evaluation of the Head Start Bilingual-Bicultural Curriculum Development Project. Designed to proceed in four phases over a three-and-a-half-year period, the evaluation is currently in its second phase (October 1978 to September 1979). During this phase, the evaluators were expected to pilot test the measurement battery for assessing program impact, program quality and consumer satisfaction. The evaluators are also expected to carry out randomization of subjects into experimental and control groups. The measurement battery was selected during the first and prior phase (1977-78). During that phase, the evaluators also made final recommendations on the sites that are expected to participate in the evaluation (replication sites of model developers). In addition, the evaluators also collected some initial pretest data from teachers. The rest of the data will be collected and analyzed during phase III (1979-80). Finally, phase IV (October 1, 1980 to March 31, 1981) will be devoted to writing a final report and shaping the knowledge distribution system that will be used to inform program decision making at the local Head Start level: a set of pamphlets that will describe each model in detail and discuss, among other things, what is required for its implementation.

Goals of the Juárez Evaluation

The guiding purpose of the Juárez evaluation is to supply ACYF with information bearing on the effectiveness of four early childhood bilingual-bicultural models for Spanish-speaking children (Juárez and Associates, 1978). Once the information is supplied, ACYF expects to use it in deciding on the feasibility of wider distribution of the models to other Head Start centers across the nation. This basic information need on the part of ACYF requires that the evaluation focus on the collection of three types of data.

First, the evaluation must find out whether it is feasible to implement successfully the curriculum models in more than one setting. To address this question, the evaluators will collect information bearing on two general factors related to program implementation: (1) the *process* required for installing the program, and (2) the program *procedures* required of the model for activating its valued message systems.[2] Among the procedural features of the models that the evaluators expect to focus on are staff, community, resource and student characteristics required by the model if it is to function as designed.

Second, the evaluation must find out whether the model objectives are being met by measuring model impact on children, teachers, and parents. The contractual agreement is very explicit as to how this kind of measurement must be carried out. ACYF has required that the evaluation employ an experimental pre- and post- test design in the measurement of model impact. At each replication site, a total of 90 four-year-old children will be randomly assigned to treatment and control groups. Following this random assignment, the children will be pre- and post- tested on a selected number of competency measures: (1) Spanish language comprehension, (2) Spanish language production, (3) English language comprehension, (4) English language production, (5) concept development, and (6) socio-emotional development.

To measure model impact on teachers, an interview schedule will be administered on a pre-post basis. This questionnaire is designed to tap background characteristics and attitudes toward, knowledge of, and competency in early childhood bilingual-bicultural education. The same procedure is being used to measure model impact on parents. There will be a pre-post administration of a questionnaire designed to tap background characteristics and attitudes toward and knowledge of general education, bilingual-bicultural education and vocational careers for their children.

Lastly, the evaluation must find out whether Head Start staff, parents and other community members have received the curriculum models favorably. This information need will be met by looking at the extent of staff and parental satisfaction with the model. Parents will be asked essentially whether the curriculum models are compatible with their views of how their children should be educated. Teachers, on the other hand, will be expected to comment on the quality, clarity, suitability and perceived effectiveness of the model.

As intimated earlier, a goal of all this research activity is the production of pamphlet summaries describing the evaluation findings bearing on each model. ACYF will then use these pamphlets to inform local Head Start centers of the options available to them when deciding on how best to meet the special needs of Spanish-speaking children. The pamphlets will describe each model, discuss what each would require for implementation, identify what each would offer in the form of programmatic strengths, and provide data on how effective each model was found to be with children, parents and teachers. It is not the intent of the pamphlets to provide a comparative analysis of four models, since a comparative analysis of the models à la Follow Through is not among the goals of the evaluation. The model comparisons are being left to the consumers of the models. At least that is the plan.

Design of the Juárez Evaluation

The design of the Juárez evaluation reduces to what Juárez and Associates call a holistic or multi-method data collection strategy. It has also been referred to as a contextual evaluation study design. For the evaluators, these terms are interchangeable, and they all imply an expansion of the experimental approach so as to include ratings, event sampling and ethnographic techniques. The inclusion of these other approaches into the evaluation design specified by the evaluation contract, the argument goes, would allow for drawing relationships between program processes (input) and outcome measures (output). As Juárez and Associates have developed it, this argument stems from four key issues related to evaluative research. All four issues relate to the need for clear and exact knowledge of: (1) program treatment, (2) program participants and settings, (3) program contexts, and (4) control group activities. In isolating these four issues, Juárez and Associates are drawing on a growing consensus among researchers that the lack of these data is likely to make research findings (particularly psychometric test results) uninterpretable. This is the kind of reasoning that has helped to shape the design of the so-called contextual evaluation study of Juárez and Associates.

There are three basic objectives to this type of study design. The first is measurement of the nature and extent of program implementation over time. In measuring implementation the evaluators hope to show whether it is feasible to expect successful implementation of the curriculum models at varying sites. Specific data will be collected on setting and material resources, individuals, schedule and program organization, attitudes and actual program activities. The data on these variables will be provided by employing a *fidelity* perspective in the measurement of model implementation.[3]

The second objective of the design is to secure the kind of observational data that might be of use in interpreting test outcomes. In this case, the qualitative data become an explanatory adjunct to quantitative results. But the more interesting feature here is the varying kind of qualitative data that Juárez and Associates have targeted for collection:

> Observations of classroom activities and situations, such as specific lessons, and language use in various situations, will be taken into consideration in the interpretation of test data. These observations will also include information on the measurement process or how the children in both the treatment and the control groups were tested, and on the experimental arrangement, including information on the control group experience and how well randomization worked. All of the above activities may have a strong influence on test results (Juárez and Associates, 1978: I-10).

The influences of ethnography and ethnomethodology are very evident here.

Finally, the third objective is to secure qualitative change data over time. The intent here is not to use qualitative data to help explain test results, but to use qualitative data *itself* as outcome data. As Juárez and Associates view it, the use of qualitative data as outcome data is a complementary and equally valid way of providing information bearing on model impact. And the strategy has the added and very attractive feature of being able to tap unanticipated outcomes. This is an important point, for it illustrates the sensitivity of the evaluation toward the very real and commonly acknowledged possibility of side effects due to explicit as well as *implicit* features of program designs (Monagham, 1976). Although important, the measurement of program side effects is an item routinely omitted by evaluation designs. In sum, among the foci of the qualitative data collection strategy are specific classroom behaviors and control group activities.

To operationalize this multi-method design, the evaluators are relying on the use of what they call a "participant researcher" (PR). This PR is very instrumental to the Juárez scheme. One reason for suggesting the presence of a PR on site is the need to eliminate the "outsider" image of evaluators. In a sense, PR might very well stand for public relations in this case. By becoming an insider, if you will, the PR is likely to get a deeper view of program processes and effects. At the same time, the PR serves to alleviate, if not eliminate, the relational strain so common to program evaluations. While on site, the PR is expected to supervise psychometric testing, conduct naturalistic observations, administer interviews to teachers, and update treatment and control group information through periodic phone calls to parents. As proposed, the use of the PR is an interesting and intriguing innovation in evaluation studies that again reflects the strong influences that ethnography and ethnomethodology are having on evaluative research generally and on the Juárez evaluation in particular.

To summarize, the Juárez evaluation design contains all that has been lacking in other federally sponsored evaluations of bilingual education. There have been four federally sponsored studies that are well known: (1) A Process Evaluation of the Bilingual Education Program, Title VII, ESEA (Development Associates, 1973); (2) Bilingual Education: An Unmet Need (Comptroller General, 1976); (3) The Condition of Bilingual Education in the Nation (U.S. Commissioner of Education, 1976); and (4) Evaluation of the Impact of ESEA Title VII Spanish/English Bilingual Education Program (Danoff, 1978). Differences in purpose, range and focus make comparisons between these evaluations and the Juárez study difficult to make. Nevertheless, a brief summary of one of the most widely cited of these studies (the AIR Title VII impact study) will help to place the Juárez study in context. The Juárez effort represents an impact study of bilingual education with many of the features one hopes for in well-designed evaluations. We would like to examine how it differs from the Title VII evaluation and then explore how these differences increase the opportunity for the current study to serve a true reproductive function.

The AIR Title VII Impact Study

The American Institutes for Research (AIR) conducted a major large-scale evaluation of Title VII programs. Interim results were released in April 1977 and the Executive Summary of the final report was released by the Office of Education in March 1978. Before long these reports were being widely cited as evidence that bilingual education was not working. When the next year's education bill was being debated, Congressman Ashbrook of Ohio proposed an amendment to abolish bilingual education, saying that "the program is actually preventing children from learning English." The evaluation findings were being used to support some lawmakers' views of public policy, but for the most part Congress has been supportive of bilingual education, increasing the budget annually.

In the fall and spring of 1975-76, thousands of students in grades two through six were tested at thirty-eight different sites across the country (in a total of 150 schools). The Title VII projects included in the study were in their fourth or fifth year of funding and presumed to be mature bilingual programs. The comparison group was selected by asking district personnel to nominate one non-Title VII classroom with students comparable to each Title VII classroom. The match was in terms of ethnicity, socioeconomic status, and grade level. AIR reported that the non-Title VII students were basically comparable to the Title VII students, and that standard statistical procedures were used to adjust for differences between groups. Standardized achievement tests were used to measure English and Spanish oral comprehension and reading, and mathematics. A student questionnaire obtained student background information and attitude toward school-related activities. A subsample of classrooms were observed, and teachers and directors interviewed to obtain information on the educational experiences of the students (Danoff, 1978).

Three different methods of analysis were used to assess Title VII's impact. Overall, "the Title VII Program did not appear to be having a consistent significant impact on student achievement in these two subjects (English Language Arts and Mathematics)." The comparisons with non-Title VII children showed that the Title VII students were performing in English worse than the non-Title VII students. In math, the two groups were performing at about the same level. An increase in Spanish reading scores was found during the year for Title VII students, but these gains could not be compared with the non-Title VII students because the number who could complete the test was too small.

The study also examined the educational goals of Title VII programs. In interviewing the directors of Title VII programs it was found that eighty-six percent reported that children remained in the bilingual project even after they were able to function in school in English. According to the AIR report, "these findings reflect Title VII project activities which run counter to the 'transition' approach strongly implied by the ESEA Title VII legislation."

One of the major difficulties of most large-scale educational evaluations is locating and maintaining an appropriate comparison group. We have the word of the AIR researchers that "classrooms" were matched in terms of SES, ethnicity and grade level. Yet the students in Title VII programs did worse on tests of English than their matched comparisons. Did AIR match the groups on initial language facility or language dominance? The report doesn't say, but it was reported that the increases in Spanish reading scores of the Title VII students could not be compared with the non-Title VII student scores because too few of the non-Title VII students could even take the Spanish reading test.

Groups were judged for comparability in 1975-76, not when the students began their Title VII program. The study also grouped all Title VII programs together with no attempt to identify and separately analyze quality bilingual programs.

Perhaps one of the major weaknesses of the study is an ambiguity in its purpose. USOE sought to discover the impact of Title VII programs (primarily on the children) when a prior question might have been, "What educational programs are being implemented under the Title VII legislation?" The politics of bilingual education in the United States are not unrelated to the politics of "basic skills," and this climate affects reaction to the study. In the current debate regarding a return to the "basics," one hears reference to the traditional American values inherent in the mechanics of reading, writing and arithmetic. In debates on bilingual education there is the parallel reference to the virtues of the traditional "melting pot" process in America. It may not be the achievement approach reflected in the responses of the Title VII program directors that concerns opponents of bilingual education.

On the Reproductive Function of the Juárez Evaluation

Aside from the judgment that the Juárez evaluation seems more promising and interesting than the Title VII evaluation, a question worth raising at this point is whether we can expect the Juárez evaluation to make a difference in shaping early childhood bilingual education policy formation. Although the question seems premature at this point, there is sufficient reason to claim that the findings of the Juárez evaluation are very likely to be used as intended. The irony here is that the substantive findings may not really matter. As we see it, the evidence seems too compelling to conclude otherwise. Notwithstanding radical shifts in administrative leadership and government policy, the evaluation findings will probably be used to legitimate federal efforts in the field of early childhood bilingual education. To expect otherwise is to overlook the reproductive function that evaluative research can and sometimes does serve. Contributing to this reproductive function is the structural linkage that exists between educational research and the institutions that sponsor it. In fact, there is no such thing as neutral research. Whether of the order of scientific interests Jurgen Habermas (1971) describes, or ideology, there are specific interests underlying all forms of knowledge production. Michael Apple describes the problem well:

> . . . what is the prevailing function of research? Isn't it merely a process of data production that tries to help us solve our day-to-day problems? I am afraid that our answer here must be no, for an affirmative answer neglects one important yet too often forgotten social fact: research creates information for use *by* somebody. It is sponsored by and affiliated with organizations that have a stake, though often not a conscious one, in the continued maintenance of their and other more powerful institutions' basic modes of operation. Thus, we must ask the political question, 'Why is this data produced?' One should not conceive of the products of educational research apart from the institutional functions they perform. Too often they perform a rather interesting role; they act to prevent committed educators from focusing on the contradictions within our institutions by forcing attention on official definitions of problems (Apple, 1977: 118).

Evaluative research is no exception to this. Indeed, nowhere is the reproductive function of research more apparent than in evaluative studies, for these essentially seek a measurement of the reproductive value of that which they study. And now that social systems generally look to scientific rationality for legitimacy (Habermas, 1970), the reproductive function of evaluative research becomes increasingly important. The national evaluation of Project Head Start is illustrative of just how important a role evaluative research can come to play in the social reproduction of a major federal program.

The controversy created by the Westinghouse/Ohio Evaluation of Project Head Start is well known. The political and methodological issues that it raised were many, and the debate was heated and long. But now that the controversial dust has settled and a number of significant events in the history of the evaluation have been reconstructed, we can see clearly that the Westinghouse/Ohio evaluation seems to have served its function well: it helped to preserve Project Head Start and deliver to its leadership what it had desired all along.

The most important feature of the Westinghouse/Ohio evaluation was not the set of findings that were generated but the *scientific legitimacy* that it produced for the internal and external expansion of Project Head Start. That Head Start summer programs were generally less effective than full-year programs and that the impact on Head Start children tended not to persist into the primary grades was of no surprise to the Head Start Project. As Lois-Ellin Datta points out:

> Evidence suggesting that summer programs were less developmentally effective than full-year programs and that academic gains of Head Start were not sustained had been available almost since the beginning of Head Start. . . . The greater benefits of full-year versus summer programs were evident also in the 1965-to-1969 data . . . most advisors cautioned that brief programs would have limited effects on language, cognition, or other aspects of intellectual development (Datta, 1976: 144-146).

The fact that this knowledge was available to Project Head Start prior to its evaluation helps to explain why the Head Start Research Council argued strongly against the design of the Westinghouse/Ohio study. Although it was unable to alter the basic design of the impact study, the Head Start Research Council at least managed to influence the study to some degree. Measures of parental satisfaction and child affect and motivation became part of the measurement battery. And to complement the study, an advisory board of experts was also established.

The reaction of the Head Start Research Council indicates that the evaluation of the project may have been feared. In light of the knowledge then available to Head Start, this fear seems justified. Nevertheless, there remained a need to legitimate expansion of the Head Start project. Such legitimation came from the Westinghouse Report in the form of findings and recommendations that were supposedly based on scientific rationality. As sources of this rationality, the roles played by the Westinghouse Learning Corporation and Ohio University cannot be underestimated. A more accurate understanding of the Westinghouse Report requires relational analysis: that the report not be examined apart from its producers, two institutions interested and committed to preserving and expanding research.[4]

That the evaluation served a reproductive function is suggested by the OCD leadership as it reconstructs the history of the Westinghouse Report:

> We used the Westinghouse and other studies constructively to reaffirm the Head Start focus on the whole child; the concerns about the summer projects were reasserted and the short-term innoculation notion was shown to be fallacious; the notion of a single magic year was also shown to be limited; and the folly of selecting as criteria stable measures of development was emphasized.
>
> Westinghouse is just the only book on the shelf about Head Start and so people point to it. But the issues debated about Head Start and early childhood education are issues we'd have been debating anyhow.
>
> Westinghouse helped justify what we wanted as early as 1966: continuity, earlier involvement, greater concern about parent involvement. And we used Westinghouse to legitimize these (Datta, 1976: 151).

It is true that the Head Start budget stabilized after the report. And it is also true that Elliot Richardson, Secretary of the Department of Health, Education and Welfare (HEW) under Richard Nixon, may have received convincing pressure from Head Start parents to preserve Head Start. But there are two factors we need to keep in mind here. First, the demonstration of Head Start parents in Washington buttressed well one of the few positive findings of the Westinghouse Report: parental satisfaction, what the Head Start Research Council insisted on adding as a measure to the study. In a sense, the report may have functioned to legitimate the action of the parents as well. Second, policies in Washington were beginning to shift as a result of new administrative leadership. The untimeliness of the report is what almost interfered with its reproductive function. The new leadership at HEW found itself holding the results of a study that it had not sponsored and therefore was not prepared to use. The evaluation had lost its political legitimacy. Here was a case of scientific rationality without political backing. The political legitimacy of the evaluation had to be reconstituted. This reconstitution of political legitimacy came in the form of both federal and grass-roots support.

In the case of the Juárez evaluation, there is a key factor strongly favoring its reproductive function. It has to do with the *structural linkage* that exists between ACYF and the evaluation. On the other hand, we have ACYF wanting to "help Head Start programs desiring to implement bilingual curricula to choose the model or models most appropriate for their circumstances and needs." This implies a very different use of information than that of making budget decisions about a national bilingual education program like Title VII. On the other hand, we have a consulting firm that has consented to address the "research" problem that ACYF has defined and to design and carry out an evaluation to resolve it. The result is an evaluation specifically designed to generate findings that local Head Start programs can survey so as to be able to judge not only how well a given curriculum model works, but under what "circumstances and needs" each works or fails to work. Although the AIR study obtained some program descriptive data, this information was not sufficiently precise to permit an assessment of what circumstances exist and under which ones particular effects would be found. Thus, we are left at the end of the AIR study with basically one, global conclusion: Title VII children do no better than, and perhaps worse than, their non-Title VII counterparts. This is the kind of conclusion that tends, at least politically, to weaken the reproductive power of an evaluation. When it happens, the loss in reproductive power then has to be restored through recommendations of some kind. But because of the different purpose and the more "open" design of the Juárez evaluation, the reproductive function of that evaluation may not need the doctoring usually found in evaluations in the form of "positive" recommendations suggesting that the program be saved.

The structural linkage between ACYF and the Juárez evaluation makes the study more focused and more limited. It focuses on a particular set of curriculum projects that were funded for a limited time period. The study is more limited in size (four sites and only hundreds of thousands of dollars spread over several years) and in no way approaches the multimillion dollar Title VII program. The Juárez findings can be used by a single agency to shape its own strategy toward bilingual children and families and does not have to serve as "the" evaluation of "U.S. bilingual education."

Furthermore, ACYF has a history of supporting program development and research efforts, which raises the probability that the findings from the Juárez study will be received positively by the agency and acted upon. In 1972, for example, ACYF (then the Office of Child Development) began Home Start, a home-based variant of Head Start and simultaneously funded an evaluation that was designed to collect both process and outcome data for judging the implementation and impact of the program. Information from the evaluation was used in modifying guidelines for the program, and when Home Start ended and more than 300 Head Start programs adopted a home-based option (usually to supplement their ongoing center-based program), ACYF instituted six regional training centers to provide training and technical assistance to Head Start programs making this change (Love, 1978). If the Juárez evaluation provides useful information about the four bilingual curriculum projects, there is every indication that ACYF will attempt to base future programmatic decisions on that information.

It seems to us that mandates to evaluate institutional policies and practices presents a very troublesome dilemma to policy makers, especially those who have an interest in preserving certain policies and practices that are considered important and worthwhile. On one hand, the policy maker has to demonstrate the worth of a given policy or program in order to justify its preservation. How does the policy maker do it without jeopardizing the policy or program? One option is for the policy maker to define clearly what he/she wants the evaluation to do in light of what is known about what evaluative research can and cannot do and then support a well thought-out evaluation design capable of delivering the kind of information that would be usable in maintaining or improving the policy or program being evaluated. That seems to be the posture reflected in the Juárez evaluation, and we submit that it is as reasonable as any other.

Toward a New Direction in Bilingual-Bicultural Education Policy Research

There is a dire need in bilingual-bicultural education policy research for engaging in relational analysis. We need to start looking at social activity as being structurally related to other forms of social activity and institutions. This also means that we need to start social actions in terms of their relations to other forms of social action and underlying principles of social organization and control. The absence of this view in bilingual education research is somewhat of an irony.

As reformers, bilingual educators have done their share to accentuate and help eliminate inequities in educational opportunity. As researchers, however, they have not given equal attention to finding out the structural reasons for these inequities. The tendency has been to rely more on developing languages of incompatibilities and bicognitivism to justify institutional amelioration rather than restructuration. The problem here is that these language systems function more as slogans and tend to fall short of what is needed in order to understand the structural relations that underlie social and cultural reproduction. What is needed is a different metaphor or language system that allows one to describe the structural relations between institutions and individuals in such a way that one can begin to see how individuals and institutions function for and against each other.

During all the debate over the Title VII findings, we have somehow overlooked the critical issue that has been raised: whether the federal government should play a mediating role in the reproduction of ethnic languages and cultures. We can't respond to that issue by pointing to a faulty evaluation design. The issue is politically charged and research design has very little to do with it. The issue relates more to a structural relation that federal support for bilingual education seems to be engendering. That's a political concern that the Title VII evaluation helped to exacerbate in that it was able to show how bilingual programs were being used for language and cultural maintenance. To alleviate the concern, federal policy makers have started a search for entry-exit criteria that could be applied to Title VII students. This search is certainly a good indicator that the Title VII evaluation has served its reproductive function rather well in certain areas. The findings have so far led to tighter monitoring and control which are, in a sense, improvements and therefore preservation of the program. It makes sense, therefore, to pay less attention to questions of faulty design and more attention to the structural reasons underlying the Title VII evaluation, because when looked at closely, the problem with the AIR evaluation has more to do with the purpose and type of questions raised than with faulty design.

To summarize, using the AIR and Juárez evaluations as contrasting examples of bilingual research, we have suggested a different direction for policy research in bilingual education. We suggest an orientation that looks at all the factors (program evaluations being one example) affecting bilingual eduation policy formation within the larger relational nexus of which they are a part. If these factors are to be accurately interpreted, we cannot afford to settle for anything less.

BIBLIOGRAPHY

Apple, M. "Politics and Research." In *The Curriculum and Cultural Reproduction.* Edited by M. MacDonald. London: Open University Press, 1977.

Arenas, S. "Bilingual-bicultural Programs for Preschool Children." *Children Today.* July/August, 1978.

Berman, P. & McLaughlin, M. S. *Federal programs Supporting Educational Change, volume 1: A Model of Educational Change*. Santa Monica, Calif.: Rand Corporation, 1975.

Bernstein, B. *Class, Codes and Control* (vol. 3). London: Routledge, and Kagan Paul, 1975.

Comptroller General of the United States. *Bilingual education: An unmet need*. Washington, D.C.: U.S. General Accounting Office, 1976.

Danoff, M. N. *Evaluation of the impact of ESEA Title VII Spanish/English Bilingual Education Program: Overview of study and findings*. Palo Alto, Calif.: American Institutes for Research, 1978.

Datta, L. E. "The Impact of the Westinghouse/Ohio Evaluation on the Development of Head Start: An Examination of the Immediate and Long-term Effects and How They Came About." In, *The Evaluation of Social Programs*, Edited by C. Abt. Beverly Hills, Calif.: Sage, 1976.

Development Associates. *A Process Evaluation of the Bilingual Education Program, Title VII, ESEA*. Washington, D.C.: Author, 1973.

Habermas, J. *Toward a Rational Society*. Boston, Mass.: Beacon Press, 1970.

Habermas, J. *Knowledge and Human Interests*. Boston, Mass.: Beacon Press, 1971.

Juárez and Associates. *An Evaluation of the Head Start Bilingual/Bicultural Curriculum Development Project*. Los Angeles, Calif.: Author, 1978.

Love, J. M. "The Impact of the Evaluation of the National Home Start Demonstration Program." In, *The Impact of Evaluation: Lessons Drawn from the Evaluations of Five Early Childhood Programs*, Edited by A. C. Granville, et al. Symposium presented at the annual meeting of the American Educational Research Association, Toronto, Canada, 1978).

Monaghan, A. C. *A Consideration of the Feasibility of a National Study of the Impact of Follow Through on the Public School System*. Cambridge, Mass.: The Huron Institute, 1976.

U.S. Commissioner of Education. *The Condition of Bilingual Education in the Nation*. Washington, D.C.: U.S. Department of Health, Education and Welfare, 1976.

NOTES

1. *Head Start Newsletter*, November/December 1978: 6.
2. The concept of message systems is a Bernsteinian notion that is used to refer to curriculum, pedagogy, and evaluation. For a detailed discussion, see Bernstein, 1975: 85-115.
3. Although the intent here is not to provide a critique of the evaluation design, there is a compulsion however, to note that the fidelity perspective as used traditionally in the measurement of implementation is problematic in securing accurate assessments of institutional change. For example see Berman, et al (1975).
4. For a treatment of the concept of relational analysis, see Michael Apple, "On Analyzing Hegemony," *The Journal of Curriculum Theorizing*, 1:1.

AN ETHNOGRAPHIC EVALUATION/RESEARCH MODEL FOR BILINGUAL PROGRAMS

Marietta Saravia Shore

In this paper I will propose a paradigm for research on the effectiveness of different bilingual program models. The suggested research paradigm is theory-based ethnographic evaluation synthesized with quantitative research which is long-term and cumulative. This evaluation/research paradigm provides for developing a knowledge base derived from testing hypotheses in actual classrooms and schools where bilingual programs are implemented.

To demonstrate the need for this research paradigm, I will review the historical factors which have resulted in the lack of a research base concerning the effectiveness of bilingual education in the United States. These factors include federal policies such as the allocation of most Title VII funds to bilingual education basic programs and the relative lack of funding for research; the lack of comprehensive guidelines for the evaluation of Title VII bilingual programs; the absence of comprehensive, long-term planning for research and, in most of the research which has been carried out, the lack of a well-developed theoretical framework for research on bilingual programs. These criticisms will be documented by R. Troike's (1978) recent review, *Research Evidence for the Effectiveness of Bilingual Education* and Zappert and Cruz' (1977) book, *Bilingual Education: An Appraisal of Empirical Research.*

To address the absence of a developed theoretical framework, various definitions of bilingual program models in the literature will be discussed, and a conceptual framework for defining models of bilingual education will be proposed.

The scope of this paper is limited to a discussion of *applied* research in the field of bilingual education. It will not deal with basic research such as that being conducted in child language acquisition by psycholinguists and sociolinguists, or research on language usage in minority communities. Rather, this paper will suggest a research/evaluation paradigm to investigate the effectiveness of bilingual education program models as they are presently implemented. This means situating first and second language learning in a specific social, legal and historical *context*: learning in actual school settings by groups of students from a particular social class. In Title VII bilingual programs, most students are of lower socioeconomic status, speak a minority home language, are of elementary school age and are members of a minority cultural group interacting with a dominant cultural group. Similarly, in educational programs developed as a result of the *Lau* decision, the groups served by bilingual programs also tend to have the same pattern of minority culture status. It is in this sociocultural context that research and evaluations of bilingual programs in the United States need to be addressed.

Several factors can be suggested for the present lack of research to inform decisions concerning the most effective models of bilingual education. Among the most significant have been the lack of federal planning and coordination of resources for comprehensive research; the low priority and low level of USOE funding for such research; the absence of an adequate theoretical framework for such research and the inadequate federal guidelines for comprehensive evaluations of bilingual programs, which, cumulatively, over a period of years, could have yielded relevant data.

Federal Policies re Funding Allocations for Research in Bilingual Education

Rudolph Troike (1978) of the National Clearinghouse on Bilingual Education has recently done a summary of the federal allocation of resources to the field of research in bilingual education. He noted that although Title VII of the Elementary and Secondary Act authorized bilingual education programs in 1968, it was not until 1974 that provision for funding research was added to the legislation (Bilingual Education Act of 1974) and it was not until 1976 that the Office of Bilingual Education, prompted by the Center for Applied Linguistics, included a request for funds for research in their budget. Only 2 million dollars of a total of 135 million dollars was appropriated for research in 1977-78, but "subsequently most of this was reallocated to other activities" (Troike, 1978: 1).

Another federal agency, the National Institute of Education, has spent more than half a million dollars in bringing together scholars and researchers to determine priorities for research in bilingual education, and spent a little more than a million dollars on actual research.

Troike concluded that less than one-half of one percent of the 500 million dollar total spent in the past ten years on bilingual education has been allocated to research. Thus, the field of bilingual education is in "critical need of research." As Troike pointed out, this lack of funding of research would never be allowed in medical or military fields and should not be tolerated in education.

Planning and Coordination of Resources

Another factor that has been contributing to the lack of a research base for bilingual education is the lack of federal planning for comprehensive research and evaluation. The New York State Consortium of Colleges and Universities in Bilingual Education–Committee on Research has stated in its position paper of April, 1977:

> Research in Bilingual Education has been fragmentary, piecemeal, and discontinuous. There has been little interdisciplinary, long-range, useful research grounded in coherent theory and methodology. Consequently, there is a lack of research to guide decisions and policy concerning teacher training and bilingual program implementation.

One exception to this fragmentation existed during the past several years when the National Institute of Education had a viable Multicultural/Bilingual Division, which is no longer in existence. The NIE Multicultural/Bilingual branch developed a comprehensive program plan (1976, 1977, 1978) for several years of research projects which not only addressed significant problems but also articulated with one another. There was coordination between NIE, OBE and the National Center for Educational Statistics (NCES) in the development and pilot testing of an instrument to assess English proficiency and utilize that instrument to determine aggregate statistics on the numbers of limited-English-speaking students across the United States (The Child English Services Survey). NIE also funded such research as the Instructional Implications of Cognitive Styles in which De Avila (1978) found variation in cognitive styles among the students from the same ethnic group, thus extending the work of Ramírez and Castañeda (1974).

NIE's Multicultural/Bilingual Division utilized a process which enabled them to develop projects as part of a comprehensive research plan. Educators and researchers were commissioned to write state-of-the-art papers on such topics as the dimensions of bilingual education research and to assemble as a group to discuss them. This process of dialogue guided by such practitioners and scholars in residence as Joshua Fishman, José Vázquez, and George Blanco, served to develop a comprehensive conceptual framework for research and to determine priorities for research projects. This process of comprehensive planning, and coordination of resources among agencies, is a model which could be usefully emulated.

Lack of Comprehensive Evaluation Guidelines

In addition to the limited selection of valid assessment procedures for language assessment, another reason that the evaluations of Title VII programs have yielded so little data on the effectiveness of different program models of bilingual education is that the federal guidelines for program evaluation were so inadequate. The United States Office of Education required only product evaluations rather than comprehensive process and product evaluations. The U.S.O.E. Guidelines require programs to:

> Describe the methods, techniques, and procedures which will be used to determine the degree to which the objectives of the proposed program are achieved.
>
> Describe the instruments to be used to conduct the evaluation.

It would seem that as much attention should be given to ascertaining whether or not the program was implemented as proposed, before evaluating whether or not the objectives of the program had been met. This would not only assist the staff involved in the program to monitor implementation but to identify gaps in the program and administrative support system so that modifications could be made on an ongoing basis. Moreover, to develop a research base for bilingual program implementation, the *processes* of bilingual programs need to be related to the products or goals of the programs, as described below.

Research/Evaluation Models

I would suggest that the lack of a viable, appropriate theoretical framework for bilingual education research and evaluation has been as detrimental as the lack of funding for research. In two separate reviews of research studies and evaluations of bilingual programs by the Center for Applied Linguistics and the Northwest Regional Educational Laboratory, the majority of research and evaluations reviewed were found to be worthless for the purpose of serving as a research base for assessing the effectiveness of bilingual education or for the improvement of bilingual programs.

The Center for Applied Linguistics reviewed 150 evaluation reports and only found 7 evaluations which met "minimal criteria for acceptability and contained usable information" (Troike, 1978: 3). Similarly, the Northwest Regional Educational Laboratory only found 3 of 108 evaluations of bilingual programs and twelve of seventy-six research studies that met their criteria for methodological soundness.

Zappert and Cruz of the Northwest Regional Educational Laboratory (1977) listed the criteria they used to determine whether or not the evaluation or research they reviewed was adequate. They found the following to be the most prevalent reasons for poor, inadequate evaluations and research:

1. no control for socioeconomic status
2. inadequate sample size (<30)
   improper sampling techniques
   excessive attrition rates
3. no baseline or comparison group data or no control group or non-relevant comparisons
4. no control for initial language dominance
5. significant differences in teacher qualifications or characteristics
   other confounding variables
6. insufficient statistical information
   improper statistical applications

Research Findings

After sifting through the evaluations and research studies, Zappert and Cruz summarized the findings of those twelve studies which met their criteria for validity and adequacy. Of the sixty-six separate findings from the twelve studies, forty-one percent were "neutral", that is, they showed no adverse effects of bilingual education on students. Students in the bilingual program were performing as well in English as their comparison group peers who had not had a bilingual education. Fifty-eight percent of the findings were positive, that is, the students were performing significantly better in some skills than the monolingually educated, while only one percent of the findings were negative.

Similarly, Troike (1978) reported that in the twelve evaluations which CAL found adequate, the students of various ethnolinguistic groups, Chinese-dominant, Spanish-dominant, French-speaking and Navajo-speaking, in various bilingual programs, were performing at or above the level of the comparison group students on such measures as the Comprehensive Test of Basic Skills and the Metropolitan Achievement Test.

One of the significant findings brought out by Troike in reviewing bilingual program evaluations was that programs reporting the cumulative effects of participation in a bilingual program over a period of three years had the most positive results. This suggests that bilingual education is a cumulative process not adequately assessed by a one-year or partial year study, and that, therefore, a longitudinal research/evaluation model would be more appropriate.

Evaluation as Research

In his review of the research evidence for the effectiveness of bilingual education programs in the U.S., Troike (1978) made this observation,

> program evaluations can be of such potential benefit to programs and . . . they are one of the few available sources of research evidence for program effectivenss. (Troike, 1978: 3)

I would like not only to support that statement but build upon it. For the purpose of answering the questions we have on the effectiveness of bilingual education and the effectiveness of different bilingual education program models, I suggest that long term, theory-based, ethnographic evaluations of actual bilingual programs may be the most heuristic research model. I contend that the experimental or laboratory paradigm of research is not so useful because it only deals with several controlled variables in an artifically controlled situation. By contrast, the interactive, ethnographic paradigm of evaluation/research takes into account the *interaction* of numerous variables *in the specific context where the learning occurs*—not in an experimental lab situation but in the actual classroom over an extended period of time.

I am not suggesting, however, that we continue to use the paradigm of evaluation most prevalent today; that is, that evaluation is synonymous with the measurement of the discrepancy between student objectives and student performance. There are two major problems with this paradigm. One is that it is reductionistic by limiting the objectives of education to changes in student *behavior*. Ralph Tyler, who first formulated *congruency* evaluation, that is determining the congruence between objectives and performance, makes this reductionism quite clear.

> The process of evaluation is essentially the process of determining to what extent the educational objectives are actually being realized by the program of curriculum and instruction. However, since educational objectives are essentially changes in human beings, that is, the objectives aimed at are to produce certain desirable *changes in the behavior patterns of the student,* then evaluation is the process for determining the degree to which these changes in behavior are actually taking place. (Tyler, 1950: 69)

Those who conceptualize the goals of education as also encompassing changes in consciousness, critical analysis, comprehension of historical relationships, and the capacity to compare value systems and become committed to one, find this behavioral reductionism extremely limited. This is particularly the case when behavioral objectives determine and limit the content of the curriculum. This is not to say that behavioral objectives are not useful in evaluation, because they are, but rather that there is a danger in defining evaluation solely in terms of student behavioral objectives and limiting curriculum objectives to those that can be observed and/or tested by paper and pencil instruments.

Again, there is a contradiction between the pluralistic goals of bilingual/bicultural/multicultural and cross-cultural education and their evaluation in terms of the Skinnerian behaviorist model of educational evaluation which can only deal with some of those goals.

The second major problem with this "product" model of evaluation has been noted above. Such a "product" evaluation, to use the economic metaphor, which only assesses student behavior, ignores the context and the processes, approaches and treatment being implemented by the bilingual program. If one of the goals of bilingual programs is cultural pluralism, then the most appropriate assessment might be a process evaluation of the program, to ascertain whether such options in learning models are provided. If one of the goals of bilingual programs is to offer the option for students to learn the skills that enable them to have access to various resources and positions within the larger society and to participate in a changing society and in changing society to meet changing needs, then the assessment might be focused on whether or not the program is being implemented in such a way that there is the opportunity for students to learn to take responsibility for their time, movement, learning and decisions (Grannis, 1975).

Depending on the goals that are agreed upon by the conflicting interest groups which decide students' curriculum and assessment, the effectiveness of a bilingual program might be assessed on the basis of what it is doing and what it is offering as well as on the outcomes of its students. Furthermore, if both the processes of implementation and the outcomes are assessed over a period of several years this will yield research data for a knowledge base on the relative effectiveness of various bilingual education program models.

There are alternatives to the product evaluation model which only assesses students' behavior (that is most often operationally defined as the selection of multiple-choice answers on a verbal paper and pencil test). One is ethnographic evaluation, which encompasses assessment of the *process* of program implementation and student learning as well as the assessment of the outcomes: the extent of student learning. This is done by observations of students in the same social contexts as those in which they have learned and through interviewing participants to ascertain the meaning of their observed behavior from their perspective. This evaluation would be documented by ethnographic and psychometric methods. That is, students would be observed informally interacting with teachers and peers, materials and problems, and documentation made of their mastery of criterion-referenced outcomes such as communicative competence in the first and second language in a naturalistic setting, as well as through criterion-reference formal tests.

Ethnographic Evaluation

Ethnographic evaluation is defined as the use of on-site participant observation and in-depth interviews of the program participants over an extended period of time informed by the theoretical framework and research findings of anthropological inquiry. Ethnographic research/evaluation is exemplified by the work of Ogbu (1974), Cole, Gay, Glick and Sharp (1971), Rist, (1973, 1977), Erickson (1977), and Lacey (1970).

The alternative research paradigm being proposed is an interdisciplinary synthesis of qualitative and quantitative evaluation research derived from anthropological inquiry and educational psychology (Rist, 1977). The methodology encompasses a sequence in which the researchers' theoretical premises interact with field-based observations of bilingual education programs leading to modifications of the original theories as well as field-generated hypotheses. These are, then, formulated as hypotheses which predict the relationship between student outcomes and specific program process variables. These program variables include teaching strategies and content/language allocation, as well as program structural variables such as classroom organization, adminstrative support, the extent of articulation between the bilingual and monolingual program and the extent to which the bilingual program pervades the school. These hypotheses guide data collection and interpretation.

The program process variables are identified, monitored and documented through ethnographic observation and recording via field notes, observation instruments, photographs and videotape. At appropriate intervals, a discrepancy evaluation is conducted to compare the hypothesized student outcomes and the actual outcomes.

This model of ethnographic evaluation/research was synthesized with the model of theory-based evaluation/research formulated by Fitz-Gibbon and Lyons Morris (1975). Theory-based evaluation provides a viable and heuristic alternative to the experimental/laboratory paradigm prevalent in most evaluations. Fitz-Gibbon and Lyons Morris note that "rarely does the evaluator present any rationale for the choice of variables . . . At present, evaluations are preponderantly atheoretical" (1975: 3). I would argue instead that evaluations are usually based on behaviorist theory, which is implicit, as exemplified by behavioral objectives determining the focus of evaluations, and program evaluation viewed as synonymous to standardized measurement of students. By contrast, in theory-based evaluations, a learning theory would predict the specific inputs or interactions which lead to specific student outcomes.

Theory-based evaluation suggests that the learning theories and teaching models on which education programs are based should be made explicit rather than remain implicit. The processes expected to result in specific student outcomes by the learning theory need to be identified and stated as hypotheses.

An approach which complements that of theory-based evaluation has been proposed by Adrianne Bank of the Center for the Study of Evaluation at UCLA. She suggests the identification of teaching models as integral to the evaluation of educational programs. The teaching model provides "a framework within which intended student outcomes, learning activities, materials and instructional settings are related to one another" (Bank 1975: 5).

The Research Question

The discussion will be limited to research and evaluations which address the questions:

1. For the students mentioned above, is bilingual education more effective than education solely through a second language?

2. Which models of bilingual education are more effective in meeting the long-term goals and short-term objectives selected by school administrators / teachers / parents / program developers / legislation: Title VII of ESEA or Title IV of ESAA?

However, before any research can determine which bilingual program models are most effective, we need to ask, what is meant by "effective"? and what is a "program model?"

What is Meant by Effective?

One of the terms most in need of clarification in bilingual education research is "effective". What are the criteria of effectiveness? Who selects and defines the criteria of effectiveness? Do the administrators of the bilingual program? Do the teachers? Do the parents? Do the courts? Does the legislature in its rules and regulations? Does the Office of Evaluation and Dissemination? Do evaluators of the program operationally define the goals of the program by defining behavioral objectives for the program in their evaluation design?

In the final analysis, will the "effectiveness" of bilingual programs be solely assessed by the results of standardized tests of *individual* achievement normed on English speaking students, but used as a *group* test for students to whom English is a second language (as did the AIR Study)? Will there be any attempt to assess the effectiveness of bilingual programs in terms of their varying goals? For there are a number of different definitions of "effective" depending on your values, goals and priorities.

In an evaluation you can make explicit a process that is usually implicit and taken for granted in most research. Evaluation, as the word implies, is based on values. Different groups may all have the goal of implementing an effective bilingual program. However, depending on their value systems, effectiveness can mean something different to separate groups of parents, and may be defined in other ways by various groups of teachers or administrators.

A mechanistic interpretation of research or evaluation skirts the difficult issue of values. Stufflebeam's (1971) model, *Educational Evaluation As Decision-Making*, seeks to make goal-setting an explicit process. In confronting this issue he noted,

> In a pluralistic society in which multiple values exist side by side, which values will be served? (1971: 19)

If we are to be consistent with the ideal of cultural pluralism, the goals of bilingual programs would be determined by the local community affected by the program. Different goals make sense for different communities. For example, Puerto Rican parents who expect to spend part of their lives on the mainland and also live for a time in Puerto Rico would have a greater concern that their children become functionally bilingual in all skill areas so that they could participate in the schools in Puerto Rico where instruction is primarily in Spanish or on the mainland where instruction is primarily in English.

Goals of Bilingual Programs

Having seen that there are different definitions of "effectiveness" depending on one's values and goals, it may clarify the options to look at the range of bilingual program goals. Table 1 summarizes some of the major educational goals of bilingual programs. These include four possible goals for the minority students' marked and unmarked language (English).

Among all four options there is a consistent goal for English: oral communicative competence and literacy are common goals. The options differ only in relation to the commitment to development of skills in the marked language (other than English). These vary from (1) complete loss and *replacement* by English, through (2) a three year limit on the use of the marked language in a *transition* from the home language to English (3) *maintenance* of the student's oral communicative competence but neglect of literacy in the home language to (4) *development* of both literacy and communicative competence in the home language as well as English.

In addition, there are related goals for the students' culture and structural status. These latter goals are usually not explicit. But there is no such thing as "benign neglect" of an ethnic culture. When the students' cultural values and interaction patterns are not an integral part of the bilingual program, the outcome is cultural assimilation and/or structural marginality.

We can further distinguish between two aspects of program goals which are often confused: *cultural* assimilation/cultural pluralism and structural integration/segregation. Cultural assimilation refers to the replacement of the *marked* culture by the cultural system of the *unmarked,* socioeconomically dominant group. Cultural pluralism, by contrast, allows for options among the majority and minority cultural values and behavior patterns, often in different domains or situations.

Further, structural integration may or may not co-exist with goals of cultural pluralism or cultural assimilation. Structural integration refers to access by minority group members to education at all levels, to economic resources, to occupations at every level of responsibility, income and prestige, and to political power to effect legislation which effects all our lives.[1] We have seen that certain minority groups which have culturally assimilated the 'mainstream' dominant white middle-class values remain structurally segregated with only token access to higher education and position of prestige, income and political power. These separate goals must be clearly distinguished. Otherwise cultural assimilation may imply structural integration when it really masks structural segregation.

Even these goals of bilingual programs are often defined differently by different interest groups. I have used the term "communicative competence" as a goal, while for many, "language proficiency" is the goal. In many bilingual programs, goals have been limited to linguistic competencies. Yet sociolinguists would define communicative competence more broadly to include social competencies, that is, the ability to use the knowledge of which social contexts and with whom, different linguistic and non-verbal repertoires are appropriate to communicate effectively.

At another level, the goals of bilingual programs are often defined by the instruments available which purport to measure those goals, for example, the extent of "language proficiency" or "communicative competence." An evaluator's selection of instruments and procedures is therefore significant. The limited development of valid assessment procedures for communicative competence as compared to the plethora of discrete point tests of specific language proficiency skills determines the emphasis of most evaluations of bilingual programs of outcomes as well as entry and

TABLE 1
POLITICAL / EDUCATIONAL GOALS

		DEVELOPMENTAL	MAINTENANCE	TRANSITIONAL	REPLACEMENT
LANGUAGES	Marked	+ literacy + oral comm. competence	+ oral comm. competence	(3 year limit)	
	Unmarked (English)	+ literacy + oral comm. competence	+ literacy + oral comm. competence	+ literacy + oral comm. competence	+ literacy + oral comm. competence
		CULTURAL PLURALISM		CULTURAL ASSIMILATION	
CULTURES	Marked	+ own value system and behavior pattern			
	Unmarked	+ value system of socioeconomically dominant group		+ value system and behavior of socioeconomically dominant group	
		STRUCTURAL INTEGRATION	SEPARATISM	STRUCTURAL SEGREGATION	
SOCIAL STRUCTURE	Marked Roles	± access to education, jobs, political power within own community	± autonomous institutions	± tokenism ± discrimination	
	Unmarked Roles	+ access to education, jobs, political power of larger society			

exit criteria. However, if the goals of bilingual programs include oral communicative competence in both languages as well as literacy in both languages, then presumably all these skills would be assessed. Since oral communicative competence is not amenable to group-administered paper and pencil assessment on an instrument which can be computer-scored, it is necessary to utilize observation and interaction in situational contexts, an ethnographic approach. As Lee in "Assessing Communicative Competence via the Repertoire Model" has suggested, "Observing children's *natural behavior* during social interchanges in semi-structures or real life settings would be recommended" (1978: 3).

While some may support the goal that there be a process of goal-setting involving interested groups in the community, that is–parents, teachers, students, and administrators–the reality we most often see is that federal and state funding agencies determine the goals of bilingual programs and then evaluators determine the operational definition of those goals by the instruments they select. Only in districts where parents have organized, and in cooperation with district community school boards and district administrative staff, have supported goals supplemental to those of the USOE and the SEA funding agencies, is there a possibility that the process of goal-setting will be more open to reflect specific community goals.

Bilingual Program Models

One of the theses of this paper is that the lack of a holistic theoretical framework for defining models of bilingual education has been one of the factors impeding research and evaluation on the effectiveness of different program models. There is a lack of consensus among researchers and practitioners as to what a "program model" is. Many "models" are defined solely by a specific language methodology i.e., (the "alternate day model," "back to back," "grammar-translation") which neglects the sociocultural context of the bilingual program. More comprehensive models, such as those of Mackey (1970) and Fishman and Lovas (1971) do deal with language in its societal context, but do not deal with other sociocultural aspects of a bilingual program. Saville and Troike (1971) also concentrate on language factors in defining their models. Only J. Gonzalez (1975) and Saravia-Shore (1977) have explicitly dealt with other factors, such as the inclusion of the history and culture of the marked language group as integral to curricular content and practice.

In Mackey's (1970) models of bilingual education, the *functional use* and *status* of each language are the most significant features. Whether a language is used as a *medium of instruction* or is only taught as a *subject* makes the critical difference in Mackey's classification. Some of the models in this classification scheme that are found in U.S. bilingual education are:

1. *Dual—Medium Equal Maintenance*
   Both languages are used as mediums of instruction and given equal treatment (method: alternate morning and afternoon or days or weeks, etc.)
2. *Dual—Medium Differential Maintenance*
   Each language has a different function in a different domain.
3. *Dual Medium Accultural Transfer*
   Initial use of both languages as a preparation for eventual exclusive use of the mainstream language of wider communication.

4. *Single Medium Irredental Maintenance*
   The marked language is maintained only as a subject, not as a medium of instruction.
   The other models which would not be considered bilingual programs under Title VII, include:
5. *Single Medium Irredental Transfer*
   Only the marked language (i.e., Spanish) is used as a medium of instruction.
6. *Single Medium Accultural Transfer*
   English as the sole medium of instruction.
7. *Dual Medium Irredental Transfer*
   ESL as a subject only; the marked language used as a medium for instruction.

Fishman and Lovas (1970), similarly attend to the *function* of each language in their quadripartite classification, adding the *extent of skills development* of each language.

Type IV *Full Bilingualism* corresponds to Mackey's *Dual Medium-Equal Maintenance Model.*

Their definition encompasses learning all linguistic skills; reading, writing, listening and speaking in both languages.

Type III *Partial Bilingualism*

Literacy in the marked language is limited to certain domains, relevant to the culture (similar to Dual Medium - Differential Maintenance).

Type II *Monoliterate Bilingualism*

Only oral fluency is expected in the marked language, while both fluency and literacy are required in the unmarked, language of wider communication.

Type I *Transitional Bilingualism*

(Similar to Dual Medium Accultural Transfer).

The marked language is used only as a bridge to English for easier adjustment to school.

Saville and Troike (1971) also focus on the function of each language in their three models, while they emphasize the variable of the extent of time in which the marked language is used. For example, in one model similar to dual medium differential maintenance, the function of English changes from that of a subject, initially ESL, to a medium of instruction after the student has adequate control of the language.

The crucial difference in these models is the speed of accultural transfer. In one model, both languages are used as mediums of instruction through grade eight. In the second model, the marked language is only maintained in a few subjects, and in the third, the marked language is phased out completely after grade three (as in transitional bilingualism or dual medium accultural transfer).

J. Gonzalez (1975) has taken into account the legal context and constrictions of bilingual programs in the United States in his five models. In addition to the *transitional* (Type A) which has a remedial/compensatory context, Gonzalez includes *bilingual (Type B)* similar to dual medium equal maintenance.

Moreover, Gonzalez has included another factor, the history and culture of the marked language group as an integral part of curricular content and methodology, in bilingual/bicultural maintenance, which is explicitly mentioned in the Title VII definition of bilingual education.

In Gonzalez' models, another significant feature is noted—the participation of all students, not only the marked language group, in a program of linguistically and *culturally pluralistic* schooling (Type E).

Still another model focuses on the bilingual/bicultural (restorationist) Type D model which applies to ethnolinguistic groups whose language has been displaced by English, as has that of many Native American peoples.

In summary, the significant instructional features of the most frequently cited bilingual program models are:

1. the *function* given each language in the curriculum: as a subject or medium of instruction
2. the *domains* of each language in the curriculum: which subjects are taught in each language; the language of classroom routines
3. the *status* of each language; as a bridge to the mainstream language or as a resource with the status in its own right, operationally defined by the *length of time the language is maintained* as a medium of instruction or as a subject in the curriculum
4. the *extent of skills development* of each language: listening, speaking, reading, writing, in the curriculum

Only González has explicitly included in a bilingual program model the *cultural* context of both languages. This is broadly defined as the inclusion of the history and culture of the speakers of the marked languages, as an integral part of the curriculum. Further, the importance of student grouping is included in the González model, that is,

5. the *participation of students who are native speakers* of English as well as native speakers of the marked language in the bilingual program. This provides the possibility of the program being a two-way rather than one-way program (Stern, 1963) in which native English speakers learn the marked language from peers instead of as a "foreign language." This model has other implications, i.e., learning of English from native-English-speaking peers as well as the teachers. The necessity for including the sociocultural context of bilingual program models is clearer if we consider a specific model.

If we examine the immersion model, some of the contradictions emerge. Ignoring the historical context of "immersion" and the SES of the students which, as we have noted, is associated with different outcomes, Bernal (1977) suggests the use of the very process which most bilingual educators in the U.S. have criticized as inadequate for lower SES Hispanic students. Instead of the use of *two* languages as mediums of instruction, the "immersion" program is limited to English—thus making this so-called bilingual program model indistinguishable from the usual practice of monolingual education in the United States for the first two years. Not until the home language is introduced as a subject, in the third year, is the program bilingual. Do we not have an operational definition of bilingual education that provides for the use of both languages as mediums of instruction and learning? Why wait until third grade to include the home language and allow a child to suffer culture shock?

This immersion model was taken from the St. Lambert Canadian experiment and its Redwood City replication. In both these programs, participating students were speakers of the higher status language and/or were middle SES. As Christina B. Paulston (1975) has noted concerning the factor of SES:

> The research findings are quite clear on one point. Upper and middle class children do perfectly well whether they are schooled in the mother tongue or in L_2 although we don't really know why. Elitist bilingual education has never been an educational problem.

The applicability of this immersion model for working-class Hispanic students is doubtful. One wonders about a model which Bernal admits involves asking teachers to try to "understand and deal with the cultural shock the children will experience" and "be supportive of the children's language and culture without addressing them in their native language."

The latter is an example of the lack of a theoretical framework leading to incompatible methodology. In the immersion model, effective materials are included to "handle concepts and attitudes toward development of cultural acceptance" and "to present an awareness of differences in cultures as an acceptable and positive concept"..." *but only in the target (second) language.*" It seems to be overlooked that the home language of the students is a crucial aspect of their culture. So are their patterns of interaction with one another and adults, such as the cultural expectation of respect accorded to parents. Thus, the immersion model is in practice inimical to acceptance of the students' culture during the first two years of the program.

The inadequate definition of the role of culture in bilingual programs is an issue that needs clarification. In both the behaviorist and the immersion models as described by Bernal, "culture" is interpreted as an external entity which can be slotted into the curriculum at specified times, instead of regarded as an on-going pervasive integrating process. For example, Bernal states:

> This involvement (by parents in ethnic-specific cultural activities) could be part of the larger program of learning and culturally enriching activities which may range from "festivities" conducted at the school to extracurricular educational experiences such as field trips. Parents of the children must take a generally supportive role although their participation in everyday classroom activities is sharply curtailed.

The inclusion of the immersion model without regard to the socioeconomic context of the students and statements such as the above suggest the need for an anthropological framework for bilingual/multicultural programs.

Theoretical Framework

Christina Bratt Paulston (1975) has long supported the importance of historical, political and structural context as the independent variable in research studies with bilingual education as the dependent variable. The studies by Skutnabb-Kangas and Toukomaa (1975, 1977), in Troike (1978), in conjunction with those of Lambert and Tucker (1972) and Andrew Cohen (1975) demonstrate the importance of this context variable and also of the theoretical framework of conflict theory from which it was derived. A conflict theoretical framework "emphasizes the inherent instability of social systems and views conflict as a commonly occurring consequence of interaction. Change is assumed to be a natural result of contact and conflict" (Arvizu, 1978: 5).[2]

These recent studies have given empirical support to the significance of socioeconomic and political contexts of bilingual programs as the most important independent variables in bilingual education research. This can be seen in the comparison that can be made between the learning of French as a second language by English-speaking Anglo-Canadians from a middle class, economically dominant group in their society (Lambert and Tucker, 1972) as compared to the learning of English as a second language by lower SES Spanish-speaking students in the U.S. and the Finnish migrant students to Sweden. As reported by Troike, (1978), Skutnabb-Kangas and Toukomaa found that the dominated minority Finnish students showed different learning outcomes depending on their length of native language learning in their own country. The Finnish students who migrated to Sweden when they were between ten and twelve years old, and thus had five or six years of education in Finnish, were "much more likely to approach the norms of Swedish" than the Finnish students who had immigrated to Sweden when they were of pre-school or primary age and had participated longer in the "immersion" in Swedish as a second language. The early "immersion" in the second language was the same process for all three groups (Anglo-Canadian, Finnish and Spanish-speaking Americans). The crucial difference seems to be the socioeconomic status of the student group.

The students from an economically dominant group in Canada fared much better than did the students from the subordinate minority group with low SES in both the U.S. and Sweden.

Bilingual Program Models

The findings of Skutnabb-Kangas and Toukomaa (1976, 1977) also point to another issue. There needs to be more specificity about the processes involved in "bilingual education." The research cited has demonstrated that students of the same ethnolinguistic group and SES who have a longer period of time to master their native language do better in learning their second language than students taught with the concurrent method of learning skills in *both* languages at the same time without first mastery of the native language.

I would suggest that bilingual education program models need to be based in specific learning theories which are compatible in order to guide the development of components which mutually support or supplement one another to become a coherent, cohesive whole. For example, the theoretical base might be Piaget's developmental paradigm of interactive learning, Gattegno's child initiated rule-generation in the "Silent Method" of language and mathematical learning, Montessori's active learning model or behaviorist reinforcement learning theory which forms the basis for the audiolingual method of second language acquisition. Each of these theories suggest a particular classroom organization and role for the student, the teacher, peer learning and interaction with materials. Several of the theories are compatible; some are in opposition. I contend that a bilingual program model, analogous to any system, needs to have components which articulate and interact compatibly toward specified goals. Two examples of integrated bilingual program models are given in the table below from Saravia-Shore (1977).

To illustrate, in a program based on behaviorist theory as in Table 2, only an English-speaking teacher is necessary to offer a model of ESL and reinforce the limited-English-speaking students' imitation of the modeled behavior. By contrast, in the program based on Piagetian developmental theory, native English-speaking students would be integrated with the English-language learners for a significant portion of the day since the theory posits that students are active learners with a purpose, to communicate with other children in the second language.

Therefore, behavioral learning theory is compatible with learning ESL as a subject in one-way programs where limited-English-speaking students are separated for most of the day (dominance segregation) and in pull-out

TABLE 2

TWO BILINGUAL/MULTICULTURAL PROGRAM MODELS, WITH CONGRUENT DISTINCTIVE FEATURES

	GOALS:	
LANGUAGES:	Developmental	Transitional
CULTURE:	Pluralism	Assimilation
SOCIAL STRUCTURE:	Structural Integration	Structural Integration
MODEL:	*CHILD DEVELOPMENTAL*	*BEHAVIORIST* (Audiolingual)
	Process-oriented Piaget, Chomsky	Product oriented following Skinner
	Teacher speaks L_1 and L_2	Teacher Models L_2
	Aide speaks L_1	Aide speaks L_1
	Dominance Integration	Dominance Segregation
	L_2 acquired from peers in natural settings	
	Two-way program	One-way program
	Ethnic culture is integral	Token cultural activities
	Parent Advisory role	Token parent involvement
	Pluralistic context	Mainstream cultural context
	Experiential, multicultural curriculum	Objective-based curriculum
	Languages separated	Languages separated
	Curriculum content learned in L_1 first	Curriculum content taught in L_2
	Integration of reading and content	ESL is a subject
	Reading learned first in L_1	Reading learned first in L_2
	Gradual intro to L_2	Rapid intro to L_2
	Language-Experience approach	L_1 is a subject
	Bilingual Program articulated with Monolingual	Pull-out program

programs. However, pull-out programs in which limited-English students only have the teacher as the model for the second language would not be compatible with the Piagetian developmental learning theory, whereas two-way programs in which students learn their second language from interaction with other students who speak that language in structured learning activities (dominance integration) would be.

The necessity for a holistic theoretical framework can be seen in the selection of a model appropriate to the political and economic context, such as the status of the marked language, the extent to which the marked language is spoken in the community and by whom. Furthermore, a comprehensive holistic model is necessary to prevent the components from working at cross-purposes, as can also be seen in Bernal's description of the immersion model in the U.S. context.

Saravia-Shore (1977) suggested considering language components as feature variations of a total bilingual program model. This was prompted by the contradictions of another perspective on bilingual program models presented by Bernal (1977) at the N.I.E. Conference on the Dimensions of Bilingual Education Research. Bernal presented five pairs of field-based models:

1. translation vs. alternation
2. "pull-out" vs. integral
3. transitional vs. developmental
4. dominance segregation vs. dominance integration
5. simultaneous introduction of second language vs. delayed introduction of second language

Bernal also suggested four theoretical-empirical models:

1. behaviorist
2. eclectic
3. immersion
4. child-centered

The labels of the five field-based models give some indication of the lack of a comprehensive conceptual framework for bilingual program models. First, program goals such as "transitional" and "developmental" are used to label some models while a specific language methodology, i.e., "translation" vs. "alternation" is used to characterize another set of "models" and *structural* factors, such as "pull-out" vs. "integral", are used to characterize two other "models". Learning theories are used for still others, "the behaviorist" and the "child-centered".

When Bernal combined these "models" into a matrix, he noted that certain models were mutually exclusive which, nevertheless, yielded a total of fifty-two separate "models." As a result of the lack of a comprehensive theoretical framework underlying these models, other contradictions which were not noted as mutually exclusive, remain.

For example, in Bernal's matrix, the "child-centered" model is presented as compatible with translation, alternation, developmental, dominance segregation, dominance integration and simultaneous introduction of second language, (delayed introduction of the second language is omitted). However, in the actual implementation of the child developmental model based on Piagetian and Chomskian approaches, how could the "translation" approach be included? Or how could "dominance segregation" be used if you expect students to acquire their second language as they acquired their first in natural language settings with peers who speak the second language? This is not to say that bilingual programs with approaches incompatible with their stated goals do not exist, because they do. But they are *not* models.

The sociocultural context of bilingual programs cannot be ignored. In the program models presented in Table 2, the alternatives of a "mainstream cultural context" and a "pluralistic context" are included. Other cultural feature variations are also indicated, such as the role of parents, either as advisory or "token" participants, and alternatives such as "token" cultural activities as compared to the ethnic culture being integral to the curriculum, in the respect shown to the values and expectations concerning interactions among adults and children, for example.

For the past ten years, bilingual education has been primarily influenced by educational psychologists and second language teachers. Behaviorist learning theory and the audio-lingual method have been prevalent in teacher training institutions. The evaluation of bilingual education programs has also been dominated by educational psychologists and behaviorism. Although the comparative cross cultural approach and the study of cultures has been the domain of anthropology, this discipline has had relatively little impact on bilingual program implementation.

Taking this situation into account, a resolution was recently passed by the American Anthropological Association concerning the need to make culture an integral part of educational planning. The resolution defined culture as:

1. Culture is intimately related to language and the development of basic communication, computation and social skills;
2. Culture is an important part of the dynamics of the teaching-learning process in all classrooms, both bilingual and monolingual;
3. Culture affects the organization of learning, pedagogical practices, evaluative procedures and rules of schools, as well as instructional activities and curriculum;
4. Culture is more than the heritage of a people through dance, food, holidays and history. Culture is more than a component of bilingual education programs. It is a dynamic, creative and continuous process which includes behaviors, values, and substances shared by people that guides them in their struggle for survival and gives meaning to their lives. As a vital process it needs to be understood by more people in the United States, a multiple society which has many interacting cultural groups.[3]

A related dimension of bilingual programs which needs to be taken into account in research is the *structural* context. In my experience, based on observation of various bilingual programs, the position of the bilingual program within the social structure of the school is important. The structural context of either articulation with the regular, monolingual education program or isolation from it, is significant. Such structural features as whether or not the program is a total bilingual school or a minischool or separate annex with its own coordinator or discrete, isolated classes which lack coordination with the monolingual program or support services available to monolingual students should be included in research on the effectiveness of different bilingual program models.

In summary, in order to build a cumulative knowledge base on the effectiveness of bilingual education program models, a holistic, ethnographic paradigm of research/evaluation synthesizing qualitative and quantitative research methodologies is suggested. The scope of research would then encompass the sociocultural context in which bilingual programs function. This sociocultural context would include the community context of the school, the SES of the students as well as the articulation of the bilingual program within the social structure of the school.

The ethnographic research/evaluation model also avoids some of the lacunae of the behavioral research/evaluation model. The latter is characterized by Bernal (1977) when he states:

> This operational definition of the Developmental Model, then, is based on its *effects;* how the school achieves this (so long as it is doing something) is only of secondary importance.

I would argue that in order to distinguish between models and to be able to replicate models, it is crucial to operationally define the procedures, methodologies and structural features of the bilingual program model being implemented.

Bilingual program models can be defined more adequately through the process of intensive on-site participant observation guided by comprehensive cross-cultural learning theory. Interviews of program developers and teachers can make their learning theory explicit. Observations of the implementation of the approaches can be made informally as well as documented in narrative, videotape and checklist form.

The structured and informal interrelationships of bilingual and monolingual teachers, administrators and students can also be better understood through participant observation, network analysis and informal interviews than through paper and pencil attitude questionnaires.

As noted by Fishman (1974), feelings and attitudes such as fears for job security among monolingual English-speaking administrators and teachers "are part of the social context of bilingual education and may well determine the success or failure of any program . . ." (Fishman, 1974: 347).

The outcomes of bilingual/multicultural/cross-cultural education programs can also be more adequately assessed through multiple methods of data gathering such as informal observation and interviews as well as criterion-referenced tests rather than solely through standardized tests of achievement. Cumulative research over several years of program participation would also more adequately assess the outcomes of different bilingual program models.

NOTES

1. Harrington (1975).
2. Conflict theory cannot be adequately covered here. For further explication see:
   Cohen, Percy S. *Modern Social Theory* New York: Basic Books, Inc., 1968.

Paulston, Roland G. *Conflicting Theories of Social and Educational Change A Typological Review,* UCIS University of Pittsburgh, 1976.

3. This excerpt is from the resolution on culture in educational planning submitted by Steven F. Arvizu and Margaret Gibson of the Cross Cultural Resource Center, California State University at Sacramento, to the Council on Anthropology and Education. The resolution was passed by the CAE and a shorter version was passed by the American Anthropological Association at its Annual Meeting in November, 1978.

REFERENCES

Arvizu, Steven F. "Home-School Linkages: A Cross Cultural Approach to Parent Participation" in Arvizu, et al. *A Cross Cultural Approach to Parent Participation.* Sacramento: Cross Cultural Resource Center, California State University, Sacramento. 1978.

Bank, Adrianne. "The Uses of Teaching Models in Planning and Evaluation." *Evaluation Comment:* The Journal of Educational Evaluation. Los Angeles: The Center for the Study of Evaluation, UCLA, Vol. 5, No. 1, 1975.

Bernal, Ernest. "Dimensions of Bilingual Education: A Look at the Real World." Washington, D.C.: Unpublished commissioned paper presented to N.I.E. Conference, February 14-16, 1977.

Cohen, Andrew D. *A Sociolinguistic Approach to Bilingual Education: Experiments in the American Southwest.* Rowley, Mass: Newbury House, 1975.

Cole, Michael; Gay, John; Glick, Joseph A. and Sharp, Donald W. *The Cultural Context of Learning and Thinking: An Exploration in Experimental Anthropology.* New York: Basic Books, Inc., 1971.

DeAvila, Edward. "Preliminary Report on Instructional Implications of Cognitive Styles." Paper read to Annual Meeting of American Educational Research Association. Toronto, Ontario, Canada, 1978.

Erickson, Fred. "Some Approaches to Inquiry in School-Community Ethnography." Washington, D.C.: *Anthropology and Education Quarterly.* Special Issue: Exploring Qualitative/Quantitative Research Methodologies in Education, Vol. VIII, No. 2, May, 1977.

Fishman, Joshua and Lovas, T. "Bilingual Education in Sociolinguistic Perspective." *TESOL Quarterly,* 4:3, 1970.

Fishman, Joshua A. A Sociology of Bilingual Education. Final Report of research under contract OECO-73-0588, Division of Foreign Studies, Dept of HEW, USOE. 1974.

Fitz-Gibbon, Carol Taylor and Morris, Lynn Lyons. "Theory-Based Evaluation." *Evaluation Comment:* The Journal of Educational Evaluation, Vol. 5, No. 1, June, 1975.

González, J. M. "Coming of Age in Bilingual/Bicultural Education: A Historical Perspective." *Inequality in Education.* No. 19 February, 1975.

Grannis, Joseph C. "Community, Competence and Individuation: The Effects of Different Controls in Educational Environments." *IRCD Bulletin.* Institute for Urban and Minority Education, Teachers College, Columbia University, Spring, Vol. X, No. 2. 1975.

Harrington, Charles C. "A Psychological Anthropoligist's View of Ethnicity and Schooling." *IRCD Bulletin,* Vol. X, No. 4, Fall, 1975.

Lacey, Colin. *Hightown Grammar: The School as a Social System.* Manchester: Manchester University Press, 1970.

Lee, Lee C. "Assessing Communicative Competence via the Repertoire Model." Paper prepared for the National Panel on Head Start Profiles of Program Effects on Children. Agency for Children, Youth and Families. 1979.

Lambert, Wallace E., Tucker, G. Richard. *Bilingual Education of Children: The St. Lambert Experiment.* Rowley, Mass: Newbury House Publisher, 1972.

Mackey, W. F. in Andersson and Boyer, M. *Bilingual Schooling in the United States.* Austin, Texas: Southwest Education Development Laboratory. 1970.

National Institute of Education. *Multicultural/Bilingual Division Fiscal Year 1976 Program Plan.* Washington, D.C.: National Institute of Education. U.S. Department of Health, Education & Welfare. 1976-78.

Ogbu, John. *The Next Generation: An Ethnography of Education in an Urban Neighborhood.* New York: Academic Press, Harcourt Brace Jovanovich, 1974.

Paulston, Christina Bratt. "Ethnic Relations and Bilingual Education: Accounting for Contradictory Data." Toronto: *Travaux de Recherches sur le Bilinguisme.* Ontario Institute for Studies in Education, No. 6, May, 1975.

Ramírez, III, Manuel and Castañeda, Alfredo. *Cultural Democracy, Bicognitive Development and Education.* New York: Academic Press, 1974.

Rist, Ray. *The Urban School: A Factory for Failure.* Cambridge, Massachusetts: M I T Press, 1973.

Saravia-Shore, Marietta. Review of "Dimensions of Bilingual Education Research: A Look at the Real World." Washington, D.C.: National Institute of Education. Unpublished commissioned paper for Conference on Dimensions of Bilingual Education Research, February 14-16, 1977.

Saville-Troike, Muriel and Troike, Rudolph. *A Handbook of Bilingual Education.* Washington, D.C.: TESOL. 1971.

Seelye, H. Ned and Navarro, Billie. *A Guide to the Selection of Bilingual Education Program Designs.* Chicago, Illinois: Bilingual Education Service Center and Department of Bilingual Bicultural Education, Illinois Office of Education. n.d.

Stufflebeam, Daniel L., et. el. Chair, Phi Delta Kappa National Study Committee on Evaluation. *Educational Evaluation and Decision Making.* Itasca, Illinois: F.E. Peacock, 1971.

Troike, Rudolph C. *Research Evidence for the Effectiveness of Bilingual Education.* Rosslyn, Virginia: National Clearinghouse for Bilingual Education. 1978.

Tyler, Ralph W. *Basic Principles of Curriculum and Instruction.* Syllabus for Education 360. Chicago, Illinois: University of Chicago Press, 1950.

Zappert, Laraine T. and Cruz, B. Roberto. *Bilingual Education: An Appraisal of Empirical Research.* Berkeley, California: Bay Area Bilingual Education League/Lau Center, Berkeley Unified School District. 1977.

THE IMPACT OF DESCRIPTIVE AND EVALUATIVE RESEARCH OF BILINGUAL EDUCATION PROGRAMS ON FEDERAL, STATE AND LOCAL PUBLIC POLICY

Lester S. Golub

The title of this paper suggests that in the world of bilingual education, where Congress has established a compensatory education program for limited-English-proficiency pupils in the public schools, descriptive and evaluative research would have been conducted on a few demonstration programs before large scale implementation and funding of these programs was begun. This is not necessarily so. A bilingual education concept has evolved which permits children and students to learn subject matter in their native language while mastering control of English. Thus federally and eventually statutorily supported bilingual education (under Title VII of the Elementary and Secondary Education Act) was born and is on its way to becoming a restless teenager. The program has been operationalized, legislated, and mandated long before assumptions underlying their worth were validated through research and evaluation. The implementation of a socially motivated, innovative, educational program, such as bilingual education, usually precedes the research and evaluation of the underlying assumption of the program. The results of formative, descriptive, and evaluative research should make an impact on a program. The major function of descriptive and evaluative research is to provide data for public policy and decision makers at the federal, state, and local levels for program implementation and modification (Alkin, Kosecoff, Fitz-Gibbon, and Seligman, 1974).

Education as a social science generally tends to implement an instructional program as determined by needs, politics, fashion, philosophy. Then, if there are funds, human resources, and the determination available, the innovative program might be evaluated in a variety of ways. The model is not an irrational one since it means development and implementation of the program, research to evaluate the program, and then, based on the research data, modification and refinement or abandonment of the program. Bilingual education as a child of the late sixties is just moving into the descriptive and evaluative research stage. Thus, in this paper, impacts on bilingual education public policy will not necessarily be attributed to the results of descriptive and evaluative research, but rather will attempt to show where public policy changes have occurred concurrently with the result of descriptive or evaluative research.

The purpose of this paper is to examine descriptive and evaluative research which attempts to answer some of the following questions: (1) Are limited-English-proficiency, (LEP), pupils in bilingual education programs achieving in reading, writing, and using oral language at a predetermined criterion level in two languages? (2) Are LEP pupils achieving in subject matter at a predetermined criterion level? (3) Are LEP pupils' attitudes toward self, home, school, and community positive or at parity with pupils in monolingual English programs in the same school or in similar schools? (4) Do pupils in bilingual education programs and in monolingual English programs have a predetermined level of awareness of the cultural groups in contact? (5) What are the effects of three models of bilingual education, (transitional, maintenance, and immersion) on the target population? (6) What is public opinion toward bilingual education in communities where local, state, and federal funding is being used to support these programs?

Not all of the above questions are directly answerable in the current research literature emanating from bilingual education. However, the above questions are those which federal and state legislators and local program decision makers ask. The answers and points of view presented here are those which are generally available and which shape attitudes and decisions of these policy makers.

The methodology of this paper consists of addressing such areas of concern in bilingual education as: (1) establishing needs and policy toward bilingual education, (2) funding sources, (3) legal statutes, legislation, and mandates, (4) teacher training, certification, and staff development, (5) program quality control and program evaluation. Where appropriate, these areas of concern attempt to convey the point of view of federal and state legislators and local program policy makers.

In order to exit from this paper with understanding, we should enter the paper with an understanding of some basic terms such as: impact, descriptive research, evaluative research, bilingualism, bilingual education, legislation, litigation, mandate and the law, program policy, and public policy, as they are used here.

Impact. The change in direction or velocity caused by one set of data or theory on another set of data or theory can be termed impact. In bilingual education, we might expect that such a program would impact the clients so that more of them would complete high school and attend college than did without the program. Data is needed to determine this impact.

Descriptive Research. Descriptive research is a legitimate form of research in education which attempts to describe a condition in a systematic way. The style is usually descriptive-narrative, and generally lacks statistical analysis although census type statistics are frequently part of a descriptive research study. An example of a descriptive research study could be the report of the needs assessment to determine the feasibility of a bilingual education program. Frequently descriptive research precedes evaluative research.

Evaluative Research. Evaluative research deals with objective measures which can be used for making decisions. Evidence of bilingual education program impact should be based on objective measures obtained from representative pupil samples. Achievement gain measures should be evident for program participants and for a comparable control group. Preprogram, baseline data or comparison with an appropriate norm-referenced group is also acceptable in evaluative research of bilingual education program.

An evaluative-research model for bilingual education should include: (1) context evaluation, a description and analysis of the program to be evaluated including its goals and objectives; (2) input evaluation, a description of the capabilities and procedures of the program agency for achieving the program goals and objectives; (3) management system evaluation, a description of the program implementation strategy; (4) process evaluation, a description of the documentation of the implementation stages of the program; and (5) product evaluation, a description of the qualitative and quantitative achievement of the goals and objectives of the program. The product evaluation should include a formative evaluation at intermediate levels of program development and a summative evaluation at a terminal state of program development.

The evaluative-research design is not a true experimental design, yet it must have either a control group, preprogram or entry baseline data, or norm-referenced data. The very nature of bilingual-bicultural education mitigates against rigorous experimental, control, and random assignment design since the Office of Civil Rights and the *Lau* remedies make it mandatory that all pupils in need of linguistic instruction in English receive it. The population is unique, culturally and linguistically. Instructional programs are typically loosely designed and measurement problems are acute.

ESEA, Title VII funding of bilingual-bicultural programs requires a quantitative estimate of pupil growth both in English, L2, and the home language, L1, (*Federal Register, 1976*). Readily accessible language tests such as the *Test of Reading, Inter-American Series* (1966) and the *Language Assessment Battery* (1976) developed by the Board of Education of the City of New York, have very limited and poorly defined norming groups. Limited-English-proficiency students may be assessed in their English proficiency by using norm-referenced English language tests, particularly English reading tests; however, such tests have been normed on native speakers of English. Little, if any, published research is available to indicate how groups of non-native speakers of English respond to these tests.

Without extensive statistical analysis, locally constructed or criterion-referenced instruments preclude non-native comparisons, and as a result will have little or no impact on federal and state legislation or even on local program policy and decision making. If federal, state, and local bilingual education public policy and decision making are to result from descriptive and evaluative research, then appropriate evaluation tools and well-coordinated information dissemination are necessary.

Bilingualism. Most persons think of a bilingual person as one who can speak two languages, each with control like that of a native speaker. Although such a definition on the surface seems reasonable, in reality it does not apply to children in a bilingual education program. A bilingual child in the sense used in this paper is one who has the potential of becoming bilingual (Foster, 1976). Such a child speaks a first language other than English and has or is obtaining some knowledge of English and is in a program which will attempt to make the child literate (listen, think, speak, read, and write) in English and possibly literate in the native language as well. Bilingualism is also considered from a socioeconomic perspective since bilingual clients in such a program are tied to the "culturally disadvantaged." The need for these children to learn English is seen as an economic need in a socially mobile society; whereas, the need for these children to use their native tongue is seen from a psychological advantage, raising the self-esteem of the child, and continuing the educational process of the child at the point of entry into the classroom. The bilingual children serviced in bilingual education programs are national minorities, Mexican-American and Puerto Ricans who generally display low achievement rates, low school holding power, overagedness, and minimal participation in extracurricular activities. Localized minorities such as Italians, Germans, Polish, French became Americanized (socialized) between 1880 and 1930. A few indigenous minorities, Eskimos, Aleuts, native Hawaiian, American Samoans, and native American Indians, though not always fluent in the indigenous language find themselves in bilingual education programs for social and psychological reasons and this can be justified on the grounds of ability grouping rather than linguistic grouping. This definition of bilingualism puts limited-English-proficiency students in bilingual education when they are considered to be the member of a disfavored class.

Bilingual Education. With the passage of the Bilingual Education Act in 1968, school districts, some with federal funds in hand and others out of pocket, provide a variety of educational structures, all conceived to meet the needs of the "bilingual" pupil. Bilingual education is a formalized response to the educational needs of "disadvantaged" national minorities who maintain a viable ethnic identity. The social and political function of the bilingual education program determines its form. If the social and political function is to have separate or integrated classes, then two languages will be recognized as a characteristic of the program. If the function of the bilingual education program is to assimilate or mainstream the "bilingual" child, then only one language will be recognized by the school staff.

No two bilingual education classrooms will look alike, but generally, bilingual education programs can be characterized as follows, depending on the function of the program:

1. mixed classes—assimilation: transition to English - not aimed at dual language skills.
2. separate classes—assimilation: This is characteristic of large urban schools where students can stay in bilingual education classes until they can be phased into the regular school program.
3. mixed classes—pluralism: This model is most often considered to be the predominant bilingual education model, even though the guidelines for federal funding require the transitional model. This is a low-keyed maintenance model.
4. separate classes—pluralism: This is the most radical maintenance model which can be found in Indian and Chicano schools where the ethnic language and culture is used exclusively for instruction. English is supplemental.

Using social and political functions of bilingual education as a description of the bilingual education program is different from the operational description of bilingual education models such as: (1) transitional (Grubb, 1976), (2) maintenance (Bequer, 1978), and (3) immersion (Beebe, 1978). In classifying bilingual education program models, look first at the social and political function and form will be clear. The separate classes, assimilation model and the mixed-classes, pluralism model are most likely to be found where there is a large population of Puerto Rican or Chicano children; the mixed-classes, assimilation model is most often used for small ethnic groups.

An optimal elementary school bilingual education classroom, as perceived by a federal or a state leigslator, after reading within the bibliography of this paper, consists of a mix of approximately sixty percent bilingual education pupils and forty percent monolingual English pupils. All pupils will be pretested in September of each year and posttested in May of each year on their English language proficiency skills of listening, speaking, reading, and writing. Appropriate norm-referenced tests would be used. The bilingual pupils will be given a parallel version of these norm-referenced tests in the native language. In programs where compensatory bilingual education classes are separate, these classrooms, for comparison purposes, should be compared with a monolingual English classroom from the target school and should be socioeconomically and ethnically mixed to represent the normal multicultural mix of the school. Criterion-referenced tests in second and native language proficiency and subject matter achievement should be given at frequent intervals during the school year.

All children will receive subject matter instruction in clear and precise English with reinforcement in the native language. Recent research (Best, 1978) has shown that monolingual English students given science vocabulary in English and Spanish did significantly better on a criterion-referenced achievement test in the science concepts taught than did monolingual English students who were given the same vocabulary in English only. Reading and writing in English will be presented according to the needs of pupils as determined by an individualized, diagnostic-prescriptive procedure. Special classes will be provided for bilingual education pupils and monolingual English pupils, upon parental request and approval, in English as a second language and Spanish for Spanish speakers. The goal of the elementary program will be to develop English language proficiency to an optimum level for each student, based upon the student's entry level and capacity.

All classroom teachers will be certified as elementary school teachers, endorsed as bilingual education teachers with native or near native second language proficiency. Aides, where employed, will know the bilingual education children's native language. Teachers, aides, and administrators will maintain an instructional management system devised and updated for each individual pupil in the program. Parents and community will be advised of the program and will participate in the "cultures in contact" awareness components of the program. In such a program, transition to the monolingual English program takes place over a period of two to four years and is based on continuous progress testing and observation of pupils.

The secondary school program presents a somewhat different model. Pupils who enter the bilingual education program at the secondary school level will be those who have had most of their elementary school experience in the native language and might have learned some English through social contact. These pupils should be placed in mixed subject matter classrooms with bilingual education trained teachers. All instruction is to be given to all pupils in clear and concise English with reinforcement in the second language. All subject matter tests are to be presented in parallel forms. The English and second language proficiency tests are administered on the same model as the elementary school program. Special subject matter support is provided on an individualized, diagnostic-prescriptive model for the bilingual education pupils in their native language. The bilingual education students will also be provided with appropriate English language proficiency classes and Spanish for Spanish speakers where requested by the student and parents. Parents and community will be advisory and participatory.

Program and Public Policy. We are judged by others by what we do. A bilingual education program is in itself a public notice which expresses the values, methods, and skills of the institution implementing the program. Policy is concerned with public and private affairs. The way a bilingual education program is managed and administered demonstrates the controlling policy. For this reason, the declaration of the policy to the public lags considerably behind the demonstration of the program.

Legislation, Litigation, Mandate, and Law. Legislation can be considered to be the enactments of a legislative body such as the U.S. Congress or the California State Board of Education both of which have enacted guidelines governing bilingual education program legislation. Litigation is the process of bringing to the judicial procedures a controversy involving adverse parties or classes of parties as in the *Lau* v. *Nichols* dispute, so that legislation could be provided to prevent large numbers of LEP pupils from not receiving equal education. A mandate, as contrasted to a law, usually has no legal support, since it is usually an order or command of a superior to an underling. The Pennsylvania State Department of Education has mandated bilingual education procedures in schools where there are twenty or more students of the same language group. However, the mandate cannot be enforced since the Pennsylvania Department of Education is not a judicial or a legislative body.

IMPACTS ON PROGRAMS AND POLICY

The following discussion of impacts will follow a thematic model rather than a chronological or administrative model. The themes investigated at the federal, state, and local levels include: (1) establishing needs for bilingual education, (2) funding sources and concern, (3) legal statutes, legislation, and mandates, (4) teacher training, certification, and staff development, and (5) program quality control evaluation.

Establishing Needs and Goals for Bilingual Education Programs

As many as 2.5 million children in the United States primarily speak, read, and write a language other than English. These children are educationally disadvantaged because they cannot understand instruction traditionally given in English. Bilingual education is designed to teach these children English and to teach them subject matter in their native language so that they can progress through school.

Bilingual education theory was relatively new when the Bilingual Education Program was established in 1968. The program administered by the Office of Education, Department of Health, Education and Welfare, HEW, was intended to be a research and demonstration program, yet it was managed and administered as though it were an educational service program. Because inadequate plans were made to carry out, evaluate, and monitor the goals of the program, the Office of Bilingual Education has made little progress toward identifying effective ways of providing bilingual education instruction, training bilingual education teachers, and developing suitable teaching materials to help prevent this problem from reoccurring. The Comptroller General (U.S. General Accounting Office, GAO, 1976) has suggested that Congress establish legislative controls over future educational demonstration programs. These controls would require that federal agencies establish program goals, objectives, and milestones, and assess the program and report periodically to the Congress on its progress. In response to the GAO report, the Office of Education has provided responses which serve as policy:

1. The Office of Education and National Institute of Education are formulating a plan for systematically developing effective ways of providing bilingual education.
2. The Office of Education is revising program regulations to establish requirements which should improve project evaluation reports.
3. The Office of Education and the National Institute of Education are undertaking and planning several actions to explain the appropriateness of test instruments.
4. The Office of Education has reviewed the issue of limiting the number of English-speaking children allowed in the program. New guidelines of the Bilingual Education Act, Public Law 95-561, Educational Amendments of 1978, Title VII reflect these considerations.

Evans' "Study of State Programs in Bilingual Education," (U.S. Congress House of Representatives, 1977: 505-511) indicates that on the whole, states are playing a limited but growing role in bilingual education. The number of states which mandate or permit bilingual education has grown to forty. Ten states are still prohibited by law from giving classroom instruction in any but the English language. The needs and goals at the state level tend to: (1) implement "transitional" bilingual instructional programs (seventeen states); (2) establish special qualifications for the certification of bilingual education teachers (thirteen states); (3) provide local education agencies with supplementary funds in support of bilingual education (thirteen states); and (4) mandate a cultural component in bilingual instruction programs (thirteen states). Unfortunately, no quality control exists to measure the effectiveness of the State Education Agencies in performing or attaining these goals.

The GAO report makes a clear statement that the Office of Bilingual Education has not been managed as an educational demonstration program. The effect of this policy shows up in the fact that local bilingual education programs were not carefully documented and evaluated, nor were needs assessments conducted and goals established. Program descriptions are generally written by a free-lance writer or a teacher hired to write an article for public consumption (Beebe, 1978; Shender, 1975; Hall, 1976; Carpenter, 1977; Bequer, 1978; Drake, 1976; Grubb, 1976). The need for a bilingual education policy on program needs assessments and goal setting at the local level is outstanding. Without this, appropriate program evaluations are impossible to conduct.

The Development Associates Incorporated study (1977, a, b, c, d) of state programs in bilingual education is exceptional in that it also includes a descriptive evaluation of fifteen case studies of noteworthy local programs or projects which appear to have been effective in a particular area of bilingual education. The assumption in describing these noteworthy local projects is that ideas about programming, the materials and methodologies developed, and the evaluation procedures of these projects can be shared with other local programs throughout the country and in many cases replicated with similar results.

Funding Sources and Participation

Because Title VII was established as a demonstration program, the Office of Education originally intended that Local Education Agenices would absorb project costs after five years. However, beginning in school year 1974-75 projects could be funded for longer than five years where exceptional potential for achieving program goals were demonstrated, but could not be funded indefinitely. Federal funds totaling $374.9 million were appropriated for the program from its inception through fiscal year 1976. Ten states received 83.5 percent of available funding: New York, 13.7%; Massachusetts, 2.4%; Pennsylvania, 2%; New Jersey, 2.5%; Florida, 3%; California, 31.7%; Arizona, 2.9%; Colorado, 2.8%; New Mexico, 4.1%; and Texas, 18.4%. The number of federally funded projects has grown from 79 in 1969 to 425 programs in sixty-nine languages in 1978. About eighty-five percent of the projects are directed toward Spanish-speaking children. Languages include: (1) American Indian languages (2) European languages-French, Portuguese, Spanish, (3) Pacific Island languages-Chamorro, Palauan, Pouapean; (4) other languages-Chinese, Eskimo, Russian.

Federal policy is politically appealing and designed to meet the needs of large numbers of limited-English-proficiency pupils. One wonders how effective and manageable such a national program with such a large number of languages represented can be, even though it is politically useful to the politicians in the ten states receiving 83.5% of the funds.

Funding and participation at the state level is neither broad nor generous. Of the nineteen states operating state bilingual education programs in the 1975-76 school year, sixteen appropriated funds specifically for bilingual education ranging from $19 to $431 per student. However, only Colorado, Illinois, Massachusetts, Utah, and Puerto Rico allocated more state funds than they received from the federal government. All sixteen of the states which financially support bilingual education operate direct service programs in contrast to demonstration or experimental programs. Clearly, states are willing to expend money on bilingual education programs if someone hustles up the federal funds for the expenditure, otherwise they are not likely to spend funds on bilingual education.

Funding of bilingual education projects at the school district level is varied. Rarely are local projects supported from just one source of funds. In addition to local and state funds, eighteen federal programs provide some financial support to bilingual education projects. Ninety percent of federal funds supporting bilingual education are provided through ESEA Title I (thirty-seven percent) and Title VII (fifty-three percent). The final financial burden for compensatory bilingual education programs falls on the local education agencies. The *Lau* decision does not accept financing inability as an excuse for not offering necessary education to students of limited-English-speaking ability, especially if there are significant numbers of these students.

Legal Statutes, Legislation, and Mandates

Although bilingual education is federally and statutorily supported, it must be remembered that education is not a protected right under the constitution. What is protected under the Fourteenth Amendment is equal protection. In the *Lau* v. *Nichols* decision, it is equal education which is being affirmed, not bilingual education, and it is equal education for significant numbers of students where there are designated exit requirements, but nondesignated entry requirements. That is, if a child enters school without a knowledge of English and is not taught the language, then the child enters at a disadvantage and never obtains the exit requirements.

The memo from J. Stanley Pottinger, Director, Office of Civil Rights, to school districts with more than five percent national origin-minority group children prescribes procedures for conforming to the *Lau* decision:

1. The school district must take affirmative steps to rectify the language deficiency of limited-English-speaking ability pupils in order to open its instructional program to these students.
2. Districts must not assign limited-English-speaking ability pupils to classes for the mentally retarded on the basis of criteria which essentially measures English language skills.
3. Any ability grouping or tracking system used for these students must not operate as an educational dead-end or permanent track.
4. School districts must notify parents of their activities and programs for limited-English-speaking ability pupils.

Twenty states (Irizarry, 1978) have adapted legislation pursuant to bilingual education: Alaska, Arizona, California, Colorado, Connecticut, Illinois, Indiana, Louisiana, Maine, Massachusetts, Michigan, Minnesota, New Jersey, New Mexico, New York, Oregon, Rhode Island, Texas, Utah, and Wisconsin. Other states have simple mandates which are generally not public policy since they have no legislative backing or financial funding. The state laws are similar in that they all propose to develop English language skills and to provide an equal educational opportunity to the populations they are intended to serve. They differ in goals for native language, population served, types of program, length of time in program, and assessment requirements. In all cases, local programs will be affected by the provisions of the state.

As public policy unfolds in the legal and legislative domains of bilingual education, it is quite clear that the federal government is adamant about providing quality, equal education for disadvantaged, limited-English-proficiency students, so adamant that they have contributed and have authorized to be appropriated hundreds of millions of dollars to the effort, and are enforcing the *Lau* remedies, even though the Supreme Court statement of "substantial numbers" is ambiguous. The federal regulations expand the description of eligible clients to limited-English-proficiency (including listening, speaking, reading, and writing) students. This definition will open program eligibility to a larger group of students; in some cases, disadvantaged speakers of regional and socioeconomic dialects of English. Local education agencies have the legal and financial obligation to comply with federal statutes and regulations. The federal offices are counting on the local bilingual education programs to supply demonstration bilingual education programs, models, materials, documentation, and evaluations. The states are caught in the middle, attempting to satisfy all of their constituencies and on the whole remaining quite silent about their attitudes and public policy toward the right of non-English-speaking children to receive compensatory language instruction in English.

Teacher Training, Certification, and Staff Development

Objective evidence is lacking on whether students perform better because they have been taught by a bilingual education teacher who by definition would have fluency in the students' native language. Nevertheless, educators including U.S. Office of Education officials agree that additional bilingual education teachers are needed. Although there is a general surplus of elementary and secondary teachers, progress in training bilingual education teachers has been hampered by the capacity of colleges and universities to "retool" in order to provide the necessary training, and previous federally funded teacher training programs which have not been successful in meeting the need for bilingual education teachers.

In March 1974, the U.S. Office of Education estimated that about 1.8 to 2.5 million children needed bilingual education, and, using classroom student-teacher ratio of 30 to 1, estimated that the number of bilingual education teachers needed would range from 60,000 to 83,000. In the GAO report to Congress (1976), of the projects they reviewed only about twenty-seven percent of the teachers were bilingual and the majority had not received college training to teach in bilingual classrooms. Most local bilingual education project directors believed that the shortage of qualified teachers adversely affected the quality of instruction in their projects.

Initial bilingual education guidelines specified that project teachers have certain qualifications and competencies including: (1) bilingual capability, (2) training and teaching experience, using the language of the target population as a medium of instruction, (3) training and experience in teaching English as a second language, and (4) an awareness of the target student's culture. Waggonner (1977) has described states certification requirements for teachers of bilingual education programs. Arizona, California, Delaware, Illinois, Massachusetts, New Mexico, and Texas have separate certification for bilingual education teachers. Indiana, Michigan, New Jersey, Rhode Island have endorsement of the regular certificate, making a total of eleven states which have certification requirements as public policy for bilingual education teachers. All require proficiency in the language of the target population; Arizona, Illinois, Massachusetts, New Jersey, and Texas require bilingual methodology; California, Delaware, Michigan, New Jersey, and Texas require English as a second language methodology, and Arizona, California, Delaware, Massachusetts, Michigan, New Mexico, and Texas require field experience. The National Association of State Directors of Teacher Education and Certification has issued ten Bilingual-Bicultural Teacher Education Standards. The U.S. Office of Education has produced competencies for university programs in bilingual education (Acosta and Blanco, 1978).

Federal support for the education of bilingual education teachers and trainers of teachers is provided under Title VII and has increased the teaching capabilities of individuals at local education agency projects; national need for bilingual education teachers is still great. As long as thirty-nine states do not require bilingual education certification or endorsement, institutes of higher education in those states will not recognize the need to spend money on such a program unless they are federally funded.

Program Quality Control and Program Evaluation

Local bilingual education project evaluations, because they are not designated to provide comprehensive objective evidence of student progress reports, have been of little use to local and federal decision makers. However, local project evaluation reports are the only source of information regarding students' academic progress and serve as a basis of identifying projects worthy of replication. Because of the latitude which the U.S. Office of Education has given local programs in the preparation of evaluation reports, these reports have been inadequate for measuring the design and quality of a program, particularly for measuring program effects on student achievement. Evaluative reports are generally weak in: (1) statistical data in tests presented in different formats, making comparisons between projects difficult; (2) attempt to measure goals which were not stated in measurable terms, such as, rectifying unequal education opportunities, improve reading ability, develop self-confidence; and (3) contain minimal amounts of documentation in the nature, strength, and weaknesses of classroom activities. All too often, local program goals do not address federal bilingual education program goals: to make the student proficient in English, and to teach them subject matter in their native language until they can make good progress in English. In some local programs, the stated goals do not even relate to academic progress: enhance students' self-image, stimulate students' awareness of two cultures. The GAO report (1976) indicates that: directors of projects recommend students be tested in academic subjects, suggest which instruments ought to be used, and specify a format for presenting the test scores.

In 1974, the National Institute of Education contracted the American Institutes for Research in the Behavioral Sciences, Palo Alto, (1977) to conduct an evaluation of the national impact of ESEA Title VII Spanish/English bilingual programs. The data was collected during the 1975-76 school year, and the interim report was dated 1977. This AIR summary of impact of Title VII projects on student achievement and attitude toward school indicates:

1. Both Title VII and non-Title VII student achievement in English language arts was at approximately the twentieth percentile at pretest and posttest.
2. Non-TitleVII Hispanic students had a higher mean score in English language arts but this was not reported as a significant difference.
3. Title VII Hispanic students generally performed better than non-Title VII Hispanic students in mathematics computation.
4. Title VII Hispanic students made gains in Spanish reading from pretest to posttest.

5. Participation in a Title VII project did not affect attitudes toward school-related activities.

Because of the sharp criticism of the student achievement data collection (Troike, 1977), it would be irresponsible to draw policy statements from this student achievement data other than large amounts of federal funds should not be allocated to inexperienced evaluators in any field, particularly one as specialized as bilingual education.

However, the AIR report does have some interesting ancillary findings which should not be ignored and are being used for public policy making:

1. Approximately seventy-five percent of students in Title VII Spanish/English bilingual education programs were of Hispanic origin; however, less than thirty-three percent had limited-English-speaking ability as judged by the teachers.
2. Almost all of the teachers and most of the aides had been involved in inservice or district workshops in bilingual education.
3. Two-thirds of the teachers and aides had two or more years experience in bilingual education.
4. Two-thirds of the teachers and aides indicated that they spoke both English and Spanish.
5. Eighty-five percent of the project directors indicated that pupils remain in the bilingual education program, even after they obtain fluency in English.
6. The per pupil cost for Title VII students ranged from $1127 to $2120 with an average of $1398.

The public policy resulting from the AIR report will be: (1) closer attention to program quality control in the form of student achievement data, (2) federal funding going to more projects, thus reducing the per pupil cost for students in Title VII programs. Many districts will have to finance their own program from regular local and state funding. (3) less federal funding going to inservice training, with more attention going specifically to training, certification and endorsement of teachers to fill the need in non-Title VII bilingual education programs.

One example of a thorough, useful and inexpensive bilingual education program evaluation of a non-Title VII program has been discussed by Golub (1978). This study sets up an evaluation design and test-time guideline. Data collection procedures are described for seven tasks: (1) measure of aural-oral language ability, Spanish and English; (2) measures of reading achievement, Spanish and English; (3) measures of achievement in subject matter, science, social studies, and math; (4) measure of knowledge of Puerto Rican culture; (5) measures of attitudes toward self, family, school, and community; (6) measures of classroom environment and classroom teaching; and (7) measures of attitudes of parents, teachers, and administrators. Pretest and posttest data, comparison between pupils in bilingual education and non-bilingual education classrooms, and achievement criterion levels were used. Since the *Lau* v. *Nichols* decision makes it illegal not to provide compensatory English language instruction to substantial numbers of LEP students, it is almost impossible to find a comparison group.

Other questions can be asked with the pupil performance data: (1) What percentage of students are transferred to monolingual English classes per year from the bilingual education program? (2) How well do bilingual pupils who are transferred to the monolingual English program function compared to their monolingual English classmates? (3) How does their percentile rank on reading test change? (4) How does the subject matter achievement of pupils in bilingual education classes compare with those in monolingual English classes? (5) How does attitude toward self, family, school, and community of bilingual education pupils change over the grades and compare with monolingual English pupils? Answers to these questions will take time to develop specifically for bilingual education programs.

In summary, although bilingual education as a federally funded concept was implemented without much research support, the whole concept of bilingual education is not alien to the national or international scene. The need was there and the method seemed obvious. Since 1968, research, both descriptive and evaluative, has taken place, slowly at first, more rapidly at present and not all of it on target. Public policy has evolved from two sources: (1) public opinion, as in the case of lagging state legislation and teacher certification bilingual education policy, and in the case of institutes of higher education where change and retraining of faculty seems to be an almost impossible or extremely time-consuming task. (2) descriptive and evaluative research which tends to produce reactionary behavior on the part of federal, state, and local officials.

Some areas of bilingual education which need descriptive and evaluative research are: (1) attitudes, self concept, cultural awareness and community impact, (2) needs assessment, proposal writing and review, (3) materials development, adaptation, and dissemination, and (4) program management and organizational communication.

In order to form public policy from descriptive and evaluative research, it is going to be necessary to set up a systematic research system directed precisely at answering reasonable, measureable, and precise policy type questions. Bilingual educators still do not have a classroom or program instructional model of bilingual education curriculum and materials. Bibliographies are available but a developmental program of study with scope and sequence within the curriculum for bilingual education is not. Individualized, diagnostic-prescriptive and management systems need development and research.

If these tasks are to be accomplished, a research and development Center of Bilingual Research will have to take on these responsibilities. The National Institute of Education is charged with the establishment of such a Center, which should be in place by 1980. The Center for Bilingual Research is designed to conduct research on language acquisition, language functioning, and bilingual education. This Center should work actively in answering the public policy type questions addressed in this paper.

BIBLIOGRAPHY

Acosta, Robert Kelly and Blanco, George. *Competencies for University Programs in Bilingual Education*. Washington, U.S. Office of Education. Superintendent of Documents, U.S. Government Printing Office, 1978.

U.S. Department of Health, Education, and Welfare, Publication Number OE78-07903.

Alkin, N. C., Kosecoff, J., Fitz-Gibbon, C., & Seligman, R. *Evaluation and Decision Making: The Title VII Experience.* Los Angeles: Center for the Study of Evaluation, University of California, Los Angeles, 1974.

American Institutes for Research in the Behavioral Sciences, Palo Alto, California. Evaluation of the impact of ESEA Title VII Spanish English Bilingual Education Program. Volume I: Study Design and Interim Findings, April, 1977 ED 138090.

American Institutes for Research in the Behavioral Sciences, Palo Alto, California. Evaluation of the impact of ESEA Title VII Spanish/English Bilingual Education Program, Volume II: Project Descriptions, ED 138091.

American Institutes for Research. Evaluation of the impact of ESEA Title VII Spanish/English Bilingual Education Programs. Los Angeles: National Dissemination and Assessment Center, California State University, Los Angeles, August 1978.

Appleton, Nicholas, *Multiculturalism and the Courts.* Los Angeles: National Dissemination and Assessment Center, California State University, Los Angeles, November 1978.

Beebe, Von N. "Spanish comes alive on La Isla Caribe." *Phi Delta Kappan,* 1978, *60*: 95.

Beezer, Bruce. "Bilingual Education and State Legislation." *Educational Forum,* 1977, *40*: 537-541.

Bequer, Marta M. A look at bilingual programs in Dade County. "Gateway to the Latin Worlds." *Educational Leadership,* 1978, *35*: 644-648.

Berdie, D., & Anderson, J. *Questionnaires: Design and Use.* Metuchen, N.J.: The Scarecrow Press, 1974.

Bernal, E. M. *Concept-learning among Anglo, Black, Mexican-American Children using Facilitation Strategies and Bilingual Techniques.* Unpublished doctoral dissertation, University of Texas at Austin, 1971.

Best, Nancy. *Effects of Spanish-English Vocabulary Instruction on Vocabulary and Content Learning, Self-concept and Social Distance in Secondary Science and Social Studies Classes With Hispanic and Nonhispanic Students.* Unpublished doctoral dissertation, The Pennsylvania State University, 1978.

"Bilingual Education - A Problem of Substantial Numbers?" *Fordham Urban Law Journal,* 1977, *5*: 561-572.

Bilingual Education Act. Rosslyn, Virginia: National Clearinghouse for Bilingual Education, January, 1979.

Bledgoe, Joseph C. "Self Concepts of Children and their Intelligence, Achievement, Interests, and Anxiety." *Childhood Education,* 1967, *43*: 436-438.

Bortin, Barbara H. Bilingual Program Evaluation: Processes and Problems. U.S. Educational Resource Information Center. ERIC Document Reproduction Service No. ED 137 350, April 1977.

Brisk, Maria Estela. Bilingual Higher Education Programs: Their Impact on Institutions and Community. Los Angeles: National Dissemination and Assessment Center, California State University, Los Angeles, October 1978.

Canedo, O. O. *Performance of Mexican-American Students on a Test of Verbal Intelligence*. Unpublished doctoral dissertation, International University, 1972.

Campell, D. T., & Stanley, J. C. Experimental and Quasi-experimental Designs for Research of Teaching. *Handbook of Research on Teaching*. Chicago: Rand McNally, 1963.

Carpenter, Iris. "Babel Reversed." *American Education*. 1977, *13*: 27-30.

Carter, David G. Brown, Frank, and Harris, J., John III. Bilingual-bicultural Education: A Legal Analysis: *Education and Urban Society*, 1978, *10*: 295-304.

Cazden, C., & Legget, E. L. Culturally Responsible Education: A Discussion of Lau Remedies II. Los Angeles: National Dissemination Center, California State University, Los Angeles, September 1978.

Center for Applied Linguistics. Bilingual Education: Current Perspectives. Volume I: Social Science; Volume 2: Linguistics; Volume 3: Law; Volume 4: Education; Volume 5: Synthesis. Arlington, Virginia: The Center for Applied Linguistics, 1978.

Center for Applied Linguistics. Guidelines for the Preparation and Certification of Teachers of Bilingual/Bicultural Education. Center for Applied Linguistics, Arlington, VA, November 1974.

Deane, Barbara and Zirkel, Perry A. "The Bilingual Education Mandate: It says schools must do something: must do it soon-and probably must find the money to get it done." *American School Board Journal*, 1975, *163*: 29-34.

DeAvilla, E. A., Sharon, C., "A Few Thoughts about Language Assessment: The Lau Decision reconsidered." Los Angeles: National Dissemination and Assessment Center, California State University, Los Angeles, March 1978.

Development Associates, Inc. Report on extra-state jurisdictions. A study of state programs in bilingual education (Supporting Volume I). U.S. Educational Resource Information Center. ERIC Document Reproduction Service No. ED 142 055, March 1977a.

Development Associates, Inc. Case studies of noteworthy project in bilingual education. A study of state programs in bilingual education (Supporting Volume II). U.S. Educational Resource Information Center. ERIC Document Reproduction Service No. ED 142 045, March 1977b.

Development Associates, Inc. Inventory of bilingual education provisions in state legislation. A study of state programs in bilingual education. (Supporting Volume III). U.S. Educational Resource Information Center. ERIC Document Reproduction Service No. ED., 142 053, March 1977c.

Development Associates, Inc. Final report on "A Study of State Programs in Bilingual Education." U.S. Educational Resource Information Center. ERIC Document Reproduction Service No. ED 142 056, March 1977d.

Drake, Diane. "Empowering Children Through Bilingual/Bicultural Education." *Educational Forum*, 1976, *40*: 199-204.

Epstein, Noel. *Language Ethnicity, and the Schools*. Policy alternatives for bilingual-bicultural education. Washington, D.C.: Institute for Educational Forum, 1976, *40*: 199-204.

Erickson, Fredrick. The Politics of Speaking: An Approach to Evaluating Bilingual/Bicultural Schools. Los Angeles: National Dissemination and

Assessment Center. California State University, Los Angeles, January 1978.

Escobedo, Theresa Herrera. Culturally Responsive Early Childhood Education Programs for Non-English-Speaking Children. Los Angeles: National Dissemination and Assessment Center. California State University, Los Angeles, April 1978.

Federal Register, Vol. 41, No. 69. Washington, D.C.: U.S. Government Printing Office, April 1977.

Fishman, J. Cooper, R. L., & Ma, R. *Bilingualism in the Barrio*. Bloomington: Indiana University, 1971.

Fishman, J. A., & Lovas, J. Bilingual Education in Sociolinguistics Perspective. *TESOL Quarterly*. 1970, *4*: 215-222.

Fong, Kevin, Cultural Pluralism. *Harvard Civil Rights - Civil Liberties Law Review*. 1978, *13*: 133-173.

Foster, William P. "Bilingual Education: An Educational and Legal Survey." *Journal of Law and Education*, 1976, *5*: 149-171.

Garcia, A. B., & Zimmerna, B. J. "The Effect of Examiner Ethnicity and Language on the Performance of Bilingual Mexican-American First Graders." *Journal of Social Psychology*, 1972, *87*: 3-11.

Golub, Lester S., Evaluation Design and Implementation of a Bilingual Education Program, Grades 1-12, Spanish/English. *Education and Urban Society*, 1978, *10*: 363- 384.

Golub L. S., Goslin, R. D., & Alemany, M. T. Opinion questionnaire for bilingual education. Questionario de Opiniones para la educación bilingue. University Park, PA: The Pennsylvania State University, 1976.

Goslin, R. E. *Language and Reading Factors as Indicators of Achievement in Science and Social Studies for Students in a Bilingual Education Program*. Unpublished doctoral dissertation, The Pennsylvania State University, 1978.

Grubb, Susan A. "Back of the Yards" Goes Bilingual. *American Education*, 1976 *12*: 15-18.

Gustafson, R. A., & Owens, T. R. The Self-concept of Mexican American Youngsters and Related Environmental Characteristics. U.S. Educational Resource Information Center. ERIC Document Reporduction Service No. ED 053 195, November 1971.

Hall, Beverly. "The Bilingual-Bicultural School." *Nation*, 1976, *223*: 519-522.

Hickey, T. "Bilingualism and the Measurement of Intelligence and Verbal Learning Abilities." *Exceptional Children*, 1975, *39*:24-28.

Horst, D. P., Tall Madge, C. K., & Wood, C. T. *A Practical Guide to Measuring Project Impact on Student Achievement*. Wasington, D.C.: Government Printing Office, 1975.

Iiams, Thomas M. "Gathering Storm over Bilingual Education." *Phi Delta Kappan*, 1977, *59*:226-230.

Ilivicky, Martin. Bilingual Education-Politics or Process. *NASSP National Association Secondary School Principals Bulletin*, 1976, *60*, 56-59.

Interamerican Research Associates. A bibliography of bilingual-bicultural preschool material for the spanish speaking child. Washington, U.S. Office of Human Development, 1977, Department of Health, Education, and Welfare, DHEW publication #ODH 77-31062 ED 142 045.

Irizarry, Ruddie A. Bilingual Education: State and Federal Legislative Mandates. Los Angeles: National Dissemination and Assessment Center, California State University, Los Angeles, California, 90032, 1978.

Language Assessment Battery. New York: Board of Education of the City of New York. Publisher, Houghton Mifflin Co., 1976.

Laosa, Luis M. "Viewing bilingual multicultural education television: an empirical analysis of children's behavior during television viewing." *Journal of Educational Psychology,* 1976, *68*: 133-142.

Law, Alexander I. Evaluating bilingual programs. U.S. Educational Resource Information Center. ERIC Document Reproduction Service No. ED 138 645, April 1977.

Lawrence, Gay. "Indian Education: Why Bilingual-Bicultural?" *Education and Society,* 1978, *10*:305-320.

Locks, N. A., Pletcher, B. A., & Reynods, D. F. *Language assessment instruments for limited-English speaking students: A needs analysis.* Washington, D.C.,: Department of Health, Education, and Welfare, National Institute of Education, 1978.

Macaulay, Ronald. Attitudes toward language and their importance for children's language learning. Los Angeles: National Dissemination and Assessment Center, California State University, Los Angeles, December 1977.

Mead, Margaret. "The Conservation of Insight-Educational Understanding of Bilingualism." *Teachers College Record,* 1978, *79*: 705-721.

Ovando, Carlos J. "School Implications of the Peaceful Latino Invasion." *Phi Delta Kappan,* 1977, *59*: 230-234.

Palomares, Geraldine D. The effects of stereotyping on the self-concept of Mexican-Americans. U.S. Educational Resource Information Center, ERIC Document Reproduction Service No. 056 806, March 1972.

Paulson, Christina Bratt. "Rationale for Bilingual Education Reforms: A Comparative Assessment." *Comparative Education Review,* 1978, *22*: 402-419.

Peleg, Ziva R. "Impact Assessment in the Evaluation of Bilingual Programs: Is it Feasible?" *Educational Technology,* 1978, *18*: 19-23.

Popham, E. J. *Educational Evaluation.* Englewood Cliffs, N. J. Prentice-Hall, 1975.

Saville-Troike, Muriel. Linguistic bases for bilingual education. Los Angeles: National Dissemination and Assessment Center. California State University, Los Angeles, September 1977.

Silverman, Robert J. and Russel, Randall H. "Relationships among three measures of bilingualism and academic achievement." *Education and Urban Society,* 1978, *10*: 347-362.

Silverman, R. J., Noa, J. K., & Russell, R. *Oral language tests for bilingual students; an evaluation of language dominance and proficiency instruments.* Portland, Oregon: Northwest Regional Education Laboratory, 1977.

Shender, Karen J. "Bilingual Education: How un-american can you get?" *Learning,* 1976, *5*: 32-41.

Smith, W. Elwood and Foley, Douglas E. "Mexican Resistance to Schooling." *Education and Urban Society,* 1978, *10*: 145-176.

Stake, R. E. "The Countenance of Educational Evaluation." *Teacher College Record* 1967, *68*:523-540.

Stufflebeam, D. I. *Educational Evaluation Decision Making.* Itasca, Ill: Peacock, 1971.

Swain, Merrill. "School Reform through Bilingual Education: Problems and Some Solutions in Evaluating Programs." *Comparative Education Review,* 1978, *22:* 420-433.

Teitelbaun, Herbert and Hiller, Richard J. "Bilingual Education: The Legal Mandate." *Harvard Educational Review,* 1977, *47:* 138-170.

Test of Reading, Inter-American Series, Levels, I, II, III, IV, V. San Antonio Texas: Guidance Testing Associates, 1966.

Troike, Rudolph C. Research evidence for the effectiveness of bilingual education. Rosslyn, Virginia: National Clearinghouse for Bilingual Education, 1978.

Troike, Rudolph C. Response to AIR study "Evaluation of the Impact of ESEA Title VII Spanish/English Bilingual Education Program." Arlington, VA: Center for Applied Linguistics, 1977.

Tyler, A. W. General statement on evaluation. *Journal of Educational Research,* 1942, *35:* 492-501.

U.S. General Accounting Office. Bilingual Education: An Unmet Need, Office of Education, report to the Congress by the Comptroller General of the United States. Washington, 1976.

U.S. Congress. House of Representatives. Committee on Education and Labor. Subcommittee on Elementary, Secondary, and Vocational Education. Part 3: Bilingual Education, Hearings, 95th Congress, 1st session on H. R. 15. June 7-9, 1977. Washington, U.S. Government Printing Office, 1977.

U.S. Congress Senate Committee on Human Resources. Education amendments of 1978: report to accompany S. 1753. Washington, U.S. Government Printing Office, 1978. 95th Congress, 2nd session. Senate Report no. 95-856.

Valverde, Leonard A. and Brown, Frank. "Equal education opportunity and bilingual-bicultural education: a socioeconomic perspective." *Education and Urban Society,* 1978, *10,* 277-294.

Waggonner, Dorothy, State certification requirements for teachers of bilingual education programs, June, 1977. Washington Education Division, National Center for Educational Statistics. Superintendent of Documents, U.S. Government Printing Office, 1977.

Waggonner, Dorothy. State education agencies and language minority students. Washington National Center for Educational Statistics, 1978.

Warren, Jonathan R. Prediction of college achievement among Mexican-American students in California. Los Angeles: National Dissemination and Assessment Center, California State University, Los Angeles, May 1978.

Worthen, B., & Sanders, J. *Educational Evaluation: Theory and Practice.* Worthington, Ohio: Charles A. Jones, 1973.

Worral, A. D. *Bilingualism and Cognitive Development.* Unpublished doctoral dissertation, University of Washington, 1970.

Zirkel, P. A., & Greene, J. F. The measurement of self-concept of disadvantaged students. U.S. Educational Resources Information Center, ERIC Document Reproduction Service No. ED 053 160, November 1961.

THE RELATIONSHIP BETWEEN STUDENT LANGUAGE GROWTH AND TEACHER CERTIFICATION IN BILINGUAL CROSSCULTURAL EDUCATION

Angela B. Garcia and Enselmina Marin

In the state of California, the passage of AB 1329, the Chacon-Mascone or Bilingual Education Act of 1976, mandated that teachers in bilingual classrooms must hold one of three certificates: a Certificate of Competency in Bilingual Crosscultural Education, a Credential in Bilingual Crosscultural Education (for graduating education students) or a Bilingual-Crosscultural Specialist Credential (for teachers possessing a valid teaching credential). The credential or certificate is awarded following recommendation from an assessor agency or institution of higher education qualified to affirm that the candidate is competent to teach in a bilingual classroom, has demonstrated mastery of English and another language (such as Spanish) as well as knowledge of the culture of students from the minority language group (e.g., Hispanic or Chicano history and culture).

Presumably this greater familiarity with bilingual methodology, language and culture will enable teachers to implement specifically bilingual teaching strategies which in turn will enable their students to achieve greater academic gains while acquiring English proficiency sooner than those students in monolingual English classrooms.

This legislation thus rests on the assumption that teachers who are specially prepared linguistically and culturally will better understand the entering level of cognitive and affective skills of limited- or non-English-speaking (LES or NES) children and will structure the classroom to build on the students' strengths and deal with the difficulties characteristic of their cultural and linguistic group.

Thus one can hypothesize that LES/NES students whose teachers hold this bilingual credential will (1) receive instruction which includes their home language and cultures to a greater extent than students with noncredentialed teachers, and (2) this instruction will enable them to improve their English and Spanish language skills or demonstrate significantly superior language gains over comparable students with the noncredentialed teachers.

Comparatively little research has been done in the area of bilingual education (Cruz, 1978). Certainly, the California legislation is much too young to have permitted examination of its impact at the classroom level prior to 1979. One can even argue that examining the relationship of a teacher's credential status and her/his classroom instructional strategies or student performance is still premature. However, preliminary research into the relationships among these three variables is highly desirable given the dramatic economic and professional impact which the legislation has had on school districts and teachers. Eventually the main concern with most educational program legislation is that of students' academic improvement; the crucial area with bilingual education laws is student language skill development.

Figure 1 presents a graphic conceptualization of the relationships among these three major variables. While all three relationships represented by lines A, B and C are critical, available data enables us to address that represented by line A.

Figure 1

The Relationships Among Student Achievement, Bilingual Strategies, Implementation and Teacher Bilingual Certification

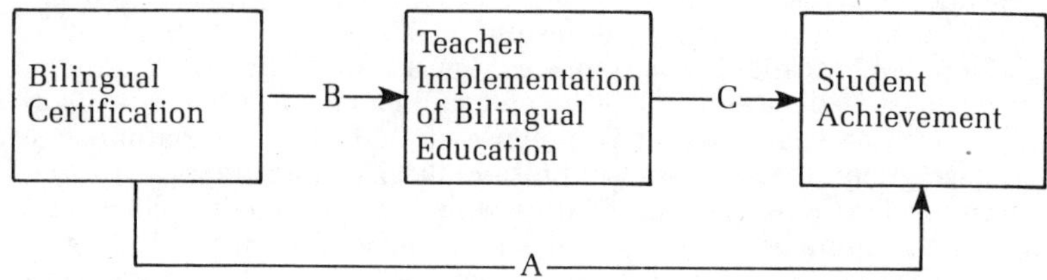

The purpose of the analyses reported herein was to determine whether students in classrooms with bilingually certified teachers gained significantly more in language skills than students whose teachers lacked this bilingual crosscultural credential. Subsequent reports will also address the necessary concommitant questions of whether teachers with this credential demonstrated higher levels of implementation of bilingual teaching strategies and whether students in classrooms with high implementation of bilingual strategies gained significantly more in English and Spanish skills than did those students in classrooms with low implementation of bilingual education techniques.

Method

Sample—The teachers included in this study comprised all of the Title VII teachers in eight school districts in the San Jose, California area. The data on classroom gains are based on all the students enrolled in these classrooms for the entire year and for whom both fall, 1977, and spring, 1978, English and Spanish test results exist. Table 1 presents the number of kindergarten to sixth grade classrooms included as well as the numbers of students with pre- and post-test scores per grade level.

While it may appear that eighty-seven classrooms were sampled, a total of sixty-eight teachers participated in this study. Twenty teachers taught

TABLE 1

KINDERGARTEN THROUGH SIXTH GRADE
NUMBER OF STUDENTS AND CLASSROOMS TESTED

	Certificated Teachers		*Noncertificated Teachers*	
Grade	Students	Classrooms	Students	Classrooms
Kindergarten	36	3	187	10
First	84	5	196	11
Second	102	7	172	9
Third	82	5	149	10
Fourth	33	3	171	10
Fifth	70	4	55	5
Sixth	143	2	57	3
Total	550	29	987	58

multi-graded classes—ten of the teachers with bilingual credentials and ten without this credential.

Instrumentation

The tests administered in October, 1977, and May, 1978, were the English and the Spanish versions of the *Language Assessment Battery* (Houghton Mifflin, 1977). Each version contained two levels—Level I for grades kindergarten through second and Level II for grades three through six. Each battery assesses speaking, listening, reading and writing skills and is on the list of instruments approved by the State of California Bilingual Education Office for assessing language proficiency.

Level I batteries are individual tests and were administered by external testers trained extensively by us. Level II batteries contain three group tests which the teachers administered to their own students in groups. Teachers also received training on test administration from us. A fourth test, an individually administered speaking measure, was administered by the external testers.

Results

Given that the research question focuses on a teacher characteristic, the classroom is the appropriate unit of analysis. Analyses of the raw scores on the total battery yielded mean class scores fall and spring. The fall score was subtracted from the spring class mean and the subsequent number served as the difference score for each classroom per grade level. Means were then computed based on all the difference scores for the certificated teachers per grade level and the resulting means were compared to the difference means of the classroom taught by noncertificated teachers.

Tables 2 and 3 present the data on these t test comparisons for English and Spanish gains. No differences reached significance on the English LAB gains. The Spanish gains analyses indicated that third graders taught by certificated teachers gained significantly more than their peers taught by noncertificated third grade teachers. All other differences failed to reach significance.

Since third grade students with certificated teachers significantly gained more in Spanish than peers with noncertificated teachers, we explored the two additional characteristics on which we had information for the third grade teachers. Supervisors or resource personnel who worked daily with these teachers were asked to rate their Spanish proficiency according to a five point scale. A rating of five indicated native fluency in Spanish while a rating of one indicated severely limited Spanish proficiency. The resulting mean Spanish language proficiency for third grade teachers with bilingual certification was five, an indicator of the highest level of command of the Spanish language, the fluency of a native speaker. In contrast,

TABLE 2

MEAN CLASSROOM GAINS ON THE *ENGLISH LANGUAGE ASSESSMENT BATTERY* WITH CERTIFICATED* AND NON-CERTIFICATED* TEACHERS

Grade	*Certificated*			*Non-Certificated*		
	n	$\overline{X}$	SD	n	$\overline{X}$	SD
Kindergarten	(4)	4.2	2.4	(9)	4.9	2.6
First	(5)	9.9	4.4	(11)	7.8	2.9
Second	(7)	6.9	4	(9)	5.1	6.6
Third	(5)	22.4	9	(10)	17.3	4
Fourth	(3)	13.4	5.1	(10)	16.3	8.9
Fifth	(3)	8.8	6.8	(6)	18.8	14.5
Sixth	(2)	6.7	.2	(3)	13.2	6.8

TABLE 3

MEAN CLASSROOM GAINS ON THE *SPANISH LANGUAGE ASSESSMENT BATTERY* WITH CERTIFICATED* AND NON-CERTIFICATED* TEACHERS

Grade	*Certificated*			*Non-Certificated*				
	n	$\overline{X}$	SD	n	$\overline{X}$	SD	t	p
Kindergarten	(4)	5.1	2.6	(11)	4.1	2.7		
First	(8)	8.1	5.5	(10)	6.5	1.9		
Second	(8)	8.1	5.7	(10)	5.1	4.6		
Third	(5)	26.3	8.4	(10)	7.6	13.5	2.9	.02
Fourth	(4)	13.0	7.6	(10)	9.3	19.8		
Fifth	(5)	9.8	12.0	(5)	9.3	15.7		
Sixth	(2)	9.5	2.9	(4)	5.2	6.6		

*These terms refer to those who have obtained the bilingual certificate credential ("Certificated") and those who lack that special certificate ("Non Certificated").

the mean rating of the Spanish language proficiency of the non-certificated teachers was 3.5, a rating indicating moderate ability in Spanish. While this group of teachers included three fluent Spanish speakers, the remainder were either non-Spanish speaking (with a rating of one) or very limited in Spanish proficiency (two).

By grouping the classroom by battery level, we can increase the n sizes and reduce the differences between the variances of the certificated and noncertificated groups (See Table 4). The results of the *t* tests on these group means are similar in the case of the English language gains, i.e., no differences in gains between the two groups reached significance. On the other hand, on the Spanish tests, the differences between Level I certificated and noncertificated groups attained significance ($p<.05$) with the certificated group demonstrating greater gains in their Spanish language skills than their counterparts in the noncertificated classrooms.

Figure 2 provides a graph of the fall and spring mean Spanish LAB scores by third to sixth graders with certificated and non-certificated teachers. The only difference in gains which reached statistical significance with these analyses was the difference between the third graders where the students with certificated teachers gained significantly more on English skills than those with teachers lacking a bilingual certificate.

The students in these analyses represented the entire range of language ability. Fluent-English-speaking students were included along with limited- and non-English-speaking pupils. Since the original state legislation evolved from the concern for LES and NES students, we can speculate that significant differences might manifest themselves only with these students. To test this possibility we divided students in every classroom into the three language ability groups—FES, LES and NES.

Fluent-English speakers were those students who in the fall scored above the third stanine on the English norms published in the LAB Technical Manual (Board of Education, 1976). Non-English speakers scored at or below a chance score of twenty raw score points for Level II and zero to three items correct on Level I. Limited-English-speaking students scored

TABLE 4

MEAN LANGUAGE GAINS BY UPPER AND LOWER ELEMENTARY CLASSES WITH CERTIFICATED AND NONCERTIFICATED TEACHERS

1977—1978

	Certificated			*Noncertificated*				
Grades	(n)	$\overline{X}$	SD	(n)	$\overline{X}$	SD	t	p
ENGLISH *LAB* GAINS								
K-2	(16)	7.2	3.8	(29)	6.0	3.3		
3-6	(13)	14.7	9.4	(29)	16.9	10.1		
SPANISH *LAB* GAINS								
K-2	(20)	7.6	4.9	(31)	5.2	3.8	2	.05
3-6	(16)	15.7	11.2	(30)	8.4	15.1		

below the fourth stanine (or the twenty-two percentile rank or lower) but above chance score.

Figure 2

Fall to Spring Means on the Spanish *Language Assessment Battery* for Upper Elementary Grades

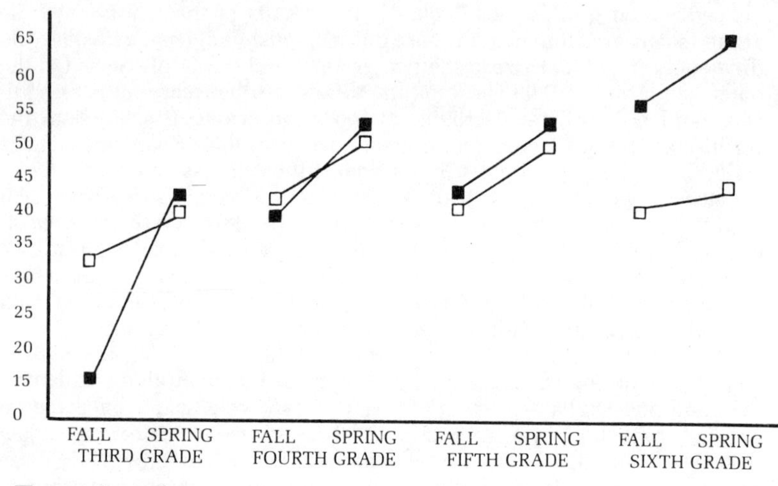

Table 5 presents the number of LES/NES students and classrooms per grade with certificated and non-certificated teachers. Although the numbers of students per grade level were very small, we conducted two sets of exploratory analyses on the data for these subgroups. For one set of analyses, we grouped both LES and NES students together by battery level and conducted *t* tests to determine the significance of differences in mean English gains between the LES/NES students with certificated and non-certificated teachers. None of the differences attained significance although both K-2 and 3-6 students with certificated teachers tended to gain more in English proficiency than their counterparts with non-certificated teachers.

A second set of analyses were conducted examining separately the gains of LES and NES students. Table 6 presents the results of those analyses on the mean English LAB gains by the four groups (LES certificated and non-certificated; NES certificated and non-certificated) per grade level. Only one difference reached significance at the $p<.05$ level. NES third graders with certificated teachers gained significantly more on English language skills than third grade NES students with non-certificated teachers.

Discussion

The assumption that students of limited- and non-English speaking ability will benefit more from instruction by a specially trained and certificated

TABLE 5

NUMBER OF LES/NES STUDENTS AND CLASSROOMS PER GRADE WITH CERTIFICATED AND NON-CERTIFICATED TEACHERS

	Certificated		*Non-Certificated*	
Grade	Students	Classrooms	Students	Classrooms
KINDERGARTEN				
LES	24	4	141	9
NES	5	4	16	7
FIRST GRADE				
LES	70	5	148	12
NES	6	3	5	4
SECOND GRADE				
LES	72	7	103	9
NES	9	4	7	3
TOTAL LEVEL I	186	27	420	44
THIRD GRADE				
LES	32	5	81	10
NES	27	5	11	6
FOURTH GRADE				
LES	20	3	82	10
NES	3	1	18	8
FIFTH GRADE				
LES	41	3	26	6
NES	7	2	13	2
SIXTH GRADE				
LES	25	2	30	3
NES	1	1	4	2
TOTAL LEVEL II	156	22	265	47

LES = Limited-English-speaking students
NES = Non-English-speaking students

teacher received tentative support from this preliminary study. The only significant difference obtained on English language gains favored children with certificated teachers.

The differences in gains on Spanish language skills more strongly favored students with certificated teachers. Analyses including all language ability students in the two types of classrooms yielded a statistically significant difference with third graders who had certificated teachers showing greater gains in Spanish skills than those students with non-certificated teachers.

On analyses by battery levels, both age groups (K-2 and 3-6th grades) showed higher Spanish language gains when taught by certificated teachers than non-certificated ones, with the K-2 difference reaching statistical significance.

While these preliminary findings suggest important differences which may exist between teachers who have obtained or lack a bilingual cross-

TABLE 6

MEAN ENGLISH LANGUAGE GAINS BY LIMITED AND NON-ENGLISH-SPEAKING STUDENTS WITH CERTIFICATED AND NON-CERTIFICATED TEACHERS

Grade	*Certificated* (n)	$\overline{X}$	SD	*Non-Certificated* (n)	$\overline{X}$	SD	t	p
KINDERGARTEN								
LES	(4)	5.3	4.8	(9)	4.8	1.2		
NES	(4)	14.8	6.3	(7)	15.1	6.8		
FIRST GRADE								
LES	(5)	9.4	1.3	(12)	8.1	8.6		
NES	(3)	18.1	1.9	(4)	21.1	16.4		
SECOND GRADE								
LES	(7)	11.1	.9	(9)	6.7	3.7		
NES	(4)	22.2	12.8	(3)	24.0	3.5		
THIRD GRADE								
LES	(5)	22.0	6.3	(10)	18.7	9.2		
NES	(5)	37.7	10.5	(6)	26.1	6.4	2.27	.05
FOURTH GRADE								
LES	(3)	10.4	7.0	(10)	18.1	7.9		
NES	(1)	58.7	—	(8)	46.3	17.3		
FIFTH GRADE								
LES	(3)	8.5	14.7	(6)	20.3	8.5		
NES	(2)	21.7	25.0	(2)	59.0	15.5		
SIXTH GRADE								
LES	(2)	10.0	.8	(3)	17.2	8.0		
NES	(1)	22.0	—	(2)	67.2	15.9		

(n) refers to the number of classrooms per grade. Numbers vary per grade level by teacher type due to the absence of LES or NES students in a few classrooms.
LES = Limited-English-speaking students
NES = Non-English-speaking students

cultural certificate, these exploratory analyses tell us nothing about the type and quality of education which the sampled students received. Several alternative explanations for the differences or, more precisely, the lack of differences between these two groups of children can be advanced. One likely explanation could be that the teaching strategies of these two particular groups of teachers were essentially the same for English instruction.

While possession of a bilingual crosscultural credential requires demonstration of extensive knowledge of the primary language, the home culture, and bilingual education methodology, the lack of such a credential does not signify a concommittent lack of knowledge of these three areas. All the non-certificated teachers in this study taught in a Title VII bilingual program. All had the services of a bilingual resource teacher. Even more important, twenty-eight were bilingual (Spanish-English speakers) and twenty-six had a Hispanic background and thus presumably possessed knowledge of the home culture of the LES/NES students. Only eighteen of the fifty-eight non-certificated teachers knew little or no Spanish *and* belonged to a cultural group different from that of their Hispanic students.

The importance of teacher proficiency in Spanish in contributing to the language development of the Title VII students is supported by the finding that the third grade students with certificated teachers gained significantly more in Spanish than their counterparts with noncertificated teachers. These certificated teachers had demonstrated native proficiency in Spanish. Thus, fluency in Spanish enables a teacher to help limited-English-proficiency students learn Spanish better than a teacher who knows little or no Spanish. This in turn may help the student learn English language skills better, a trend evident from the finding that these same students showed greater gains in English also (although not statistically significant).

Systematic classroom observations of essential bilingual education components with these students and teachers could reveal not only whether the teachers differ in their language usage, and instructional methodology, but, more importantly, what relationships emerge between bilingual teaching practices and student achievement (Line C in Figure 1) and credentialing and implementation of bilingual education methodology (Line B in Figure 1). Our subsequent reports will present the results of our current research in this area.

REFERENCES

Board of Education. "Language Assessment Battery Technical Manual." New York: Board of Education, 1976.

Cruz, B. Roberto. "The need for sound and quality empirical research in bilingual education controlling for intervening variables and shortcomings." In *American Institutes for Research Impact Study on Bilingual Education.* CABE President Report to California Assembly Education Committee. San Mateo, California: November 9, 1978.

BILINGUAL EDUCATION IN THE RECEPTION OF POLITICAL IMMIGRANTS: THE CASE OF CUBANS IN MIAMI, FLORIDA*

Silvia Pedraza-Bailey and Teresa A. Sullivan

Congress appropriated funds for bilingual education beginning in 1968 (81 Stat. 816), and the judicial mandate for bilingual education came about in *Lau* v. *Nichols* (1974). But federally funded bilingual education was in fact born in 1960-61, fourteen years before it was legally mandated, as part of a program to receive Cuban political refugees in Dade County, Florida. This paper describes the elements of that prototype bilingual education program.

THE REASON FOR THE PROGRAM

Bilingual education was only part of a comprehensive program to receive the Cuban refugees. Americans are familar with comprehensive refugee reception programs because of the coordinated efforts made to receive recent Indochinese refugees. However, when the Cuban political immigrants began arriving in 1960, the United States had had only limited experience in providing for refugee needs. The comprehensive program was as much an innovation as its bilingual education component was.

The United States had been seen as a haven for the political dissidents of Europe in the 1700s and 1800s, but the restrictive immigration legislation of the early 1900s affected political and economic immigrants alike. The national quotas established in the 1924 Immigration Act (43 Stat. 153) were not waived to receive refugees from Hitler, not even children (Smith, 1966). The policy toward refugees began to change after World War II.

The first World War II refugees were admitted by executive decree of President Harry S. Truman in 1945. He led a political fight to pass the Displaced Persons Act of 1948 (62 Stat. 1009), which admitted refugees by "mortgaging" national quotas (Eckerson, 1966: 13). In the next twelve years there were six additional laws to admit political immigrants.[1] Later acts overlooked the quotas; the Refugee Relief Act of 1953 (67 Stat. 400) even provided visas for Asian refugees. Asian immigrants had been all but excluded from the United States since 1924.[2]

---

*This research was funded by Grant No. 21-17-78-03 of the Employment and Training Administration, U.S. Department of Labor, to the National Opinion Research Center. Because grantees conducting research and development projects under Government sponsorship are encouraged to express their own judgment freely, this paper does not necessarily represent the official opinion or position of the Department of Labor. The authors are solely responsible for the contents of this paper.

None of these statutes provided a comprehensive program for the needs of the refugees, but through a process of accretion, most of the elements for a comprehensive program were there by the time the Cubans arrived. The Displaced Persons Act was implemented by state level Commissions for Displaced Persons, laying the groundwork for federal-state cooperation. The provision of temporary services was foreshadowed by the housing the federal government provided to Hungarian refugees at Camp Kilmer, New Jersey. A whole range of services was demonstrated by the Netherlands government, which paid for the resettlement of Dutch-Indonesian refugees in the U.S.. The assistance provided included financial aid, health and accident insurance, job retraining, English classes, and orientation to U.S. history and culture (Smith, 1966).

The Cuban refugee migration dwarfed the others in size, and the program to receive them dwarfed the others in scope and imagination. The first effort was the creation, by President Eisenhower in December, 1960, of the Cuban Refugee Emergency Center in Miami, Florida. It received an allocation of $1 million to provide initial relief (food, clothing, health care), to help the refugees find jobs, and to initiate a resettlement program for employable refugees that would distribute them to other areas. In addition, in February, 1961, President Kennedy directed that a Cuban Refugee Program ($4 million allocation for fiscal year 1960) be established under the Department of Health, Education and Welfare. The program was a cooperative one involving the Public Health Service, the Employment Service of the U.S. Department of Labor, the Florida State Department of Public Welfare, the Dade County Health Department, the Dade County Public Schools, the University of Miami and voluntary agencies, both in the Miami area and nationally.

In the beginning funds were allocated to the program from presidential discretionary funds. Permanent authority for the program was provided by the Migration and Refugee Assistance Act (76 Stat. 121) effective June 28, 1962 (Prohias and Casal, 1974), which provided for: (1) transportation costs from Cuba; (2) financial assistance to needy refugees; (3) financial assistance to state and local public agencies which provided services for refugees; (4) costs of resettlement outside of Miami; (5) employment and professional training courses for refugees. From the beginning of the Cuban Refugee Program until the end of fiscal year 1973, about $867 million was spent on the program. Table 1 presents program expenditures per year. Table 2 shows that, for only the years 1969 to 1972, 90,000 persons received financial or medical assistance under the Cuban Refugee Program.

The comprehensive nature of the program, set out in outline in the Migration and Refugee Assistance Act, was realized in its implementation. Ultimately the Program would do all of the following:

1. help voluntary agencies to provide daily necessities, to resettle, and to find jobs
2. gain private and government agency cooperation to provide job opportunities
3. provide funds for resettlement, including transportation and adjustment costs in the new community

TABLE 1

ASSISTANCE TO CUBAN REFUGEES BY THE CUBAN REFUGEE PROGRAM, 1961 THROUGH 1974
(In millions of dollars)

Fiscal Year	Program Administration		Welfare Assistance (includes health services)		Resettlement		Education		Movement of Refugees		Fiscal Year Total
	Amount	Per-cent	Amount	Per-cent	Amount	Per-cent	Amount	Per-cent	Amount	Per-cent	Amount
1961	0.2	4.9	2.3	56.1	0.5	12.2	1.0	24.4	—	—	4.1
1962	0.6	1.6	28.5	74.0	3.8	9.8	5.5	14.2	—	—	38.5
1963	1.0	1.8	41.9	75.0	3.7	6.5	9.5	16.9	—	—	56.0
1964	1.0	1.8	33.2	72.2	2.2	4.7	9.7	21.0	—	—	46.0
1965	0.9	2.9	20.7	63.6	1.3	4.0	9.6	29.5	—	—	32.5
1966	2.0	5.6	18.9	52.8	4.5	12.6	10.4	29.0	0.9	1.0	36.2
1967	2.0	4.3	23.5	49.5	5.8	12.7	14.3	31.3	0.6	1.3	46.2
1968	2.0	3.6	30.5	54.7	4.9	8.8	17.8	31.9	0.6	1.0	55.8
1969	1.9	2.7	44.5	63.0	4.8	6.7	18.8	26.9	0.6	0.9	70.6
1970	2.3	2.6	59.3	67.8	4.7	5.4	20.5	23.4	0.7	0.8	87.4
1971	2.6	2.3	81.5	72.7	5.5	4.9	21.6	19.2	0.9	0.8	112.1
1972	2.4	1.8	113.0	82.7	2.9	2.1	17.8	13.0	0.5	0.4	136.7
1973 (est.)	2.0	1.4	125.3	86.5	1.3	0.9	16.0	11.0	0.3	0.2	145.0
1974 (est.)	1.6	1.8	73.3	81.1	1.0	1.1	14.0	15.6	—	—	90.0

SOURCE: U.S. Budgets. In Prohias and Casal, 1974, Table 45.

TABLE 2

NUMBER OF PERSONS RECEIVING FINANCIAL AND/OR MEDICAL ASSISTANCE UNDER THE CUBAN REFUGEE PROGRAM

End of Year	Number of Persons			Florida as Proportion of Total
	Florida	Other States	Total	
1969	27,738	25,002	52,740	52.6
1970	32,500	33,600	66,100	49.2
1971	32,400	45,300	77,700	41.7
1972	35,600	55,100	90,700	39.2

SOURCE: Appendix to the Budget for Fiscal Years 1971-1974. In Prohias and Casal, 1974, Table 40.

4. furnish financial assistance for basic maintenance in Miami and communities of resettlement, administered through federal, state and local channels, based on standards used in communities involved
5. provide essential health services
6. furnish federal assistance for local public school operating costs related to the Cuban impact
7. initiate measures to augment training and educational opportunities, including physicians, teachers, and those with other professional backgrounds
8. provide financial aid for unaccompanied children
9. undertake surplus food distribution administered by the Dade County (Miami) Welfare Department (Prohias and Casal, 1974)

The sixth function, the assistance to the local public schools, formed the basis for Miami's bilingual education experiment.

IMPACT OF THE CUBAN REFUGEE PROGRAM ON THE PUBLIC SCHOOL SYSTEM

Joe Hall, superintendent of the public schools of Dade County, began most of his annual reports on *The Cuban Refugee* by recalling the problems the school system faced:

> It was early in 1960 that the public schools of Dade County began to experience a problem which was unique not only to the local school system but probably in the entire history of education in the United States. This was the first time that thousands of persons, forced to flee from their native homeland because of political upheaval, had sought refuge in the United States and brought with them their children to enroll in the local school system. Although a few settled in other areas of Florida and elsewhere in the United States, the overwhelming majority stopped at the closest port of entry, Miami and Dade County, and brought their children to the public schools. Thus, because of an accident of geography the citizens of Florida and of Dade County accepted responsibility for these refugees for the entire nation.
>
> Because the influx of these Cuban refugees in such large numbers was unexpected and because most of the children and the adults

spoke no English, they created special problems for the community and for the school system.

The county was incapable of educating the Cuban refugee children without substantial federal aid.

Beginning with the school year 1960-61, the Cuban Refugee Program allocated funds to the Dade County public school system through annual "agreements" signed by the Dade County School Board and the U.S. Office of Education. (For the detailed annual agreements, see Dade County, Florida, Board of Public Instruction, Department of Administrative Research, *The Cuban Refugee in the Public Schools of Dade County, Florida,* annual reports, 1960-61 through 1972-73.)

The first contract between the federal government and Dade County was negotiated during the 1960-61 school year. The federal government agreed to pay half of the cost of educating all Cuban refugee students. The cost per Cuban pupil was estimated to be twenty percent higher, due to the language barrier, than that of the regular student. Thus federal payment per refugee student was set at sixty percent of the estimated Dade County operating cost per student. The sixty percent rate was in effect until the 1965-66 school year in which the federal government, based on the fact that Cuban refugees had become tax paying members of the community, tried to reimburse Dade County for only those children of families receiving public assistance. Dade County objected and a compromise agreement was worked out in which federal participation was set at sixty percent of the cost of refugee students from families receiving public assistance, but only forty-five percent for all other refugee pupils.

On October 3, 1965, President Johnson announced the "open door" policy in response to Fidel Castro's offer to let the Cubans emigrate, and a second major wave of Cuban immigration began. This new stage, regulated by the "Memorandum of Understanding" between the U.S. and Cuban governments, brought a new influx of Cuban students to Dade County public schools. In addition, some of the refugees who had been resettled throughout the country earlier began to filter back into Dade County. As the superintendent of the school system expressed it, "There is no end in sight." On October 11, 1965, eight days after the Open Door Policy was announced, the Dade County School Board stopped the admission of Cuban refugee children. "The county was financially pressed with no provision for classrooms or teachers without assurance of federal assistance" (Dade County, Florida, Board of Public Instruction, Report No. 12). Once again the federal government stepped in to aid the Cuban refugees. A new working agreement was reached between the government and the public school system for those students entering the U.S. after October 3, 1965 (see Table 3), which included 100% reimbursement for those entering after that date. The increasing number of Cuban refugee children in the schools by year can be seen in Figure 1. The second wave of Cuban immigration presented a dramatic increase in the number of refugee children in the schools.

With the dramatic increase in the number of new Cuban pupils in the second major wave of immigration, additional educational services were necessary for their education. The Dade County School Board agreed to provide the following services and personnel required for their education:

TABLE 3

FEDERAL PARTICIPATION IN THE DADE COUNTY, FLORIDA, PUBLIC SCHOOL SYSTEM THROUGH THE CUBAN REFUGEE PROGRAM

School Year	Proportion of Dade County Operating Cost per Student Paid on Behalf of the Cuban Refugee Students Who Arrived:	
	Before October 3, 1965	After October 3, 1965
1960-61 thru 1964-65	60% for all students	
1965-66 thru 1967-68	60% for students in families receiving assistance and 45% for all other students	100% for all students
1968-69	30% for all students	60% for all students, up to 5 years in the school system
1970-71—	None	Same as during 1969-70 school term

SOURCE: General Accounting Office, 1971. In Phohias and Casal, 1974, Table 54.

one Cuban teacher aide for each 60 new children; one visiting teacher-counselor for each 500 new children; one psychological caseworker for each 1,000 new children; four clerks for record-keeping of the new children; one supervisor of bilingual education; one Class 14 secretary; and special teaching materials for the new children. The federal government agreed to pay for the salaries of these necessary personnel and for the materials to perform the specialized educational services. After the 1969-70 school year, payments were discontinued for "old" refugee pupils as well as for a growing number of "new" students who had been enrolled in schools in the United States for five consecutive years. As pupils became ineligible, their census records were merged with the general file. Thus total membership data for Cuban refugees are not available after June, 1970 (Dade County, Florida, Board of Public Instruction, Report No. 12). The total number of Cuban refugee pupils in the schools from 1961 to 1970 can be seen in Table 4.

The federal government also assisted the education of Cuban adults beginning in 1962-63 when it was agreed by the Dade County School Board:

> that payment was to be made for Cuban refugees attending the Dade County Junior College at the rate of ninety-six cents per class hour of instruction, computed on the basis that each class hour of junior college instruction was equivalent to two classroom type hours in the adult education program as previously specified. Hours of instruction for refugees in the Junior College program were to be included in the hours of classroom type instruction provided under the adult and vocational education program.

Cuban refugee adults taking adult and vocational courses were furnished with the needed textbooks, workbooks, manuals, library services, instructional materials, shop materials, and equipment usage. Class and shop fees were not charged for Cuban refugee adult and vocational students.

Figure 1:

Cuban Refugee Pupils in Grades 1-12, 1960-61 through 1968-69, Dade County Public Schools, Miami, Florida.

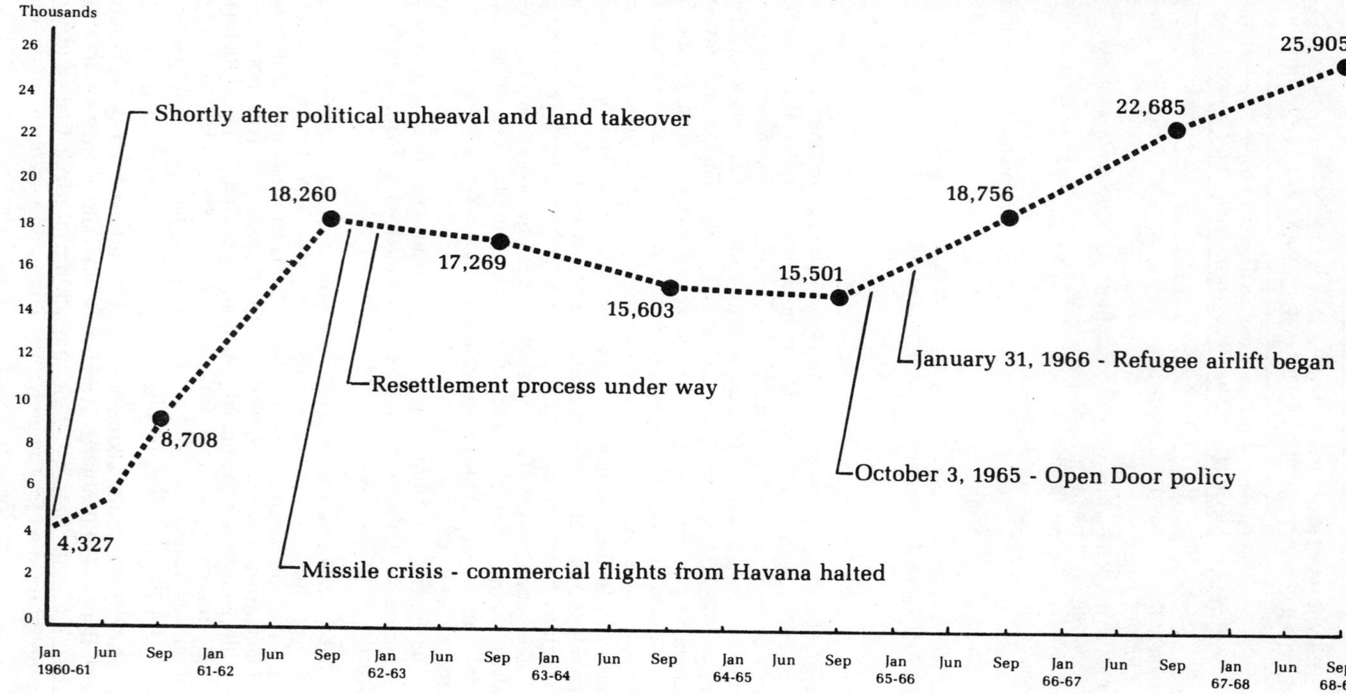

TABLE 4

NUMBER OF CUBAN REFUGEE PUPILS IN THE DADE COUNTY PUBLIC SCHOOLS, 1961-1970, AND THEIR PROPORTION OF THE TOTAL NUMBER OF PUPILS IN THE SCHOOL SYSTEM

Date of School Census	Total Pupils in School System	Cuban Refugee Pupils	Cuban Pupils as Proportion of Total
1/26/61	166,828	4,327	2.59
1/24/62	178,975	11,735	6.56
1/25/63	189,338	17,865	9.44
1/24/64	194,093	16,641	8.57
1/22/65	197,976	15,566	7.86
1/20/66	203,481	16,209	7.97
1/26/67	211,051	19,719	9.34
1/25/68	219,997	23,504	10.68
1/23/69	233,508	27,011	11,57
1/27/70	243,006	31,230	12.85

SOURCE: Adapted from Dade County, Florida Board of Public Instruction. *The Cuban Refugee.* Report No. 12.

The federal contribution to the Dade County public school system was sizable.[3] From 1960 to 1972, over $117 million dollars was paid by the federal government to the Dade County school system under the Cuban Refugee Program. These payments represented about seventy-five percent of all the money Dade County spent on education, and about twenty-five percent of the total Cuban Refugee Program expenditures from 1960 to 1972. Table 5 provides a breakdown of the federal contribution by the type of educational program, plus the total number of children in grades one to twelve and the number of adults in the vocational and adult programs.

PROGRAMS OF INSTRUCTION

The federal funds to the Dade County public schools provided three kinds of bilingual education: preparatory programs, the program for grades one to twelve and adult education.

Preparatory Programs

For many years the public schools of Dade County had operated an extensive summer recreational and academic program involving thousands of students. By agreement with HEW in the summer of 1961, the school system began to provide an entirely new program of conversational English designed for and available only to the Cuban refugee children. The programs were established in those school centers where a high percentage of Cuban refugee children lived. English classes and recreational programs were held five days each week for the total school day. The program was supervised and coordinated by a bilingual principal who

TABLE 5

FEDERAL PARTICIPATION (IN DOLLARS) FOR CUBAN REFUGEE PUPILS IN DADE COUNTY, FLORIDA, PUBLIC SCHOOL SYSTEM, BY TYPE OF EDUCATIONAL PROGRAM, 1960-61 THROUGH 1972-73

School Year	Federal Participation (In Dollars)			
	Grades 1-12 Program	Vocational and Adult Programs	Summer Programs	Total Expenditures
1960-61	$ 623,500	$ 50,000	$ 26,078	$ 699,578
1961-62	3,076,284	882,740	30,187	3,989,211
1962-63	5,953,586	1,651,457	80,317	7,685,360
1963-64	5,763,669	1,140,315	44,858	6,948,842
1964-65	5,261,318	1,154,386	81,987	6,497,691
1965-66	5,832,646	1,039,727	102,390	6,974,763
1966-67	9,427,135	990,786	100,374	10,518,295
1967-68	13,000,819	891,995	158,718	14,051,532
1968-69	13,519,220	904,623	160,000	14,583,843
1969-70	15,588,598	876,667	159,997	16,625,262
1970-71	13,512,238	935,204	159,914	14,607,356
1971-72	12,814,069	919,177	99,471	13,832,717
1972-73	12,638,552	833,195	—	13,471,747
TOTAL	$117,011,634	$12,270,272	$1,204,291	$130,486,197

SOURCE: Dade County, Florida, Board of Public Instruction. *The Cuban Refugee.* Report No. 12.

served during the regular school years as principal of an elementary school in which large numbers of refugee children were enrolled. The program provided orientation, which made for an easier transition in September, and it helped to build English vocabulary.

Beginning in 1964-65, the school system also agreed to provide a three hour a day pre-school program for five-year-old Cuban refugee children. This was due to the fact that, as the superintendent of the school system stressed, "A problem remains, however, at the first grade level where many pupils enter who know little or no English." So, for them a special language and reading program was designed using materials of the *Miami Linguistic Readers Series*, which were developed there under a Ford Foundation grant.

Program of Instruction for Grades One to Twelve

Miami had long offered conversational Spanish, even at the elementary level. But beginning in 1960-61 the instructional program for children in grades one to twelve was reorganized so that it became a prototype for current efforts in bilingual education.

In schools which had a large number of Cuban pupils, a Spanish-speaking secretary was provided and in several schools an orientation teacher was provided through the Special Education Department of the school system. The orientation teachers worked with the pupils in small groups to help them adjust to the program and customs of their new school and to teach them English. In some schools the orientation classes were organized at the elementary, intermediate and advanced levels. Many schools made use of the "buddy" system by which the non-English-speaking pupils were paired with bilingual pupils. Parents of the refugee pupils were involved through the P.T.A., Mother's Clubs, and in other ways, and bulletins and programs for parents were developed in both English and Spanish. One P.T.A. employed a bilingual teacher to instruct parents in English.

Two bilingual visiting teachers were employed to serve schools having the greatest number of refugee children. The instructional program was reorganized to provide for a team consisting of one American teacher and two bilingual Cuban refugee teacher aides.

Because the norms of the tests used in the regular standardized testing program did not provide a valid basis for making judgments concerning the abilities or achievements of the Spanish pupils, all of them were excluded from the standardized testing program. Until the time when they could read and comprehend material in the substantive fields, the teachers did not grade the students in these areas. When they were proficient enough to be transferred to the regular program, they were placed in the regular program and taught like the "independent" students. This reorganization

> facilitated improvement of the instructional program for the thousands of Cuban refugee pupils. It also alleviated many of the objections which had been raised by some of the citizens of the county who had objected to the placement of the Cuban refugee pupils in the regular schools and objections voiced by some teachers who had complained about the downgrading of the quality of instruction (Dade County, Florida, Board of Public Instruction, Report No. 1).

Substantial revisions were made in the elementary curriculum, although not in the junior high and high school curricula. Starting in September 1963, as a result of a three-year Ford Foundation grant, the Board of Public Instruction approved participation in a Project in Bilingual Education of Cuban Refugee Pupils. This project provided for the revision of instructional materials originally developed in Puerto Rico and the development of beginning reading materials to be developed for bilingual children. "It was anticipated that the materials to be developed would have wider application than to the Dade County situation" (Dade County, Florida, Board of Public Instruction, Report No. 2).

This same Ford Foundation grant partially supported the bilingual school which began functioning in September 1963 at Coral Way Elementary. Each year the program was expanded one grade so that by 1966 both English- and Spanish-speaking children were offered an instructional program in both languages in all grades, where half the day was spent in studying the regular curriculum in the native language (English or Spanish), and the other half of the day was devoted to studying in the second language.

Significant efforts were made to institute bilingual education not only at the level of instruction, but also organizationally. The staffing of the program employed a unique team teaching situation:

> A team of three is assigned to teach 60 pupils—one certified American teacher and two Cuban aides recruited from among the refugee teachers living in Miami. The certified teacher develops the instructional program, but the aide participates in the planning and execution of the program. These former Cuban teachers serve as an invaluable liaison between the Spanish-speaking community and the school. Training of the staff members for this job is also an important feature of the program (Dade County, Florida, Board of Public Instruction, Report No. 6).

Training workshops existed both for the American teachers and the Cuban aides—for the former an English-SL inservice workshop, and for the latter a Spanish-S inservice workshop. Through their participation in these workshops, over 150 teachers and aides were able to develop a functional understanding of the instructional needs of non-English-speaking pupils at primary, intermediate, and secondary levels. "As a result of the workshops, the schools which received a large number of refugee pupils had trained staff members able to develop and carry out a sound instructional program" (Dade County, Florida, Board of Public Instruction, Report No. 6).

It can be seen that the Miami program combined aspects of both the "transition" and "maintenance" models of bilingual education.

> Faced with the deluge of Cuban refugees, our school system chose to meet this problem head-on, as a legitimate challenge to the professional competence and ingenuity of its educational forces. This challenge was met on at least three levels—organizational, instructional and materials development. Decisions made in each of these areas were predicated on the conviction that the principal educational objective in programs for non-English speaking students must be to teach them English as effectively and efficiently as possible.
>
> . . . all non-English speaking pupils in grades 1-12 are classified into one of three categories: non-independent, intermediate, or independent, which refer only to ability to speak and understand English. In no way do these refer to intelligence or academic achievement.
>
> In both elementary and secondary schools the non-independents have approximately 3 hours of English as a second language each day. The rest of the day they participate in areas of the regular curriculum where lack of proficiency in English is not a serious handicap.
>
> . . . Spanish-S is a course offered only to native speakers of Spanish in grades 4-12. The purpose of this is to develop the Spanish-speaking child's literacy in his native language.
>
> (Dade County, Florida, Board of Public Instruction, Report No. 6).

Adult Education

In addition to programs for children, three kinds of adult programs were offered: conversational English, vocational training, and English-language "retooling" courses for Cuban professionals.

Beginning in the fall of 1961, an accelerated conversational English program for adults was instituted, again backed by federal funds. A unit of training consisted of five hours a day for a ten-week period. On the average there was one teacher for every ten students, and a higher than normal ratio of administrative and supervisory personnel. Approximately 200 persons received training every ten weeks.

In the first year of operation, the school year 1960-61, about 9,000 adult students were enrolled. By 1962-63 the number attending had climbed to about 20,000. In 1963-64 and 1964-65, it reached 30,000 each year. In 1966-67 it stabilized at about 20,000 a year, where it continued until 1972-73.

The classes were of two types, intensive and part-time. The intensive classes met for two-and-a-half hours a day, five days a week, for twelve week periods. The part-time classes met two nights a week, three hours each night, for sixteen weeks. The classes were taught by two teachers, one an American and the other a Cuban teacher aide. They both taught two sessions a day, of fifty students each. Classes were offered in seven centers throughout the county. In the intensive classes English was offered at both the beginning and intermediate levels. At both levels the emphasis was on aural perception and oral reproduction. When as many as thirty students indicated a desire to take English, a new class was begun to accommodate them. Beginning in the summer of 1963, an inservice workshop was also added as orientation for the teachers. In this workshop the teachers received instruction in the theory of language teaching, and had actual classroom practice with groups of non-English-speaking pupils.

An instructional program in English on open circuit television was initiated for half an hour, twice a week. This program was viewed in the adult high school centers, where a viewing room instructor was employed for each fifty students in these T.V. classes. After the telecast, the students returned to classrooms for a follow-up and review of the telecast. "Since this program was on open circuit T.V., it was viewed by many in their homes and thus fulfilled a public service as well as meeting the needs of those who were able to attend the class sessions." As the superintendent of the school system expressed it,

> It was found that if the refugees remained in the English classes for as long as sixteen weeks on the average, they were able to communicate sufficiently to take their place in the community or to attempt other learning activities in the vocational shops and extension classes. Many entered the business education classes which provide secretarial training (Dade County, Florida, Board of Public Instruction, Report No. 1).

English language classes often provided a transition to vocational education. There were a number of classes in the areas of business, general and distributive education, "shop", adult high school, reading, office work, home economics, and the like. The hours, length of these classes, and meeting times of the English classes were arranged to fit any schedule needed by the adult students. As the superintendent of the school system put it, "These students mastered the language rapidly and many enrolled in the adult high school, business education, and other vocational shop or interest classes." The agreement between the Dade County public schools and the federal government required that the program of vocational training given Cuban refugees be coordinated with the program of the Cuban Refugee Emergency Center, and that officials of this center should approve all vocational training except the English classes.

Professional "retooling" was especially important for professionals who needed to pass American licensing examinations. The retraining program for Cuban physicians is of particular interest. It consisted of twelve weeks of instruction, with lectures simultaneously translated into Spanish, and with the teaching of English medical terminology. In 1972 thirty members of the University of Miami School of Medicine were lecturing in the program. By 1966, 1,263 Cuban physicians had completed the program of instruction, including language and English medical terminology instruction, provided by Barry College. As of 1974, over 2,000 Cuban physicians had graduated from this course and gone on to become full-fledged practitioners in the U.S. This program definitely helped the effective utilization of Cuban medical manpower in the U.S. (Moncarz, 1969).

It is interesting to note that although this program was initiated for Cubans, since its inception physicians from other Latin American countries have also enrolled in it, without U.S. government tuition assistance. They constitute about twenty percent of the enrollment since 1964. Although the Cuban physician program was not paid for by funds to the Dade County schools, it was paid for through federal appropriations. These appropriations also helped retain other professionals, including bilingual teachers.

TEACHER RETRAINING PROGRAMS

John F. Thomas (1963), Director of the Cuban Refugee Program, was keenly aware of the barriers to the structural assimilation of immigrants imposed by citizenship, training and certification requirements, even for those immigrants of higher social class of origin:

> One common requirement affecting employability in certain professions is U.S. citizenship, or a declaration of intent to become a citizen, a requirement which cannot be met by the vast majority of the refugees because of their immigration status. Data published by the American Immigration and Citizenship Conference in its "Guide to Occupational Practice Requirements in the U.S.A. for Foreign-Trained Architects, Dentists, Engineers, Lawyers, Librarians, Musicians, Nurses, Physicians, Teachers, Veterinarians" (July 1961) show that citizenship or a declaration of intent is a requirement for licensing as follows:
>
> | | |
> |---|---|
> | Architects | 24 states |
> | Dentists | 45 states and D.C. |
> | Lawyers | most states |
> | Professional nurses | 22 states, Puerto Rico and V.I. |
> | Practical nurses | 28 states, Puerto Rico and V.I. |
> | Physicians | 41 states and Puerto Rico |
> | Public-school teachers | most states |
> | Veterinarians | 29 states |
>
> Other requirements also affect certain professionals. Six states do not accept any foreign-trained physicians. Dental studies pursued in a foreign university receive virtually no recognition in the United States. The same is true of law studies pursued in countries such as Cuba that do not base their legal system on English common law (p. 11).

The Cuban Refugee Program helped to institute programs that retrained selected groups of skilled and professional Cubans—largely teachers, college professors, doctors and lawyers, for whom the barriers of lack of American certificates would have meant that they could not have practiced the careers they had been trained in, in the United States.

The Cuban Teacher Retraining Program at the University of Miami was initiated in 1963 when a large number of Cuban teachers and an even larger number of Cuban children were coming into the United States. The program was designed to meet the needs of both the teachers, by providing them a means of meeting Florida licensing or certification requirements, and the students, by providing them with bilingual teachers. By 1973, ten years after the inception of the program, nearly 500 Cuban teachers had completed the program and been certified.

The Cuban Teacher Retraining Program was composed of personnel from the Dade County public school system, the Cuban Refugee Program, the State Department of Education, and the University of Miami. The guiding philosophy of the program was to immerse the Cuban teachers as much as possible in the culture of the United States, and especially in its educational system, in a systematic and gradual way, in order to help them make the transition to teaching in the U.S. Its aim was to enable Cuban teachers to meet the licensing and certification requirements of their profession. As Sevick (1974: 14) has stressed:

> There were several problems facing such teachers before their talents could be employed: first, they themselves needed to learn English before their talents could be helpful in an American school—they had to become bilingual; secondly, to teach in the public schools Cuban teachers needed to be certified by the state of Florida which required citizenship; thirdly, those teachers with university degrees from Cuba would need to validate their degrees through a North American institution.

With respect to the latter, the Florida State Board of Education requires that a person with a degree from a non-accredited institution must validate that degree through an accredited institution before the degree will be recognized for certification purposes in the state of Florida.[4] In order to do this the state Department of Education specified that one had to: (1) gain unconditional admission to candidacy for an advanced degree in the graduate school of a standard institution of higher learning; (2) earn in residence at one standard institution having an approved graduate division, a total of twelve semester hours of graduate credit in an approved degree validation program to merit full recognition of the degree earned at the non-accredited institution.

The language problem was one of the most difficult obstacles for the teachers to overcome. As was explained earlier, federal assistance was provided to help in learning English in the programs provided by the Dade County public schools' adult programs. In addition, the teaching of English became a significant community activity, with various religious groups and voluntary associations organizing English classes for the refugees. Barry College in December, 1960 began providing free English classes, and special English classes were added for doctors and lawyers. "In 1963 Barry College began offering a free course, Methods of Teaching Spanish to English-speaking students, to enable Cubans, especially lawyers whose legal training was virtually inapplicable in the United States, to obtain teaching positions. Most found Spanish teaching positions outside of Florida" (University of Miami, 1967: 112).

Another obstacle was the citizenship requirement for teacher certification in Florida. The Florida Department of Education regulation stipulated that in order to obtain a certificate one had to be a citizen of the United States, or a citizen of a nation not antagonistic to democratic forms of government, which, it was deemed, did not include Cuba. After numerous negotiations, the state of Florida allowed Cuban refugee teachers to obtain provisional certification before obtaining citizenship.

In addition to the program conducted at the University of Miami, eight other institutions sponsored similar programs to enable teachers from Cuba to resume their profession in this country, and to enable members of other professions, such as lawyers, to become retrained as teachers. The following is a list of the other institutions conducting programs, and the years of the programs (Sevick, 1974: 20):

Cooperating Institutions	*Years of Courses*
State University of Iowa Iowa City, Iowa	1963, 1964, 1965
Indiana State University Terre Haute, Indiana	1963, 1964
College of Great Falls Great Falls, Montana	1964
Kutztown State Teachers College Kutztown, Pennsylvania	Summers of 1964, 1965
Fairleigh Dickinson University Rutherford, Teaneck and Madison, New Jersey	1965, 1966, 1967, 1968, 1969, 1970
Kansas State Teachers College Emporia, Kansas	1964, 1965, 1966, 1967, 1968
College of Mount St. Mary Los Angeles, California	Summers of 1965, 1966, 1967, 1968

At the program of the State University of Iowa, participants of the program were selected in Miami through the cooperation of the Cuban Refugee Center. Tuition, room and board were provided to participants. Participants were already hired by school districts in Iowa before beginning their studies. Hence they were assured of employment after completing their studies. As the Director of the Institute for the Orientation of Cuban Refugee Teachers in Iowa expressed its aims:

> We believed that our program would serve a dual purpose: it would be beneficial to the State of Iowa by facilitating the extension and enrichment of foreign language instruction in the public schools of Iowa; it would also help the Cuban refugees by giving them an opportunity to rebuild their lives and regain economic security (Sevick, 1974: 21).

At Indiana State University, 105 teachers from Cuba participated in the programs conducted during the 1963 and 1964 school years. Kansas State Teachers College conducted both a teacher education program for Cuban teachers, and also courses in library education for Cuban professionals, most of whom were formerly lawyers in Cuba with law degrees from the University of Havana. This program lasted over four years and enabled over 100 persons to begin professions in the United States in teaching or library work. The program at the College of Great Falls, Montana, arose out of the need for language teachers in the western states at that time, and their curriculum was aimed to meet the certification requirements of the western states.

The largest teacher retraining program was that of the University of Miami. This program was instituted when an agreement contract was reached between the federal government and the University of Miami "to provide professional retraining in the American educational system to Cuban refugee teachers to enable them to pursue their careers in the United States" (Department of Health, Education and Welfare Grant No. OE 78-19-0210-105.0, in Sevick, 1974: 25). All the study done through the program was aimed to meet this primary purpose of enabling Cuban educators to resume their professions in the United States. A second objective was to provide bilingual teachers and teacher aides for the increasing number of Cuban students in the Dade County public school system.

The pilot program for teacher retraining at the University of Miami was conducted from January, 1963 to August, 1963, with thirty students. To meet the Florida requirements for validation of their Cuban degrees, they took twelve credits of graduate work in philosophy and history of education; curriculum and school organization; general methods of teaching; and testing and educational psychology. No tuition or fees were charged to the participants. All the participants held a Doctor of Pedagogy, Doctor of Philosophy and Letters, or other degree which was considered equivalent to the B.A. in the United States. Their Cuban university degrees were validated by the University of Miami upon completion of course work in the program. Elementary or secondary school teaching experience was also a prerequisite for admission to the program, as was an adequate command of the English language. Provisional certification in Florida was obtained by the participants after the citizenship requirement for provisional certification was waived. The graduates were placed in full-time teaching positions, with a regular teacher's salary. As Sevick expressed it, "the most important effect of the pilot program was the fact that professional talent, which would otherwise have remained unused or unusable, was now enabled to be productive and capable of making a contribution to the schools of this country" (1974: 34).

With the success of the pilot program in retraining teachers and finding them jobs, a second program was initiated during 1963-64, the emphasis of which was again to help Cuban educators to return to professional status in this country. A new aspect was now introduced to the program, the employment of graduates of the program in other states than Florida, as schools other than those in Dade County needed bilingual teachers. The basic curriculum was expanded beyond the previous education courses to include course work in English composition and humanities, as well as a course in methods of teaching Spanish using the audio-lingual approach.

All these courses were intended to be helpful in eventually meeting full certification requirements.

In the third year of the program, 1964-65, another innovation was introduced. The first two years of the program had been limited to students who had completed the equivalent of the B.A. in Cuba and needed to validate that degree for American certification purposes. In the third year the program was expanded to include those persons who had completed two or more years of Cuban university work but had not yet obtained their degrees when they left Cuba. "A new aspect of the program had developed: the possibility of obtaining a North American university degree by those teachers who had not completed their degree work in Cuba. Completion of a degree at the University of Miami School of Education would bring Florida certification automatically in the teaching major. Certification in other states would be easily available also" (Sevick, 1974: 38). Hardin's (1965) evaluation of Cuban education was used in evaluating Cuban transcripts. Those seeking a degree took one to two-and-a-half years of course work, depending on the amount of Cuban university work that had been completed. In addition, starting in this year, the participants began to be enrolled in the regular sections of courses of the University of Miami instead of in sections composed only of program participants. A further change introduced in this year was that participants began to incur tuition charges which were financed through the Cuban Student Loan Program.

Another important innovation was introduced in the fourth year of the program, 1965-66. It was recognized that there was a substantial number of former Cuban teachers who had completed only the teacher training program of the *escuela normal* (normal school) in Cuba. In Cuba the *escuela normal* program followed elementary school training and was intended strictly as preparatory for teaching. Hence it was specified that "although this training may not be considered to be equivalent to high school or college in this country, the normal school training will be acceptable as a high school diploma" (University of Miami School of Education. Sevick, 1974: 41).

Up until then the Cuban teacher aide working in the Dade County public schools with a *escuela normal* background in Cuba had no way of obtaining eventual certification except by undertaking a complete bachelor's degree program in an institution in this country. With this innovation, they were allowed to be admitted to the Cuban Teacher Retraining Program and the University of Miami as degree-seeking students, with a major in elementary education, that enabled them to obtain full certification as teachers.

The University of Miami program was notified by the Cuban Refugee Program that funds would no longer be available after the 1977 fiscal year and no new applicants were accepted after the spring of 1973. But as Sevick stressed, the program "has been a unique educational experiment, for never before have so many teachers from a foreign country been "retrained" as a group to teach in the United States" (1974: 17).

Without setting out to design a bilingual education program, the Cuban Refugee Program nevertheless provided, through federal funding and the co-operation of state and local agencies, a comprehensive program for receiving Cuban political immigrants. The program provided for both children and adults, and for teachers as well as students. The program surmounted obstacles that today are still with us: standardized testing, community resistance; and lack of qualified teachers. Further study and evaluation of the Miami experiment is an important research area for bilingual educators.

NOTES

1. The six statutes were the Refugee Relief Act of 1953 (67 Stat. 400); Act of September 11, 1957 (71 Stat. 639); Hungarian Parolees Act (72 Stat. 419); Azores and Netherlands Refugees Act (72 Stat. 1712); Act of September 22, 1959 (73 Stat. 644); Refugee-Escapees Act (74 Stat. 504).
2. During World War II, an annual token quota of 105 was allowed for Chinese as a wartime concession. The attempts to restrict Asian immigration began with the Chinese Exclusion Act of 1882 (22 Stat. 58).
3. Only two other school systems in the U.S., those of Union City and West New York (both in Hudson County, New Jersey) received some funds from the federal government through the Cuban Refugee Program. The amount that they received was not comparable to the federal contribution to the Dade County school system, but since 1970 they have each received roughly $1 million dollars per year. Cuban students represent fifty percent of the total student body in Union City and West New York, and they are the overwhelming majority of all Spanish-speaking students enrolled in these school systems.
4. A non-accredited institution was one which had not been granted academic accreditation by one of the following accrediting associations: the Southern Association of Colleges and Schools; the Middle States Association of Colleges and Secondary Schools; the New England Association of Colleges and Secondary Schools; the North Central Association of Colleges and Secondary Schools; the Northwest Association of Secondary and Higher Schools; the Western College Association.

BIBLIOGRAPHY

"Cuban Student Loan Program." *Higher Education* 20 (March): 14. 1964.

Dade County, Florida. Board of Public Instruction. Department of Administrative Research. *The Cuban Refugee in the Public Schools of Dade County, Florida.* Annual Reports. No. 1—1960-61 through No. 12—1972-73.

Eckerson, Helen F. "Immigration and National Origin." *The Annals* 367 (September): 4-14. 1966.

Florida State Department of Education. *Requirements for Teacher Certification.* Tallahassee: Florida State Department of Education. 1968.

Gray, R. B. "Aid to Cuban Refugees in Florida." *Governmental Research Bulletin* 1 (March): 1-4. 1964.

Hardin, Henry N. *Evaluating Cuban Education.* Miami: University of Miami Press. 1965.

"Iowa Si! Training Program for Special Teachers." *Newsweek* 62 (August): 75. 1963.

Lau v. *Nichols.* 94 S.Ct. 786, 414 U.S. 563, 39 L.Ed. 2nd 1. 1974.

Moncarz, Raul. "A Study of the Effect of Environmental Change of Human Capital among Selected Skilled Cubans." Ph.D. dissertation. Florida State University. 1969.

Prohias, Rafael J. and Lourdes Casal. *The Cuban Minority in the U.S.: Preliminary Report on Need Identification and Program Evaluation, Final Report for Fiscal Year 1973.* Washington, D.C.: Cuban National Planning Council. 1974.

Rogg, Eleanor Meyer. *The Assimilation of Cuban Exiles: The Role of Community and Class.* New York: Aberdeen Press. 1974.

Sevick, Charles V. *A History and Evaluation of the Cuban Teacher Retraining Program of the University of Miami 1963-1973.* University of Miami Ph.D. thesis. Coral Gables, Florida. 1974.

Smith, Richard Ferree. "Refugees," *The Annals* 367 (September): 43-52. 1966.

Thomas, John F. "Cuban Refugee Program." *Welfare in Review* 1 (September): 1-20. 1963.

U.S. Cuban Refugee Program. *Professional Manpower: A New Way to Meet the Need.* U.S. Department of Health, Education and Welfare.

United States General Accounting Office. *Analysis of Federal Expenditures to Aid Cuban Refugees.* Washington D.C.: Government Printing Office. 1971.

U.S. Office of Education. *United States Loan Program for Cuban Students, Guidelines for Borrowers.* Washington: Government Printing Office.

University of Miami School of Medicine. "International Medical Education: A Program Blossoms." *Spectra* II, no. 4.

University of Miami Center for Advanced International Studies. "The Cuban Immigration 1959-66 and its Impact on Miami-Dade County, Florida." Coral Gables, Florida: The University. 1967.

BILINGUAL EDUCATION AND PUBLIC POLICY: THE CASES OF THE AMERICAN INDIAN

Bea Medicine

As the name for the original inhabitants of this country has vacillated (Indian to American Indian, Indian-American to First Americans, and presently, Native American), governmental policy as it relates to education and the very life-styles of these tribal peoples have evidenced the impingement of public sentiment and public pressure upon the policy decisions which have affected them for generations. Numbering less than a million persons, whatever the name applied to them, public policy has conveniently obscured the numerous tribal entities, and multifarious educational policies have been pressed upon powerless peoples. Historically and unilaterally, the thrust of all educational programs has been towards assimilation and eventual amalgamation into a larger, dominant, and mainly white society.

The final report of the American Indian Policy Review Commission notes that, "A total of 289 tribes and bands live on 268 'federally recognized' reservations or otherwise defined 'trust areas' in 26 states." (1977: 90). Of immediate significance for bilingual education is the fact that an estimated 206 different languages and language dialects are still spoken among these native peoples. Wallace Chafe provides a sense of language utilization in Indian communities when he estimates that 49 of these languages have less than ten speakers aged fifty or over while 6 of these languages have more than 10,000 speakers in all generations representing language fluency. Fluency in the remaining 152 languages falls somewhere within these polarities. (Chafe, 1962: 162-171). Data of this nature points to the diverse need in terms of maintenance, transitional or revitalization programs involving Native American groups.

Most Native American tribal aggregates view themselves as independent nations within a multi-cultural superstructure. Nationhood at the time of the signing of treaties has given most tribes a unique trust relationship with the federal government which is reflected in the requirements for education. Generally, Indians as tribal aggregates and as individuals hold that federal provision for their education is a treaty right for many of them and see it as an important aspect of a trust relationship. Each treaty is viewed as an important mandate for each tribe. When Congress halted treaty-making with tribes in 1871, Indian policy was determined unilaterally. This established a pervasive trend to generate and generalize public policy of overriding dimensions whatever the cultural background of the peoples involved.

This paper seeks to present an ethno-historical overview to enhance awareness of these superimposed directives in the field of bilingual education as they relate to tribal peoples in the United States. It posits a nexus of policy and its implementation which should yield new insights into contemporary research needs and strategies for Native Americans.

Recent articulations by Indian militants, testimony-givers in countless congressional hearings on Indian "problems" accross the country, and by members of innumerable "Task Forces" set up to deal with educational concerns, have mentioned the loss of ancestral Indian languages. What scope and precision these losses have entailed are seldom articulated for tribally distinct groups. Language loss has been mainly verbalized in rhetoric, polemics, and possible guilt-inducing attempts for policy planners.

Most current studies on American Indians contain scattered references to the loss of native languages and the inefficient use of English. Perspectives on the use of languages—ancestral and new—in specific tribes or communities are seldom delineated. A stringent analysis of language policy as intertwined with the entire process of education for a specific group of natives is a research need of high priority. There are several reasons for this absence in the arena of language use and ethnicity. Historically, overarching governmental policy has not given credence to idiosyncratic reactions of tribes to the policy. Evaluative frames have not been applied in any equitable fashion. More recently, the deficit model as it has been applied to Indians has co-opted linguistic research into probing problems such as dropout rates, reading difficulties, and insensitive teachers. Sociological and historical aspects in juxtaposition with the contours of speech communities must be perceived for Native American groups. Despite generations of propulsion to assimilation and concerted efforts for cultural change enacted via the educational process, each tribe has maintained some type of cultural base by virtue of ecological isolation (reservations) or socioeconomic constraints (race and class) or by simple choice. Thus, despite superordinate governmental dictates and decision making which has been external to the native community, tribes have maintained some aspect of cultural and linguistic integrity. Therefore, in assessing public policy and tribal enactment of the rules and regulations, an ethnographic sophistication and an awareness of the interface between two different modes of social organization is essential.

The wide range of cultural types exemplified by native societies and the differential reaction to language policy may best be exemplified by cross-cultural comparisons. Indeed, if only a careful analysis of one tribe is done, it can show the dynamics of language use, retention, and change. Moreover, it can highlight the areas for current and future research.

The American Indian Policy Review Commission presented a report on one of the "five civilized tribes." Referring to the Cherokee:

> In the 1820's, (*sic*) that tribe established a peaceful, thriving, self-sustaining community whose governing elite actively promoted constitutionalism, commercial farming, education, and Christianity. The United States virtually denied the abundant evidence of Cherokee success, deliberately assaulted the administrative integrity of the Cher-

> okee government, and fostered enduring tribal factions—all in a successful effort to secure a treaty for tribal lands in Appalachia.
>
> Few tribes in the nineteenth century went as far as the Cherokees in trying to accommodate to the government's notion of civilization. But nearly all received their education for civilization in the context of an overall plan of action that deprived them of their most valuable resources, displaced them from their homes, attacked and subverted their chosen leaders, and denigrated their religious and ceremonial life, family relations, dress, *language*, and sexual division of labor. (Final Report, 1977: 61). (Italics are mine.)

The Cherokee had chosen accommodation and used the same criteria which the conquerors had. Indeed, they had become literate in their own native language, using a syllabary said to have been developed by the Cherokee, Sequoyah. Thus, most of the pinnacles of civilization had been achieved on native terms. Yet, in the forced displacement from the Southeastern United States to Indian Territory (now Oklahoma), the more "full blood" descendents of this Cherokee group are considered illiterate and "unacculturated."

Wahrhaftig and Thomas describe the Cherokee context in the Oklahoma area:

> Prominent whites say with pride, "We're all a little bit Indian here." They maintain that real Cherokees are about "bred out." Few Cherokees are left who can speak their native tongue, whites insist, and fewer still are learning their language. In twenty years, according to white myth, the Cherokee language and with it the separate and distinctive community that speaks it will fade into memory.
>
> Anthropologists visiting us in the field, men who thought their previous studies had taught them what a conservative tribe is like, were astonished by the Cherokees. Seldom had they seen people who speak so little English, who are so unshakably traditional in outlook. (in Bahr, Chadwick, and Day, 1972: 80-81).

Qualitative contours of this contemporary community are again illuminated by this excerpt from the same authors, Thomas (a Cherokee) and Wahrhaftig:

> Before 1907, the entire area was part of the Cherokee nation. Today, 12,000 Cherokees live there, 9,500 of them in traditionally structured, small, Cherokee-speaking settlements. The educational level of these Cherokee Indians is one of the lowest in the United States and their dropout rate is one of the highest. Of the adult Cherokees 40 percent are functionally illiterate in English. Approximately one in three heads of Cherokee households in country Cherokee settlements cannot speak English. Cherokees attended their own schools for half a century and the school system of the State of Oklahoma for sixty years thereafter. Even so, the Cherokee community of eastern Oklahoma is one of the least educated in our nation. (In Wax, Diamond, Gearing, 1971: 231-232).

Recent effects of policy decisions which have affected this group have not yet been clarified—effective utilization of Title VII and other bilingual attempts are yet to be documented. One can state that the Oklahoma Cherokee represent one example of the effects of forced relocation, cultural isolation, factionalism, loss of community control over schools, and educational policies to move a powerless people into a projected middle-class existence in an area which heretofore has been economically deprived. Recent emphasis upon the disadvantaged peoples of Appalachia in federal funding programs will also have implications.

Though many Native American individuals speak of treaty obligations, one finds that the younger generations seldom know the obligations of the federal government that is often outlined in the treaties and which form the basis for the relationships between tribe and federal government. To give the essence of "treaty talk," one famous agreement was examined for requirements on education. The 1868 Treaty with the Sioux, Brule, Oglala, Miniconjou, Yanktonai, Hunkpapa, Blackfeet, Cuthead, Two Kettle, Sans Arc, and Santee bands (and Arapaho, an Algonkian speaking Plains tribe), is quite explicit. Parenthetically, the Standing Rock Tribal Council published the text of all treaties pertaining to the Sioux for the tribal members in 1973. The section delineating education is as follows:

> Article #7: In order to insure the civilization of the Indians entering into this treaty, the necessity of education is admitted, especially of such of them as are or may be settled on said agricultural reservation, and they therefore pledge themselves to compel their children, male and female, between the ages of six and sixteen years, to attend school; and it is hereby made the duty of the agent for said Indians to see that this stipulation is strictly complied with; and the United States agrees that for every thirty children between said ages who can be induced or compelled to attend school, a house shall be provided and a teacher competent to teach the elementary branches of an English education shall be furnished, who will reside among said Indians, and faithfully discharge his or her duties as a teacher. The provisions of this article to continue for not less than twenty years. (Treaties and Agreements and the Proceedings of the Treaties and Agreements of the Tribes and Bands of the Sioux Nation, 1973: 94).

This directive is specific as to age, sex, type of education, provision of school house and teacher for a stated number of pupils. Of significance is the equating of civilizing the Sioux Indians, a nomadic, warrior society, with an "English education." It also predicated a sedentary life with an agricultural base.

The following policy statement, though lengthy, gives a more detailed rationale for the linguistic education of Indian people and exemplifies the over-arching formation of language policy:

> Longer and closer consideration of the subject has only deepened my conviction that it is a matter not only of importance, but of necessity that the Indians acquire the English language as rapidly as possible. The government has entered upon the great work of educating and citizenizing the Indians and establishing them upon homesteads. The adults are expected to assume the role of citizens, and of course the rising generation will be expected and required more nearly to fill the measure of citizenship, and the main purpose of educating them is to enable them to read, write, and speak the English language and to transact business with English-speaking people. When they take upon themselves the responsibilities and privileges of citizenship their vernacular will be of no advantage. Only through the medium of the English tongue can they acquire a knowledge of the Constitution of the country and their rights and duties thereunder . . . Nothing so

> surely and perfectly stamps upon an individual a national characteristic as language . . . Only English has been allowed to be taught in the public schools in the territory acquired by this country from Spain, Mexico, and Russia, although the native populations spoke another tongue . . .
>
> Deeming it for the very best interest of the Indian, both as an individual and as an embryo citizen, to have this policy strictly enforced among the various schools on Indian reservations, orders have been issued accordingly to Indian agents . . .
>
> It is believed that if any Indian vernacular is allowed to be taught by the missionaries in schools on Indian reservations, it will prejudice the youthful pupil as well as his untutored and uncivilized or semi-civilized parent against the English language, and, to some extent at least, against Government schools in which the English language exclusively has always been taught. To teach Indian school children their native tongue is practically to exclude English, and to prevent them from acquiring it. This language, which is good enough for a white man and a black man, ought to be good enough for the red man. It is also believed that teaching an Indian youth in his own barbarous dialect is a positive detriment to him. The first step to be taken toward civilization, toward teaching the Indians the mischief and folly of continuing their barbarous practices, is to teach them the English language. The impracticality, if not the impossibility, of civilizing the Indians of this country in any other tongue other than our own would seem to be obvious, especially in view of the fact that the number of Indian vernaculars is even greater than the number of tribes. Bands of the same tribes inhabiting different localities have different dialects, and sometimes can not communicate with each other except by sign language. If we expect to infuse into the rising generation the leaven of American citizenship, we must remove the stumbling blocks of hereditary customs and manners, and of these language is one of the most important elements. . . . (House Executive Document No. 1, 50th Congress., 1st sess. serial 2542: 19-21) reprinted in Prucha, 1975: 174-176).

This extract from the Annual Report of the Commissioner of Indian Affairs of 1887 indicates the official position of the Department in viewing the English language as one of the chief modes of bringing civilization to the Indians. J. D. C. Atkins interprets this directive which then could be re-interpreted down the bureaucratic ladder. The foregoing also brings into focus the extreme ethnocentrism and superior attitudes of those individuals dedicated to bringing a new life style to Indian peoples. The tone and thrust of this policy formed the cornerstone of Indian education until the effects of the Collier administration were felt in the 1930s.

In an effort to give an epic view of this process of language repression, several statements from Siouan life histories are included. Throughout Indian country, from the Winnebago in Wisconsin (also a Siouan-speaking group) to the Makah (Wakashan-linguistic affiliation) in the Northwest on the Washington coast, a standard practice was to wash the mouth of the student who "reverted" back to speaking the native tongue with "strong yellow laundry soap, you know, the kind that comes in bars." (Quote from Pearl Warren, (Makah), Medicine, field notes, 1972). The trauma of this experience was still evident in this sixty-five-year-old woman as her eyes filled with tears. Most often in the history of language change, the recipients of the program's internalization of those superimposed policies are seldom considered.

Luther Standing Bear, describes his meeting with his father at Carlisle Indian School:

> When I got downstairs, my father was in the center of a large crowd of the boys, who were all shaking hands with him. He was so glad to see me, and I was so delighted to see him. But our rules were not to speak the Indian language under any consideration. And here was my father, and he could not speak English!
>
> My first act was to write a note to Captain Pratt, asking if he would permit me to speak to my father in the Sioux tongue. I said, "My father is here. Please allow me to speak to him in Indian." Captain Pratt answered, "Yes, my boy; bring your father over to my house." (1928: 149).

Later, Standing Bear notes, "He allowed the boys to talk to him in the Indian tongue, and that pleased the boys very much." (ibid., 150). Luther Standing Bear, who entered Carlisle Indian School in 1897, recalls his father's conversation after Captain Pratt took the elder Standing Bear on a trip to Boston, New York, Baltimore, Philadelphia, and Washington.

> After he returned from the trip, he spoke to me in this wise: "My son, since I have seen all those cities, and the way the Long Knife people are doing, I begin to realize that our lands and our game are all gone. There is nothing but the Long Knives (or white people) everywhere I went, and they keep coming like flies. So we will have to learn their ways, in order that we may be able to live with them. You will have to learn all you can, and I will see that your brothers and sisters follow in the path you are making for them."
>
> This is the first time my father had ever spoken to me regarding acquiring a white man's education. He continued: "Some day I want to hear you speak like these Long Knife people, and work like them." This was spoken to me by my father in the Dakota tongue, but it meant so much to me. He was so serious in his conversation along this line that I felt quite 'puffed up.' I wanted to please him in everything—even to getting killed on the battlefield. Even that I was willing to endure. (ibid., 151-152).

This statement is all the more remarkable since Luther volunteered to attend Carlisle without his father's permission for he had heeded his admonishment "to die in battle, meeting the enemy." He viewed going to school in the East as "meeting the enemy," it seems. As Standing Bear had made an autonomous decision, his father agreed. Other data detailing the trauma of a forcible language learning experience is given in Appendix I. Noteworthy to mention at this time is the dearth of life history material for women. This is especially significant for it reflects the male-bias of early ethnographers, but also indicates that, among the Sioux, for example, women were kept away from these investigators. It is possible to examine the roles of women in the socialization process by looking at life histories (see Medicine, 1975). This lack of data in language studies is especially crucial as it is the mother and mother surrogate who is so important in the early language acquisition of children. The full effects of cultural genocide and the psychic toll on native individuals have not been part of the investigative priorities of early researchers. Fragmentary references and anecdotal statements must be carefully honed out of the ethnographic record.

A cogent analysis of the numerous educational attempts forced upon the Indians, parochial and governmental, should be examined in the entire area of bilingual education for Indians. The translation of native languages into religious items—Bibles, hymnals, and prayer books—is seldom acknowledged. These are important means by which many Native Americans, under the guise of Christianization, were able to retain their indigenous languages. Indigneous statements are forerunners and should be examined when current reference is made to "Indian English" (Leap, 1973) or when novelists, (Ruth Beebe Hill, 1979) speak of "archaic" Dakotah languages and exploit Indian languages for profit.

The influence of John Collier in the New Deal era was enormous in charting new directions in Indian education. His thesis was that education should develop, rather than diminish, group loyalties and that the unique cultural backgrounds of the tribes be acknowledged, enhanced, and emphasized via the learning processes. His policy "insisted that Indians have religious and social freedom in all manners where such freedom was not directly contrary to public morals." (Philp, 1972: 69). After his appointment as Commissioner of Indian Affairs, he obtained, in June, 1934, the passage of the Indian Reorganization Act. This act rejected the traditional policy of assimilation and "Americanization" of the Indians in favor of a policy of cultural pluralism.

As a part of cultural revitalization, bilingual readers were developed for some tribes. The readers for the Sioux included such books as *Brave Against the Enemy (T'oka wan itkip'ip Ohitike kin he)* by Ann Nolan Clark and Helen Post.

Thus, the prolonged period when "The Indian Bureau tried to Americanize Native American children by sending them to boarding schools where they were taught to despise their culture" (Philp, 1973: 22) drew to a close. An element not sufficiently treated in historical analyses of Indian education is that of native language use. Sociolinguistic studies of language use and retention and its utilization in native communities are sadly lacking for this period. Basic to Collier's emphasis on cultural awareness via native religious expression, development of Indian arts, crafts, and music, was the seldom mentioned role of language as a medium by which religious ritual and expressive elements of native cultures were fostered.

A succinct statement must suffice for this period:

> There is also in press a series of books in Sioux and English. Here the problem is different. More of the Sioux speak English. They are more familiar with the world beyond the reservation. But their language is the one used in their own world. Owing to the labors of missionaries over many years, many of the Sioux are able to read and write their own language now. Here we need only take advantage of the work that has been done, and provide opportunities for its use. Our major departure has been to work in the dialect that has the greatest number of speakers—Teton—whereas most of the printed material used today is in the eastern dialects. Since they are all mutually intelligible, this is a matter of economy. (Kennard, in LaFarge, 1942: 114).

The comparative stance here refers to the Navajo, who were, and are, the tribe evidencing the largest degree of monolingualism in their native language of the Athabaskan stock.

Forty-one years after the bench-mark Meriam Report of 1928 which presaged the 1969 Senate Committee report entitled *Indian Education: A National Tragedy—A National Challenge,* the subtle pressures toward cultural homogenization to white European language and values continued. Indians were still being victimized by an alien educational process. The well-funded study by Havighurst and Fuchs (1972) indicates the scope of bilingual education. Although they indicate no unanimous opinion regarding native language use, they state . . . "the National Study found considerable support among Indian youths and their parents for instruction in the native languages themselves, as subjects of study, within the schools, both at the elementary and secondary level." (Fuchs and Havighurst, 1972: 213). As the Bureau of Indian Affairs is now contracting their schools to tribal groups in an effort to sponsor community control and self-determination, the decisions regarding the impact of bicultural and bilingual education for Indians may have a new emphasis. Parent Advisory Councils which are mandated by proposal requirements plus such native organizations as the National Indian Education Association and the Coalition of Community Controlled Schools are means of obtaining the much-overworked phrase "Indian input" into the curricula.

The negation of the ideal of a homogeneous American society plus the valuation of ethnicity in current contemporary American life styles has in general given a new perspective to language use in most native societies. The resiliency and adaptiveness of American Indians and Alaskan Natives, as the identity now goes, can be seen in the efforts to strengthen the imperative that culture and language are wedded together and form a more positive identity. The enhanced aspects of being a native in a white world will have some interesting connotations for future researchers. From a viewpoint of interaction in native communities, the apparent interest seems to be increasing.

We can, therefore, turn to recent public policies which have been responsible for this heightened interest.

The Indian Education Act of 1972 (P.L. 92-318) has authorized and given great impetus for innovative and compensatory programs in BIA, public schools, community-controlled schools and in adult education and higher education programs. This legislation stresses the allocation of decision-making powers to native tribes and groups. It also established an Office of Indian Education in the United States Office of Education under the supervision of a National Advisory Council on Indian Education appointed by the President. The Council consists of fifteen Native Americans who are of varied tribal backgrounds.

Local level political systems were acknowledged with program review and veto powers given to Indian citizen groups. An outstanding feature of this legislation is a provision to serve all Native Americans whether or not they are affiliated with a federally recognized tribe.

The Amendment of Title VII of the Elementary and Secondary Act of 1965, Bilingual Education (P.L. 93-380) August 21, 1974 has added great impetus to the funding of bilingual programs for native peoples.

William Demmert, first Deputy Commissioner of Indian Education and former Director of Indian Education in the Bureau of Indian Affairs writes in an article in *American Education:* "It is absolutely imperative that Indian parents and communities participate in forming the cultural, psychological, physical, intellectual, and language base upon which schools must later build." (Aug.-Sept. 1976: 8). He further indicated the scope of these Acts when he stated: "In FY 1976, some 278,000 Indian students in over a thousand school districts are benefiting from Part A grants, which are supporting bicultural-bilingual enrichment activities that include the development of cultural awareness curriculums (*sic*) in reading and mathematics and such supportive services as guidance counseling and transportation." (ibid.: 8)

What is empirical evidence of the need for bilingual education for Indian children?

The National Indian Training and Research Center was contracted by the Bureau of Indian Affairs to conduct an assessment of the bilingual education needs of children. Data was collected by use of questionnaires completed by officials at all BIA, contract, or public schools receiving Johnson-O'Malley funds. There were great variations in the ways in which bilingual education was defined and the regulations interpreted. Only thirty-three percent of the schools had conducted needs assessments to give data for program planning. Parents actually favoring the approach were not significant. The study indicated that of 169,482 Indian children enrolled in BIA schools, approximately one-third evidenced bilingual education needs while almost one-fourth indicated need for this special program which at that time (1973) was not being met.

One report indicates that "Before 1970 there would have been few bilingual programs to observe in Eskimo and Indian communities. Now there are more than thirty-five programs, some new and some that have been going on for several years, some in only certain grades in a single school, some in many schools in an area." (Bank Street School of Education Report, 1976: 253).

Recent discourse—academic, legalistic, and popular—has focussed upon the larger populations of minority peoples involved in the bilingual education dilemma. The unique cases of the numerically smallest, yet most culturally diverse of these groups has been ignored in recent research.

What then are the patterns of language use in the lives of contemporary Native Americans? In some areas, i.e., the Pueblos in the Southwest, language has persisted and is closely tied to religious ritual and esoteric language. In many instances, the community people, especially the ritual leaders and religious practitioners, often resist bilingual education on the grounds that teaching a native language in the school might reveal their religious beliefs and allow non-Pueblos to learn the native tongue and gain access to cultural data. This rationale also has implications for utilization of cultural content in curricula. Santo Domingo Pueblo (a Keresan speaking group) is an example.

However, among the numerous Navajo, there is a strong commitment to the use of the native language which is deemed essential for monolingual children or those who have little exposure to English to become bilingual with the least possible psychic stress to the individual. Many successful school situations, staffed by qualified Navajo educators with sound involvement of communities, (i.e., Rough Rock) are exemplary experiments in bilingual education. The Navajo school at Rock Point is an excellent example of a language maintainence program where bilingual education is carried from kindergarten through the eighth grade. The enormous population growth of the Navajo seemingly coincided with more tolerant views regarding Indian education and a corollary training program for Navajo teachers. There factors may be credited for a more efficacious education program which is also attuned to the needs of this segment of the Indian population. The continued effectiveness of the Navajo language programs needs further evaluation.

An example of a retrieval-revival program is that of the Onieda (an Iroquoian-speaking group) in Wisconsin. This group is presently engaged in the revival of native religion, the establishment of a tribal museum and archives, and increased interest in oral history. Much of this cultural revitalization may be tied to land claims.

The Makah (a Wakashan-speaking group) in northwestern Washington state have a large federal grant to revive their language. This nativistic movement is also to revive other expressive elements of culture as music, dance, and tribal dress.

Within the entire range of bilingual education programs for Native Americans, there is a pervasive idiosyncratic expression of language use. Some parents and parental surrogates (as grandparents) feel that the sooner the children learn English well, the easier it will be for them to adapt and function effectively in a predominantly English-speaking world. Others have stated, "I don't want my children to have the 'hard time' (difficulty) I had learning the English language" and will speak only "Indian English" to them. These individuals very often use a native language in communicating with their aged cohorts and in community affairs. This attitude is typical in many Lakota Sioux communities, where the degree of bilingualism is difficult to determine. Language use in the native vernacular may, in these, and other Indian communities (i.e., Yakina) be seen as a means of adding "funding" to an educational base. In many contemporary native communities, the parents and parental age-mates feel that education should begin in the child's first language with a gradual but effective transition to competence in English and the mastering of the school's curriculum. Others feel that a complete break with the community's language and culture is a prerequisite for adaptation in a white school and society.

A great majority of the current Indian population resides in cities or off-reservation communities. This group often holds their parents responsible for not teaching them their native language. This trend can possibly be reflected in the inclusion of the teaching of native Indian and Inuit (Eskimo) languages in some universities and colleges.

The effects of the Bilingual Education Act (Title VII) undoubtedly will have some consequences for the future direction of education for American Indians and Alaskan natives. The Indian Self-Determination Act of 1977 with a clearly mandated issue of indigenous control will present interesting directions in the field of language and culture. Presently, there have been few attempts to evaluate those bicultural and bilingual programs which have been in operation since the funding base has been applied to native communities.

The decisions made by a superordinate decision-making body in the execution of policy determining language use and the educational process has had dire effects upon the linguistic skills of contemporary natives. The language policies have been tied to the civilization process based upon the destruction of native language and lifestyles.

The basic policies have been set and then reinterpreted by bureaucrats and decision makers in the numerous federal and state agencies which impinge upon native life. Thus, a certain capriciousness is evident in the ethnohistoric record which can be seen in the idiosyncratic relationship of each tribe to their treaties and the Indian agent. More recently, this pattern of financial dependence is seen in the composition of advisory boards, interpreters of present language policy, and proposal readers.

At this juncture, several points can be made regarding contemporary programs. Most of the schools involved in bilingual education have been seen as "model" schools with the expectation that their continuity would be assured by the community. In most instances, due to monetary restrictions and dependence upon Title VII as the "funding" source, many of the bilingual programs have been abandoned after five years. In many communities, due to the historical restrictions on language use documented previously, many of the programs have assumed a cultural and language retrieval aspect. In almost all communities, local level politics entered the picture and oriented the programs. In many instances, the individuals most competent to teach native languages and culture have been the most inept in the political machinations of school boards, parent advisory councils, and public school politics, and were merely shunted aside for other more "acceptable" (from the administrative point of view) native peoples.

What is evident in this brief paper is the fact of a super-subordinate situation in which language policy has, and is, being formulated at another level and being shifted upon the educational processes of powerless peoples of all tribes.

APPENDIX

Francis LaFlesche, gives an interesting view of language learning among the Omaha (also a Siouan language):

> From the earliest years the Omaha child was trained in the grammatical use of his native tongue. No slip was allowed to pass uncorrected, and as a result there was no child-talk such as obtains among English-speaking children,—the only difference between the speech of old and young was in the pronunciation of words which the infant often failed to utter correctly, but this difficulty was soon overcome, and a boy of ten or twelve years was apt to speak as good Omaha as a man of mature years.
>
> Like the grown folks, we youngsters were fond of companionship and of talking. In making our gamesticks and in our play, we chattered incessantly of the things that occupied our minds, and we thought it a hardship when we were obliged to speak in low tones while older people were engaged in conversation. When we entered the Mission School, we experienced a greater hardship, for there we encountered a rule that prohibited the use of our own language, which rule was rigidly enforced with a hickory rod, so that the newcomer, however socially inclined, was obliged to go about like a little dummy until he learned to express himself in English.

All the boys in our school were given English names, because their Indian names were difficult for the teachers to pronounce. Besides, the aboriginal names were considered by the missionaries as heathenish, and therefore should be obliterated. No less heathenish in their origin were the English substitutes, but the loss of their original meanings and significance through long useage had rendered them fit to continue as appellations for civilized folk. And so, in place of Tae-noo-ga-wa-he, came Philip Sheridan; in that of Wa-pah'-dae, Ulysses S. Grant; that of Koo'-we-he-ge-ra, Alexander, and so on. Our sponsors went even further back in history, and thus we had our David and Jonathan, Gideon and Isaac, and, with the flood of these new names came Noah. It made little difference to us that we had to learn the significance of one more word as applied to ourselves, when the task before us was to make our way through an entire strange language. So we learned to call each other by our English names, and continued to do so even after we had left school and had grown to manhood.

Referring to his vignettes, La Flesche continues:

In the talk of the boys I have striven to give a reproduction of the peculiar English spoken by them, which was composite, gathered from the imperfect comprehension of their books, the provincialisms of the teachers, and the slang and bad grammar picked up from uneducated white persons employed at the school or at the Government Agency. Oddities of speech, profanity, localisms, and slang were unknown in the Omaha language, so when such expressions fell upon the ears of these lads they innocently learned and used them without the slightest suspicion that there could be bad as well as good English.

The misconception of Indian life and character so common among the White people has been largely due to an ignorance of the Indian's language, or his mode of thought, his beliefs, his ideals, and his native institutions. Every aspect of the Indian and his manner of life has always been strange to the White man, and this strangeness had been magnified by the mists of prejudice and the conflict of interests between the two races. While these in time may disappear, no native American can ever cease to regret that the utterances of his father have been constantly belittled when put into English, that their thoughts have frequently been travestied and their native dignity obscured. The average interpreter has generally picked up his knowledge of English in a random fashion, for very few have had the advantage of a thorough education, and all have had to deal with the difficulties that attend the translator. The beauty and picturesqueness, and euphonious playfulness, or the gravity of diction which I have heard among my own people, and other tribes as well, are all but impossible to be given literally in English (LaFlesche, 1963).

REFERENCES

American Indian Policy Review Commission. *Final Report,* Vols. 1 and 2. Washington: United States Government Printing Office, 1977.

Beebe Hill, Ruth. *Hanta Yo—An American Saga.* Garden City, New York: Doubleday and Co., Inc. 1979.

Chafe, W. L. "Estimates regarding the present speakers of North American Indian Languages." in *International Journal of American Linguistics* 28: (1962) pp. 162-171. ibid corrected estimates 31: (1965) pp. 345-346.

Clark, Ann and Post, Helen. *Brave Against the Enemy (I'oka wan itkik'ip ohitike kin he)*. Lawrence, Kansas: Haskell Institute Printing Department, 1944.

Demmert, William G., Jr. "Indian Education: Where and Whither?" in *American Education*. Office of Education, Health, Education and Welfare 112:7 (1976) pp. 6-9.

Fuchs, Estelle and Havighurst, Robert J. *To Live on this Earth*. Garden City, New York: Doubleday and Co., 1972.

LaFlesche, Francis. *The Middle Five*. Madison: University of Wisconsin Press, 1963.

Leap, William. "Language Pluralism in a Southwestern Pueblo: The Evidence from Isleta," in *Bilingualism in the Southwest*. ed. P. R. Turner, pp. 274-294 Tucson: University of Arizona Press, 1973.

Kennard, Edward A. "The Use of Native Languages and Cultures in Indian Education," in *The Changing Indian*; ed. Oliver LaFarge, pp. 109-115 Norman: University of Oklahoma Press, 1942.

Medicine, Bea. *Native American Women: A Perspective*. Las Cruces, New Mexico: Eric/Cress, 1978.

Philp, Kenneth R. "John Collier and the American Indian, 1920-1945," in *Essays on Radicalism in Contemporary America*. ed. Leon B. Blair pp. 63-80 Austin: University of Texas Press, 1972.

__________. "John Collier and the Crusade to Protect Indian Religious Freedom." *Journal of Ethnic Studies*. 1:1 (1973) pp. 22-38.

Prucha, Francis Paul. *Documents of United States History*. Lincoln: University of Nebraska Press, 1975.

Standing Bear, Luther. *My People, The Sioux*. Boston: Houghton Mifflin Co., 1928.

Survey of Bilingual Education Needs of Indian Children. Research and Evaluation Report, Series No. 36. Albuquerque: Indian Education Resources Center, Bureau of Indian Affairs. October, 1975.

Thomas, Robert K. and Wahrhaftig, Albert L. "Indians, Hillbillies and the Education Problem." in *Anthropological Perspectives in Education*. Wax, Murray L., Diamond, Stanley, and Gearging, Fred eds., New York: Basic Books, Inc. 1971.

Treaties and Agreements and the Proceedings of the Treaties and Agreements of the Tribes and Bands of the Sioux Nation. Fort Yates, North Dakota: Standing Rock Sioux Tribe, 1973.

Trimble, Joseph E., et al, *Review of the Literature on Educational Needs and Problems of American Indians*. Seattle: Battelle Memorial Institute, 1977.

Wahrhaftig, Albert L. and Thomas, Robert K. "Renaissance and Repression: The Oklahoma Cherokee." in Bahr, Howard M., Chadwick, Bruce A., and Day, Robert C., *Native Americans Today: Sociological Perspectives* pp. 80-89 New York: Harper and Row, 1972.

Zimiles, Herbert, et al. *Young Native Americans and their Families: Educational Needs Assessment and Recommendations*. New York: Bank Street School of Education, 1976.

LANGUAGE ATTITUDES IN A NEW YORK PUERTO RICAN COMMUNITY

John Attinasi

This essay is concerned with the opinions, attitudes and aspirations of a group of Puerto Rican residents of *el barrio*—East Harlem, New York City. The sample contains ninety-one persons over twelve years old, chosen after a year of participant-observation. The sample, technically a *purposive sample,* represents the main social networks in an urban, low-income residential block. A language attitude questionnaire provided the basis for this report. It was administered in a sociolinguistic interview which lasted about two hours. (For more detail on the method and rationale of this study, the full report of the sociolinguistic investigation should be consulted. In that report, [Language Policy Task Force: 1979], an orientation to language attitude studies and a review of their relevance to the Hispanic and Puerto Rican community may be found).

This attitudinal study forms one component of the integrated ethnographic-linguistic-attitudinal research undertaken by the Centro de Estudios Puertorriqueños. Description of the neighborhood, its members and their networks of interaction provides the community context; the sociolinguistic studies of verb structures, nominal and verbal realization of the plural in sentences, and the alternation of languages in fluent speech (code-switching) offer evidence regarding skills found among speakers; this language attitude report discusses the recognized and desired features of the sociolinguistic situation. Together, these studies form the empirical part of the wider goal articulated by the Centro and the National Puerto Rican Task Force on Educational Policy (see Bonilla and del Valle articles in this volume) to formulate and implement a language policy for Puerto Ricans in the United States.

Bilingual education policy in the U.S. at the present time, and the language planning that exists in general, have been legislated "from the top," and presented to communities by policy makers who are distinct from both affected community members and policy-oriented researchers (Lynn 1978). Current legislation provides for "bilingual education" whose primary goal is not bilingualism but transition into English. Our critique of imposed transitional bilingual education—of any language or educational policy—contains two aspects. At a theoretical level, the principle of national self-determination (about which much has been written, e.g., Language Policy Task Force 1978: 19-20), implies respect for national tradition and requires policy control from within the cultural group affected. At the practical level, the implementation of policy requires community acceptance to insure its success (Haugen 1966: 60-64; Jernudd & Das Gupta 1971; Kelman 1971: 27).[1] Therefore, the determination of the resources, attitudes, needs and goals of the community regarding education and language in general is crucial.

In presenting and interpreting the views of the community, caution against popularism and other erroneous tendencies is appropriate. Not everything the populace says should become a platform for policy. Three negative tendencies have been noticed in at least some cases: "alienation of spirit," that is often infatuated with the values of the oppressor (see footnote 33); "cultural-nationalist" idealism that views culture as immutable, thinking that every change is a threat; and "apathetic personalism," that values the comfort of the individual, ignoring the social interdependence that is the cornerstone of human, and therefore national, existence. A theory which encompasses political economy, cultural and linguistic rights, and ultimately the health and self-creativity of a society—though such a theory is but implied in this treatment—provides an objective standpoint in the search for a community-based language policy, and offers a means of judging the assumptions and implications of material in this survey.

The above is, in brief, the rationale for this study, asking key questions related to the following issues for the community: the choice of Spanish or English or bilingualism; the existing resources of the community in terms of skills and usage; linguistic issues in education and the relationship of language to cultural and national identity.

The sample is similar to the Puerto Rican population in the United States in terms of age, birth, employment and other factors (see the Introduction; and Pedraza 1979; also see Bureau of Labor Statistics 1975). Respondents were carefully chosen to represent typical speakers and lifestyles in the community studied. While it is not certain that *el barrio* is "the most" Puerto Rican community in the continental United States, it may be claimed that it is one of the most important communities for understanding migration and other effects of the colonial relationship between the U.S. and Puerto Rico because it is one of the oldest, largest and most dense communities of Puerto Ricans.

El barrio may be considered a case that allows the testing of extremes for Spanish in the United States. Its ethnic density would tend to maintain the language (Giles 1977: 312ff, Gaarder 1977: 107ff). The long-term residence of many in the community might, on the other hand, favor linguistic assimilation (if ethnic integrity is strong here, then in more recently established communities, attachment to Puertoricanness should be even more salient). In fact, one finds a continuum of Puerto Ricans in the United States, with recent arrival, cyclic migration, and residence with other ethnic and linguistic groups as some of the characteristics to be weighed in order to understand the dynamics of language and culture across the nation and through time. (This report does not attempt to speak about the language situation nor about bilingual education in Puerto Rico—that would require a separate treatment since the issues are different and the history is complex (see Language Policy Task Force 1978). We see this work as pertinent to the Puerto Rican population in the United States, without assuming anything about the nature of the differences between Puerto Rican culture in the U.S. and in Puerto Rico (see Bonilla and Colon 1979).

The American possession of Puerto Rico, periods of imposition of the English language, and the consequential migration to the United States have put critical stresses on Puerto Rican culture. Unemployment is more than double the national average;[2] many live in inadequate housing and have income below the "poverty level"[3] and educational failure is rampant.[4] Language policy is not the panacea for all social ills, but clearly educational failure and community attitudes are related to contemporary social life.

How culture relates to language in the community is also at issue in this study. The present dynamics of the community are not part of a general "everything changes" process. Rather, television, consumerism, inflation, unemployment and intensified migration are powerful new elements in twentieth century struggles which involve both economics and nationality. These elements in turn, affect cultural expression. Given such conditions, and acknowledging Puerto Rico's status as a direct colony of the richest nation-state in the world, the situation and solutions of the Puerto Rican community possess a wider relevance for understanding the world emerging at the last part of this century.[5] On the one hand, resources have become more precious, information more available and communication (including transportation) has shrunk the distance between nations. On the other hand, the national groups in the United States are attacked for not assimilating, their ethnicity is considered intransigence and a sign of future problems, their bilingual character is considered pathological.[6]

Thus the findings of this study—values and beliefs about language, and about culture—relate not only to policy but the survival of a community.[7] The community's views on language, when articulated with wider social and economic needs, can enter the legal and educational struggle as grassroots evidence in the formulation of meaningful policy. Also at issue are the development of critical and intellectual skills, access to formal varieties of language, and the improvement of schooling.

But these wider concerns cannot be resolved without a clear assessment of the sociolinguistic values and norms of interaction that are present in the community. By implication, cultural and educational issues can be better addressed in more focused study based upon this basic research. (The Language Policy Task Force has undertaken such lines of research observing classroom and student interaction in East Harlem, and interviewing a sample of teachers and parents for language attitudes.)

PERSONAL AND SOCIAL CHARACTERISTICS

Demographics

The demographic characteristics of the ninety-one persons from *el barrio* in this study match well those of the U.S. Puerto Rican community. Briefly, Puerto Ricans are on the average, young (one-half are under twenty-five years of age), and educated to about junior high school level. Many are poor (one-third are below the poverty level). Puerto Ricans are becoming established as long-term residents of the United States. Ninety percent of the persons in this sample have lived in the U.S. over ten years.

The sample in this report represents a community with greater ethnic density than that of most Puerto Rican settlements in the United States. Even in New York, only about one in five Puerto Ricans live in neighborhoods like *el barrio,* in which they are in the majority. The mean population density in most Puerto Rican neighborhoods is about twenty-five percent.

The attitudinal sample is also slightly older than the general population because we aimed at an adult view of language attitudes, systematically excluding from the interviews children under twelve years of age. The sex distribution of the sample is weighted toward men, largely due to the public orientation and participant methodology of the fieldwork. A preliminary analysis, however, showed that sex of the respondent did not appear as a factor in the correlation of attitudes. Greater evenness in male-female proportions might even show a greater attachment to Spanish, more balanced bilingualism in code-switching and higher indicators of cultural identity.

The makeup of the sample may be seen in Table 1. See page 445. In addition, younger males and older females are lacking in the sample due to unwillingness of the former and difficulty in interviewing the latter.

Birthplace

Only about half (fifty-five percent) were born in Puerto Rico, a characteristic which reflects national trends (Waggoner 1978). Birthplace is a useful independent variable for many attitudinal items. But as we shall see, another variable, age of arrival in the U.S. for those not born here, is a useful factor in distinguishing the diversity in the community regarding many items of attitude. Table 2 shows a correlation between the present demographics of the community and the migration process. Nearly all the adolescents were born in the U.S., while about a third of the young adults were born here and another third came before age five. The drop-offs in the higher age of arrival categories for young adults indicate the stability of the East Harlem population, and relate to migration figures that peaked approximately twenty-four years ago (History Task Force 1979).

Street Orientation

The variable "street orientation" was used to indicate the observed use of public areas for social activity. Whereas some persons "hang out" regularly, others do not frequently socialize on the sidewalks and stoops. After observation, it appeared that about half the sample is "street-oriented," the majority of whom are young people. It is our interest to see if public use of language when correlated with attitudinal and linguistic studies of the "street oriented" sector of the sample can illuminate the patterns of sociolinguistic variation and communicative values held by the community as a whole.[8]

Against the backdrop of these general figures for the Puerto Rican population in New York and the U.S., it can be seen that the sample in this study is similar in terms of age, education, birthplace, time in the U.S. for migrants, urban location and housing. The sample reported here lacks correspondence with the general population of Puerto Ricans in the United

States, chiefly in the low representation of older women and the high ethnic concentration. In a sample that is different in ethnic density and historical depth (Hartford, Ct.), but similar to the East Harlam sample under discussion, Zirkel (1973) found many of the same aspirations and attitudes as in this study. Especially striking are (1) the permanence of Spanish oral conversation among younger people despite greater overall skills in English, (2) the interest in education, especially bilingual-bicultural education and (3) an extremely favorable attitude toward bilingualism: English for the pragmatics of living and Spanish for cultural identity. Let us now turn to the views of this sample.

Cultural and Political Views

Friendships. Most of the people in the sample have mainly Puerto Rican friends. Table 3 displays the patterns of friendships by ethnic group. As can be seen, the community seems largely connected to other Puerto Ricans, and secondarily to blacks (who share a similar social position and many of the same neighborhoods in the city).

Cultural Identity in Family Life. Two brief questions were asked concerning how much emphasis was put on identity as Puerto Ricans when the speaker was a child, and how much interest the person has in teaching Puerto Rican culture to his/her own children. As can be seen in Figure 1, emphasis on Puerto Rican culture is strong in both cases.

Puerto Rican Identity and Image. When asked what it meant to be Puerto Rican, most were unable to say much beyond birth or parentage. Others said Puerto Ricanness is a visible thing: one said, *"Lo tienen en la cara"*; another said, "It's written all over their face." In these responses the physical face is the head-meaning for a whole taxonomy of physical features, facial muscle articulation, gesture, and of course, ways of speaking that are characterized by kinetic, melodic or syntactic subtleties, as well as special lexical items and turns of phrase.

Since we could not expect our respondants to answer questions that are unresolved even among scholars, we approached ethnic identity through a set of questions. In it we wanted to get at the components of Puerto Rican nationality. Responses to these questions may be seen in Table 4.

The two features judged important by nearly all and "very important" by more than forty percent were parents and pride. They were considered equally important, even though one is genetic, a matter of parentage and the other is affective, a matter of feeling. Note that nearly half say it is not necessary to be born in Puerto Rico (exactly forty-eight percent of this sample was not born in Puerto Rico). Adolescents consider Puerto Rican birth and Spanish language maintenance to be less important than do the adults. Yet values and traditions were held to be more important by youths than by adults. The adolescents also consider struggle to be an important characteristic of Puerto Rican identity more than do other age groups. The concept of "struggle" is not foreign to the community, neither economically (jobs, housing), nor linguistically, (consider the stigma attached to both the Spanish and English spoken by Puerto Ricans, and the controversy about the mixing of the languages). A Puerto Rican who is not struggling or not working-class would still be Puerto Rican, even though these features are part of the historical context of a colonized national group. Most of the community rated items of this historical type (8-11 in Table 4) as not important to ethnic identity, although a more ideologized position would be that these are important aspects of the evolution and survival of the culture and important to coherence and unity.

It would be worthwhile to ponder the implications of these results in group discussion or in future studies: Why do the adolescents, who have the least knowledge of Puerto Rican values and traditions, and the briefest concrete experience of the struggle we have noted, consider these elements to be more integral to the culture than do older people who are the carriers of the culture?

The most striking result is that the Spanish language is not evaluated by any group as extremely important for Puertorricanness. That is, a person who has Puerto Rican parents but does not speak Spanish, is nonetheless Puerto Rican. The implication is that "you don't have to speak Spanish to be Puerto Rican." Half, however, consider Spanish to be "important." Some seem to interpret the question about the necessity of the Spanish language to Puerto Rican identity, (this question was phrased: "Is it necessary to speak Spanish in order to be Puerto Rican?" *¿Es necesario hablar español para ser puertorriqueño? ¿Cree que una persona tiene que hablar español para ser puertorriqueño?),* as asking whether Spanish is "sufficient," rather than "necessary." They respond that many Latin Americans, and even North Americans, know Spanish. When asked bluntly how important "language" (with no specification of Spanish or English) is to group solidarity, most (ninety percent) considered it to be very to extremely important.

Moreover, eighty-nine percent felt English is no threat to Puerto Rican identity. Everyone, in responding to a related question, "can you speak English and be part of Puerto Rican culture?" said yes. Nearly as many (ninety-five percent of eighty-six persons) said it is possible to speak Spanish and be part of American culture. For this community, as for many theorists in social science, language is a key component of culture and an important element in group cohesion. Yet it is not of paramount importance, as many cultural idealists would hold (see Fragoso manuscript for a review of this controversy among Puerto Rican poets). The Spanish language is not an essential symbol of Puerto Rican culture for this sample of people. Rather, Puerto Rican identity is seen as expressible in English, and American culture is compatible with the Spanish language. This is a serious statement by a segment of community which is not involved in either intellectual or political debate. More will be said about the implications of this independence of language and culture in our conclusions. For the moment, refer to some striking raw statistics in Table 5.

Puerto Rican Status, and the Status of the Languages

Several direct questions approached the self-definition of persons by labels of nationality, the esteem of outsiders, and several items that are crucial to the status of the Spanish language. Most respondents said they feel they are part of both the United States and Puerto Rico, and give their nationality in terms that reflect participation in two national cultures (Table 6). A substantial portion (thirty-eight percent) consider themselves pure Puerto Rican. Nearly no one said they were American. Although only fifteen percent said they feel themselves to be part of Puerto Rico, in another question ninety-three percent said it is necessary for Puerto Ricans to remain distinct as a group. Thus national sentiment is high. See Figures 2 and 3 for the breakdown of nationality by age group.

Political leaders of every stripe are dissatisfied with the present political status of Puerto Rico.[9] Yet sixty-five percent of the interview sample favor some form of commonwealth status for Puerto Rico. Thirteen people (fourteen percent) favor independence, and an equal number (fourteen percent) favor statehood. When asked why they preferred the status they favor for Puerto Rico, over seventy-two percent gave no response. Some had no reason for their view, others found it difficult or were disinclined to discuss such a complex issue in the interview context.

When asked "How do non-Puerto Ricans feel about us?" fifty-three percent said they felt disliked, twenty-two percent said they thought others were indifferent. On a seven point scale the social image of Puerto Ricans was placed low-to-medium by most (ninety percent) of the sample. In a study conducted early in the peak period of migration, (Siegel et al., 1954), a Puerto Rican population in Philadelphia that was somewhat different from the East Harlam sample (more in the Philadelphia sample were born in Puerto Rico, had recently arrived in the U.S., and half had lived in New York for at least a short time) preceived lack of acceptance in social institutions, neighborhoods, and to a lesser degree, in the workplace. In fact the attitudes of most of their American neighbors (both black and white) were more severely prejudiced than Puerto Ricans thought they were. This underestimate of unfavorable acceptance, which is perhaps a defense, prevents confrontation and can delay organization to change the social situation.

Two-thirds think the present social position is unjustified. About half feel that language is related to the present social position. Most said that it is not just to evaluate social position or image according to language. Puerto Ricans clearly sense the stress on their national culture in terms of the esteem of outsiders and in their own position of neither having a sovereign nation nor having full equality as Americans. A majority feel they are part of both cultures, American and Puerto Rican, and reject "complete separation" (independence) as well as full incorporation (statehood) into the United States. For the majority, the distinction between resolving the conflict between two cultures (by being bicultural, see Lambert 1972) and being caught in it (neither Puerto Rican nor American) is subtle, requiring finer analysis than we have at present. The term Puerto Rican-American may connote any point in the resolution of that conflict, just as the term Nuyorican may have either negative connotations (cf. Americanized), or symbolize a positive new identity (cf. Algarin and Piñero 1975: 18, "A new day needs a new language or else the day becomes a repetition of yesterday . . . ordinary life for the Nuyorican happens in two languages.").

Cultural and Ethnic Composites

Two composites were constructed from various questions which dealt with emblems of Puerto Rican identity and cultural activity. The cultural identity composite is aimed at overt signs of Puerto Rican cultural life: food, friends, music, desire for the acquisition of Puerto Rican culture. Three-fourths of the community scored high in cultural identity according to the composite, and no independent or other composite variable was seen to correlate with it. This indicates a strong sense of cultural identity within every group, and unity in the sample. The language-culture relationship in this regard deserves brief treatment.

Those people with fluency in Spanish score higher on the cultural identity composite than all others. However, those who have high English skills are not negatively correlated with cultural identity. This is not a paradox. A positive correlation of Spanish language with cultural identity means that those with more Spanish have a greater score on the index, and that those with less have a lower score, but not that more English implies less cultural identity. The bilingual users in the high English areas also correlate well with cultural identity. This relates back to ideas about the non-necessity of language choice, and the lack of division in this regard in the community. We should not say that knowing English is poorly correlated with cultural identity, but that not having Spanish is. Bilingualism correlates best of all.

The second composite consists of several questions related to Puerto Rican concerns, ethnic pride and reported nationality.[10] As shown in Table 7 the young adults are highest in ethnic identity of all age groups, the adolescents are lowest.

Another factor which shows a positive correlation is Puerto Rican birthplace. Language use shows a correlation as well, evident in both the Spanish choice factor and in the language resource variable. In the latter measure, two-thirds of the nearly monolingual Spanish speakers are among the highest scorers for ethnic identity. The economic support variable shows that the persons who derive support from outside but use it within the block are highest in the index for ethnic identity. Next highest are those who remain internal in earning and spending, followed by the group who work outside the block, and finally the dependent persons (a value which interacts with age, birthplace, dominant language, age of arrival and total time in Puerto Rico—mainly composed of younger persons).

Whereas the cultural identity composite illustrates attitudes towards external cultural traits, the ethnic identity composite touches deeper emotional attachments and self-definition. In the former, all age groups are high, with language as a relevant variable only in the lack of Spanish perhaps related to less access to friends and the Spanish expression of cultural elements. On the other hand, the ethnic identity composite correlates with age, showing the young adults to be leaders in the assertion of Puertorricanness.

A central issue that these results bring into focus is the role of the young adults in the affirmation of Puerto Rican culture, and their choice to be bilingual. On several scales the young adults appear to assert Puertorricanness above all other groups. They are highest of every age group in the ethnic identity composite. They are lowest in the self-ascription Puerto Rican-American, highest in the self-ascription Nuyorican.[11] The young adults report the greatest increase in the use of Spanish, and in comparison with their greater English skills, seem to be speaking a great deal of Spanish. The young adults may be seen as a group, then, which symbolizes the assertion of Puerto Rican culture in the United States.

The struggle over language and culture constantly affects the process of social and linguistic transformation.[12] The young adults, rather than retreating from the process and the debate that affects it and tries to direct it, are spearheading it. They seem to reject the usual choices of separation or assimilation. Rather, they are searching for a new cultural definition and choosing bilingualism as a means to communicate with the Latin-American world in Nueva York.

LANGUAGE BACKGROUND, USE AND MAINTENANCE

Language Background

Over three-quarters of the sample learned Spanish as their first language, including persons born and raised in the U.S. The adolescents and about half of the young adults learned Spanish in the United States. Most of the persons over thirty learned Spanish in Puerto Rico.[13]

The importance of parents as teachers of Spanish becomes obvious when we consider that parents, who are overwhelmingly Spanish dominant, account for eighty-six percent of the responses to the question "Who was the most important teacher of Spanish?" By contrast, the responses to "most important teachers of English" were widely spread over several categories, such as friends, relatives, co-workers, etc. with parents having a major input in English learning only for adolescents (and to a lesser extent, young adults). Ninety-five percent have learned the English they control in the U.S.

Language Use

Habitual language use in several channels of communication: reading, television and radio, was investigated without the formal assessment of competence. Self-report, which has been seen to be valuable in macro-sociolinguistic studies of this type (Fishman, Cooper and Ma, et al., 1971: 494) seemed to be the most natural way to derive such information and keep the interview more like a conversation than a test. In addition, we asked general questions about the language that feels most comfortable and the dominant language in the speaker's own judgment. Lastly, a set of hypothetical domains attempted to elicit which persons and situations were most likely to be spoken to in Spanish, English or some form of bilingual usage.

The respondents are fairly evenly divided in reported language dominance (forty percent bilingual, thirty percent Spanish, and thirty percent English dominant). All the older people said they were most comfortable in Spanish. On the other hand, none of the adolescents are; of the forty-three persons (forty-seven percent) who said they were most comfortable in English, almost half were adolescents. Generally, the language that would be spoken to a Puerto Rican whose ethnicity, but not language ability was perceived would be Spanish for thirty-eight percent of the sample (only seventeen percent of the adolescents said it would be Spanish; most of the mainly Spanish-speaking people would choose Spanish); it would be English for twenty-seven percent (half are adolescents). Twenty-one percent said they would code-switch or mix the languages. The bilinguals would mix the two (thirty-four percent), speak English (twenty-six percent), speak Spanish (twenty-one percent), or determine what to speak situationally (eighteen percent).

Speech in Domains

Language use reports were used to determine who spoke which language in various situations. Non-response was noted in many cases due to inappropriateness of question or situations.[14]

From the table of self-report (Table 8) the correlation between age and Spanish can be clearly seen in the domains of family and neighborhood: older people are generally addressed in Spanish, particularly by other adults. Young adults on the other hand report more bilingual behavior. With teenagers (Table 8, items 13 and 16), English is most used, along with substantial amounts of Spanish code-switching. More Spanish is used by children than teenagers. Looking at some other domains of reported language use, a pattern of language use that is connected to both who is speaking and to whom the speech is addressed begins to appear. The general category of "socializing" (item 20) implies interaction with one's friends and age-set.[15] Note in Table 9, that nearly one-half the adolescents use English with their peers, one-half the young adults code-switch with their peers and the older people tend to use Spanish.

Code-switching

Although we do not have assurance that the category "mixed, or code-switching" means the same to the respondent as it does to a linguist, there can be little doubt that mixing the two languages in speech is a real category. In the section on valued varieties it is seen that most people (eighty percent) considered the mixing of the two languages to be very widespread. By contrast only about one-third think there are many bilinguals who keep the languages separate.

Observed code-switching occurs mostly in young adults and to a considerable extent among mature adults; only about one-fourth of the adolescents and older people are observed code-switching. Because the older groups are mainly Spanish speaking, and the younger group is mainly English speaking, while the adults groups report bilingual ability, the connection between code-switching and bilingual ability is implied. The following patterns emerge: code-switching occurs from an English base more prevalently than from a Spanish base; and it occurs among U.S.-raised persons more than among those who arrived after age six. Not clear in these data are the subtle distinctions in degree of bilingualism, ethnic function and kind of code-switching. In addition, the conclusion that complex intra-sentential code-switching (as opposed to switching for isolated words, exclamations and whole sentences) correlates positively with balanced bilingualism, is treated in another paper (See Poplack 1979 for a typology of code-switching among twenty speakers selected from this sample).

It appears that mixed usage, or code-switching is perceived and reported as a variety of speech with nearly as much strength as the natural languages Spanish and English. In the seven questions that show the least non-response in the domains report, code-switching is reported six times as frequently as other forms of bilingual behavior. Code-switching is reported as frequently as speaking in English, and nearly as frequently as speaking in Spanish. Here the three prongs of language investigation in *el barrio* show the same social fact in various lights. The attitudes of the community indicate that code-switching is something like a natural language. Earlier, Pedraza had observed mixed usage as a norm of interaction not only signalling ethnic identity, but as an intensification of communication. At the same time the linguistic investigations, first of a single speaker then of twenty speakers, tell us about the types and syntax of code-switching. Bilingual speech is descriptively undeniable, whatever prescriptive grammarians may claim.

What we are calling code-switching (with reservations about its strict linguistic character in these self-report items) is clearly a recognized variety, used by all to children and teenagers, and especially used (by all to all) in neighborhood interactions (See Table 8, items 12-14).

The correlation between age and Spanish, postulating that older people use Spanish and younger people use English, is not at all simple; neither for speakers, nor hearers (those who receive speech). Whereas one can see the trend of more use of Spanish to adults, more use of code-switching by young adults and English by adolescents, Spanish is used to and by children for initial language acquisition. The use of English in higher proportions when speaking to adolescents than to children may indicate either a strategy of bilingual maintenance or a tendency toward language shift. Thus, the "American Immigrant Model"[16] wherein the grandparents (first generation) speak the non-English national language, the parents (second generation) are bilingual and the children (third generation) are monolingual in English is inappropriate. The figures on competence in the next section begin to illustrate the bilingual resources that could be developed in this community.

Small children begin to learn language in Spanish; through childhood and adolescence they acquire more English, in school and with peers. The crucial point is whether the Spanish of these young people will reactivate after adolescence, to yield a stable bilingual community. The young adults show that this has been the case.

Reported Language Competence

Self report of competence in both Spanish and English related to the four specific language skills (understanding, speaking, reading, writing, Table 10) indicate the bilingual character of the community. The correlations between Spanish and age, and English and youth are present, but not so strongly that a generational split should be posited. Rather, adults should be seen as Spanish dominant, and younger people should be seen as competent in Spanish (especially in the passive skills of reading and comprehension of spoken Spanish), with developed verbal skills in English.

The bilingual character of the community is evident from Table 10. A high incidence of oral skills appears in both languages across age groups, with correlation between age and Spanish particularly evident in speaking skills. Both age groups report higher percentages of literary skills in English than in Spanish. Here, too, the age-language correlation shows the adolescents tending to possess greater English skills, though they are not without Spanish skills.

Overall competence in each language was also rated by speakers. The results are presented in Table 11.

Speak Good, Live Good

Although the concept of "good language" is shaky, vague and based on many criteria, some non-linguistic, and some totally subjective, most speakers did not question the terms "good Spanish" and "good English". The questions concerned who, in general and in the neighborhood, speaks "good" language and whether the speaker considered himself/herself to speak good Spanish/English.

From the results in Table 12, it can be seen that Puerto Ricans are considered to be, in general terms, good speakers of Spanish. Good language is in general connected to ethnicity, education, occupation, and to age. Time of residence in either Puerto Rico (for Spanish) or in New York (for English) did not receive much emphasis. When asked to speak from experience rather than in general, focusing on the neighborhood, the ethnic factor diminished. Younger people in general are seen as speaking good English by forty-two percent of the sample, and older people are seen as speaking good Spanish by forty-three percent. For people in the neighborhood, high level of education or occupation was seen as associated with good English by twenty percent (for Spanish this figure went down to only five percent perhaps because the Spanish speakers in *el barrio* for the most part do not have prestigious jobs or educational credentials). When asked "Just what is meant by good language?", one quarter of the respondents thought that pronunciation was the key to good language; about fifteen percent each thought that vocabulary, comprehensibility or a combination of factors were vital. (Less than ten percent gave other opinions about "good" language and nonresponse was about fifteen percent for each). The bilinguals, the young adults, better educated persons, and those who work locally are higher than the general sample in self-assessment of good language (see Table 13).[17] Persons born in Puerto Rico, mature adults, those who claim Puerto Rican nationality, and both those with little education and those with high school or beyond are higher in self-estimate of good Spanish.

Language Maintenance

The community is in favor of the maintenance of Spanish without equivocation. One hundred percent want their children to speak Spanish, ninety-nine percent want Spanish maintained in the Puerto Rican community in New York.[18] All but one person (again ninety-nine percent) think bilingual education should be used for the maintenance of Spanish. People say Spanish should be maintained since it is the national language and because it is part of the culture of Puerto Rico. When asked how it should or could be maintained, the role of the family in Spanish maintenance became clear.

A combination of all factors (i.e., parents, grandparents, family, older people, school) was considered responsible for maintaining Spanish in the community by about forty percent; another forty percent signalled parents and family specifically. Fewer than fifteen percent said the school should be responsible. Schools and bilingual education programs then, are seen as important but not responsible for the maintenance of Spanish. Responsibility rests in the home environment.

What should a child be taught, in terms of language? Only ten percent thought the Puerto Rican child's first language should be English. Thirty percent thought it should be Spanish. But most striking is the majority opinion (fifty-nine percent) that children should acquire both Spanish and English initially.[19] This result is striking, first in its departure from the census and sample figures that show Spanish as the overwhelming first language of the community; second in the transcendence of the myth of "language choice," that in effect, a person (especially an American) can only really have one language; third, in the positive evaluation of both Spanish and English, and to the overt use of bilingual modes of speech.

Before turning to the direct and implied ways that the values of language forms are expressed in the New York Puerto Rican community, it might be valuable to list the raw results of several more key questions. These results will serve as a reference point for much of the discussion which follows concerning both attitudes and reported competence. In the final analysis, these attitudes of importance and value may relate to recommendations for policy. From Table 14 it can be seen that both languages are useful and valued, and that neither language is considered either a threat to identity nor a barrier to participation in either Puerto Rican or American culture and society.

Valued Varieties: Perceptions about the Language of the Community.

A complex series of questions was to be asked to determine indirectly how persons viewed the language varieties found in the community. Six varieties were used. They may be divided into three "pure" and three hybrid types, as in Figure 4. It was thought less useful to include other more finely distinguished dialectal forms, such as Jíbaro Spanish, black English, Castilian, and refined English. These would have complicated the routine which was already quite complex. Besides multiplying the choices, it was foreseen that it would be hard to know how people would interpret some of these terms.

The results clearly support the notion that the community is bilingual, without rigorously separating the languages, and that Spanish retains a strong presence in the community. Although it would be premature to infer that these varieties are valued in the order that they are recognized, such recognition does indicate a view of their prevalence in the community. The attitude measure derived indirectly from an estimate of quantity appears similar to other attitudes more directly elicited. Ranked first in Table 15 is bilingualism of the 'mixed' type (vaguer than, but similar to, code-switching). Below that, Spanish is ranked above English.

When asked if there exists a form of communication called 'Spanglish," only ten persons said no (eleven percent). This is an emotion-laden term and a controversial topic. For linguists, "Spanglish" is a useless word because so many phenomena have been referred to by this single and unclear term. For the community, it is difficult to pinpoint the intention of the term. Some, with very positive emotion in their voice said, "Yes, this is a new form of speech." Others said yes, matter-of-factly, accepting that the two languages are used in non-isolated ways. Some were negative, some were skeptical; but nonetheless most acknowledged that communication often freely draws on the two languages nearly simultaneously. One person had a theory which is too close to our studied analysis to be dismissed merely as a typology from folk meta-linguistics:

> I think there's three different types. One is where half the word is in English and half is in Spanish, right? Also that some of the Spanish words are direct translations from English. And the other thing is, that you say half your sentence in Spanish and half in English.

This woman (LS) seems to be talking of three important contact phenomena: loanwords with phonological incorporation, calque (relexification), and intra-sentential code-switching. Her assumption in all the examples she gives is that the speaker of "Spanglish" is basically an English speaker found in New York at the present time.

Bilingual Education

The community largely holds a positive attitude toward education in any form and the practical skills education purports to bring. The positive general attitudes toward education, and bilingual education in particular, however, are not matched by either confidence in, or acquaintance with, existing programs of bilingual education in the community. On one side, bilingual education is seen as a means of maintenance and cultivation of the Spanish language. But along with the view of the possible benefit to the cultural and linguistic interests of Puerto Ricans, there are not many strongly expressed attitudes favoring the programs currently available and operative.

Twenty-three percent of the sample feel the purpose of bilingual education should be to teach the Spanish language and the culture of Puerto Rico to Puerto Ricans. Groups of about the same size (i.e., one-fifth of the sample) say bilingual education should be used to teach general academic subjects (twenty-two percent); to teach Spanish and English (twenty percent); and, a group of twenty-two percent say they do not know what the purposes of bilingual education are. (Lesser percentages not given). It is interesting to note that the three main categories are all issues of importance: (1) the preservation of ethnic identity through continuation of the Spanish language and familiarity with the culture and history of Puerto Rico; (2) the general need for educational excellence (whatever language is used as the medium, the principle objective is that the pupil acquire information and skills); and (3) the cultivation of bilingualism, so that Puerto Ricans may be fluent in both Spanish and English.

In speaking of the actual utility of bilingual education, the non-response category more than doubles. Fifty-four percent say they don't know the actual usefulness of bilingual education, and sixty-two percent did not want to comment on the success of present bilingual education programs. About one-fifth of the sample did rate bilingual education as successful.

The impression that there is a great amount of nonresponse regarding specifics, but a great expectation as to the value of bilingual education in the abstract, was confirmed in the composition of an index for bilingual education. Ninety-four percent scored high in an index that neutralized the effect of nonresponses. Further evidence of the generally positive orientation toward bilingual education are seen in the following raw results.

1. Ninety-nine percent want to see schools help maintain Spanish.
2. Ninety-nine percent want both Spanish and English as languages of instruction.
3. Ninety-five percent want Spanish as a school subject.

In addition ninety-nine percent favor bilingual education in non-Puerto Rican communities. Ninety-seven percent feel communities should have the choice of bilingual education. Eighty-eight percent feel that within the Puerto Rican community, both Spanish and English speakers should have bilingual education. Finally, eighty-one percent feel that bilingual education should provide basic educational skills.

The conclusion is clear. Despite the high rates of nonresponse, (a kind of nonresponse that reflects more on outreach on the part of the schools than on the community), and despite the general discrepancy between the abstract goals of educators and the concrete practice in the schools, the community nonetheless wants bilingual education. Such bilingual education will best serve the community if it provides Spanish and English skills to both Spanish-speaking and English-speaking children aiding in maintaining and increasing the bilingual skills of the Puerto Rican community.

Change in Language Use

Another area of self-report concerns the increase or decrease in the use of the languages. All groups, except the adolescents, report the greatest use of both Spanish and English at the present time. Adolescents report greater use of Spanish at an earlier age.

The majority report that they are speaking more English, (two-thirds of the sample regardless of language resources). One-third reports using more Spanish. Given the status of Spanish as first language acquired by most of the community,[20] and recognizing the pressures and incentives to use English in the United States, one would expect increased use of English to be reported, even by older people, as is the case (note that their use of Spanish is the same). But most interesting is the high report of increased use of Spanish by young adults (see Table 16). The variation by resource group shows bilinguals to be lowest in reporting increased English and highest in reporting increased Spanish (see Table 17).

The initial ethnographic research in this neighborhood of *el barrio,* the subsequent sociolinguistic studies, especially of code-switching, and the figures in this report indicate that the sociolinguistic situation in the New York Puerto Rican community is one of societal bilingualism (Fishman, et al., 1971: 539-611. See also Kelly 1969). Although Fishman states that bilingualism without diglossia (i.e., a society in which the two languages have neither specific status nor domains of differentiation) usually comprises a transitional stage, Pedraza argues that this situation exists and is stable[21] in Puerto Rican communities such as *el barrio*. No diglossia means for Pedraza that in every domain of social interaction, whether school, church, home or neighborhood, even in official interaction and in the workplace, Spanish and English may be heard. Yet individual speakers may choose to interact in one or the other language (or to use both), depending on the language of family members or co-workers, their church affiliation or other factors, yielding a compartmentalization at a microlinguistic level that does not appear in the macrolinguistic measurement. At present it appears that English is more widespread, if not superordinate, in this stable societal bilingualism. Looking beyond the Puerto Rican community to the increasing Latin American speech community in New York, and considering socioeconomic as well as linguistic patterns, (residence and job-market especially) an increase in both the need for Spanish and positive evaluation of abilities in Spanish is quite probable. For both national and international reasons, then, this work projects a societal bilingualism in which English is the primary and Spanish the subordinate language. The pressure of peer groups and cultural commodities (music, movies, magazines and television) which favor the English language must be recognized. The adolescents, though they have many of the same Spanish-oriented characteristics as the adults in their language background, are consistently observed as having or habitually using less competence in Spanish. The question to which we must return, in this report and years hence, is: Do the characteristics of the adolescents represent a stage in their development (only one phase), or do they provide a view of the future adult community? Some further analysis of the linguistic census material is provided in the next part of this report to approach just that issue.

THE LINGUISTIC COMPOSITE SCORES

Composites for Language Use

Spanish use is higher among those with more experience in Puerto Rico, among older people and among those with less orientation to the streets. Spanish users report less code-switching (and the sociolinguistic studies show that their switching is less sytactically complex; see Poplack, 1979). Nine persons who were born in the U.S. and three who arrived before the age of six report a great amount of Spanish use. (Table 18).[22]

The overall pattern of reported Spanish use is not the reciprocal opposite for English use. In other words, English use does not correlate with youth and U.S. birth the way Spanish use correlates with age and Puerto Rican birth.

When English use is tabulated by age of arrival in Table 19, there appear to be nearly even proportions among the U.S. oriented group (twenty-five vs. thirty), in contrast to the wide disparity (forty-three vs. twelve) for Spanish use. We expected that three-quarters to all of the adolescents would report a great deal of English use, yet the proportions are only about half and half. Eleven report low English usage; only twelve report a great deal of English usage. The same is true for birthplace as an independent variable; only eighteen of those born in the U.S. report a great deal of English usage; twenty do not. All these figures indicate that bilingualism, especially the use of Spanish by those with high English skills, is a major pattern in the community.

Regarding other variables, pro-statehood supporters are a little higher than all other favored political status groups in reported use of English. Street orientation for social interaction also correlates with report of English usage.

Those observed to code-switch are higher in reported English use than those who do not. Those who work nearby the neighborhood are highest in Spanish usage, followed by those who derive income from social services and exchange that income for goods and services locally. Those who work outside the block are high in both indices, and the dependent group composed mainly of adolescents is similar in English report to the group who hold jobs outside the block, but lower than them in Spanish report.

The bilingual use composite contains scores that are quite low. Only twelve people report very high bilingual usage, and another twelve report medium-high bilingual usage. Of these twenty-four persons, twelve are young adults. Eleven are street-oriented in their interactions, but thirteen are not. Eleven, not the same eleven necessarily, are observed code-switching frequently. Twenty of the twenty-four persons are analyzed as bilinguals in the composite for main resources. Nineteen of these twenty-four have high English resources, and ten have high Spanish resources. Fifteen were born in the United States; six arrived before the age of six from Puerto Rico. Fourteen favor the political status quo; seven favor independence. These seven pro-independence people represent more than half the thirteen in the whole sample who favor independence. (Sixty-five percent of the sample favor the commonwealth, fourteen percent favor independence, fourteen percent statehood).

In general, Spanish use is higher than English use in the composites. The bar graphs in Figure 5 indicate the percentage of the sample in four divisions of the scoring for three use indices.

Spanish Choice over English: Triangular Model For Language Use

To avoid interaction between the scores for language use and to compensate for nonresponse, a triangular pattern was derived by constructing a single scale for Spanish vs. English report, and cross-tabulating it against reported bilingual usage. The model is as shown in Figure 6, with the triangle on the left indicating the general features of the model, and the triangle on the right indicating the placement of the ninety-one speakers in the sample within that triangle. An explanation of each alphabetically-keyed group follows.

A. Bilingual, some switching
B. Bilingual, little switching
C. Spanish Monolingual
D. English Monolingual
E. Bilingual Code-switchers

A. A large part of the sample is bilingual. Thirty-five persons (thirty-eight percent) are in the middle ranges of bilingual report and in the middle ranges of the Spanish-English choice variable. Of these, twenty-four (twenty-six percent) lean toward English in their reported use and eleven (twelve percent) toward Spanish.

B. Another group is ranged in the central area of the Spanish choice variable (twenty-one persons, twenty-three percent), but report little or no bilingual behavior; i.e., they report using the two languages, but in separate domains, or to distinct interlocuters. Thirteen of these lean toward reporting English usage; eight lean toward more Spanish usage.

C. Sixteen persons (eighteen percent) report mostly Spanish usage and very little bilingual usage. These are the monolingual Spanish speakers in the sample.[23]

D. Three persons claim nearly no bilingual usage and very little Spanish usage. This three percent may be considered the English monolingual group. They are mostly adolescent.

E. Fourteen persons (fifteen percent) report about equal amounts of Spanish and English use and report a great deal of bilingual usage. We may think of this group as rather coincidental with the best (i.e., intrasentential) code-switchers on the block.

The 100-cell table is given in Figure 7, the clusters are presented formally in Table 20.[24] This "Use Triangle" was then subjected to a number of filters (age of arrival, birthplace) yielding patterns visible at a glance for various sub-groupings (Table 21).

Note, for example, the incidence of English tendency *and* bilingualism among those born in the U.S., and the strong component of bilingual use among those who arrived as babies. The other displays show tendencies away from bilingual report and toward monolingual Spanish report as the age of arrival of the respondent increases.

Age as a factor clarifies one aspect of this triangular display. Generally, adults are high (i.e., to the right) in spanish choice, and adolescents low (to the left); young adults, however, are found along the entire range of the variable. They share with the adults the frequent use (or report of use) in Spanish, but also share high English choice and bilingual report with the adolescents. Again the young adolescents emerge as an important group in community bilingualism. This role is underlined by the demographic strength of the younger adult population in general, as well as in the present sample. A tendency toward Spanish is related to Puerto Rican birth; birth in the United States indicates a tendency toward English. The raw figures in these tables confirm Pedraza's observation that bilingualism of an English-dominant character is becoming more prevalent in the community, especially as more Puerto Ricans are born in the U.S.

Language Resources

Just as interesting as the distinction between report and behavior is the distinction between ability and behavior. In this section, we compare what people can do with what they do. In the previous section, the report of behavior was displayed in triangular patterns generated from the various questions regarding language spoken to various interlocutors. In the following pages, the concept of language as a resource (Jernudd and Das Gupta 1971: 196-197) is the rationale for composite scores regarding skills and the acquisition of skills.

Parallel questions were asked for English and for Spanish to avoid interaction among the responses (a positive answer for one item does not automatically indicate a negative answer for its counterpart). Reported skills in listening, speaking, reading and writing, main teachers of the languages, age and place of language acquisition, and self-rating of competence comprised the score for resources. In all, ten distinct questions were used for each language. Over half the sample scored in the very high ranges for each language resource: fifty-three percent for Spanish; fifty-seven percent for English. In Table 22, cross-tabulating the two resource indices, the descriptive significance of the composites can be most clearly seen. In cell A there are six persons (seven percent) who are low in both resources. Our point is not to prove the performance of speakers. They might be seen as having low skills in both languages, or as bilinguals of low competence. This is a very small group. The other cells contain persons who have more skills, background and general resources in one language than in the other. Thirty-seven such persons (forty-one percent) have greater resources in English, and thirty-three (thirty-six percent) have greater resources in Spanish (cells B and C). Fifteen persons (cell D) (sixteen percent) have high resources in both languages.

In Table 23, the two language resource composites (in four levels) are used to generate a sixteen cell table. The key table gives a guide to the cells. Note how many of the young adults are strong in bilingual resources (i.e., they cluster in the lower cells to the right). The mature adults are bilinguals who tend toward greater strengths in Spanish. The older group is higher in Spanish resources and quite low in English resources.

When the adolescents are filtered out of this general cross-tabulation of resources, two trends become clear. First, there is a correlation between youth and English—nineteen of the twenty-three adolescents are in cell B (High English-Low Spanish resources). Two-thirds of the adults are in the row for high Spanish resources. Second, bilingualism among the adults is widespread. Nearly all the high resource bilinguals in cell D are adults.

As for birthplace, there is no surprise (see Figure 8).[25] The U.S.-born are higher in English resources; the Puerto Rican-born are higher in Spanish resources. But note the even proportions of all groups in medium-high resources.

Age of arrival correlates inversely with English resources; most (ninety percent) of these with high English resources came as babies, or were born in the U.S. Similarly, most (ninety percent) of those with low English resources came to the U.S. later in life, so later arrival implies lower resources in English. On the other hand, only three persons who arrived after the age of six (three out of thirty-four) are low in Spanish resources. There are fifty-five persons who were either born in the U.S. or came before the age of six.[26] They may be best considered New York City-raised. Forty-six of them (eighty-four percent) are high in English resources. More than half are bilingual (by the measure Main Language Resource, below); the rest are mainly English speakers, except for two who are mainly Spanish speakers. Thus the experience of living in Puerto Rico enhances resources in the Spanish language (thirty-one out of thirty-four). The experience of living in the United States, at least for Puerto Ricans in *el barrio,* tends to result in bilingualism for slightly more than half (twenty-eight out of fifty-five, and English dominance for somewhat less than half (twenty-five out of fifty-five).

Main Language Resource

The composite index Main Language Resource is a variable constructed by hand and judgment after many passes over the scores for each individual on language resources for Spanish and English, on language use and skills, and dominance reports both by speakers concerning themselves and from observation by the fieldworker. This material was reviewed case-by-case for each individual and thus produced a total view of each person's language strengths. Discrepancies were settled in team consultation, and a few marginal cases were assigned to one category of main language resource.

The variable is named Main Language Resource because it does not attempt to measure degree of competence, nor to resolve the controversies of the definition and assessment of dominance. These difficulties, partially empirical and partly due to the distance between the researchers and their knowledge of individuals (often multiplied in large scale anonymous research), were not problematic for the present work. Clearly there are variations in ability, fluency and creative use of Spanish and English; but personal experience and a number of different scales of report and observation allowed us to place the members of the sample into one of the following categories:

1. twenty-seven percent mainly English speakers n=25
2. thirty-one percent mainly Spanish speakers n=28
3. forty-two percent mainly bilinguals n=38 (Total n-91)

The most striking correlations in Table 24 appear along the (upper left to lower-right) diagonals of nearly every table: consistently one-quarter of the sample shows up in the Spanish-by-Spanish cell, about one-third appears in the bilingual-by-bilingual cell, and one-fifth in the English-by-English cell. Thirty-four percent of the sample have become bilingual after first learning Spanish, but these bilinguals for the most part read and write in English, and the majority feel most comfortable speaking English. About half of the bilinguals have been categorized as being bilingual by the participant observer. This may be an effect of the public setting in which the fieldwork was carried out. It seems that this situation of bilingualism tending toward English strengths is not a misobservation on the part of Pedraza.

Several cross-tabulations of factors relate language resources to language background, use and skills. Three-fourths of the sample learned Spanish first. But only about a third want their children to learn Spanish first, and nearly two-thirds want their children to acquire both languages simultaneously.

The tables in Table 24 cross-tabulate several key items in language background and use against the measures of language dominance by the speaker's own report and main language resource by our analysis. The first set of tables (D1, R1) thus plot one against the other to note goodness of fit and provide the initial correlation of the two variables. The first pair of tables are merely ninety-degree rotations of one another to establish for the reader the main lines of each table to follow in the horizontal row scores concerned with Spanish, bilingualism and English. There follow parallel sets of tables for the reported first language, for habitual language of literacy, for most comfortable language, and for the ethnographer's (Pedraza's) rating of language dominance.

The proportions are nearly the same for both measures (though the individuals do not entirely coincide): about forty percent are bilingual, about thirty percent each are mainly Spanish and mainly English-speaking persons. The non-coincidences of the measures (D1,R1) show that nine percent of the sample overreport English dominance, though their scores on the resource index show them to be bilingual. A smaller number (six percent) overreport bilingualism, though they are analyzed to be mainly English speakers. These noncoincidences, small in size, indicate that only a few persons are overreporting Spanish ability.

Characteristics of Bilinguals

The set of persons whose main language resources are bilingual coincides with bilingualism by other dominance-related factors.[27] Insofar as these characteristics are typical or prevalent, stable bilingualism is viable as an alternative to either containment within monolingual Spanish speech communities, or assimilation into monolingual Anglo-America.

Considering the use of the media,[28] language of literacy, most comfortable language and the prevalence of English in the schools and workplace,

English-tending bilingualism appears to be the strategy the community is taking as a means to retain the Spanish language. Remember that on the maintenance of Spanish, the community is unanimous.

Let us further characterize the bilinguals. These persons, for the most part, acquired Spanish first, then became and remain bilingual. But they read and write mostly in English (Table 24, R3, B3, Row B). This group might be further subdivided between one-quarter who are most comfortable speaking and reading in English, even though they are bilingual, a group consisting of six who are bilingual with no preference for either language, and a smaller group, perhaps one-tenth of the sample who are bilingual but prefer Spanish.

What are the age-related figures for bilingualism? One-fourth of the adolescents, three-fifths of the young adults, one-half of the mature adults and one-tenth of the older people are bilingual. Note again the importance of the young adults. They have lived and been educated in the United States; this gives them the English skills many of the older persons do not have, but in contrast to the adolescents their maturity connects them to the adult Puerto Rican community.

Other characteristics reinforce the view that the community is stably bilingual. Whereas ninety-six percent of the mainly Spanish speakers were born in Puerto Rico, and eighty-eight percent of the mainly English speakers were born in the USA, the bilinguals were, about half and half, born in both Puerto Rico and the U.S. Bilinguals born in Puerto Rico came to the U.S. before the age of twelve (see Table 25). The mainly Spanish speakers were educated in Puerto Rico; English speakers and bilinguals were educated in the US. (From these results, conclusions can be drawn either that U.S. education is conducive to bilingualism, or more realistically, that some persons, the bilinguals, preserve Spanish despite U.S. education). Pedraza surmises that lack of educational success explains why a few of the persons in the sample, despite long presence in the U.S., have remained nearly monolingual in Spanish. Thus, the educational system could be an important factor in the bilingualism of the community, as these findings show, and as the community has indicated it desires it to be. It turns out that most of the people who have been educated past junior high school are indeed bilingual (see Table 26). In brief, there are more bilinguals with high English resources than bilinguals with high Spanish resources; and there are more mainly English speakers who use Spanish than there are mainly Spanish speakers who use English.[29]

A key point emerges here: persons are either over-reporting Spanish usage in relation to their Spanish skills, or—as we conclude—many members of the community are speaking more Spanish than their abilities would indicate. In effect, the community has greater skills in English at the present time, and this situation might continue, or increase, as birthplace, schooling and work in the continental U.S. likewise increase. Nonetheless, the community desires to retain Spanish, and continues to speak Spanish and bilingually.

The table on economic support (Table 28) shows that there is no correlation between main language resources and involvement in the economy, with the exception that English correlates with dependence on others, (and this is an artifact of the adolescent group who largely make up the dependent group). This is an important negative finding. The general conclusion emerges that main language resources are independent of many aspects of the society. Some of these are: there is no correlation between main resource language and level of occupation, no correlation with favored status for Puerto Rico, nor with degree of participation in the political/electoral system in the U.S., no correlation with the index for ethnic identity, nor for the index of cultural identity, and no correlation with the bilingual education index.

These findings should be connected to attitudes, especially the report by the community about the independent relationship of Puerto Rican identity to the Spanish language. At the overt level, the community says that English is compatible with Puerto Rican culture, Spanish with American culture and that Spanish is not necessary to either self-image or ethnic definition. Covertly, many factors in the social make-up of the community correlate equally well with all language resources. Thus the articulated culture and the facts of society show the same situation: Spanish is desired and important, not essential. As one teacher recently interviewed outside this sample said:

> not that a child of Puerto Rican parents who does not speak Spanish is not Puerto Rican; there's just a certain richness and connection to the culture, the music, the jokes, the interaction, that they miss.

A distinctive social pattern is becoming evident. It needs careful analysis, for its implications are momentous. The attitude that Spanish is not necessary does not necessarily imply assimilation into English-speaking America; nor the transculturation of Puerto Rican life.[30] But it does signal a transformation of language and culture, and an ongoing struggle of symbol and expression. In the words of a self-ascribed Nuyorican poet:

> There is at the edge of every empire a linguistic explosion that results from the many multilingual tribes that collect around wealth and power. (Algarín 1975: 15)

The stakes are high: On the one hand the community may lose both the Spanish language and important parts of its culture, especially its verbal literature, music and lore—a fear expressed by many poets and intellectuals oriented toward Puerto Rican tradition. On the other hand, a specifically New York Latin culture with bilingualism and strong connections to both Hispanic and Anglo streams may be evolving, with powerful consequences for the United States and for history.

A former mayor of the town of Guayama, Puerto Rico, who describes himself as "a member of the Partido Popular because it is the least bad," indicates the irony in the colonial relationship, and hints at its as yet unclearly understood implications:

> Nosotros no fuimos a los Estados Unidos a decirle que nos cogiera. . . . Estaba hablando con una americana, que me decía, 'Yo no se como Ustedes pretenden de vivir en una colonia de los Estados Unidos.' Le contesté, '¿Pero cuál es la colonia? Usted dice que es americana. Yo me considero ciudadano americano igual que Usted. Y fíjese que Usted

> no puede decir que es puertorriqueña, porque Usted no lo es, Yo, si— Puedo decir que soy puertorriqueño y americano tambíen. Porque mire: colonia son Ustedes de nosotros, porque nosotros vivimos de Ustedes.*

Jose Luis González, a writer associated with abhorrence of the deterioration of the Spanish tongue due to English, commented thus about Bernardo Vega's notion of *patria*, the embodiment of national culture:

> no podía ser mito ahistórico ni mística elitista, sino realidad humana y social concreta y viva. Patria es la comunidad de hombres y mujeres que a lo largo de un proceso histórico conforma una manera de vivir la vida en constante evolución y cámbio.**
>
> (*Memorias de Bernardo Vega* 1977 p.24)

This perceptive view of culture and political allegiance, when applied to language yields a concept similarly dynamic, quite unlike the cultural-nationalist position. Language in an evolving culture must all the more be "a living concrete social reality." The means of cultural expression and transmission must evolve as does society or "fatherland;" for language is spoken by the same "community of men and women who mold a manner of living (and speaking) through a long process of constant evolution and change."

Possibly the "Nuyoricans" are New Ricans, new in their cultural innovation, ahead of the native Puerto Ricans in birthplace and in ideas, as Jaime Carrera suggests (Fragoso, ms.) But there is also the loser's side of the gamble: to be *entre lenguas*, between languages, is to be foreign in both lands, speaking a hermetic language that is intelligible only to the insiders of the group. Incomplete bilingualism ("Two languages coexisting in your head as modes of expression can either strengthen your alertness or cause confusion." Algarin 1975: 18), and even bilingual education that does not provide cultural continuity and self-esteem, contains just these risks.

If the quantitative findings in the sociolinguistic studies may be interpreted in this connection, the strength of the Spanish grammatical system in verbal forms and meanings, in plural retention and concord, and in the syntactic regularity maintained in code-switching, indicate that bilingualism is no risk to Puerto Rican culture or language. On a more general level many bilinguals appear to be bicultural; participating in two (or

---

*"We didn't go to the U.S. and tell them to take us over. . . ." "I was talking with an American, and she was saying, 'How can you be content to live in a colony of the U.S.?' I answered, 'But which is the colony? You say you are an American. I consider myself an American citizen just as you do. And think about it: You can't say you're a Puerto Rican, because you are not. But I am. I can say that I am a Puerto Rican and an American. So look: You are a colony of ours, because we live off you!' "

**"Fatherland" should not be interperted as an ahistorical myth nor an elitist mystification, but rather as a living, concrete and social human reality. Fatherland is the community of men and women which through historical process forges a constantly evolving and changing manner of living.

more) of the many variants of American culture and Puerto Rican culture that exist under (or in opposition to) American domination.

LANGUAGE AND CULTURE

Language Dominance

In many ways, the concept of "language dominance" contains premises that are inherently problematic. Insofar as has been possible, the issue of dominance has been purposely avoided in this report for many reasons:

1. For the implementation of bilingual education under current legislation, "dominance" is an arbitrary level of language ability determined by sometimes questionable instruments. The number of non-English or Spanish-dominant students in a school directly determines educational funding. A developed alternative to "dominance" is needed, including better measurement of language resources (in this report attitudinal, not empirical resources were computed), recognition of community attitudes, coupled with more objective assessment of the value and possibility of language cultivation.[31]
2. In Spanish, *dominar* in regard to language means to control or have a command. In this sense many persons in the community "dominate" Spanish and English, even though they may have greater skills in one language. From the standpoint of the English non-equivalent cognate *be dominant,* in the sense of "have a superior capacity," an "English-dominant" person may actually "dominate" both languages. Of course, strictly speaking no one person can control all the varieties, structures and lexical items that exist in even one of the world-wide languages designated under the umbrella terms Spanish and English.
3. Even language *capacity* itself is a difficult term, related not only to grammatical competence, or the ability to produce sentences. Habitual use, as well as comfort in speaking, and range of stylistic variation should also be considered.
4. Since such linguistic quality and quantity evolves through time, the culture of a society and its linguistic habits may change. In another sense then, it is possible to say that a language no longer *dominates* the culture. For Irish and many Native American cultures, and for segments of Puerto Rican culture in New York, the English language predominates at the present time.
5. On the other hand a cultural group may influence the habitual use, even the evolution of a language and thus dominate, in the sense of prevail over the language (Latin American Spanish, Haitian, and black American post-Creole English are examples).
6. Finally, *domination* implies subjugation to external authority. Hence in language and language policy the concept connotes a relationship we do not espouse (*informant, peasant,* indeed the terms *Island* and *Mainland* are likewise subtly elitist terms). This sense of dominance (superiority-inferiority) relates especially to the cultural conflict alluded to previously. Language domination figures in the cultural struggle, especially in the popular media (Note how the key phrases—*bilingual danger* and the *threat of English*—indicate that language is a major weapon in the arsenal of the intellectual battle). Other battlegrounds in the cultural struggle are often confused with language: these are interpersonal friction, political colonialism and economic monopoly. Such issues, though ex-

pressed in language and argued with words, are social, not verbal issues (see Bills 1979).

Note the root, *dom,* in all these terms, related to "lord and liege, king, master" and other terms which pragmatically are defined by the subordination of people for the economic benefit of a ruler.[32] Such assumptions of inequality are fundamentally contradictory to principles underlying this investigation.

In this discussion, we are seeking, however tentatively, a middle level method of analysis and interpretation that connects the methodology of our research (empirical hypotheses) to "the method" of the historical-economic interpretation of all social life. (Yartseva et al, 1977: 14).

The Opinion Conflict

In the Puerto Rican sociolinguistic situation in New York many of the senses of *dominance* co-exist: ability, prevalence, authority and subjugation. These senses are watchwords in the various views and interests in the continuous interdependence of language and culture. Cultural nationalists view linguistic change as the erosion of autonomy. The Nuyorican poets assert they are creating a new language to express a new culture. A few feel that there is only benefit to be gained in rejecting Spanish. Alienation is visible in parents who proudly say: "*mi hija está en escuela privada, y habla nada mas que Ingles.*"[33] Others, indicating that culture is wider than language and that language is flexible have said, "You can speak anything you want. If you're Puerto Rican, *you are Puerto Rican*!"

Dynamically connected to economic and social history (which are processes, not things), culture and language are also processual. To say that "Language is the vehicle of culture," is not, as has been intended, the equivalent to, nor proof that "Spanish is absolutely essential for Puerto Rican culture." Rather, in the abstract it means that culture implies language. No culture can exist without language. Practically, it means that earlier forms of Puerto Rican culture, up to the present, have been expressed and transmitted in Spanish. From the processual standpoint it is evident that cultures and existing *language varieties* change and embody new symbolic values, even though human *language itself,* the prime means of communication and cultural interchange, retains its characteristic qualities of expression, social unification and community definition.

In 1978, after extensive institutional use of English in Puerto Rico during eighty years of American possession and nearly thirty years of intensive migration to the English-speaking continental United States, Spanish is still considered to be the language of the Puerto Rican community, though not without qualification. The general opinion of language and culture is that each language has greater value in its home culture.

Seven out of ten in this sample feel that Puerto Ricans have a better opinion of a Spanish speaker and a poorer opinion of an English speaker (eight out of ten think Americans have a poorer opinion of a Spanish speaker. Table 5, items 9-12). English monolinguals pose more division in the Puerto Rican community than do Puerto Ricans who only speak Spanish (Table 14). In all, however the majority opinion is that monolinguals do not divide the community.

The community would prefer societal bilingualism, and the bilinguals in this sample appear to score high in many of the cultural and linguistic items. Still, a bilingual society with monolinguals of each language does not appear to be a threat.

It is not easy to interpret the opinion by eighty-four percent that the Spanish language is not necessary to cultural identity.

Among those who said "A person does not have to speak Spanish to be Puerto Rican" (=Spanish is not necessary to cultural identity), the following opinions were heard:

1. "English exists among Puerto Ricans today."
2. "Many times you have to speak English and that doesn't stop you from being Puerto Rican."
3. "You can learn other languages and speak whatever you want."
4. "Americans, blacks and other Hispanics know Spanish and they are not Puerto Rican."
5. "Nationality is separate from language."

The speaker who voiced the last comment is a young adult and considers himself Puerto Rican by nationality. Below is the reasoning he gives, asserting the importance of Spanish and its dynamic in the New York Puerto Rican community:

Q. "Do you have to speak Spanish in order to be Puerto Rican?"
A. "No."
Q. "Why?"
A. "Because you're Puerto Rican by itself. That's a nationality: you're Puerto Rican. I know that Spanish is a tradition in Puerto Rico, but it's not necessary [to speak Spanish] to be a Puerto Rican."
Q. "So nationality is separate from language, that's what you're saying? For the Puerto Rican community to remain Puerto Rican in the future, it has to speak Spanish?"
A. "I would say, yeah, even though I said that nationality is separate from language. It's something that keeps up the spirit of Puerto Ricans. I mean, you could have two or three individuals who don't speak Spanish at all, but they could be Puerto Rican. But if the whole community was to, you know, stop, it wouldn't be the same as if it was to speak Spanish. Other people wouldn't think of them as a nationality. Let's say the old people, years from now, they die. When the young guys, like, let's say, me—if I was to forget Spanish and like the rest of all the teenagers was to grow up and not know Spanish at all, then their kids wouldn't know Spanish at all . . . then you would have a community that hardly speaks Spanish. Now if I teach my children my Spanish language—I would teach my kids even though they are learning English. That would keep the community together, in the Spanish way."

It appears that Spanish is highly valued, yet the members of the community would not exclude others who by birth or parentage are Puerto Rican, though they might not speak Spanish. The culture has other aspects to it than language alone,[34] but what Puerto Rican culture would be like without Spanish is a speculation that most do not want to venture. Rather, one hundred percent feel that Spanish should be maintained not only in Puerto Rico but in the community in New York, and in the U.S. generally.

In this sample, only fifteen percent assumed, as many more with ideologized positions do, that Spanish is an essential and indispensable part of the culture. One said, "*La forma de distinguir entre los latinos es por el acento.*" "Accent distinguishes the various Latin American groups." He clearly emphasized not only the importance of Spanish but also the regional variation which enables recognition of cultural specifics even within the generic term "Hispanic."

A few others said, "People will not recognize you as Puerto Rican if you don't speak Spanish." And several said, "The heritage of Puerto Ricans has traditionally been expressed in Spanish."

Of course, Spain itself was a colonizer, and two other cultures, indigenous and West African must be recognized as "traditional" in Puerto Rico, though they are often relegated a lesser role. Thus the presence of English monolinguals is a further facet of cultural imposition, but not a totally new issue in the definition of the national culture and history of Puerto Rico. Nationhood in the sense of "political sovereignty" was only for a brief period coincident with Puerto Rican nationality. Then, perhaps even more than now, mainly the upper class Spanish tradition was recognized as traditional Puerto Rican heritage. Bernardo Vega's dynamic concept of *patria,* "Fatherland," has added relevance when proletarian culture and the impact of English are brought into the discussion of what Puerto Rican culture is as the end of the twentieth century approaches.

To return briefly to the questionnaire results regarding language and cultural identity, more people feel that it is necessary for the community to continue to speak Spanish (fifty-five percent), than feel that it is necessary for an individual to speak Spanish in order to be Puerto Rican (fifteen percent). This implies the need for Spanish to remain an aspect of the culture in the future, as the reasoning of the young man transcribed above illustrates. It is puzzling that this result is positive in just slightly over half the sample, whereas other questions on maintenance were unanimous. In fact, the young adults more than all other groups combined express the attitude that Spanish is very important to Puertorricanness, and are second to the older people in emphasizing the importance of language to group solidarity.

The age-group breakdowns on these and many other items concerned with language resources, invite the following speculative scenario for the sociolinguistic cycle in the present community:

The younger children learn Spanish and English and hear both from separate speakers and from those who combine them in various ways. The older children and adolescents speak (and receive communication) increasingly in English. This accords well with their position as students and as members of peer groups which include non-Hispanics. As the school experience ends and employment responsibilities begin in young adulthood (successfully or unsuccessfully), the use of Spanish increases in mixed usage and in monolingual speech to older persons. Young adults then reactivate the Spanish skills acquired in childhood and then left rather passive in adolescence. Mature adults speak both languages. At present older persons are Spanish monolingual or nearly so.

From these results emerge views of Puerto Rican identity that are different from views that are often presented:

1. that the community is assimilating and losing Spanish
2. that the community is recalcitrant and does not want to speak English

3. that the community wants to retain in New York everything that is in Puerto Rico
4. that the community is creating a new, creole life and creolized language.

Spanish is not seen as integral to the community's identity, though it is desired by all and considered important by more than half. English, also, is desired; and Puerto Rican culture is seen as compatible with English (though never to the exclusion of Spanish). Traditions are not accepted uncritically, and life in Puerto Rico is not romanticized. In fact, neither living in Puerto Rico, nor living in a Puerto Rican neighborhood like *el barrio,* is considered more than partially important in being Puerto Rican. Many feel that aspects of New York Puerto Rican life are unique, but in regard to language, the dichotomy between Spanglish as contamination and Spanglish as a new Rican language is not valid. Rather, the two languages, Spanish and English occur in many ranges of usage, with norms of interaction that are unique or distinctive, in either language and both simultaneously, fluidly and within a single speaker situation or sentence. But this speaking though a separate mode or way of interacting, does not cease to be comprised of Spanish and English, just as its speakers do not cease to be Puerto Rican. The sense of the Puerto Rican at this time is intertwined with U.S. culture and economy, with U.S. experience and also with the traditional culture of Puerto Rico.

Seeing the bilingual resources so high in the community should not encourage complacency, much less should parents and cultural leaders in the Puerto Rican community turn their backs on the sociolinguistic situation, saying, "*Bueno,* the community is doing fine. English is strong, Spanish is strong. What else do we have to do?" The attitudes both within and toward the community are often not positive; reading scores and dropout rates are staggering (Silverman 1978). There is much to be done to cultivate raw language resources into elaborated skills, to be intellectually critical of the prevalent cultural and linguistic expression in both languages, to be able to deal competently and innovatively in the literary standard forms (especially syntax and orthography) of both, and be willing to recognize and develop valuable oral skills, appropriate to community norms of interaction.

Plain Talk: Is Spanish Necessary?

At the beginning of this research we puzzled over whether Spanish is essential to the Puerto Rican community. Like Wittgenstein's example of philosophers stumbling over metaphysical wordings we asked, "Is Spanish necessary, sufficient, integral, indispensible, valued, essential . . . ?" Someone on the block, early in the interviews, said, "*El español no es necesario porque hay mucha gente bilingue.*"

If we knew then what we know now, we could have closed the study at that point. Essentially, that is what we have learned: Spanish is the assumed basis of community interaction; to say that bilingualism "proves" that Spanish is not necessary only reaffirms the valued permanence of Spanish, along with English. But without the hours of making other contacts to interview other people, coding the 177 questions into 300-plus variables and composites, programming the computer runs and reading mountains of long printout paper, we wouldn't have known whether to believe that speaker, or another who said, "Of course, Spanish is necessary, it's the Puerto Rican language."

Now we know who to believe. But we don't know if it's right. So we present these findings for discussion and comparison, in order to ground the debate about language, education, policy and the sociolinguistic condition of the community in the concrete speech patterns of an important Puerto Rican speech community.

Stable societal bilingualism is a goal inferred from this study, but not an easy one. Societal bilingualism is indeed rare (Canada, Belgium and other multi-lingual societies are not societies with a bilingual majority, for example. Indigenous languages in Latin America, to take another example, can only survive in diglossic situations). The argument in the ethnography of the Puerto Rican neighborhood here investigated is that bilingualism exists with no domain of speaking that is neither totally Spanish nor totally English. Such bilingualism without diglossia is usually temporary, lasting a few generations at best. Language vitality depends not only on societal factors, such as demography, status and institutional support. In a bilingual situation such as the Puerto Rican case in New York, the continued vitality of Spanish depends also on a performative niche in the speech ecology "where English just will not do."[35]

In status, Spanish is a world language, with its académia and literary tradition. Within the community there is prestige ascribed to Puerto Rican styles of speaking, although both the language itself (as opposed to French) and the variety (as opposed to Argentinian or Castillian) have lower status when viewed by others. Demographically, the number of productive, fluent speakers is great, and in the segregated neighborhoods where Hispanics live, population density of speakers again favors vitality. Institutional support exists in schools, neighborhood organizations and in some bilingual education programs. Attitudes as well favor not only Spanish retention and maintenance, but bilingualism.

What then is the prognosis for societal bilingualism that is not temporary? In the major domains, school, home, neighborhood, work and official negotiation, both languages exist. Yet in specific speech situations within these domains there are events and participants that require Spanish. For example, the migration from Puerto Rico and Latin America generally presents numerous interpersonal occasions when Spanish is not merely optional but mandatory; and in many interactions involving bilinguals, the Spanish speaker and use of Spanish is accommodated. Even with dispersal away from population concentrations like *el barrio,* segregation and social cohesiveness still result in speech communities that interact primarily Hispano-to-Hispano, in places like Worcester, Mass., Rochester, N.Y. and Lancaster, Pa.. The sociolinguistic life cycle presented above also provides for certain societal niches where English and Spanish are differentiated situationally, though not by domain. Lastly, certain cultural niches exist where nothing is quite like the use of Spanish; and these are not only domestic and face-to-face situations such as emotion, cooking, and courting, but in music, poetry and debate as well, which are more intellectual aspects of culture.

To the question: Should Spanish be retained among Puerto Ricans? we adopt a three-quarter stance, raising the chin but not the eyelids, and respond, as did many: "*¿Y porqué no?*" The question is not will Spanish survive, but in what way will the community continue to use it?

We end with questions that should open the conversation among Puerto Ricans, Hispanics generally and other national linguistic minorities. What is socially desirable in these findings? What positive aspects should be retained, what developed? What is to be changed through the intervention of the community in its own condition? What are the implications for a self-determined policy?

ACKNOWLEDGEMENTS

This work was sponsored by the Ford Foundation.

Pedro Pedraza conducted field interviews to gather the data in 1977 and 1978. The manuscript has benefitted from close reading by Frank Bonilla and the Language Policy Task Force (Pedro Pedraza, Alicia Pousada, and Shana Poplack). A word of thanks goes out as well to Robert Terdiman, Donald Hindle and Robert Cooper for assistance in data processing. The hard work of coding and machine manipulation of the data was carefully carried out by Felix Toledo. Zunilda Lopez typed the many versions through which this manuscript has passed.

Without these many people, this work would not have whatever merit it contains. All errors remain my responsibility.

J.J.A. (June, 1979)

NOTES

1. In a review of bilingual education programs in fourteen nations, thousands of schools, and research derived from a quarter of a million students, Coffman and Lei-Min (abstracted in Fishman 1976: 137) note that general achievement is related mainly to reading and that reading is directly related to home environment. Fishman comments: "Thus the importance of home and community is once again confirmed. . . . Rather than view bilingual education as a means of changing home and community characteristics (as many American spokespersons and educators are inclined to do), . . . bilingual education should be governed by these characteristics and therefore require home and community support for its success."
2. Twenty percent (Bureau of Labor Statistics 1975).
3. Eighty-five percent, according to the 1970 Census, live in designated poverty areas.
4. Dropout rates from high school range from fifty-seven percent to eighty-one percent for major U.S. cities according to Aspira (1977). Generally Hispanic dropoutism is four times as high as Anglo rates (Silverman 1978).

5. "One thing that has been brought home with increasing forcefulness in the course of these reflections is the richness of the Puerto Rican case as a historical instance of a global movement that has been a part of world capitalist development for nearly two hundred years. Puerto Rican migration is perhaps unique in the duration and relative magnitude of the population displacement, the depth and scope of related changes in the Island's economy, class configuration, and political organization. With the intensification in recent decades of the legal and illegal flow of workers from formerly colonized and peripheral economies to metropolitan centers, the case takes on a special pertinence, not only for countries that may be at various stages in a similar process of associated development and population exchange with the United States, but also for migration from all labor surplus industrializing regions to metropolitan centers." (History Task Force 1979: 9-10).
6. Many editorials, articles and columns in the mass media *N.Y. Times* editorials 11/22/76, 7/4/79; Tom Bethell, *Harper's*, Feb. 1979; Carl Tucker *Saturday Review* 5/12/1979; Philip Quigg "My Turn" *Newsweek* 10/16/78. Note also that many bilingual programs are funded under "remedial" auspices and that for many schools the bilingual program is considered a residual or "dumping" area for problem students (and less desirable teachers).
7. "Our knowledge of demographic trends, the history of Puerto Rico and our community in the United States, the Constitutional and legal issues raised by the thrust of linguistic or ethnic claims in this country, as well as the changing configuration of capitalist production on a world scale all lead us to believe that language issues will constitute a primary focus of policy contention in the next few decades. As a community whose survival may hang in the balance, we must strive for a realistic sense of the full complexity of the processes involved and for reasoned judgments about desired outcome and lines of action within our reach" (National Puerto Rican Task Force on Educational Policy 1977: 7-8).
8. This did not prove to be useful in the present study, not because the concept is invalid, but because subtle measures of street behavior are not available in this type of (survey) research. The raw material of the interviews, hundreds of hours of tape, may provide clues to such values. Here, of course, novelists have been as successful as ethnographers in portraying speech variation and interaction. The problem is to abstract patterns from such performance.
9. "Even the defenders of Puerto Rico's present status, formally adopted in 1952, now call for a new dimension of sovereignty that will give the island the maximum plenitude of autonomy." Jose A. Cabranes. "Puerto Rico: Out of the Colonial Closet," *Foreign Affairs*. Winter 1978-1979, 33: 67.
10. Each question was given a maximum of three points except for the nationality question, 'Puerto Rican' was given 4 points, 'Neo-Rican' was given 3 points, because it was felt this designation was more affirmative of a non-American alternative culture, in other words more of a national minority than an immigrant group assimilating, or assimilated as the next designations imply. "Puerto Rican American" 2 points; American 1 point. When three divisions are made, ten persons

(11 percent) scored 'low' (5-9 points); fifty-seven persons (sixty-four percent) scored in the medium range (10-13 points), and twenty-two (twenty-five percent) scored high (14-16 points). Since the middle group was so large and the peripheral groups (especially the low) were so small, it was thought wise to split the middle group putting those who scored 10-11 with the 'low' group, the others with the 'high', this enabling the results to be seen more graphically.

11. The term Nuyorican, in the continental United States especially, implies a rejection of the process of melting into the American middle class, adherence to Puerto Rican identity, yet a rebellion against many traditional and colonized ideas prevalent in Puerto Rico. None of the Nuyoricans in this sample are Spanish dominant; nine of the sixteen are bilingual. Puerto-Rican-American could mean many things, related mainly to questionable concepts such as pluralism or even downright assimilation. (cf. Chicano vs. Mexican-American).
12. The community's unanimous response on the maintenance of Spanish along with its willingness, almost demand, for bilingual education indicate that there is a possibility for community organizing to serve as the basis for assertion of the national culture both in policy and in practice, and more modestly, to serve as a basis for community involvement in education.
13. Sixty-three percent were educated in the United States, twenty-one percent in Puerto Rico, eight percent in both places, six percent elsewhere. The language of education in New York schools was English for sixty-six percent. Only three persons (three percent) were educated in Spanish; eight (nine percent) were educated in both. In Puerto Rican schools the medium of education was the Spanish language for twenty-nine percent, was both for nine percent and was English for only two people (two percent).
14. Although the choices presented were several: "Spanish," "English," "mixed (code-switching)," "both languages separately," "both with more English," "both with more Spanish," as well as "I don't know," "no response" and "not applicable," the latter three can be collapsed into a category of nonresponse because the subtleties in the differences between no response and not applicable are not so crucial here, and the three previous to that can all be collapsed into "bilingual" behavior.
15. All groups except the young adults have nonresponse in "dancing," and they report mixing the two languages. The "bodega" shows little English, but the question is loaded by having the domain introduced by a Spanish term. Older persons engage less in active sports.
16. See Fishman's introduction to *International Migration Review*, Vol. VI, No. 2, 1971.
17. Even though the general frequencies are under half for good language, within one's own main resource language the self assessment of good language is about sixty percent.
18. Ninety-seven percent think Spanish should be maintained in Puerto Rico. In a related question, forty-seven percent say Spanish should be the sole official language of Puerto Rico and fifty-two percent say Puerto Rico should be officially bilingual. In either case, Spanish maintenance is favored nearly unanimously.

19. The opinion that bilingual acquisition is detrimental to the cognitive formation of the child has been requestioned in recent years by some of the foremost researchers in the field (Lambert 1972, 1974; Giles 1975). Although the research has not been without class-based and methodological biases, it appears that bilingualism may enhance the symbolic manipulation skills necessary for successful language acquisition.
20. Half the sample also learned English at the early stage of language acquisition (age two to seven); another quarter of the sample learned English between the ages of seven and fourteen.
21. Pedraza (1979) underlines the role of cyclic migration as key to Spanish maintenance at the present time. Whereas the young adults may have been constrained to speak Spanish as they grew up during massive in-migration, adolescents and children may need to use Spanish in social contexts of children and adults who circulate between New York and Puerto Rico.
22. The twelve U.S. born persons who report the frequent use of Spanish were examined more closely, case-by-case, revealing that all spend a great deal of time in public interaction (a feature which correlates more, however, with English use). Of the four adolescents, three are young adults who interact frequently with older, Spanish-speaking men in the Gavilanes and Banca networks. One seems to be frequently out of work. He exemplifies a pattern observed by Pedraza, that sometimes even U.S.-born men are Spanish to the exclusion of ability in English. Often these are people who had a less-than-successful school experience and who are frequently out of work. One of the persons reporting a great amount of Spanish use does not fit that pattern. He has spent all his life in New York, is a fluent bilingual and says, "I respect both my flags." Another frequently spent one year in Puerto Rico and the next in New York, in a pattern of cyclic migration throughout most of his life. Two are over-reporting, from followup observation. (Cases No. 1, 5, 10, 11, 25, 27, 32, 51, 61, 64, 78, 80).
23. Two more report some bilingual usage, but choose Spanish over English, i.e., they do not report to use English. These should be included with the Spanish monolinguals, with qualification, bringing the percentage to twenty percent for mostly Spanish monolingual persons.
24. Raw = absolute number, RPT—percentage for the entire table, RCP = column percent, RPR = row percentage, ERF—expected raw frequency, based on the proportion of each column and row that any given cell might ideally represent. Readers might wish to derive other patterns from these displays.
25. Birthplace is not part of the composites, but given the weighting for place of acquisition and age of acquisition of the languages, one would expect Spanish to correlate with Puerto Rico as birthplace.
26. For this question there are only eighty-nine cases, not ninety-one, due to missing information.
27. The term Main Language Resource as opposed to a measurement of self-report of dominance, means an assessment of personal history, reported skills and use, as well as personal observation of language interaction. It is a derived measure, but one that compensates for the misreport that is inherent in linguistic auto-observation. No formal

measures of dominance, whether testing of skills, observation of fluency, or of use-time have been carried out. These measures are both worthwhile and problematic. Language resource as here used is, like many linguistic concepts, a fuzzy-edged set. It indicates the location of an intangible that is both difficult and theoretically dangerous to define.

28. Results not presented here, but overwhelmingly English language oriented except for strong use of Spanish radio.
29. Filtering the triangular use tables by Main Resource languages shows only nine of the mainly English speakers using mostly English. On the other hand, most of the mainly Spanish speakers report nearly monolingual Spanish (refer to the top row of Table 27). The bilinguals tend toward English, but no bilingual appears in either the far left (English monolingual) or far right (Spanish monolingual) column. The table also shows more bilingual usage among the English speakers than among the Spanish.
30. Two studies in bilingualism in the *barrio* recognized this. Hoffman (1971: 231) asserted, "It is inaccurate to say that all Puerto Ricans are on their way to acculturation." Fishman (1971: 60-61) noted, "no grand ideology in defense of Spanish is felt to be necessary," among intellectuals he interviewed who are in some ways the standard-bearers of the culture.
31. The Office of Bilingual Education of the City of New York intends to replace the LAB test with a more reliable instrument (A. Orta, personal communication). On the West Coast, some bilingual projects have resulted in positive views of Mexican culture, without the devaluation of Anglo culture, more positive attitudes toward school generally, among students; and among parents, views have been recorded that bilingual education is both symbolically (culturally) and instrumentally (economically) beneficial (Cohen 1975: 262ff). Cohen also notes that bilingual education "is turning the tide against cultural stripping" which is prevalent in monolingual education. Attitudes expressed in *el barrio* tend in the same direction: the aspiration that bilingual education will promote bilingualism, for cultural self-respect, for general knowledge and for occupational opportunity.
32. This root is also the same as that in "domestic," the male honorific in Spanish "don", and "dome" meaning round roof, cathedral. The root is derived from the greek *domo* "house" and the Sanskrit *dam* "tame." Thus the history of the word like the social aspect of its referent contains various meanings, from household leadership to more complex forms of authority and control.
33. "My daughter is in private school and only speaks English." Phonetically, [mi.ha.ˀta.neh.kwe.la.pri.βa.i.ya.bla.maˀ.kiŋ."gle]
34. Unlike the Albanian-Greek case (Trudgill 1977) in which language is the only distinguishing characteristic of the group.
35. These thoughts owe much to the closing remarks "On the Future of Spanish in the United States," by Gary Keller, editor of *The Bilingual Review/La Revista Bilingue,* and Dean of the Graduate School at Eastern Michigan University (Sixth Annual Conference on Hispanic Linguistics, July 22, 1979, Adelphi University).

BIBLIOGRAPHY

Abrahams, R. D., and R. C. Troike. *Language and Cultural Diversity in American Education.* Englewood Cliffs: Prentice Hall, 1972.

Agheyisi, Rebecca, and Joshua Fishman. "Language Attitude Studies: A Brief Survey of Methodological Approaches," *Anthropological Linguistics,* XII, 5, (1970) pp. 137-157.

Algarín, Miguel, et al. *Nuyorican Poetry,* New York: William Morrow, 1975.

Amastae, John, and Lucía Elías-Olivares. "Attitudes Toward Varieties of Spanish." The Fourth LACUS Forum. Columbia, S.C.: Hornbeam Press, (1977) pp. 286-302.

Aspira. *Social Factors and Educational Attainment among Puerto Ricans in U.S. Metropolitan Areas, 1970.* New York: Aspira of America, 1976.

Bills, Garland. Review of Dittmar, Norbert. *A Critical Survey of Sociolinguistics. Language* 55, 2, (1979) pp. 454-457.

Bonilla, Frank and Hector Colón. "Puerto Rican Return Migration in the '70s," *Migration Today,* April, (1979) pp. 7-12.

Coffman, W. E. and Lai-Min Paul Lee. "Cross-National Assessment of Educational Achievement: a Review." *Educational Researcher* 3, 6, 13-16 (see Fishman 1976: 137 F) 1974.

Cohen, Andrew D. *A Sociolinguistic Approach to Bilingual Education.* Rowley, MA: Newbury House, 1975.

Cooper, Robert L. *Language Attitudes II, International Journal of the Sociology of Language, 6* (= *Linguistics,* No. 166), 1975.

__________. *Language Attitudes I, International Journal of the Sociology of Language, 3* (= *Linguistics,* No. 136), 1974.

__________. and J.A. Fishman. 1974. "The Study of Language Attitudes." in Cooper 1974.

Cordasco, Francesco, and Eugene Bucchini, eds. *The Puerto Rican Community and its Children on the Mainland.* A sourcebook for Teachers, Social Workers and other Professionals. Metuchen, NJ: Scarecrow Press, 1972.

Fishman, J.A., ed. *International Migration Review* (issue on language and migration), Vol. V, No. 2. (1971).

__________. R.L. Cooper, and Roxanna Ma. *Bilingualism in the Barrio.* Bloomington: Indiana University Press (Language and Science Monographs, 7), 1971.

__________. "Intellectuals from the Island," in Fishman, Cooper and Ma 1971. Bloomington: Indiana University Press (Language Science Monographs, 7), 1971.

__________. and Charles Terry. "The Validity of Census Data on Bilingualism in a Puerto Rican Neighborhood." *American Sociological Review,* (1971) pp. 636-650.

Fishman, J.A. *Bilingual Education: An International Sociological Perspective.* Rowly, MA: Newbury House, 1976.

Flores, J. "The Insular Vision: Pedreira's Interpretation of Puerto Rican Culture." History Task Force, Centro de Estudios Puertorriqueños, CUNY. Cultural Working Paper #1, 1978.

Fragoso, Victor. (ms.) "El Encuentro del Español y del Ingles en la Literatura Puertorriqueña." Culture Task Force, Centro de Estudios Puertorriqueños.

Gaarder, A. Bruce. *Bilingual Schooling and the Survival of Spanish in the United States.* Rowley, MA: Newbury House, 1977.

Giles, H., and P.F. Powesland. *Speech Style and Social Evaluation.* London: Academic Press, 1975.

__________. *Language, Ethnicity and Intergroup Relations.* London: Academic Press, 1977.

__________. R.Y. Bourhis, and D.M. Tucker. 1977. "Towards a Theory of Language in Ethnic Group Relations," in Giles (1977), pp. 307-348.

History Task Force. *Labor Migration under Capitalism: the Puerto Rican Experience,* New York: Monthly Review Press, 1979.

Hoffman, Gerald. 1971. "Life in the Neighborhood," in Fishman, Cooper and Ma 1971, pp. 199-232.

Kelly, L. G., ed. *Description and Measurement of Bilingualism,* Toronto: U. of Toronto Press, 1969.

Kloss, Heinz. "Language Rights of Immigrant Groups," *International Migration Review,* V(2), (1971) pp. 262-264.

Lambert, Wallace. 1972. "A Social Psychology of Bilingualism." in Abrahams and Troike 1972, pp. 197-200.

Language Policy Task Force. "Language Policy and the Puerto Rican Community." *Bilingual Review,* V, 1-2, pp. 1-40. Also, Centro de Estudios Puertorriqueños, CUNY. Language Working Paper #1, 1978.

Lauria, Antonio. 1964. " 'Respeto', 'Relajo' and Interpersonal Relations in Puerto Rico." *Anthropological Quarterly,* 37, pp. 53-67. (Reprinted in Cordasco, F. and E. Buccioni, 1972, pp. 36-48.)

Lee, Richard R. 1971. "Dialect Perception: A Critical Review and Re-evaluation." *The Quarterly Journal of Speech,* LVII, 4, (1971) pp. 410-417.

Lynn, Lawrence, ed. *Knowledge and Policy: The Uncertain Connection.* Washington, D.C.: National Academy of Sciences, 1978.

Macías, R.F. *Mexicano/Chicano Sociolinguistic Behavior and Language Policy in the United States.* Georgetown University dissertation, 1979.

Mintz, Sidney W. 1966. "Puerto Rico: An Essay in the Definition of a National Culture." *Status of Puerto Rico.* Selected background studies prepared for the United States-Puerto Rico Commission. (Reprinted 1975, NY: Arno Press, pp. 339-434.)

Pedraza, P. (ms.). "Ethnographic Aspects of a Block in El Barrio." Language Policy Task Force, Centro de Estudios Puertorriqueños, CUNY.

Pedreira, Antonio S. *Insularismo.* San Juan: Biblioteca de Autores Puertorriqueños, 1934.

Poplack, S. "Linguistic Structure and Ethnic Function of Code-Switching." Language Policy Task Force, Centro de Estudios Puertorriqueños, CUNY. Language Working Paper #2, 1978.

Poplack, S. "Typology of Code-Switching." Language Policy Task Force, Centro de Estudios Puertorriqueños, CUNY. Language Working Paper #4, 1979.

Pousada, A., and Poplack, S. (ms.). "No Case for Conversion: A Study of the Puerto Rican Verbal System." Language Policy Task Force, Centro de Estudios Puertorriqueños, CUNY.

Rogler, Lloyd. "A Better Life: Notes from Puerto Rico," *Transaction*, II, 3, 1965.

Ryan, Ellen Bouchard, and Miguel Carranza. 1975. "Evaluative Reactions of Bilingual, Anglo and Mexican American Adolescents Towards Speakers of English and Spanish." in Cooper 1975, pp. 83-104.

__________. 1977. "Ingroup and Outgroup Reactions to Mexican American Language Varieties." in Giles 1977, pp. 59-82.

Shuy, R.W., and R.W. Fasold, eds. *Language Attitudes: Current Trends and Projects.* Washington: Georgetown University Press, 1973.

Siegel, A., H. Orlans, and L. Greer. 1954. *Puerto Ricans in Philadelphia.* (Reprinted in the Puerto Rican Experience series, NY: Arno Press, 1975.)

Silverman, Leslie. "The Educational Disadvantage of Language Minority Persons in the United States, Spring 1976" National Center for Educational Statistics Bulletin, July 26 (78 B-4) U.S. Department of Health Education and Welfare/Education Division, 1978.

Smith, David. "Language, Speech and Ideology: A Conceptual Framework." in Shuy and Fasold, (1973) pp. 97-112.

Spolsky, B., and R. Cooper. *Frontiers of Bilingual Education.* Rowley, MA: Newbury House, 1977.

__________. *Case Studies in Bilingual Education.* Rowley, MA: Newbury House, 1978.

Trudgill, P., and G.A. Tzavaras. 1977. "Why Albanian-Greeks are not Albanians: Language Shift in Attica and Biotia." in Giles 1977, pp. 170-184.

United States Department of Commerce, Bureau of the Census. New York Tract. #166. Washington, D.C.: Census of Population, 1970.

United States Department of Labor. *A Socio-Economic Profile of Puerto Rican New Yorkers.* New York: Bureau of Labor Statistics, 1975.

Waggoner, Dorothy. "Geographic Distribution, Nativity, and Age Distribution of Language Minorities in the United States." Spring 1976, and "Place of Birth and Language Characteristics of Persons of Hispanic Origins in the United States: Spring 1976." National Center for Educational Statistics Bulletin 78 B-5, 78 B-6, U.S. Department of Health Education and Welfare/Education Division, 1978.

Williams, Frederick. 1974. "The Identification of Linguistic Attitudes." in Cooper 1974, pp. 21-33.

__________. *Exploration of the Linguistic Attitudes of Teachers.* Rowley, MA: Newbury House, 1976.

Wolck, Wolfgang. 1973. "Attitude Toward Spanish and Quechua in Bilingual Peru." in Shuy and Fasold 1973, pp. 129-147.

Wolf, Eric. "Aspects of Group Relations in a Complex Society: Mexico." *American Anthropologist*, LVII, 4, (1956): 1065-1078.

Wolfram, Walt. 1973. "Objective and Subjective Parameters of Language Assimilation Among Second Generation Puerto Ricans in East Harlem." in Shuy and Fasold 1973, pp. 148-1973.

Yartseva, Victoria, et al. *Theoretical Aspects of Linguistics.* Editorial Board of "Social Sciences Today," Moscow: USSR Academy of Sciences, 1977.

Zirkel, Perry A. "Puerto Rican Parents: an Educational Survey," *Integral Education* 11:6 (1973) pp. 20-26.

TABLE 1

AGE AND SEX OF ATTITUDINAL SAMPLE

#	Age Group	Age Range	M	F	
23	Adolescents	12-18 years of age	7	16	25%
33	Young Adults	19-30 years of age	17	16	36%
25	Mature Adults	31-50 years of age	18	7	27%
10	Older Persons	50+ years of age	9	1	11%
n= 91			51	40	n=91
			56%	44%	100%

TABLE 2

AGE OF ARRIVAL BY AGE GROUP

	Age of Arrival						
	Baby 0-5	Young 6-12	Adol 13-19	Adult 20-98	Born USA	Total N	%
N	17	10	10	14	38	89	
Adolescent	2	—	—	—	24	23	26
Young Adult	11	6	6	1	13	33	37
Mature Adult	6	6	4	9	4	26	23
Other People	—	—	1	16	1	10	11
Total %	19	11	11	16	43		100

TABLE 3

REPORTED FRIENDSHIPS BY NATIONALITY

Friendships %	All/Most	Some/Few	None
Puerto Ricans	94	5	—
Black Americans	7	78	15
Anglo Americans	3	70	26
Other Latin-Americans	1	65	21
Other Nationality	—	37	59

Fig. 1

Family emphasis on Puerto Rican Cultural Identity

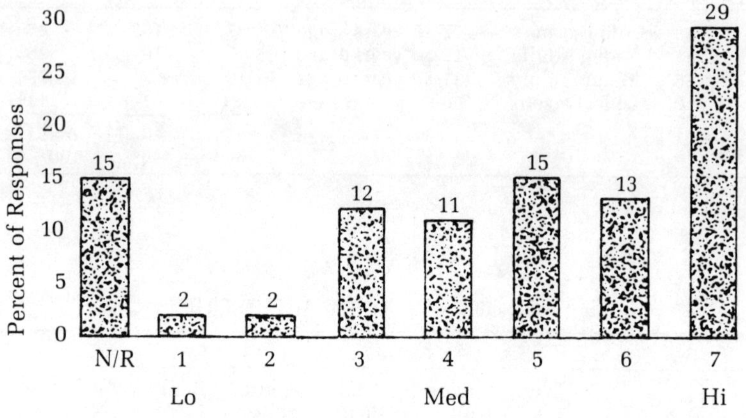

Q. Do you want your children to learn Puerto Rican History and Cuture?

	Y.	No	ABS
%	97	3	0

TABLE 4

PUERTO RICAN ETHNIC TRAIT PERCEPTION

Trait	Very Impt	Impt	Not Impt
"Which of the following are necessary for Puertorricanness?" or "Which are important for someone to be Puerto Rican?"			
	%	%	%
(Elements of Paternity)			
1. Puerto Rican Parentage	40	47	10
2. Puerto Rican Birth	22	29	48
(Elements of Patrimony)			
1. Pride	43	46	10
2. Puerto Rican Concerns	22	55	20
3. Values and Traditions	27	52	20
4. Spanish Language	21	47	30
5. Live in Puerto Rico	5	27	65
(Elements of history or coincidence)			
1. Struggle to make a living	14	30	55
2. Be Working Class	10	26	63
3. Talk like a Puerto Rican	5	33	60
4. Barrio life	3	23	73

TABLE 5

SOME RAW STATISTICS ON LANGUAGE AND CULTURAL IDENTITY

	% YES	% NO	% ABS
1. Is Spanish necessary to cultural identity?	15	83	—
2. Is Spanish necessary to the N.Y.P.R. community?	54	45	—
3. Is language important to group solidarity?	90	10	—
4. Does speech hold the community together?	75	22	3
5. Does one kind of speaking feel most Puerto Rican?	52	48	—
6. Is Spanish an important part of P.R. culture?	87	13	—
7. Is English an important part of American culture?	87	13	—
8. Is English important to integrate into American society?	92	8	—
9. Do P.R. have a better opinion of Spanish speakers?	70	29	1
10. Does Anglo society have a better opinion of English speakers?	60	38	2
11. Do Puerto Ricans have a better opinion of English speakers?	27	70	3
12. Does Anglo society have a better opinion of Spanish speakers?	15	80	5

TABLE 6

SELF-REPORT OF CULTURAL DETERMINATION AND NATIONALITY

		Puerto Rican	Both	USA
What do you consider yourself to be a part of?		15%	65%	20%
	Puerto Rican	Nuyorican	Puerto Rican American	USA
What is your nationality?	38%	18%	42%	2%

Figure 2

Model for four designations of Nationality (n=91).

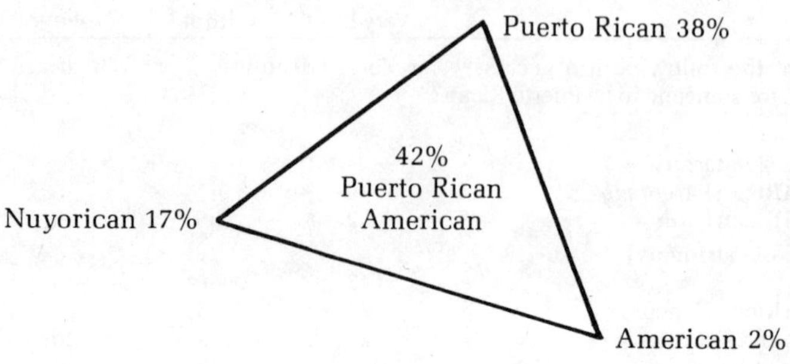

Figure 3.

Age Division of Self Report of Nationality (in percentages)

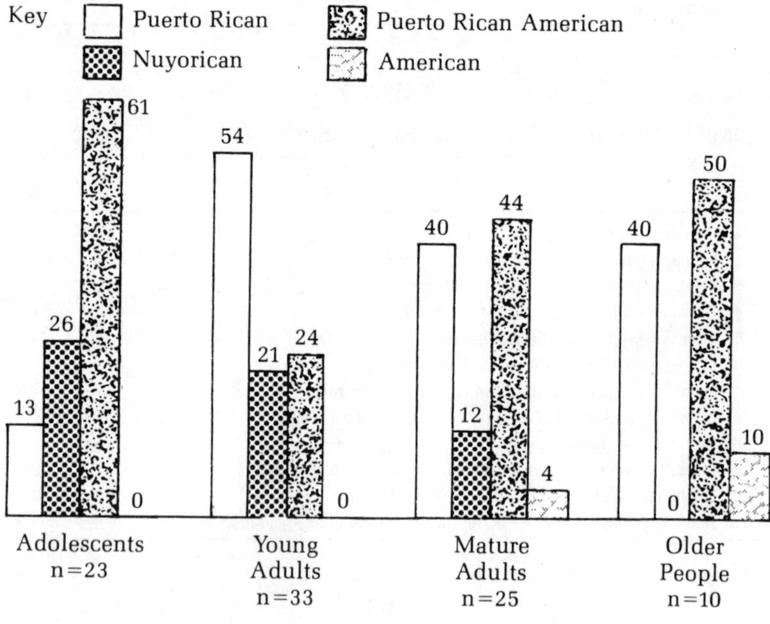

TABLE 7
ETHNIC IDENTITY COMPOSITE BY AGE, RAW AND COLUMN PERCENTAGE

ETHNIC IDENTITY	AGE GROUP	Adolescents	Young Adults	Mature Adults	Older People	Totals
LOW	Raw n	19	12	13	6	50
	Column %	83%	36%	52%	60%	55%
HIGH	Raw n	4	21	12	4	41
	Column %	17%	64%	48%	40%	45%
	Total n	23	33	25	10	91

TABLE 8
SELF REPORT OF LANGUAGE CHOICE IN SOCIAL DOMAINS

Language Used	% Spanish	% English	% Code-switching	% Other Bilingualism	% Non-Response
I. *Workplace*					
1. with co-workers	11	19	13	6	51
2. with boss	3	38	3	3	52
II. *Family*					
3. with mother	29	3	9	10	49
4. with father	22	5	7	5	60
5. with siblings	7	26	14	7	46
III. *School*					
6. w/school friends	—	13	13	6	67
7. w/teacher	—	24	4	4	67
8. w/principal	—	23	1	5	70
IV. *Church*					
9. w/adults in church	23	13	7	2	54
10. w/teenagers "	4	30	4	4	56
11. w/children "	10	16	8	10	56
V. *In the Neighborhood On the block*					
12. w/adults	51	10	25	14	—
13. w/teenagers	18	41	32	8	2
14. w/children	24	35	26	13	1
VI. *Family*					
15. w/adult relative	71	8	13	8	—
16. w/teen relatives	22	43	27	8	2
17. w/child relatives	26	31	33	9	1
VII. *Social Life*					
18. in active sports	5	33	22	2	37
19. in sedentary games	34	24	26	4	11
20. socializing	31	30	32	7	1
21. in bodega	69	5	20	4	1
22. while dancing	20	12	32	3	33

TABLE 9
LANGUAGES USED IN SOCIALIZING

	Spanish	English	CS	Other Biling	Attrition	Total
Adolescents	9	47	30	9	4	100
Young Adults	18	24	48	9	—	100
Mature Adults	48	24	24	4	—	100
Older People	80	20	—	—	—	100
Totals N	28	27	29	5	1	91
%	31	30	32	5	1	100

TABLE 10

SELF-REPORT OF GENERAL LANGUAGE SKILLS ENGLISH AND SPANISH

	Understanding Spoken Speech						
	English				Spanish		
%	Yes	Some	No	%	Yes	Some	No
Adolescents	100	—	—		96	4	—
Adults	86	13	1		100	—	—
Total(N=91)	89	10	1		99	1	—
	Speaking						
	English				Spanish		
%	Yes	Some	No	%	Yes	Some	No
Adolescents	100	—	—		87	13	—
Adults	76	19	5		100	—	—
Total(N=91)	82	14	3		97	3	—
	Reading						
	English				Spanish		
%	Yes	Some	No	%	Yes	Some	No
Adolescents	100	—	—		52	26	22
Adults	84	10	6		76	9	15
Total(N=91)	88	8	4		70	13	16
	Writing						
	English				Spanish		
%	Yes	Some	No	%	Yes	Some	No
Adolescents	96	4	—		39	13	48
Adults	66	15	19		63	13	24
Total(N=91)	74	12	14		57	13	30

TABLE 11

SELF REPORT OF COMPETENCE

	English				Spanish		
%	Hi	Med	Lo	%	Hi	Med	Lo
Adolescents(n=23)	87	13	—		26	70	4
All Adults(n=67)	32	55	13		53	47	—
Young Adults(n=32)	41	55	3		44	56	—
Mature Adults(n=25)	24	56	21		44	56	—
Older People(n=10)	20	50	30		100	—	—
Total(n=90)	46	44	9		46	53	1

TABLE 12

GOOD SPEAKERS OF SPANISH AND ENGLISH

Good Spanish (in general)	Good English (in general)
Puerto Ricans 23%	White (Anglo) ethnicity 30%
Prestige dialects 20%	Educational or Occupational level 30%
Educational or Occupational level 20%	Younger generation 19%
Older generation 20%	
Long residence in Puerto Rico 4%	Long residence in U.S.A 2%

TABLE 13

SELF ASSESSMENT OF SPEAKING GOOD SPANISH AND GOOD ENGLISH (IN PERCENTAGES)

Independent Variable	Main Language Resource			Age Group				Sex		Birth-Place		Education			
ALTERNATIVE	SPAN	BILING	ENG	ADOL	YADUL	MADUL	OLDER	M	F	PR	US	4 YRS.	JR.H.S.	H.S.	COLL
N in each group	N=28	38	25	23	33	25	10	51	40	50	41	7	56	18	9
Do you speak															
GOOD SPANISH	%60	58	16	21	45	72	50	53	40	58	34	71	32	72	67
GOOD ENGLISH	% 7	59	64	57	52	32	30	35	55	30	60	14	34	56	100

Percentage of each group reporting "good Spanish" and "good English" for Main Language Resource, Age, Sex, Birthplace and Education

Independent Variable	Nationality by Self Report				Economic Support				General Sample 91	
ALTERNATIVE	PR	USA	PR-AM	NUYORICAN	LOCAL	OUTSIDE	XCH	DEP		
N in each group	N=35	2	38	16	10	24	25	29	YES	NO
Do you speak										
GOOD SPANISH	%54	50	42	43	60	54	60	31	47	45
GOOD ENGLISH	%34	50	47	56	60	33	36	55	44	45

Percentage of each group reporting "good Spanish" and "good English" for Self report of Nationality and Economic support.

TABLE 14
SEVEN KEY QUESTIONS OF LANGUAGE VALUES
(IN PERCENTAGES)

Raw Frequencies on Seven Key Questions of Language Value	% YES	% NO	% ABS
Can you speak English and be part of Puerto Rican culture?	100	—	—
Can you speak Spanish and be part of American culture?	95	5	—
Is English a threat to Puerto Rican identity?	10	90	—
Do monolingual Spanish speakers divide the community?	13	86	—
Do monolingual English speakers divide the Puerto Rican community?	32	68	—
Is English important for good job positions?	99	1	—
Is Spanish important for good job positions?	57	43	—

FIGURE 4
SPEECH VARIETIES OF SPANISH AND ENGLISH

Spanish monolingual
more Spanish/
less English

English monolingual
more English/
less Spanish

Bilingual/
mixed

Bilingual/separate

TABLE 15
ESTIMATES OF QUANTITY OF SPEAKERS OF VARIOUS VARIETIES

Number of Speakers in the N.Y. Puerto Rican community	% Many	% Some	% Few
Bilingual (mixed or C/S)	80	3	16
Spanish w/little English	77	5	18
Monolingual Spanish	71	5	23
English w/little Spanish	59	4	36
Monolingual English	47	4	48
Bilingual, but separate	37	7	54

TABLE 16
SELF REPORT OF CHANGE IN USE OF SPANISH AND ENGLISH BY AGE GROUP

	Increase or Decrease in Spanish			English		
	% More	Same	Less	% More	Same	Less
Adolescents (n=23)	26	4	70	83	9	9
Young Adults (n=33)	52	18	30	67	15	15
Mature Adults (n=25)	36	40	20	52	20	20
Older Persons (n=10)	—	80	20	80	10	
Total (n=91)	35	27	36	68	14	13

TABLE 17

RESOURCE GROUP PERCENTAGES FOR REPORT OF USING MORE SPANISH AND ENGLISH

	More Spanish	More English
Spanish	28	71
Bilingual	42	52
English	32	88
Total	35	68

TABLE 18

AGE OF ARRIVAL BY SPANISH USE INDEX

	Age of Arrival	
	Born in USA or arrived before age 6	Arrived after age 6
Low Spanish Use	43	8
High Spanish Use	12	26

TABLE 19

AGE OF ARRIVAL BY ENGLISH USE INDEX

	Age of Arrival	
	Born in the USA or arrived before age 6	Arrived after age 6
Low English Use	25	28
High English Use	30	6

Figure 5.
Percentages for Language Use Indices

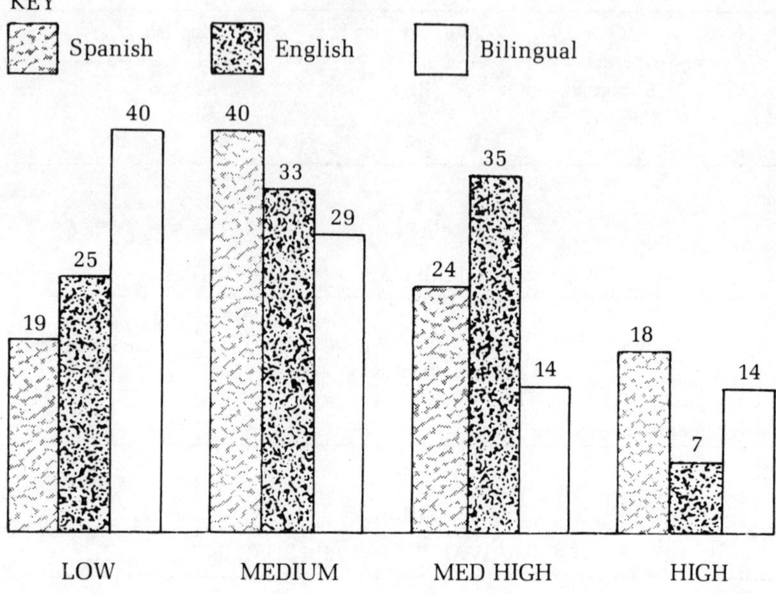

Figure 6.

Reported Use Triangle, in model and with absolute number for the sample.

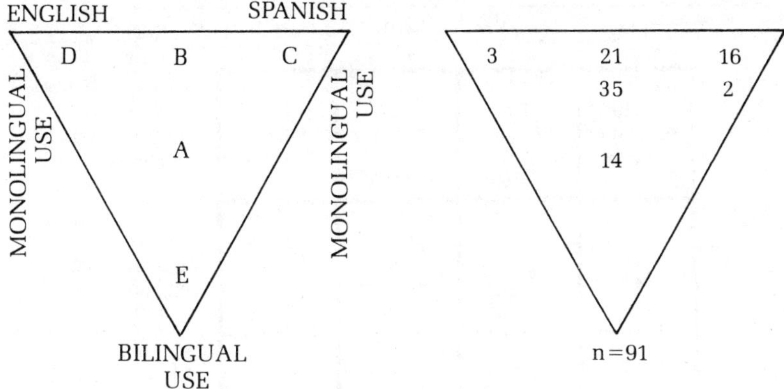

Figure 7.

Complete tabulation of Spanish choice by Bilingual Report in absolute numbers.

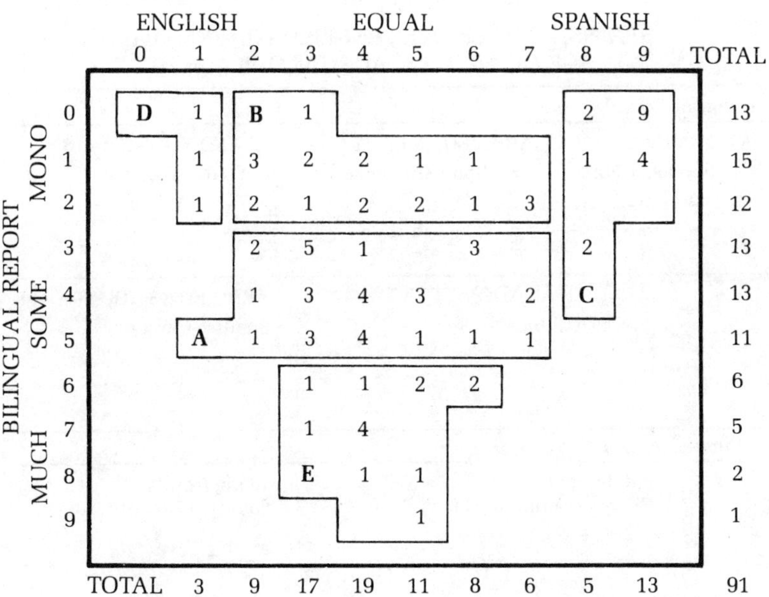

SPANISH CHOICE OVER ENGLISH

BILINGUAL REPORT		ENGLISH 0	1	2	3	EQUAL 4	5	6	7	SPANISH 8	9	TOTAL
MONO	0	**D**	1	**B**	1					2	9	13
	1		1	3	2	2	1	1		1	4	15
	2		1	2	1	2	2	1	3			12
SOME	3			2	5	1		3		2		13
	4			1	3	4	3		2	**C**		13
	5		**A**	1	3	4	1	1	1			11
MUCH	6				1	1	2	2				6
	7				1	4						5
	8				**E**	1	1					2
	9						1					1
TOTAL			3	9	17	19	11	8	6	5	13	91

TABLE 20
SPANISH CHOICE OVER ENGLISH BY BI-REPORT

Rows = Biling Report — Columns = SP Choice Over English

	VLO 0-1	MLO 2-4	MHI 5-7	HI 8-9	Row Sums	Key
VLO 0-2	3	13	8	16	40	RAW
	3.297	14.286	8.791	17.582	43.956	RPT
	100.000	28.889	32.000	88.889	43.956	RPC
	7.500	32.500	20.000	40.000	100.000	RPR
	1.3	19.8	11.0	7.9	40.0	ERF
MED 3-5		24	11	2	37	RAW
		26.374	12.088	2.198	40.659	RPT
		53.333	44.000	11.111	40.659	RPC
		64.865	29.730	5.405	100.000	RPR
	1.2	18.3	10.2	7.3	37.0	ERF
HI 5-9		8	6		14	RAW
		8.791	6.593		15.385	RPT
		17.778	24.000		15.385	RPC
		57.143	42.857		100.000	RPR
	0.5	6.9	3.8	2.8	14.0	ERF
Col Sums	3	45	25	18	91	RAW
	3.297	49.451	27.473	19.780	100.000	RPT
	100.000	100.000	100.000	100.000	100.000	RPC
	3.297	49.451	27.473	19.780	100.000	RPR
	3.0	45.0	25.0	18.0	91.0	ERF

TABLE 21
SPANISH CHOICE OVER ENGLISH FILTERED BY AGE OF ARRIVAL, AGE, BIRTHPLACE

I. Age of Arrival

BORN IN USA n=38

Bi-Report / Spanish Choice				
	2	9	1	—
	—	15	5	—
	—	3	3	—

ARRIVED AS BABY n=17

Bi-Report / Spanish Choice				
	1	1	1	1
	—	6	2	—
	—	5	2	—

ARRIVED YOUNG n=10

Bi-Report / Spanish Choice				
	—	1	2	—
	—	3	1	1
	—	—	2	—

ARRIVED AS ADOLESCENT n=10

Bi-Report / Spanish Choice				
	—	—	4	3
	—	—	2	—
	—	—	1	—

ARRIVED AS ADULT n=14

Bi-Report / Spanish Choice				
	—	—	—	12
	—	—	1	1
	—	—	—	—

II. Filtered by Age

Adolescents — Spanish Choice n=23

Bi-Report / Spanish Choice				
	2	8	—	—
	—	8	1	—
	—	2	2	—

Young Adults — Spanish Choice n=33

Bi-Report / Spanish Choice				
	—	3	3	4
	—	11	5	—
	—	4	3	1

TABLE 21—(Cont.)

SPANISH CHOICE OVER ENGLISH FILTERED BY AGE OF ARRIVAL, AGE, BIRTHPLACE

	Mature Adults Spanish Choice n=25					Older People Spanish Choice n=10			
Bi-Report	1	2	4	6	Bi-Report	—	—	1	6
	—	5	3	1		—	—	2	1
	—	2	1	—		—	—	—	—

III. Filtered by Birthplace

	Puerto Rico n=50 Spanish Choice					U.S. n=41 Spanish Choice			
Bi-Report	—	4	7	16	Bi-Report	3	9	1	—
	—	8	6	2		—	16	5	—
	—	4	3	—		—	4	3	—

TABLE 22

ENGLISH RESOURCES BY SPANISH RESOURCES (IN PERCENTAGES)

Spanish Resources	English Resources Low-Med-Med-Hi	Very High	Total
Low-Med-Med-Hi	7[a]	41[b]	47
Very High	36[c]	16[d]	53
Total	43	57	100

TABLE 23

SIX SIXTEEN-CELL TABLES FOR LANGUAGE RESOURCES (WITH KEY)

SPANISH RESOURCES	ENGLISH RESOURCES: LO	MLO	MHI	VHI
LO	1 A-Lingual	2	3 Mono English	4
MLO	5	6	7 English Dominance	8
MHI	9 Mono	10	11	12
VHI	13 Spanish	14 Spanish Dominance	15	16 Perfect Bilingual

Sixteen-cell Resource Table Key

Total Sample n=91

SPANISH	ENGLISH			
			6	5
		3	12	5
	6	8	17	10
	7	7	5	

Adolescents n=23

SPANISH	ENGLISH			
			3	4
			5	4
		1	2	4

All Adults n=68

SPANISH	ENGLISH			
			3	1
		3	7	1
	6	7	15	6
	7	7	5	

TABLE 23—(Cont.)
SIX SIXTEEN-CELL TABLES FOR LANGUAGE RESOURCES (WITH KEY)

	ENGLISH					ENGLISH					ENGLISH			
SPANISH			1	1	SPANISH			1		SPANISH			1	
		1	4	1			1	3				1		
	1	3	10	5		2	2	5	1		3	2		
	1	3	2			4	4	2			2			
	Young Adults n=33					Mature Adults n=25					Older Adults n=10			

Figure 8.
Language resources by Birthplace (in percentages)

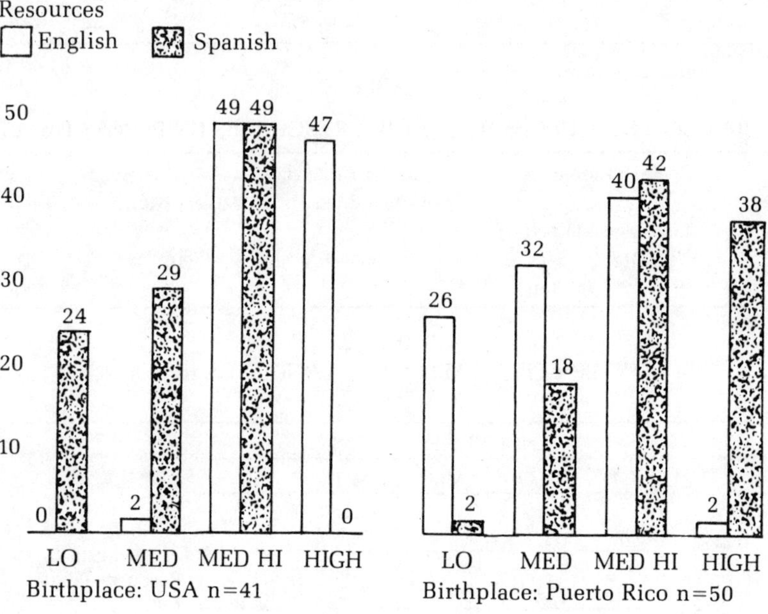

TABLE 24
DOMINANT LANGUAGE TABLES

KEY	NAME OF VARIABLE	VAR. CODE
S = Spanish	First Language	52
B = Both bilingual	Dominant Language (By Self Report)	66
MB = Both, but mixed	Habitual Language of Literacy	67
SB = Both, but separate	Most Comfortable Language	104
E = English	Observed Dominance	315
T = Total	Main Resource Language	766

TABLE 24—(Cont.)

DOMINANT LANGUAGE TABLES

DOMINANT LANGUAGE BY SELF REPORT TABLES
(in percentages)

DOMINANT SELF REPORT	DOM LG ANL S	B	E	T
S	26	2	1	30
B	3	31	6	40
E	1	9	20	30
T	31	42	27	100

TABLE D1 DOMINANT SELF REPORT BY MAIN RESOURCE

MAIN RESOURCE LANGUAGE TABLES
(in percentages)

MAIN RESOURCE LANGUAGE	DOM LG SELF REPORT S	B	E	T
S	26	3	1	31
B	2	31	9	42
E	1	6	20	27
T	30	40	30	100

TABLE R1 MAIN RESOURCE BY DOMINANT SELF REPORT

DOMINANT SELF REPORT	FIRST LANGUAGE S	B	E	T
S	29	1	—	30
B	29	8	3	40
E	19	7	4	30
T	77	15	7	99

TABLE D2 DOMINANT SELF REPORT BY FIRST LANGUAGE

MAIN RESOURCE LANGUAGE	FIRST LANGUAGE S	B	E	T
S	31	—	—	31
B	34	7	1	42
E	12	9	7	27
T	77	16	8	100

TABLE R2 MAIN RESOURCE BY FIRST LANGUAGE

LANGUAGE OF SELF-REPORT TABLES
(in percentages)

DOMINANT SELF REPORT	HABITUAL LANGUAGE OF LITERACY S	B	E	T
S	23	2	4	30
B	3	3	33	40
E	—	1	29	30
T	26	7	67	100

TABLE D3 DOMINANT SELF REPORT BY HABITUAL LITERACY

MAIN RESOURCE TABLES
(in percentages)

MAIN RESOURCE LANGUAGE	HABITUAL LANGUAGE OF LITERACY S	B	E	T
S	25	1	4	31
B	1	5	36	42
E	—	1	26	27
T	26	7	67	100

TABLE R3 MAIN RESOURCE BY HABITUAL LITERACY

DOMINANT SELF REPORT	MOST COMFORTABLE LANGUAGE S	MB	SB	E	T
S	26	2	—	1	30
B	4	8	5	22	40
E	2	3	1	23	30
T	33	13	7	47	100

TABLE D4 DOMINANT SELF REPORT BY MOST COMFORTABLE

MAIN RESOURCE LANGUAGE	MOST COMFORTABLE LANGUAGE S	MB	SB	E	T
S	22	2	1	—	31
B	6	9	6	22	42
E	—	2	—	25	27
T	33	13	7	47	100

TABLE R4 MAIN RESOURCE BY MOST COMFORTABLE

DOMINANT SELF REPORT	OBSERVED DOM LG S	B	E	T
S	25	4	—	30
B	3	17	20	40
E	—	3	26	30
T	29	25	46	100

TABLE D5 DOMINANT SELF REPORT BY OBSERVED DOMINANT

MAIN RESOURCE LANGUAGE	OBSERVED DOM LG S	B	E	T
S	28	2	—	30
B	1	20	21	43
E	—	2	25	27
T	29	25	46	100

TABLE R5 MAIN RESOURCE BY OBSERVED DOMINANT

TABLE 25

AGE OF ARRIVAL BY MAIN LANGUAGE RESOURCE
(IN PERCENTAGES)

	Baby 0-5	Young 6-12	Adol 13-19	Adult 20-98	Born USA	Total N	Total %
	17	10	10	14	38	89	
Spanish	1	2	11	16	1	28	31
Bilingual	11	9	—	—	20	36	40
English	7	—	—	—	21	25	28
Total	19	11	11	16	42		99

TABLE 26

MAIN LANGUAGE RESOURCES BY HIGHEST GRADE IN SCHOOL
(IN PERCENTAGES)

	Highest Grade in School					
	4 or less	Jr.H.S.	H.S. grad	College	Total N	Total %
N=	7	56	18	9		
Spanish	7	18	6	—	28	31
Bilingual	—	20	11	10	38	42
English	—	24	3	—	25	27
Total	7	61	20	10	91	100

TABLE 27

"USE TRIANGLE" FOR MAIN RESOURCE LANGUAGE

	Resource Language													
	English (n=25) Spanish Choice					Bilingual (n=38) Spanish Choice					Spanish (n=28) Spanish Choice			
Bi-Report	3	6	—	—	Bi-Report	—	7	3	—	Bi-Report	—	—	5	6
	—	12	1	—		1	12	6	—		—	—	4	2
	—	3	—	—		—	5	5	—		—	—	1	—

TABLE 28

MAIN LANGUAGE RESOURCES BY ECONOMIC SUPPORT

(IN PERCENTAGES)

	Economic Support					
	Nearby	Outside	Xchange	Dependent	Total N	Total %
N=	10	24	25	29		
Spanish	5	13	10	3	28	31
Bilingual	5	11	16	10	38	43
English	1	3	2	20	24	26
Total	11	27	28	33	91	100

COMPARATIVE ETHNIC FACTORS IN BILINGUAL EDUCATION: THE UNITED STATES AND ABROAD

Jacob L. Ornstein-Galicia

In his work *Bilingualism as a World Phenomenon* (1968), William F. Mackey emphasizes that in the world there are more areas marked by linguistic diversity or pluralingualism than by monolingualism.[1] Even so, if only "one language" is spoken in a country, there may be a diglossic situation, as in Greece, where *katharevusa* or the high form, co-exists with the *dimotike* or low, informal, variety, creating all sorts of problems in the media and in the public sector and education. Again Mackey and the writer (1977) in their essay "Revolt of the Ethnics" (1977: 121-22) point out that there are barely 250- odd sovereign nation-states in the world, housing, willingly or not, over 5,000 living languages, and an uncounted number of dialects. The question appropriately raised in this volume as we go into the seeming decade of mandated public bilingual-bicultural education (henceforth BE) is not so much whether each of these thousands of ethnic groups has an "inalienable right" to bilingual-bicultural education, but rather what factors, demographic and otherwise, favor or disfavor the securing of such schooling.

Few educational movements have aroused such passions and polarization of public opinion as BE, due in large part no doubt to America's general assimilationist orientation and our former blind faith in the efficacy of the "melting pot" ideal. As social philosopher Michael Novak points out in his *Rise of the Unmeltable Ethnics: The New Political Force of the Seventies* (1971), all this has been rudely shattered in the past few decades. By way of compensation, perhaps, an almost mystic cult has grown up regarding BE, which many bilingualists view as a sacred crusade capable of righting long-time ethnic wrongs committed by preceding generations. There are sobering voices, however, and I note that a participant in these forums, Amador Bustos (1979), expresses misgivings in his paper of the dangers of misplaced confidence in the movement as a sure guarantor of social change. Likewise Geraldo Kaprosy and Robert St. Clair, in their essay "Order Versus Conflict Societies: The Dilemma of Bicultural Education" (forthcoming) develop in detail a similar thesis reflecting serious doubts that BE can do all that is expected of it by way of changing society. Although I am hardly in agreement with the entire content of the latter writing, it is well that those of us who do believe in BE shed our rose-colored glasses in its regard, and adopt a more realistic orientation.

All this is by way of saying that the writer basically accepts a conflict model or basis for BE, and indeed for most enlightened educational innovations. Whatever the political system, it would appear, the application of pressure appears to be more effective than the purity and nobility of ideas—although I would be the last to dismiss idealism as a great creative force. Yet we live and function in a world of *Realpolitik* where concessions are rarely gained without some sort of struggle. Accordingly, the *raison d'être* of this paper is less whether ethnic group X has an "inalienable right" to BE, but rather, under what conditions BE can be achieved. What are, specifically, the recurrent sociopolitical and linguistic factors? One might say, as was the case with the animals of George Orwell's *1984*, some minorities, in the harsh world of realities, appear to be "more equal" than others.

Addressing this issue, we have tried to identify the leading sociolinguistic characteristics or factors which maximize (or diminish) the probabilities of securing BE, given a favorable political context. Our consideration belongs squarely in the field of language planning and language policy, an interdisciplinary sub-field of sociolinguistics which has developed vigorously in the past fifteen or twenty years, and for which a considerable bibliography already exists.

The basis for the selection of the factors is, in this first approximation, empirical observation and considerable research and writing by the author in this field. His extensive files on the subject include materials culled both from popular and scholarly periodicals and books. Some of the material may be seen in the pages of the volume co-authored with William F. Mackey and titled: *The Bilingual Education Movement* (1977).

Language issues have severely troubled not only educators but social planners and politicians, particularly since World War II, which has seen the birth of some 200 new nations, and the emergence of strong drives for civil rights and ethnic self-determination, virtually the world over. Reports of study groups are a rich source of insight into these problems. For example, the dozen or so volumes of the Canadian Royal Commission on Bilingualism and Biculturalism (Ottawa: Queen's Printer). The most complete guide to the languages employed in each nation of the world are the files and reports of the ongoing project Linguistic Composition of the Nations of the World, being conducted by Heinz Kloss, Grant D. McConnell and Henri Dorion, at the International Center for Research on Bilingualism, Laval University, Québec. The first two volumes, under the same name as their project, on North America, and on Central and Southwestern Asia respectively have already appeared (1974, 1975). The best single source of up-to-date bibliography, as well as a great deal of information on language policy is the *Sociolinguistics Newsletter*, published by Scholar's Press, University of Montana, Helena.

The selected factors or variables have been gathered into a matrix along two dimensions, the first sociopolitical, the second linguistic. Thus our methodology, in this stochastic device intended as a heuristic, has been to extrapolate from observable past and present experience of ethnic groups in the United States and abroad. The predictive power of the different variables obviously must vary, and, in fact, just as is the case with economic forecasts, there is no certainty that a cluster of factors would necessarily yield the same results as in the past. Bilingualists have as much right to err as do economists and others who attempt prognostication!

Two Dimensions of a Tentative Predictive Matrix

In elaborating the schema or matrix which is presented in the appendix, we have found that, in order to make any sense at all, the different component items ought to be applied as need be, both at the micro- or local, and the macro- or national (even supra-national) levels. We are here pretty much following terminology given currency by Joshua Fishman in his extensive writings on the "sociology of language" (cf. for example, Fishman, 1971: 221; 1972). In other words, in most cases there must be a mix of favorable factors both at the community and the national levels, for a decision to be made in favor of BE and its continuation.

The matrix at the appendix is meant as the first entry, the name of a specific ethnic group whose possibilities for BE are being considered. At this stage we have no relative weightings or numerical scores, and perhaps never can reach such a point of quantification. Ratings for each variable are based on a positive-negative binary opposition, expressed as plus-minus respectively, although in some cases, a ± or plus and/or minus marking is possible, depending upon whether the factor mostly applies or the opposite. At this point, a simple majority of plusses, in our projection, ought to indicate favorable chances for BE. As in economic predicting, however, the adverse effect of one powerful variable, often new and not predicted, or an unfavorable turn of events may nullify such chances. The similarity to "war games" strategy or a game of chess is unmistakable!

Along the Sociopolitical Dimension

Demographic strength, item 1, is by and large a strongly positive factor, and we have so couched it that it refers as much to the impact of a group upon the nation, as to absolute numbers. In the United States, Spanish-speaking Latinos, the largest foreign-language (or "other language") minority numbering easily 17 million, have been foremost in exerting the political pressure resulting in the passage of Title VII as an amendment to the Elementary and Secondary School Act, in 1967. Most probably, a decade earlier no one but a madman would have considered possible the passage of such legislation in such a unilingually oriented nation.

BE is by now funded for some seventy different ethnic groups, with the great majority of projects being Spanish-English, and with Amerindian-English programs second by a very wide margin. In the latter case we are dealing not with a homogeneous group but rather with numerous tribes, some genetically related and others unrelated. What about the remainder of the more than a hundred immigrant languages brought here by settlers from every continent? Some are presented in the funding, while others such as Danish or Magyar do not claim enough younger speakers to qualify. It would seem that for the public schools, they may only receive minus ratings.

Nevertheless, despite the bleakness of the picture painted above, there is a respectable amount of BE being conducted under parochial, fraternal and private auspices. This topic is currently being researched by Fishman and associates through a recently funded project.

At the same time numerical strength is not always paramount. In the case of Ethiopia, neither the majority people, the Galla or Sidomo-speakers, nor any of a half-dozen other groups, constitutes the ruling elite. This is made up of the Amharas, a minority people, who have managed to retain power and, for all practical purposes, to block formal representation of the others in language and culture.

In the next variable, number 2 or territoriality, we borrow the terminology from De La Garza, Arciniega and Kruszewski, and their book *Chicanos and Native Americans: The Territorial Minorities* (1974). These workers, all social scientists, emphasize the extreme importance that this has had for U.S. ethnic policy, since most immigrant groups have been only vaguely associated with specific locations. We would like to expand the term to signify also that when a group is co-terminal, that it is in an area bordering a country where the language is official or dominant, and opportunities for maintenance, ethnicity and BE are increased. The Spanish of the Chicano speech community of the Southwest is especially reinforced in its maintenance by the presence of a 2,000-mile border with Mexico, and constant interchange. By the same token the Acadian or "Cajun" minority of Louisiana lacks any proximity either to Canada or France, and this variety of French is virtually threatened with extinction despite sincere efforts being made to maintain it.

In the case of Mexican-Americans, the entire package of goals of the Chicano movement enjoys all the more credibility because of their ability to claim longer residence in the five-state area of California, Colorado, Arizona, New Mexico and Texas than do Anglos, and that the terms of the treaty following the Mexican War in 1848, particularly as regards language and culture, have been shoddily observed. There are indeed elements in the movement that, inspired by the Parti Québecois and its demand for an independent Québec, also have separatist pretensions. A case in point is the heavily-researched article by Ray Castro, writing from Harvard, in the *Bilingual Review* (1976), who concludes that the bilingual movement can give little to Chicanos, and who recommends the setting up of autonomous Chicano monolingual Spanish-speaking regions in the Southwest. There are precedents for this in post-Versailles Europe, India and the U.S.S.R. Still speaking of the Southwest, it should also be recalled that the two legislators who probably did most to insure passage of the Bilingual Education Act, Senators Yarborough of Texas and Montoya of New Mexico, served a constituency with a high proportion of territorial bilinguals.

By the same token, the absence of territoriality tends to weaken ethnic aspirations. The sordid existence of Yiddish-speaking Jews in the East European ghettoes, the Holocaust, the sufferings of the Armenian diaspora, the decimation of many American Indian tribes by action in the nineteenth century, the threat by the bulldozer to the Xingu and other Tupi-Guaraní tribes of the Brazilian Amazonian jungle, are just a few instances of the defenselessness of small peoples not firmly rooted in a specific area, or who are displaced.

The history of irredentist claims, in just the nineteenth and twentieth century, would include many familiar and unfamiliar peoples such as the Armenians, Kurds, Macedonians, and many others, filling many volumes. What is important here is that territoriality relates strongly to the principle that possession is nine-tenths of the law. (On "territoriality" cf. also McRae, 1975).

Cultural-religious distance, or differentiation of an extreme sort, the third item in this dimension, may substantially cut off an ethnic group from the mainstream. A case in point are the German-speaking "plain people sects" including Amish, Hutterites (South Dakota), and certain Mennonite believers. In such instances, adherence to a rigid religious or philosophical code proscribes participation in the "worldly" mainstream. A situation of this sort may favor bilingualism and the maintenance of a separate culture if the group depends upon the mainstream for earning a living. If not, monolingualism may be the result for the majority. Indeed such sectarians are among the few immigrant groups which have maintained a strong bilingual tradition in America.

As numerous sects also eschew public schools, they are obviously poor candidates for this framework. Recent Supreme Court and other legal decisions have begun to be more liberal in granting such groups exemption from public education and the right to conduct their own schooling. All in all, most of these groups, if they speak a foreign language, would qualify for a plus rating on our scales. Let it also be noted that the Mennonites of the state of Chihuahua, Mexico, have also continued to maintain both their bilingualism (German-Spanish) and their separate way of life.

Turning to more conventional groups, this factor may be significant, or not. Andersson and Boyer (1970, II: 127) in discussing German-Americans, neatly illustrates the complex interplay not only of religious but also other sociopolitical factors with BE and other language issues. The German immigration to the U.S. constitutes our largest component, and one which in the past was highly interested in maintaining their language along with English. Our source observes:

> The rural population was made up almost entirely of "Church Germans" (Roman Catholic, Orthodox Lutherans, and other Protestants). The urban German element were to a large extent liberals, or what were called "Club Germans." Roman Catholics and Orthodox Lutherans soon stressed the bilingual aspect, and the Old Lutherans tried to maintain the predominance of German over English in their schools. The other Protestants and the secularized Liberals were less tenacious. They gradually abandoned their own German schools because, since the 1860's, as we have seen, much was being done to foster German in the public elementary schools which served communities with large German American populations.

As Andersson and Boyer emphasize, from 1830 to 1848 German-Americans successfully exerted pressure to have German bilingual instruction in the public schools, a breakthrough which saw Cincinnati, Ohio become the focus of uninterrupted bilingual instruction from 1840 to 1917 (ibid.). Other cities with large German concentrations, such as Milwaukee, Chicago and Cleveland followed suit.

In the German-American instance, as we note above, the factor of religious preference was highly plus for Catholic and Lutheran Germans, and from low plus to minus for others. Thus, if we decided to adopt a five-point scale for our measure, the former would receive four or five, while the remainder would receive from three downwards, or minus.

Religious preference, or some other cultural feature, then, may or may not be an influential factor strongly linked with BE.

The following factor, number 4, or ethnicity/ethos, concerns group solidarity, based on that whole gamut of beliefs that make up the self-perception of the group, usually embracing a strong body of legend or "ethos" and traditional view of its unique identity—and often superiority to other groups. Language often is regarded as the ultimate symbolic system and concepts in it considered unique.

Although numerous groups have become extinct in human history, through aggression or assimilation, students of the subject have rarely ceased to wonder at the ability to survive unfavorable odds, geographic and social, shown by various peoples, including Jews, Armenians, Kurds, Basques of Spain, Bretons and Occitanians (Provençal-speakers) of France, Romanes (popularly known as Gypsies), and others.

At the same time, except for completely assimilated persons with little feelings for ancestral roots, it is dangerous to randomly assume low ratings for ethnicity, as the melting pot experience of the United States, constantly resurfacing manifestations of identity in strongly authoritarian regimes such as those of U.S.S.R. and Yugoslavia tend to manifest.

For U.S. groups, extremely significant work continues to be done by the indefatigable Joshua Fishman, who has given currency to the very term "ethnicity," in large part through his monumental *Language Loyalty in the United States* (1966). His ongoing project on BE outside of public school auspices, will probably make us aware of a great deal of latent ethnicity which merely may go unnoticed due to low visibility.

As for U.S. Latinos who particularly concern us here, it is too early to predict the lasting effect of Chicano attempts to build up a sense of special identity, through the concept of a legendary birthplace in Aztlán, a growing body of folklore territorially marked, and affirmative demands for recognition of Chicano Spanish as a legitimate medium of communication. There is no question but what this is promoting much more of a positive self-image than was the case formerly. At the same time cultural components heighten the awareness of Chicano or Latino identity, with no loss to the ideals of American citizenship. The case of Boricuas and Cubans differs considerably and will not be discussed immediately here.

Unfortunately, funding and thrust for legislation like the Ethnic Heritage Bill has been inadequate, so that the best public support for ethnicity comes indirectly, ironic as this may sound, through BE programs which are actually for the most part transitional.

Proceeding now to number 5, or socioeconomic status (SES), curiously enough, bilingualism and BE are viewed most positively at the top and bottom of the economic ladder. Upper-middle and upper income persons are more likely to travel extensively, and have interests abroad, while lower-income foreign-language groups, particularly foreign-language immigrants, are forced to become bilingual to survive. Typically, the former arrange for BE through private schools and tutors, while the latter are often dependent upon the good offices of the respective government.

At the opposite end of the SES scale, persons of foreign-language ancestry, using this term in the sense of "anything but English" in the United States, especially those of rather recent immigration, encounter basic lack of mainstream language skills as a formidable barrier of an educational and vocational nature. Hence school authorities may either take a hard-nosed stance of "learn the dominant language or else," or take steps to encourage the introduction of BE.

Throughout the world the patterns vary widely, and both postures described in the preceding paragraph may be found. In Western European countries normally thought of as bastions of democracy, the hard-nosed stance has been typical, and only lately have, for example, the West German authorities admitted *arbeiter* or foreign workers, and slowly taken some measures toward BE for children of Turkish, Yugoslav, Greek, Italian and other nationalities (For the situation in Germany and Scandinavia, cf. Dittmar et al, 1978).

In the United States, the attitude toward BE is very ambivalent, and although bilingualism is admiringly regarded among the, let's say, diplomats and jet-setters, "institutional bilingualism" is viewed as a necessary evil for children of the "culture of poverty."

Hence, the ratings for a given group may well be ± and here as with other variables SES may be an infra-ethnic differentiator.

Few factors would, by any formulation, generally receive heavier weighting along this dimension than item number 6, mobilization, adopting here the term made current by political scientist Karl Deutsch, an authority on nationalism and statehood. Deutsch (1967: 47) singles out various ethnic groups such as the Finns, whose language slightly more than a century ago was little except a vernacular, that is, used merely for oral everyday purposes. However, through their high ethnicity, and ability to mobilize socially and politically, they were ready for statehood when the Russian Czarist Empire crumbled in 1917, vigorously developing their language into what Heinz Kloss (1968) terms an *Ausbau* or elaborated medium, capable of dealing with communication needs in an advanced technological society. Previous to this, as the former notes, the language for formal, written purposes (sometimes called the "court" language) was Swedish.

It should be added that the term "politicization" is more commonly employed today than "mobilization" when speaking of contemporary ethnic groups. Whatever is used, one may thus view the ascendancy of the "dominant" or "mainstream" ruling elite as the result of struggles and conflicts between different ethnic and other segments of the population. The language of that ascendant group and its culture will accordingly mark the culture of an emergent nation, and as Kloss, who accepts Deutsch' formulation observes: "In fact language is a variable dependent on political factors" (1968: 104), and he adds:

> To estimate, therefore, whether future nationalism will be based in Bolivia in Spanish or Quechua or Aymara, in the Philippines on Tagalog, English, Spanish or the various local languages, it is essential to determine at what rates traditional people are being 'mobilized' into each of these groups (1968: 105).

Although the concept of mobilization as a means for gaining benefits and recognition is widely accepted by social scientists and linguists, this is not universally so. For example, a younger political scientist (mentioned as editor of *Language Problems and Language Planning*[2]), Jonathan Pool (1972), attacks Deutsch' concept and its common acceptance. He points out correctly that in a number of cases ethnic advantages and language rights were achieved without mobilization. We shall see, in discussing favorability at the macro-level, or highest government instance, that benefits like literacy, and cultural expression may be accorded by fiat, or by the same token, negated out of hand (cf. also Nahir, 1977).

Now, completing the listings in this dimension, we posit numbers 7 and 8, favorable micro-level and favorable macro-level, respectively. In the former we regard the local/regional situation, where variation can cover a broad spectrum. If we were to contrast two widely divergent micro-levels in the United States, probably a grass-roots rural town in Appalachia, barely subsisting, would do quite well for a negative rating. In a context like this, no matter how many foreign-language speakers there might be, innovations like BE tend to be regarded as useless "frills." (Analyses of the community level may be seen in Benavides 1979; Martínez 1979 this volume).

Highly positive ratings would very likely be assigned to solidly middle-class suburban communities, for instance, near Washington, D.C., New York City, Philadelphia, particularly the East Coast where foreign languages are most acceptable and desirable. Moving down the Atlantic Seaboard, probably the outstanding example of a favorable micro-level would be Miami, Florida, where refugees from Cuba precipitated the first federally-funded BEM programs (properly Dade County), and where a strongly middle-class population of Latinos, Jews, Anglos and others have been most supportive of BE not only for ethnic children, but for monolingual Anglos. By contrast, lower SES parents often fear education in anything but English as simply another device to keep them economically and vocationally deprived.

Much attention has correctly been paid to community involvement by Title VII and companion legislation. In its best form it has often produced parental involvement where formerly fear and trepidation toward school "authorities" was the rule. A growing number of writers are addressing these problems, including some of those present at the two forums at Eastern Michigan University.

Ratings, then, would vary from area to area. What is to be done, however, where BE is regarded with intense hostility or where only federal intervention will force the issue? One trembles for the quality of education which is liable to result. Very clearly, some sort of vigorous informational campaign would be desirable, even essential. Mackey and Ornstein have argued against premature introduction of BE, merely as an act of faith, since nothing undermines the possibilities for a viable project than the resounding collapse of a jerry-built program (1977: 31-32).

Indeed the situation at the community level includes a vast number of sub-variables, in addition to psychological attitudes, and embracing economic, sociological, linguistic and other conditions. In the United States, how the school system exercises local option, and in France, how it implements the uniform national education policy, would be germane. All in all, unfavorable factors at this, the micro-level, could conspire to delay BE or somehow prevent its introduction. If overridden, as has occurred in various communities already, more or less subtle means may be employed to sabotage a program, no matter how well conceived.

Finally, as we have seen in the continued conflict for civil and ethnic gains during the past quarter century, the highest instance of power (Supreme Court, etc.) may be the ultimate arbiter of demands for redress in the public sector. Hence, it is fitting that the final entry in the socio-political dimension should be favorability at the macro-level, be it a relatively democratic or a rigidly controlled authoritarian or dictatorial framework. There are apparently few nations today where somewhere at the top level of governmental authority, a BE program, national or local, could not be either mandated or rejected (Regarding BE and the U.S. federal echelon of government, cf. Stoller, 1976).

With this as a generally acceptable political fact, the micro-level, then, must be, for our purposes, if not favorable, at least not unfavorable. Nevertheless, BE, if one looks at the global picture (cf. Mackey and Ornstein, 1977: esp. 1-21), we become strikingly aware that large segments of the world's populations, residing in a nation where macro-level disfavors anything but one official and "dominant" language, simply have no opportunity for BE facilities, barring some sort of change.

An example of this has historically been Iran, where despite the relative tolerance of their historical Cyrus the Great, at least under the Pahlavi dynasty, one and only one language (and culture)—Farsi—was allowed. Demographically, however, Iran has sizeable minority groups, including Kurds, Azerbaijani and other Turks, Turkomani Baluchí, Jewish, Armenian, Arab and a distinctive religious minority, the Bahá'í. During the recent Khomeini Islamic revolution, some of these minorities seeking redress, have engaged both in military action against the Ayatollah's forces,* and against one another. Recurrent newspaper reports stress that ethnic frictions are a great stumbling block for the new regime, whose ethnolinguistic policies do not yet seem crystallized. Thus, one would assign a minus factor for any language in Iran other than Farsi. Other examples are numerous.

In an opposite direction, as mentioned previously, the macro-level, representing a concentration of power, may bestow ethnic benefits, including BE upon unmobilized groups, large or small, by mandate or fiat, thus bypassing or not reckoning with most of the other variables among the sociopolitical dimension. Perhaps one of the best case studies of this may be seen in Peru, where beginning as early as 1945 a series of military juntas opted to empower the Ministry of Education to implement programs of BE for the speakers of the seven dialects of Quechua, as well as other indigenous languages. A leading role was also played by the Universidad Mayor Nacional de San Marcos, and such eminent linguists as Alberto Escobar, as well as the Summer Institute of Linguistics, a missionary-linguist group headquartered in the United States and functioning in numerous continents. In addition, well-known linguists such as Donald Solá of Cornell and Wolfgang Wölck of State University of New York, Buffalo, performed certain tasks. The ambitious target of eventually making all Peruvian citizens bilingual in Spanish and Quechua has apparently been reduced to lesser proportions. At any rate, the story is fascinating, espe-

*According to an Associated Press report, some 2,000 Kurdish rebels attacked government forces near Narivan, Iran (close to the Iraqi border) on 26 July, 1979, with resultant casualties.

cially as we read a statement reported by Burns, an SIL linguist, and which was made by General Alfredo Arrisueño speaking as Minister of Education in his inaugural speech at the thirty-ninth International Congress of Americanists, Aug. 1970, Lima:

> And, in closing, let me state that the deep interest which the Military Revolutionary Government has in the problems of the Quechua-speaking masses and other language groups, problems so well known by the distinguished specialists gathered here, has prompted the official incorporation into the new educational system and establishment of special priority for BILINGUAL EDUCATION (Burns, 1971, 27 fn.). (For fuller details cf.: Burns 1968, 1971; Wise 1969; Ministry of Education, Peru, 1972; Pozzi-Escot 1972; Solá 1979).

Indeed, partially supporting Pool's thesis that ethnic benefits and language choice are not necessary concomitants of mobilization and economic development accepted pretty much also by Fishman and Kloss (cf. Pool, 1972; Fishman and Kloss, 1967), we find numerous cases in history of minorities equipped with the tools of literacy and BE simply because, through previous struggles of other groups and the establishment of an over-all policy, this became automatic. For example, in the Soviet sphere, the Gagauzy, a small Turkic group in Rumania, who were accorded literacy and BE some twenty years ago (cf. Ornstein, 1964) and the Wends or Lusatians of the German Democratic Republic, a vestigial Slavic-speaking minority, enjoy the same privileges, and although the youth are switching heavily to German, government efforts promote Wendish culture, folklore, and, of course, BE (ibid.). Political dissent in whatsoever tongue, is, however, another matter.

As for the U.S., this has also occurred with groups such as the Basques, largely sheepherders scattered throughout the Rocky Mountain states. It must be said, however, lest this be seen as condescending, that although geographically dispersed, this group rates extremely high on any measures of group solidarity and ethnic loyalty/ethos. Whether the language can, nevertheless, be maintained in future generations is an open question.

Probing the Linguistic Dimension

Although inevitable overlap with factors in the first dimension exist, we have attempted to assign factors here which are strongly language-linked. The gratifying burgeoning of the interdisciplinary field or sub-field of sociolinguistics in the past two decades reveals that, more than ever, language is being recognized for the social act that it is, an act incapable of occurring in an abstract vacuum.

First of all, we identify item number 9, or vitality of the language, utilizing here Stewart's concept (1968). Without any diabolical machinations, languages are born and die or become extinct as a normal societal process. One might mention some of the Indian languages of the United States, or abroad, the Pamir group in the U.S.S.R. At the same time, a language that is becoming extinct, or which has become little used may still be chosen as a national, official language by a new nation, or it may be selected to be taught bilingually. This was the case in the Irish state (Eire) where Irish Gaelic was spoken only in the Gaeltacht, comprising a few counties. Since 1921, Gaelic has been elaborated into a "sociologically complete" medium and is taught along with English, although the latter tongue is the common language of most citizens. The case of Hebrew is similar, and belongs also to the "revival" category in language planning. Both languages rated high in historicity and continuity of use.

By and large, however, an active body of speakers affects possible BE adoption positively, and vice versa.

Another factor number 10, is the historicity of tradition of the language, here again adopting one of Stewart's notions (1968). Ordinarily this would refer to formal, written tradition, due to the association of writing with prestige and authority. Some peoples, including certain Amerindian tribes, hold strong taboos regarding writing, or sharing their language with outsiders, but nonetheless display well-developed oral traditions.

Others, by contrast, have enthusiastically welcomed it, participating very actively in devising a writing style, and in developing materials. In line with tradition, storytellers are often part of a BE program, presenting stories and legends of the tribes. Perhaps "community involvement" due to the uniqueness of the Amerindian situation, is greater among Native Americans than elsewhere. (cf. also: Medicine 1979).

The following item, number 11, degree of standardization and codification, might well be merged with historicity in a future revision. In any event, it is a positive factor in considering BE, that language X has a unified written form, and a readily acceptable standard. Languages like English, French, German, Italian, Russian have been standardized for some centuries, although most of the world's languages have not even been committed to writing. The task of materials preparation may and often is rendered increasingly difficult by disputes among members of the community or by teaching personnel, as to what is "acceptable." In the case of Navajo, for example, there are several written forms, and controversy has not ceased.

As for Italian, although long standardized *la quistione della lingua* (in effect "the standard language problem") still is argued by speakers and writers of the language. Spanish is the official or dominant language of nineteen nations—more than any other language. Here again the problem of which variety to teach inevitably raises its head. In Navajo, as noted, several distinctive writing variants cause disagreements as to what should be followed in bilingual projects. Modern Greek is in effect two languages, while the complex linguistic situation of Norway has been penetratingly analyzed by Haugen, where the disputes between traditionalists who prefer the Danish-modeled *bokmål,* waxes still furious with liberally-oriented partisans of *lands-mål,* based on West Norwegian rural dialects.

Thorny problems exist, however, even with such languages as German, Spanish, French and Italian, since most U.S. speakers of these languages usually realize them in a dialectal form, making the formal standard almost a foreign language in some cases. In the case of Spanish, although speakers of U.S. varieties are, with minor lexical exceptions, mutually highly intelligible, the fact is that all Puerto Rican, Cuban and Chicano Spanish are spoken as special U.S. varieties, with their own norms, resulting from contact with English, generous borrowing and reconstruction or reshaping of the items, as in Chicano Spanish: *suera* "sweater;" *breca* "break". (cf. also: Elías-Olivares 1979; Bowen 1972; Ornstein 1972).

The unwillingness to utilize and teach these varieties along with standard Spanish has also proved a serious stumbling block, in large part owing to deeply rooted normative, prescriptive, traditional ideas, and the naive notion that there is a "pure" form in every language. Used as a vernacular mostly, especially among poorer Chicanos and Boricuas, the association of Spanish with poverty-stricken, uneducated individuals is a minus factor for these languages, as is the association of French speakers in New England with Canadian French, again despite the position of these languages as highly literate "international" languages of wider communication, much used outside their borders.

Hence the fact that a language is highly standardized is not always a great boon. In early programs here the use of imported texts had to be abandoned, so alien were they in content and spirit.

In speaking of language distance, number 12, we do not have in mind merely genetic relationship, since some languages, although similar in structure, differ vastly in their lexicon, which may have been heavily borrowed from a language or languages of another stock. This is the case with English, which has been called by the great Danish scholar Jespersen as a language Germanic in structure, but with a Romance (i.e, of Latin origin) vocabulary. Thus it is that languages sharing the international Latin-Greek vocabulary of English, particularly such as the West European ones, seem "easier," and in many ways they are, and thus more acceptable to learners, especially those as language-resistant as our compatriots!

Aside from this, grammatical structure, including such phenomena as complicated case and gender structures, tend to discourage learners. Likewise, any strange alphabet, even the Slavic Cyrillic one used by Russians (which may be mastered in an hour or so), tend to provide minus loading, since laymen are convinced that they are a kind of "Chinese writing." When it comes to syllabaries such as those used by Amhuric or Asian Indian languages, or character-writing systems, employed by Chinese, Japanese or Korean, the gigantic task involved in their partial mastery compounds the negative nature of possible involvement with them. By and large, bilingualists have been wise to stick to romanization in such cases, although careful to explain the rudiments of the formal systems, so that the learners might ultimately make the decision to undertake them later. Here again the difficulties of the graphemic or writing system are compounded, in Chinese, by a highly complex phonology or pronunciation system, and in most leading Oriental languages including Vietnamese, the fact that there is so little common vocabulary to English-speakers.

At the same time, such obstacles mentioned should not and apparently do not deter the setting up of one BE program after another in Oriental languages. Nevertheless, foreign language enrollment statistics at all levels of school show the highest mortality rates in the United States for precisely these languages of the "most difficult" group, in which these fall. Accordingly, this provides all the more opportunity for innovation and for creativity in counteracting the magnitude of the pedagogic complexities, and for effecting a change to a lamentable system of exposing all too few young Americans to too few languages, and even these, with too little exposure too late in their cognitive development.

We are now about to shift to factors which have little to do with the intrinsic shape, the structure or features of human language. In item number 13, the language situation, actually a technical term coined by Ferguson (1962), one confronts a sort of orchestration of a number of widely divergent factors, or sub-variables, if one wishes.

First of all, the situation either at the macro-level or the micro-level can be quite disparate, hence pulling in opposite directions, which would be negative for BE. Of tremendous importance is the distribution and numerical strength of the individual languages, and of course, the type of commitment which the macro-level entertains toward ethnolinguistic pluralism—favorable, for example, in Switzerland, unfavorable in Iran in recent years. The prestige of different languages, and particularly the sociopolitical clout of their speakers (e.g. the Amharas of Ethiopia) can spell representation in multilingual schooling or not.

In general, a language spoken in a context of high linguistic diversity, as in India or Nigeria, has less chance for representation in these terms than one in a nation with low diversity, which is committed to "cultural pluralism." The language policy of the national government is, of course, part of this and it may be implicit, as it is in many democracies, or spelled out in constitutions, as it is in the U.S.S.R., South Africa, and other lands.

Returning to numbers, we repeat that in countries like Nigeria and India, with between 100 and 200 distinct languages, or the U.S.S.R. (whose language solution is in many ways similar to that of India) so-called "minor" languages may simply be left out of the running, to continue as vernaculars, or to disappear. One should not underestimate the practical difficulties and expense involved in the bilingual teaching in several languages. We have witnessed in the last few years the exacerbation of ethnic relations in Belgium and Canada, committed to only two-language bilingualism in the public sector and education. Hence linguistic "equality" can be extremely complex, and costly—a problem to be kept in mind in the United States in view of the Proposition 13 type of atmosphere which is coming to be more common. In stating this, I hasten to qualify that I speak here only as a sort of "devil's advocate." (Discussion of delegates from twenty-seven nations at a U.N. conference on these problems are reported in Mackey and Verdoodt 1975.)

Somehow plurilingual countries manage, although this may require not education in a "language-pair" but in a "language-set," two terms coined by the writer (1974). An example is India where, if a child comes from a home not speaking one of the languages of the individual states (for example, Marathi, Malayalam, Tamil), it usually receives schooling in the larger local (regional) medium, the state language, and Hindi, the over-all official lingua franca, as well as, at a later stage, instruction in a completely foreign language such as English, French, German, Russian.

Our scope here does not permit us to analyze all facets of the language situation, since as noted, it involves so many different elements, psychological, sociological, political as well as linguistic.

With the emergence of so many multilingual new nations, a great deal is being written about language choice, not only in new, but also in older lands. A number of new nations, in Africa particularly, unable to reach agreement among so many rival tribes or peoples, seek a "neutral," "exoglossic" arrangement (Fishman, 1972), resorting to non-native languages such as English, French, or both. Others are able to apply an "endoglossic" or "native language" solution. Some decide upon a mixed formula, such as Somalia, with its official languages Somali and Italian. The plurilingual nation of Indonesia, has rejected Javanese, its largest but most status-ridden language, choosing instead Bazaar Malay, a former vernacular, which has been "engineered" into what Kloss terms a "sociologically complete" language (1972).

Language attitude(s) constitutes the fourteenth factor on this dimension, and as such it is one that is dependent on one group's perception of its language or that of others. For example, in the famed masked-guise test administered by Canadian social psychologists such as Wallace Lambert and Richard Tucker, English-speakers were more favorably viewed by subjects listening to tape recordings (made by the same fluent bilingual!) than French-speakers (1967), a factor sure to influence motivation in approaching one of the "language-pair" or "language-set."

This has special implications for bilingual studies, since most pupils in BE programs come from homes where parents usually speak, not the formal standard, but rather a dialect, some more or less stigmatized variety. As noted, in the U.S., this is a cause of constant friction in the school programs where, in particular, prescriptively-minded teachers insist that only "book" Spanish or French should be employed. Nevertheless, the varieties of such languages overwhelmingly used here are those which have developed in contact with English, and are full of interferential features (some call the code-switching form a separate variety, or mode, which is linguistically tenable).

Research on language attitudes has flourished in recent years, and is being applied fruitfully to the bilingual sector as well. In an extensive sociolinguistic survey conducted by the writer at the University of Texas, El Paso, some rather dismaying results were gleaned on the way in which Southwest (Chicano) Spanish variety is viewed, even by students at various points in their college careers. Our institution is located almost immediately on the U.S.-Mexico border, and claims the largest Chicano enrollment of any senior institution (i.e., with graduate school) of any in the fifty states, and probably with the highest proportion of bilinguals, well over a third.

Questions regarding perceptions of regional Spanish (and English) were included in the *Sociolinguistic Background Questionnaire* (Brooks, Brooks, Goodman, and Ornstein, 1972). From an array of four choices; "formal, educated," "informal, everyday," "southwest dialect," and "border slang," a mere five percent of the Chicanos believe that "formal educated style" was heard in the Southwest, and no Anglos did. The most frequent response, to our displeasure, was "border slang," representing thirty-one percent of the Mexican-American respondents and fifty-one percent of Anglos. The second most popular choice, was quite correctly, "informal, everyday" language selected by thirty-two percent Anglos, and forty percent Chicanos, while "formal educated" accounted for only seven Chicanos, or two percent.

At the same time, Spanish-English bilinguals contradicted themselves when they responded to a question asking them which of the above types they spoke, with forty-eight percent claiming "formal, educated," while more than half claimed "informal, everyday" language, with ten percent acknowledging control of "southwest dialect" and almost no one admitting to "border slang." At the same time a large number of Chicanos expressed loyalty and attachment to Chicano Spanish, probably in part a reflex to the prestige brought to it by the Chicano movement (Goodman and Renner, 1978; Ornstein, 1976, 1975). As regards linguistic attitudes, the point to be stressed here is that all too many Chicanos themselves, as the above reflects, still entertain the attitude that Southwest Spanish, any U.S. Spanish variety, is quite highly stigmatized, as the perjorative term "slang" connotes.

A great deal has been written about "language loyalty," since Fishman submitted the concept in 1966 through his significant volume *Language Loyalty in the United States*. Great ambiguity exists since, if professed "loyalty" to a language is not implemented by an active commitment to maintaining it, which usually means speaking it in the home at least, there is perhaps little but symbolic significance in this.

In our research study at El Paso, which involved both the aforementioned questionnaire and a writing and speaking fluency test (the latter an open-ended oral interview), we could find very little significance between professed loyalty to Spanish and to "Mexican-American culture" and actual performance in Spanish. This and other evidence exists which would deter one from assuming that language loyalty is a corollary of ethnicity. For example, Jewish people have maintained a high degree of ethnicity in the Diaspora yet this is not dependent upon any one spoken language. Until Israel's founding, Hebrew had been viewed as a mostly religious medium (In connection with Hebrew vs. Yiddish, cf. Fishman, 1972).

Another aspect of language attitudes is that which concerns the functionality of a language, and in an even broader sense, the motivation for studying it. Again social psychologist Wallace Lambert, of McGill University, has coined the convenient set of oppositions "integrative" and "instrumental" motivation for undertaking a language. The former refers to the desire of the individual to make the language and its use part of his life style, while the latter concept refers to the practical, utilitarian value, the extrinsic value perceived in it. We could in the future collapse both these terms into my own, I belive, namely "functionality."

By any standards instrumental motivation for persons to become functional or "bilingual" in the "languages of wider communication" such as English, French, Spanish, Arabic, Chinese, Russian, Hindi-Urdu, would be high, since this can be translated very often into vocational opportunity and the like. By contrast, language like Albanian, Macedonian, Latvian, Southern Paiute (with no disparagement intended), must rest on more "integrative" grounds, with identification with certain groups, or domestically with a desire to communicate with members of the nationality.

This completes the factors along the linguistic dimension, which in general, can be overridden by the sociopolitical ones. Nevertheless, they can be highly significant. The double-edged sword of the Marxist-Leninist insistence on cultural self-expression of the nationalities in the Soviet Union may be seen in the constant resurgence of expressions of ethnic loyalty at the micro-level, in the Baltic republics, Central Asia and elsewhere. (cf. Ornstein, 1968; Lewis, 1972).

Finally, recognizing the unique importance that sociopolitical events may have for such developments as BE, we posit a new concept in "favorable conjuncture," number 15. In this we adopt a term found in comprehensive English-usage dictionaries, but which is used in the sense of "combination" or "convergence" of events, mostly in Europe (cf. German and Swedish, "*konjunktur*, Russian *kon'ÿunktura*, Serbo-Croat *konjunktura)* and is frequently employed in the sense of "crisis."[3]

Hence, the last item, all other factors along both dimensions being mostly favorable, and given a favorable constellation of events, chances for BE by our formulation would, then, be favorable, or vice versa. This was an independent one, number 15.

This was the backdrop for the passage of the Bilingual Education Act in 1967, and is the type of scenario that continues to unfold, granted with variations, throughout a world whose extreme abundance of languages represents an *embarras de richesse.*

Some Directions

In a programmatic approach such as the foregoing we can hardly boast of firm conclusions, or results validated by our formulation. At this juncture, the most we can do is to appeal for a dialogue with colleagues who may perceive enough merit in the approach to test it out themselves and share findings so that the schema can be progressively improved in future approximations.

The schema and discussion, as noted previously, have been motivated stochastically, and namely for forging an instrument which has some predictive value in determining which conditions, social and linguistic, maximize the introduction of BE as well as its maintenance. Is this a feasible heuristic, or should a set of discovery criteria be elaborated along quite different lines? Time will tell. Another open issue regards the extent to which relative weighing and quantification of the factors is possible.

Beyond possible utility of the schema itself, we genuinely hope that interest in comparative BE structures might be stimulated in developing this as a legitimate object of discussion both in scholarly and pedagogic writing. While there have been a series of international conferences on the description and measurement of bilingualism, we still await the organization of a multinational forum on comparative bilingual-bicultural national systems.

It is difficult to deny that, BE is at present so beleagured an innovation in the public sector, bilingualists should therefore speak with some conviction and passion from their own vantage-point. Nevertheless, now that we are well into the second decade of contemporary BE, perhaps it is time that we shed the parochialism and even "provincialism" that mark so many discussions, and extend our parameters of vision. Could we not all benefit from a broader exchange of experience and insights gained from other continents? *Podemos contestar, en forma bilingüe, que poco se podría perder así y mucho se podría ganar. Por ende, "al buen entendedor le bastan pocos palabras."*

Appendix

MATRIX FOR PREDICTING FAVORABILITY OF ETHNIC FACTORS FOR BILINGUAL/BICULTURAL EDUCATION (FIRST APPROXIMATION)*

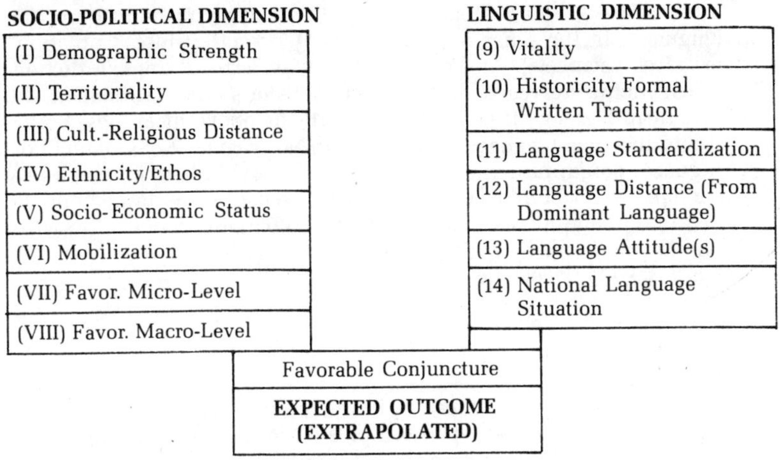

SOCIO-POLITICAL DIMENSION	**LINGUISTIC DIMENSION**
(I) Demographic Strength	(9) Vitality
(II) Territoriality	(10) Historicity Formal Written Tradition
(III) Cult.-Religious Distance	(11) Language Standardization
(IV) Ethnicity/Ethos	(12) Language Distance (From Dominant Language)
(V) Socio-Economic Status	(13) Language Attitude(s)
(VI) Mobilization	(14) National Language Situation
(VII) Favor. Micro-Level	
(VIII) Favor. Macro-Level	

Favorable Conjuncture
EXPECTED OUTCOME (EXTRAPOLATED)

**N.B.*

1. *Rate + or - within each cell, avoiding ±*
2. *Blank cell = "non-applicable"*
3. *A simple majority of pluses=favorability, and vice versa.*
4. *Supplementary sheets may be attached with descriptive detail on each factor*

NOTES

1. It is impossible to mention by name all who have in some way made helpful suggestions toward the improvement of the present paper. Helpful comments were made regarding the matrix or schema, by Bonnie S. Brooks, Department of Educational Psychology and Guidance, and Thomas Price, Dept. of Political Science, both of this University, while John H. Haddox (Jr.), a student here, actually prepared the sketch. Space forbids us from enumerating all forum participants who so kindly remained until the very last moment on Saturday, June 23, 1979, providing animated and useful feedback both for my paper and that of the other speaker on the morning's program. I am very grateful also for written remarks handed me by Donald F. Solá, Cornell University, and the joint (written) comments furnished by Andrew Cohen, Center for Applied Linguistics, Israel, and Reynaldo Macías, National Institute for Education, Washington, D.C.
2. *Language Problems and Language Planning,* whose editor is Richard E. Wood, Department of Foreign Languages, Plymouth State College, Plymouth, N.H. 03264, has an international Editorial Board. Published

in Rotterdam, Netherlands, it is available through Walter de Gruyter, Inc., 3 Westchester Plaza, Elmsford, N.Y. 10523.

3. The term *conjuncture,* and its Latin-derived counterparts in other languages has a concrete denotation of "juncture joint" and the like. In more abstract connotations, it tends to be used in many European languages in the sense of either "covergence of events," "situation" or "circumstance(s)," or very commonly as "crisis." English dictionaries, including recent editions of Webster's International or the American Heritage Dictionary report all the above meanings. Equivalents in other languages: Danish and Norwegian, *Konjunktur;* Portuguese, *conjuntura;* Italian, *congiuntura;* in Polish, interestingly enough, when employed in an abstract sense it has undergone semantic change almost exclusively to "economic boom" (the latter pointed out to me by Z. A. Kruszewski and confirmed in authoritative *Kościuszko-Berkeley* dictionary lexicons.

Addendum

Extensive and constructive feedback was received from participants following presentation of the paper and of the Matrix for Predicting Favorability of Ethnic Factors for Bilingual-Bicultural Education at the conclusion of the Ethnoperspective Forum on 23 June, 1979. No more can be done here than to touch upon some of the issues raised. As I am depending upon written notes rapidly taken, I apologize for any misrepresentations, which will be corrected in the future.

In general, approbation was registered of approaches attempted to identify and categorize factors influential in determining probabilities of successful establishment and maintenance of BE programs. Armando Valdés raised the possibility of classifying variables, according to their potency, perhaps under rubrics of "weak, medium and strong." José Rosario saw a need for "teasing out" factors of particular relevance, in terms of their frequency, to mention one aspect, in different and numerous situations conducive, or not, to BE. Along these same lines Juan Halcón perceived the need for generalizing and systematizing "BE situations" and their characteristics, much as has been done by scholars of the phenomenon (or phenomena) of bilingualism, such as Einar Haugen and Uriel Weinreich. In a similar vein, Alfredo Benavides recommended deeper and more explicit study on the multicultural contexts throughout the world of BE, utilizing such seminal research findings as those in Gedzie's volume on international education, or Woolcott's work on the culture of the Canadian Kwiakutl, as well as Hostetter's work on the Amish. In the United States itself, it was suggested that an examination be conducted of the setting and forces operative in such a small city as Crystal City, Texas, where in recent years 3 million dollars in government funds were allocated to serve a variety of cultural, social and educational needs, including BE. This case was all the more remarkable because at one point in time virtually the entire "power structure" was constituted by Mexican-Americans exercising political, social and educational functions of official nature.

Opinions appeared rather divided on the desirability of quantifying the different ethnic factors in the matrix, or similar ones. Frank Bonilla saw a danger in such attempts or in the effort itself to claim too much by way of the "diagnostic" value of individual variables, thereby building up an application of such models as this. Certainly whoever utilizes such variables must know in depth what they really stand for. Bonilla insisted rightly that in many cases, the influence of one single factor might unpredictably nullify the force of all the others. One observer described such vagaries as the "see-saw" of variables.

Andrew Cohen appeared to be somewhat optimistic about possibilities for quantification of models like this, and for the application of statistical procedures including regression analysis. He suggested that it might be desirable also to match up factors in the present Matrix with factors in a given BE program in operation.

A contribution to the portion of the matrix titled "Expected Outcome," regarding the probable resolutions which would fill this cell was made by Reynaldo Macías, and reported to me in written form at the conclusion of the Ethnosperspective Forum, by Andrew Cohen, who had also discussed this orally with the former. Accordingly, the following outcomes might be predicted:

1. A BE program would be confronted by insurmountable odds.
2. A BE program of type X will self-destruct after *Y* years.
3. A BE program of type X will maintain itself over time.
4. (Unlikely) A BE program will expand to include the non-target groups (e.g. mainstream groups).

I am, of course, deeply grateful to these colleagues for exerting such efforts in behalf of this paper, in the true spirit of a symbiotic forum. There are, of course, other possible predicted outcomes, such as:

5. A BE program might be feasible when and if variable(s) x (y, z, etc.) change(s) in a direction supportive or favorable to BE basic requirements.

As sociopolitical and even linguistic conditions are constantly in a process of change, albeit often slowly, outcome five might be realistic. Meanwhile one through four appear to cover the main possibilities. Further dialogue, written or oral, on this and other particulars of this essay is invited. (cf. also Macías, 1979).

Cohen, in a written note, added the following:

> "Note that your model is taking bilingual education as a single phenomenon, but, as you're well aware, it is a variety of things, e.g., if we're still able to refer to 'transitional' BE (although Rudy Troike thinks it's hurting the movement to contrast this with 'maintenance' programs), then we may well be eventualizing its demise."

Donald Solá, among other observations, pointed out that attempts such as mine, in which a set of specific factors are isolated, are reminiscent of and somewhat cognate with approaches in the field of linguistics, particularly the "distinctive features" model elaborated by Morris Halle of MIT and Roman Jakobson of Harvard. These features are then applied to the nature of human languages in general, with sub-categorical variations noted in analyzing a specific language.

REFERENCES

Andersson, Theordore and Mildred Boyer. *Bilingual Schooling in the United States.* 2 vols. Wash. D.C.: U.S. Gov't. Printing Office, 1970.

__________. *Bilingual Schooling in the United States.* rev. ed. Austin, Tex.: Nat'l Educ. Laboratory Publishers, 1978.

Brooks, Bonnie S., Brooks, G. D., Goodman, P. W., Ornstein, J. *Sociolinguistic Background Questionaire: A Measurement Instrument for the Study of Bilingualism.* rev. ed. El Paso: Cross-Cultural Southwestern Ethnic Study-Center, Univ. of Texas, El Paso, 1972.

Burns, Donald H. "Bilingual Education in the Andes of Peru." in *Language Problems of Developing Nations.* J. A. Fishman, C. A. Ferguson, and J. Das Gupta, eds. New York: John Wiley and Sons, 1968.

__________. "Five Years of Bilingual Education in the Andes of Peru." Inter-Branch Quechua Workers' Conference of Summer Institute of Linguistics," Lima. May 3-10, 1971 (Typescript).

Bustos, Amador S. "Bilingual/Bicultural Education in the Context of National Public Policy." Paper presented in partial fulfillment for Doctor of Education Degree. School of Education., U. Of California, Berkeley. 1979.

Castro, Ray. "Shifting the Burden of Bilingualism: The Case for Monolingual Communities." *Bilingual Review.* 31: p. 3-28. (Jan.-Apr.) 1976.

De la Garza, Rudoph., Kruszewski, Z. A. and Arciniega, T. *Chicanos and Native Americans: Our Territorial Minorities.* Englewood Cliffs, N.J.: Prentice-Hall, 1974.

Dittmar, Norbert, Haberland, H., Kutnabb-Kangas, T. and Teleman, U. eds. Papers from the *First-Scandinavian-German Symposium on the Language of Immigrant Workers and their Children.* Roskilde, Denmark: Roskilde Universitetscenter (Postbox 260).

Deutsch, Karl. W. *Nationalism and Social Communication.* New York: John Wiley and Sons. 1953.

Elías Olivares, Lucía and Valdés, G. Fallis. "Language Diversity in Chicano Speech Communities: Implications for Language Teaching." Sociolinguistic Working Paper No. 54. (Jan.). Austin, TX.: Southwestern Educational Development Laboratory. 1979.

Ferguson, Charles A. "Diglossia." *Word.* 15: (1959) 325-340.

Fishman, Joshua A., et al., eds. *Language Loyalty in the United States.* The Hague: Mouton. 1966.

__________. ed. *Readings in the Sociology of Language.* The Hague: Mouton. 1968.

__________. "Bilingual Education in Sociolinguistic Perspective." *TESOL Quarterly.* (1970): 215-222.

__________. Sociology of Language: An Interdisciplinary Social Science Approach to Language in Society." in *Advances in the Sociology of Language* II. J. Fishman, ed. The Hague: Mouton. (1971): 215-222.

Fishman, J. A., Cooper, Robt. C., Ma, Roxana *et al.* 1968. *Bilingualism in the Barrio.* Final Report on Contract OEC-1-7-062817-0297. to HEW (New York, Yeshiva Univ.): also Bloomington, Ind. rev. ed. Indiana University Press, 1971.

Haugen, Einar. "Planning for a Standard Language in Modern Norway." *Anthropological Linguistics.* 1.3: (1959) pp. 8-21.

__________. *The Ecology of Language.* Essays by E. Haugen. Cambridge: Harvard University Press, 1972.

Kaprosy, Geraldo and St. Clair, Robt. "Order vs. Conflict Societies: the Dilemma of Bicultural Education." In *Social and Educational Issues in Bilingualism.* ch. 2. eds. R. St. Clair, G. Valdés-Fallis and J. Ornstein. forthcoming.

Kloss, Heinz. "Notes Concerning a Language-National Typology," in *Language Problems.* J. Fishman, ed. 1968. pp. 69-86.

__________. *The Bilingual Tradition in the United States.* Rowley, Mass.,: Newbury House. 1976.

__________. and McConnell, Grant D. *Linguistic Composition of the Nations of the World.* II. North America. Québec: Presses de l'Université Laval, 1975.

__________. *Linguistic Composition* II. *Central and Western South Asia.* Québec: Presses de L'Université Laval, 1974.

Lambert, Wallace. "The Social Psychology of Bilingualism" in Bilingualism in the Modern World. John Macnamara, ed. *Journal of Social Issues* vol. XVII, No. 2 (1967): 21-109.

Lewis, E. Glyn. "Migration and Language in the U.S.S.R." in *Advances in the Sociology of Language.* Fishman, ed. (1972) p. 310-341.

Macias, Reynaldo. Mexicano/Chicano Sociolinguistic Behavior. Ph.D. dissertation. Washington, D.C.: Georgetown University, 1979.

Mackay, Wm. F. and Ornstein, J. *The Bilingual Education Movement: Essays on its Progress. El Paso: Texas Western Press (University of Texas) 1977.*

__________. *Sociolinguistic Studies in Language Contact: Methods and Cases.* Mouton and W. de Grutter: The Hague and Berlin, 1979.

Mackey, Wm. F. and Verdoodt, Albert, eds. *The Multinational Society.* Rowley, Mass.: Newbury House, 1973.

McRae, Kenneth D. "Bilingual Language Districts in Finland and Canada: Adventures in the Transplanting of an Institution." *Canadian Public Policy/Analyse De Politiques.* 4.3: (1978) 331-51.

__________. "Political Dynamics of Bilingualism and Biculturalism: Lessons from the Royal Commission Reports." in *Bilingualism and Bilingual Education: Readings and Insights.* J. Ornstein and Robt. St. Clair, eds. San Antonio, Tex.: Trinity University Press (Trinity University) in press.

Ministerio de Educación. *Política nacional de educatión bilingüe.* Lima, Peru: Dirección Cen. de Publicaciones, 1972.

Nahir, Moshe. "The Five Aspects of Language Planning—A Classification." *Language Problems and Language Planning.* (1977) 107-23.

Ornstein, Jacob L. "Africa Seeks a Common Language." *Review of Politics.* 26.2: (1964) 205-14 (Apr.)

__________. 1964b. "Patterns of Language Planning in the New States." *World Politics.* 17.1: 40-49 (Oct.)

__________. A Sociolinguistic Study of Mexican-American and Anglos Students in a Border University. (Occas. Paper. No. 3 Border-State Consortium for Latin American Studies. Will Kennedy, ed. S. Diego: S. D. State Univ., Inst. of Publ. and Urban Aff. Press, 1975.

__________. "A Cross-Disciplinary Sociolingual Investigation of Mexican-American Bilinguals/Biculturals at a U.S. Border University, Language and Social Parameters." *La Linguistique* (Paris). 12.1: (1976) pp. 131-145.

__________. "Soviet Language Policy: Continuity and Change." in *Ethnic Minorities in the Soviet Union.* Erich Goldhagen, ed. New York: Praeger. (1978) pp. 121-46.

Pool, Jonathan. "National Development and Language Diversity" in *Advances* II, Fishman, (1972) pp. 214-230.

Pozzi-Escot, Inés. "El uso de la lengua vernácula en la educación" *Seminario Nacional de Educación Bilingüe.* (Jan. 17-22, 1972) pp. 1-9.

Rustow, Dankwart. "Language, Modernization and Nationhood." in *Language Problems,* Fishman, et al. (1968): 87-106.

Solá, Donald. "A Flexible-Technology Model for Bilingual Education." presented at annual meeting, National Association of Bilingual Educators," 8 May, Seattle, Washington, 1979.

Stewart, Wm. A. "Sociolinguistic Typology for Describing National Multilingualism." in *A Reader in the Sociology of Language.* J. A. Fishman, ed. The Hague: Mouton. (1968) 531-45.

Stoller, Paul. "The Language Planning Activities of the U.S. Office of Bilingual Education." *International Journal of the Sociology of Language* vol. 11 "Language Planning in the United States." Joan Rubin, issue editor. (1976) pp. 45-60.

Veltman, Calvin. "Les leçons étonnantes des statistiques sur l'assimilation linguistique aux Ètats-Unis et au Canada." *Le Devoir* (Montréal) 9 Aug. 1976: 5-6.

__________. "The Evolution of Ethno-Linguistic Frontiers in the United States and Canada" (typescript, Dept. of Sociology, State Univ. of New York, Plattsburgh) submitted for publication. 1977.

CAN BILINGUAL TEACHING TECHNIQUES REFLECT BILINGUAL COMMUNITY BEHAVIORS?—A STUDY IN ETHNOCULTURE AND ITS RELATIONSHIP TO SOME AMENDMENTS CONTAINED IN THE NEW BILINGUAL EDUCATION ACT

Rodolfo Jacobson

Recent studies concerning the implementation of bilingual education programs have shown that the success of these programs depends to a large extent upon the social, cultural and attitudinal conditions prevailing in the immediate neighborhood of the school hosting such a program. "It would be a mistake," argues Rolf Kjolseth (1972: 95)

> to overestimate what any school can accomplish or to overvalue the significance of a student's performance, if it is restricted only to the domain of the school itself. The school is only one domain in the life space of individuals and communities. Language cannot "live" there, although it may receive important impulses. *The life of a language depends first and foremost upon its use in other domains* [Italics, mine].

It is for this very reason that Andrew D. Cohen begins his chapter entitled "Research Design and Procedures" with a sociodemographic description of the city where the bilingual program with which he was associated was located (1975: 68-74). On the other hand, it may be useful to closely examine, not only demographic and socioeconomic factors, but also certain interactional norms present in the community and to consider which of these can be adapted to suit pedagogical objectives. Finally, it is the community alone that can provide us with information concerning the hopes and expectations parents have for their children, and that schools must take into account. In sum, there is a rich source of information in the community that we must tap and bring into closer relationship with the school so that we may generate a more realistic climate in our classrooms.

One of the most striking behavioral patterns observable in communities where two languages are in contact is the language alternation, or better, code-switching, that occurs when bilingual members of those communities interact with one another in an informal and relaxed situation. The American Southwest, in particular in the proximity of the Mexico-U.S. border, Ontario, Canada, and Alsace-Lorraine in Europe are well known for the switching practices of their inhabitants who switch with remarkable ease from English to Spanish, from French to English or from French to German. Examples like:

> I lose my temper *porque a mí me da mucho coraje*
> or
> (wife to mother) *Con la misma chaqueta por cuatro años* and (wife to husband) You are the one wearing the same jacket

have been recorded in South Texas and show how speakers alternate at times within the same sentence and at other times in the transition from one sentence to the next. Similar switching samples have been heard in Ontario and Alsace-Lorraine:

> *M'a* [*je m'en vais*] runner *mon bicyc' pour une coupe de* minutes *s'a* [*sur la*] *Main pi m'a r'tourner* back *à maison pour* watcher *'a* game *de* hockey *sur le Canal* 25*
>
> "Bois ton verre vide" [Trink Dein Glass leer]*

I have tried to show in several articles that the switching between two languages is not a random process but occurs as an obvious response to a definable source found in the speaker himself or in his immediate environment. To account for this consistency in code-switching practices, I have recently proposed the following classificatory framework, where I distinguished lexical (semicode-switching) from syntactic switching (true code-switching) and attempted to show that certain psychological and, in particular, sociological factors are responsible for switches from one to the other language.

Five psychological factors, or rather psychologically-conditioned categories, tend to trigger the switch from one to the other language. One of these, *substratum*, reflects the subconscious intrusion of the speaker's dominant language; another, *emotion*, justifies the switching because of the speaker's emotional involvement in the described event. *Hesitation*, that is, the gaps within utterances while the speaker searches for the appropriate word or phrase, is variably realized depending upon his language dominance, whereas the *false start* in L1 tends to produce a new start in L2. To be sure, not all switches can be justified and it just may be that a speaker prefers *(preference)* to use one rather than the other language at a given moment.

TABLE 1

A SYSTEM OF CODE-SWITCHING CATEGORIES

Semi-code-switching	True code-switching	
	Psychologically conditioned	Sociologically conditioned
1. Borrowing	1. Substratum	1. Code
2. Terminology	2. Emotion	2. Domain
3. Calque	3. Hesitation	3. Culture
4. Access	4. False Start	4. Interpersonal relations
	5. Preference	5. Topic
		6. Metaphor

*These examples were supplied by participants at the Seminaire Internationale de Sociolinguistique, Perpignan, France, July 1977.

TABLE 2

SOCIOLOGICALLY CONDITIONED VARIABLES

1. Code	2. Domain	3. Culture
(a) Initiation of response	(a) Home/family	(a) Geographic environment
(b) Continued speed (after (SW)	(b) Church	(b) Culture conditioned attitude
(c) Prior code use	(c) Employment	(c) Language-locale association
(d) Code as topic	(d) School	(d) Cultural bias
(e) Anticipatory embedding	(e) Business	(e) Persons as cultural exponents
(f) Quote		(f) Cultural heritage
(g) Classification		(g) Social/political institution
(h) Precoining		(h) Language as culture
		(i) Culture-related custom

4. Interpersonal relations	5. Topic	6. Metaphor
(a) Siblings	(a) Occupation	(a) Contrast
(b) Spouses	(b) Financial matters/ numbers	(b) Emphasis
(c) Peers	(c) Mechanical interests	(c) Humor
(d) Acquaintances	(d) Food	(d) Parenthetical remarks
(e) Employer-employee	(e) Time-related experiences	
(f) Teacher-student	(f) Imaginary content	

The six sociologically-conditioned categories that I have so far identified seem to cover all the switching events encountered in my research. They are however rather broad categories and it has become necessary to break each one down into subcategories. A brief description of the major categories shall here suffice but examples for each of the subcategories can be found in the appendix. *Code* stresses the fact that certain decisions concerning language choice are conditioned by several language-related facts. What language, for example, is appropriate for a response, if one interlocutor chooses English as a medium of communication but the other wishes to use Spanish; or how should one quote, when speaking, say, in Spanish, a person who made his comment in English? Also, does a request for clarification mean that the partner in communication has not heard well or has failed to understand what was said because of the language used? Finally, how do we handle a saying coined in one language when we talk in the other language? All these are language-related decisions and they tend to trigger the switching under favorable circumstances.

Domain conveys, as we all know, the notion that there is a close correlation between the major social institutions of our society and the language variety that is appropriately chosen when our talk relates to one of them. What language variety tends to be triggered when the bilingual speaks about his home, his family or his neighborhood? When talking about one's employment or his school or university, does the bilingual usually find a switch to the mainstream language warranted? Also, does the church equally trigger one or the other language or does this domain generate variable language choices, depending upon whether it is seen as a keeper of language and culture or a supraethnic institution? If one language is predictable here but is not the language spoken at the moment, then the codeswitch is most likely to occur.

Culture, because of the bilingual-bicultural person's identification with the vernacular culture at certain times and with the mainstream culture at others, is an important source for triggering language switching. In other words, the close-knit relationship between language and culture brings that language to the foreground that best reveals the cultural idiosyncracies in question. Hence, the reference in Spanish to a location may evoke in the speaker quite a different image from the one that underlies its English counterpart. By the same token, whenever cultural loyalty is emphasized, the language variety chosen will differ from the one that is appropriate when acculturation comes into play. Sociopolitical issues, on one hand, and different customs, on the other, often make the person switch to the other language, just to get his point across more effectively. After all, is there a better code than English for a person to "take the fifth amendment;" and Spanish to criticize a speaker who asks "*¿qué?*" and not "*¿mande?*" when he seeks clarification?

Interpersonal relations are equally important to the monolingual and the bilingual person. They help the speaker select the appropriate style and, if he is bilingual, the appropriate language. In a gathering, the speaker will undoubtedly alternate between languages, depending upon whom he addresses. If we always address a person in L1 only, it is certainly quite unusual, even if we know that he also speaks L2, to switch to the latter code. Hence, it requires the speaker to make a careful analysis of the addressee(s) in order to select the code that will meet with the approval of the person addressed.

The *topic* of discussion represents another important cue for code selection. Conversations exploring or dealing with money amounts, automechanics, and numbers usually trigger a language other than the home variety in which matters concerning foodmaking, housekeeping, gardening, etc. are expressed more meaningfully. Also, events concerning the remote past do not always require the same code as do current happenings, in particular when the past evokes the association with a different culture.

For contrast or for emphasis, speakers tend to style shift or code-switch metaphorically. *Metaphor,* then, is one more category within the proposed framework that explains why a bilingual speaker would at times repeat word by word in the other language what he has just stated in the first one. Obviously, it was not meant for better comprehension as his partner in communication is as bilingual as he is. The reader may of course have noted that some of these categories overlap with others, so that the investigator often wonders whether he should classify a switch as an instance of topic or interpersonal relations or of culture or domain. On the other hand, if we treat the categories as variables, and assess, regardless of some overlapping, the relative weight of one as opposed to the other, we can arrive at some reasonably accurate conclusions.

At the outset of the investigation that led to the elaboration of the preceding framework, I realized that three dichotomies have a bearing upon the direction that the analysis of code-switching events would take: (1) Are we seeking conventional linguistic or psycho-sociolinguistic information?, (2) Is the lexicon or the (morpho-) syntax our main concern? and (3) Does the switch occur at sentence or discourse level? Important as conventional linguistic studies concerning code-switching are, I have given priority to the psycholinguistic and sociolinguistic aspects of the switching and considered syntax to be far more revealing than the lexicon. Because of the nature of the data gathered, I have also devoted more attention to intrasentential code-switching. There is little doubt as to which type is more common but within the constraint of this paper, I shall refer mainly to intersentential code-switching and argue that it lends itself most effectively to serve as a teaching technique in bilingual education. Since the switching from one code to the other, whether intrasentential or intersentential, is common practice in borderland areas, its incorporation and adaptation to pedagogy constitutes a significant rapprochement between community behavior and school model. With the recent emphasis that we have awarded to the neighborhood where a school is located, the inclusion of community norms in a school program is to add very significantly to the success of the program.

Code-switching as a teaching strategy is known as the Concurrent Approach, however prior research on the topic is scarce. As a matter of fact, except for the favorable treatment of the closely related free alternation approach described by William Mackey in his fine monograph "Bilingual Education in a Binational School," a study of the bilingual method implemented in Berlin's J. F. Kennedy School, we only find a few general comments concerning the approach in the work of Andersson and Boyer (1970), Cordasco (1977) and a few others. The discussions of these latter authors do not reflect a deeper knowledge of the goals of the approach nor are their evaluations based on any known implementation of a program design where the concurrent approach had been chosen as a bilingual teaching mode. Their criticism is mainly based on two unproven assumptions; (1) Bilingual teachers, who usually are dominant in either one or the other language, cannot control their language choice and will speak more often in one rather than the other language; in other words, they cannot achieve a fifty-fifty ratio and (2) Teaching the child in both languages concurrently will confuse him/her and ultimately contribute to his/her mixing the two languages, thus making it too difficult for him/her to speak in one language at a time. It is my contention that teachers *can* be trained to distribute their two languages allowing equal time to both and that children *can* learn to speak one language exclusive of the other when their feeling for language appropriateness is properly developed.

My recent work done in Laredo in association with the local director of a bilingual education program has permitted me to develop the approach and to test it out with students, teachers and administrators. Thanks to the support received by the local staff, I attempted to specify what the constituent elements of the approach should be and how the bilingual teacher could be trained to implement it effectively. To specify the nature of the approach I first developed a general theme that I labeled the "Prestige of Codes." This theme stresses the belief that both languages are equally effective and valuable means of communication. Thus, the attitudinal perspective is at the heart of the matter and the success of the approach is contingent on the self-awareness of both the teachers and the students. The actual decision, however, when one or the other language should be chosen is ruled by a series of cues to which the individual participants in the school experience are expected to respond. These cues are grouped within four broader areas: interpersonal relationships, language development, curriculum, and classroom strategies. Each of the cues marks a specific source that may trigger a language switch at a given moment, and the inventory of the cues serves as a guideline for the teacher to follow in order to balance out both linguistic codes.

Four classroom strategies seem to benefit from intersentential switching. A concept taught in language A can be reinforced more effectively if this is done in language B. A lesson taught in language A can be reviewed in language B to add a new perspective to the review lesson. The switch from language A to language B is an effective strategy, just like Gumperz' metaphorical switching (Gumperz, 1971: 294-96), in order to recapture the attention of one or more children whose mind(s) wandered off unexpectedly. To praise a child or to reprimand him is often done more convincingly in the child's dominant language. Hence, *conceptual reinforcement, review, capturing of attention* and *approval/disapproval* are being suggested as strategies where the switching from one to the other language is very effective.

The bilingual child is expected to become sensitive to those switches that occur because one language is more appropriate than the other at a given moment. By the same token, regardless of school subject, he can react more enthusiastically to certain areas in content in Spanish and to others in English. Finally, bilingual children must be encouraged to read about the same subject in both languages. They will do better in class discussion, if they are allowed to talk in Spanish about what they read in that language and, in English about what they read in the mainstream language. In sum, *language appropriateness, content,* and *text* are three important cues that trigger switches whenever curricular matters are of concern. Language is not only developed in the language arts class but also at other moments of the instructional process. Whereas the language arts class is restricted to the language that is being taught, the various school subjects allow the teacher to have the child who needs more proficiency in one language express himself in that language. Furthermore, he may wish to help the child in expanding his vocabulary range in the weaker language as well as have him acquire some expertise in rendering in language B what was just said in language A. *Variable language dominance, lexical enrichment,* and *translatability* are therefore thought of as powerful goals in the language development of the bilingual child.

Not everything in the class is geared to the acquisition of information. There also occurs a great deal of interpersonal relationship between teacher and students that requires the former to make some meaningful decisions as to which language is more appropriate during the verbal interaction. Is this interaction rather intimate or is it formal? Is the preference of one over the other language a matter of courtesy or one of free choice? Is the child fatigued or does his self-awareness need to be strengthened? Are we talking about the usual teacher-student relationship or one where the teacher wishes to establish an almost peer-like rapport with one or more of her students? The presence of any one of these cues may suggest a language switch to achieve a more satisfactory bilingual performance. Therefore, *intimacy-formality, courtesy, free choice, fatigue, self-awareness,* and *rapport* have been proposed as cues under "Interpersonal Relationships" in order for the teacher to react to them by making a language choice decision that is most conducive to producing a truly bilingual atmosphere. To summarize, in stressing the equal prestige of the two languages, the author is emphasizing the importance of the affective domain in bilingual education, whereas in asking teachers to respond linguistically to certain cues, he is promoting sociolinguistic sensitivity. Both the affective and the sociolinguistic awareness require some specialized training that can be imparted to the balanced bilingual teacher in a reasonably short training session as shown below.

Staff development is an important phase of any bilingual program. However, for the implementation of the concurrent approach, it is crucial that teachers be trained in its use. First of all, they must learn to monitor themselves as to how they use language and how they distribute the two languages in a bilingual program. A training session should include theoretical facts, class observations, coding sessions, advanced planning, videotaped performances and peer critiques. The full understanding of its rationale and the actual implementation during token lessons tend to convince teachers of the feasibility of the approach. Workshops of this nature have been conducted in Laredo and elsewhere and were organized with the following seven segments in mind:

1. the rationale of the concurrent approach and its conceptual framework: the prestige of codes and the system of cues
2. the cue-response analysis: audio- and videotaped mini-lessons to be studied, transcribed and coded
3. advanced planning of language distribution: lesson plans in two languages with adequate switch rationalizations
4. lesson drafts for approval
5. video-taped mini-lessons
6. peer critiques: lesson replay and instant evaluation
7. special topics, such as "Spanish terminology" and "Role of the monolingual teacher in a team approach."

The rationale of the approach and its conceptual framework (1) has already been mentioned and need not be discussed any further. It may be in order however, to briefly comment on the remaining six segments. The cue-response analysis (2) is intended to make teachers aware of the significance of language switching as a pedagogical strategy. By the same token, teachers are familiarized with the underlying reasons for this language alternation by first listening to audiotapes or watching videotapes of demonstration lessons and then transcribing those parts of the lessons that contain switches from one to the other language. Finally, they are asked to rationalize why and how the switching has occurred; that is, what pedagogical objective may have induced the demonstration teacher to switch and how the children responded. This coding process is done by assigning the appropriate number-letter combination identifying area and cue. For example, if the switching is justifiable as a *classroom strategy* and intended to achieve *conceptual development,* the teacher identifies the switch from L1 to L2 as *1a* (*1* for classroom strategies and *a* for conceptual development). After the cue-response analysis session, the teachers are ready to plan their language distribution for a given class by writing out pertinent lesson plans (3). These plans are submitted on special forms on which the teachers write out what is to be taught in one language and what in the other and why the language switch is expected to achieve better results. These tri-partite lesson plans are then approved (4) but with the understanding that changes may still become necessary as the lesson is actually taught. Children may just not respond as anticipated or teachers may identify, in the actual class, a cue that they were unable to predict when the lesson was planned. The teachers are now ready to implement their lesson before a video camera (5). The teachers are then grouped in teams of two in order to allow for a closer peer relationship as the lessons are first filmed and then replayed for instant evaluation (6). Although the workshop evaluators view the instant replay with the teams, their role as critics is minimal and, at best, indirect, whereas the two peers in each team criticize one another quite freely. The video sessions usually make the teachers aware that there are still many unresolved questions, such as the familiarity with specialzed terms to be used during the Spanish portion of certain content classes (e.g. math or science) or the role of the monolingual teacher in the bilingual team approach (7). These and other issues are then discussed in a special topics session during the final stage of the workshop. This kind of one-week workshop generally turns out satisfactorily to motivate teachers to use the mentioned technique and to ensure their competency in controlled switching. Reactions to this practice-oriented workshop were very positive and later class observations showed that teachers had indeed become more effective in the way in which they integrated the switching technique in their classes.

The balanced distribution of the two languages in teaching any one of the school subjects other than language arts, suggests to the learner that switching between languages is for him a way to cope with the bicultural-bilingual setting in which he functions. By the same token, the concurrent use of the two languages suggests to him that, at least while the bilingual program is in operation, a full maintenance program is being implemented. On the other hand, since bilingual programs are not normally included in the children's education beyond the elementary school, the question arises in regard to what should be done to avoid the attrition of the vernacular language as the child moves from the bilingual program into the monolingual program.

It may be appropriate at this point to examine some recent amendments to the Bilingual Education Act known as Public Law 95-561, Education Amendments of 1978, Title VII. In Section 703a the law defines "programs of bilingual education" and regulates their implementation in Paragraph 4 A-D as follows:

> (A) The term 'program of bilingual education' means a program of instruction, designed for children of limited English proficiency in elementary or secondary schools, in which, with respect to the years of study to which such program is applicable—
>
> "(i) there is instruction given in, and study of, English and, to the extent necessary to allow a child to achieve competence in the English language, the native language of the children of limited Eng-

lish proficiency, and such instruction is given with appreciation for the cultural heritage of such children, and of other children in American society, and, with respect to elementary and secondary school instruction, such instruction shall, to the extent necessary, be in all courses or subjects of study which will allow a child to progress effectively through the educational system; and
"(ii) the requirements in subparagraphs (B) through (F) [(E) and (F) regarding applications for Federal funding and parents' advisory councils are not reproduced here] of this paragraph and established pursuant to subsection (b) [not relevant to our discussion here] of this section are met.

(B) In order to prevent the segregation of children on the basis of national origin in programs assisted under this title, and in order to broaden the understanding of children about languages and cultural heritages other than their own, a program of bilingual instruction may include the participation of children whose language is English, but in no event shall the percentage of such children exceed 40 per centum. The objective of the program shall be to assist children of limited English proficiency to improve their English language skills, and the participation of other children in the program must be for the principal purpose of contributing to the achievement of that objective. The program may provide for centralization of teacher training and curriculum development, but it shall serve such children in the schools which they normally attend.

(C) In such courses or subjects of study as art, music, and physical education, a program of bilingual education shall make provision for the participation of children of limited English proficiency in regular classes.

(D) Children enrolled in a program of bilingual education shall, if graded classes are used, be placed, to the extent practicable, in classes with children of approximately the same age and level of educational attainment. If children of significantly varying ages or levels of educational attainment are placed in the same class, the program of bilingual education shall seek to insure that each child is provided with instruction which is appropriate for his level of educational attainment.

The law of Novemer 1, 1978 stresses the fact that the native language be used only "to the extent necessary to allow a child to achieve competence in the English language." Contrary to the ultimate objective of the concurrent approach to maintain or preserve the vernacular language, the law seems to address itself only to the acquisition of the English language, leaving, by implication, the preservation of the native language, if so desired, to agencies other than the federal government. Seen from the viewpoint of second language instruction, this emphasis oddly contradicts the principles of ESL methodology that restricts the use of the native language while teaching the target language. What is probably meant here—and was expressed in the earlier definition more clearly—is that the native language can serve as a medium of instruction in the teaching of content as long as the imperfect knowledge of the mainstream language still stands in the way of successful school performance. If this is indeed the avowed purpose of bilingual instruction, then the child participates in a program that is potentially maintenance-oriented, contingent upon the means that are found to continue his bilinguality after he has exited from the federally funded program. Accordingly, we may have to distinguish between material and ideological support by the federal government in the sense that bilingual education, when federally funded, seeks to bring about proficiency in the English language but, when funded through other sources, can lead to the preservation of the vernacular language if language maintenance is a desirable goal for the community where such a program is located.

This interpretation of the federal law is also supported, indirectly, by the admittance of English-dominant children to the bilingual education as stated in Paragraph (B) of the same section (see above). If children whose language is English are allowed to participate, up to a forty percent enrollment of such children, in a bilingual program in order to prevent segregation and, most importantly, "in order to broaden the understanding of children about languages and cultural heritages other than their own," it would be senseless to prevent them, after grade three or five, from further developing their newly acquired bilingualism or biculturalism. I just cannot believe that the law is written to encourage English-dominant children to become bilingual during the first years of their school experience and, once this goal is achieved, to encourage them to lose their bilinguality and biculturality.

Bilingual instruction shall be implemented "with appreciation for the cultural heritage of such [Limited English Proficiency] children, and of other children in American society" (see (i) of 4A). This statement still seems to reflect a condescending attitude toward American minorities and therefore falls short of a full commitment to biculturalism or multiculturalism as a viable philosophy for those whose ethnic roots differ from those of the mainstream society. We may learn to appreciate what is basically foreign to us but we seek to identify with the values we call our own, whether they represent our ethnic heritage or, in Fishman's words, our "symbolic integration" with the entire nation (1970: 30). The official wording could be paraphrased like this: It is all right for you to be a Mexican-American—or a Native American or a Black American or an Asian American—as a matter of fact, we respect and appreciate your heritage but you better leave your roots behind and become one of us as members of the mainstream society. Whereas most of us have come to accept some degree of cultural democracy, the federal government has merely updated, glorified if you will, the melting pot theory—still a far cry from the so-called *salad bowl!* However, even here the wording is not entirely clear and allows for variable interpretation, creating a kind of continuum that stretches from a human interpretation of the melting pot toward the implantation of cultural democracy leaving it then up to the individual to place himself on this continuum according to how he views American society. Although more guidance would have been desirable, the flexibility assures those who believe in the maintenance of two languages and two cultures that they are on ideologically sound grounds also, as far as the federal government is concerned.

To summarize the previous discussion, it might be fair to assert that, even though the 1978 amendments to the Bilingual Education Act are not overtly supportive of stable bilingualism and of cultural democracy, the achievement of such goals are viable whenever community support is available. Acculturation and linguistic assimilation are of course, viable objectives for some communities and there is no intent here to suggest that the U.S. as a whole should become a bilingual nation. Some other communities, because of the presence there of groups that are ethnically, culturally and/or linguistically different, may instead seek a double allegiance as a means to cope with past traditions and modern mainstream values. When I proposed to write this paper, I intended to focus on the conflicting views between the cultural-linguistic goals of multicultural communities and the current legislation. As the paper developed I have become increasingly aware that Law 95-561 lends itself, because of its lukewarm support of any kind of bilingual maintenance, to promoting the degree of bilingualism and biculturalism that is justifiable in terms of the community itself. Our responsibility then lies with the community. Thus it becomes more important than ever to correlate educational programs with community objectives and orient bilingual programs toward assimilation or maintenance as such trends in a given community support it. I do not know whether or not this flexibility was actually intended but it does lend itself to promoting bilingualism and biculturalism in areas like South Texas and, by implication, stresses the legality of the maintenance program when it is supported by the community. Therefore the future of the concurrent approach, like maintenance programs in general, is in the hands of parents and other community persons.

I have attempted to show that the concurrent use of two languages is far from being a random behavior or flipflopping of sorts, but a strategy used by bilinguals under certain circumstances and explainable on the basis of psycholinguistic and sociolinguistic criteria. I have furthermore attempted to show that these strategies can be adapted effectively to bilingual teaching. The teachers using the code-switching approach, that is, the *concurrent approach,* are promoting a feeling of prestige in regard to both languages and are developing in their children language proficiencies as school subjects are being mastered. I have shown, in addition, what kind of inservice training teachers need in order to implement the approach successfully. Finally, I have discussed some recent amendments of the Bilingual Education Act which at first sight, seem to conflict with the implementation of a maintenance-oriented model like the *concurrent approach* but in the final analysis, can be interpreted as justifying the goals of a maintenance program if the community, where such a program is in operation, is willing to support it, at least ideologically. The future will tell the degree to which not only ideological but also financial backing is required. I hope that I have been successful in showing the mutual relationship between bilingual community behaviors, bilingual teaching techniques and current legislation.

APPENDIX

EXCERPTS FROM CODE-SWITCHING DATA

1. –And I tell you another thing *que* I'd shoot anybody . . . (FM-1.14) [Substratum]
2. –I lose my temper *porque a mí me da mucho coraje* . . . (FM1.15-16) [Emotion]

3. – . . . she would tell me things like—*este*—you know (FM-5.11) [Hesitation]
4. –It takes—*Es más despacio la manera esa.* (EC-24.14-15) [False Start]
5. – . . . I wished they'd come more often!
   –*You ought to get on the phone*—y dijo mamá que vinieran a visitar,¿ves? (EC-3.20-23) [CODE: Initiation of response]
6. –Sabe lo que me gusta a mí ¡ves. Man! *That's all kinds of beers ahí!* (EC-25.10) [CODE: Continued speech after switching]
7. – . . . ¿Le borro y le pongo "speak?" (M-3.1-2) [CODE: Prior code use]
8. –Ah, no—it's not a sound problem, it's more of a like *como donde acentúa uno la palabra.* (VC-12.9-10) [CODE: As topic]
9. " . . . si no 'biera ella dicho eso, WE WOULD *TAKE FOR GRANTED* THAT IT WAS THE LAST SATURDAY, . . . [CODE: anticipatory embedding (specialized terms)]
10. "¿Bueno, pos, IS THERE ANOTHER *MOTION?*" [CODE: anticipatory embedding (specialized terms)]
11. –"*How long have you been here?*" Pos le decía "*twenty-nine, thirty years.*" (EC-10.1-2) [CODE: Quote]
12. –No he podido grabar la conversación.
    ¿Qué es que dijo?
    –*I was unable to record the conversation.* (RJ-memory) [CODE: Clarification]
13. – . . . *un hombre precabido vale por* dos.—Ahora digo yo *si toca la de malas,* OK but I did what I could to prevent it. (FM-2.5-7) [CODE: Precoining]
14. –*Mis sobrinas* are the typical—you know—they can understand it, . . . (FM-4.12-13) [Home/Family Domain]
15. –¿No?
    –Sí. *He is going to be training for a manager right now.* (EC-6.7-9) [Employment Domain]
16. –Oh, sí. Si porque *I notice que if I write something down I can remember it better.* (EC-28.7-8) [School Domain]
17. –A hijo. Me están haciendo garras, cousin.
    –*Insurance*—Oye y *those guys are going to raise the rates,* ¿verdad? (EC-23.10-11) [Business Domain]
18. –It was the day you went *al parque.* (R-1.6) [Culture: Environment]
19. –Cuando comenzó esto todos los que andaban mechudos, *they believe that they were no good* . . . (EC-9.16-18) [CULTURE: Attitude/Bias]
20. –*Los doctores que vienen de México igualmente.* Hacen lo mismo after being here for a while. (FM.-6.10-11) [CULTURE: Language-locals]
21. –Andale, that's probably the best bet. (EC-22.5) [CULTURE: Loyalty/acculturation]
22. –I went only for one sole reason to Mexico—*porque no me contaran como era.* I went when I was twenty a la capital. (FM-9.22-23) [CULTURE: Heritage]
23. –Well, you do a lot of P.R. *Cuando vienen las mamases muy bien, tienes que calmarlas.* (VC-1.3-5) [CULTURE: Persons]
24. –Ah . . . bueno, como me estás grabando—*I'll take the fifth amendment—on that one.* (VC-1.12-13) [CULTURE: Social/Political institution]

25. –And maybe it's part of the culture, too, because, you know, like *con nosotros* "¿qué?," you know, se oye *muy mal*. I mean, *en mi casa todo el tiempo es "mande."* (VC-13.19-21) [CULTURE: Language]
26. –En México si un three or four year old—you have them recitando. (FM-12.10-11) [CULTURE: Customs]
27. –(to sibling) X, *get it*.
    –Es pa' é-. A estas horas—es pa.él. (EC-3.1-2) [Between siblings]
28. –(Wife to mother) Con las misma chaqueta por cuatro años.
    –(Wife to husband) *You are the one wearing the same jacket*. (EC-7.19-21) [between spouses]
29. –Pos maybe a Chevrolet or Ford. See how they compare, con el *Toyota—el five-speed Toyota-long bed*. ¿Cómo la ves tu con los pickups? . . . EC-152-4) [between peers]
30. –Otra vez! Otra vez! A ver!
    –(to interviewer) *She knows that she can do it* (EC-2.14-15) [between acquaintances]
31. –*And when you're talking to Mrs. Green or . . . do you feel uncomfortable with her?*
    –Uh-huh.
    –*Because it has to be all English*. (VD-11.18-21) [between employer & employee]
32. – . . . *We started out with 900 . . . about 950 kids.*
    –¿Y ahora?
    –*And we've got . . . 'mm, what? 530 . . .*
    –*¿De veras? Casi, casi casi la mitad.*
    –*Yeah, we've got 530 . . .* (VC3.14-19) [TOPIC: Occupation]
33. –It's gonna cost me—por las placas *three hundred*.
    –Bastantito.
    –Y cobra como *twelve dollars* cada . . . (VC-8.5-7) [TOPIC: Financial matters]
34. –Pero estaba pensando *about the maintenance* (EC-15.21) [TOPIC: Mechanical matters]
35. –It was good meat *con mushroom sauce y otra salsa blanca que no sé que sería. Pero la carne estaba suavecita, suavecita.* (FM-14.14-16) [TOPIC: food]
36. –*Forty-two miles* fíjate. (EC-21.10-11)
    –Sí, estoy pagando *five hundred* y pico por año. (EC-23.12) [TOPIC: Numbers]
37. –Tengo el complejo de que la mamá mexicana siempre estaba amasando, haciendo tortillas. Cuando me casé, I promised myself I wouldn't. (FM-16.2-4) [time-related topics]
38. –"There was no way the City could have picked it [a broken branch] up, you could have still seen, ah, QUE ESTABA UN PEDAZO, ESTABA QUEBRADO—UN CACHO QUE ESTABA QUEBRADO but there was nothing." [Imaginary content: mystery]
39. –". . . You saw her face in the egg?
    –"Exact replica, I mean, just like having a picture, you know, Y VIDE A LA SENORA [witch] ESTA Y ESTA MUJER NO LA CONOCIA YO . . . [Imaginary content: brujería]

40. "DESPUES, she turned him over on his stomach Y LE ESTIRO EL CUERITO DE LA ESPALDA PA' QUE LE TRONARA . . ." [Imaginary content: curanderismo]
41. –¿Me aprobó mi sopa? *Ah, that's good.* Este no es macaroni de la bolsa. [METAPHOR: For contrast]
42. – . . . , íbamos allí siempre cada año. *We went there every year.* (VC-6.506) [METAPHOR: For emphasis]
43. –*Dice* "Why is that?" *Dice* "because if you would stop snoring, then I would be able . . ." (CL-15.18-19) [METAPHOR: Parenthetical remarks]

BIBLIOGRAPHY

Andersson, Theodore and Boyer, Mildred. *Bilingual Schooling in the United States.* Southwest Educational Development Laboratory, Austin, Texas, 1970.

Cohen, Andrew D. *A Sociolinguistic Approach to Bilingual Education.* Rowley, Mass.: Newbury House, 1975.

Cordasco, Francesco. *Bilingual School in the United States: A Sourcebook for Educational Personnel.* New York: McGraw-Hill Book Company, 1977.

Fishman, Joshua. *Sociolinguistics.* Rowley, MA: Newbury House, 1970.

__________. *Bilingual Education: An International Sociological Perspective.* Rowley, MA: Newbury House, 1976.

Fishman, Joshua and John Lovas. 1972. "Bilingual Education in a Sociolinguistic Perspective" in B. Spolsky.

Gumperz, John J. *Language in Social Groups.* Stanford, California: Stanford University Press, 1971.

Jacobson, Rodolfo. "How to Trigger Codeswitching in a Bilingual Classroom" in B. Hoffer and B. L. Dubois, eds. *Southwest Areal Linguistics Now and Then.* San Antonio, TX: Trinity University, 1977.

__________. "Anticipatory Embedding and Imaginary Content: two newly identified codeswitching variables," in A. G. Lozano, ed., *Bilingual and Biliterate Perspectives.* Boulder, Colorado: University of Colorado, 1978a.

__________. "The Social Implications of Intra-sentential Codeswitching" in R. Romo and R. Paredes, eds., *New Directions in Chicano Scholarship.* San Diego, CA: University of California, 1978b.

__________. "Codeswitching in South Texas: Sociolinguistic Considerations and Pedagogical Applications." *The Journal of the Linguistic Association of the Southwest,* Vol. III, Nos. 1 and 2, 1978c.

__________. "Beyond ESL: The Teaching of Content other than Language Arts in Bilingual Education." Austin, TX: Southwest Educational Development Laboratory and ERIC Microfiche ED162525, 1979a.

__________. "Can and Should the Laredo Experiment be Duplicated Elsewhere? The Applicability of the Concurrent Approach in Other Communities." Paper delivered at the 1979 NABE Conference, Seattle, Washington, 1979b.

Kjolseth, Rolf. "Bilingual Education Programs in the United States: For Assimilation or Pluralism" in B. Spolsky, 1972.

Mackey, William. *Bilingual Education in a Binational School.* Rowley, MA: Newbury House, 1972.

National Clearinghouse for Bilingual Education. *The Bilingual Education Act*. Rosslyn, Virginia, 1979.

Spolsky, Bernard, ed. *The Language Education of Minority Children*. Rowley, MA: Newbury House, 1972.

STATE MANDATED COMPETENCY TESTING: A CATCH-22 FOR BILINGUAL STUDENTS

Rosa Quezada

A growing concern over increasing numbers of ill-prepared students graduating from high schools across the country has spurred the current movement toward minimal competency testing. The catylyst for this movement is fear that increased numbers of students were graduating from high schools without acquiring skills necessary for success in the adult world. This fear is accelerated within the bilingual community through disproportionate grade retention and drop-out rates. The focus of this paper will be on minimal competency testing and the bilingual student. The benefits, constraints, and legal considerations related to such programs of testing will be presented with an emphasis on the two alternatives available for bilingual students; inclusion in minimal competency testing programs or exclusion from such programs. In addition, some recommended actions for parents for each of the alternatives will be presented.

The minimal competency movement has gained momentum throughout the nation with twenty-eight states presently mandating some form of competency testing. Of these, fifteen are linked in some way to high school graduation as in Florida, North Carolina, and Oregon (Thompson, 1979). It is interesting to note that the responsibility for learning has been placed on the student while that of teaching has been removed from the instructor. In a sense, the concept of "blaming the victim" for his/her poor education is the result. If bilingual students have not received an appropriate education resulting in a high school diploma, it is their fault and the students will be negatively reinforced for their failure through the receipt of the certificate of attendance. This in turn will insure their failure as they seek employment in the adult world and find their certificates equated with the perception of them as undereducated, illiterate, and incompetent.

Definitions

One of the problems related to minimal competency testing is the confusion of terminology related to the movement, such as "competency," "minimal," and "life skills." It is important to clarify some of these terms. Haney and Madaus note that in referring to the word "competency," it sometimes seems to be used according to one of its dictionary definitions, "sufficient means for a modest livelihood." All students should have sufficient means for a modest livelihood by the time they leave high school.

Often it seems to connote ability to get along in late twentieth century America, hence we find, as in the Oregon competency based education program, allusions to the abilities each student must attain "in order to function in society."

Spady (1977) in his discussion of competency based education in Oregon defines competencies as "indicators of successful performance in life role activities (be they producer, consumer, political citizen, driver, family member, intimate friend, recreational participant, or life-long learner) and distinguishes them from discrete cognitive, manual, and social capacities (such as reading and computational skills, and motivation) that, when integrated and adapted to particular social contexts, serve as the enablers of building blocks on which competencies ultimately depend." Spady notes that the issue of definitions related to "required minimums" and "desirable maximums" is one that must be reviewed. How can "minimums" or "maximums" be set concretely? In practice, the setting of minimum scores seems to be the result of compromise between judgements of what minimum seems plausible to expect within the Anglo community and judgements about what proportions of failure seem to be politically tolerable (Haney and Madaus 1978).

It appears that at present there simply is no scientific basis for deciding what "minimum" points should be; the decisions involved in setting them are political rather than scientific. The implications of these decisions for bilingual students will be discussed below.

Attempting to define "life skills" appears to be nebulous as well. Henry Brickell, Director of Policy Studies in Education, a Division of the Academy for Educational Development in New York City analyzed the questions related to this issue and attempts to clarify the definitions of school vs. life skills as follows: "School skills relate well to future school skills; life skills reflect those needed to succeed in later life." However, several questions arise when one delves deeper into this definition. First, it is not easy to secure agreement upon the adult roles with which the schools should be concerned. Second, it is not easy to agree upon what constitutes success in adult roles. Third, it is difficult to draw a connection between school-trained capacities and adult role competencies. And finally, even if capacities could be linked to those competencies which are deemed important, there is no evidence that introducing programs of minimal competency will help students whom the schools are now failing, particularly bilingual students.

Benefits of Mandated Competency Testing

Proponents of minimal competency testing believe that it is positive and necessary. Cawelti (1977) states that some of the more positive outcomes related to programs of minimal competency testing are the development of a clear set of goals and objectives for the school system, and the opportunity to fundamentally re-examine the nature of general education for secondary students.

It has also been alleged that through the above procedures, a consistent curriculum for students will be established which theoretically could help to equalize educational opportunities for all students. Finally, advocates of such testing programs claim that their establishment will eliminate the present practice of issuing "fraudulent" high school diplomas. They charge that schools are "pushing" students through the system without requiring minimum standards for graduation. Proponents site cases where students who have graduated from high school are ill prepared to function in society and lack basic mathematical, reading and writing skills. It is their hope that minimal competency tests will ensure a "standard" education which will prepare students for the future.

A fifth benefit cited by its advocates revolves around the potential for strong remediation programs. These programs would be established for students who have not achieved the "minimum" standards set by local competency tests. Students would be identified early and appropriate remedial work would provide them with skill development in deficient areas. These types of programs would permit all students to achieve the necessary skills for graduation with a high school diploma.

Some states have opted to issue two categories of diplomas. One would be the traditional diploma which would certify that the student had indeed completed twelve years of education and was capable of completing a minimal set of standards which will allow the student to perform successfully as an adult. The second category would provide a "certificate of attendance" to those students who have completed twelve years of education but who have not been able to pass a minimal competency test.

Minimal Competency Testing in Connecticut

In Connecticut, Public Act No. 78-194, an Act Concerning Education Evaluation and Remedial Assistance went into effect on July 1, 1978. This act states that annually each public school student enrolled in grades three, five and seven will be examined in basic reading, language arts and mathematics skills. It provides for programs of remediation for those students who are unable to pass competency tests in the areas of reading, language arts and mathematics. However, major questions derive from Connecticut's law in the areas of cut-off points and remediation programs for those students who fail the test.

Questions related to testing *per se* are: How does one determine a cut-off point? Does one use a percentage, the bottom quartile, or select those students who are below one standard deviation? Should one standard be established for all children or different standards for children of high or low socioeconomic status? What kind of test is warranted (normed vs. criterion referenced)?

The following questions relate to programs of remediation: Will the Local Education Agency (LEA) be responsible for developing a remediation plan for each child? What are the components for good remedial programs? What is the effect of testing on the curriculum? If you test in grades three, five, seven, and nine, can you remediate in grades four, six, and eight? What are the implications of different amounts of funding for defining the remediation program? How do you demonstrate instructional improvement? And finally, how do you know that the money awarded to LEA's for such programs is actually used for remediation? For the bilingual educator it is important to note that Public Act No. 78-194 makes two exceptions from mandated minimal competency testing: special education students and students enrolled in programs of bilingual education. This exclusion of bilingual students from mandated minimal competency testing in the public schools of Connecticut has implications for the direction such testing may take in other states with large percentages of bilingual students. Exclusion from such programs will clearly have detrimental effects on bilingual students in three critical areas: programs of remediation, possible classroom neglect, and the denial of high school diplomas.

The most apparent effect of exclusion from the testing program will be that students enrolled will not be eligible for state-funded programs of remediation. According to the law such students would not be eligible for inclusion in any accounting the LEA may present to the State Board of Education for funding purposes. It would seem then that any bilingual student who would potentially benefit from remediation in English reading skills, for example, could not receive such assistance from a program funded by the state for those students unable to meet competency standards. Is this to be considered equalization of educational opportunities as some advocates of minimal competency testing have proclaimed? A second effect of exclusion from competency programs is that such bilingual students may be neglected by classroom teachers who know their students are excluded from the testing program. Some teachers may devote time and assistance to those students who will have to perform well on the tests since they may equate their student's success with their own success in teaching. For example, a teacher may spend more time with student "A" in her bilingual classroom who is a native speaker of English, developing those skills needed to pass the test. Student "B" in the same class, who is bilingual and not eligible for the testing program may receive less attention in skills development than his or her English-speaking peer. Student "B" who may need more intensive skills development in English would actually receive less. Clearly the potential for classroom teacher neglect of excluded students exists.

Finally, will exclusion from such a testing and remediation program result in the awarding of certificates of attendance rather than high school diplomas for bilingual students? The receipt of such a certificate will carry with it implications of an "inferior" student or at least of a student who will not be "successful" in the adult world. Does this imply then, that state funded and monitored programs, such as those in bilingual education, are inferior to "regular" classroom programs? Has the intent to equalize educational opportunity through a bilingual program been lost through faulty planning and assessment by the State Board of Education?

These are but three areas of concern which the author points out in order to move to the broader issue. If, in states such as Connecticut, the bilingual community defends the inclusion of its students in minimal competency testing programs, what options will result?

Critical Issues for Bilingual Students

Several negative effects of minimal competency testing programs on bilingual students are also issues which may affect the student population as a whole. Opponents to the minimal competency testing movement have stated that it will be disastrous. Three critical issues for bilingual educators and students deal with the tests themselves, programs of remediation for those students who fail to meet the "minimum" standard and the effects this type of testing program may have on the curriculum of the public schools.

A number of problems have arisen regarding the testing process itself. Critics have argued that there is no arbitrary manner by which one can establish a "cut-off" point.

Glass (1978) reports that he has "read the writings of those who claim the ability to make the determination of mastery or competence in statistical or psychological ways." They can't. At least they cannot determine criterion levels or standards other than arbitrary ones. It appears that the criteria for establishing cut-off points are based on value judgements. Although statistical procedures may help reduce error in determining whether a student reached the cut-off point or not, they cannot do away with the subjectivity involved in setting cut-off scores.

Others question whether minimal competency tests are a reliable means for making decisions about individual students. Real concern exists regarding whether the tests can be made free of cultural bias. The issue of cultural bias has already affected the minority student, as some testing programs have already demonstrated. For example, Cawelti (1977) found that in one Florida district, eight percent of the Anglo students failed on the Adult Performance Level Test administered in one Florida district while fifty-six percent of the minority students failed it. As a result the NAACP has announced its intention to file suit to prevent further administration of Florida's proficiency examination on the grounds that it is culturally biased.

The results of a culturally biased test for bilingual students is compounded by language differences. It is important to note that nowhere in minimal competency legislation has it been mentioned that bilingual students will be tested in their dominant language. Further, it will be difficult to convince some legislators that this is necessary. As we all know, direct translations of existing tests in English are invalid. To use translated tests as competency measures is unacceptable.

With present "drop-out" or "push-out" rates for high school Hispanics set as high as eighty-five percent in some areas of our country, it may very well be that competency testing will increase these numbers. Culturally biased tests with "unfair" cut-off points will virtually guarantee failure for Hispanic students.

Opponents of the movement note that progams of remediation for those students who fail competency tests also have inherent detrimental effects. Critics cite increased grade retention rates of bilingual students as a probability. If bilingual students cannot pass such tests in early grades, that may be sufficient justification for their nonpromotion. Cawelti (1977) points to research that demonstrates the futility of retaining students. His citation of research as early as 1911 demonstrates that "a majority of students who are retained in grades as a result of failing competency tests will either not improve their performance or will actually do worse if left back."

Further, competency testing may result in the tracking of bilingual students. Students may be grouped according to test results, with those receiving the lowest scores grouped together for "intensive" remediation. This point has already been noted by many minority residents of North Carolina where minimum competency testing has been implemented. As a result of the program a boycott of the state-wide competencies test has been advocated by minority group leaders. A recent Southern Regional

Council report suggested that tracking based on competency test results may become the new segregation.

A reoccuring theme in arguments against minimal competency programs is that of its relationship to the curriculum. In order for the test to be instructionally valid, topics in the curriculum must actually have been taught to the students tested. It is apparent that educators will have to begin to take a closer look at what should be learned that is not now being learned, and what should be taught that is not now being taught (Haney and Madaus).

Some educators fear increased curricular imbalance due to the demands of competencies to be tested vs. those things being taught at the present time.

An increased stress on "teaching for the test" may disastrously affect the general curriculum. Schools may opt to limit range of offerings presently available to students. This may lead to the elimination of such areas as cultual pluralism and social diversity within the curriculum as these subjects may *not* be measured by the tests. Further, this may result in termination of bilingual programs as their objectives may not be in concert with items tested.

Wise's (1978) warning that "those who care about the education of minority children not fall into the trap of confusing the equalization of educational opportunity with the need to raise academic achievement" is well taken. He predicts that the diversion may well mean less racial integration, less equalization of resources, and less access. Surely the picture he paints for the culturally different student is most depressing.

Finally, the cost implications of testing arouse concerns as well. Arasian, Madaus, and Padulla have estimated that the costs of administering a test can range from 15¢ to $13.00 per pupil. If one includes the costs for developing the tests and for the remedial classes needed for all students who do not pass it, and possible legal expenses, the real costs of minimum competency testing program could soar well beyond $15.00 to $20.00 per pupil (Haney and Madaus, 1978). Some educators worry that, due to heavy costs accrued by initial testing programs, little financial assistance will be provided for remediation programs. In the case of the bilingual students, then, all deficient students will be identified as such but prospects for improving their condition may appear bleak.

Some Legal Implications

The issue of minimal competency testing has resulted in legal action in several states. Wise (1978) suggests that it is likely that legal actions will be initiated against states which institute minimal competency testing programs and that the following four legal theories are likely to be raised in such cases:

1. *A denial of equal protection of the law.* (The Fourteenth Amendment.) This theory contends that because of unequal educational opportunity for minority students and cultural biases of the minimal competency testing program, minority students will be negatively affected by such programs. If one views statistics from states such as North Carolina where minimal competency testing programs have been instituted, the differences are apparent. Forty percent of the black high school juniors who took the test failed to

answer seventy percent of the reading questions correctly, compared with nine percent of the white students. In mathematics, eighty-five percent of the blacks answered less than seventy percent correctly, compared with thirty-eight percent of the whites. It is clear that tracking of minority students based on test scores is inevitable.

Wise points out that, in order to clearly prove denial of equal protection, the "plaintiff must establish three elements: (1) that racial imbalance exists between the tracks, (2) that placement in lower tracks results from substantial reliance on scores from a culturally biased test, and (3) that students are injured because of an inadequate remedial program that permanently keeps them in the lower tracks. He does conclude however that the courts probably will distinguish competency testing from tracking as long as remedial instruction is provided to promote equal educational opportunity and upgrade academic performance. However, in order to prove a denial of equal protection, one must prove that it was the interest of the state to discriminate against a particular minority group or that such an action "bears no rational relationship to any legitimate state interest." In North Carolina, the courts have decided that minimal competency testing programs have evolved in order to ensure that *all* students graduate from high school programs with literacy skills. They deny any intent to discriminate against any minority group *per se*. Plaintiffs will have a difficult time attempting to prove denial of equal protection of the law.

2. *Title VI.* A second theory suggests that minimal competency testing may be a violation of Title VI of the 1964 Civil Rights Act which states that "no person in the United States shall on the grounds of race, color or national origin, be subjected to discrimination under any program or activity receiving federal financial assistance." HEW's position is that Title VI is violated by any practice or procedure that has a disproportionate racial impact. It is ironic that the *Lau* v. *Nichols* case has been cited as the authority for the proposition that competency testing programs are invalid because of Title VI standards on racial imbalance. Because *Lau* provided special remediation education through a temporary tracking system for Chinese-speaking students, it appears to support minimal competency testing programs. However, if large numbers of minority students are identified and provided with programs of remediation to eliminate the effects of unequal educational opportunities, then it may prove valid.
3. *Procedural Due Process.* A third theory which minimal competency testing programs may challenge is the Fourteenth Amendment declaration that no state shall act to deprive its citizens of life, liberty, or property without due process of law. Challenges brought against minimal competency testing programs under procedural due process could be based upon the premise that a student who is denied a high school diploma, may have had his or her procedural rights violated if he or she had not received proper notification (Carter, 1979). Carter argues that notifying students during their first or second year of high school is not adequate notice of a minimum competency requirement for receiving a diploma. On the other hand, if the courts support the denial of a high school diploma until the student has actually mastered appropriate academic skills in a remedial program in order to pass the tests, the

courts may defer to education policies and find that no hearing is required (Wise, 1978).

4. *Substantive Due Process.* Finally, competency testing may deprive students of an interest in liberty or property without substantive due process under the Fourteenth Amendment. Three major points are generally charged: (1) critics of minimal competency testing claim that it is unfair to require minimal competencies after the student has been in school for ten or eleven years. It can be argued that a student who had been notified of such standards earlier in his or her academic career could have adapted new study skills which could ensure success in passing such a test in order to graduate. (2) The validity of the tests themselves is questionable. Is it fair to assume that those skills being tested are actually being taught in school? Haney and Madaus note that precedent has already been established for bringing suit on such an issue (Learner, 1978). (3) Confusion exists as to definition of competency. Critics charge that because the term itself is so subjective, requiring "competencies" for receipt of a high school diploma may violate substantive due process of the law. As pointed out earlier in this paper, it is difficult for experts in the field of education to concur on the definition of such terms as "competency," "minimums" and "maximums." Can the court decide for experts in the field of education? It appears unlikely.

An Action Plan For Parents

Minimal competency testing for bilingual students has serious implications. But how can parents of bilingual students be prepared to make decisions regarding such testing programs for their children?

In those states where students enrolled in bilingual programs are excluded from such testing programs it may be important for parents to support such exclusion. Upon reviewing the constraints and uncertainties presently surrounding minimal competency testing it may be in the bilingual students' best interest to be exempted from such confusion. However, parents should be aware of the following:

1. Parents of bilingual students should take action which will ensure that their children will receive a high school diploma upon completion of high school and *not* a certificate of attendance if their children are excluded from such testing programs.
2. Parents should demand information on evaluation reports from which their children presently receive services, for example, Title I reading and mathematics programs. Are these programs improving their children's academic skills?
3. Parents should actively participate in Parents Advisory Committees which are required for federal and many state funded projects which serve bilingual students. These Parents Advisory Committees will assist in clarifying parent-student rights and laws related to bilingual education.
4. Parents should actively seek information regarding the bilingual program, its objectives, and evaluation. Research has indicated that those bilingual programs where parents are actively involved are those which are must successful.

On the other hand, in those states where bilingual students will be included in minimal competency testing programs, other types of parent action are necessary. Some of the issues which need to be addressed for these students include the following:

1. Appropriate adjustments must be made to ensure that minimal competency testing will be administered to bilingual students in their dominant language. These tests should not be mere translations of English versions, but tests which will measure the competencies required in the dominant language of the student.
2. Selection of culture-fair tests. Perhaps a panel could be created at the state level to ensure such test development.
3. Remediation programs in the dominant language of the student should be provided for those bilingual students who have not passed the tests.
4. Issuing of a high school diploma upon graduation and not a certificate of attendance, for those bilingual students who pass the test in their dominant language.

In the political arena, it is crucial that both bilingual parents and educators become involved in legislative committees reviewing minimal competency testing legislation. Along with the issues discussed above, items of broader implication include:

1. The review of cut-off points for failure. How do these arbitrarily set cut-off points affect bilingual students? Are there disproportionately high numbers of bilingual students failing such tests if such specific cut-offs are instituted?
2. The review of information relevant to achievement in files of students who do not pass minimal competency tests. Will this information be used for identification only, resulting in teaching of bilingual students? Will it be used as criteria of eligibility for a remedial program?
3. Will students receive a high school diploma or a certificate of attendance?
4. The review of the type of remedial programs for those bilingual students who have not passed the test. Will the state provide sufficient funds for a remedial program or will students be identified and tracked but not serviced with appropriate remediation?
5. The review of drop-out rates of the bilingual community. A study should be undertaken to assess the results of failure on minimal competency testing. Are increased numbers of bilingual students leaving school because of the tests?
6. Finally, the review of policy for minimal competency testing in private schools. Is it equivalent to that of the public school system? Or is it possible that those who can afford a non-public school education will be assessed on different criteria than those students attending public schools?

To summarize, the minimal competency testing issue will effect bilingual children. Whether legislation is at the national or state level, it appears that parents as well as teachers should be taking an active role in the development of any plans for such testing. We must also seriously consider the nature of the remedial program conducted with students who do not meet the performance standards, as well as develop a more systematic program of evaluation and reporting. Wise (1977) states that minimum competency testing does nothing to improve teaching or learning. If this is so, clearly one result will be to hold the student responsible for the failure of the educational system, again a case of "blaming the victim." Cawelti (1977) warns all of us touched by the educational system in this country that "any attempt to return to an elitest form of education that cuts off low income, culturally disadvantaged or alienated youths from the mainstream is counter to our democratic ideals."

BIBLIOGRAPHY

Andrews, Richard L. "How Sound Are The Assumptions of Competency-Based Programs?" *Educational Leadership.* (Jan. 1974).

Carter, David G. "Competency Testing: An Emerging Legal Issue." *Education in an Urban Society* (Aug. 1979).

Cawelti, Gordon. "Requiring Competencies for Graduation—Some Curricular Issues" *Educational Leadership* (Nov. 1977).

Gable, Robert. "Minimum Competency Testing: NEAR's Rule" *Northeastern Educational Research Association Annual Meeting at Ellenville, N.Y.* (Oct. 26, 1978).

Gallagher, James and Ramsbotham, Ann. "Developing North Carolina's Competency Testing Program." *School Law Bulletin,* Vol. IX, No. 4, (Oct. 1978).

Haney, Walter and Madaus, George. "Making Sense of the Competency Testing Movement." *Harvard Educational Review,* Vol. 48, No. 4, (Nov. 1978).

McClung, Merle Steven. "Are Competency Testing Programs Fair? Legal?" *Phi Delta Kappan* (Feb. 1978).

McClung, M. "Competency Testing: Potential for Discrimination." *Clearinghouse Review,* Vol. 2, (1977).

Pipho, C. "State Activity Minimal Competence Testing." *Educational Commission of the States at Denver, Colorado* (May 1978).

Reilly, Wayne. "Competency Based Education: Some Educational, Political and Historical Perspectives." *Ford Foundation Fellows in Education,* (Sept. 1, 1977).

Smith, Michael R. "Legal Considerations of Competency Testing Programs." *School Law Bulletin* Vol. IX, No. 4, (Oct. 1978).

Spady, William G. "Competency Based Education: A Bandwagon in Search of a Definition." *Educational Research* Vol. 6, No. 1, (Jan. 1977).

Taylor, Robert L. "Effects of Minimum Competencies on Promotion Standards." *Educational Leadership* (Oct. 1978).

Thompson, Scott. "Current Status of Minimum Competency Testing in the United States" *American Association of Colleges for Teacher Education* (Mar. 1, 1979)

Wise, Arthur E. "On the Limits of Reforming the Schools Through Educational Measurement." *Cross Reference* Vol. 1, No. 4, (Aug. 1978).